REFORMATIONAL THEOLOGY

Reformational Theology

A New Paradigm
for Doing Dogmatics

Gordon J. Spykman

WILLIAM B. EERDMANS PUBLISHING COMPANY
GRAND RAPIDS, MICHIGAN

Copyright © 1992 by Wm. B. Eerdmans Publishing Co.
255 Jefferson Ave. S.E., Grand Rapids, Mich. 49503
All rights reserved

Printed in the United States of America

Library of Congress Cataloguing-in-Publication Data

Spykman, Gordon J.
    Reformational theology: a new paradigm for doing dogmatics /
Gordon J. Spykman.
        p.   cm.
    Includes bibliographical references and index.
    ISBN 0-8028-3701-8
    1. Theology, Doctrinal.   2. Reformed Church — Doctrines.
I. Title.
BT75.2.S67 1991
230'.42 — dc20   91-41815
                                                         CIP

Contents

PART THREE: SIN AND EVIL

PART FOUR: THE WAY OF SALVATION

PART FIVE: THE CONSUMMATION

Preface

Manuscripts, it seems, are never "all done." They always beg for a few more finishing touches. Finally, however, one must simply drop the pen and go to press. For this project that time has now come.

From the start I envisioned the working out of this handbook on dogmatics as my major project for the 1980s. Now, looking back upon that decade of research and writing, I wish to discharge the debt of gratitude I owe to many along the way who offered a helping hand. My sincere thanks to librarians at Calvin and "the Free" for good services rendered, to the college administration for the sabbaticals and reduced teaching loads which created the blocks of time needed for such an undertaking, to John C. Vander Stelt of Dordt College for his careful reading of the manuscript, and especially to Donna Quist and Esther Vander Tuig for their unfailing patience, expertise, and cordial spirit in processing numerous drafts of this manuscript. And to my wife, Eleanor, as ever, "Thanks!" for sharing in the ups and downs of this project.

As this work now enters the marketplace of theological ideas, whatever in it proves to be good I dedicate to the memory of my father, Albert, in recognition of his unceasing support, his sound though un-schooled theological sensitivities, and the lively interest on his part which contributed to the completion of this "new paradigm for doing Reformed dogmatics."

Autumn, 1991   GORDON J. SPYKMAN

PART ONE

FOUNDATIONS

Chapter I

Rationale and Prospectus

I. 1. Accounting for This Project

In the introduction to his book *Christian Faith* (English translation, 1979), Leiden professor Hendrikus Berkhof drops the comment that writing dogmatics is "a rather lonely adventure" (p. xii). If this is true of the broader Reformed community in Europe (which can boast of very substantial studies in dogmatics by Karl Barth, Emil Brunner, G. C. Berkouwer, Otto Weber, and Helmut Thielicke, among others) and South Africa (Adrio König), it is even more glaringly true of the Reformed community in North America. Louis Berkhof stands out as one of our "lonely adventurers." His standard work, *Systematic Theology* (1947), holds an almost uncontested place, joined along the way by Herman Hoeksema's *Reformed Dogmatics* (1966) and Carl Henry's series *God, Revelation, and Authority* (1976ff.). A few other titles may deserve honorable mention. All told, however, our century leaves us with a rather meager record.

Though duly appreciative of this legacy, we must nonetheless come to terms with Hendrikus Berkhof's further comment that "classic dogmatics gave profound answers to questions that no one asks anymore" (p. xvii). Can this judgment simply be dismissed as a case of overstatement? Or does it reflect a penetrating insight into the current state of affairs? Throughout modernity, and especially during the decades since World War II, Western culture has undergone radical changes. Reformed dogmatics must therefore now consider the challenge of how to renew its address to the perennial issues of the Christian faith as we approach the close of this twentieth century.

This is so for at least two reasons. First, there is the current crisis situation which we all face as Christians living in a post-Enlightenment culture. Western Christianity is being literally swamped by the tidal wave of modern secularism. The older, deeply entrenched dualist structures of traditional theologies had the effect of promoting, or at least of preserving, the idea of a "sacred" realm alongside, above, or beyond the "secular." But now these long-standing dualisms of the past are making way for the new monisms of contemporary process theology. These monisms of recent decades are out to dismantle the "upper room" where the "sacred" still survives. A "radical secularity" is emerging in which the "sacred" is reduced at best to a depth dimension of our "secular" world of experience as its "Ground of Being." For Reformed theology, therefore, one of the challenges of our age is to reformulate a Christian dogmatics which can stand as a real and respectable alternative to both the older dualist and the newer monist traditions.

A second reason for reworking Reformed dogmatics is a more perennial one. It is rooted in the very nature of a biblically Reformed understanding of the nature of Christian living. The life of faith is a life of ongoing sanctification. Doing theology is one way of living out this call to sanctification. Its claim rests on us as an abiding task. Each succeeding generation is called to build anew on foundations laid by earlier Christian thinkers. Such a renewal effort will surely bear the unique benchmarks of our time and place in history. But in the measure that it responds faithfully to the steadying norms of God's Word, it is also bound to reflect certain abidingly relevant insights. The credibility of such a venture depends therefore on its manifest continuity with "the faith of the fathers" . . . "once for all delivered to the church." Of a faithful theologian, as of any faithful scribe, it must be said that "he brings forth from his treasure things old and new." Thus the call to engage in dogmatics lures us ever onward as a theoretical way of "working out our salvation with fear and trembling." It is a systematic way of "giving an account of the hope that is in us" — to all who will stop long enough to look and listen, both within the church and outside. In this light we can recognize theologizing as a redemptively updated way of making good on the cultural mandate which has accompanied us from the very beginning as both a benediction and an obligation. It therefore holds for *theologia* as for *ecclesia* that *reformata* must lead to *semper reformanda est* — theology, once reformed, must constantly undergo reformation.

In these waning years of the twentieth century the fertile field of Reformed dogmatics once again lies open before us. A number of Reformed scholars believe that a new harvesttime has arrived, an opportune moment to reap some of the ripened fruit of past and present biblical, philosophical, and theological labors within the Reformed tradition on both sides of the ocean. In seeking to open up some new insights, new horizons, new perspectives, and new directions for dogmatics, I aim to stand within and work from out of the best in the Reformed tradition, even while seeking also to advance and further reform it.

In this project I envision no more than a dogmatics in outline. I wish simply to sketch the broad contours of the theological landscape which lies before us, without detailing every landmark or fully exploring every point along the horizon. This will leave room aplenty for further elaboration. In making this first move I am extending an open invitation to my colleagues to help flesh out this initial probe — cooperating, critiquing, and contributing, as they see fit. I wish also to acknowledge the deep debt of gratitude I owe to many students who over the years have helped to shape these ideas.

I. 2. Standing within a Venerable Tradition

Tradition is the very lifeblood of theology. Detached from tradition, theology is like a cut flower which, severed from its roots and subsoil, soon withers in one's hand. No healthy theology ever arises *de novo*. By honoring sound tradition, theological continuity with the past is assured. At the same time tradition creates the possibility of opening new doors to the future. As the proverb puts it, "Tradition is the prologue to the future." Every dogmatics worth its salt must therefore take its stand squarely within one or another confessional tradition.

These observations hold for this project too. At the outset, therefore, there is good reason to lay the relevant cards on the table. Nothing is to be gained by trying to obscure one's tradition. Not that tradition is the ultimate norm for doing theology. The norm for dogmatics, as for all of life, remains the Word of God. Yet tradition is nonetheless crucially important. It is the bearer of a community's identity, the stimulus for its enterprising spirit, the shaper of its habits of thought, the forum for its theological reflections. Tradition is the historical-cultural channel within which Christian theologians respond to the claims of God's Word on their dogmatic undertakings. Both a certain stability and a certain tentativity, therefore, accompany all theology, the present work as well as those of the past.

Within which mainstream tradition do I intend, then, to locate this project? As already indicated, it is meant to take its place within the Reformed-Calvinist wing of the Protestant Reformation — in distinction, for example, from the Lutheran, Anglican, Zwinglian, and Anabaptist traditions, and clearly also from the Roman Catholic and Eastern Orthodox traditions. It acknowledges its primary indebtedness, moreover, to the Reformation as it came to expression in the Dutch Reformed tradition in distinction from that of Scottish Presbyterianism. But this tradition, too, is far from homogeneous. It has a checkered legacy, with all the ups and downs characteristic of most theologies from the sixteenth century to the present. Through all these zigzag movements there is, nevertheless, a discernible line of continuity in reformational thinking. It is not, to be sure, an unbroken tradition. But in it lies a recoverable line of development, one which can be reconstructed. That is the line I wish to follow and now briefly sketch as a way of introducing the lineage out of which this renewal project in Reformed dogmatics is born. Perhaps this can be done best by painting a picture with a few bold strokes of certain leading representative spokesmen who stand in this Reformed tradition.

Historically I take my point of departure in Calvin's theology, as expressed especially in his most definitive work, *The Institutes*. Calvin was not the kind of person to accept the views of even the most esteemed fathers (for example, Bernard of Clairvaux, one of his favorites) unless he found them to be in agreement with the Scriptures. The genius of his theology was, accordingly, its strong appeal to Scripture. His basic hermeneutic principle (which, it seems, he himself was not always able to honor fully) was this: try to say no more than Scripture, for this is speculation; try also to say no less than Scripture, for this is to impoverish God's Word. Methodologically, biblical revelation sets the parameters for theological reflection. With this commitment Calvin reached back over a millennium of disparate theologies to Augustine (whom he quotes with approval more often than any other church father) and through Augustine back to the teachings of Paul and the rest of Scripture.

Starting with John Calvin (1509-1564), we take a long leap forward into the nineteenth century. We are thus bypassing more than two centuries of Reformed orthodoxy as it took shape in Protestant scholastic theology. Accordingly, our focus falls next on the leader of the neo-Calvinist revival, Abraham Kuyper (1837-1920). Most important for our purposes is not his dogmatics but his biblically Reformed worldview, within which dogmatics finds its place. This Calvinian tradition in dogmatics proper has come to more lasting expression in the time-tested work of Kuyper's colleague, Herman Bavinck (1854-1921). He stands out as the seasoned systematic theologian of the neo-Calvinist movement around the turn of the century. In more recent times this tradition has been enriched by the works of Klaas Schilder (1890-1952) and Cornelius Van Til (1895-1987).

It was, however, the *Systematic Theology* of Louis Berkhof (1873-1957) which made the deepest and most lasting impact on the present-day Reformed community in North America. His dogmatics represents the tempered end product of a long-standing scholastic tradition in Reformed theology. Since the middle of this century, however, it has become increasingly apparent that this scholastic mold of theologizing is losing its appeal. The needed impetus for renewal came then from the extensive series "Studies in Dogmatics," which flowed from the pen of G. C. Berkouwer (1903-). Berkouwer's dynamic theology liberated many of us from the scholastic concepts which dominated the theology of Louis Berkhof. It reinvigorated dogmatics with the fresh winds of a more original Calvinist dogmatics and updated the thinking of Bavinck for our times. Berkouwer, however, leaves us with a long row of about twenty monographs, but not a comprehensive, well-rounded systematic theology.

That is roughly where we find ourselves today. With mixed feelings, gratitude interspersed with sympathetic criticism, we seek now to draw on this tradition. Calvin, Kuyper, Bavinck, Schilder, Van Til, Louis Berkhof, Berkouwer — of them the biblical admonition holds, "Honor your forebears." For they were all servants of the Lord to help us become better servants of the Lord, also in this theological enterprise called Reformed dogmatics.

Last but not least, this preliminary statement of rationale and purpose also calls for a comment on Christian philosophizing. The fruits of contemporary Christian philosophy, growing out of the biblical world-view, also play an important role in identifying the historical-theological tradition within which this renewal project in Reformed dogmatics is being launched, resulting in a "world-viewish theology" (Arthur Holmes, *Contours of a World View*, pp. 34-38). Seeking to do theology without a self-conscious philosophical orientation is an "impossible possibility": possible in the sense that some theologians (Karl Barth and others) may pretend to do so; but impossible in the sense that philosophical reflection can never be effectively excluded from dogmatics. Dogmatics is too important to be entrusted to theologians who are unclear about their philosophical orientation. Apart from philosophy, theology becomes a narrow, shallow, and largely vacuous undertaking. This renewal effort in Reformed dogmatics seeks to avoid that pitfall. Fortunately, there is a Christian philosophy to which we can appeal — the Philosophy of Law-Idea. Its roots lie in the work of D. H. T. Vollenhoven (1892-1978) and Herman Dooyeweerd (1894-1977) at the Free University in Amsterdam over the past half century. To them we owe the original definitive formulation of a cosmonomic philosophy. Their work is not, however, a closed system — as no philosophy or theology can ever be. It invites ongoing review by contemporary Christian thinkers. Yet its fundamental ideas and basic contours are sufficiently clear and firm to offer a very helpful context for doing theology within the Calvinist tradition today. The widespread influence of this philosophy in recent times is a further contributing factor to making the present an opportune time to attempt a restatement of Reformed dogmatics. For this Christian philosophy has much to offer to theologians and other Christian thinkers in opening up insights into the meaning, structure, and direction of our life in God's world. These objectives, says Andre Troost, "can be worked out with a certain assurance of justification only in the context of a theology that proceeds from a biblical worldview and is philosophically Reformed" — adding that "to date, as far as I know, there is no such theology" ("Circular of the International Conference of Institutions for Christian Higher Education," no. 18 [April 1980], p. 2).

I. 3. Capitalizing on Recent Biblical Studies

This project is based, moreover, on the thesis that fruitful interaction is possible between biblical and systematic studies within the larger field of theological scholarship. In the past, high and almost insuperable walls of separation have often been erected between them. This has led to serious breakdowns in communication between those engaged in these two branches of learning. Often they have gone their separate ways, each group defensively staking out its own field of inquiry, each laying claim to its own distinctive methodology, each holding its own exclusive conferences, each calling the academic respectability of the other into question. Often there has been a glaring lack of cooperation between dogmatics and biblical studies. Students often sense this tension most keenly.

In introducing his *Evangelical Faith* (1968-1974) as a work devoted to "doctrinal totality," Helmut Thielicke addresses these strained relationships within the ranks of theological scholarship. "In an age which publishes little more than collections of theological essays," he says, ". . . it might seem presumptuous to set forth here the first part of a complete dogmatic system." Though my totality picture differs markedly from his, my feelings about this "venture" are strangely akin to his as he sketches them anecdotally in the following scenario.

> Perhaps for the moment we are indeed in a position only to put individual stones in the mosaic, and I have every respect for theological colleagues whose important monographs help to do this so impressively. Yet I myself must make the venture of recapturing the total picture or at least of recalling it, of giving a reminder of its existence. I do not want to miss the woods for the trees. To those hard at work in the woods I will perhaps look like a passing hiker, possibly even a happy-go-lucky fellow who is looking around in all directions instead of concentrating on a particular growth (although this kind of journey can often be the most strenuous). I greet

them all with friendship, gratitude, and respect, even if they may view me with a certain indignation, and I am aware that the more or less passable trails are due to their labors. If these foresters and their associates, however, are kind enough to spare the forest rambler a few glances, they will perhaps notice that he has had to take note of their work, for otherwise he would not be here and would never have reached this part of the forest. The rambler is simply seeking in all modesty to give a first report on what is going on in this forest, on what he has seen in it, and on why he regards it, not as the aggregate of felled or stricken trees or trees standing alone, but rather as a vast and inviting forest. (Vol. I, pp. 16-17)

Dogmaticians tend to berate biblical theologians as eclectic thinkers engaging in fragmented scholarship, expending their energies on isolated bits and pieces of biblical data. Biblical scholars, in turn, tend to disdain dogmaticians as theological system-builders obsessed with grand designs and master plans of rational coherence. Each tends to discredit, if not the right of existence, then at least the legitimate reason for existence of the other. Bold pretenses to superiority emerge on both sides. Biblical scholarship often claims to represent theology in its purest form, at its most fundamental level, giving dogmatics the cold shoulder as ethereal speculation. Meanwhile systematic theology often unfurls its banner as the most erudite and finished product of the theological enterprise. Cornerstone or capstone — often that has become the "to be or not to be" question of theological irritation between these two disciplines.

The appropriate time to set aside this false dilemma is now. As within every science, so too within theology, there is a certain division of labors which coincides with certain natural lines of demarcation within the field as a whole. A certain differentiation of tasks is clearly discernible. Of both biblical theology and dogmatics, therefore, let it be said that each has its own identity and integrity. Each has its own object of study, its own organizing principles and methodologies. Both are, of course, called to be "biblical" in the sense of being true to the Bible. The fact that biblical theology works more directly with biblical givens is no assurance that it is therefore more true to Scripture than dogmatics, even though the latter may work more indirectly with biblical givens. Together they must bow before the authority of God's Word as the norm which holds for both disciplines. Both are theological responses to that abiding norm. Yet they are different in their areas of inquiry, in their tools of research, in the outcomes of their respective studies. These differences must be honored.

At the same time, there is an underlying unity between work in biblical and systematic theology. Differentiation of tasks may not be allowed to negate the basic religious unity which binds them together. They stand in coexisting and proexisting relationships to each other within the larger arena of theological scholarship. This project in dogmatics aims to draw heavily on this relationship of mutual interdependence. It seeks to bring biblical and systematic theology into a closer working relationship by incorporating more clearly and directly the fruits of biblical research into its dogmatic reflections. In fact, as a central organizing principle, I will lean heavily on the basic motifs of creation-fall-redemption-consummation as they are unfolded historically within the drama of biblical revelation.

The past several decades have witnessed very intensive, productive work in the area of biblical theology. Unfortunately, its results do not add up to an unmixed blessing. There is evidence aplenty of large-scale capitulation to historical-critical methods, evoking strong reaction along the lines of crassly biblicist ways of interpreting Scripture. There is, however, also a third way. A strong tradition of reformational hermeneutics stands as a real alternative to the controversial liberalist-fundamentalist polarity which for so long has forced itself on us as the dominant frame of reference for interpreting the Bible. In the wake of the recent resurgence of biblical studies in Reformed circles, new insights have been opened up. Old Hellenist, medieval, and scholastic patterns of listening to the Bible have been largely overcome. Stimulating ways of reading Scripture more meaningfully lie at our fingertips. The time is now ripe to integrate these findings into a renewed and updated Reformed dogmatics.

Let us take inventory briefly of some of these key biblical ideas:

- renewed appreciation of the creation order as the abiding framework for all ongoing revelation as it sheds its light on cosmic history;
- more dynamic understanding of man* as imager of God;
- mounting dissatisfaction with Hellenist anthropologies which divide human beings into sharp body/soul dichotomies, accompanied by the recovery of a more holist biblical view of man;
- deepened realization of the profound reality of man's fall into sin and its radical and sweeping effect on life as a whole;
- clearer insight into the interrelatedness of revelation in creation and redemption;
- better grasp of the unity of the Old and New Testaments, related as promise and fulfillment;
- more consistent development of the linear view of history which runs through biblical revelation;

---

* I use the word *man* here and in what follows as meaning "human being," whether male or female. When the word *man* is used in this generic sense, pronouns referring to *man* must also be understood as having this generic sense.

- growing recognition of the idea that the biblical message is anchored in redemption history, which, as unfolding acts in a drama, highlights the mighty acts of God, centered in Jesus Christ.
- rediscovery of the abiding relevance of Old Testament legislation for a renewed life-style in our times;
- more profound recognition of Israel as corporate personality reaching its fulfillment in Christ and his body, the church, the new Israel;
- rehabilitation of a literary analysis of biblical narratives, with greater openness to the priority and normativity of its literal sense and canonical meaning;
- eager assimilation of the contributions of archeology to a clearer reconstruction of the historical setting and cultural context of biblical revelation;
- grateful recognition of the work done in comparative language studies in shedding new light on the meaning of obscure concepts in the Scriptures;
- growing repudiation of the tendency to read Greek philosophical ideas into the New Testament, replaced by a greater appreciation of its Hebrew background.

In all these valuable insights, reemphasized by much of recent biblical scholarship, we can discern a golden thread weaving its way through the total fabric of biblical revelation, lending it a coherent perspective on life. Perhaps for Reformed dogmatics it can be captured most succinctly in the pervasive biblical teaching on covenant and kingdom. Covenant and kingdom are like two sides of a single coin. Accordingly, we may say that in creation God covenanted his kingdom into existence. After the fall, God renewed the covenant with a view toward the coming of his kingdom. The ultimate goal is the restoration of all creation in the renewed earth. Thus, the original covenant stands forever as the abiding foundation and norm for life in God's world. Similarly, in the beginning God created his kingdom — "the heavens and the earth," the realm over which he rules. Mankind, then, as servants of the King, rebelled; but God came back, renewing the kingdom in a proleptic way through Israel, and then reestablished it decisively with the coming of King Jesus. The kingdom, therefore, now stands as a settled reality securely anchored in God's past acts of salvation ("the kingdom is at hand"), as an abiding, present, coming reality (the redemptive "already" in Christ), and as an assured hope based on the promise of a future fully restored reality (the eschatological "not yet" on the way to its consummation). In this sense covenant and kingdom are two ways of viewing the one all-embracing reality of God's way with his world. Covenant is kingdom looking back to its original and abiding charter given with the

11

creation. Kingdom is covenant looking forward programmatically toward its promised goal of perfect renewal. Along the way this vision gives meaning and hope to our common call to covenant faithfulness and kingdom service.

This project, therefore, aims to make these biblical perspectives more serviceable in Reformed dogmatics. Structurally, this involves rearranging the themes of the traditional *loci* method of organizing systematic theology, ordering them instead along the lines of the biblical story line of creation-fall-and-redemption on the way to the final consummation of all things. Within the context of a Reformed worldview these central biblical motifs will be cross-referenced with a doctrine of the Trinity which views the Father as Initiator, the Son as Mediator, and the Holy Spirit as Enabler. These are the organizing principles I have chosen in shaping the basic contours of this systematic theology.

Chapter II

Prolegomena*— An Historical Survey: Philosophy and Theology as Partners?

II. 1. Thesis

At the very outset, let me state the thesis which will emerge from this prolegomenal survey. Built into this chapter with a kind of cumulative force is a conclusion concerning the relationship of theology to philosophy which stands as the central thesis toward which the following overview moves. The thesis is this: rightly understood, theology and philosophy form a partnership in the sense that the best prolegomena to Christian theology, more specifically to Reformed dogmatics, is a Christian philosophy. (Cf. Gordon J. Spykman, "Christian Philosophy as Prolegomena to Reformed Dogmatics," 'N Woord op sy Tyd, pp. 137-56.)

II. 2. Disconcerting Advice

Some issues, it seems, never really get settled. One would think that by now, with nearly two thousand years of Western Christian thought behind us, we could point to a rather solid consensus on the question of the relationship between theology and philosophy. This expectation turns out, however, to be little more than wishful thinking. For in reality one finds an enormous lack of unanimity. The many disparate views tend, however, to fall into certain basic patterns. Some thinkers devise ways

* In this section and those which follow the focus is on prolegomenal issues, literally "things to be said in advance," commonly called Introduction to Systematic Theology and described by Thielicke as "clearance work in a cluttered situation" (Evangelical Faith, Vol. I, p. 11).

13

to fuse philosophy and theology. Others merely tolerate the presence of philosophy as an unworthy intruder into the sacred courts of the "queen of the sciences." Others openly oppose philosophy as an adversary of the gospel. Others erect artificial, misleading barriers between these two branches of learning. Still others simply ignore the question.

During my student days I wondered from time to time about these connections. Both philosophy and theology were required disciplines in our prescribed program of studies. Both sought shelter under the common umbrella of Christian higher education. Yet as fellow guides on our academic pilgrimage they seemed to be elbowing each other rather vigorously at almost every significant turn along the way. How were we to integrate meaningfully the lectures in Room 32 (philosophy) with those in Room 35 (theology)? There was a good deal of talk, in those days already, about the integration of Christian faith and learning and about the unifying effect of a biblically Reformed world-and-life view. On this point, however, the trumpets issued uncertain sounds. There was little clarity, only an abundance of confusion.

Occasionally I would read a dash of Bavinck's theology. I was struck there by repeated references, seemingly at random, often within a single paragraph, to theologians like Schleiermacher and Harnack alongside of philosophers like Kant and Hegel. What was a fledgling scholar to make of such complexities?

Armed with such questions, with due respect, and, I suspect, with undue docility, I seized various opportunities to approach my professors, looking for help. The answers I received were strikingly uniform. Well, you see — so I was told — this is the way it is: theology deals with matters of faith, philosophy with matters of reason. But — so I thought — certainly some measure of rationality goes into theologizing too. Otherwise simply believing would be enough. Why then all these years of mental exertion in preparation for ministry in the church? Nor, certainly, can faith be absent from philosophy.

Again, in answer to my continued proddings, the answer came back: philosophy operates on the plane of general revelation, theology on the plane of special revelation. But this answer also failed to satisfy my curiosity. It seemed unthinkable that in Christian philosophizing the Bible should function as a closed book. Moreover, the philosophers did in fact work with the Scriptures. So, persisting in my inquiry, like a broken record, I heard another variation on the same tune: philosophy is concened with issues in the realm of common grace, theology in the realm of special grace. Shades of the long-standing medieval dilemma, I thought. Thomas Aquinas was still alive and well deep into the twentieth century, and he could claim disciples in Reformed as well as Roman Catholic circles.

14

These dualist answers simply did not help. They served only to create more problems. But my uneasiness with these strikingly similar answers was largely intuitive. For by virtue of deeply ingrained inclination and formative training this split-level mind-set was part and parcel of my own makeup. The spirit of the Secession* is not easy to shake off. Thus this haunting sense of dissatisfaction with the standard answers was not simply an academic problem which I could lay on the table and discuss with my teachers in a somewhat detached, dispassionate way. It also found its echo in my personal struggles to arrive at a deeper and fuller unifying perspective on life as a whole.

As I look back now, I see clearly that such dualist outlooks involve serious departures from the holist worldview and life-vision which is given with creation and illumined by biblical revelation. Such dichotomies (meaning literally "to cut in two") create false dilemmas for Christian scholarship. They betray a misconception of the nature of the antithesis — a confusing mixture of the structures of reality with the conflicting spiritual directions present in the world. They therefore trouble us needlessly with false antinomies so that, looking out on the world as it were with bifocal glasses, we always see things in bipolar tension (body and soul, realm of nature and realm of grace, daily bread and spiritual bread). We are in fact led to think that this is the way things really are. We then fail to realize that such bifocal glasses cause us to read into reality dualisms which actually are not there at all. Such misconstructions of the relationship between theology and philosophy are anchored in underlying dualist misconceptions of created reality itself. They result inevitably in the loss of biblical single-mindedness in Christian scholarship. For such dichotomies violate the integral unity which is woven into the richly variegated fabric of the creation order as well as the religiously whole sense of what being human means for our life in God's world.

II. 3. A Colossal Obstacle

According to Helmut Thielicke, "The present intellectual and spiritual situation is marked by a distinctive dualism" (*Evangelical Faith*, Vol. I, p. 11). This dualist problematic is not, however, a newcomer. It has been with us a long, long time. It is older than my instructors, older also than Thomas and his fellow medievalists, much older therefore also than its reembodiment in the similar mind-set of Protestant scholastic thought

* A nineteenth-century revival movement in Dutch Reformed circles, deeply affected by the typically modern dichotomy between rationality and morality.

during the modern period. It has in fact dogged Western Christianity at almost every step of its nearly two thousand-year history. Thinking in terms of two realms has posed the most "colossal obstacle" (Dietrich Bonhoeffer) to a "unified field of knowledge" (Francis Schaeffer) for Christian scholars in every generation. Critical reflection on our Christian past forces on us, almost incontrovertibly, the conclusion that nearly all our basic problems stem from false dilemmas occasioned by a wholly dubious "Christ/culture" (H. Richard Niebuhr) way of addressing the fundamental issues of a Christian worldview. Thus we get locked into the enduring problem of a dual normativity.

Consider Bonhoeffer's very incisive commentary on "thinking in terms of two spheres":

> Since the beginnings of Christian ethics after the times of the New Testament the main underlying conception in ethical thought, and the one which consciously or unconsciously has determined its whole course, has been the conception of a juxtaposition and conflict of two spheres, the one divine, holy, supernatural and Christian, and the other worldly, profane, natural and un-Christian. This view becomes dominant for the first time in the Middle Ages, and for the second time in the pseudo-Protestant thought of the period after the Reformation. . . . In the scholastic scheme of things the realm of the natural is made subordinate to the realm of grace; in the pseudo-Lutheran scheme the autonomy of the orders of this world is proclaimed in opposition to the law of Christ; and in the scheme of the Enthusiasts the congregation of the Elect takes up the struggle with a hostile world for the establishment of God's kingdom on earth. In all these schemes the cause of Christ becomes a partial and provincial matter within the limits of reality. . . . However great the importance which is attached to the reality in Christ, it still always remains a partial reality amid other realities. The division of the total reality into a sacred and a profane sphere, a Christian and a secular sphere, creates the possibility of existence in a single one of these spheres, a spiritual existence which has no part in secular existence, and a secular existence which can claim autonomy for itself and can exercise this right of autonomy in its dealings with the spiritual sphere. The monk and the nineteenth-century Protestant secularist typify these two possibilities. The whole of medieval history is centred upon the theme of the predominance of the spiritual sphere over the secular sphere, the predominance of the *regnum gratiae* over the *regnum naturae;* and the modern age is characterized by an ever increasing independence of the secular in its relations with the spiritual. So long as Christ and the world are conceived as two opposing and mutually repellent spheres, man will be left in the following dilemma: he abandons reality as a whole, and places himself in one or other of the two spheres. He seeks Christ without the world, or he

seeks the world without Christ. In either case he is deceiving himself. Or else he tries to stand in both spaces at once and thereby becomes the man of eternal conflict, the kind of man who emerged in the period after the reformation and who has repeatedly set himself up as representing the only form of Christian existence which is in accord with reality. (*Ethics*, pp. 196-97)*

II. 4. Charting the Course

To make good on this critical appraisal of dualist tendencies as they bear on questions of prolegomena, I invite you to a fast tour of some major epochs within the mainstream of Western Christianity. Obviously this cannot be a comprehensive survey of all the classic theologies and philosophies coming down from the past. Limitations of space and time, as well as competence, demand a more focused resumé. This rapid review, accordingly, takes the form of a spot-check. It will, however, be honest, I trust, to the facts at hand, convincing in its principle of selection, and broadly representative of the true course of events. It centers on the question of how Christian theologians have construed the relationship between their task and that of the philosophers.

To help keep our intent and purpose clearly in mind, here are the issues of primary concern: a) as already indicated, the relationship between philosophy and theology; b) paralleling that, the relationship of prolegomena to the rest of dogmatics; c) the recurring problem of casting these issues into the form of a nature/grace dualism; d) consequently, the dialectical tension which arises from such a dual (complementary and/or competing) normativity; and e) the effect of these patterns of thought on life in the Christian community.

II. 5. Second-Century Crisis

The roots of these stubbornly persistent issues are most clearly traceable to the second century. With the emergence of a fourth and fifth generation of Christians, we witness the dramatic transition from the original apostolic proclamation of the gospel to the earliest forms of Christian theol-

---

* Bonhoeffer's loose conception of "ethics" and his Christomonist understanding of "reality in Christ" are open to criticism — but that is not the point here. The point is his very candid and succinct indictment of dualist thinking and living.

ogizing. To understand the genius of this early Christian theology we must look at the kind of people engaged in it. The majority were not Christian thinkers of Jewish origin. They were Greco-Roman converts, younger Christians. Moreover, in contrast to medieval theologians who were mostly monks, and modern theologians who are mainly university professors, these early Christian theologians were largely pastors and bishops of local congregations and regional churches. Understandably, therefore, they produced basically a very practical theology, oriented strongly to the mission of the church in a hostile world and to the immediate crises of faith and life within the Christian community as it evolved from its Hebrew beginnings and moved increasingly outward into the Greco-Roman culture of the empire. Accordingly, the tracts of the early fathers were not only very catechetical and doctrinal but also pointedly apologetic and polemical. For the church and its theologians found themselves headed on a collision course with the prevailing spirits of those times, descendant from various schools of thought in Greek philosophy (Platonism, Aristotelianism, Stoicism, Epicureanism — the greatest threat being neo-Platonism, the wellspring of early Gnostic heresies).

Together with the eighteenth century, the second century stands out as perhaps the most decisive turning-point in charting the course of Western Christian theology. Its thinkers had to wrestle with such questions as these: How should one view the relationship between Christian theology and Greek philosophy, doing justice to the latter while preserving the integrity of the former? And how is one to negotiate the differences and bridge the gaps between the gospel and pagan ideology? The early fathers had little in the way of clear precedent on which to draw. There was no standing tradition to which they could appeal. They had only the witness of the Old Testament prophets and the New Testament evangelists and, growing out of this, the testimony of the first disciples and early martyrs as this took shape in their own living experience. Not surprisingly, therefore, they offered very diverse and often conflicting answers to the crucial question of the stance Christian theology should take over against Greek philosophy.

On its negative side, the most forcefully stated world-negating answer was formulated by Tertullian (150-225) in his well-known rhetorical question, "What has Jerusalem to do with Athens?" — to which the clearly implied response was "Nothing!" Separation, isolation, "get out from among them" — this was his answer. This withdrawal motif took shape in one wing of early Christianity. Recognition of the tremendously seductive powers of surrounding pagan cultures and the comparative weakness of the early church lent to this black-white solution a large measure of plausibility. Of course, it also brought with it clear-cut implications for the theology/philosophy issue. These are discernible by comparing this very negative stance in the later Tertullian, during the Montanist stage in his life, with the more accommodating references to Greco-Roman ideas in his earlier career. However attractive Tertullian's memorable position and whatever its long-range impact on Western Christianity, as embodied, for example, in the monastic movement, this was not the worldview which eventually won the day in Christian theology.

The outlook which ultimately triumphed was that developed by another branch of early Christian thinkers led by Justin Martyr (?-165), together with Clement (150-215) and Origen (185-253) of the Alexandrian school. This wing of early Christian theology advocated a more affirmative approach to Greek culture. Seeking accommodation, it developed a complementary model of the relationship between philosophy and theology. As reason is subservient to faith, it was argued, so Greek philosophy can serve as a preparatory stage in developing a Christian body of truth. Like the proverbial Trojan horse, Christian theology opened its gates to admit and make room for Greek philosophy to play a servant role in the formulation of Christian doctrine. Philosophers were enlisted as "handmaidens" to theologians. So complete was the presumed conquest of theology over philosophy, so fully did some Christians believe that they had assimilated into their own theological systems the "natural light" of pagan thinking, that in A.D. 529 the last remaining schools of Greek philosophy were closed.

Increasingly, however, the victor became the victim. The philosopher-servant became the master architect who reconstructed the house of Christian theology. Major Christian thinkers freely adopted Greek forms of thought to shape the content of the Christian faith. The dualist worldview so typical of Hellenist thought was embraced as the basic frame of reference for delineating the contours of Christian theology (note, for example, the antinomy in Augustine between the "City of God" and the "City of the World"). Such dualist-synthesist approaches reflect quite generally the theological models which emerged from the early era of Western Christianity. There was still a large measure of instability and fluidity in understanding the reciprocating relationship between theology and philosophy. The trend, however, was in the direction of viewing the latter as prolegomena to the former. Officially, Greek philosophy had been declared dead. In actuality, however, it was kept alive by the grace of Christian theology. Christian thinkers compromised their biblical distinctiveness by assimilating into their theological structures dualist religious motifs borrowed from the very Greek philosophy which had presumably been vanquished. Thus distortions appeared in Christian theology, in its fundamental starting points as well as in its overall format.

II. 6. Medieval Synthesis

For centuries this accommodation of alien viewpoints, burdened by an irresolvable inner dialect, was able to maintain itself only as an unstable synthesis. It continued to cry aloud for greater internal consistency. For methodologically dualist axioms refuse to yield unifying conclusions. So the search went on for a theory capable of forging a unified totality picture, one capable of incorporating the basic contributions of both Greek philosophy and Christian theology. This ongoing reflection took place, however, without critically reexamining the basic givens as inherited from the past.

In the thirteenth century the historical situation was finally ripe for a new initiative. Greek philosophy in the form of Aristotelian logic, which had managed to survive the "dark ages" largely through the work of Boethius (480-525), experienced a vigorous resurgence, thanks in part to Mohammedan scholarship. Earlier Christian thinkers had relied most heavily on the "vertical," hierarchical structures of Platonic thought. But now, drawing on the more "horizontal," cause-and-effect categories of Aristotelian thought, Thomas Aquinas (1225-1274) bequeathed to Western Christianity a masterful synthesis. While updating the ancient problematic, he at the same time projected his restatement of it down through the medieval, Reformation, and modern eras, and on into our times. Instead of the biblical teaching that grace renews and restores nature, Thomas, in continuity with many mainline early church fathers, held that grace complements and elevates nature. Thus the directional antithesis between judgment and redemption as taught in Scripture was turned once again into a structural antinomy between rival sectors of reality held together in bipolar tension. The end product was a split-level view of reality, with nature as a lower and grace as a higher order. Nature, despite sin, was viewed as still basically good; but grace was far better. Philosophy, accordingly, was viewed as belonging to the natural realm of reason, and theology to the supernatural realm of faith.

Clearly, however, the desired organic unity of perspective was still not achieved within the structures of the Thomist blueprint of reality. The inherited dualist dialectic was not relieved in any essential way. Thomism offers at best a functional unity embodied in the career of a philosopher/theologian like Thomas himself and in the convergence of both temporal and eternal qualities in the institutional church. As the two swords, the swords of earthly and heavenly authority, ultimately come to rest in a single magisterial hand, so also both the knowledge of natural things (philosophy) and of supernatural things (theology), each in its own way, come to be viewed as subordinate to the magisterial authority of the church. Within the arena of Christian scholarship, therefore, philosophy engages in theoretical reflection on natural things. Its norm is natural law. It operates by unaided human reason, which remains basically intact, unaffected by the fall into sin, leaving Thomism with the notion of an "incomplete fall" (Schaeffer). Appeal to revelation is not an essential trait of philosophy. It stakes its claim to credibility on universal laws of logic common to all rational men of goodwill. Thinking out the implications of the classic rational proofs for the existence of God enters significantly into such a pursuit of philosophy. Thus philosophy, in the form of a natural theology, serves as prolegomena to theology proper, which in turn is viewed as the theoretical contemplation of supernatural truths. Philosophical argumentation lays a rational basis for Christian faith. As such, it also carries with it an apologetic thrust — the rational defense, justification, and vindication of the positive theology which builds on it.

The Thomist worldview was designed to reconcile age-old tensions, including those between theology and philosophy. It did so by undertaking the magnificent yet futile task of seeking to distil a unified perspective on reality from a dualist starting point (nature/grace). The result was a pseudo-unity which yields little more than a comprehensive yet precarious synthesis of the very bipolar problematic with which it began, held together in a new tension-laden dialectic. The outcome was a no-win situation. Both theology and philosophy proved to be losers. For Thomism undercuts the very possibility of a truly Christian philosophy. Instead it inserts natural theology as a substructure underneath its theological superstructure. Thus it renders impossible an authentically biblical prolegomena. Theology itself also came out a loser. Spiritualized, it drifted off into the ethereal realms of the beatific vision. Thus it severed itself from meaningful contact with the down-to-earth life of God's people in his world.

II. 7. The Reformation: A New Departure

The Reformation marks a new beginning. Its original impetus proved, however, to be rather short-lived. Yet, while it lasted, it offered Western Christian theology its first decisively different approach to the issue at hand since the close of the apostolic era. As an historical point of departure in developing a new paradigm for doing Reformed dogmatics, we shall take up the story of John Calvin in Geneva during the decades straddling the middle of the sixteenth century.

Calvin belongs to the second generation of the Reformers. Despite his differences with Martin Luther (1483-1546), Calvin still regarded the

21

Wittenberg Reformer as his spiritual father. Basically they stand or fall together. Luther is thinkable apart from Calvin; but Calvin cannot be understood apart from Luther. As a feisty pioneer Reformer, Luther found little time for restful, undisturbed study. His was a colorfully stormy career. He was compelled to do theology on the run, opportunistically, addressing a flurry of critical issues as occasion demanded. Understandably, therefore, his theology is not a well-rounded whole but a power-packed complex of dialectically interrelated insights. Note, for example, his ideas on *Deus revelatus* and *Deus absconditus,* on law and gospel, on the kingdom of God and the kingdom of the world.

Calvin was able to carry on his labors under the more settled conditions which followed in the aftermath of Luther's ground-breaking achievements. His theology accordingly reflects a more self-conscious and deliberate methodology. It has a more comprehensive, architectonic wholeness to it. His final definitive edition of *The Institutes* in 1559, the seasoned end product of about a dozen earlier editions involving successive revisions, augmentations, and refinements on that original "little booklet" of 1536, encapsulates much of the best of Reformation theology.

In his work Calvin was reaching back over a thousand years of errant theology to recapture central ideas embedded in the theology of Augustine. He was at the same time drawing anew on the heart of Pauline teaching, and in it the meaning of biblical revelation as a whole. Thus the line of development in Christian theology which I intend to follow runs from the Scriptures through Augustine to Calvin, taking Calvin then as an historical starting point for the further development of a Reformed dogmatics.

Prior to the crisis of the sixteenth century, the medieval church had allowed various competing schools of theology (Augustinian, Thomist, Scotist, Nominalist) to develop rather freely. However, at the Council of Trent (1545-1563), the confessional voice of the Counter-Reformation, the situation called for a common front against the Reformers on the part of the mother church. Trent therefore felt compelled to adopt a stance inclusive enough to embrace the various Roman Catholic schools of thought, yet exclusive enough to pass judgment on the Reformers.

Calvin's theology represents a decisive departure from the prevailingly dualist patterns of these medieval and Trentine theologies. It therefore represents a breakaway toward a new evangelical future. On a number of points, however, Calvin fell short of a consistent follow-through in developing the full potentials of his rearticulated reformational doctrine. His theology is, therefore, not the last word. But it certainly is a promising first word. Its virtue lies in pointing out new directions for a more integrally coherent approach to reformational theologizing and philosophizing.

II. 8. Reaction

Before long, however, this new momentum ground to a halt. Seeds of renewal, sown in the original era of reformation, had germinated. Seedlings had sprung, offering promise of continued growth. The future appeared hopeful for a continuing process of inner reformation on the part of both philosophers and theologians. Soon, however, these seedlings were choked out before bearing their ripened fruit.

Two interrelated developments go a long way in accounting for these dashed hopes. On the one hand, reformational theology was thwarted by the strong reactionary spirit of the Roman Catholic Counter-Reformation movement. With it came the aggressive reassertion of traditional Thomist patterns of thought on the philosophy/theology question. On the other hand, the promising beginnings embedded in Calvin's thinking were frustrated before the sixteenth century had even run its full course by contrary influences within the reformational tradition itself on the part of theologians like Theodore Beza (1519-1605), Calvin's successor as rector of the Geneva Academy. To counteract the Counter-Reformation, a protestantized version of medieval scholasticism appeared on the scene. Thus the old dualisms were revived. In somewhat revised forms they were handed down through the seventeenth, eighteenth, and nineteenth centuries, and on into the twentieth century.

Let us turn now in sequence to the two sides of this reactionary movement.

II. 9. Counter-Reformation

In the wake of the Reformation movement the Roman Catholic Church converted itself increasingly into a beleaguered fortress. A siege mentality set in, not only in its continuing response to the Reformation but also in response to the secularizing, antiauthoritarian, revolutionary crisis situation which eventually come to a head within its own ranks in the nineteenth century. To offset the spirit of modern liberalist thought, Rome entrenched itself repeatedly behind the time-tested dogmas of the Thomist and Trentine tradition. In 1879 Thomas was canonized as the "angelic doctor," the patron saint of Roman Catholic centers of learning. During the twentieth century, in the face of a menacing modernism, in the face of historicist and existentialist ways of explaining the development of dogma, in the face of biblical criticism, in the face of renewal movements which threatened to shatter the monolithic image of the church, at first even in the face of the contemporary "New Theology" which eventually triumphed at Vatican II, the papacy repeatedly called its thinkers back to Thomas as a sure guide.

At the climactic center of this hold-the-line mentality stands the First Vatican Council, convened in 1869-1870. There, in unambiguous terms, the basic structure of the Thomist dualism-seeking-synthesis outlook was promulgated, backed by the full weight of papal authority. Note the following declarations.

The Twofold Order of Religious Knowledge:

The Catholic Church with one consent has also ever held and holds that there is a twofold order of knowledge, distinct both in principle and also in object; in principle, because our knowledge in the one is by natural reason, and in the other by divine faith: in object, because, besides those things which natural reason can attain, there are proposed to our belief mysteries hidden in God, which unless divinely revealed, cannot be known.

Reason and Faith Cannot Be Contradictory:

But although faith is above reason, there can never be any real discrepancy between faith and reason, since the same God who reveals mysteries and infuses faith has bestowed the light of reason on the human mind, and God cannot deny himself, nor can truth ever contradict truth. The false appearance of such a contradiction is mainly due, either to the dogmas of faith not having been understood and expounded according to the mind of the Church, or to the inventions of opinion having been taken for the verdicts of reason.

II. 10. Scholasticism Revisited

As we have seen, the dualist-dialectical synthesis of Thomas became dominant first in the medieval era. It became dominant again in the pseudo-Protestant thought of the early modern period in its reaction to the Counter-Reformation. As a result, much of the heritage regained in the sixteenth century was lost during subsequent centuries. Protestant theology came under heavy pressure from a resurgent Thomism. This was also true of theology as carried on in the Reformed wing. It, too, abandoned the newly rediscovered evangelical style of theologizing so characteristic of the work of Luther and Calvin. It opted instead to counteract the reactionary theology of Roman Catholicism with a reactionary theology of its own. As a result, instead of growth, stagnation set in. Even worse, Reformed thinkers reverted to pre-reformational ways

24

of doing theology arising out of Constantinian, Augustinian, and Thomist worldviews. Of these, the nearest at hand and most fully developed was Thomism. Thus, Protestant scholastic thinkers found themselves opposing the older Thomism with a newer Thomism of their own making. In effect, this meant pouring Protestant wine into Roman Catholic bottles. They relied on the overall dualist structures, together with the forms, categories, and concepts of medieval scholastic theology. This led to seemingly endless, spiritually exhausting rounds of running encounters which pit this latter-day scholasticism against an older version of the same. Both sides armed themselves with strikingly similar ammunition. Structurally the arguments and counterarguments were much alike, since both drew heavily on Aristotelian logic.

The results are not surprising. They have a clear ring of familiarity about them. Ancient dualist patterns of thought recur: the nature/grace scheme, the reason/faith dichotomy, the nature/supernature antinomy. Even the typically Lutheran law/gospel dialectic was often forced into this dualist mold. Accordingly, philosophy is consigned to a lower and theology to an upper level. Theology is enthroned as "queen of the sciences," with philosophy as her "handmaiden." Philosophy gets absorbed into natural theology, which is made subservient to theology proper, serving an undergirding purpose. Its task is to lay a rational foundation for Christian doctrine, to argue its plausibility on the basis of universal laws of logic, to verify its credibility, to offer a reasoned apologetic for Christian faith, and thus to articulate a prolegomena which can serve as the substructure on which the theological superstructure can rest.

This modern scholastic way of doing theology did not confine itself to one or another tradition within Protestantism. It emerged as a widely diffusive movement which exerted a pervasive influence on all major post-Reformation traditions. The Reformed tradition was no exception. Within it this dualist mind-set informed the way theologians and non-theologians alike thought and talked and wrote about general and special revelation, reason and faith, common and special grace, law and gospel, inner and outer covenant, body and soul, sometimes even in a dispensational way about Old and New Testament, certainly about philosophy and theology, and accordingly about the relationship of prolegomena to dogmatics as well as the relationship of apologetics to the rest of theology. Indeed, "the problems of dualism are our problems. They create a plague that still afflicts us. Dualism distorts our reading of the Scriptures and hampers our lines of obedience. But the most devastating effect of dualism is that it necessitates a double allegiance. It forces us to serve two masters" (Brian J. Walsh and J. Richard Middleton, *The Transforming Vision: Shaping a Christian World View*, p. 113).

II. 11. Full Circle

With this very sketchy overview, focused on the philosophy/theology issue, we have now come full circle. We are back to my student days. Against this historical background I now understand more clearly the questions I raised and the answers I received. But now it is also clear, I trust, that the answers given are really not solutions at all but only reinforcements of the problem, and why this is so.

II. 12. Radical Revolution

Before moving on toward the concluding thesis which emerges from this survey, we must step back a century or two into the era of the Enlightenment. Along with the second century, the eighteenth century stands out as perhaps the most decisive turning point in the unfolding drama of Western Christian theology. One can hardly conceive of a more radical religio-cultural revolution. With full force it exploded on the streets of Paris in the French Revolution of 1789. It was not, however, an overnight occurrence. Its roots are traceable to the humanist ideas of Renaissance thinkers in the fourteenth and fifteenth centuries. Its initial impact was held back for a time by the revival of historic Christianity in the Reformation. It regained its momentum, however, with the rise of Protestant scholasticism during the post-Reformation era with its strongly rationalist tendencies. In the Enlightenment, therefore, the humanism of the Renaissance and the rational orthodoxy of Protestant and Catholic thought reached their climactic expression. With gathering force a radical and sweeping shift in Christian thinking was taking place.

    This revolutionary shift can be illustrated by reference to Augustine and Calvin. Both held that true knowledge consists in knowing God and ourselves in an interrelated way (*Institutes*, I.1.1), a conviction they held in common with historic Christianity. Prior to the Enlightenment every major Western Christian tradition — whether Roman Catholic, Lutheran, Calvinist, Zwinglian, Anglican, or Anabaptist — recognized within this relationship the priority of knowing God. Divine self-revelation was accepted as the basic and unquestioned reality. Self-knowledge is secondary. The reality of God's Word is sure, firm, beyond doubt. Any room for uncertainty or insecurity must be sought on the side of human response.

    The Enlightenment, however, overturned this fundamental tenet of the Christian faith. Question marks were placed on God's side and exclamation marks on man's side. Increasingly the center of gravity in

26

theology drifted from <u>God to man</u>. The sovereignty of God made way for the pretended autonomy of man. Recall the raucous creed of the French Revolution: "No God, no master! Man the measure of all things." God was eclipsed. The greatness of man was celebrated. Theocentric thinking was pushed into the background, anthropocentric thinking into the foreground. Theology became a refined form of anthropology. Transcendent norms were pulled down into the world and into the historical process. The biblical idea of the kingdom of God was transposed into an ideology of human achievement. Increasingly theology concentrated its attention not on ontology (the creation order), but on epistemology (the possibilities of human knowledge). This in turn gave rise to the fascination, even obsession, of modern and contemporary theology with rational processes of interpretation. All significant theological issues were increasingly reduced to hermeneutic problems. One of the most important by-products of the Enlightenment movement was therefore a growing concern with history. This led to the steady awakening of the modern historical mind during the eighteenth and nineteenth centuries, and on into the twentieth century. Doors were opening wide to contemporary historicism. If earlier theologies (over)stressed "being," modern theologies began increasingly to (over)stress "becoming." The existential situation, evolutionary process, fluctuation, change, contingency, immanence — these were embraced as the accepted hermeneutic keys to unlock the meaning of life. Understandably, therefore, historical-critical methods became widely acclaimed as the proven way of bringing "the assured results of the scientific method" into theology.

II. 13. The Liberalist Dream

Concurrent with the emergence of historicism came the impact of Darwinism in all branches of study. It, too, reflects deep dependence on the rise of historical consciousness during the modern era. A remarkable convergence then takes place. Once the anthropocentric dogmatics of the Enlightenment and the historical mind of modern man get linked with Darwinian evolutionism, the result is modern liberalism. Its basic tenets are well known: the inherent goodness and perfectibility of mankind, a rational Christianity, a religion of "facts" rather than "faith," its notion of "the spark of the divine in us all," its identification of God with the ultimate outcome of human destiny, its cultural optimism based on the idea of "the kingdom of God in America in this generation" — and more of such (im)pious platitudes and superficial prattle. World War I came as a serious setback to such religious utopianism. But that was to be "the war to end all wars!" In Europe this spirit of the nineteenth century ended abruptly around 1914 when all these pretty dreams turned into nightmares in the gas-filled trenches of the Siegfried and Maginot lines. In North America such optimism dies harder. But in recent decades we find here, too, that these man-centered ideals born of a liberalist religious fantasy, like lovely castles in the sky, have come crashing down on us in a thousand irreparable pieces. The bubble has burst. This entire ill-fated scenario is unthinkable apart from the lasting influence of Enlightenment thinking.

Like all major theologies, classic liberalism worked within the framework of the long-accepted dialectical tension of a sacred/secular, faith/reason dualism. Its concern was to articulate the Christian faith in a way acceptable to the modern mind. Liberals sought thus to retain a certain aura of respect for the sacred dimension in life, a time and place for holiness and piety, an "upper room" for spiritual experiences. The sacred and the secular were allowed to coexist, be it in uneasy tension. The emphasis fell, however, on some form of this-worldly secularity, while still trying to preserve room for the sacred.

The sworn enemy of liberalism was fundamentalism. Structurally, however, it, too, shared the prevailing commitment of modernity to dualist thought patterns. Only it struck out in a very different direction. It could not repudiate completely the secular, the needs of the body, and some involvement in the life of the world. But it viewed such entanglements as necessary evils, concessions made with a guilty conscience. For at heart it was otherworldly. It concentrated on sacred things, spiritual retreats, and mountaintop experiences.

Whatever their differences, and however furious the raging controversy between them, both liberalist and fundamentalist theologies were developed from within the jointly accepted framework of a sacred/secular dichotomy. With this common starting point, they then moved out in opposite directions. They are, nevertheless, but variations on the same dualist tune. Very strange bedfellows indeed, but bedfellows nonetheless.

II. 14. Monism: the End of Dualism

A further stage in the development of Enlightenment theology is now being enacted before our eyes in the monist theologies which have become dominant since around the middle of this century. Perhaps we are witnessing a final act in this unfolding drama. For the next move, if carried out consistently, would appear to signal the very destruction of theology itself, at least if theology is thought of as involving meaningful reference to God or revelation. For the idea of the otherness of God and of revelation as a normative Word from beyond our world of experience is steadily being crowded out to make more room for immanentist theologies.

In the monist theologies of the past few decades the plot thickens. Liberalism was a compromise, a halfway house between the "sacred" and the "secular." Monist theologies show determined signs of going all the way with the downward drift generated by the Enlightenment. One highly publicized expression of this was, of course, the "God is dead" theology. Its heyday was short-lived. Its long-term significance, however, lies in the trend which it signals. For presently emerging secular theologies are prepared not simply to abandon the upstairs (the "sacred") while letting it stand, but to dismantle it thoroughly and take up permanent residence in the downstairs (the "secular"). Or better: they wish to collapse the upstairs into the downstairs. We are no longer to think of the divine as being "up there" or "out there," but as being "in here" (J. A. T. Robinson). He is the "Ground of Being" (Paul Tillich) — of all being and therefore also of man's way of being human. God no longer dwells in the "heights"; he is the "depth dimension" of our own life. He is assimilated with us into the historical process, a participant in our open-ended venture into the future. In the various forms of process theology, secular theology, or monist theology — by whatever name — the movement of thought is not *von oben* (from above) but *von unten* (from below). The revolutionary thrust of the Enlightenment movement is well on the way to running its full course. Ancient dualisms have devolved into modern monisms. Secularist movements seek to erase the Creator-creature distinction itself, absorbing the former into the latter as factors in an impersonal process. "Man is then not God's partner, but only his product, . . . [for] then the possibility of facing each other in a personal relationship is excluded" (Hendrikus Berkhof, *Christian Faith*, p. 153).

II. 15. Maker of the Modern Mind

The great mastermind of the Enlightenment was Immanuel Kant (1724-1804). His synthesis was as formative for the modern period as that of Thomas for the medieval era. In him nearly all subsequent philosophy and theology take their point of departure. All of us walk in his shadow. In his *Critique of Pure Reason* Kant forged a synthesis between the idealist and the empiricist traditions. In his *Critique of Practical Reason* he set out to salvage a place for religion conceived of as morality. This dual critique exposes the basic thought structures of the worldview which has shaped the modern mind. Pure reason is conceived of as the realm of hard facts, the phenomena, the empirical data of sense perception, of reasoned theorizing bound by the ironclad laws of logic and the scientific method. Beyond it lies the realm of noumenal ideas, of religion, ethics, morality, and value judgments. Here we experience God, freedom, and immortality. Such religious ideas are, however, no more than the postulates of autonomous human reason which commend themselves to us as moral imperatives. They have only an "as if" status — we must act as if their validity were firmly established. For the total meaning of life is dependent on human rationality, as Kant explains in his *Religion within the Bounds of Reason Alone*. Within this universal frame of reference the long-standing and persistent dualist scheme emerges anew as the fundamental internal structuring principle for dealing with life. It is merely given a new twist: Kant recasts the nature/grace dualism into the science/morality, fact/value, or nature/freedom dichotomy. Science deals rationally with the firm facts of reality. Theology belongs to the religious domain where men contemplate sacred things, act morally, and make value judgments. Theology, therefore, can no longer be regarded as a science. Perhaps at best it is an "art." In the realm of science "what is" is all that matters; in morality only the "why" and the "whereunto" count. The sciences, including philosophy, deal with hard facts in a value-free way. Theology, on the other hand, has no firm factual basis nor a rational method, but is limited to making moral value judgments. It operates not by (pure) reason, but by moral intuition. Thus in one fell swoop Kant, while drawing on more than a millennium of Western Christian theology, radically overthrew it. He exploded the idea of natural theology, of philosophy providing a rational foundation for theology, of faith supported by reason, and of reasoned prolegomena as introduction to dogmatics. In the process Kant swept aside and thoroughly discredited the classic rational proofs for the existence of God as philosophical underpinnings for Christian theology.

Thus traditional theology came to be divorced from all other branches of scholarship, including philosophy. It was left to stand alone as a house without foundations. Underneath were only the shifting sands of reason sublimated into moral ideals.

II. 16. Father of Modern Theology

With Kant as grandfather of the modern mind, Daniel Schleiermacher (1768-1834) then follows as the undisputed father of modern theology. His great achievement lies in this, that he adapted Kant's philosophical vision to theology. It is no exaggeration to say that "the entire nineteenth century belongs to Schleiermacher" (Karl Barth). After Kant, modern theology was destined never to be the same again. He had demolished the long-standing rational arguments on which theology had traditionally rested its case. How then could theology still be rescued? That was the Herculean challenge to which Schleiermacher addressed himself. What new substructure could be laid as a prolegomenal base of support for a systematic exposition of the Christian faith?

Schleiermacher attacked this problem by accepting the Kantian conclusion that the objects of religious belief have no "objective" status. They are postulates of the human mind. Christian doctrine must therefore rest on some "subjective" basis. The idea of *Gefühl* ("feeling") filled this need. It became the hermeneutic key to doing theology — "feeling" in the sense of "pious self-consciousness," finite man's "feeling of absolute dependence" on Another who is infinite. According to Schleiermacher, this deep-seated religious intuition is a universal phenomenon. All men participate in a common quest after God, to which each community bequeaths its own unique spiritual experiences. Christianity, however, represents the highest stage in the development of mankind's ethical aspirations. As such it merits the allegiance of all rational moral people. Accordingly, he interpreted the Old Testament as the record of Israel's communion with Yahweh, and the New Testament as eulogies on Jesus by his earliest disciples. Along these lines Schleiermacher developed a reconstructed apology for Christianity as reflected in his well-known fervent appeal to the people of his age, his *On Religion: Discourse to Its Cultured Despisers.*

Schleiermacher believed that he had offered new grounds on which to construct a Christian theology. His approach was, however, just as man-centered and subjectivist as Kant's. True to Kant, however, Schleiermacher refused to justify it on the basis of rational argumentation. He appealed rather to the phenomena of religious experience. The result was Christian faith rooted in finely attuned spiritual feeling. The task of theology is to offer a systematic exposition of this universal *Gefühl.* Its base of support is the scientific study of the phenomena of human religions, which serves then as the prolegomena for a study of the Christian religion.

II. 17. Twentieth-Century "Church Father"

Against this background it is not difficult to understand why around 1920 the newly emergent theology of Karl Barth (1886-1968) fell like a bomb into the playground of the theologians. Barth was educated for the ministry at the feet of some of the best exponents of Schleiermacher's nineteenth-century liberalist theology. Committed to it, he began his preaching career in 1911 in the small town of Safenwil in his native Switzerland. During the agonizing years of World War I, however, he came to realize the spiritual bankruptcy of classic liberalism. His haunting problem was the weekly sermon. During the crisis years of 1914-1917 Barth discovered the impotency of liberalism to proclaim a meaningful message to a world in deep trouble. Desperately he searched for a new way to go. Out of these spiritual struggles came his earliest publications, his *Römerbrief* (1919, 1921; English translation *Epistle to the Romans,* 1950) and his *Theology of the Word of God* (1922). A world in need responded quickly to this new direction in theology. Barth's explanation of this "breakthrough" was self-effacingly simple: "Climbing the steep stairs of the church tower during a storm, my feet slipped. Stumbling, my flailing arms reached out for some support to break my fall. Suddenly I caught hold of the belfry rope. Hanging on for dear life, the bell began tolling, and it kept on ringing until people came running to see what was going on."

This anecdotal explanation reflects a certain post–World War I state of readiness for a new theological initiative. It also helps account for Barth's sustained efforts in bringing about a reversal in theology. As an alternative to both Thomism and liberalism he appealed to the ideas of the Reformation, seeking to update them for our times by offering what he regarded as a twentieth-century reinterpretation of Calvin's theology. Moving out from there, Barth unleashed on the world a veritable avalanche of theological literature. The capstone is his voluminous *Church Dogmatics.* As with every great thinker, it seems, so here, it is possible to speak of the earlier and later Barth. Taken as a whole, however, his theology is variously called "crisis theology," "dialectical theology," "neoorthodox theology," even "neo-modernist theology" (Cornelius Van Til). Under whatever label, Barth's prolific work stands as a frontal assault on both the medieval scholastic and the modern liberal traditions. Structurally Barth held that both are guilty of the same heresy. Both accept some form of philosophical base for Christian doctrine — whether that be reason or feeling. Both are alike unacceptable. For both assume that there is in the world of historical reality and human experience some sort of continuous hierarchy of being *(analogia entis)* extending from man to God which offers a point of contact for the Christian faith. Their common error, Barth holds, lies therefore in their false notion of the possibility of providing some sort of prolegomena as a substructure for Christian dogmatics. At bottom, both mistakenly embrace some notion of a natural or general revelation. On this ground, then, a natural theology is constructed as the underpinning for theology proper. With this traditional line of reasoning Barth intends to make a clean break. He therefore rejects out of hand any kind of positive role for philosophy in carrying out our theological calling. For the very nature of philosophy militates against an authentic Christian theology. It is in essence antagonistic to Christian theology. The very idea of a Christian philosophy is a contradiction in terms. (In passing, the question may well be asked whether Barth is not actually more deeply indebted to philosophy, particularly to existential philosophy in the line of Kierkegaard, than he would be willing to admit. Is theology ever possible apart from philosophical reflection?)

Barth, then, repudiates the subsumptions of both scholasticism and liberalism, and does so on basic methodological grounds. In their prolegomena, he holds, the former presupposes a rational basis for Christian faith, the latter an experiential base. Both arise out of human subjectivity. Both violate the otherness of God, revelation, and faith. Both seek to blaze a trail from man to God. Both are rooted in human potentiality. Both pursue theology *von unten.*

In his attempt to turn the tide Barth made a radical switch to the "other side." Rejecting all immanentist approaches to theology, he allows the full emphasis to fall on the absolute transcendence of God. God is the "wholly Other." If past theologies had tended to pull the norm down into man and his world, Barth was determined to locate the norm over and beyond man in God alone. Within the framework of the long-standing two-factor God/man problematic, which Barth appears to accept, it now seems that, just as other modern theologies overloaded the human circuit, Barth's theology overloads the divine circuit. Either way, the biblical message gets short-circuited and we end up blowing our theological fuses.

Instead of doing theology *von unten,* Barth insists on doing it *von oben.* This radical reversal in methodology with respect to the direction and movement of theological thought helps to account for Barth's major role in drafting the Barmen Declaration (1934). "German Christians" living under Hitler's Third Reich were, in Barth's view, succumbing to the temptation of striking up a coalition between the Christian faith and the religion of national socialism. But true faith, he insisted, is one thing, human religion another. Never can the two be merged. That which is from above cannot be embodied in that which is from below — the more so, as in this case, when dealing with a modern form of paganism. Barth's resolute stand on this issue resulted in banishment from Germany back to his native Switzerland.

In Christian dogmatics, according to Barth, the flow of thought must be exclusively *von oben.* It must be completely open to that which is beyond. It must start with God and his revelation in Jesus Christ. It must rest on its own ground, not some alien basis, such as a rational philosophy, natural theology, or an experiential apologetic. Christian faith must start with itself. There is no prolegomena to Christian dogmatics. It must rather honor the ancient adages, *credimus ut intelligamus* ("we believe in order that we may know" — Augustine) and *fides quaerens intellectum* ("faith seeking understanding" — Anselm). All pre-theological groundwork is therefore contraband. Prolegomena cannot consist of a word *vorauf* ("beforehand"). At best it is a word *zuerst* ("to start with"). Rejecting all rational apologetics, natural theology, religious phenomena, experiential reflection, philosophical groundwork, or any other kind of introductory approach to theology, Christian dogmatics, according to Barth, must stand on its own feet, be true to itself alone, and begin with its own starting points.

This radically new departure also helps to account for Barth's bitter controversy with his early colleague, Emil Brunner (1889-1966), which led to their prolonged estrangement. The conflict between "the elephant" and "the whale" — descriptions of these two giant figures in contemporary theology — centered precisely on these issues. Barth had earlier commended Brunner as "the first man [in 1924] writing against Schleiermacher whose premises were really different, really free of him," adding the critical comment "(even if they were perhaps only relatively free of him!)." But by the 1930s these two great theologians became enmeshed in a bitter conflict and, as a result, parted ways for over three decades.

Both Barth and Brunner agreed that theology must grant divine initiative the priority in Christian doctrine. For Barth, however, this divine sovereignty was absolute and exclusive; for Brunner it was relatively so. Brunner's theology allowed for some recognition of human creatureliness in our responses to general revelation as a ground for our receptivity of saving revelation. He advanced his eristic apologetics as a form of pro-legomena to dogmatics. Accordingly, he argued that man is able at least to ask the questions to which revelation offers the answers. To Barth this appeared to be opening the door once again to natural theology as a basis for Christian dogmatics. It meant returning to the "fleshpots of Egypt" (traditional theology) after crossing over into "the promised land" (neoorthodox theology). To change the analogy, both agreed that "the lightning bolt" of divine revelation descends directly and decisively from the other side, charged with a radical verticality. Brunner held, however, that on our side there are "lightning rods" to receive the divine message. Barth's rejoinder was, as it were, that the lightning carries with it its own rods. There is no point of contact on our side. We must expect everything from God. He creates his own arena of confrontation and encounter. This divine "breakthrough" must ever remain the one and only starting point for Christian theology. No prolegomena can precede it. If prolegomena is to be given a place within theology at all, it must be nothing more than theology's first words about itself.

Barth's approach represents a needed corrective on traditional theologies which called on rationalist and experientialist types of prolegomena to serve a preliminary function in laying the foundations for Christian dogmatics. It was a healthy reaction. But a reaction is seldom an authentic or decisive resolution. Barth sensed rightly that the traditional relationship between philosophy and theology, between prolegomena and dogmatics, harbored a disjunction between the two which made general revelation an independent source of knowledge and thus led to natural theology. At the same time it failed to do justice to the full reality of special revelation. Barth's reactionary corrective is itself, however, equally unacceptable. To clear the decks of the old problematics he swept overboard the historic Christian doctrine of general revelation. And, as consistency demanded, Scripture was also reduced from its traditional status as special revelation ("a paper pope," Barth called it) to the role of primary witness to revelation. For revelation itself is, by definition, only and always a personal act of the self-disclosing God. This was realized exclusively and fully in Jesus Christ. Thus Barth arrived at his Christomonism.

Reformed theology must be sensitive to the healthy correctives in Barth's dogmatics. It need not, however, follow him in repudiating every form of prolegomena. It can learn from Barth and yet go a better way, if it is willing to recognize that prolegomena is a completely integral part of theology as a whole, that faith is the common starting point for prolegomena as well as dogmatics, that creational revelation does not imply natural theology, and that the long-standing nature/grace and reason/faith dichotomies are not normative for defining the relationship between prolegomena and dogmatics.

A final point: Barth rejects traditional dichotomies between prolegomena and dogmatics without rejecting the basic antinomies which undergird them. This is evident from the fundamental structure of his theology as a whole. The way he holds eternity and time, superhistory and ordinary history, together in dialectical tension is reminiscent of older grace/nature schemes. In Barth, however, despite his protestations to the contrary, the relationship between these antinomies is colored by the influence of earlier voluntarist (William of Occam) and later existentialist (Kierkegaard) philosophical thought. Therefore his formulation of this nagging problematic is more dynamic and action-packed, less rigid and predictable than the static form it usually took in earlier theologies. Momentary flashes of sudden, uncontrollable intervention from beyond into our otherwise ordinary way of life create an overlay of grace in the form of sporadic divine-human encounters within this natural world, both judging and justifying it, but without basically altering its spiritual direction or renewing it. Thus, despite his radical critique of earlier dualist patterns of thought, Barth was unable to escape the trap into which the others had also fallen. Like the others, he took up residence in the same old split-level house, only he made some major adjustments within it, drastically rearranging the furniture and altering its flow of traffic.

II. 18. Transition Figure

Dietrich Bonhoeffer (1906-1945) is a crucial transition figure in the movement which was launched in the Enlightenment and which is now being realized increasingly in our times — the movement from the older dualisms to newer monisms. Despite the urgings of evangelical Christians in America in 1939 to accept their hospitality, and thus to avoid the impending outbreak of war in Europe and to pursue his theology at a safe distance in the New World, Bonhoeffer was conscience-bound to return to Germany. Inner peace returned only after he boarded the boat back to Germany. There he joined the resistance movement. He became an active participant in the underground movement, a clandestine seminary, and the plot on Hitler's life, for which he finally suffered a martyr's death.

As an early disciple of Barth, Bonhoeffer discovered that his teacher's theology paralyzed Christian efforts at renewing culture. Barth's concept of grace merely cuts through or bounces off nature, but does not redirect or transform it in obedience to God. It calls Christians to pray for change and witness against evil, but it offers no incentive for Christian societal action aimed at restoring the public order to greater conformity to the will of God. Barth's "wholly other" God never really becomes an active partner in a strategized program of reformation. Bonhoeffer also discovered that his background in Lutheran pietism (gospel for the church, law for the world) failed him on this score. It led to withdrawal into the worshipful atmosphere of the sanctuary with no carryover power into the existential struggles which the confessing church of Germany faced at that time. This is "cheap grace."

Traditional grace-against-nature and grace-above-nature schemes proved impotent. The power of divine grace, Bonhoeffer concluded, must be experienced precisely in, under, and with the down-to-earth life of mankind in bread-and-butter terms at the very crossroads of secular affairs. He therefore called for a "worldly Christianity." He spoke of "God in the midst" and "Christ at the center" of reality. In Christ God entered the world and allowed himself to be fastened to a cross. It is precisely by this self-sacrificing powerlessness of God that he sets out to conquer mankind. Christ is the Man for others. In him God loses himself in the world. "Before God, and with God, we live without God" (*Letters and Papers from Prison*, p. 360). In seeking to liberate himself from the paralyzing stranglehold of the old nature/grace schemes, in effect — we are limited here to educated guesses, since his premature death left Bonhoeffer's theology in an unfinished state, allowing for a variety of conflicting interpretations of and contradictory appeals to his work — Bonhoeffer collapses grace into nature and with it, apparently, opens the door to the possibility of collapsing transcendence into temporal reality. Thus his theology, quite unintentionally, it seems, lends impetus to the rise of the various monist and process theologies which have arisen in the decades since World War II.

II. 19. Resumé

Through all the varied acts in this moving historical-theological drama, which we have allowed to pass in hurried review, a single rather sharply focused cluster of themes keeps repeating itself, namely, the issue of philosophy/theology, reason/faith, prolegomena/dogmatics, nature/grace, natural theology/theology proper. With it the urgent question confronts us of choosing between a single and a dual normativity. In conclusion, let us now look at the impact of this problem on our current ways of doing Reformed theology in the service of the Christian community.

II. 20. Closer to Home

Around the turn of this century a dispute arose between the Princeton school of apologetics and the theology of Kuyper and Bavinck at the Free University in Amsterdam. At stake was once again the question of the relationship of reason and faith, and with it the role of prolegomena in theology. The Princeton position represents a form of rationalism; the Amsterdam position has been called fideism. According to the former, as expressed by Benjamin B. Warfield (1851-1921), apologetics constitutes the very essence of prolegomena. Its task is foundational to that of dogmatics. By means of "objective" rational reflection, appealing to universally valid laws of logic, and suspending one's faith commitments or at least holding them in abeyance momentarily for the sake of argument, the Reformed theologian as apologist in his prolegomenal work must establish beforehand the basic tenets of the systematic theology which follows. This burden of proof holds for such doctrinal questions as the reality of God, of revelation, and of man as respondent to the Word of God.

In explaining the Amsterdam position, Kuyper criticized the Princeton apologetics as one more example of natural theology rooted in a false conception of natural reason. It minimizes the radical effects of the fall and fails to do full justice to the renewing power of God's work of redemption in Christ. It overlooks the spiritual line of demarcation which the Bible draws between faith and unbelief, between man's fallen and regenerate state. Thus it erases or at least blurs the antithesis between "two kinds of people" and accordingly between "two kinds of science." On Kuyper's view prolegomena, like all theology, can proceed from no other starting point than faith alone. Rather than viewing a reasoned apologetics as the foundation for the total structure of theology, he assigned it to one of the side rooms in the house of theology. It is a spin-off of theology proper, subservient to the task of theology as a whole. It is a focused and specialized explication of Christian theology in confrontation with its critics. Warfield countered that if apologetics is thus reduced to a mere appendage to systematic theology, then, after the positive exposition of Reformed doctrine is completed, the question might well arise whether, perchance, all these teachings are after all mere "fancy" rather than firm "fact."

It is clear that here, too, we are confronted with profoundly different approaches to theology. The differences here are basically the same as those we encountered throughout the two thousand-year history of Christian theology. Only in this case they come to expression within the mainstream of Calvinian thought, setting Dutch Reformed and Scotch Presbyterian traditions against each other. Much more is involved than the question of where to locate apologetics — before or after or within the main body of Reformed dogmatics. At bottom the dispute touches directly on the very nature of prolegomena.

In this renewal project in Reformed dogmatics I shall proceed on the working assumption of the basic rightness of the Kuyperian perspective on this issue. Accordingly, prolegomena is indeed introductory, but not in the sense that one can pass through it and then leave it behind. It is not a rationally argued substructure undergirding a faith-qualified theological superstructure. Its task is not to justify dogmatics from the outside, but to initiate an explanation of it from within one's own tradition. Prolegomena is therefore integral to the rest of dogmatics in taking a believing response to God's Word as its ongoing starting point. It, too, is rooted in a biblical worldview. Worked out more theoretically,

38

such a worldview takes on shape and form in a Christian philosophy. Theology calls for such a theoretical frame of reference, and it is precisely the task of a Christian philosophy to offer such a totality picture. As we move along, therefore, I shall delineate the basic contours of such a Christian philosophy as the theoretical doorway into and perspectival context for doing Reformed dogmatics. In this sense it is foundational. Christian philosophy serves to clarify the underlying presuppositions of dogmatics, its accepted paradigm of created reality, its theological method and hermeneutic, its normative reference points, and its basic concepts. This, I submit, is the most authentic, positive, and useful service which a prolegomena can render.

Chapter III

Contemporary Dilemmas

III. 1. First Things/Last Things

Show me your prolegomena, and I will predict the rest of your theology. This is a defensible thesis, assuming, of course, a reasonable measure of consistency. So close is the connection between "first things" and "last things." This helps to account for the renewed attention currently being devoted to prolegomenal issues in their far-reaching significance. The realization is growing that fundamental starting points are enormously important in determining the entire shape of dogmatics. If protology runs amuck, then ultimately eschatology will suffer too, and every doctrine in between as well.

In Reformed dogmatics, therefore, "first things" must be given high priority. Accordingly, "the first word" (protology), "the things which must be said first" (prolegomena), must be anchored in God's "first Word" for the world given with creation. Detaching prolegomena from its creational base means that redemption, as the restoration of the fallen creation, is left hanging in thin air. Then the promised consummation of all things in a renewed world gets reduced to an idealized, vacuous goal, which beckons us onward toward a future as nebulous as the sentimentalized versions of a "sweet bye-and-bye" located "beyond the blue horizon" on some "beautiful isle of somewhere." If the biblical foundations of the creation order are allowed to crumble, then sooner or later the whole house of Reformed dogmatics will collapse like a deck of cards.

40

III. 2. Dual Normativity

The historical-theological overview sketched in the preceding chapter demonstrates the tight stranglehold that two-factor ways of thinking (God and man, with nothing in between) have held on most theologies in the Western Christian tradition. This stubbornly persistent outlook continues to plague us down to the present time. At bottom it raises the question of normativity: Where are we to locate the norm for doing theology? In God and/or in man? In the realm of grace and/or in the realm of nature? In the "sacred" and/or in the "secular"? In its origins this problem is traceable to Greek philosophical influences on early church fathers in the second century. We shall deal with it now in its more contemporary forms.

III. 3. Godless World, Worldless God

It is Kant's definition of the age-old problem which controls most of modern thought. Few theologians have succeeded in extricating themselves from his dilemma as set forth in his *Conflict of the Faculties*. He states his case something like this: there are but two universes of rational discourse, that of pure reason (science) and that of practical reason (religion understood as morality). God, and theology as a study of the things of God, must therefore belong to the one realm or the other. If God is thought of as belonging to the world of verifiable factuality, then he is not the God of Christian faith. For, as Spirit, he is not subject to empirical research. If, on the other hand, we conceive of God as existing outside this world of scientific reality, then too, quite obviously, he cannot be the object of theoretical reflection. He belongs to the realm of noumenal things. This is the quandary of modern theology.

Kant opts clearly for the second horn of this dilemma. Accordingly God is viewed as an ethical postulate of reasoning man, as the point of reference for moral values. Since his existence is "supernatural" he has no place in the natural, rational order. The world is, therefore, Godless, and God is worldless. In this way Kant seeks to salvage a place for religion. God, faith, Scripture, theology, and the like all have only a hypothetical status. They are not rationally demonstrable, since they lie outside the realm of sense perception and therefore of scientific verification. They enjoy only an "as if" status: we must act "as if" the objects of religious-theological reflection were rationally ascertained, and therefore "as if" the related moral imperatives have the binding force of divine sanction.

41

Thus, both theology in general and dogmatics in particular are sublimated into an ethereal realm beyond secularity. Thus also, prolegomena, understood traditionally as a purely reasoned avenue of approach to dogmatics proper, is rendered untenable. For, on Kant's view, there is only a "practical" route which leads from the phenomenal world to God, from science to theology. Kant's dualist restatement of the traditional philosophy/theology, prolegomena/dogmatics problem remains the formative backdrop for all modern theologizing.

III. 4. Accommodation

The modern period in theology has witnessed many ingenious variations on this Kantian dilemma. Few theologians, however, were able to break with this basic pattern and launch a radically new departure. Granting its subsumptions, the viable ways of relating the two halves of Kant's theoretical world are really quite limited. The following possible models come to mind.

First, there is *accommodation*. The most prevalent approach was to revise the Kantian paradigm in an attempt to make it more acceptable to Christian sensitivities. Seeking to bridge the gap between Kant's hard view of science and his soft view of religion, theologians sought to forge a firmer place for belief in God, for a reasoned prolegomena, and for dogmatics proper. This method is epitomized in Schleiermacher and his disciples. Basically they were trying to clear a path from the world to God. They accepted Kant's discontinuity between these two universes of discourse. At the same time they developed a variety of arguments to recover a certain continuity. Traditional Roman Catholic theology appeals to the *analogia entis* in support of this upward movement. Most modern theologians, however, rejected the ontology implied in this approach. Instead, they resorted to more existentialist methodologies developed by such disciplines as philosophy of religion, cultural anthropology, historical criticism, phenomenology, and positivist science. Almost without exception these approaches have resulted in very tenuous balancing acts, with little consensus among their adherents. Not surprisingly, therefore, some accommodationists faithfully follow the dualist line in Kant. Others exploit the monist potentials in his thought system. Still others resort to a combination of the two, tending toward synthesis, either in the form of a complementary or a dialectical relationship between science and religion.

III. 5. Confrontation

A second major model is that of *confrontation*. Its chief exponents are Barth, Brunner, and other representatives of neoorthodox theology. Despite Barth's repeated disavowal of philosophy, his theology, too, betrays the strong background influence of Kantian thought patterns, filtered through the categories of existential philosophy. For the two-factor perspective lies close to the heart of his dogmatics too. Only he travels a route diametrically opposed to that of Schleiermacher. Instead of building bridges from man to God, as in Schleiermacher, Barth posits an infinite unbridgeable gulf between them. There are no ladders by which to climb from human experience upward toward the divine. God, as it were, pulls all the ladders up behind him into heaven. God and the world, therefore, stand in a confrontational relationship. God is "the Wholly Other." The world is "the far country" into which he sends his Son. Christ is the only point of contact, God's only word for the world, the only bridge, the only ladder. All movement is from the other side. Revelation, faith, proclamation, and church are all exclusively the products of divine initiative. Theology is therefore not in any sense from beneath, but only from above. Barth's position allows no room for prolegomena in the sense of a reasoned approach to or way into Christian dogmatics.

III. 6. Complex Developments

Barthian exclusivism stands in sharp contrast to the inclusivism of the Schleiermacherian tradition. Together they represent the two dominant, but rival, theological models of our times. The roots of both are traceable to Kant. Nearly all modern theologians, accordingly, find themselves walking in the shadow of this eighteenth-century giant. Throughout the nineteenth century, and well into the twentieth century, the whole field of theology was dominated by Schleiermacher as the transmitter of Kantian thought. As Barth put it, "The first place in a history of the theology of the most recent times belongs and will always belong to Schleiermacher, and he has no rival. . . ." What Schleiermacher said of Frederick the Great, says Barth, can also be said of Schleiermacher himself: "He did not found a school, but an era." During our century, however, Barth and his cohorts set out to turn the tide.

Now, however, and increasingly since mid-century, it appears that the Barthian interlude is past. Following the temporary holding action of neoorthodoxy, the onward march of Schleiermacherian methodologies is evident in the reemergence of classic liberal theology in the form of contemporary secular theologies, now in the monist molds of process theologies. Instead of prolegomena laying a foundation for dogmatics by working its way "upward" toward God, it seeks to do so by working its way "backward" toward God as some indefinable starting point in the historical process, or "inward" toward God as the "Ground of Being," or "forward" toward God as the future goal of history. The theoretical potentials for this very complex development, with its cacophony of theological sounds, are still deeply embedded in the profoundly formative thought patterns of Kantian philosophy.

III. 7. Theology "from Below"

As noted, the basic pattern of Schleiermacher's theology keeps coming back in a variety of ways. It therefore merits further scrutiny. In his work *Christian Faith,* Schleiermacher honors the Kantian dogma which places God outside the rational world of theoretical reflection. On what grounds is it then still possible to speak meaningfully about God? Schleiermacher's answer is that God can be known from reflections on the religious experiences of the human race. In all men there is a certain "feeling of absolute dependence," a feeling of "pious self-consciousness." Proceeding on this conviction, Schleiermacher analyzes universal religious phenomena. By a comparative study of world religions Schleiermacher seeks to establish a certain ascending order of religious experiences, Christianity being the highest stage in mankind's religious evolution. While other religions may attain to some idea of salvation, Christianity offers the world a "Savior."

Those who lock themselves into a two-factor view of reality, refusing to accept revelation as the starting point and centering norm for theology, have no choice but to accept some version of this approach. Though burdened with inner contradictions and beset by horrendous problems, in a secularized world this method continues to exert a magnetically attractive power. In it prolegomena plays a crucial, if not indispensable role. Its task is to provide a rationale for Christian dogmatics. Yet the phenomena at hand are unable to sustain the needed weight of evidence. Its positivist method, moreover, lacks adequate criteria to justify its assessment of human religiosity. Its intent is obviously to escape the ironclad logic of the Kantian dilemma, which argued that, if God be God, then he cannot be part of our world of experience or an object of theoretical reflection. In the end, however, Schleiermacher joined Kant in resting his case on an equally, though different, humanist line of reasoning. He, too, shifted the norm for theology from the God-side to the man-side. Human response was made normative for dogmatics. This leaves us with an essentially nonrevelational base for religion. By defining "religious feeling" as naturally present to human consciousness, Schleiermacher opens the floodgates to the primacy and autonomy of human experience. His "feeling of absolute dependence" replaces the biblical doctrine of creation. The result is, instead of theology, a form of anthropology. Schleiermacher's theological method stands or falls with its assumption of an unbroken continuity between world religions and Christian faith which allows for comparing them as movable points on the same spectrum, with no substantial breaks between them.

Finally, however, in the second edition of his *Christian Faith,* Schleiermacher abruptly, yet substantially, alters this uniformitarian ideal. His synthesis begins to fall apart. He concedes that "für die christliche Glaubenslehre ist die Darstellung zugleich die Begründung" (11.5) — that is, the very setting forth of Christian doctrine is its own foundation. It therefore does not need the extensive religio-phenomenological undergirding on which he had expended so much effort. This concession, coming later, would have necessitated drastic changes in his entire theological approach, if he had gone back and revised his dogmatics in the light of it. But there it stands as a glaring inconsistency, an inner contradiction, left unresolved. Schleiermacher had begun to turn the tables on his own method.

III. 8. Theology "from Above"

Barth's theological method, along with that of Schleiermacher, is so overwhelmingly important that it, too, calls for additional emphasis and critical comment. His "breakthrough" represents modernity's most radical departure from the Schleiermacherian approach. Nevertheless, like most others, Barth was unsuccessful in shaking off the Kantian problematic. It may even be argued that he accentuated it by his emphasis on the absolute otherness of God. In doing so, however, in his own unique way Barth did manage to shift the center of gravity in theology from Schleiermacher's historical pole to his own suprahistorical pole, from "subjectivism" to "objectivism," from man to God, from human religion to divine revelation, from doing theology *von unten* to doing it *von oben.* Because Barth offers a substantial alternative to the prevailing methodology of most modern theologies, his views continue to serve as a crucial sounding board for all major trends in contemporary theology. Positively or negatively, nearly all leading theologians now feel compelled to define their positions in relation to his.

As we noticed earlier, Schleiermacher eventually conceded that "Darstellung ist zugleich Begründung." This idea was fundamentally alien to Schleiermacher's system of thought. He was therefore unable to incorporate it integrally into his theology. Yet in this passing reference he at least tacitly admits that Christian doctrine is uniquely Christian. What stands there as a remarkable concession in Schleiermacher becomes the very starting point for Barth. He holds that it is impossible to pave a road from religion in general to Christian doctrine. For Christian theology is its own justification. It must take as its point of departure that which is distinctively Christian, namely, the Word of God, God's personal act of revelation in Jesus Christ, faith as a sovereign gift of God, and the church as a divine creation. Accordingly Barth rejects both the modernist idea of prolegomena as rooted in human potentiality and the Roman Catholic idea which roots it in a hierarchy of being. The orientation of theology can and must be always and only from above.

Instead of Schleiermacher's unbroken continuity, Barth posits a radical discontinuity. Instead of starting with the universal phenomena of religion, or with rational proofs for the existence of God, or with Brunner's eristics (assuming historical points of contact for revelation), or with Tillich's answering theology (philosophy posing the questions to which theology offers the answers), or with any apologetic designed to vindicate in advance the Christian faith — instead of any such thing, Barth contends that dogmatics must start and end with that which is specifically its own. He therefore advocates strictly a theology of the Word of God. He consistently repudiates all traditional definitions of prolegomena. "The prefix *pro* in prolegomena," he says, "is to be understood in an unreal sense: it deals not with things which are to be said beforehand *(vorher),* but at the beginning *(zuerst)*" (*Church Dogmatics,* I/1). The norm for theology is transcendent, not immanent. Christian faith finds no points of contact with anything around us. It has no horizontal orientation; it is radically vertical in its orientation. Its passwords are therefore "encounter," not "evolution"; "Christ," not "culture"; "God-to-man," not "man-to-God"; "invasion from Beyond," not "a ladder leading upwards"; "self-identity," not "solidarity"; "confrontation," not "accommodation"; "otherness," not "similitude"; "divine event," not "human achievement." Thus Barth built "a China wall" around dogmatics with no prolegomenal gateways leading in or out. Methodologically, he locked Christian theology up in its own house. The only possible introduction to dogmatics is from within the enclosed circle of dogmatics itself. Only in the actual doing of theology does an entryway open itself up to us. Prolegomena as the way into dogmatics is located within the very bounds of dogmatics. Its starting point is revelation; its goal is proclamation.

Barth makes this clear in the following paragraph:

> In order to give an account of the way of knowledge pursued in dogmatics, we cannot take a position which is somewhere apart from this way or above the work of dogmatics. Such a place apart or above could only be an ontology or anthropology as the basic science of the human possibilities among which consideration is somewhere given to that of faith and the Church. But any supposed reality of the Church in which the decision of the Lord of the Church is already anticipated can only be viewed as such a place apart or above. In both cases, i.e., in both Modernist and Roman Catholic prolegomena, it can be known and said in advance, before actually embarking on dogmatics, what will be the proper way of knowledge. Evangelical dogmatics cannot proceed along these lines. It can only venture to embark on its way, and then on this way, admittedly perhaps as its first task, yet genuinely on this way, concern itself with the knowledge of the correctness of this way. It knows that there can be no entering the self-enclosed circle of this concern from without, whether from a general human possibility or an ecclesiastical reality. It realizes that all its knowledge, even its knowledge of the correctness of its knowledge, can only be an event, and cannot therefore be guaranteed as correct knowledge from any place apart from or above this event. In no circumstances, therefore, can it understand the account which is to be rendered in prolegomena as an attempt to secure such a guarantee. This account can be given only within, even if at the beginning of, the dogmatic work which is not guaranteed from that point apart or above. (*Church Dogmatics,* I/1)

Agreeing with Barth on this point, Otto Weber says that "the *starting* point of every dogmatics is implicitly given in its *central* point." There is therefore "no real pro-legomena to dogmatics" (*Foundations of Dogmatics,* Vol. I, p. 5).

Accordingly, a Barthian understanding of the object of dogmatic study may be defined as follows: the church's proclamation of the Christ of Scripture as expressed in the dogmas of Christian faith. In unpacking the meaning of this compact definition, we may accent the following elements built into it. "Church" — this is the *locus* of dogmatics; it must be done in, for, and by the church; hence Barth's *Church Dogmatics.* "Proclamation" — living as we do "between the times," proclamation is a present form of the Word of God, a secondary witness to it. "Christ" — revelation being always and only a personal act of intervention from beyond, Barth's Christomonism follows as a consistent conclusion. "Scripture" — as the primary witness to God's Word in Christ, the Bible serves as our pointer to revelation. "Dogmas" — Barth's theology lent renewed emphasis to the proposition that historic Christian doctrines are (after the doctrinal indifference typical of liberalism) still of immense importance.

The final link in the chain which makes up this definition, namely, dogma, raises an interesting point. In terms of theological method, is Barth here, like Schleiermacher, also making a major concession, one which calls into question the possibility of maintaining consistently the radicality of his own chosen approach to dogmatics? "Dogma" conjures up the idea of a certain Christian tradition coming up out of the past, a certain line of historical continuity. Is this then, after all, a horizontal factor which compromises, or at least tones down, his appeal to radical verticality? Does the development of dogma within the church of all ages serve then as Barth's form of prolegomena built into the body of his dogmatics? Is the historical process of dogma formation then an implied *vorher* in Barth's theology, even though he wishes to grant it no more than a *zuerst* status? It certainly appears to function as a way of moving from the outside into the inner circle of his encounter theology. We are therefore led to wonder whether structurally, in terms of his theological method, dogmatic tradition plays a prolegomenal role in Barth which is roughly analogous to the study of comparative religions in Schleiermacher. It seems that Barth's original emphasis on discontinuity (revelation apart from historical reality) may be just as untenable as Schleiermacher's original emphasis on continuity (human religious experience as a way into revelation).

III. 9. A Limited Number of Viable Options

We see, then, that the history of Christian theology yields three basic models of the relationship of prolegomena to dogmatics proper. First, there is the traditional *rationalist* model. This approach maintained its dominance throughout the early and medieval periods, and on into the modern period. Its leading exponents stood in the Roman Catholic and Protestant scholastic traditions. It erected a foundation for dogmatics by appeal to Greek philosophy and natural theology, capitalizing on the classic rational proofs for the existence of God.

In the wake of Kantian philosophy this method became discredited and fell into disuse. Under the impact of the Enlightenment, rationalist ways of doing prolegomena lost their power to convince the modern mind. For these rationalist methods implicitly assume what they presumably set out to prove — namely, the Christian faith. Since the secular spirit of modernity could no longer share these underlying assumptions, the conclusions drawn from them also failed to carry weight.

The Enlightenment therefore generated a second type of prolegomena, whose chief architect was Schleiermacher. It abandoned the deductivism of the rational model in favor of a more inductive approach. It led to the emergence of an *historical* method. Like its predecessor, this approach also tries to work its way upward from the world to God. It bases its case, however, on existential arguments, on human experience, on an analysis of general religious phenomena, utilizing the tools of positivist science. But this method has also suffered erosion. For the data it amassed proved insufficient to sustain the argument. Growing secularism effectively blocks every road upward, outward, or beyond.

Both the traditional rationalist model and the modern historical model operate within the perspective of a two-factor theology — God and man, and nothing else. Both view prolegomena as a reasoned movement from man toward God. Methodologically, both also presuppose that in prolegomena Christian theologians must adopt a certain "pre-Christian" mind-set, a certain unbiased predisposition. A studied effort must be made to avoid "showing one's hand" prematurely. Both agree, therefore, that dogmatics calls for a certain kind of introduction beforehand. Sharp differences remain, however, on its precise nature. Yet the basic impulse to do theology from below remains intact.

The only alternative model, substantially different from the other two, is that of Barth. He swept aside both the medieval model, based ontologically on the *analogia entis,* and the modern model, based anthropologically on an analysis of religious experience. After Kant, the rationalist model has been largely abandoned. The two main contenders for dominance in contemporary disputes on prolegomena are therefore Barth and Schleiermacher. Given a two-factor frame of reference in theology, it is nearly impossible to avoid lining up on the one or the other side in this ongoing debate. These contrary methods therefore impose an agonizing choice on contemporary theologians. For, on the one hand, a consistent application of the Barthian method makes it extremely difficult to lend any substantial content to the doctrine of a "wholly other" God. A Schleiermacherian approach, on the other hand, leads to filling Christian doctrine with humanist ideas, re-creating God in the varied images of man. The Barthian tradition makes God the great Subject and man the object of divine activity; that of Schleiermacher sees man as the subject and God as the object and goal of human potentiality.

This is the seemingly insurmountable dilemma facing contemporary theology. Every responsible address to prolegomena must somehow come to terms with this fundamental choice imposed on us by our long history of two-factor theologies. So whose lead shall we follow in rethinking the question of a prolegomena to Reformed dogmatics? The

current status of the question appears to allow for no third possibility
— or does it?

III. 10. Mediating Positions

Many contemporary thinkers sense keenly the force of this harsh
dilemma. For Reformed theologians working on prolegomenal issues in
dogmatics neither option is appealing. For theologians with biblical
antennae, the neoorthodox method seems too "objectivist," the liberal
method too "subjectivist." If this is so, where do we go from here?

Recent trends reflect a movement toward an intermediate position
— a tendency to draw from both sides of the dilemma and then to come
down in the center. In doing so it is possible, of course, to find support
in both Schleiermacher and Barth. For, as observed earlier, both compromised their basic positions by making concessions in the opposite
direction. In seeking to travel a middle-of-the-road route, contemporary
mediating theologians wish naturally to avoid the quandary of a *tertium
quid* solution involving a simplistically blended mixture of the two. At
the same time, however, their middle point lacks a firmly structured place
in their dogmatic outlines. It tends to hang suspended somewhere in
space between heaven and earth, between God and man. Those advanc-
ing this view give the impression of wishing to claim the best of both
worlds. The result is a fence-straddling act, covered by an almost indefinable concept called "relationality." Such reconstructions overlook the
confusion inherent in the very distinction itself between "objectivity" and
"subjectivity" as applied to divine revelation and human response. For
this distinction holds only for intracosmic reality, not for the relationship
between the Creator and his creation.

III. 11. "God with Us"

An instructive case in point is the report by the Reformed Churches
of the Netherlands on the nature of scriptural authority entitled *God
with us* (*God met ons*, 1980). It advocates a new "concept of truth."
Instead of the traditional polar tension between an "objective concept
of truth" and a "subjective concept of truth," this report calls for a
"relational concept of truth." It rejects the former as too receptive and
passive, though acknowledging that such objectivity recognizes quite
rightly a transcendent norm. While the latter is right in engaging man

actively in the process of revelation, it, too, is defective. For subjectivity easily allows human initiative to decide the question of truth without taking seriously any external normativity. Therefore, "anyone who limits truth either to the objective or to the subjective relativizes it and depreciates its fullness." Objectivity and subjectivity must go hand in hand. "The objective element is more clearly revealed precisely in and with the subjective aspect," and conversely, "the subjective comes to its own more fully precisely in and with the objective." Thus the report argues for "a relationship between subject and object" described as an "interaction by which both really begin to become clearly depicted." "If it is handled well," the report adds, "then our talk about from above *(van boven)* will not get watered down, but will rather come to its own precisely through an accent on from beneath *(van beneden)*." Despite the apparent ambivalence of this "third way," the report maintains that "this shift in the concept of truth toward a relational understanding of it [the objective as present in the subjective, and also the other way around] can give us a richer view of the truth of Scripture" (pp. 9-23).

III. 12. "Correlation Motif"

A similar trend toward "relational" solutions to the long-standing two-factor problem is evident at a more theoretical level in many contemporary theologies. To illustrate this point let us reflect briefly on the works of three Reformed theologians — G. C. Berkouwer, Hendrikus Berkhof, and Harry Kuitert.

This crucial issue was a matter of constant concern to Berkouwer. His career in theology, covering more than half a century, reflects a three-stage shift in emphasis with respect to the "objectivity/subjectivity" issue. The early Berkouwer accents the "objectivity" of revelation, whereas later he stresses its existential, "subjective" dimension. The middle Berkouwer I shall take as representative of the high point in his very productive career, epitomized in the major works of his monumental series entitled "Studies in Dogmatics." In these writings the idea of relationality is woven tightly into the overall fabric of his theology. It is not an incidental idea standing on the periphery of his dogmatics, but a key concept at the very center. Berkouwer refers to it consistently as the *correlatie motif* (the "correlation motif"). It functions as a linking concept, located at the very point of intersection of the God/man relationship. It is meant to hold together the grace of God, on the one side, and man's response of faith, on the other. Berkouwer refuses adamantly to construe this "correlation motif" in a cooperative, complementary, or competitive way. It is rather the ever present religious pivotal point of man's encounter with his Maker and Redeemer. It is the hinge on which all of Berkouwer's dogmatics turns.

Berkouwer has left us no work on prolegomena, and therefore with no explanation of his basic methodology, except perhaps in the opening chapter of his *Faith and Justification*. Yet his "correlation motif" can be construed as a promising movement in the direction of a three-factor dogmatics: God/the "correlation motif"/man. Yet this crossroads concept fails to function in a clearly structured way. Perhaps this is due to Berkouwer's aversion to philosophical reflection, rooted, as he says, in "a metaphysical system for explaining the world." As a result this "correlation motif" continues to oscillate back and forth as though still caught in the bipolar tension of a two-factor theology. The center of gravity in his dogmatics is therefore open to noticeable shifts from an early magnetic pull toward the "objectivity" pole to a later drift toward a "subjectivity" pole. Along the way the "correlation motif" hangs suspended on the high-powered tension line between these two polar magnitudes.

III. 13. A Mixed Method

A similar pendulumlike problematic is evident in Hendrikus Berkhof's work *Christian Faith* (1979). His approach to the issue at hand reflects a greater degree of methodological self-consciousness than that of Berkouwer. From start to finish prolegomenal issues play a decisive role in Berkhof's thinking. He deals with them very explicitly and offers a step-by-step, reasoned account of his procedures. In the process he faces up squarely to this watershed decision in dogmatics: whether to side with the subjectivist and inclusivist approach of Schleiermacher or the objectivist and exclusivist approach of Barth. Berkhof's statement of the problem is, however, more clear-cut than his answer. For we find him drawing his theological impulses from both sources. The result is a mixed method.

Which approach prevails? Berkhof creates a mood of suspense by holding off on an answer to this question. Popular theological literature may take its cue, he says, from intriguing ideas in vogue at a given time in history. However, a handbook on doctrine calls for different standards.

> In view of the derailments observable in dogmatics, we must proceed in prolegomena from that area of reality where Christian faith once grew up or "touched down" (which of these two words is correct can only be made clear later), namely, the area of "religion." Thus we shall combine a phenomenological with an historical approach. In doing so we are joining

that century-old tradition which, ever since that break known as the Enlightenment, has moved forward strongly under the leadership of Schleiermacher and others. This choice may seem a bit unfortunate during an era such as ours which is often described as "religionless." But even at such a time honesty requires that we do not deny the origins of the Christian faith in the world of religion. (P. 5)

Berkhof here follows the line of Schleiermacher, but not to the exclusion of the Barthian approach. Moving along, a synthetic method emerges. His points of contact arise from the concessions made by both Schleiermacher and Barth. He appeals to Schleiermacher's concession that continuity in world religions is finally broken by the need to "step over" to the Christian faith, and Barth's concession that the vertical "breakthrough" does after all carry with it a horizontal holding power. Thus, despite Barth's adamant objections, Berkhof says: "We choose for the full legitimacy of a prolegomena" (p. 4). How then are we to construe its content? This is his answer: "From out of the broad and universal world of human reality we shall choose religion as our port-of-entry in order to catch a vision of what the Christian faith can and must mean within the whole of reality" (p. 6). Thus, on the relationship between prolegomena and dogmatics Berkhof acknowledges his indebtedness to the Schleiermacherian method.

Yet there is also an attempt to honor Barth's emphasis on the unique and distinctive character of the Christian faith. Unlike Schleiermacher, Berkhof viewed the purpose of prolegomena as not to amass evidence to demonstrate the superiority of the Christian faith, but only to locate it in relationship to religion in general.

Berkhof's theology presupposes two magnitudes: earthly reality and divine redemption — and the relationship between them. The question then arises, with Barth, whether prolegomena is even necessary as a way to move from the one to the other. Is not a straightforward exposition of Christian doctrine sufficient? If so, "then there is very much to be said for the dogmatics of the Reformation era which tended to simply open the door and enter" (p. 4) — thus, no introduction at all. Why not follow this example? Berkhof's answer to this question betrays a certain affinity for Barth's approach, which in turn reflects that of Reformation dogmatics. Prolegomena in the traditional sense, as rational, phenomenological, or historical verification, is not essential to dogmatics. In this Berkhof distances himself from the Schleiermacherian tradition. In the end, however, he sides with Schleiermacher. For ultimately, according to Berkhof, prolegomena rests on more pragmatic considerations. As he puts it:

If we do not emulate the wise restraint [of the Reformers] it is because we live in other times. Between us and the Reformation lies the Enlightenment and all that followed it. In lieu of this man has become infinitely more self-conscious, and at the same time God has become more dubious. Redemption and reality have drifted apart: reality has become increasingly fuller and redemption increasingly vaguer. Even the believer cannot withdraw from that spiritual climate. If doctrine is to clarify and deepen faith, then its practitioner may not forget the climate in which he works. Starting right out with dogmatics, which may at certain times in history be experienced as a form of liberation, would come across in our times as downright merciless. It would promote the idea that faith is a separate world alongside our normal, real world. Therefore, we make room for prolegomena. (Pp. 4-5)

Berkhof appears thus to adopt the pattern of a mixed model — an analysis of world religions (prolegomena) on the way to a statement of Christian faith (dogmatics). This suggests a certain continuity. Yet there is also a decisive discontinuity. For faith rests on an encounter with God which springs, not from our surroundings, but from divine initiative. Dogmatics is, accordingly, "systematic reflection on the content of the relationship which God establishes with us in Christ" (p. 35). Such relationality is the focal point of dogmatics. For such "reflection is not directed toward human states of feeling, nor immediately toward God himself, but toward the encounter between God and man, in which faith confesses God as the initiator" (p. 35). Standing within this encounter, the theologian thinks backward (prolegomena) to his "pre-Christian" condition, to those who still do not make the good confession, to the *why*-in-the-world of Christian faith. Standing there, he also thinks forward (dogmatics) to the implications of the encounter, to life after taking "the big step," to the *what*-in-the-world of the Christian faith.

In Berkhof's dogmatics, therefore, the plot thickens. Schleiermacher becomes Barth's ally in death as he never was in life. Through it all, however, there is the same age-old bone of contention: What are we to do about prolegomena? The current trend is to interchange the two opposing approaches. The net effect of such synthesis is internal conflict. For what Schleiermacher makes the very heartbeat of dogmatics, namely, prolegomena as a foundational word spoken beforehand, Barth wishes to eliminate altogether, or at most to incorporate into dogmatics as a first word. This modern jockeying for position is more than merely a question of where and how to locate prolegomena. At bottom it involves a profoundly pretheological decision: Is prolegomena to take its normative starting point in divine revelation or in human religious response? Is its reasoned movement to be *von oben* or *von unten*? A further question is this: Is not this "objectivity/subjectivity" dilemma itself inherently faulty? For while the concepts "objective" and "subjective" are appropriate in analyzing intracosmic reality, they are inappropriate in understanding the God-man relationship. This raises the further question: Are not all attempts to reconcile this tension actually misleading? Does not the current impasse ultimately call for a new initiative in the form of an authentic "third way" which can offer a real alternative?

III. 14. Experiential Theology

We are offered another bridging-the-gap model in Harry Kuitert's book *Wat Heet Geloven?* (1977). This work is devoted to a respectful but sustained and intensive critique of Barth's "supernaturalism" which, Kuitert argues, ends in total "mystification" of God, man, revelation, the world, everything. The other half of the modern dilemma, a Schleiermacherian form of "naturalism" which enslaves theology to positivist science, has also suffered shipwreck. So what is left? Is there a way out of this impasse which can reopen the possibilities for meaningful "God-talk"?

In answering these questions, Kuitert's emphasis falls on prolegomena as a form of apologetic. Its task is to create room for communication

> between Christians and non-Christians; between Christians and other Christians; and between the two halves which make up a Christian — the half which gladly believes the truth and the half which has difficulty with it, the half which moves forward from assurance to assurance and the half which finds "How do you know?" a valid question. (P. 232)

What test of truth can we apply to Christian doctrine? By what means can we verify and justify it scientifically to the satisfaction of our fellowmen?

To surmount the Kantian dilemma Kuitert seeks to establish a vantage point behind and beyond it. This standpoint he calls a "meta-position" — a philosophical approach to dogmatics which serves as his prolegomenal point of view. From this perspective he engages in a doggedly tenacious lingual analysis of such doctrinal "is-statements" (*is-zinnen*) as "God is Creator and Redeemer." Theoretical reflection of this sort calls for an examination of the assumptions, possible meanings, and implications of our theological propositions. Frontally it is Barth's theology, but more obliquely it is nineteenth-century liberal theology which serves as the foil for Kuitert's thesis that, given the failures of the latter and the shortcomings of the former, the only plausible way to treat

Christian dogma is within the framework of a mediating model centering on man. Anthropology is therefore the hermeneutic key to unlock the meaning of dogma — man as "mediating factor" in revelation. Thus Kuitert arrives at an "experiential theology" *(ervaringstheologie)*, with nature, culture, the historical opening up process of God's future, and the final consummation of God's involvement with the world as the criteria for validating Christian belief. Developments since Kant leave us with the predicament, says Kuitert, of choosing between history and kerygma, of either a theology which brings faith down into earthly life where it makes a difference but runs the risk of tainting it with secular, humanist connotations, or a theology which seals it up in heaven where it makes no earthly difference.

Facing this impasse, Barth opts forthrightly for absolute transcendence over against the prevailing nineteenth-century emphasis on immanence. His theology, therefore, according to Kuitert, stands at "the crossroads of a multitude of routes," so much so that it represents "that point at which one must begin in order to understand the theological developments of our times" (p. 194). He goes on to say that

> . . . within the context of the dilemma posed by Kant, namely: either God is in our world of experience, but then he is not God; or he is God, but then not in our world of experience — one can hardly make another choice than Barth's, if one wishes not to surrender the Christian faith. Such then is the attractive power of Barth's theology, as long as one confines himself to Kant's dilemma. Given this dilemma, his is the only way to rescue theology from the impoverishment of the science-ideal of positivism. But is this dilemma valid? Rather than taking refuge in a supernatural concept of revelation, one could set out to undermine the dilemma itself. For God and human experience do not by definition exclude each other. On the contrary, it is experience itself to which Christians appeal for their knowledge of God, since [cumulative] experience is the avenue by which the Christian Church has come to its [rough draft of the] knowledge of God. Naturally such a statement of the case runs the risk of making God completely the predicate of our experience. It seems to me, however, that it comes down to choosing the one or the other: either the little word "God" remains empty, or it draws its content arbitrarily from human subjectivity, or it receives its content and predication from [historical] experience. (Pp. 228-29)

Thus the choices are clearly stated: we either take the side of Barth (supernaturalism) or of Schleiermacher (subjectivism) or of Kuitert (history). The question remains, however, whether Kuitert's thesis offers us a substantial alternative, a real "third way." Referring to Schleiermacher and Barth, Kuitert holds that "it is these two . . . which stand at the cradle of our modern problematic. Both wish to preserve what they consider to be a fundamental given of the Christian faith; both also thrive on the shortcomings of the other; and therefore the conflict between them never ceases" (p. 197). Most modern theologians, therefore, have tried to seek "a way which avoids supernaturalism without falling into naturalism" (p. 198). This leads Kuitert to propose an approach which sees human experience as the medium of revealed truth. His proposal takes distance from Barth. But is it more than a revision of Schleiermacher?

In the Anselmian approach which Barth develops in his *fides quaerens intellectum* he argues that dogmatics must find its starting point in revelation itself. It must therefore stand on its own feet, not seeking prolegomenal support in creation, history, human experience, religion, or any other earthly potentiality. On this Kuitert comments as follows:

> We do not wish to detract anything from Barth's intellectual acumen or disrespect the way he develops *fides* as his starting point. We might go even further and say, Is any other starting point possible? Can Christian theologians ever assume their point of departure in anything else than *fides*? And can theology ever do anything else than move out from there toward *intelligere*? The question seems to practically answer itself. Yet the objections to it are so formidable that we can do nothing else but come to this conclusion: It cannot be so, nor does it have to be so. Theology before Barth never went at it this way. . . . It never condemned theology to let go of its faith at the start of its theologizing; but it also never compelled the theologian to turn his theology into an explication of his faith in Jesus Christ. (P. 64)

According to Kuitert, this is the Achilles' heel of Barth's dogmatics. It allows for no prolegomenal justification of Christian belief since "God cannot be verified, precisely because he is God" (p. 189). Barth's theology is a closed house, without doors or windows, cutting off all possibility of communication from within or from without. God is made to dwell in absolute transcendence. Revelation is a closed circle, for God is himself both the Subject and the Object as well as the Mediator of his own self-disclosure. It allows for no human, historical, earthly mediation. According to Kuitert, this should spell the end of all theology, except — there stands Barth's long row of imposing books on dogmatics.

Kuitert recognizes clearly how thoroughly the Kantian dilemma pervades the structures of contemporary theology. Like many others, he wishes to escape this modern impasse. Appeals to something "in between" *(tussen-in)* becomes the heart of the current struggle, resulting in a form of "mediating theology" *(bemiddelingstheologie)*. The question remains, however: Is it possible in this way to close the gap?

Kuitert argues that his thesis is in accord with classic theology. For the latter began not with its own established position, as Barth does, but "with a common fund of insights and truths shared by Christians and non-Christians." Thus it was able "to erect a platform *(vloertje)* of commonly held truths upon which the structure of a Christian account of its faith could finally be constucted. . . . This common ground *(vloertje)*, which makes communication and argumentation possible, can be located best in the area of anthropology." With such an approach, "not only will the dialogue between the Christian and the non-Christian be honorably reinstated, but it will be located precisely at a point which will make argumentation and control equally possible for all partners in the dialogue" (pp. 111-13).

Not surprisingly, therefore — again contrary to Barth — Kuitert says, "I can appreciate the case for Christians beginning with faith in Jesus Christ, also in their theology; but taking such faith as a starting point and turning it into a 'methodological principle' seems to me indeed like building a house without doors" (p. 217). For accepting "a normative concept of faith" (p. 63) as one's presuppositional starting point breaks off all communication with those holding to other convictions.

Kuitert comments that Hendrikus Berkhof's move toward "middle ground" comes across to him as "an inconsistent revision of the Barthian foundation" (p. 210). Berkhof might well wonder in turn whether Kuitert's drift toward "middle ground" is not likewise an inconsistent revision of the Schleiermacherian foundation. How does Kuitert's method differ essentially from nineteenth-century approaches? He affirms forthrightly the reality of revelation (p. 222). That is indeed a big difference. Methodologically, however, revelation is not allowed to play a decisive role in his prolegomena. The actual, operative norm in dogmatics is located in our common critical reflection on cumulative historical experience. Thus the pieces of the puzzle of two-factor theologizing have been reshuffled and rearranged once again. But the basic problem remains unresolved.

We must, of course, take history seriously. It is God's way with his world — his way, through fall and redemption, of redirecting the potentials of creation toward the coming of his kingdom. Our cumulative historical fund of experiences, however, is not revelation, and is therefore not normative. If human culture is taken to be the criterion for prolegomena to dogmatics, then human response becomes normative for doing theology. Then the danger of refined forms of historicism, cultural relativism, and scientism begins again to loom large. Moreover, without a firm creational base, the only choice left to Christian theology is to take flight into an eschatological openness to God's future for man.

III. 15. Restating the Issue

Our present concern is with sorting out contemporary issues in prolegomena. The fundamental question is: Where are we to locate the norm?
Current trends do not differ fundamentally from past thinking on this
issue. Christian theology continues to reflect a persistent inability or
unwillingness to break with the established pattern of two-factor perspectives. Even though older, more static, ontologically conceived worldviews have made way for newer, more dynamic, existentially conceived
ones, the same knotty problem continues to haunt us: Is the prolegomenal
norm for dogmatics "up there" or "down here"? It is along this battle
line that the major skirmishes are being reenacted; but with this difference, that the front line of conflict tends to drift steadily toward a kind
of no-man's-land somewhere in between. Given a divine horizon and a
human horizon, the drift is toward a "fusion of horizons."

The result is a waffling concept of normativity which bounces back
and forth between divine revelation and human response. Instead of
pushing the norm up into heaven or pulling it down to earth, the norm
gets suspended tenuously along an indefinable high-tension line between
this dual polarity. The result is complexity compounded: instead of
locating the pivotal point in one or the other of these two *relata,* God
or man, laborious efforts are expended to locate the focal point in an
ambivalent *relatio* concept. This trend reflects an implicit dissatisfaction
with two-factor solutions. Yet the dialectic inherent in it is still generally
assumed to be the proper way to state the case. At the same time, however,
this stumbling movement toward a "middle ground" reflects the felt need
for a mediating norm. A feverish yet largely inarticulate search is under-
way for such a "missing link."

Instead of maintaining a clearly focused distinction between revelation and response, contemporary theology projects a blurred image of
the two poles. The human pole, however, tends magnetically to pull
things in its direction. Our historical situation, our cultural context, our
human experience is viewed as somehow determinative of revelation
itself. So the questions multiply: Does human response participate in
divine revelation? Do earthly relationships contribute to the relationship
of God to the world? And, if so, how? Is divine activity then also subject
to historical development, just as ours is? Are human responses *consti-*
tutive of and *normative for* God's relationship to us? Or are human
relationships normative only for our understanding of the primordial
God-man relationship? If our experience of Jesus Christ is constitutive
of and/or normative for who he really was and is, are we then not
compelled to follow the lead of *Gemeindetheologie* ("Church Theology")
in distinguishing between the Jesus-who-was and the Jesus-who-is, the

historical Jesus of Galilee and the deified Christ of later Christian reflection? To say, with Calvin (1 Corinthians 2:7), that God accommodates *(attemperat)* his revelation to our understanding is one thing. To say that our understanding is constitutive of and/or normative for revelation is quite another. Caught in the pressure cooker between this "down draft" and "up draft," contemporary theology seeks shelter in some indefinable center.

In the meantime the theological winds of doctrine are blowing increasingly into the future. The gravitational center is therefore shifting steadily from "above" to "below" to "up ahead," from the God-pole to the man-pole to a future-pole, from divine transcendence to human immanence to eschatological self-transcendence, from faith to love to hope. In it all, however, there is little looking back to an original and abiding reality behind the resurrection, the cross, and the fall. Creation gets absorbed into the process of salvation history. Biblical witness to the creation order is bypassed in favor of existentialist views of reality. The results are upon us. For when creational revelation gets eclipsed, the meaning of salvation here-and-now and of the ultimate re-creation of all things also gets eclipsed.

We see, then, that contemporary mediating theologies carry with them an intuitive though inarticulate impulse in the direction of a three-factor theology. This is a hopeful sign. There is little inclination, however, to take full advantage of this opportunity. Movement continues toward some ambiguous and oscillating idea of a mediating center, but without granting it a normatively structured place in theology. What therefore others appear unwittingly to be groping for is precisely what lies at the heart of this renewal effort in Reformed dogmatics. Its intent and purpose is to explicate the meaning-full-ness of the Word of God as the pivotal point, the normative boundary and bridge between the revealing God and his responding creatures.

III. 16. A Three-Factor Alternative

In pressing for a three-factor approach to dogmatics as an alternative to the prevailing two-factor approaches, we are dealing with more than abstract theoretical issues. The choices we make at this point have far-reaching practical implications as well. For theory and practice are tightly interconnected. They should not be played off against each other. This often happens in two diametrically opposed ways. The man on the street often thinks, on the one hand, that by its very nature theory always gets bogged down hopelessly in ethereal, vacuous, dubious speculation, while, on the contrary, only what has practical value really matters. On the other hand, there are those, both inside and outside academic circles, who pin their hopes on scientific-theoretical knowledge to solve our problems, thinking that practical knowledge is at best guesswork. Both views misrepresent the matter. Both are based on misunderstandings of the relationship between theory and practice.

Often a certain position is rejected with the comment: "It's great in theory, but no good in practice." If that is truly the case, if a given view of reality is indeed impractical, then it is also poor theory. For theory is not some independent entity standing over against practice. Theory (theology) and praxis (piety) are two equally legitimate ways of knowing reality. Practical knowledge, however, is primary — for example, knowing God by faith in Jesus Christ. Theoretical knowledge is secondary — that is, reflecting critically on such faith-knowledge. Praxis funds theory. Confessing the authority of Scripture is practical; theologizing on this confession is theoretical. Theory involves taking a certain distance from such faith-knowledge, holding it at arm's length, in order to gain a more critically reflective and fuller in-depth understanding of what such faith-knowledge involves. Thus, rightly understood, theory seeks to give a reasoned account of the data presented to it by everyday practical living in God's world.

The point is this: two-factor theologies run stuck repeatedly in seeking to give a theoretical account of the things we experience in the daily praxis of Christian living. The counterthesis is this: a three-factor theory of reality offers more adequate and satisfying answers to the practical questions we face in our life together in the world. Let us look at three examples.

a) Christian View of Marriage. On a two-factor view, one must hold that the norm for marriage lies either in God or in man. It is accordingly rather commonplace for Christians to affirm the former by saying, "Marriages are made in heaven." But if this is so, how do we establish contact with that norm? For "God dwells in light unapproachable." The real signing and sealing ceremony then takes place behind the scenes, hidden in God's eternal decree. Thus we overload God's side, and man loses out. How then do we get a handle on marital problems? For the norm is placed beyond our reach. Marriage then becomes divinized. How can we then still assume responsibility for it? And if the marriage goes wrong, must we then blame God?

On the other hand, if the norm gets pulled down into history, we must then conclude that "marriages are made on earth." But is there nothing more to it than that? If that is all, then marriage becomes secularized. It is then merely a form of social contract between two people, with no "third party" involved.

61

A three-factor alternative recognizes a third dimension: there is a Word of God, given as a creation ordinance, which functions as the norm for marriage, calling for fidelity. Thus, marriages do indeed take place "on earth" and nowhere else; yet always "before the face of God." This *coram Deo* perspective is anchored in God's mediating Word. By it he maintains his claim on marriage. Through it, also, the divinely established norm for marriage is made accessible and responsibly real in daily practice.

b) Christian View of Civil Government. On a two-factor theology, once again, the norm for political life must be located either "upstairs" or "downstairs." If one opts for the former, the same familiar problem recurs. Existing governmental establishments can then be defended with an appeal to divine will. The status quo gets canonized, allowing for no meaningful address to an accessible norm in support of a call for political reforms. The specter then arises of rulers shielding themselves from public accountability by an appeal to "the divine right of kings." This approach offers an all-too-easy answer to the question of civil disobedience — it is always wrong.

If, however, we choose to sit on the other horn of this sacred/secular dilemma, then the norm for government gets leveled out to the idea of popular sovereignty. The *vox populi* then becomes the *vox Dei*. The basis for political life is then located in the will of the people, taking shape in a social contract, with public policy determined by majoritarian rule. Political practice can then rise no higher than a patriotic salute to "government of the people, by the people, and for the people."

Here, too, a three-factor view of reality offers an alternative. The norm lies neither in the hidden recesses of an inscrutable divine will nor in the arbitrary judgment that "the people have spoken," but in the mediating Word of God for public justice, given with creation, reaffirmed in the redeeming work of Christ, and illumined by the witness of the Scriptures. This view holds revelation and response together, each retaining its identity, yet always in a religiously charged relationship.

c) Predestination — Election and Reprobation. Given a two-factor theology, this doctrine falls prey to similar bipolar tensions. The sharp controversy between supra- and infralapsarians stands as a dramatic illustration of it. If, on the one hand, predestination is understood as an historical rerun of a prewritten script traceable to a set of decrees in the eternal mind of God, then dark and ominous shadows fall over biblical teachings on election and reprobation. Instead of assurance and comfort, this expression of the sovereign grace of God then engenders only a gnawing sense of insecurity and anxiety. To avert the theoretical speculation and the practical agony and passivity which flow from this view, some seek to locate the norm for election and/or reprobation in the arena of human responsibility within the historical horizon of our life-experience. This leads to a form of refined humanism.

As an alternative, a three-factor theology of predestination finds its normative focal point, not in the inner being of God himself, nor in human spirituality, but in God's Word as the covenantal bond between God and his creatures. This perspective offers promising methodological possibilities for restructuring the doctrine of election and reprobation. Accordingly, God holds himself to his covenanting Word, and he holds us to it as well. We can then speak more meaningfully of God's covenant faithfulness: God is true to his electing and reprobating Word. On the response side, too, covenant faithfulness (election) and covenant unfaithfulness (reprobation) come to their own more fully both as assurance and imperative.

Chapter IV

Clarification of Basic Categories

IV. 1. Introduction

The preceding chapters belabored the point that the leading theologies of the past are overwhelmingly dualist in their thought patterns. Such dualist views of life find their deeper backdrop in two-factor worldviews. These two views of reality go hand in hand. For facing the choice of locating the norm for life either "upstairs" or "downstairs," their biblical sensitivities induce Christians intuitively to opt for the former. But then the question arises: How can we get a handle on it? They are then led to pull the norm down into our world of experience to make it more accessible. The result is a dual normativity: God as the primary norm and the church or the pope or personal spiritual experience as a secondary norm. Thus a "Christ and culture"-type sacred/secular dialectic emerges. For dualist starting points never yield the integrally unified outlook which all reflective people intuitively desire — not even in the monist world-views of process theologies, which internalize the dialectic by assimilating it into the vortex of history. But the question remains: What precisely constitutes a dualist-dichotomist approach? To clarify this issue it may be helpful to contrast dualism with two important theological distinctions which should not be construed as dualist in nature.

IV. 2. Creator/Creature Distinction

The first is the Creator/creature distinction, which is fundamental to biblical religion. On this view, God and the world are two uniquely distinct realities. The difference between them is not merely quantitative but qualitative. God is not simply more of what we are. There is an

64

essential discontinuity, not just a shade of difference, nor a gradual, more-or-less distinction, as though God has only a "running head start" on us. God is absolutely sovereign, "the Other," not simply "Another." Even the biblical teaching on man as imager of God may not be allowed to eclipse the radical otherness of God. There is indeed a *relatio* between these *relata* — a two-way relationship, a covenant partnership, anchored in the mediating function of God's Word. But that Word stands as the boundary line as well as the bridge between the Creator and his creatures. Every inclination, therefore, to humanize the divine or to deify the human is contraband. Let God be God, and let man be man. Thus, every notion of an *analogia entis* is fundamentally ruled out. The point is this: it is unwarranted to regard such recognition of the Creator/creature distinction as a dualism. Therefore, to regard every couplet, every reference to two *relata* — in this case God and man — as an instance of dualism or dichotomy is confusing and misleading. Duality is not the same as dualism.

IV. 3. Antithesis

Dualisms take place within creation, not between the Creator and the creation. Yet, not every historical instance of over-againstness, of a duality or couplet, should be construed as a dichotomy. Speaking of the differences between, say, male and female, Jew and Gentile, East and West as dualisms only blurs the picture.

Clarity demands, therefore, that we recognize a real antinomy at work within the world which may also not be called a dualism. Such is the case with the biblical idea of antithesis. Think of "the seed of the woman" and "the seed of the serpent" (Genesis 3). Recall the words of Moses: "I hold up before you this day blessing and cursing, the way of death and the way of life — therefore, choose life" (Deuteronomy 30:15, 19). Recall Joshua's parting message: "Choose you this day whom you will serve — the gods of your forefathers or Yahweh" (Joshua 24:14-15). Recall Elijah's challenge to Israel: "How long will you go halting between two positions; if God be God, serve him; if Baal, then serve him" (1 Kings 18:20). Think, too, of the New Testament's repeated emphasis on the choice between God and Mammon, the "broad way" and the "narrow way." Christ speaks, furthermore, in word pictures of "wheat" and "tares" growing up side by side in the same field, and of "sheep" and "goats."

In biblical teaching the antithesis points to a spiritual conflict which cuts across all of life. World history demonstrates this running encounter between two opposing forces — the "kingdom of light" and the "kingdom of darkness." Both the awesome judgment and the renewing grace of God are big-as-life realities all around us. At heart men are either Christ-believers or disbelievers. Yet the line of the antithesis also cuts through the very life of Christians. The "old man" and "new man" are locked in mortal conflict within our bosoms. Listen to Paul: "The good I would I do not, and the evil I would not, that I do. O wretched man that I am!" (Romans 7:15, 24). Christians therefore are not strangers to the heart-rending cry for help: "Lord, I believe, help my unbelief" (Mark 9:24).

But again this is not a dualism. For the antithesis represents a spiritual warfare between good and evil which knows no territorial boundaries. It is not geographically, locally, or spatially definable. The enmity between these two hostile forces does not coincide with two parts of reality, as though one sector of life were holy and the other unholy, or one bloc righteous and the other unrighteous. It is a directional antithesis which runs through all the structures of life. Sin is totally pervasive. Grace, too, lays its claim on all reality. The antithesis may therefore not be dualistically misconstrued as though it drives a wedge between soul and body, faith and reason, theology and philosophy, church and world — with the former viewed as good and the latter as evil.

In the beginning God established his thesis for the world — covenant faithfulness and kingdom obedience. After the fall, he reestablished this thesis in Christ. But "the enemy" continues to launch his antithetical counterattacks. Therefore, to set the record straight, we should not label Christian organizations and institutions as "antithetical" or "separate." The opposite is true. Christian causes stand in principle behind the thesis that Christ is Lord of all. So-called "neutral" organizations and institutions, which are in reality humanist and secular, are in principle "antithetical" and "separate." For they fail to stand on the side of the biblical thesis. They have in effect separated themselves from the renewed order of reality, namely, that "God is in Christ reconciling all things to himself" (2 Corinthians 5:19). So now the basic question we all face is this: Are we for Christ or for some anti-Christ? This thetical/antithetical decision is radical and all-embracing in its impact. But again it is confusing and misleading to call this a dualism.

IV. 4. Dualism

What, then, are we to understand by dualism? If not the Creator/creature distinction, and if not the antithesis, what then? At a deeply religious level dualisms blunt the sharp edge of the antithesis. Instead of moving us wholeheartedly in the one spiritual direction or the other, dualism allows for a divided allegiance. Instead of leading to single-mindedness, it draws a line through the world and opts for walking on both sides of it, though with uneven pace. Dualism gives the spiritual antithesis onto-logical status by defining some parts, aspects, sectors, activities, or realms of life (the ministries of the church) as good and others (politics) as less than good or even evil.

In very practical terms, for example, dualisms allow us to regard Sunday as the Lord's day. But to whom, then, do the other days belong? Tithe money is considered dedicated to the Lord, while the rest we can do with as we jolly well please. A dualist note also finds an echo in the gospel hymn, "Take time to be holy. . . ," forgetting that the biblical idea of holiness is not something limited to certain moments. We may take time to eat, sleep, and play, but not to be holy. Holiness is a religious orientation which holds for life in its total extent and in all its parts. Every dualism, however, breaks up the religious oneness of life by pitting faith against reason, grace against nature. It forces false choices. It tries to keep one foot in the so-called sacred realm and the other in the secular. It fails to recognize that the Christian life as a whole is sacred in the sense of being dedicated to the Lord, and that at the same time all of life is also secular in the sense of engagement in down-to-earth reality.

Dualism grants sin a built-in ontological status. Some parts of our life in the world are considered inherently, innately evil. At least they have a lesser status than other parts. Some callings are higher and holier than others. Celibacy is purer than marriage; theology proper is more honorable than its reasoned prolegomena or philosophy or the other sciences; evangelism is more saintly than social work. In some things faith counts, but not in others, or not as fully. Some sectors of life are religious; others are religiously neutral. Such fact/value dichotomies con-tinue to slay their thousands.

At bottom, therefore, dualism may be defined as a confusion of structure and direction. It is a view of reality in which two earthly magnitudes are conceived of as standing in opposition to each other, and this opposition (antithesis) is read back ontologically into the very struc-tures of creation. Accordingly, some life-activities and historical struc-tures are regarded as redeemable, others as only remotely redeemable at best. In light of our earlier historical-theological analysis, all this has a ring of long-standing familiarity about it.

In some world religions this dualist conflict between good and evil is projected back on the gods themselves. It assumes the form of an ultimate dualism — as, for example, in Greek mythology with its conflict between Zeus and the Titans; or in the superstitions of many ethnic religions with their belief in hostile and friendly spirits which pervade the world; or in Manichaeism with its view of the good God of the spirit standing over against the evil Demiurge of matter. Within Western Christian theology, too, we encounter hints of such an ultimate dualism, as in Luther's *Deus revelatus* and *Deus absconditus*. Reformed theology, too, has not always been free of such dualist tendencies.

In dualisms the divine norm is always either kept at a distance, a step removed from everyday living ("upstairs"), or it is identified with some aspect of life ("downstairs"), or it takes the form of a dual normativity which wavers dialectically between the two. Dualism is a deceptive attempt to reject life in the world (in part) while at the same time also accepting it (in part). It tends to break rather than to absorb the tension between the "already" and the "not yet" in the biblical vision of the coming kingdom: some parts of life are viewed as "already" under the rule of Christ, others "not yet." Christian faith is often related only extrinsically to scholarship. All such dualisms make it impossible to do justice to the biblical message of creation/fall/redemption as holist realities. For they disrupt the unity of the creation order. They legitimatize the reality of sin in one or another realm of life. They limit the cosmic impact of the biblical message of redemption. They confine Christian witness to only certain limited sectors of life.

Summarizing, we may say that the Creator/creature distinction is an abiding ontic reality. The antithesis stands as a present historical reality. Dualism is, however, a conceptual distortion of reality.

IV. 5. Village/Town/City

The distorted picture of reality, painted by people wearing dualist glasses, has issued in a rather widely held reconstruction of the history of mankind. Perhaps this picture reflects descriptively the actual course of historical events. But to present it as a normatively developing state of affairs, as is often done, is another matter.

On this reconstruction of our human odyssey, the generations of mankind have evolved through three basic stages of religious commitment. First, there was the "village." During this primitive phase all of life was viewed as sacred. A sacral view of reality pervaded all communal relationships. Later a middle stage of development emerged, identified with the "town." At this juncture in history a mixed model of society was dominant. Life was viewed as divided rather clearly into two parts, the sacred and the secular, grace and nature. The sacral monism of the "village" made way for the sacred/secular dualism of the "town." Modern man, so the argument goes, has now entered the third (and final?) phase of his pilgrimage, called the "city." The pendulum has now swung all the way from the sacral pole, through the dualist middle ground, to the secular pole. The result is the "secular city." All life in our technological society is now being inundated by the tidal wave of secularism.

Some may curse this evolutionary shift. Others acclaim it as a normative development, as a sign that at last "man has come of age." However that may be, the point is clear: This reconstruction of Western history presupposes a dualist worldview. It builds a dualist definition into all three categories by which it describes the course of events. Accordingly, this scenario represents a distorted paradigm of reality imposed on world history.

IV. 6. A Calvinist Alternative

A significant alternative viewpoint lies in the Calvinist tradition as articulated by such theologians as Herman Bavinck. In his treatment of the dualism issue Bavinck continues to make use of the traditional Thomist concepts of nature and grace. He defines and handles them, however, in an untraditional, more reformational way. According to Bavinck, "the great question which returns always and everywhere" is this: "How is grace related to nature, . . . what is the connection between creation and re-creation, . . . between humanity and Christianity, between that which is below and that which is above?" Basic differences among Christians stem from this fundamental problem. For

> . . . we err continually on the side of the right or on the side of the left. One moment we sacrifice the Christian to the human, and the next we sacrifice the human to the Christian. On the one side looms the danger of worldliness, on the other side that of otherworldliness. And yet we hold fast to the conviction that the Christian and the human are not in conflict with each other.

According to Bavinck this problem is especially acute in Roman Catholic theology, which holds that nature is of a lower order than grace. Grace complements and elevates nature, but does not restore it. Thus an "eternal dualism" remains, since "Christianity does not become an immanent and reforming principle" in life. According to reformational thinking, however, "Christianity is not a quantitative entity which hovers transcendently above the natural, but a religious and ethical power which enters immanently into the natural and banishes only that which is impure." Thus, "grace does not serve to take man up into a supernatural order, but to liberate him from sin. Grace is not opposed to nature, but only to sin." Given this perspective, "the Reformation came into collision at virtually every point" with the dualism and supernaturalism so characteristic of other systems of thought. This is true especially of Calvin, since

> in the powerful mind of the French Reformer, re-creation is not a system which supplements creation, as in Catholicism, not a religious reformation which leaves creation intact, as in Luther, much less a new creation, as in Anabaptism, but the joyful news of the renewal of all creatures. Here the gospel comes fully to its own, comes to true catholicity. There is nothing which cannot and ought not to be evangelized. Not only the church, but also the home, school, society and state are placed under the dominion of the principle of Christianity.

Bavinck holds, accordingly, that the message of the gospel is "grace alone," which "does not abolish nature, but affirms and restores it." For "Christ came, not to destroy the works of the Father, but only those of the devil." Grace is the *reparatio* of a fallen nature. For "the *materia* of all things is and remains the same, but the *forma* given in creation was deformed by sin, to be once again completely reformed by grace." The result is a tremendous sense of relief, liberation, and responsibility; for "if you are a Christian, a Christian in the full sense of the word, then you are not a peculiar, eccentric human being, but you are fully human. To be Christian means to be human. It is man's humanity which is redeemed" (Jan Veenhof, *Nature and Grace in Bavinck,* pp. 4-24).

This approach by Bavinck offers a real alternative to other major modern theologies. It corrects the persistent dilemmas arising out of Kant's impact on modern thought. It reaches beyond the old dualisms. It leads to a radical redefinition of the age-old problem. It opens up new directions in theology. It alters refreshingly the very contours of dogmatics. It creates a strikingly different approach to prolegomenal issues. This, then, is the alternative method to which this project is committed.

IV. 7. Locating the Norm

The decisive question in theology is that of normativity. No theology is ever self-justifying, self-explanatory, or self-vindicating. At bottom every theology stands or falls ultimately with its appeal to some normative authority. The fundamental question is, therefore, where to locate the norm. If we bypass the covenant Word as the mediating third factor between God and man, opting instead for the familiar two-factor structures in theology, various troublesome possibilities present themselves.

We may hold, on the one hand, that God is the norm — that the norm must lie somewhere in the divine realm. Thus the norm is located not on man's side, but on God's. Choosing for this side of the two-factor dilemma means pushing the norm away from life and upward toward God, locating it in some transcendent sphere. To all practical intents and purposes the norm is then placed beyond our reach. This renders it inaccessible and inoperative as a constant steadying factor in theology. It opens wide the door to the idea of divine arbitrariness, with revelation coming over us as sporadic breakthroughs. Or it leads to a kind of mystic withdrawal from creation in search of beatific visions. Dogmatics is then turned into a form of metaphysical speculation (a la Barth).

The other alternative which a two-factor theology offers is to pull the norm down into history. It then slips from God's side to ours. The norm then gets located somewhere in man and his world of experience. Human response takes on the form and force of revelation. Something creational becomes normative for theologizing (a la Schleiermacher).

A two-factor theology keeps us trapped inextricably in the age-old familiar dilemma. Consistency demands that we then either eternalize the norm or historicize it. Either it gets frozen on the other side or it gets absorbed into the historical process with its flux and flow. Thus we are left with the choice between a refined form of deism and a refined form of humanism.

Neither of these alternatives offers a happy prospect. Understandably, therefore, dogmatics has expended great energy in trying to forge a "third way." Theologians have become professional bridge builders. Western Christian theology is a veritable showcase filled with such bridging models: *analogia entis,* divine breakthroughs, emanations of deity into earthly reality, evolvements of the world toward its divine destiny, Gnostic ecstasies seeking contact with higher realms of being, correspondence theories of knowledge, beatific visions, and more. As long, however, as theology begins by locking itself into a two-factor perspective it will never succeed in breaking this dialectical tension in which the divine and the human act as mutually limiting factors, as competitors, or as cooperators. Unity then remains an illusive ideal. Instead, a tug-of-war situation develops between man and his Maker. Either we eclipse divine sovereignty, Arminian style; or we eclipse human responsibility, labeling it hyper-Calvinism. The only way out, then, is some form of waffling in-between position. In all such stratagems, however, the biblical witness to the Word of God as the normatively structured boundary and bridge between the Creator and his creatures goes largely unrecognized and undeveloped. The same must then be said for the Word of God as the covenantal bond which establishes the relationship of promise and obligation between God and man, as the key to understanding revelation in its unity and diversity, and as the norm for all human response, including dogmatics. The Word of God is the final resting place in theology's restless search for the "missing link."

IV. 8. Unattractive Options

Continued adherence to two-factor thinking drives us into some very unenticing impasses. Attempts to escape those snares fall into the following basic patterns.

a) Deism. Since in this theory the linking power of God's Word is absent, the Creator and the creature are allowed to drift apart. Deists are, however, not atheists. They still formally acknowledge a Supreme Being, a higher Hand, as the original source of the world. But once created, the world is ascribed an independent existence over against its Maker. God becomes an absentee landlord on a rather permanent holiday. He may indeed occasionally pay a surprise visit. We call such supernatural visitations miracles. For the rest, however, mankind, endowed with certain "inalienable rights," acts autonomously. Once the great clockmaker designs, constructs, and winds up his masterpiece, the clock then runs on its own according to natural law. The result is practical atheism.

b) Pantheism. This theory drifts in the opposite direction. In the absence of God's Word, which fixes the borderline between Creator and creature, God and the world are allowed to converge. Pantheism is a modern form of ancient neo-Platonism, except that, whereas in the latter the movement is from God downward into the creation, in modernity the movement is upward from the creation into God. The world tends toward a higher spiritual unity, evolving into divinity. Men possess within themselves a "spark of the divine" which can be fanned into full flame. The noblest in creation is man, and the noblest potentiality in man is God. God is thus a symbol of the destiny of all creation at its highest level of achievement. By an evolutionary process pantheists view man and all creation as either actually or potentially divine — thus wiping out the Creator/creature distinction.

c) Gnosticism. As indicated above, the neo-Platonic system of thought, instead of seeing creation as evolving toward God, sees it as devolving from God. God is pure Spirit. Inasmuch as creation is material, it is of a lower order, enslaved to an alien power. Material things are to be avoided by fleeing the world. The spiritual in creation and in man, which is good, is viewed as the sole avenue of communion with the divine. Thus, in Gnosticism too, whether in its ancient or contemporary expressions, there is no clear line of demarcation between the revealing God and the responding creature, as located in the mediating power of God's Word.

d) Voluntarism. On this position, too, there is no room for a covenantal bond between God and the world. Unlike deism, however, voluntarism ascribes literally every activity in the world to the immediate and arbitrary intervention of God. Creation has no significant reality of its own. For this would constitute a threat to the sovereignty of God. God is everything, creation nothing. The world has no real integrity. Its history is a marionette show. Creational activity is a direct extension of the will of God. Every important creaturely action is at bottom a divine action. The divine will is the unmediated cause of all culturally formative happenings. The result is quietism.

e) Monism. This contemporary worldview is a kind of inverted form of pantheism — inverted in the sense that, instead of creation evolving toward divinity, the divine is assimilated into the historical process. God has no identity or integrity apart from the world, nor the world apart from God. Yet the two cannot simply be fused. There is duality (the sacred and the secular) within a unitary process — captured in the concept "pan-entheism." God's existence is therefore no longer describable in terms of "up there" or "out there," but only "down here" and "in here." He is deeply enmeshed in the unfolding historical process, which, as a closed continuum, spirals open-endedly toward its future. That future represents the full eschatological unfolding of the reality of God-and-man-together. Monism, a form of radical historicism, like pantheism and Gnosticism, finally demands a thoroughgoing restatement of the Creator/creature question, since in the end both parties lose their unique identities. The two merge pan-entheistically into one. There is therefore no longer a vis-à-vis relationship of revelation/response between God and his creatures, that relationship on which theology is called to reflect.

IV. 9. Theological Language

None of these various options offers any promise of a unified life-vision. They all presuppose a two-factor worldview. The impasse created by them has generated a heated semantic controversy over the currently popular topic of "God-talk" with its profound implications for biblical hermeneutics, theology as a whole, and especially dogmatics. The question which arises is this: What status, nature, and weight can we attach to the way we talk about God? How does the language we use in referring to God relate to who God really is? In current discussions three main schools of thought have emerged. These three views are as follows.

a) Some hold that our language about God is *equivocal.* God and man stand at such a distance that human language is incapable of speaking about him with any degree of certainty. No direct, explicit statements are possible. For God and man have nothing in common, no link, no bond. Emphasis here falls on discontinuity. There is nothing in between except a yawning chasm which language cannot bridge. All "God talk" is therefore at best only conjectural and dubious. The equivocalist view leads to skepticism or agnosticism.

b) Others hold that our language about God is *univocal*. This view presupposes a substantial commonality between God and man. They are drawn so close together as to make possible a number of shared qualities, such as being, time, rationality, and language. The Creator-creature distinction tends toward overlap. Our "God talk" therefore corresponds quite exactly to who God really is in a roughly one-to-one relationship. Our language is essentially of the same order as God's. Emphasis here falls on continuity. To call God our "Father" means that he is Father in a sense quite identical with our human conception of fatherhood. The univocalist view represents an overstatement of how God relates to his creatures. It tends either to underrate divine sovereignty or to overplay human potentiality, thus leading in the end toward a form of lingual historicism — taking human language, which is a creational potential arising in response to the Word of God, and normatizing it with reference to God.

c) A third view holds that our language about God is *analogical*. It involves a break with two-factor thinking, comporting best with a three-factor outlook. It is more than a simple blend of the other two views, though it does seek to recognize the element of truth in both the equivocalist and univocalist perspectives. It stands, however, as a genuine alternative. For it locates the norm neither in God, which pushes it too far away, nor in man, which pulls it too close, but in the mediating Word of God which holds God and man together in a communicating relationship of revelation and response. Everything hinges on revelation. God's Word is the *logos* of John's gospel.* Our conversations with God and about God stand in a relationship of analogy to that Word. That holds for theological discourse too. The equivocal view offers too little knowledge of God's ways, the univocalist view presumes too much. Contrastingly, the analogical view holds that what we can know and say about God is not exhaustive or comprehensive, but it is sufficient, true, and trustworthy. For his Word is not only the boundary, expressing limitation, but also the bridge, expressing communion. God is true to his Word. And his Word faithfully reveals him. There is doubtless more to God than what is revealed through his Word. But all that lies beyond it is

---

* The idea of God's mediating Word within this three-factor worldview — wherever it occurs throughout this work — should not be confused with the "logos" doctrine espoused by a number of early church fathers.

more of the same. The analogical view, therefore, seeks to honor the biblical call to both humility and assurance in our knowledge of God and in our theological language.

IV. 10. Word of God as Norm

There are many ways to silence the Word of God in theology. The above models have the effect of doing precisely that. One can push the revelational norm so far away that it fades out. One can also pull it into our world of reality so thoroughly that it gets muffled amid surrounding sounds. That choice appears to be the fate of all two-factor theologies. Only a three-factor theology, in which the Word is recognized as holding a normatively structured place at the heart of the covenantal relationship between God and the world, can avoid these pitfalls. Revelation must be honored in its integrity as God's Word, and human response in its integrity as our answer to it. Response, however, may not be normatized. It is fully and truly human, just as revelation is fully and truly divine. We may never humanize the divine Word, nor deify the human word. To paraphrase ideas borrowed from the Chalcedonian Creed: The Creator and his creatures coexist "unseparated" and "undivided," but at the same time "unchanged" and "unconfused." Only in some such way can we avoid either secularizing the world by pushing the norm of God's Word off to an irrelevant distance or sacralizing the world by absorbing the norm into it. The impact of these considerations is to urge on us the importance of a three-factor worldview: God/his mediating Word/and the world. In this paradigm God's Word stands as both the boundary and the bridge between the Creator and his creation.

A picture is often worth a thousand words. Perhaps therefore a simple sketch, depicting a bit more graphically the intent of a three-factor view of reality, may be helpful:

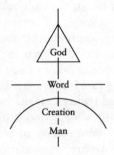

Chapter V

Prolegomena:
New Directions in Dogmatics

V. 1. New Paradigm

It is time now to turn a new corner. Earlier chapters repeatedly exposed the dualist anomalies which arise from two-factor theologies, creating inescapable dilemmas both in practice and in theory. These problems generated by traditional ways of stating the issue argue strongly for a new paradigm. We move on now to consider such an alternative paradigm as the frame of reference for a renewed statement of Reformed dogmatics. The central concern in this venture is a three-factor view of reality. I have already hinted broadly at this approach. It now remains to elaborate it more fully.

V. 2. *Sola Scriptura*

The key position in a three-factor view of reality belongs to the Word of God. It is the religious bond, the unbreakable link which binds the Creator and his creatures together in covenant partnership. But where do we turn for instruction concerning the place and role of God's Word for our life together in the world? Given the reality of our radical fall into sin, there is only one noetic point of departure, the Bible (cf. *Belgic Confession,* Article II). Scripture is the noetic key to a right understanding of the ontic order of created reality. It is the indispensable pair of glasses (Calvin, *Institutes,* I,6,1) which we with our sin-blurred vision must now wear in order to discover the meaning of creation, history, Christ, religion, and all the rest. If we are serious about the search for truth as related to the Truth, we cannot bypass this Book. For "all Scripture is inspired by God, and is therefore profitable for instruction, for rebuke, for correction, and for training in righteousness, that the man of God may be perfect, equipped for every good work" (2 Timothy 3:16-17) — including that work called doing dogmatics.

Choosing for Scripture as our port of entry excludes, of course, other choices. Modern theology, as we have seen, offers a number of other possible approaches. In saying "yes" to the reformational idea of *sola Scriptura* we are thereby saying "no" to a host of other noetic starting points — such as a priori commitments to human reason, natural law, historical methods, religious phenomena, and scientific testing. All of these approaches have been explored very intensively and extensively in such disciplines as philosophy of religion, cultural anthropology, psychology and sociology of religion, and historical criticism.

In adopting *sola Scriptura* as our epistemological vantage point, it is important to be clear on what we are saying. The affirmation of *sola Scriptura* does not mean that Scripture is God's only revelation. This was *Sola Scriptura* not the original meaning of this byword as coined by the sixteenth-century Reformers. For clearly Calvin, Luther, and others held that God reveals himself in creation and in Christ as well as in Scripture. Moreover, their appeal to *sola Scriptura* was not meant to deny the importance of church tradition, theology, philosophy, the church fathers, or the sciences and arts. All these have their rightful place in the life of the Christian community. The question, however, is this: By what unimpeachable standard is Christian faith to be evaluated? What is our central criterion of judgment? The answer is *sola Scriptura,* which, in the ablative case, means "by Scripture alone." This password of the Reformation conveys the idea of means or agency. That is, by the light of Scripture alone we are to judge all things and "hold fast to what is good."

This *sola Scriptura* accent therefore holds with equal force for Christian theologizing. Given the reality of sin with its profound and sweeping effect on our minds, it is now "by Scripture alone" as Word of God that we can begin to arrive at a renewed understanding of God's Word for creation and his Word incarnate in Christ. It belongs to the very genius of the Reformed tradition to seek to do justice to the full range of divine revelation, both creationally and redemptively, and in all the forms in which it comes to us, claims our allegiance, and elicits our response.

Theology is beset on every side with reductionist tendencies. Classic liberalism, if it leaves room for revelation at all, reduces it to the exemplary personality of Jesus. In a far more profound way neoorthodoxy also reduces God's Word to the once-for-all revelation of God in Christ Jesus. For divine self-disclosure is by definition always and only a personal event. Such Christomonism involves a severe denigration of creation and Scripture as primary modes of revelation. Evangelical Christians, too, are often guilty — in practice, if not in theory — of reductionist tendencies. Creation is often regarded simply as a natural given. Jesus Christ is honored as personal Savior and Lord. The concept of revelation, however, is reserved quite exclusively for the Bible alone.

Reformed dogmatics, as it takes its place within this polyglot universe of theological discourse, must recognize that it stands or falls with its adherence to "every Word which proceeds from the mouth of God" (Matthew 4:4). It may, therefore, not allow the *sola Scriptura* motif to be weakened by any reductionist connotations. Scripture does not close the doors to other forms of revelation. Rather, it serves as our open window on the full cosmic dimensions of our Father's world. As Cornelius Van Til puts it, "God's revelation in nature, together with God's revelation in Scripture, forms God's one grand scheme of covenant-revelation of himself to man" (*The Doctrine of Scripture*, p. 4).

The following thesis therefore defines our noetic stance: Taking Scripture seriously as Word of God leads us to recognize that there is more to the Word of God than Scripture alone. For the Bible itself points to realities beyond itself which it identifies as Word of God. To corroborate this thesis let us reflect on the biblical witness concerning the full reality of God's Word.

V. 3. God's Word for Creation

There is, first of all, God's Word for creation. Scripture illumines God's way with his world. As we tune in on its message, eavesdropping as its redemptive drama unfolds, paying careful attention to the text itself, and, as it were, "reading between the lines," this is what we hear as we highlight its testimony to creation. In the beginning, day in and day out, God put his Word to his world again and again. Ringing through the biblical account of origins is the constantly repeated refrain, "And God said, 'Let there be! . . . ,'" and so it was. His Word is never mere wishful thinking. It does what it says. His Word is powerful, active, dynamic, creative, purposeful. This mission-accomplishing thrust of the creational Word in Genesis is reinforced in God's encounter with Job, where he says:

> "[I] prescribed bounds for [the sea],
> And set its bars and doors,
> And said, 'Thus far shall you come, and no farther,
> And here shall your proud waves be stayed.'
> Have you commanded the morning since your days began. . . ?" (Job 38:10-12)

This passage points clearly to the power of God's Word as it holds for all created reality. The psalmist adds this commentary:

> By the Word of the LORD were the heavens made,
> And all their host by the breath of his mouth. . . .
> For he spoke, and it came to be;
> He commanded, and it stood forth. (Psalm 33:6, 9)

Western thinking often distinguishes sharply between "words" and "deeds." Words are cheap, deeds are what really count. This contrast clearly finds no support in Scripture, as is evident from the above passages. For God's words and his works are equivalents. Repeatedly they are used interchangeably. By his worded work and by his working Word God brought all things into existence, giving them their established structures, interrelated order, meaning, and direction. That Word has lost none of its efficacy:

> "As the rain and the snow come down from heaven,
> and do not return to it without watering the earth
> and making it bud and flourish, so that it yields
> seed for the sower and bread for the eater,
> so is my Word that goes out from my mouth:
> It will not return to me empty but will accomplish
> what I desire and achieve the purpose for which I sent it." (Isaiah 55:10-11)

The Psalms are punctuated liberally with this accent on the Word of God *(dabar)* by which he created all things, and now sustains, governs, and directs them to their appointed ends. That Word is subservient to God himself. At the same time it transcends the creation. As Psalm 119:89 puts it:

> Forever, O LORD, thy Word
> Is firmly fixed in the heavens.

The Word is the Word *of* God. It is therefore distinguishable from God himself. At the same time it stands transcendently above and holds for all creation. Perhaps we can capture this biblical emphasis best by saying that God's Word, that is, the Will of God *for* creation, is revealed *in* creation. This, it seems, is the thrust of Psalm 19:1-4:

> The heavens declare the glory of God;
> The skies proclaim the work of his hands.

Day after day they pour forth speech;
Night after night they display knowledge.
There is no speech or language where their voice is not heard.
Their voice goes out into all the earth,
Their words to the ends of the world.

This perspective is echoed in the following doxologies of the Psalmist:

He sends forth his command to the earth;
His Word runs swiftly.
He gives snow like wool;
He scatters hoarfrost like ashes.
He casts forth his ice like morsels;
Who can stand before his cold?
He sends forth his Word, and melts them;
He makes his wind to blow, and the waters flow.
He declares his Word to Jacob,
His statutes and ordinances to Israel.
He has not dealt thus with any other nation;
Praise the Lord! (Psalm 147:15-20)

Praise the LORD from the earth,
You sea monsters and all deeps,
Fire and hail, snow and frost,
Stormy winds fulfilling his Word. (Psalm 148:7-8)

The rich variety of terms scattered throughout the Psalms — word, command, statute, ordinance, precept, decree — with their different shades of meaning, all emphasize this central point: God is the Origin and Lord of all, and he mediates his sovereign rule through his Word. These Old Testament passages are, of course, poetic in form. We are therefore sometimes tempted to regard their elegant expressions ("His Word runs swiftly," Psalm 147:15) as mere figures of speech, reflecting poetic license, rather than as pointed references to reality. To do so, however, is to shortchange revelation. In their cumulative thrust, these richly variegated word pictures are reality-laden affirmations of the Word of God for creation. They make a forceful claim on the way we give structure to the biblical doctrine of creation.

What, then, is the relationship between "general revelation," understood as God's Word for creation, and our various scientific enterprises? In doing science, theology included, we may say that all created reality reveals the holding power of God's Word *reflexively*. The Psalm 19 passage might then be paraphrased along these lines: The heavens declare God's glory by revealing how his Word holds for the movement of heavenly bodies. Similarly, the magnetic force of gravity declares God's glory by revealing how God's Word holds for falling objects. Again, the scientific notion of capillary action declares God's glory by revealing how God's Word holds for the life of trees. The Word of God as such is transcendent. Thus it is not directly accessible to human investigation. It is therefore misleading to say without qualification that creation *is* divine revelation — that it *is* Word of God. Such expressions carry pantheist overtones. Creational revelation is rather a *reflexive, responsive* concept. We gain insight into the "knowledge of God" as Creator (Calvin) by observing how his various creatures respond to the holding power of his Word, each creature "after its kind." This holds for every aspect of created reality: migrating birds, land use, human rationality, child development. In theology this holds for reflection on our faith-life. Theoretical inquiry therefore calls for studying the *reflexive* impact of creational revelation as it impinges on each creature's way of answering to the *response* side of God's Word for creation.

In Proverbs the creational Word of God meets us personified as "Wisdom." She was there "at the beginning," serving as the divine planner and standard bearer and blueprint maker through whom the Creator ordered the life of his creation. We are told that "Wisdom has built her a house, she has set up her seven pillars" (Proverbs 9:1) — a poetic reference to Wisdom's role in God's creating activity. Even more eloquent is Wisdom's testimony to her involvement in creation and her executing role in it in Proverbs 8:22-31:

> "The LORD possessed me at the beginning of his work, before his deeds
>   of old;
> I was appointed from eternity, from the beginning, before the world
>   began. . . .
> I was there when he set the heavens in place, when he marked out the
>   horizon on the face of the deep,
> When he established the clouds above and fixed securely the fountains
>   of the deep,
> When he gave the sea its boundary so that the waters would not
>   overstep his command,
>   and when he marked out the foundations of the earth.
> Then I was the craftsman at his side.
> I was filled with delight day after day, rejoicing always in his presence,
> Rejoicing in his whole world and delighting in mankind."

God's Word for creation is revealed not only in calling all things into existence, but also in the divine wisdom which infuses the ongoing life of his creatures. Think of Isaiah's parable of the God-instructed farmer (28:23-29). His good insight into plowing and threshing, sowing and harvesting, "comes from the LORD of hosts" who is "wonderful in counsel and excellent in wisdom." We may assume that this farmer works diligently by the light of whatever Scripture he has. But his instruction in agrarian practices is not derived directly from the inscripturated Word. It comes rather from the wisdom of God embedded in seed and soil, which the farmer attains through years of hands-on learning experience. By being thus attuned to God's Word for rain and sunshine, for the coming and going of the seasons, the farmer is "instructed aright," for "his God teaches him."

This Old Testament witness to creational revelation is confirmed by the testimony of the New Testament. In the prologue to his gospel John sets in sharp focus the centrality of God's Word *(logos)*, first in creation, then in redemption. In terms reminiscent of the Genesis narrative, John says concerning the Word that "in the beginning . . . all things were made through him, and without him was not anything made that was made" (John 1:1-3). A more forthright disclosure of the mediating role of God's Word for creation is hardly conceivable. The author of Hebrews, twice within a single passage, reaffirms this same cardinal truth with respect not only to God's redemptive but also his creational and providential acts:

> In many and various ways God spoke of old to our fathers by the prophets: but in these last days he has spoken to us by a Son, whom he appointed the heir of all things, through whom also he created the world. He reflects the glory of God and bears the very stamp of his nature, upholding the universe by his Word of power. (Hebrews 1:1-3)

This emphasis on the mediating function of the Word of God also comes through with unmistakable clarity in Hebrews 11:3: "By faith we understand that the world was created by the Word of God, so that what is seen was made out of things which do not appear."

Turn finally to the second letter of Peter. To scoffers who blindly pretend that the world will simply continue to pursue its present course without divine intervention, Peter issues this stern reminder — emphasizing anew the centrality of God's Word:

> They deliberately ignore this fact, that by the Word of God heavens existed long ago, and an earth formed out of water and by means of water, through which the world that then existed was deluged with water and perished. But by the same Word the heavens and earth that now exist have been stored up for fire, being kept until the day of judgment and destruction of ungodly men. (2 Peter 3:5-7)

From beginning to end, therefore, our world is unthinkable apart from the mediating function of the Word of God. By the Word it was created. By that same Word it is being preserved and its history is being directed toward its eschatological destiny.

V. 4. The Word Incarnate

There is but one Word of God, not two or three. From beginning to end God issues a single Word, a consistent message, an unaltered will. He does not engage in "double talk" or "triple talk." Nor does he "change his tune" along the way. His threefold Word is like a triple variation on a single theme. Consider this crude analogy: H_2O, we say, represents water. We experience water, however, in three states — as liquid, solid, and gas. Yet, in whatever state, it remains the same H_2O, water.

Similarly, God's single Word impinges itself on our lives in three ways. First and foremost, according to Scripture, is God's fundamental and abiding Word for the world, spoken concreationally — with and in and for creation. In the aftermath of sin, God in these last days "spoke to us by a Son" (Hebrews 1:2). Christ is the Word of God personified, incarnate. For "the Word became flesh and dwelt among us, full of grace and truth" (John 1:14). This original designation of Christ is the triumphant title he continues to bear even in the biblical vision of the end times. The apocalyptic Rider on the white horse is called "Faithful and True," and his name is "the Word of God" (Revelation 19:11-13). Christ is God's *alpha* and *omega* as the Word preincarnate, then incarnate, in his exaltation as well as humiliation. Paul, therefore, never tires of anchoring the full sweep of all God's purposes with creation, the mystery of his will, the gospel of salvation, and the glorious inheritance of the saints "in Christ" (*en Christō* — Ephesians 1:3-23). This christologically focused perspective is breathtaking in its cosmic scope:

> He is the image of the invisible God, the first-born of all creation; for in him all things were created, in heaven and on earth, visible and invisible, whether thrones or dominions or principalities or authorities — all things were created through him and for him. He is before all things, and in him all things hold together. He is the head of the body, the church; he is the beginning, the first-born from the dead, that in everything he might be pre-eminent. For in him all the fulness of God was pleased to dwell, and through him to reconcile to himself all things, whether on earth or in heaven, making peace by the blood of his cross. (Colossians 1:15-20)

83

Christ Jesus as Word of God is therefore the key to the meaning of creation. In "all things" *(ta panta)* he is central and dominant. He is also the heartbeat of the biblical message from the first word to the last. Without him the Old Testament remains a closed book (cf. Matthew's repeated emphasis on "fulfillment"; also Luke 24:25-27; John 5:39; Acts 8:35). His life, death, and resurrection are the very core of the New Testament gospel (John 20:30-31).

The centrality of Jesus Christ is given added impetus by the familiar analogy employed by Augustine, Calvin, and others, depicting him as "the mirror" of all God's purposes with the world. He is God's ultimate Word. We have no Word beside or beyond this Word. He fully mirrors the Father's heart and will. God's Word revealed in Christ is the boundary line in revelation: thus far you shall come and no farther. He is himself also the sure bridge between God and man. For there is only one mediator between God and men, even Christ Jesus. "No man comes to the Father" — also in settling theological issues — "but by me," says Christ of himself. He who has seen Christ has seen the Father. We need not and cannot look past him. He is God's first, middle, and last Word for the world. All God's dealings with the world — creation, preservation, judgment, redemption, consummation — are through Christ. "All authority" — also in dogmatic matters — "is mine," says Jesus. There is "no other name under heaven given among men" to which we can turn for answers. His person and work is the hermeneutic key to the meaning of life in the world. Only a Christ-mediated, Christ-centered theology will do. "What do you think of the Christ?" is the initial, interim, and final issue.

Christian scholarship, theology included, is therefore called to discern the norms of God's creational Word for our life in his world, illumined and directed by his Word in Scripture, under the regal authority of his Word incarnate, so that thus we may learn to "lead every thought captive in obedience to Christ" (2 Corinthians 10:5).

V. 5. Closer and Closer

Throughout history God accommodates his Word to the human predicament. Originally the Word for creation, inaudible and invisible, yet clearly discernible in its effect (Psalm 19:1-4), was sufficient for our needs — reinforced by a more direct communication in the Garden (Genesis 2:15-17). The original impact of God's creational Word has lost none of its force. It is still as real and vivid as the latest sunrise and the next sunset.

All this is now noetically obscured, however, by our sinful propensity to "suppress the truth" of God's "eternal power and deity" by exchanging it for self-concocted ancient and modern lies (Romans 1:18-23). To counteract the effects of the fall, God in his condescending grace drives his Word home to us, closer and closer, in successively unfolding stages of revelation. Eventually, in the fullness of the times, God goes all the way. He identifies his Word with us. The "Wisdom" of Proverbs, crying aloud in the streets, becomes the "Logos" of John's gospel. The Word is personified, incarnate in Jesus of Nazareth, like us in all things except for sin — all this for us and our salvation. The Mediator of creation is now also the Mediator of redemption.

Along the way, as it were, God walks with us a second mile in the Scriptures, and then a third mile in his Son incarnate. In the witness of the prophets (proleptically) and apostles (fulfillingly) to Jesus Christ, God brings his Word very close to us. The creating Word, spoken in the beginning, is now cast into the form of an historical document. God, as it were, lays his Word in our laps, black on white, the Word of God in the words of men. In this lingual mode of revelation, somewhat analogous to its incarnate mode, God addresses us in a fully and truly divine, but also fully and truly human way. As Moses put it, God's Word is now easily within our reach:

> "For this commandment which I command you this day is not too hard for you, neither is it far off. It is not in heaven, that you should say, 'Who will go up for us to heaven, and bring it to us, that we may hear it and do it?' Neither is it beyond the sea, that you should say, 'Who will go over the sea for us, and bring it to us, that we may hear it and do it?' But the Word is very near you; it is in your mouth and in your heart, so that you can do it." (Deuteronomy 30:11-14)

If that was already true for Israel, how much more decisively so for us who are heirs to the completed canon.

V. 6. A Single Message

Searching the Scriptures in this way leads to a recognition of the three-fold Word of God. God accommodates his Word to our changing situations. It meets us where we are in order to bring us back and onward to where we ought to be. Therein lies the redirecting power of the good news proclaimed in both law and gospel. But God's Word not only responds to changing situations. God by his Word also repeatedly creates radically new situations. By the "mother promise" (the *protevangelium*

— Genesis 3:15) God intercepts our fall into sin. In calling out Abraham he creates a new peoplehood. In Christ, the Word made flesh, he ushers in the new age: "The old has passed away, behold, the new has come" (2 Corinthians 5:17). The appearance of God's Word in Christ at the crossroads of world history is the redemptive link binding together the testimony of the prophets and the apostles, the covenant in its old and new dispensations, the forward-looking Messianic message of the Old Testament, and the witness *(martyria)*, teaching *(didachē)*, and procla-mation *(kērygma)* of the New Testament. God's Word exercises its nor-matively steadying power from creation, through fall and redemption, onward toward the re-creation of all things in Christ Jesus. The full sweep of cosmic history stands under the holding and healing power of God's Word.

In the march of time the mode of revelation changes. But its essential meaning remains constant. There is no inner tension or contradiction between the creational Word, the inscripturated Word, and the incarnate Word. His Word with and for creation from the beginning was "trust me, love me, serve me." This same call to obedient living constitutes the heart of biblical revelation. Then at the center of the centuries, in a profoundly personal way,

> God said it best in Him who came
> To bear for us the cross of shame.

In its threefold expression the Word carries a single message — unity in diversity. For there is one God, one world, one Mediator, one covenant, one will, one way of salvation, one coming kingdom.

Scripture offers pointers to scenarios which lie behind its narratives. Leading up to its inscripturation, the Word came directly to the prophets — "the word of the LORD came to me, saying, 'Speak unto Israel. . . .' " The Word was also communicated directly by Christ to the apostles — "He opened his mouth, saying, . . ." Such direct revelation is certainly Word of God. But it is no longer accessible to us in its original form. We are now dependent on its faithful embodiment in the Bible. Therefore in our lives today, to all intents and purposes, these various modes of revelation (e.g., dreams, visions, direct utterances, theophanies, the in-carnate presence) are now fully focused in the Word of Scripture.

Moreover, when the pulpit faithfully proclaims the gospel, we may also leave the assembly of the congregation, saying, "Today we heard the Word of God." Then, as Sunday turns to Monday, and as worship equips us anew for service, we may go our way to work and witness in God's world supported by the conviction, "Thus saith the LORD." This proclaimed Word is, however, not really a fourth form of God's Word.

It is the written Word exegeted, interpreted, translated, and applied. Its validity is dependent on its faithful communication of the biblical message. The Word rightly proclaimed is an echo of Scripture. It is always appellable to the Word inscripturated.

V. 7. Scripture Is the Key

Epistemologically, therefore, it all comes down to Scripture. This Book is the indispensable guide for our knowledge of the way of salvation. It confronts us with the Word incarnate in Jesus Christ. It is also the hermeneutic key for our knowledge of the enduring norms of God's creational Word in its holding power for our life together in the world. Given our present human predicament, only in the light of that redeeming and liberating Word in its lingual form can we gain insight into the meaning of created reality.

The creational Word remains God's first Word for the world. It is also his lasting Word. God has not withdrawn it. It stands firm and will endure to the end. It has lost nothing of its original holding power and clarity. The trouble lies on the response side. Therefore, though that first Word is still sufficient for its original intent and purpose, it is no longer sufficient for our present need. So, thanks to God's condescending grace, that first Word is not God's last Word. He reiterates his creational Word in his Word of redemption. There is no divine retraction. God did not retreat from his original stand. The beginning was this: "God created the heavens and the earth" — the Genesis story. In the end he will usher in "the renewed earth, in which righteousness dwells" — the story of Revelation. In the redemptive sweep of history the primeval Garden becomes a City, the "New Jerusalem." The Paradise created, and lost, will be regained and fulfilled. The plan of redemption is not a different plan, replacing the original plan of creation. The original blueprint still holds. Redemption is, as it were, a "mid-course correction" — God pursuing his abiding goal in a sin-infested world via a "detour." Creation and redemption are together directed to the same end — that we may "glorify God and enjoy him forever." Only now it takes place along an alternative route. As Bavinck puts it,

> The covenant of grace [redemption] differs from the covenant of works [creation] in the road, not in its final destination. . . . The point of arrival returns to the point of departure, and is simultaneously a high point elevated high above the point of departure. (Jan Veenhof, *Nature and Grace in Bavinck*, pp. 19-20)

Thus the Word of redemption addresses us as a reaffirmation and republication of the Word of creation. The vision of final redemption beckons us onward and summons us to become coworkers with Christ in that kingdom project which is aimed at the restoration of God's original intent for the creation, which, though fallen, is now judged and redeemed, and is being renewed (Romans 8:18-25).

V. 8. Bi-unitary Revelation

The most fundamental issue in Reformed dogmatics is, therefore, a right understanding of the relationship between creation and redemption. In the terminology of classic theology, it is the relationship between general and special revelation. Despite sin, there is a basic *continuity* which holds for our life in the world with respect to the *structures* of creation — which classic theology ascribes to "common grace," perhaps better expressed as conserving or preserving grace. Our lives also manifest a radical *discontinuity* with respect to their *direction* — the renewal of which classic theology ascribes to "special grace." God's redemptive Word in Scripture witnesses in Christ to the redirection of our misdirected lives. The biblical story line therefore reveals the movement from formation (creation), through deformation (fall) and reformation (redemption), toward consummation (restoration).

In this unfolding drama Scripture plays its uniquely decisive role. Its good news links creation and re-creation. Its message is qualified by the prefix *re,* the "re-" factor. It is a redemptive *re*-publication of God's enduring Word — "Heaven and earth may pass away, but my Word abides forever" (Mark 13:31). It is a second, revised edition of God's creational Word, now in lingual form. The law of God, his Word in imperative form, was not promulgated for the first time on Mt. Sinai. Nor was it revealed for the first time in the Pentateuch, or in the prophets, poets, or apostles. It is "as old as the hills." From the beginning God's Law-Word served as the criterion for the creation order. The law, therefore, was not "born," but "re-born" at Sinai. It was there reformulated on stone tablets, rearticulated, reiterated, restated in the language of prohibitions, reflecting the more negative side of God's positive purposes with Israel and the world.

Christ demonstrates pointedly the abiding normativity of God's Word in setting the record straight on the question of marriage and divorce (Matthew 19:3-9). In refuting the casuistry of the Pharisees of his day, he appeals to the law of Moses, affirming its perennial authority for married life. When his critics then seek a loophole in the law, Jesus acknowledges that in the face of marriage breakdowns, as a second-best solution, in order to avert further antinormative devastations of family life, Moses allowed certain concessions in the application of the law. This was, however, because of "the hardness of your hearts." As an ultimate appeal, however, Jesus reaches back to the original normative Word of fidelity, declaring that it still stands:

> "But from the beginning of creation, 'God made them male and female.' 'For this reason a man shall leave his father and mother and be joined to his wife, and the two shall become one.' So they are no longer two but one. What therefore God has joined together, let not man put asunder." (Mark 10:6-9)

Marriage is meant to be for good and for keeps. There are, therefore, no first-order "biblical grounds" for divorce, and, by that token, since God's Word is steadfast, no creational grounds either. Divorce can only be a second line of defense against further breakdowns.

Common parlance often leads us to talk of an "order of creation" and an "order of redemption." This idiom is, however, very misleading. It allows us to think of these two "orders" as two quite different realms. Such thinking leads us back into the old dualist traps. Scripture opens up a better perspective. Perhaps we can formulate it best in terms of the structure/direction distinction. Across the centuries the structures and functions of creation remain intact, thanks to the constant holding power of God's Word by which he graciously sustains the works of his hand, even in the face of sin's disrupting effects. Rain still falls and the sun still shines on the just and the unjust alike (Matthew 5:45). Marriage is still marriage, work continues, night still brings rest to tired limbs, and all people still worship at some altar. Sin, however, results in massive distortions in the way we exercise our creaturely functions and relate to each other within the structures of creation. This realization has been captured in the idea of "total depravity." Redemption aims at the renewal and redirection of our creaturely functioning within these various structures. Creation and redemption are therefore not competing or complementary sets of realities. They are rather two deeply interwoven ways of coming to know the one and only world there is: one from the viewpoint of God's creating work, the other from the viewpoint of his redeeming work. This twofold work of God must be honored in its interrelated wholeness. All that is covered by God's Word for creation is recovered by his word of redemption — "already" in principle, but "not yet" in perfection.

Recognition of this bi-unitary revelation is more than merely an article of faith, more also than an important point for theological inquiry.

It is a liberating, life-renewing experience. It unlocks the biblical idea of Christian freedom, of Christian witness, of Christian calling in the world. In the measure that we miss the mark at this point we also stray from the right path at every other point along the way, ultimately pitting God against himself. We must therefore honor the historical religious story line of creation/fall/redemption/consummation as the sequential, now also interacting pattern which stands at the heart of the unfolding biblical drama. And all four of these biblical motifs must be honored in their fully cosmic and holist dimensions. It is becoming increasingly clear that the way one responds to these cardinal biblical ideas serves as a hermeneutic test case for judging contemporary theology.

V. 9. Pilgrimage

The venerable concepts "general revelation" and "special revelation" are deeply embedded in our theological vocabulary. One may then be inclined to ask, Why move beyond this bi-unitary to a tri-unitary way of reflecting on revelation, that is, to speaking in terms of God's threefold Word — his Word for creation, in Scripture, and in Christ? In partial answer to this question, I invite you to retrace a pilgrimage which I and others have made over the past few decades.

It is, of course, still possible and meaningful, and as a starting point perhaps even indispensable, to discuss revelation under the traditional headings of general and special revelation. That tradition is in fact the very matrix out of which the idea of the threefold Word of God emerges. Without an initial firm commitment to this tradition advance is impossible. Standing within it, therefore, the tri-unitary view of revelation represents a self-conscious, deliberate effort to work out more fully its implications, relieved of the tensions latently present in these traditional concepts.

My pilgrimage can be reconstructed along the following lines. Going back to my student days, the concepts general and special revelation were part and parcel of our theological vocabulary. But questions arose. For this twofold way of thinking and speaking about revelation often tended to slip over into the same dualist patterns examined earlier on the question of the relationship between philosophy and theology. Often the integral unity between these two modes of revelation was eclipsed. Instead of a unified view of reality, a dichotomist outlook emerged. I began to wonder, moreover, about the meaningfulness of the terms themselves. What is so "general" about general revelation? The term sounded so nondescript, so purely formal, so short on content. "The heavens declare the glory of God" — that is God's general revelation in creation. But is that not indeed something very "special"! And special revelation — is it not "general" in the sense of being intended generally, universally, for all? Thus the ambiguity of the concepts, though not the reality to which they point, left me with a cluster of questions.

Carrying these unanswered questions with me, I settled down to my studies in Amsterdam. Reading around, I encountered the book *Het Dogma der Kerk*. Its chapter on revelation nudged me a step further along the way on my pilgrimage. There I found general and special revelation discussed under the rubrics of "fundamental" and "redemptive" revelation. This terminology created new possibilities. It broke with the rather nondescript, formal, abstract character of traditional terminology. The bi-unity of revelation came into clearer focus. It helped overcome the tendency toward dualist misconceptions. "Fundamental revelation" — this is God's foundational, abiding revelation in his work of creation. "Redemptive revelation" — this, after sin, is God's renewing revelation in Scripture and in Christ for the restoration of the fallen creation. With this new insight into an old truth the pilgrim went his way rejoicing.

Then came my fourth Christmas season in the ministry, serving a Canadian congregation. Having sermonized on the advent theme for the so-manyeth time, I was in search of fresh ideas. Turning to my bookshelf, I pulled down Klaas Schilder's work *Licht in de Rook*. There I came across his sermon notes on Matthew 2, "The Wise Men and Word of God." With that, another new day dawned. There it was, in good Calvinist fashion — three points. First, the Wise Men were "attracted by God's Word in nature" — the light of the advent star. Second, they were "redirected by God's Word in Scripture" — Micah 5:2, correcting their initial misconception by leading them from Jerusalem to Bethlehem. Finally, having thus been drawn magnetically by God's revelation in creation and having been redirected by the prophetic Word of the Old Testament, these foreign visitors reached the climax of their long journey, God's surprising fulfillment of his long-standing promise: They "worshiped the Word made flesh" in Jesus Christ. That Christmas discovery pushed me another step forward. An open road now lay before me, leading to an increasingly fuller recognition of the tri-unitary character of the Word of God. Schilder had traveled that road before me. Soon I found other travelers moving in the same direction. The Reformed tradition had born the fruit of ongoing reformation.

This renewed vision on divine revelation recommends itself for a number of reasons. It helps, first of all, to capitalize more fully on the fundamental unity of God's various ways of making known his will to men. With this approach we stand a better chance, moreover, of avoiding the dualist tendencies which often accompany traditional ways of discussing general and special revelation. For in the many ways God comes to us we hear his one, steadfast, covenantal call to obedient living. Finally, articulating the doctrine of revelation in terms of the threefold Word helps us adhere more faithfully to the concrete language of Scripture itself. Rather than relying on the more abstract categories general and special revelation, a step or two removed from Scripture, we can theologize with our ears attuned more closely to the very text of the Bible. Working hand in hand, biblical and dogmatic studies can then enter into a more reciprocal working relationship, bearing richer fruit for the ministry of the church and the service of God's people in the world.

V. 10. Covenant Partnership

The heart of the matter is, therefore, a three-factor theology. Its pivotal point is the mediating role of the Word of God. A perusal of leading Reformed theologians is enough to convince one that this outlook is not foreign to the reformational tradition. On every hand there is overwhelming evidence of an intuitive awareness that we are called to reckon with three great realities: the revealing God, man as responding creature, and revelation as the abiding link between them. What we are now doing, therefore, is nothing more than stating explicitly as a normative structuring principle what is already implicitly present in the mainstream of Reformed thinking. As Kuyper put it: "All revelation assumes (1) one who reveals Himself; (2) one to whom He reveals Himself; and (3) the possibility of the required relation between these two" (*Principles of Sacred Theology,* p. 257).

What this calls for is not only a continuing recognition of the reality of God and man as *partners* in an ongoing relationship of revelation and response, but also a firm recognition of the Word of God as the covenant bond which establishes a *definitive* partnership between them. Older theologies tended to stress the two *relata,* the related parties, God and man — often at the expense of the mediating *relatio.* This led to rather abstract, isolated, ontological treatments of "the doctrine of God" and "the doctrine of man," followed by "the doctrine of Christ" as Mediator. Newer theologies tend to blur the reality of God and man (the two *relata*) by assimilating them into an only vaguely definable *relatio* called "encounter," "confrontation," "crisis," or "moment of decision." In view of these developments the words of the traditional Form for Baptism are meaningful: "As in all covenants there are contained two parts . . ." (perhaps better: "two parties"), so also a right understanding of the

92

covenantal bond uniting these "two parties" is essential to a biblical worldview, to Christian faith, and to Reformed dogmatics. It is therefore crucially important to seek to do justice to the two *relata* in *relatio*.

God's Word is his way of coming out to us his creatures. By way of his Word, God, as it were, moves out of "his world" of eternal trinitarian fellowship toward the flesh-and-blood reality of the cosmos. His Word is the communicating *bridge* which undergirds his communion with us and ours with him. But it is also the *boundary* between God and the world, the borderline which sets the horizon to all creaturely upreach. In reflecting on God's mediating Word we are therefore moving along the outer limits of our theological potentials, touching on the very periphery of mystery. On this side of his Word are the "revealed things" of the Lord; on the other side are the "secret things." Along this revelational line we are pressing the distinction between the "secret Will" and the "revealed Will" of God. The former lies on "his side" of the Word, the revelational side; the latter on "our side," the response side. It should not surprise us, therefore, that in thus skirting the extremities of our knowledge our theoretical constructs begin to falter and our language becomes inarticulate. In company with Calvin (*Institutes,* I,1-5) and other theologians we must exercise great care in distinguishing between God as he is in himself *(ad intra)* and God as he comes out to us in his Word *(ad extra)*. His decreeing Word is extrinsic to God, not intrinsic. It belongs to his outgoing work, not to his inner essence. We must accordingly posit a certain distance between "the reality of God as he necessarily is and the reality of the decree" (James Daane, *The Freedom of God,* p. 77). Or, as Herman Hoeksema puts it: God is "absolute, sovereignly above all laws and relationships; and we must forever deal with the relative, because we are under law." Accordingly, "there can never be any knowledge of Him if we must establish the connection necessary for such knowledge." But "the Infinite did reach out into the finite. In this revelation we have an adequate *medium* through which . . . we derive real knowledge of God" (*Reformed Dogmatics,* p. 6).

The Word as the *relatio* between God and the world clearly has suprahistorical dimensions to it. This is the testimony of Scripture: ". . . and the Word was God" (John 1:1). But God's Word also has an outgoing creational side to it. It is *con*creational — that is, it is given along *with* created reality. Biblically speaking, therefore, the Word is unthinkable apart from creation, just as creation is unthinkable apart from the Word. It is therefore speculative to think of God's Word for creation prior to creation. It was "with God . . . from the beginning." Through the Word "were all things made" (John 1:1-2). And in Christ "the Word became flesh" (John 1:14). Here we are touching on the mystery of the Trinity. Christ the Word *is* God. He is also the Word *of*

God. This confession is meaningful only within the context of the *relatio* between God and man, conceived of as both boundary and bridge between the Creator and his creation. Theologizing must therefore begin and end with a deep sense of wonderment. It rests on childlike trust that the mediating Word is the religious lifeline which links God and man together in a lifelong, all-embracing covenant relationship of revelation and response.

Calvin's theology moves strongly in this direction. He opens *The Institutes* with these lines: "Nearly all the wisdom we possess . . . consists of two parts: the knowledge of God and of ourselves" (I,1,1). If this were Calvin's last word instead of his first, or if this were his only word, then these "two parts" could be construed as two parties, God and man, with nothing in between. We would then have to struggle with the yawning chasm between two unrelated factors of reality. In fact, however, Calvin protests the implications of such a view. He rejects, on the one hand, all pretended ignorance of God, since "the universe is for us a sort of mirror in which we can contemplate God, who is otherwise invisible" (I,5,1). He also rejects speculation, holding that "we ought not to rack our brains about God; but rather, we should contemplate him in his works" (I,5,9). We therefore know God not as he is in himself, but as he manifests himself in his outgoing words and works. The question is therefore not that of the scholastics, Who is God in his essence? But, Who is God in his relationship to us? The best understanding of Calvin is that which sees God's revelation as the abiding covenantal bond between man and his Maker. His view of the Christian religion therefore calls for the recognition of a three-factor worldview: God, his Word, and the world. As Hendrikus Berkhof puts it, "Between God and creation lies a decision of the will" (*Christian Faith,* p. 152). God's Word for creation, further revealed in Scripture and in Christ the Mediator, is the dynamic bond uniting the Creator and all his creatures, just as the Holy Spirit is the living bond (the "second Mediator") uniting us to the incarnate and glorified Word made flesh. Calvin's thinking is pervasively relational. Accordingly, every truth about God has an anthropological correlate, and every truth about man has a theological correlate.

The central importance of God's Law-Word as the norm for all created reality, to which God freely binds himself, and to which he holds us, is aptly expressed by Herman Bavinck in the following words:

The Christian worldview holds that man is always and everywhere bound by laws set forth by God as the rule for life. Everywhere there are norms which stand above man. They find a unity among themselves and find their origin and continuation in the Creator and Lawgiver of the universe. These norms are the most precious treasures entrusted to mankind. It is God's decree that these divine ideas and laws be foundations and norms, the interconnections and patterns for all creatures. To live in conformity to these norms in mind and heart, in thought and action, this is what it means most basically to become conformed to the image of God's Son. And this is the ideal and goal of man. (*Christelijke Wereldbeschouwing*, pp. 90-91)

V. 11. Recontextualizing Reformed Dogmatics

At this juncture a few explicitly methodological comments are in order.

a. Theologizing cut loose from tradition is like taking a leap in the dark. The theological traditions of the past accompany us into the present and sustain us as we move along into the future. Rejection of time-tested traditions results in cut-flower theologizing. Severed from its roots, its blossoms soon wither in our hands. Ongoing renewal of Reformed dogmatics must therefore be tempered by a deep sense of indebtedness to master theologians from the past, whose works constitute a massive legacy of insights and interpretations. Sorting out, working our way through, and coming to terms with even the major strands in this tradition is an enormous undertaking. The theological mills may grind slowly, but they do grind very finely. The restless, creative minds of the fathers appear to have left no stone unturned in explicating Christian doctrine. There is good reason to conclude, therefore, that by now all the countless pieces of this giant theological puzzle must certainly lie before us on the table. There is very little which is really new that we can bring forth under the sun. In view of this, the current situation appears to cry aloud not so much for new ideas, but for a catalytic agent to assist us in forging anew from this vast array of ideas a more unified, integrally coherent, and meaningful totality picture. Within the prolegomenal parameters of this project, then, the urgent challenge is to sketch the basic contours of a biblical worldview within which constructive theology can do its work more fruitfully. Locating dogmatics within such a frame of reference, recontextualizing it, and reshaping its structures accordingly, is a matter of high priority which motivates this present work.

b. This venture is therefore not motivated by some latter-day rationalist impulse for a closed system. Such theological imperialism would collapse under the sheer weight of its own intellectual arrogance. It is rather a matter of seeking to listen anew to the Word of God. Even our most penetrating analyses can never fully capture the cosmic sweep of the mighty acts of God in creation and redemption, together with the baffling disparities in human response. It may be possible, however, to integrate our theologizing into the basic contours of the classic Reformed worldview and life-vision in such a way that we can deal more fruitfully with the teachings of Scripture. If such a venture should do no more than relieve us of the dubious constructs of both scholastic "objectivism" and existential "subjectivism," that alone would be a significant gain. If, in addition, it should help make dogmatics more serviceable to the Christian community, so much the better. This project proceeds on the conviction that such a recontextualizing of dogmatics is possible and can indeed contribute to theologizing with greater openness to God's Word.

c. In various branches of learning it is customary nowadays to speak of model building and paradigm construction. Theologians also resort to such imagery. They draft theoretical blueprints which seek to account for the data of daily experience. Not everyone agrees, however, on the meaning and import of such models and paradigms. Therefore, on this point too, clarity is important. It is possible, for example, to claim too little for such constructs, as well as too much. They claim too little, and thus underestimate the work of Christian scholarship, who repudiate the truth character of their findings. There is a tendency among such thinkers to allow their models and paradigms only a certain pragmatic value. Their sole virtue lies in being helpful for predicting results in further experiments. On the other hand, they claim too much who cling doggedly to their hypotheses as the last word. All theoretical reflection, theology included, is, after all, but human work. As such it is always open to critical review, revision, and ongoing reformation. Recognizing this does not, however, rule out clear affirmations and forthright position taking. Conviction is not the same as arrogance. We must remember, however, that our theological models and paradigms are but responses to revelation, and not themselves revelation. Dogmatics is interpretation of God's Word, and not the Word itself. It is fitting therefore that we press our claims tentatively and with humility, however convincingly we seek to state our case.

d. There is more to dogmatics than just jumping in and doing it. Getting off on the right foot calls for a prolegomena of some sort — a word *vorauf* ("beforehand"), or at least a word *zuerst* ("as a starter"). For every theology proceeds on the basis of certain pretheological assumptions and operates inescapably within certain philosophical perspectives. Failure to clarify these basic contextual issues prolegomenally means leaving their rough edges exposed along the way, only to be deciphered later by others or explained in a postscript. "Right order of teaching," as Calvin would say, calls for dealing with such matters up front. For theology cannot stand by itself as an independent, isolated enterprise. There are always pretheological, confessional, hermeneutic, philosophical issues, issues of religious stance, of faith commitment, of worldview and life-vision, for which we must render account as we move into dogmatics. That is precisely the major concern of this prolegomena. Dogmatics is too important to be left to theologians who are unclear about their philosophical underpinnings.

e. A hasty survey of some leading contemporary theologies reinforces this point. Knowingly or not, theology always moves within the larger mainstream of some philosophical tradition. Modern Roman Catholic theology, for example, especially that which predates the rise of the "New Theology," assumes the basic structures of Thomist philosophy. The Reformed theology of the Princeton school is deeply influenced by Scottish Realism. Rudolf Bultmann openly acknowledges that his theology is indebted to the existentialist philosophy of Heidegger. Much of the heavy emphasis on language analysis and verification procedures in present-day theology is traceable to the impact of philosophers such as Wittgenstein, Russell, Whitehead, and others. Finally, to close out this brief list of examples, the Marxian analysis found in many of the liberation theologies of our time has been shaped largely by the philosophy of Hegel and the Neo-Hegelians. What is true of these theologies holds structurally for all others too.

Theology simply cannot get on with its task very well without philosophical reflection. Some may regard theology itself as an adequate substitute for philosophy. But this view suggests an expansionist notion of theology. For philosophy deals with the more general, theology with the more specific. Philosophy paints a totality picture within which theology explores in depth a community's faith-life and confessional expressions. Philosophy surveys the house of theoretical reflection as a whole. Theology, including dogmatics, occupies one room of the house. It makes sense, then, to view the house as a whole, and the street on which it stands, before moving into one of its rooms. Philosophy ought therefore to be included as a very strong foundational component in a good theological education. Arthur Holmes emphasizes the importance of philosophy for doing theology in these words:

> Philosophy . . . has a different focus than theology, a focus on concepts and arguments basic to all areas of life and thought, including but not confined to religion and theology. It therefore contributes to an understanding of foundational issues (epistemology, metaphysics, and axiology) that underlie science and history and art as well as theology, so that the integration of one's thought proceeds at a basic theoretical level that all disciplines have in common. (*Contours of a World View*, p. 39)

f. This renewal project in Reformed theology is dedicated to locating dogmatics within the Reformed worldview and the Christian philosophy developed within the neo-Kuyperian tradition. Standing within a

Calvinian tradition, Abraham Kuyper himself already recognized clearly the importance of such a larger philosophical setting for doing theology. Such contextualizing of dogmatics came to even clearer and more long-lasting expression in the work of Bavinck. The fruits of this tradition are discernible in the dogmatic studies of Berkouwer.

Kuyper's view on the integral relationship between theology and philosophy is evident in the following excerpt adapted from his major work on theological methodology:

> The task of theology is "to take up the ectypal knowledge of God, as it is known from its source, the Holy Scripture, into the consciousness of re-created humanity and to reproduce it." But "philosophy has an entirely different task." It "is called to construct the human knowledge, which has been brought to light by all the other sciences, into one architectonic whole, and to show how this building arises from one basis." Accordingly, the necessity of philosophy "arises out of the impulse of the human consciousness for unity." Therefore, to say that "a Christian is less in need of philosophy [than a non-Christian] is only to exhibit spiritual sloth and lack of understanding."

> A Christian philosophy is necessary since "philosophy which reckons only with natural data will always vibrate between a pantheistic, deistic, and materialistic interpretation, and will never do more than form schools, while Christian philosophy, whose theistic point of departure is fixed, is able to lead to unity of interpretation within the circle of regeneration. But for this very reason theology is able to go hand in hand with a Christian philosophy." It is the task of philosophy "to arrange concentrically the results of all the other sciences, and if non-Christian philosophy ignores the results of theology, as though it were no science, theology is in duty bound to enter her protest against this. If, on the other hand, the philosopher himself is regenerate, and is historically and ecclesiastically in union with the life of regeneration, then of course in his studies he includes the results of theology, together with the results of all the other sciences, and it is his care, architectonically, to raise such a cosmological building that the results of theology also find their place naturally in it." (*Principles of Sacred Theology*, pp. 614-15)

V. 12. Biblical Worldview and Christian Philosophy

Kuyper's greatest contributions to the renewal of the Calvinist tradition around the turn of this century are rooted in his dynamic rearticulation and practical implementation of a biblically directed, Reformed world-and-life view. Much like his spiritual father, Groen van Prinsterer (1801-1876), Kuyper (1837-1920) grew up as a child of his times. The nineteenth century was a bleak era for historic Christianity. Modern liberalism, fathered by Schleiermacher, dominated Western theology. For Kuyper, like Groen, the decisive turning-point came with his conversion from liberalism to the faith of the Reformers. From then on he drew his theological strength mainly from the work of Calvin. The heritage of Calvin had been handed down, however, in a seriously revised form, reshaped by post-reformational scholastic theology. The rationalist imprint of this Protestant orthodoxy is also evident in Kuyper's dogmatics. He often takes over quite uncritically some of the dualist thinking so typical of scholastic thought. Kuyper failed to bring the renewing impact of his reformational worldview to bear fully on his systematic theology. In dogmatics, therefore, Bavinck reflects the Calvinist tradition more clearly than Kuyper. His work remains a better guide than that of Kuyper.

For all three, however — Groen, Kuyper, and Bavinck — theological issues were part of a much larger picture. At stake was the very future of Western Christianity as a viable culture-shaping force. Could it survive the devastating effects of the French Revolution? Could biblical religion be revived in the face of prevailing Neo-Protestantism? Could the Reformed faith still have a redeeming influence on the direction of the Western world? Kuyper drew the lines of conflict sharply in his classic treatise on the Calvinist worldview in these words:

> From the first, therefore, I have always said to myself [that] "if the battle is to be fought with honor and with a hope of victory, then principle must be arrayed against principle; then it must be felt that in Modernism the vast energy of an all-embracing life-system assails us; then also it must be understood that we have to take our stand in a life-system of equally comprehensive and far-reaching power. And this powerful life-system is not to be invented nor formulated by ourselves, but is to be taken and applied as it presents itself in history. When thus taken, I found and confessed, and I still hold, that this manifestation of the Christian principle is given us in Calvinism. In Calvinism my heart has found rest. From Calvinism have I drawn the inspiration firmly and resolutely to take my stand in the thick of this great conflict of principles." (*Calvinism*, Stone Lectures, p. 11)

It is against the background of his keen sensitivity to this all-out struggle for the hearts and minds and lives of men, a struggle which goes beyond theological reflection, that we must understand Kuyper's call for a Christian philosophy. Such an undertaking, he held, is a matter of high priority, precisely in order to undergird theology and give it a clearer orientation. For theology finds its place within the larger contours of a biblical worldview explicated in a Christian philosophy.

Kuyper's call for a Christian philosophy went largely unanswered during his lifetime. He himself was a theologian, not a philosopher. Moreover, until well into the twentieth century the Free Reformed University in Amsterdam, which Kuyper served as a founding father, rector, and instructor, could not boast a chair in philosophy. This vacuum was filled in 1926 with the dual appointment of D. H. T. Vollenhoven and Herman Dooyeweerd.

Early in their careers the direction of thought in these pioneering philosophers was captured in a publication entitled "In Kuyper's Line." Kuyper had given ringing affirmation to his central commitment in the unforgettable confession: "There is not a single square inch of the entire cosmos of which Christ the sovereign Lord of all does not say, 'This is mine!' " Vollenhoven and Dooyeweerd then set out to open up this life-vision more fully in terms of a penetrating and coherent philosophical analysis of the structures and functions of created reality. In doing so they also sought to overcome the remnants of scholastic (dualist and synthesist) thinking still present in the theology of Kuyper and his contemporaries. That was the intriguing challenge confronting Vollenhoven, Dooyeweerd, and eventually a larger circle of like-minded Christian thinkers during recent decades. Over the span of roughly half a century their work has come to be known as "The Philosophy of Law-Idea" or "Cosmonomic Philosophy." Their analysis, critique, and reconstruction of pressing life-issues now stands as a monumental contribution to Christian scholarship. A philosopher of law who does not share Dooyeweerd's religious outlook paid him this tribute: "Without exaggeration Dooyeweerd can be called the most original philosopher Holland has ever produced, even Spinoza not excepted" (G. E. Langemeijer, "An Assessment of Herman Dooyeweerd," in L. Kalsbeek, *Contours of a Christian Philosophy,* p. 10).

This development in Christian philosophizing represents a further step in the historical unfolding of the Reformed tradition in theology. The day is now past that Reformed dogmatics can afford to be unaware of the importance of a Christian philosophy for its theology. The renewal of Reformed dogmatics now calls for a more explicit delineation of its philosophical foundations and context. To neglect the Christian philosophy associated with the names of Vollenhoven and Dooyeweerd is to impoverish Reformed theology.

The fundamental premise of this Christian philosophy lies in its commitment to the biblical teaching that all reality is so ordered by the creative work of God that his Word stands forever as the sovereign, dynamic, redeeming law for all of life. Accordingly, it repudiates the modern dogma of the pretended autonomy of human reason; it seeks to uncover the deeply religious roots and motivations which undergird its own and other systems of thought; it affirms the centrality of the human heart, out of which flow all the issues of life; and it therefore works in the firm conviction that life as a whole is religion. This unifying view on our callings in God's world, including our task in theology, lends to Reformed dogmatics a deeper sense of life-relatedness, a more firmly structured place among the scholarly disciplines, and a more responsible directedness, thus opening new doors to the possibility of ongoing theological reformation.

V. 13. Christian Philosophy and Theology

Despite Barth's protest, there appears to be a growing recognition that ". . . any attempt to formulate orthodox theology wholly apart from philosophical interests runs counter to the Christian heritage as far back as Augustine and even earlier" (Carl Henry, *God, Revelation, and Authority,* Vol. I, p. 189). Because "philosophy permeates systematic theology, . . . to avoid using philosophy is simply impossible" (Winfred Corduan, *Handmaid to Theology,* pp. 22-23). Barth's negative judgment on philosophy, however inconsistent his adherence to it, is, of course, understandable. For in the past, almost universally, philosophical prolegomena functioned as an antecedent and independently grounded system of thought. It therefore created irresolvable tensions between prolegomena and dogmatics. The former was viewed as providing the rational underpinnings for the superstructure of faith erected on it. Most prolegomena, therefore, according to Barth, "do not so much lead up to the real work of dogmatics as lead away from it" (*Church Dogmatics,* I/1). The fathers of Vatican II sensed this problem too, declaring that "in the reform of ecclesiastical studies, the first object must be a better integration of philosophy and theology" (*The Documents of Vatican II,* "Priestly Formation," Article 14). Prolegomena must be of a piece with dogmatics proper. For "the theologian will not remain true to the faith he professes if the philosophical framework he adopts is not consistent with that faith" (Stuart Fowler, *What Is Theology?,* p. 9).

Such integration is possible only if philosophical prolegomena and dogmatic theology are viewed as sharing a common footing. Though differentiated in function, prolegomena and dogmatics must be perspectivally unified. The major thesis at this point is therefore that the most fitting prolegomena to a Reformed dogmatics is a Christian philosophy. The noetic point of departure for both is Scripture. It provides the revelational pointers, the guidelines, the "control beliefs" (Nicholas Wolterstorff) for shaping a biblically directed philosophy as well as a Christian theology. The deeper background to both is a communally held Christian worldview, which binds scholars and the rest of the Christian community together as partners in faith. This jointly held worldview plays a bridging role between commitment to Scripture and the scientific enterprise in both philosophy and theology. It serves to integrate biblical faith and theoretical reflection. There is thus a kind of normative movement from faith through worldview to philosophy and theology, with reciprocal interactions in and among them. Structurally this holds not only within the Christian tradition, but in others as well. As Albert Wolters puts it:

> A worldview is a matter of the shared everyday experience of humankind, an inescapable component of all human knowing, and as such it is non-scientific, or rather (since scientific knowing is always dependent on the intuitive knowing of our everyday experience) prescientific, in nature. It belongs to an order of cognition more basic than that of science or theory. Just as aesthetics presupposes some innate sense of the beautiful and legal theory presupposes a fundamental notion of justice, so theology and philosophy presuppose a pretheoretical perspective on the world. They give a scientific elaboration of a worldview. (*Creation Regained: Biblical Basics for a Reformational Worldview,* p. 9)

Thus biblical religion shapes the basic contours of a Christian worldview. As this commonly held Christian worldview is worked out along the lines of a critical analysis of the structures and functions of created reality, it yields a Christian philosophy, whose task it is to investigate and seek to account for the empirical data of daily experience in its profound unity as well as rich diversity. The Cosmonomic Philosophy, developed within the reformational tradition, seeks to formulate the norms which hold for these well-ordered dimensions of life in a paradigm known as the "modal scale" (cf. L. Kalsbeek, *Contours of a Christian Philosophy,* pp. 95-108). Such a philosophical hermeneutic is, of course, as with all theoretical constructs, always open to ongoing review and revision. It has a status more tentative than the Christian worldview which it explicates, certainly less settled and binding than the biblical revelation to which it appeals. Nonetheless, it offers valuable insights into the identity and integrity of theology and the other scholarly disciplines, together with their coherent interrelatedness, yielding a unifying overview on the encyclopedia of learning as a whole.*

Within this perspective, we come to recognize theology as one

---

*See B. J. Van Der Walt, *A Christian Worldview and Christian Higher Education for Africa,* pp. 23-37.

discipline among others. Each has its own unique object of study. Each focuses on its own peculiar aspect of reality. Yet all of them together are coherently interrelated. Within this panoply of sciences theology is no longer to be revered as the "queen of the sciences." Where Christ is King of all there is no need of a queen. Theology is rather that discipline which focuses on the faith-life (in distinction from, say, the political-, aesthetic-, economic-, or ethical-life) of a given Christian (or non-Christian) community. While theology touches life as a whole, it views life through its own specific window. It should not attempt to be all things to all men. It is indeed a "happy science" (Barth). But its joy is largely lost if it fails to respect its own uniquely important yet limited role in the life of the Christian community. It is a special, concentrated, peculiarly focused science. It should therefore not seek to usurp the role of philosophy as a general overview science. Nor may theology invade the peculiar field of inquiry of its partners in science. It cannot cover the entire waterfront.

All too often, however, this is precisely what happens. It is a commonplace mistake to think of theology as dealing with everything "spiritual" — God, revelation, Bible reading, prayer, faith, in short, all "religious" matters. Such conventional notions involve a serious confusion of categories. For these so-called "spiritual"/"religious" realities lay their claim on nontheological studies as well as theology. They are therefore not helpful in defining the unique field of inquiry in theology. Such imprecise understandings of theology foster, moreover, the false dichotomy between a sacred and a secular realm, as though every "Christian" approach to the issues of life falls into the theologian's lap. When this happens, the concept "theology" gets misapplied, as in political, liberation, and feminist "theologies" — many of which are not specifically theological studies at all. Such practices overload our theological task. The only fundamental corrective on such encyclopedic misnomers is the inner reformation of all the sciences by means of a Christian philosophy.

Theology's specific mandate is to focus on the confessional (pistic, faith) aspect of life — leaving the biotic, psychic, social, lingual, and other aspects to scholars in other disciplines. It is called to explore life's "ultimate concerns" (Tillich), the "Here I stand!" (Luther) certainties which play a leading role and serve a formative function in shaping the Christian life, worldview, and philosophy. The central concern of biblical theology, for example, is not with the Bible as great literature or as a record of ancient history (though these aspects are never wholly absent); these considerations are ancillary to the pervasive stress on confessional certainty which is at the heart of the biblical message. Again, the historical theologian does not seek to cover the full sweep of world history, but concentrates on confessionally qualified documents (creeds), institutions (churches), practices (worship), persons (popes), and movements (revivals). These samples reflect theology's particular angle and slant on life. Since theology's object of study cannot be some "uncreated reality beyond the creation, . . . a theology that does not take seriously the world-relatedness of faith is not worth having" (Fowler, *What Is Theology?*, pp. 6, 8).

John C. Vander Stelt has broken new ground in further clarifying and refining the field of inquiry for theological reflection. In place of the traditional concept "theology" (literally "the study of God"), he makes a strong case for calling this branch of study "pistology," rooted in the biblical word *pistis,* meaning "faith" (thus "the study of faith"). At first glance, this strange-sounding nomenclature may arouse unfavorable impressions. However unusual, Vander Stelt holds that "the word 'pistology' is actually not any stranger than psychology, biology, or even theology." For the latter terms also betray their ancient lingual lineage. The only significant adjustment in replacing "theology" with "pistology" is long-standing conventional usage in favor of the former. However, allowing for acceptance of this new terminology, Vander Stelt goes on to define "pistology" as ". . . a theoretic analysis of the nature, norms, role, and scope of the subjective and objective pistical dimension of creaturely existence" ("Theology or Pistology?" in *Building the House: Essays on Christian Education,* pp. 115-35). "The object of theological investigation is no longer God, revelation, or religion. . . ," says Vander Stelt; for, from a Christian viewpoint, these three realities hold for all the sciences. What distinguishes theology from the others is its focus on "faith as a unique feature of creaturely existence."

Within this perspective Vander Stelt then distinguishes four meanings of faith. One of its most common usages is based on passages such as Ephesians 1:8: "For by grace you have been saved, through faith; and this is not your doing, it is a gift of God." Accordingly, faith is

> . . . a divine gift of grace through which sinners are converted and enabled to believe the right things again. Sinners are *un*believers, *dis*believers, not *non*believers; they believe the wrong things. They do not lack belief, but their belief is idolatrous. True faith has its origin in the miracle of God's grace.

In this most profound sense, understood as radical renewal, "faith cannot be the object of theological investigation." As act of God, it lies behind and beyond rational scrutiny. It is the deeper experiential background to all Christian life and scholarship. Drawing on such saving faith is not unique to theology; rather, it determines "whether it is a Christian or a non-Christian theology" — and for that matter whether any other scholarly enterprise is Christian or not.

But there are three biblical senses in which faith is the proper object of theological inquiry. First, faith may be understood as "a conscious, intentional human act of believing or confessing. . . ." This act of faith is often called *fides qua* — "faith by which" (Hebrews 11). Second, "faith can be used in the sense of the content of what is believed. . . . For Christian believers this content consists both of God's revelation in creation, incarnation, and inscripturation and of what men and women of God in confessional obedience (and disobedience) have done with this revelation." This content of faith is often called *fides quae* — "articles of faith" (Jude 3). Third, we experience faith

> . . . in the sense of aspect, namely, the pistical aspect of all created reality, including the nonhuman world. Through a careful, theoretical analysis of this dimension, it will be possible to begin to lay bare the intricate structure of faith as activity and faith as content, and thus to make clear how faith-life is integrally related to the rest of reality. (Pp. 128-30)

These very promising insights can spare Reformed dogmatics the agony of trying to make too much of theology (expanding it to the study of religion) as well as too little (limiting it to a study of the Bible). (Cf. Louis Berkhof, *Introductory Volume to Systematic Theology*, pp. 17-26.)

V. 14. Dogmatics as a Branch of Theology

Just as popular parlance should not be allowed to dictate the meaning of theology, so too with dogmatics. Conventional usage often associates it with high- and heavy-handed pronouncements which have the effect of forcefully silencing other points of view. ("He always speaks with such an air of dogmatic authority!") Theologians have often earned the dubious reputation of engaging in such "dogmatic" imperialism, though, as a form of arrogance, it is not limited to them. The point, however, is this, that such "dogmatism" has nothing to do with defining dogmatics.

How then are we to understand the nature, scope, and task of this enterprise known as dogmatic theology — also called systematic or constructive theology? Dogmatics is, of course, related to its root word, "dogma." Both concepts, "dogma" and "dogmatics," carry a wide range of meanings, the former having a longer history than the latter. The concept "dogma" is traceable to classical Greek thought. Philosophically it referred to a firmly grounded theoretical idea. In legal matters it stood for an authoritative command, such as a royal edict. The concept "dogma" also found its way into the New Testament. Its usage there is far broader than its typical significance in dogmatic theology today. There it refers variously to an imperial decree (Luke 2:1; Acts 17:7) or a divine ordinance (Ephesians 2:15; Colossians 2:14) or the official decisions of a church assembly (Acts 16:4).

During the early centuries of the Christian era the established teachings of the Greek schools of philosophy continued to be called dogmas. As increasingly the gospel penetrated the Greco-Roman world, Christian dogma, now proclaimed as the truth of the Scriptures, moved onto a collision course with the accepted dogmas of the empire. In the wake of the great ecumenical councils, as early Christianity became increasingly ecclesiasticized along hierarchical lines, dogmas became defined more and more as doctrinal declarations by church assemblies. They were regarded as roughly equivalent to the creeds and confessions of Christendom. This usage was carried over generally into the medieval era.

Throughout the ancient and medieval periods, however, no branch of Christian scholarship assumed to itself the title of dogmatics. This development is of comparatively recent origin. It emerged in the aftermath of the Renaissance and the Reformation during the seventeenth century. With the dawn of modernity the study of dogmas (dogmatics) was extended to embrace not only the study of creeds and confessions (symbolics), but also the theological "sentences" of the fathers. Moreover, as theology gravitated steadily away from its churchly confines into the heady atmosphere of the modern university, dogmatics took on an increasingly stronger scientific and theoretical character. Given the intensely rationalist methodologies of the scholastic tradition in Protestant orthodoxy, dogmatics was viewed increasingly as the capstone of all the other theological disciplines. Biblical studies, church history, and the other fields of theological study were to supply the building blocks with which the dogmatician could engage in "system building."

It is now past high time to lay to rest such triumphalist pretensions. For dogmatics is called to play a coexistent and proexistent role within the larger academic community. Like all other Christian scholars, dogmaticians are called to fill a servant role, ministering to the needs of the Christian community. Such an attitude could go a long way toward dismantling troublesome barriers between dogmaticians and other theologians, as well as between theologians generally and philosophers and other scientists. It could also foster better relations between the academy and the church, between the pulpit and the pew, between Sunday's worship and Monday's work, as well as lending support to Christian organizations in society. This partnership view of dogmatics also raises some important questions for theological education; for example, should dogmatics be conducted within the interdisciplinary setting of the college/university or in the more withdrawn setting of the seminary? or both?

Dogmatics is here understood as a study of the faith-life of the Christian community as formulated in dogma(s). Christian faith is, of course, more than dogma. But dogma is one expression of it. It is the cognitive, reflective side of faith as it takes shape in a body of basic beliefs and doctrines. This includes the creeds and confessions of Christendom, other statements of faith, the doctrines and traditions of the church, together with the theological schools of thought which have grown up around them. This project in Reformed dogmatics is committed to a biblically directed restatement of the major dogmas of Western Christianity. It seeks to honor their time-tested value while at the same time reevaluating their relevance for our times. This calls for critical dialogue which is subservient to spiritual growth and theological development. Such a critically affirmative dogmatics must stand on a solid confessional foundation, while being also ongoingly reformational. Dogmatic indifference is contraband. For such an attitude is incapable of contributing anything constructive to the settlement of contemporary theological issues. As Regin Prenter puts it:

> Settlement can take place only when the dogmatician places himself within his own understanding as he has received it from that confession. . . . Standing there he must first of all seek to acknowledge with what understanding of the message of the biblical writings he has the right to stand where he does. Through constant study of the biblical writings he must then be willing to correct this understanding in the degree that the content of the biblical witness compels him to do so. The result will be a readiness on his part to listen to the questions which other understandings of the biblical writings might address to his understanding. The presupposition for our being able in the ecumenical discussion to take a different standpoint is that we under no circumstance are indifferent to our own standpoint. There is nothing which stands in the way of an understanding of the concerns of other confessional bodies quite so much as dogmatic indifference to one's own confessional body. (*Creation and Redemption,* p. 29)

V. 15. Hallmarks of a Christian Philosophy

To restate my major thesis: Christian philosophy, grounded in the biblical faith and a Christian worldview, offers the most promising prolegomena to Reformed dogmatics. Such an approach creates open doors to dogmatics proper, laying its foundations and locating it within the larger context of Christian thought. What, then, are the fundamental tenets undergirding such a philosophical prolegomena? Note briefly the following formative principles.

a) A hallmark of the Calvinist tradition is its steady insistence on a firm and clear distinction between the *Creator* and his *creation*. This principle of separateness resists all tendencies to blur the divinely established boundary lines, not only differentiations within creation (for example, between male and female, worship and politics), but primordially the distinction between God and man. It rejects all notions of ontic continuity: God is transcendent and sovereign and all creatures are subject to his will. Such a profound and reverential sense of distance and otherness is a basic, nonnegotiable tenet of a Christian philosophy.

b) This does not exclude, however, communion and communication between God and man. For God discloses his sovereign will and elicits our responses to it by his mediating *Word*. God's Word is his way of coming out to us and meeting us where we are. As boundary and bridge, it is describable in biblical language as "decree," "statute," "ordinance," and "command"; or theologically as "creation order," "Law-Word," and "cultural mandate." The Word of God, so understood, impinges itself on all creatures. It holds compellingly in nature (for example, the law of gravity). In human affairs (for example, art, science, music, trade, health care) it appeals to our sense of responsibility. God's Word is no less normative for the work of dogmatic theology. It is likewise the major hinge on which Christian philosophy turns, and is therefore crucially important in a Reformed conception of prolegomena.

c) A further principle is the idea of *creatio ex nihilo*. All things originate in an absolutely sovereign, outgoing work of God. He is the Initiator of all that is. His finished work "in the beginning" delineates the arena for responsive living under his Word, defines the parameters of our theoretical potentialities, and establishes the normed horizon of every earthly enterprise.

d) A further distinction, integral to the biblical worldview and therefore also to Christian philosophy and Reformed dogmatics, is that between "the heavens" and "the earth." We read that "in the beginning God created the heavens and the earth" (Genesis 1:1). The biblical drama, as it unfolds, then focuses primarily on the earthly domain. For Scripture is addressed to us, human beings, within our habitat, not to the angelic realm. Yet the mysterious heavenly realm is never very far away. Again and again it reenters the picture. Scripture presents heaven, not as a never-never land of mythological happenings, but very concretely as the deeper background to earthly history. For beyond the "heaven" of our immediate atmosphere ("the birds of the heavens"), and beyond that of interstellar space ("the hosts of heaven"), there is "the heaven of heavens." This "third heaven" is the intracreational abode of God and his "ministering spirits" (Hebrews 1:14). In their comings and goings we catch a glimpse of that mysterious free-flowing traffic (Job 1:6; 2:1) which moves between the heavenly throne of God and the earth as his footstool (Isaiah 66:1). Repeatedly the interaction between these two arenas of created reality enters the purview of biblical revelation. Especially at crucial turning points in the history of redemption, heavenly messengers appear on the earthly scene to announce new developments and usher in new events.

These and similar biblical givens lead us to distinguish between the heavenly, invisible kingdom and the earthly, visible kingdom (Colossians 1:15-20). In both kingdoms all things were created through Christ (John 1:3). Over both God rules as sovereign Lord. Yet the agenda of the heavenly realm transcends our normal experience (apart from certain exceptional "third heaven" experiences, 2 Corinthians 12:1-6). Apart from the modern secularist mind, there is no warrant for dismissing these "heavenly places" (Ephesians 1:3) as the mythological fantasies of a prescientific age. The heavenly kingdom is real. It has its own history. The downfall of Satan (Luke 10:18) and the angelic victory over demonic powers (Revelation 12:1-17) are backdrops to the earthly triumph of God's grace in Christ Jesus. While being always open to this heavenly perspective, biblical revelation concentrates on the earthly scene. This larger cosmic openness cautions us, however, against the claims of secularism that our earthly horizon exhausts created reality and that world history is a closed continuum. For there is always more to life than meets the naked eye.

e) History is God's way with his world, his way, through its "downs" and "ups," of unfolding the potentials of his creation. He is Lord of all. Viewed from the response side, history is the drama of the *cultural mandate* — either faithfully or unfaithfully pursued. We are called to open up and develop ("have dominion" and "subdue," which means rendering tender, loving, stewardly care) the creational resources along multifaceted lines — farming, linguistics, architecture, dogmatics — as God's representatives, to his glory, and as a blessing to our fellowmen.

f) In the aftermath of Adam's sin and of redemption in Christ, reformational thought honors the important distinction between *structure* and *direction*. Structure refers to the orderliness of creation as it originally was and as God's Word still impinges on it, calling it back to what it is still meant to be and to what it will one day become. Direction refers to creational life as it is now distorted and misdirected through our fall into sin, and as it is now also in principle renewed and redirected to obedience in Christ. The divinely ordained structures *for* creation stand forever. But the structures *of* creation are fallen in Adam. Yet by his preserving (common) grace God still upholds and maintains the structures and orders of creation (marriage, work, rest, intellectual prowess). Apart from Christ, however, our life within them remains misdirected. In Christ we can begin anew to experience the restoration of our lives and, within these structures and orders of creation, to redirect them to obedient service. Sensitivity to these directional issues keeps us aware of the spiritual antithesis which cuts through our very hearts and lives, including the world of scholarship.

V. 16. Dogmatics: Partnership and Servanthood

The field of dogmatics is not an inaccessible island. At numerous points there are open bridges to and from other areas of life, carrying a lively flow of two-way traffic. Let us explore some of these connecting links.

a) A healthy dogmatics must be firmly rooted in the deeply religious faith-life of the Christian community. "Life is religion"(Evan Runner) — life in its entirety. The way we live it, our life is our religion. Dogmatics is the calling of some within the Christian community — but not all. For while all are religious, not all are theologians, not even occasionally — just as politics enters the life of every citizen but not everyone is a political theorist; or just as all of us engage in business transactions but not everyone is an economist. So theology, including dogmatics, as a scientific enterprise is not every Christian's business. It is dependent, however, on the everyday practical faith-knowledge of God's people, even as it opens up the Christian faith to theoretical reflection. Its mandate is therefore to explicate, deepen, enrich, defend, and when necessary to reform the church's understanding of that fund of dogmas which is an integral part of its living tradition.

It is crucially important, thus, to distinguish between faith and theology. They are as different as dogma and dogmatics, worship and liturgics, evangelism and missiology, sermons and homiletics. Without this distinction every theological problem runs the risk of creating a faith crisis. No theology has canonical status. That belongs to God's Word alone. Even confessions are appellable to the Word. Theology is even more tentative. It should be possible to change one's theology more readily than one's confession. A certain playfulness, room to experiment with new ideas, should be tolerated in dogmatic theology, without immediately incurring suspicion or charges of heresy. Theology is no less prone to error than any other human activity. It must therefore always be open to ongoing reformation. Dogmatics is not right simply because it is a theological activity. It can be right or wrong, detrimental or beneficial, believing or unbelieving, or, as often, a mix of both. How wrong it is, then, to place our faith in some theology. This is a form of idolatry. Theology is called to expose the idols of our time, not add to their number. Faith, however, is qualitatively different: It is "a sure knowledge . . . and a firm confidence" (Heidelberg Catechism, Q. & A. 21).

Bavinck is quoted as having said on his deathbed, "My dogmatics doesn't help me now; it is faith that counts." Was he in these words denigrating his life's work? Not at all — he was simply accentuating the priority of faith. Faith and works, including theological works, must be distinguished but not divorced (James 2:14-26). Faith funds dogmatics, as its field of inquiry. On the basis of our faith-life, and in the light of our faith-knowledge, dogmatics is called to study the acts and contents of faith. This is its stupendously profound task. For among the rich diversity of aspects which make up the wholeness of our lives, the faith aspect plays a leading role. It points upward, relating all our historical acts responsively to the Word of God.

If by faith we confess that "Christ is Lord of all," then this confession of faith sets the tone for all our other life expressions — morally, politically, economically, socially, and in every other life relationship. In the measure that the rest of our life conduct is consistent with our confession, this "vertical" faith dimension then also lends direction to our way of life as a whole. Disciplined reflection on the dogmas of this confession is the theoretical focus of dogmatic theology. As such it can play a crucial servant's role in partnership with its sister sciences. To paraphrase an ancient adage: In his work every dogmatic theologian serves God, or some god or gods; in so doing he is transformed into the image of his god or gods or God (Psalm 115:8); he then constructs a dogmatics in his own image. This cluster of truths reflects the religious depth dimension of doing dogmatics, lending it (like other branches of Christian scholarship) a compelling sense of earnestness, exhilaration, and joy. Thus faith and dogmatics go hand in hand. Faith possesses a carryover power which shapes dogmatics, so that the mind of faith also infuses one with a mind for doing dogmatics.

b) Dogmatics (like all other disciplines) is a normed science. By what norm, criterion, standard of judgment is it to operate? The history of dogmatic theology *(Dogmengeschichte)* is strewn with a motley assortment of norms. To mention just a few of these competing courts of appeal: There is the legacy of apostolic authority among the early church fathers, papal tradition in Roman Catholicism, spiritual experience in pietism, the scientific method in modern liberalism, and historical reality and praxis as a "second source of revelation" in contemporary forms of process theology. In the face of these options Reformed dogmatics, standing in the reformational tradition of Luther and Calvin, embraces the

Word of God as its "rule for faith and life," for all of life, and therefore also for theologizing. The inscripturated Word, in conjunction with the creational revelation and in its pervasive witness to Christ, is the working principle and ultimate norm for dogmatics, governing, judging, and redeeming it — for theology, too, needs redemption. God's Word is the dynamic power which lays its claim on the heart and soul and mind and strength of all faithful and obedient scholars. Scripture by itself, however, when reduced to a set of propositions to be mastered, cannot save us or our theology. Only the Christ of Scripture can. This was the forceful rebuke which Jesus administered to the Pharisees of his day (John 5:30-47). Vaunted reliance on "dotting the i's" and "crossing the t's" of Scripture without submission to the living Lord of Scripture is bibliolatry. The Christ who comes to us "clothed with the Scriptures" (Calvin) is the sole vindicator of all our dogmatic reflections. It is in this sense that God's Word is the steady norm for orthodoxy and orthopraxy.

c) Dogmatics must keep the lines of communication open to the institutional church in its variegated ministries. The mission of the church is to equip believers in practical ways for their life together in God's world (Ephesians 4:11-16). Dogmatics works at a more theoretical level. It must never forget that such theorizing is of secondary importance. The faith-knowledge which informs the life of the Christian community is primary and its priority must be honored. Remembering this, theology can offer valuable assistance if in rendering self-effacing service it places itself at the disposal of God's people. Dogmatics has no explicit place in the pulpit or in the council chambers of the church or in its catechism classes. But by standing as a servant at the nexus of faith, proclamation, and praxis, dogmatics, in cooperation with its coexisting theological disciplines, can play a supporting role in the church's ministry of preaching, teaching, administration of the sacraments, diaconal assistance, pastoral care, fellowship, and outreach.

d) In coalition with other Christian scholars, dogmatic theologians are obliged to keep their study windows open to the larger challenges of the Christian community and society at large. Their critical tools of analysis can assist the people of God in developing a more mature Christian mind on the pressing problems of the day. Their work should be so shaped by a kingdom strategy as to penetrate the marketplace of ideas and the arena of daily practice with the reforming impact of the gospel. The competencies of other scholars enable them to help God's people think and act more biblically in political, economic, social, and educational ways. Those active in dogmatics should do the same in confessional and theological ways. They should remain ever alert to opportunities to lend a helping hand to Christian organizations and action groups in society. Recall how in their own very divergent ways Walter

Rauschenbusch influenced the world with his social gospel, Karl Barth in drafting the Barmen Declaration, and Jürgen Moltmann in forging some of the theological underpinnings for contemporary liberation movements. Dogmatics may not be allowed to withdraw into an "ivory tower" seclusion.

V. 17. The Canonicity of Scripture

Scripture is the rule for all Christian living. As such it is also the canon for doing dogmatics. At this point, then, we turn in summary fashion to the question of biblical canonicity. It is not easy in retrospect to reconstruct the history of canon formation during the early Christian era. The root meaning of the word *canon* is a "measuring stick," a "criterion of judgment." One finds a few references to this idea in the Pauline epistles (2 Corinthians 10:13-17; Galatians 6:16), indicating not so much an official set of writings as the established parameters of Christian conduct and the standard of Christian belief. Still the New Testament church did embrace "the sacred scriptures" (2 Timothy 3:15) of the Old Testament as its inherited canon. This commitment lived on in the early church. At first it followed the Palestinian canon, which was made up only of the books of the Old Testament ratified by the Jewish council in Jamnia (A.D. 98), rather than the Hellenist canon, which also included the Apocrypha. Later, however, despite Jerome's cautionary note in the Vulgate (A.D. 385), the apocryphal writings were also accepted as deuterocanonical books. This tradition continued until Luther revived the issue of their canonical status with his German Bible of 1534. We are confining ourselves here to the New Testament story of canon formation.

In retracing this course of events, the following historical factors appear to have played an important role.

a) About ten *persecutions* broke out in the early centuries of the Christian era, some local, some empire-wide. Under pagan pressure some Christians "lapsed" from the faith. Others faced the prospect of a martyr's death. Confronted with this grim possibility, they were often driven to the ultimate choice: Recant of these sacred books or else. Such crises forced the issue: Among the many early church writings in circulation, for which books must we stand firm even on penalty of death?

b) *Heresies.* Like most people, when hard pressed to defend their cause, heretics, too, seized on whatever sources were available to justify their views. So the question arose: Which books carry divine authority? To which books may we appeal in order to establish Christian doctrine and practice?

c) Rival Canons. Gradually various sets of New Testament writings emerged in the early church. Notable among them was the rather standard listing of the Muratorian Fragment (c. 200), following on Marcion's gnostically inspired, intensely anti-Semitic version of the canon, reducing it to Luke's gospel and ten epistles of Paul (c. 150). Posing an opposite threat was the Montanist movement (c. 200), which expanded the canon to include the oracles of its prophetic leaders. Facing such options Christians were pressured to decide which canon to follow. Which books belong to the scriptures of the New Covenant? Thus, in the crucible of repeated conflicts the New Testament canon gradually took shape.

Looking back we may now ask: What were the normative considerations which entered decisively into this process of New Testament canon formation? Three points stand out.

a) Apostolicity. The idea of canonicity came to be viewed as essentially synonymous with apostolic tradition. Basically it was a matter of source and authorship. To be received into the canon a given book had to be directly traceable to the apostles or their immediate disciples. As firsthand eye- and earwitnesses to the life, death, and resurrection of Jesus, his words and his works, they were the living links between Christ the Head and his body the church. Canonical books were viewed as those representing the apostolic succession of Christ's gospel in the life of the church.

b) Coherence. The idea of canonicity was linked closely to the principle of consistency. To qualify, a given book had to bear clear evidence of its coherence in content with other canonical books. Apostolic writings as a whole, moreover, were embraced as Word of God on the basis of their agreement with the witness of the prophets. This criterion of coherence caused lingering doubts regarding some books — not only the Apocrypha, but also Hebrews, 2 Peter, James, Jude, and Revelation. The basic stance among the patristics remained, nevertheless, the principle of the analogy of Scripture, issuing in the rule that Scripture interprets Scripture. Questions concerning the inner consistency of Scripture arose with renewed urgency in the sixteenth century, especially in light of Luther's emphasis on "what promotes Christ" *(was Christum treibt)*, leading to his making disparaging remarks about James, Jude, and 2 Peter, to his elevation of John (stressing the words of Jesus) as "the principal gospel" above Matthew, Mark, and Luke (stressing his works), and to his eulogizing of Psalms as a "little Bible" and Romans as "the most important document in the New Testament." Generally, however, the Reformers recognized that a fundamental canonical coherence is intrinsic to the Scriptures, over against Rome which tended to look to the *magisterium* (the official teaching office of the church) as the guarantor of coherence among Scripture, the apostolic witness to Christ, and tradition.

114

c) Universality. Early Christians believed that biblical canonicity is reflected in its ecumenical address. A flood of documents had found its way into the church. Many were written by regional bishops to meet local needs and thus enjoyed a high degree of local esteem. Several versions, for example, of the "acts of the apostles" were making the rounds. To be recognized as canonical, however, a given book had to reveal clearly the relevancy of its message for the life of the church as a whole. Based on this criterion of universality, letters written by Clement of Rome to Corinthian Christians (c. 95) and by Ignatius to various Christian communities (c. 110) came to be regarded, not as canonical, but as edifying literature.

Despite widespread criticism of the canon in our times, there is little impetus to either expand or reduce the limits of the New Testament writings from the twenty-seven traditionally accepted books. Instead, contemporary critical scholarship, whether in biblical, historical, or dogmatic studies, tends to accommodate the "received text" to its own hermeneutic principles. This approach usually results in seeking to salvage a core of abiding truth by retreating into "a canon within the canon" (Gerhardt Maier, *The End of the Historical-Critical Method,* pp. 26-49).

In retrospect, we may ask, What principle of interpretation best explains what was happening in this process of canon formation? Answers to this question involve more than historical judgments. They reflect profound views on the nature of biblical canonicity itself. Four major views have been proposed.

a) Some appeal to a form of *providentia specialissima* — a series of very special providential acts of God by which he confirmed the Scriptures in the life of the early church — divine interventions bordering on the miraculous. Evidence in support of this view is singularly lacking. The story of the canon reflects a large measure of uneven development, not only between the East and the West, but also within the West. There were lingering differences, sometimes heated controversies, which only gradually yielded a solid unanimity.

b) Others seek justification for this emerging canonical consensus in the idea of *inspiration.* It is argued that the Spirit, whose inspiring activity guided the apostles in penning the Word, was also active in the life of the church, inspiring it to receive the Word. This view, however, extends the idea of inspiration beyond its meaning in Scripture. There it refers uniquely to holy men of God writing as they were moved by the Holy Spirit (2 Peter 1:20-21; 2 Timothy 3:16-17). This view therefore has a leveling effect on the historic doctrine of biblical inspiration. It blurs the important distinction between inspiration and illumination. Only the latter applies appropriately to the church's receiving, reading, interpreting, and practicing the biblical message.

c) A third view, historically and theologically far more influential than the previous two, grounds the canon in the authoritative actions of *episcopal succession and church councils*. This is the traditional stance of medieval and modern Roman Catholicism. Appeal is then made to the Easter Letter of Athanasius (c. 297-373), more decisively to the Councils of Hippo (394) and Carthage (397), and ultimately to the Council of Trent (1545-1563). At stake is the question of priority: Is the church primary or the canon? Catholic dogma holds that, though the canon has ontic authority in itself, noetically its authority for us is dependent on the consent of the church. Apostolic authority, vested hierarchically in the magisterial voice of the Roman bishop, is the concrete historical guarantor of biblical trustworthiness. The sacred writings were born out of the bosom of the church. The church can therefore claim a certain priority over Scripture. It is the custodian of truth. In this sense the living tradition of the church acts as a canon above this canon.

Appeal often goes out to Augustine's recollection of the voice which led to his conversion, "Take and read!" It is argued that this was the voice of the church confirming the Scriptures. Added to this is Augustine's later comment, "I would not believe the gospel unless moved by the authority of the Catholic Church," together with his additional comment, "You cannot have God as your Father unless you have the Church as your Mother."

These memorable words of Augustine occasioned vigorous debate during the Reformation era. Rome tended to hear in these words the voice of Augustine the churchman. The Reformers understood them in the light of Augustine the Christian thinker. Are there, then, "two Augustines"? According to Calvin, the church is indeed "the mother of believers." She exercises, however, not a canonical, but a pedagogical authority in "aiding," "helping," and "assisting" her children to live the Christian life. He therefore ascribes a ministerial task to the church,

> . . . into whose bosom God is pleased to gather his sons, not only that they may be nourished by her help and ministry as long as they are infants and children, but also that they may be guided by her motherly care until they mature and at last reach the goal of faith. . . . [Changing the metaphor, he adds that] . . . our weakness does not allow us to be dismissed from her school until we have been pupils all our lives. (*Institutes,* IV,1,1 and 4)

Calvin holds that Augustine is not teaching that "the faith of godly men is founded on the authority of the church" or that "the certainty of the gospel depends upon churchly assent," as though "Scripture has only so much weight as is conceded to it by the consent of the church." Its canonicity does not rest on "the determination of the church." Citing Paul's words that the church is "built upon the foundation of the prophets and apostles" (Ephesians 2:20), Calvin concludes that "if the teaching of the prophets and apostles is the foundation, this must have had authority before the church began to exist." Augustine therefore meant that "the authority of the church is an introduction through which we are prepared for faith in the gospel." Thus, though "the church receives and gives its seal of approval to the scriptures, it does not thereby render authentic what is otherwise doubtful or controversial." Thus the church plays a subservient role, subject to the canon which justifies it, judges it, and empowers it (*Institutes,* I,7,1-4).

While Luther places less emphasis on the "mothering" task of the church, Calvin and he agree that canonical certainty rests not on some infallible ecclesiastical decree, but on the inner testimony of the Holy Spirit. In the words of Luther, "God must say to you in your heart, 'This is God's Word'; otherwise it is uncertain." As Calvin puts it, since "the Word is not quite certain for us unless it be confirmed by the testimony of the Spirit," therefore "God sent down the same Spirit by whose power he had dispensed the Word, to complete his work by the efficacious confirmation of the Word," so that "the certainty it deserves with us is attained by the testimony of the Spirit" (*Institutes,* I,9,3; I,7,5). Thus the sixteenth-century Reformation marks a decisive crossroad in Western Christianity's understanding of biblical canonicity.

The early church was indeed the historical matrix within which God's Word was given in the lingual form of the gospel. But the very reason for existence and right of existence of the church derives from the antecedent Word which calls it into existence. The church's commitment to the canon rests not on an authoritative voice arising from within its ranks, but in the self-authenticating power of the Word itself, inseparably linked to the testimony of the Spirit.

This position, fundamental to the Reformers and elaborated in the later reformational tradition, found support in the very words of the Apostles' Creed: While we believe *that* there is "one holy catholic church," we believe "*in* the Holy Spirit." Accordingly, the church proclaims *what* is canonically true. The Holy Spirit, reinforcing his own Word, is the answer to the question *why* it is so. Paraphrasing the simple song of childlike faith, once quoted by Barth as a personal testimony, we sing, "Jesus loves me, this I know. . . ," ultimately not because of the church, but because ". . . the Bible tells me so."

One of the Reformation creeds addresses this question of canonicity succinctly and with great clarity. Note carefully the sequence of its three points and the carefully chosen words introducing each.

We receive all these books [the sixty-six of the Old and New Testament], and these only, as holy and canonical, . . . *not so much* because the church receives and approves them as such, but *more especially* because the Holy Spirit witnesses in our hearts that they are from God, and *also* because they carry the evidence thereof in themselves. (Belgic Confession, Article V)

The first point confesses the *pedagogical,* instrumental role of the church; the second the decisive, *convincing* testimony of the Spirit; the third the after-the-fact-of-faith *confirmational* appeal of theological argumentation.

d) The fourth major view on canon formation is already implicitly evident in the preceding discussion. Calvin spoke basically for the Reformation as a whole in affirming the *"self-authenticating"* character of Scripture (*Institutes,* I,7,5). This view precludes appeal to any agency over, beyond, or outside the canon itself. Under the promised leading of the Spirit (John 16:12-15) the Word does its own good work in the world. In the writings of the New Testament, accordingly, the early church, and the church of all ages, has heard the Word of the Good Shepherd as nowhere else. This Word was itself the motivating force in the process of canon formation. It won for itself a settled place in the believing consciousness of the church. The canon was mediated through the church, but not determined by it. The church has but a secondary authority, appellable to the Word and subservient to it. Even in the face of expanding claims for episcopal authority in the early church ("what the bishops have always and everywhere taught"), it was the inner dynamic of the biblical testimony itself which proved decisive.

What, then, happened at Hippo and Carthage? The church fathers gathered there were not faced with an open canonical choice. Apart from a few lingering doubts, the New Testament canon was no longer a matter of unfinished business. These councils inherited an accomplished fact. The unfolding drama of canon formation had by then run its full course. All that was left was to ratify the "self-authenticating" impact of Scripture. In effect the church was submitting its authority to that of the Word. It is this reformational view of canonicity which Reformed dogmatics seeks to honor.

V. 18. Contemporary Hermeneutics

Keeping dogmatic studies close to the Bible is a major aim of this work. This calls for a clear recognition of the noetic importance of Scripture for a right understanding of the ontic order of created reality. For Scripture is the key to all true knowledge. It is therefore also the norm for all theoretical reflection, including theology. In its total extent and in all its integrally related parts, Scripture speaks with divine, redemptive authority. It sheds its renewing light on every sector of life. This includes dogmatics as one way of hearing and knowing and doing the truth.

Given this stance, the question of how to interpret Scripture takes on crucial importance. We are therefore driven to a consideration of biblical hermeneutics, understood as the theory of exegesis, as principles and methods for understanding and communicating the historical-redemptive, Christocentric message of biblical revelation. Biblical hermeneutics therefore remains a basic touchstone for Reformed dogmatics.

Given the radical shift during the past two centuries toward anthropological theologies, accompanied by an almost obsessive concern with epistemological problems, all of which was given tremendous impetus by the Enlightenment movement, hermeneutics has become increasingly the pivotal point in almost every theological discussion. Every issue, it seems, turns out at bottom to be an hermeneutic issue. Sooner or later the password, "Show me your hermeneutic," rises to the surface as the litmus test in theological decision-making. Our aim here in this Reformed dogmatics is to articulate a confessional theology supported by a confessional hermeneutic, one which does justice to the Reformed confession concerning the nature of biblical authority. What shape and form can we give such a biblical hermeneutics?

The theological landscape of our times is crowded with a host of competing hermeneutic models. The past century has been dominated by many variations on the historical-critical method. In its most radical form this method assumes a secular-humanist view of reality. The world is viewed as a closed system governed by the cause-and-effect nexus of natural law. The scope of historical possibility — for example, *creatio ex nihilo,* a virgin-born incarnation, the resurrection — is circumscribed by the law of analogy. Modern man's view of Scripture, and accordingly his choice of a biblical hermeneutic, is based on "the assured results of the scientific method." On this view the Old Testament is reduced to a mosaic of Israel's religious experiences in its restless quest after Yahweh. Similarly, the New Testament is read as a patchwork commentary by early Christians on the Man of Nazareth. With this mind-set liberal theology employed its hermeneutic tools in the confidence that by scrutinizing these ancient prescientific documents from the vantage point of our present higher-critical stage of development, it is still possible to uncover and reconstruct from these biblical narratives "what actually happened." In the process we are able to reconstruct "the real historical Jesus" of Galilee.

The fundamental presuppositions, principles, and perspectives of such historical-critical methods are foreign to the classic Reformed view of Scripture. Little wonder therefore that traditionally Reformed thinkers were nearly unanimous in repudiating it. Of late, however, attitudes have

119

changed. Historical-critical methods, it is argued, can be used in a limited way. For Scripture is an historical revelation. It is therefore open to historical scrutiny, though not at the expense of its redemptive message. Thus careful efforts are put forth to say both "Yes" and "No" to this method in a single breath. Its underlying assumptions and overall perspective on life evoke a negative response. At the same time its tools and techniques of research elicit a qualified affirmation. This more approving approach is based on the contention that the scientific procedures of the historical-critical method are relatively "neutral" operations common to all scholars.

Such a mixed hermeneutic results in strong tensions between faith commitment and theological method, between confession and interpretation. There are those who confess that Scripture is God's Word while at the same time employing a method which fails to incorporate that confession. As a Christian, so the argument goes, one embraces Scripture as divine revelation. As a theologian engaged in an historical-critical study of the text of the Bible, however, one must methodically set aside this faith commitment. The scientific rules of the game require holding personal beliefs in abeyance in order to give the historical method free play. For religious beliefs lie outside the purview of such theological methodologies. As a matter of personal faith one may, for example, confess the resurrection of Christ. As an historical theologian, however, the most one can say is that certain people, such as the apostles, believed it and acted accordingly.

On this approach one can recover a commitment to the redemptive message of Scripture only by a leap of faith. Such a divided allegiance excludes the possibility of an integrally unified confessional theology. It embraces a dialectical tension between faith and theology which sets confession and hermeneutics at odds with each other. It is indeed true that faith and theology, confession and hermeneutics can and must be distinguished. For, as argued previously, this means recognizing the difference in priority between faith-knowledge and theoretical reflection. But to divorce them, to drive a wedge between them, leaves one with a "house divided against itself." Release from such schizoid mind-sets and the reconstruction of a more holist approach are possible only by a confessional hermeneutic pervasively shaped by the built-in, carryover formative power of its own confessional starting points.

V. 19. Biblical Pre-understanding

Every interpreter of the Bible brings a certain pre-understanding of Scripture to bear on his work. We always take ourselves with us. This requires no apology. Yet we sometimes hear people defend as ideal the notion that in reading the Scriptures we must first empty ourselves of all pre-conceptions and simply allow Scripture to write its message on our open and empty minds as on a clean slate. This is an impossible possibility — possible in the sense that some may try it, but impossible in the sense that no one can live up to it. For we can never escape ourselves, or divest ourselves of our convictions, or turn ourselves off. It is always we who are intimately involved in the act of interpreting the Bible. We approach Scripture with a certain sense of anticipation — expecting something. In searching the Scriptures we all wear "glasses" of one kind or another — moralist glasses, allegorical glasses, historical-critical glasses, kerygmatic glasses, neo-Marxist glasses, dispensational glasses, charismatic glasses, historical-redemptive glasses, or glasses of some other kind. The question is not whether we wear some such hermeneutic glasses, but what sort of glasses we wear. Most crucially the question is whether the glasses we wear in biblical interpretation have been borrowed from Scripture itself, whether they are true to Scripture, whether they have been ground and polished by constant interaction with Scripture itself, whether they can therefore stand the test of Scripture. The best hermeneutic "objectivity" is an honest-to-God's-Word "subjectivity."

If, then, a biblical viewpoint is essential in reading the Bible aright, are we then not "locked into a hermeneutic circle"? Indeed, that is so. But that is not something uniquely Christian or evangelical or Reformed. That holds for every man — the humanist, the secularist, and the rationalist too. All men live and think and act, implicitly or explicitly, on the basis of an appeal to some normative authority. The decisive question is, Which authority? To acknowledge therefore that we are "caught" in a biblically defined hermeneutic circle is nothing else than a profound recognition of our creaturely dependence on the overarching authority of God's Word. We cannot rise above our creatureliness to reach some supracreaturely vantage point. We cannot "get on top of things." We stand under the very Word of God which makes theoretical reflection on it possible.

Already in the sixteenth century Calvin recognized the importance of a right pre-understanding of the Bible. Emerging from centuries of gross neglect, he and his fellow Reformers dedicated themselves to putting Scripture back into the hands of the people of God. But how could the long-standing spiritual vacuum be filled? What was needed to prepare believers for reading this "strange book"? To reset their sights? To teach them what to look for in Scripture and what to expect of it? Calvin answers these questions briefly in the introduction to his *Institutes*. There he says that this "little book" is intended to serve as a handbook to aid Christians in studying the Scriptures. It was to be a hermeneutic guide to God's Word, to predispose its readers to a believing and obedient response to God's will. Calvin apparently felt completely at home within this hermeneutic circle. Positioning himself within it, he works out his basic rule of biblical interpretation: Try to say no more than Scripture, for this results in idle speculation; and try also to say no less than Scripture, for this is to impoverish God's Word.

V. 20. Doctrine of Scripture

Methodologically, a confession of "faith seeking understanding" (Anselm) must govern our theological explorations of the inspiration, infallibility, and authority of the Bible. On these three aspects of the doctrine of Scripture, however, the Christian tradition leaves us with a number of alternative viewpoints.

Inspiration refers to the mysterious process by which the books of the Bible were inscripturated. Theological reflection on it moves out in three sharply contrasting directions. At one extreme is the "mechanical" or "dictation" theory. On this view the human authors served merely as passive instruments of the Holy Spirit in the inscripturation process. They were but pens in the Spirit's hand, or (in more contemporary imagery) typewriters/word processors on which he punched out his message. The emphasis falls here in a radically exclusive way on divine activity. Even variations in literary genre, grammar, style, vocabulary, and diction are ascribed to the overriding influence of the Holy Spirit. Divinity eclipses humanity and historicity. The result is a docetic revelation. This view has a history about as long as Western Christianity itself.

A very opposite view, arising from typically modern post-Enlightenment developments, is the "dynamic" theory of inspiration. Its emphasis shifts radically to the side of human insight and achievement. The Bible ranks high on the list of the world's great sacred literature. It is a masterful historical document. But it is not a Book which stands in a class by itself. Human genius eclipses the divine origin and content of Scripture as Word of God.

These two conflicting views of inspiration reflect once again the false dilemma we have encountered repeatedly. For implicit in these polarized positions is the inescapable problem of all two-factor theologies. They require that the norm be located either in God or in man. Both "mechanical" and "dynamic" theories of inspiration are, therefore, the consistent though contradictory outcomes of a shared commitment to two-factor outlooks on reality. Structurally "conservatives" and "liberals" hold to a common starting point, even though they develop their views in very opposite directions.

122

A three-factor theology is helpful in relieving this otherwise irre-solvable tension. Implicit in it is a third view on inspiration, known as the "organic" theory. Those holding this position seek to avoid playing the divine and the human, the historical and the transhistorical, off against each other. They begin by bowing before the divine/human mystery of Scripture, rather than seeking to resolve it. The "organic" view rests on the confession that in the Bible we hear the Word of God in the words of men. Accordingly, Scripture is fully and truly divine as well as fully and truly human. This position points to the mediating Word as its normative focal point. For through the superintending activity of the Holy Spirit, God condescends to accommodate his transcendent Word to our creaturely and sinful understanding by casting it into lingual form through the active agency of Hebrew and Greek writers. Just as this "organic" view holds for inspiration, so it also holds for the concomitant doctrines of biblical infallibility and authority. Every divine activity in producing the Scriptures is qualified by human engagement, but is not limited by it.

Since Reformation times much theological dialogue has also been expended on the four "marks of Scripture" — namely, its necessity, suffi-ciency, perspicuity, and authority. Too often these vital truths are reduced to abstract concepts. Actually they are deeply religious insights forged in the crucible of an intensely dramatic spiritual struggle. In the conflict situation of the sixteenth century, whereas Rome asserted the prime necessity of the "mother church" for salvation to the detriment of Scrip-ture, the Reformers proclaimed the fundamental necessity of Scripture in illumining the way of life. Whereas Rome compromised the sufficiency of Scripture by its doctrine of the two sources of revelation, Scripture and tradition, the Reformers affirmed that Scripture alone is sufficient for true knowledge, and that even tradition itself must be tested by it. Whereas Rome made the clarity *(perspicuitas)* of Scripture dependent on the teaching office of the church (the *magisterium*), the Reformers held that, under the leading power of the Spirit, Scripture is its own interpreter *(analogia Scripturae),* so that its central and comprehensive message is unmistakably clear to the body of believers. Since, then, Scripture is necessary, sufficient, and perspicuous, we are to submit humbly and obediently to its redemptive authority, to which the church itself must yield.

A confession of the authority of the Bible, and theological reflection on it, is pervasively qualified by a divine-human mystery which we can never fully fathom. Scriptural authority comes from God. In its total extent and in all its parts Scripture is the inspired, and thus also the infallible and authoritative Word of God. What Paul says, God says. As the message of salvation in Jesus Christ it sheds its light on world history,

123

calling us to renewed service in the full range of all our life relationships. Scripture reveals the full counsel of God through the agency of its human authors.

Given the fallen creation, now in principle renewed and being redeemed in Christ, not only does God's Word come to us continuously "by the creation, preservation, and government of the universe," but God also "makes himself more openly known to us by his holy and divine Word, as much as we need in this life, for his glory and for the salvation of his own" (*Belgic Confession,* Article II). This confession is true to Scripture's claims concerning itself. Throughout his earthly ministry Jesus teaches and demonstrates that the "Scripture cannot be broken" (John 10:34). By his own testimony he came not "to abolish the law and the prophets, . . . but to fulfill them" (Matthew 5:17). Everywhere in Scripture he stands central. Unabashedly he presents himself as the fulfillment of all the long-standing promises of the Old Testament writings: "It is they that bear witness to me" (John 5:39). Quoting Isaiah 61, he announces to his hometown people, "Today this Scripture has been fulfilled in your hearing" (Luke 4:21). When Jesus opened the Scriptures to the wayfarers to Emmaus, we are told that "beginning with Moses and all the prophets, he interpreted to them in all the scriptures the things concerning himself" (Luke 24:27).

All Scripture rings with redemptive authority. In the words of Paul, the "sacred writings . . . are able to instruct you for salvation through faith in Christ Jesus," for "all Scripture is inspired by God and profitable for teaching, for reproof, for correction, and for training in righteousness, that the man of God may be complete, equipped for every good work" (2 Timothy 3:15-17). In a classic passage Peter writes: "First of all you must understand this, that no prophecy of Scripture is a matter of one's own interpretation, because no prophecy ever came by the impulse of man, but men moved by the Holy Spirit spoke from God" (2 Peter 1:20-21). Thus, what Scripture says, God says. The God who once spoke and still speaks his Word for creation, who "in many and various ways spoke of old to our fathers by the prophets," and who "in these last days has spoken to us by a Son" (Hebrews 1:1-2), also speaks on every page of Scripture.

Whenever, wherever, however God speaks, he speaks as God, and therefore with full divine authority — in creation, in Christ, and also in the written Word. Scripture's authority is plenary and verbal, just as it is also plenarily and verbally inspired and infallible. It is therefore the trustworthy guide for faithful living as well as the reliable norm for theology. This holds not for the words of Scripture as discreet verbal symbols or isolated syllables, but for its words in their ordered sequence as communicators of its redemptive message. The inspiration, infallibility, and authority of biblical revelation are accordingly subservient to and qualified by its life-transforming message of salvation. All these cardinal attributes of Scripture are thus related directly to its specifically redemptive content and purpose.

This view of Scripture can be further clarified by drawing a comparison with God's revelation in creation. With respect to its nature and extent, what is true of biblical revelation in its own unique way also holds for creational revelation in its own unique way. By his original and abiding Word for creation God imparted his good order and direction to life in the world. Despite sin, by that Word he still maintains the structures and functions of the cosmos. Then, to overcome the misdirecting effects of sin, God republished his Word in lingual form to redirect our lives to their original intent and purpose. In extent, therefore, both modes of revelation are global in authority. They are coterminous. Both are comprehensive and exhaustive in their coverage. They differ, however, in their message and in the nature of their authority, a difference analogous to that between redemption and creation. In the one God speaks with full authority as Creator, in the other as Creator-Redeemer. Even when Scripture speaks of creation and of God as Creator — as it certainly does — it does so within the perspective of redemption. In the creative works of his hands, no less than in the re-creative words of Scripture, God's will impinges itself on us with full authority and infallibly — though inspiration can be aptly ascribed only to Scripture. Moreover, the other attributes of Scripture — necessity, perspicuity, and sufficiency — can also be applied to God's fundamental and abiding revelation in creation. It, too, is still necessary, since by his Word for creation God maintains his abiding claim on all creatures. Its message is still perspicuous. Any lack of clarity lies on our side, not God's. It results from the noetic distortions of sin, whereby we fail to grasp the bifocal revelation of God, his goodness which goes back to the beginning, and his severity which came in response to sin. Creational revelation is also still sufficient for its originally given ends. Blame for its present insufficiency lies not on the side of divine revelation, but on the side of human response. It is still sufficient to hold men without excuse (Romans 1:20). Thus creational revelation covers the entire cosmos. Scripture re-covers the same ground. But it does so as a saving revelation, unfolding redemptively the central motifs of creation, fall, and redemption, looking forward to the consummation. The biblical message is, therefore, not partly redemptive and partly something else. The entire Scripture is fully redemptive, as it republishes and reinterprets the meaning of life in creation. Any dualist pattern of interpretation imposed on Scripture is therefore alien to its message.

V. 21. Biblical Message and Method

This saving message of Scripture is revealed in the progressively unfolding stages of salvation history running through the Old and New Testaments. Biblical hermeneutics must therefore reckon seriously with these developing acts in the biblical drama. In retracing the flow of biblical revelation, it must take into account in concretely situational ways what God says, how he speaks, when and where, with whom he is dealing, and under what circumstances. In this way Scripture narrates the history of redemption, interprets it, reflects on it. Its writings participate in and help to shape salvation history. Its redemptive events do not happen all at once. There is onward movement, action and reaction, address and response, promise and fulfillment, all moving toward, centering in, and flowing from the cross and the empty tomb. Chapter after chapter we meet God in his Word and by his Spirit deeply involved in the down-to-earth affairs of the life of his people over many centuries.

Scripture makes no pretense to offering total coverage of every significant fact, event, or person within its purview. It operates with a certain principle of selection. This is true also for its narratives on the life of Christ. It offers not a biography, but the image of Jesus Christ, as expressed in the following apostolic witness:

> Now Jesus did many other signs in the presence of his disciples, which are not written in this book — . . . were every one of them to be written, I suppose that the world itself could not contain the books which would be written . . . — but these are written that you may believe that Jesus is the Christ, the Son of God, and that believing you may have life in his name. (John 20:30-31; 21:25)

The biblical message of redemption is rooted firmly in historical reality, not ancient myth. In classical mythology the important "events" which shape the life of the world happen not in the arena of human history, but in the ethereal realm of the gods. By contrast, all biblically appellable methods of interpretation must faithfully represent the historical reality of the redemptive events therein recorded. Scripture jealously guards its antimythical character. For without its historical foundation the biblical message loses its meaning. The accent therefore falls repeatedly on the on-the-scene, firsthand reporting of its eye- and earwitnesses.

> That which was from the beginning, which we have heard, which we have seen with our eyes, which we have looked upon and touched with our hands, concerning the word of life — the life was made manifest, and we

126

saw it, and testify to it, and proclaim to you the eternal life which was with the Father and was made manifest to us — that which we have seen and heard we proclaim also to you, so that you may have fellowship with us; and our fellowship is with the Father and with his Son Jesus Christ. And we are writing this that our joy may be complete. (1 John 1:1-4)

The true meaning of Scripture can only be disclosed contextually. The basic rule for biblical interpretation is therefore this: first, last, and always consider the context — the immediate context, the extended context, ultimately the context of God's Word in its fullness. Piecemeal, fragmentary, proof-textish exegesis of loosely dangling bits of biblical information does violence to the narrative flow in the history of redemption. Those who choose to engage in such malpractice forfeit all claim to biblical support in their hermeneutic undertakings. For the authority of any given passage in Scripture is bound up intimately with its creationally based, covenantally focused, kingdom-oriented, Christ-centered thrust. Woven into the fabric of its many stories is its single story. And that biblical message must define our biblical method.

Our methods of biblical interpretation can, therefore, rightfully claim to honor Scripture's unique claim to authority only when they deal with its rich diversities within the framework of its unifying message. This holds true even when we recognize that biblical teachings do not apply to us today in the same way as to their original recipients — as, for example, with God's command to Abraham to sacrifice his firstborn, only, beloved son Isaac (Genesis 22) or with the laws of Moses given to Israel. All Scripture is abidingly normative. Its *norms* are regularly given, however, in *forms* which are historically related to the teleologically directed movements in the history of redemption. Accordingly they are passing in their direct and immediate application. Recall how the Old Testament sabbath moves along, gets fleshed out, is often distorted by the Pharisees; but it is then updated, reinterpreted, and fulfilled by Christ, and it eventually gets taken up into the Lord's Day of resurrection victory in the life of the New Testament church. The same dynamic principle of interpretation holds for the more specifically New Testament injunctions. We no longer feel duty-bound to greet one another by exchanging a holy kiss, to carry on the practice of footwashing, or to require women to wear a veil in worship. Yet these passages, too, remain authoritative and normative. In interpreting such injunctions, however, we must take into account the distinction between what God's Word meant then and there and what it continues to mean here and now. Biblical *norms,* couched in their ancient forms, must find an appropriate *form* of response in the life of the Christian community today. In the words of a Reformed creed, though . . .

the ceremonies and symbols of the law ceased at the coming of Christ, and all the shadows are accomplished, [nevertheless] in the meantime we still use the testimonies taken out of the law and the prophets to confirm us in the doctrine of the gospel, and to regulate our life in all honourableness to the glory of God, according to His will, [because] the truth and substance of them remain with us in Jesus Christ, in whom they have their completion. (*Belgic Confession,* Article XXV)

Anyone who refuses to employ this Christ-centered key to the meaning of Scripture thereby fails to submit to the real authority of Scripture. All such faulty preaching, teaching, theologizing, and living stands under the judgment of Christ himself. For we can claim biblical authority only when we embrace the One to whom Scripture testifies. Otherwise Christ's protest against the Jewish leaders of his day also falls on us: "You search the Scriptures because you think that in them you have eternal life, and it is they that bear witness to me; yet you refuse to come to me that you may have life" (John 5:39-40).

The Christ who is central in the work of creation is also central in the work of redemption as recorded in the Bible. Scripture is therefore not a record of isolated and unrelated mighty acts of God, but a sustained and integrally unified narrative. From beginning to end there is a single plan of salvation. From near the dawn of history to the final coming of the kingdom, the drama of salvation moves toward and then moves outward from Jesus Christ onward toward the "New Jerusalem." He is the leading Player in the biblical drama of redemption. His saving work is its central theme. His victory, "already" assured but "not yet" fully accomplished, is our hope.

V. 22. A Confessional Hermeneutic

It is possible now to take a few additional steps along this same path of biblical interpretation. Recent studies make clear that one's hermeneutic finds its place and plays its role within the larger scope of one's worldview. The hermeneutic of the Wellhausenian school, for example, is hardly thinkable apart from a typically modern evolutionary model of history. The neo-Marxist hermeneutic employed in many contemporary liberation theologies is oriented strongly to a typically Hegelian view of societal development. One cannot fault these schools of thought for a lack of internal consistency. The crucial point of confrontation is rather their worldview and philosophical outlook. As an alternative to these and other current hermeneutics, let us consider a method of interpretation more in line with the biblical worldview, the Reformed confessions, and Christian philosophy. I shall call it a "confessional hermeneutic."

A fundamental starting point is the biblical idea of "heart," out of which, says Scripture (Proverbs 4:23), flow all the issues of life. From this spiritual fountainhead, therefore, spring also the issues of theology in general, more particularly of dogmatics, and specifically now of hermeneutics. Accordingly, theologizing is an activity of the "heart," the miniself, the religious concentration point of our entire selfhood. The "heart" engages the whole man. Thus the Christian scholar is bound to respect his work as an activity rooted in the "heart" which, in response to God's Word, seeks to lead every thought captive in obedience to Christ Jesus (2 Corinthians 5:10). Given this religious orientation, how shall we then give shape to our principles and methods of biblical interpretation? What sort of hermeneutic paradigm shall we adopt? In answer to these questions, consider the confessional model of hermeneutics.

To forestall possible misunderstandings, "confessional" should not here be construed in a subjectivist way, as though Scripture were man's confession about God. Rather, it refers to the faith aspect of created reality, the "confessional" aspect as one way of knowing and communicating truth. In explicating this method of interpreting the Bible let us focus on that genre of biblical literature which stands at the center of discussion in our times — the historical narratives in biblical revelation. How are we to read, understand, and interpret them?

A scripturally directed view of created reality brings with it the recognition that historical events are, first of all, whole events. They come across to us intuitively and frontally in their wholeness — such events, for example, as the exodus, the resurrection, the French Revolution, Hiroshima. On further careful analysis, however, these whole events within our historical horizon can also be examined from a variety of viewpoints. Woven into the unified fabric of every historical episode is a highly diversified cluster of moments of meaning. Take, for example, Hitler's Third Reich. German society of the 1930s can be analyzed theologically in terms of its confessional stance: What was the basic belief system of the "German Christians"? But its psychological, social, economic, and political values are also open to scrutiny. All historical events have built into them these various aspects of meaning.

This created pattern of a diversity of ordered aspects within the unity of whole events holds true for biblical history too. In the mighty redeeming acts of God which constitute the very heart of biblical revelation there are clear indications of this aspectival diversity. Yet in, under, through, and with all the varied aspects which are woven into the fabric of these biblical happenings is a central, leading thread which binds them together — a dominant focus. Scripture speaks confessionally. One could, for example, analyze the *political* aspects of David's rule or the *economic* aspects of Solomon's administration. Scripture offers some intriguing insights into such things. But they are incidental to its real message. They do not open up the central focus of Scripture. Again, one could reflect on the apostle Peter from the point of view of his *psychic* makeup. Or one could study Paul's mission to Jews, Greeks, and Romans in terms of a *lingual* analysis: What languages did he use in proclaiming the gospel? Something interesting and instructive could be said about these contextual aspects of biblical revelation from what we know about Bible times. The central focus of the biblical message, however, is not political, economic, psychic, or lingual. From what point of view, then, is the history of redemption told? Which aspect stands out? Scripture touches on these and many other things within a *confessional* focus.

The various other aspects of historical reality are indeed there. Otherwise the events in the history of redemption would not be real and whole events. They all play their important roles. Now this aspect, then that one comes to the fore, but always subservient to the Scripture's central focus. It is important to recognize these other aspects, for otherwise the confessional focus would come through in an empty and docetic way. David did engage in some dramatic political activities; Solomon did establish certain ill-fated economic policies; Peter was moved by certain psychic impulses; Paul did use the Greek and Aramaic languages in his preaching. But such considerations are not central in Scripture. They are all subservient to its central focus. In its most pregnant sense Scripture is really not "about" David, Solomon, Peter, and Paul; it is all "about" Jesus Christ. What is primary is Scripture's concentration on the confessional meaning of its chain of events in their relatedness to Christ.

Scripture testifies to real historical-redemptive events, but not as "objective" chronicles. It is not ordinary historiography. It is prophetic history, interpreted history, history with a point. It explicates the meaning of the unfolding drama of redemption, one act after another, always within this confessional focus. What binds one historical event after another together into a unified pattern of Christocentric revelation is the Bible's sustained emphasis on the confessional significance of these events.

Look briefly at a few more biblical samples, chosen at random. Archeology is now able to paint a picture of Omri, king of Israel, far more detailed and illustrious than the very sober account given in the Bible. His international fame was apparently so great that foreigners referred to the nation of Israel as "the house of Omri." Yet Scripture passes all this by in silence. It disposes of Omri in seven brief verses (1 Kings 16:21-28). How do we account for that? Such treatment of a royal personage reflects the kind of book the Bible is. It sets Omri's reign in Scripture's own unique perspective. Within the historical context of buying the hill of Samaria and fortifying it, what we read of him is this: "Omri did what was evil in the sight of the Lord; he did more evil than all who were before him. For he walked in all the ways of Jeroboam, in the sins by which he made Israel to sin, provoking the LORD, the God of Israel, to anger with their idols" (1 Kings 17:25-26). That is the Bible's way of focusing in on the reign of Omri, stating in confessional language what is really of lasting importance about him, his (negative) contributions to the unfolding history of redemption on the way to the coming Christ.

Take another case. In the New Testament King Herod is presented as a despicable character from the point of view of that which is christologically important in biblical revelation. He is an agent of the dragon of Revelation 12 which stands ready to devour the Man-Child. Yet, from what we know about the political history of those times, Herod was a rather effective puppet ruler within the Roman regime. Why this sharp contrast in emphasis? Once again, it is a matter of the Bible's unique focus. Scripture does not deny Herod's military prowess, his architectural accomplishments, his psychic problems. There are, in fact, allusions to these things in the Gospels. But Scripture passes a different kind of judgment on those who play their supporting roles in the drama of redemption. Through it all Christ is the central and leading Player. From the viewpoint of the confessional focus in Scripture what is most crucial about Herod is his embodiment of the spirit of the anti-Christ.

The same holds true for Pontius Pilate and the Pharisees, and more positively for Abraham, Moses, Elijah, John the Baptist, Jesus' mother Mary, and the apostles. In each case the Bible deals with the real lives of real people who as whole persons take part in whole events. Accordingly Scripture hits on one aspect of these events after another. Sometimes it even plays up a certain aspect quite strongly. Take, for example, the psychic disorders in the later life of King Saul. But again this is for the sake of sharpening Scripture's confessional focus on Saul as an antitheocratic king. Saul's psychic state of mind is not an independent theme. This aspect of his life, together with the political, economic, and cultic aspects, is there as the concrete historical framework for driving home this confessional message: "To obey is better than sacrifice. . . ." Therefore we miss the main point if we seek to derive psychological theories from the Saul passages. This is not the intent and purpose of Scripture. But Scripture does teach confessionally that no man, like Saul, can say "No, no, no" to God's clear "Yes, yes, yes" — over against David — without such defiance taking its heavy toll in one's life ("an evil spirit of the LORD came upon him"). God is not mocked. Such rebellion leads finally to the door of the witch of Endor's house.

We give expression to this same "confessional" focus in many of our birth announcements. We thankfully proclaim in our printed cards: "The Lord has given us a child." By this confessional statement we do not deny that sexual intercourse took place, nor that there was a nine-month waiting period, nor that a doctor attended the delivery, nor that medicines and expenses were involved, nor that the state issued a birth certificate. These varied aspects of that great event are real. Yet after all is said and done, we mean to say that all the various aspects involved in that event are gathered up in the confession, "The Lord has given." That is our way of speaking biblically about childbirth. It takes the deepest meaning of the event and puts it into a true and clear confessional focus. This stands in sharp contrast, for example, to birth announcements which reduce this event to economic categories: "Announcing a new income tax exemption."

Scripture never speaks in such reductionist terms. Sometimes, indeed, Scripture plays heavily on the biotic motif, as, for example, in the untimely, unexpected, even "impossible" birth of Isaac to the aged Abraham and Sarah. Sometimes political affairs loom large, as in the persistent strife between the Judeans and Samaritans in rebuilding the temple. Sometimes the aesthetic gets large attention, as in descriptions of the grandeur of Solomon's temple. Sometimes ethnic and social relations play an important role, as in the conflict between Jewish and Gentile Christians in the early church. Nevertheless, to reduce the biblical message to one or another of these aspects is to miss the mark hermeneutically. All these aspects play a role subservient to the central, leading, dominant confessional focus of Scripture, namely, the consistent witness of all Scripture, in its total extent and in all its parts, to the redeeming work of God in Jesus Christ. As a ray of light passing through a prism gets refracted into a brilliant spectrum of colors, so — in reverse fashion — Scripture takes these diverse rays of light and concentrates them in this confessional focus: "God was in Christ reconciling the world unto himself."

This confessional hermeneutic also finds strong support in the message of Psalm 127: "Unless the LORD build the house, those who build it labor in vain; unless the LORD watches over the city, the watchman stays awake in vain." The Psalmist is not spiritualizing this building project. Real lumber and brick and mortar are involved. Nor does the Psalmist deny that it takes a lot of down-to-earth planning, saving, and working to get the job done. All kinds of physical, economic, asesthetic, social, political, and even ethical considerations enter into such an undertaking. Yet, with its own unique focus, like an X-ray exposure, Scripture cuts through all the hard realities of human toil and gets at the heart of the matter by proclaiming: Without the blessing of the Lord all the sweat and tears (of joy and hardship) are in vain, empty, without content and meaning. Without God's blessing the house defeats its real purpose for existence. The house (its foundations, walls, roof) may still stand, but it no longer stands for obedient service in family living. The same is true for guarding a city. Woe to the watchman who falls asleep at his post! Yet even if the watchmen stand guard day and night, and even if the guard is doubled and tripled, all these extra precautions will not help unless the Lord watches over the city to protect it. This is the confessional focus of the biblical message.

Such a confessional hermeneutic offers real help in seeking to do justice to Scripture both as *history* of redemption and as history of *redemption*. It offers a hermeneutic key to help unlock the centrally and comprehensively Christocentric meaning of biblical revelation. It brings with it some built-in safeguards against reductionist interpretations of the Bible, whether they be the moralist reductionisms of the exemplary method or the historical reductionisms of the historical-critical method — as well as tendencies toward rationalism, pietism, or legalism. It offers promising possibilities for a confessional theology, that is, a theological hermeneutic which is in harmony with the Reformed confessions concerning the nature of biblical authority. It helps overcome the ever present dualist-dialectical tensions between confession and theology. In this hermeneutic method faith and theology can be kept together in an integrally unified and meaningful working relationship which honors and gives free play to the conviction that the Bible is the Word of God in the words of men.

V. 23. Review

Looking back now, what does a prolegomena to Reformed dogmatics come down to? What is its place and role? How does it relate to the theology proper which lies ahead? It serves, of course, as an "Introduction," which is another name for the same thing. By way of summary, a more substantial answer can be offered by relating prolegomena to the following three ideas.

a) Tradition. It is apparent from the history of Christian dogma-formation that every dogmatics stands within a certain larger religio-philosophical tradition. To act as if the full meaning of such larger movements is exhausted in their theologies is to overinflate theology. To act, on the other hand, as if these theologies can be adequately understood in isolation from their larger traditions is to deal with theology narrowly and superficially. Prolegomena, accordingly, sketches a theology's "family tree" — its ancestry, lineage, pedigree, and spiritual heritage. This renewal effort in dogmatics therefore acknowledges its indebtedness to the

Reformation tradition in the Calvinist line as further developed in our times through the neo-Kuyperian movement.

b) Location. A second closely connected task of prolegomena is to locate dogmatics in relationship to other branches of theology, to other disciplines within the academic enterprise, and to other practical and theoretical dimensions of life as a whole. Whether this takes the form of a word *zuerst* (a beginning word), as in Calvin, or a word *vorher* (a word beforehand), as in Bavinck, its stance must be consistent with the overall tenor of the dogmatics which it introduces. Unity of thought cannot tolerate a leap, for example, from reason to faith in moving from prolegomena to dogmatics proper — as though one travels "second class" part of the way and then transfers to "first class" the rest of the way home. Perspectivally, prolegomena and dogmatics proper are of one piece. Prolegomena serves to locate the house of dogmatics within the larger neighborhood in which it resides and is at home.

c) Perspective. Incorporating these reflections on tradition and location, this prolegomena reflects the biblical worldview and Christian philosophy developed within the Reformed movement over the past one hundred years. With it come the presuppositional (from *pre-sub-ponere:* "that which is put underneath in advance") starting points, principles (from *principia,* "points of departure"), insights, and outlooks which serve to locate Reformed dogmatics within the larger contours of our life in God's world. As such, it helps to sharpen our perspectival bearings.

V. 24. Preview

Looking forward to the road ahead through the heartland of Reformed dogmatics, we pause at this point to chart our course. To gain an overview of the lay of the land a little map may be helpful. In traveling through a province of Canada or one of the states in the United States, for example, it is advisable first to find an atlas and locate that province or state within the larger context of the country as a whole. If, by analogy, we take that province or state to be Reformed dogmatics, then such wide-ranging geographical orientation is comparable to the task of prolegomena. Once this preliminary work is done and we have gotten our bearings, we are ready to move in on our target area. Accordingly, we are now about to explore that theological province or state called Reformed dogmatics. In covering this ground, too, a regional or local map may be helpful. As a prospectus to the way ahead, therefore, consider the following simple sketch as a guide to our further reflection.

PROSPECTUS

```
                   Creation      Fall      Redemption Consummation
                     F  D       D  M        R  R
                     O  I       E  I        E  E
Father: Initiator —— R  R ——    F  S ——     F  D ———— "All
                     M  E       O  D        O  I
Son: Mediator ————   A  C ——    R  I ——     R  R ——— in
                     T  T       M  R        M  E
Holy Spirit: Enabler— I  I ——   A  E ——     A  C ———— All"
                     O  O       T  C        T  T
                     N  N       I  T        I  I
                                O  I        O  O
                                N  O        N  N
                                   N
```

This approach represents a notable revision on the traditional "six loci" method with its sequential treatment of the doctrines of God, man, Christ, salvation, church, and "last things." These six themes are not lost in the present reconstruction of Reformed dogmatics. They are, however, significantly "repackaged." I am doing this not as a matter of change for the sake of change. This reordering of basic dogmas aims at overcoming the abstract and rationalist way of dealing with Christian doctrines which is inherent in the older "loci" method, betraying as it does the influences of Protestant scholastic thought.

This renewed method of dealing with classic Christian doctrines is intended as a consistent follow-through on the spirit and thrust of the preceding prolegomenal discussion. It seeks to give the historical-redemptive pattern of biblical revelation a firmer place in Reformed dogmatics. Accordingly I intend to reshape dogmatic reflection along the lines of the key biblical motifs of creation, fall, and redemption, on the way to the consummation. This final motif, usually treated under the heading "eschatology," is not a doctrine which can simply be reserved for the final chapter in a book. In a very real sense the entire biblical story line has an eschatological thrust. The Bible is not a "conservative" book, holding history back. It carries with it a built-in forward-looking impulse. There is always more to come, bigger and better things.

This work also seeks to take advantage of the trinitarian pattern of the Apostles' Creed. This ordering principle has born rich fruit in many classic Christian theologies, notably that of Calvin's *Institutes*. Accordingly, as indicated in the prospectus sketched above, this project seeks a renewal of dogmatics by cross-referencing the crucial biblical motifs with a trinitarian pattern of theologizing. In this way it seeks to honor the classic theological idea of *perichoresis* ("mutual interpenetration"), which recognizes that while the work of creation, redemption, and consummation involves *pervasively* all three Persons of the Trinity, yet through it all each Person is ascribed a work which is *prevailingly* his own.

Finally, the major concern of the preceding prolegomena was to lend support to a shift from two-factor to three-factor theologizing. This intent is reflected in the above prospectus: Christ, the Son of God, serves as the mediating Word in the ongoing covenantal relationship between God and the world — in creation, in redemption, and as we now move along toward the *eschaton*.

PART TWO

THE GOOD CREATION

Transitional Comments

The foundations for this project in Reformed dogmatics were laid in the preceding prolegomena. It remains now to build on them. The commitments made must now be honored with respect to the direction, parameters, and contours of this study.

Implied in the stance taken is the methodological decision not to begin dogmatics proper with a separate discussion of the existence and being of God, or of his knowability and attributes, or even of the doctrine of the Trinity. To reflect on these issues in advance, prior to and apart from their contextualized reality in the biblical doctrine of creation, opens the door to abstract theorizing. We know God, as Calvin argues, not as he is in himself *(ad intra),* but as he comes out to us in his revelation *(ad extra).* As Otto Weber puts it, "We cannot know God's nature in any other way than through his works" *(Foundations of Dogmatics,* Vol. I, p. 463).

The way to the knowledge of God in theology does not differ essentially from that which holds for the faith-life of the Christian community. The latter is shaped by the down-to-earth, experiential concreteness of the biblical narrative. Dogmatics, as disciplined reflection on the dogmas of that faith-life, can only deepen and enrich it. Therefore it cannot travel another, more speculative route. For methodologically it is a highly precarious, problematic, and even presumptuous venture to discuss the existence, being, knowability, attributes, and Person(s) of God in isolation from the realities of life in the creation as illumined by Scripture's confessional focus on God's covenantal dealings with his creatures under his kingly rule.

Implied accordingly is also, more positively, an adherence to the central story line of biblical revelation, namely, creation–fall–redemption–consummation. These are Scripture's crucial historical turning points. This pattern in redemptive revelation is woven into the very fabric of world history. Along this route we come, as Calvin argues in *The Institutes,* to a knowledge of God both as Creator and Redeemer. Since the Word of God is the norm for dogmatics, a faithful theological response calls for structuring our work in accord with the biblical story line.

Thus we arrive now at the doctrine of creation. We shall deal with it under three rather traditional headings:

First, cosmology (creation as a whole)
Second, anthropology (human beings)
Third, history (providence as the unfolding of creation)

Chapter I

Cosmology

I. 1. A Work of the Triune God

All the mighty acts of God in creation are mutually a work of the triune God — Father, Son, and Holy Spirit. Abraham Kuyper speaks accordingly of ". . . the sovereignty of the triune God over the whole cosmos" (*Lectures on Calvinism,* p. 79). Classic Christian dogmatics seeks to express something of this mind-boggling truth in the concept *perichoresis* — the idea of divine interpersonal cooperation. On this revelational insight, all the works of God are viewed as *pervasively* the work of all three Persons of the Trinity. Father, Son, and Holy Spirit are involved jointly in every act along the biblical story line of creation, redemption (including sanctification), and consummation. From another point of view, each of these clusters of divine activity is *prevailingly* the work of either Father, Son, or Holy Spirit. As the Holy Spirit plays a prevailing role in sanctification, and the Son in redemption, so the origination of all things is prevailingly the work of God the Father. Paul points in this direction in 1 Corinthians 8:5-6, reasoning that

> . . . although there may be many "gods" and many "lords" — as indeed there are many "gods" and many "lords" — yet for us there is one God, the Father, from whom are all things and for whom we exist, and one Lord, Jesus Christ, through whom are all things and through whom we exist.

This idea of *perichoresis* is reflected in the trinitarian formula which shapes the Apostles' Creed, beginning with its opening line: "I believe in God the Father, Almighty, Maker of heaven and earth." Such trinitarian confessions and the theologies to which they gave birth, rooted as they are in the biblical message and affirmed by the ecumenical creeds and the doctrinal standards of the Reformation, have always held an honored place in Reformed dogmatics.

Take Calvin: he concedes that the Latin and Greek concepts used to clarify the oneness and threeness in the various divine activities are of only limited value, given their often conflicting and confusing use among the church fathers. He therefore wishes to avoid "bickering," "wrangling," and "quarreling over words," so as not to become "such a stickler as to battle over mere words." He then adds concerning these trinitarian terms of distinction that "I could wish they were buried, if only among all men this faith were agreed on: that Father, Son, and Holy Spirit are one God, yet the Son is not the Father, nor the Spirit the Son, but that they are differentiated by a peculiar quality" (*Institutes,* I,13,5). Yet, apologetically, Calvin holds that the use of traditional trinitarian formulations is necessary in order to ward off heresy. Such confessional clarity is essential to "unmask false teachers," who, like "slippery snakes glide away," evading the truth by their "devious shifts" as they "cloak their errors in layers of verbiage" (*Institutes,* I,13,4).

Reflecting more positively on the essential points in the biblical doctrine of the Trinity Calvin says: "It is this: to the Father is attributed the beginning of activity, and the fountain and wellspring of all things; to the Son, wisdom, counsel, and the ordered disposition of all things; but to the Spirit is assigned the power and efficacy of that activity" (*Institutes,* I,13,18).

Restating the thrust of this biblical, confessional, and theological tradition, Louis Berkhof puts it in these words: "All things are at once *out of* the Father, *through* the Son, and *in* the Holy Spirit" (*Systematic Theology,* p. 129). Accordingly, this section on creation is governed by the following fundamental guidelines.

First, God the Father is the *Initiator* of all things. We hear the worshipers in John's apocalytic vision chant these words:

> Worthy art thou, our Lord and God,
> to receive glory and honor and power,
> for thou didst create all things,
> and by thy will they existed and were created. (Revelation 4:11)

Calvin echoes this refrain in saying,

> How can the thought of God penetrate your mind without your realizing immediately that, since you are his handiwork, you have been made over and bound to his command by right of creation, that you owe your life to him? — that whatever you undertake, whatever you do, ought to be ascribed to him? (*Institutes,* I,2,2)

Second, God the Son is the *Mediator* of all things. John's gospel speaks with unmistakable clarity on this point: ". . . All things were made through him, and without him was not anything made that was made" (1:3). In Calvin's theology the mediatorial role of the Son in creation, though latently and implicitly present in various passages, is developed only in passing. But note the following suggestive excerpt: "Even if man had remained free from all stain, his condition would have been too lowly to reach God without a Mediator" (*Institutes,* II,12,1).

Third, the Holy Spirit is the *Enabler* of all things. In the beginning already we find that "the Spirit of God was moving over the face of the waters" (Genesis 1:2). Commenting on this passage, Calvin says that it shows

> . . . not only that the beauty of the universe (which we now perceive) owes its strength and preservation to the power of the Spirit, but that before this adornment was added, even then the Spirit was occupied with tending that confused mass. . . . For it is the Spirit who, everywhere diffused, sustains all things, causes them to grow, and quickens them in heaven and in earth, . . . transfusing into all things his energy, and breathing into them essence, life, and movement. . . . (*Institutes,* I,13,14)

In what follows we wish to honor this comprehensive and balanced trinitarian approach first in the doctrine of creation, but then also through the fall and on into the doctrines of redemption and consummation. This outlook should serve as a safeguard against unwarranted tensions which arise when theologians exploit one of the three major articles of the Apostles' Creed at the expense of others. There is no good reason to play Theocentricity, Christocentricity, and Pneumacentricity off against each other. A biblically directed trinitarian dogmatics makes it possible to echo the classic Christian emphasis on God the Father *for* us, God the Son *with* us, and God the Spirit *in* us. This basic theme grows out of the well-known Pauline teaching: "For *of* him [initiation], and *through* him [mediation], and *unto* him [enablement] are all things — to him be the glory forever. Amen" (Romans 11:36). Commenting on this passage, Kuyper says: "The operations here spoken of are threefold: first, that by which all things are originated (*of* Him); second, that by which all things consist (*through* Him); third, that by which all things attain to their final destiny (*to* Him)" (*The Work of the Holy Spirit,* p. 20). Appealing to the church fathers, Kuyper concludes, stressing the same triadic perspective: "The operations whereby all things originated proceed from the Father; that whereby they received consistency from the Son; and that whereby they were led to their destiny from the Holy Spirit" (*ibid.,* p. 20). Belaboring this point, as though to emphasize its great importance,

Kuyper restates the thesis: ". . . In every work effected by Father, Son, and Holy Spirit in common, the power to bring forth proceeds from the Father, the power to arrange from the Son, the power to perfect from the Holy Spirit" (*ibid.*, p. 19).

I. 2. The Good Creation as Starting Point

It is true that "every section of dogmatics includes, in its own way and from its own point of view, the whole of dogmatics within itself" (Otto Weber, *Foundations of Dogmatics*, Vol. I, p. 349). Given his indebtedness to Barth, Weber doubtless has in mind here something more and different than can be readily conceded. He is nevertheless right in the sense that, barring inconsistencies, the central motifs of a given dogmatics play a formative role at every turn along the way. Successive chapters do not cover unrelated topics.

As indicated previously, this project in Reformed dogmatics rests on a self-consciously and deliberately chosen position on the side of a literal understanding of the biblical story line. This stance is taken even in the face of the contrary winds of doctrine now blowing strongly out of major corners in contemporary theology. Our point of departure is accordingly the biblical teaching on creation, viewed not only as a series of divine acts in the beginning, but also as the ongoing, ever present creational reality which lends life its continuing meaning. The pristine creation in its original form is no longer accessible to us. The original paradise is forever lost. Even redemption is not repristination — a return to the way it was in the beginning. It is rather the present and future restoration of the fallen creation to all it was meant to be. Still, it is religiously and theologically of utmost importance to allow our thinking to be normatively shaped by the biblical witness to a good creation, both as an original state of affairs and as an eschatological hope. Otherwise we will be hard-pressed to honor the biblical witness to the absolute goodness of God the Creator. For the bottom line in the drama of creation is this: "And God saw everything that he had made, and behold, it was very good" (Genesis 1:31). This leading motif returns in the vision of the renewed creation in these words: "But nothing unclean shall enter . . ." (Revelation 21:27). This pervasive biblical witness to the untainted goodness of God's original work of creation is undermined by contemporary dialectical, process, and monist theologies which collapse the fall and redemption backward into the creation itself. The result is a creation with built-in dialectical tensions between good and evil, a creation needing redemption from the very start.

In face of these developments it is of utmost importance to reaffirm the biblical teaching on the essential goodness of the original creation. This is so even as we recognize that from our present vantage point our understanding of it is filtered through the effects of the fall in Adam and redemption in Christ. All three crucial turning points in biblical revelation therefore now impinge themselves on our dogmatic reflections constantly and simultaneously as the cumulative impact of three unfolding acts in the scenario of world history. We therefore now look backward, and then forward, on the good creation with a vision which suffers from the distorting effects of sin. Though this vision is now in principle corrected as we don the spectacles of Scripture, yet we see these things only "as in a mirror dimly." This is the perspective of biblical revelation itself. It retells the creation story from the later standpoint of our fallenness and our redemption. Our theology of creation is therefore now colored by the concomitant realities of life in both the "old Adam" and the "new Adam."

This intermingling perspective is exemplified in Calvin's thinking. In Book One of *The Institutes* he sets out to discuss the "knowledge of God the Creator." Yet, even in this creational setting, both the force of sin and the counteracting "knowledge of God as Redeemer" repeatedly enter into the picture. Any well-constructed theology nevertheless needs certain ordering principles by which to sequence its thoughts. Accordingly we are here following the pattern of the biblical story line: first creation, then the fall, moving on to redemption and the consummation. We must remember, however, that such theological structures are only relatively binding. They may not suppress the biblical message. At the same time, we cannot deal with everything all at once without ending in confusion. So in focusing first on creation, these other relevant truths will indeed crowd in on us. Yet, methodologically, we are adopting the canonical order of Scripture, beginning with the Genesis narrative, which itself begins with the creation.

I. 3. "Right Order of Teaching"

We are therefore beginning where the Bible begins, proceeding then to retrace its redemptive commentary on the course of cosmic history, and ending eventually where the Bible ends. In taking the Genesis record as our point of departure, we are once again moving against some of the strongest currents within the mainstream of many contemporary biblical theologies. Conventional thought in many theological circles takes as its port of entry the later biblical narratives of Israel's encounter with the

Redeemer God who elects the patriarchs and liberates their descendants from Egyptian bondage. These great experiences of deliverance are then projected backward on the beginnings of the universe. This approach then yields the confession that the work of the Redeemer God of the Hebrews coincides with the work of the Creator God of the heavens and the earth.

Existentialist theologies also break with the canonical order of the biblical story line. Creation, fall, and redemption are viewed not as unfolding stages in God's way with the world, but as "existential moments" which converge in "everyman's" experience. These basic turning points are thus lifted out of their biblical order and relocated within the consciousness of mankind's universal religious experience. Take Karl Rahner as a case in point. In speaking of evil in the world, of human guilt, and of provision for salvation such that "by the redemption of Jesus Christ [the world] then becomes essentially different in an empirical and tangible way," he contends that we must not "attach any temporal sequence" to these things. For "at least methodologically we have to say first of all that such notions may not be connected in any temporal sequence" (*Foundations of Christian Faith*, p. 90). These "moments" along the biblical story line do indeed all converge as constitutive factors in our present daily experience. But to view them as intrinsic dimensions of created reality, inherently present in the structure of things from the beginning, is to rewrite the message of Scripture.

Methodologically it is helpful at this point to recall Calvin's approach to the question of the relationship of creation and redemption. In Christian experience, he holds, the knowledge of God as Creator and as Redeemer are intimately and inseparably intertwined. In our faith-knowledge they are accordingly never distinct. For Christ is Mediator of redemption as well as creation (*Institutes*, II,12,1). For "after the fall . . . no knowledge of God apart from the Mediator has power unto salvation" (*Institutes*, II,6,1). Yet for purposes of theological analysis they are distinguishable. Noetically, given the effects of sin, we must now come to know God as Redeemer in Jesus Christ as the avenue by which we come to a true knowledge of God as Creator. Ontically, however, the order of things runs in the opposite direction. Redemption presupposes creation. This is the historical order of biblical revelation. It is this ontic order which Calvin adopts as "the order of right teaching" (*Institutes*, I,2,1; I,6,1; II,1,1; II,6,1) — that is, for theological instruction. Accordingly, the "Four Book" division of Calvin's *Institutes* follows basically the trinitarian pattern of the Apostles' Creed — the First Article: God the Father and creation; the Second Article: God the Son and redemption; the Third Article: God the Holy Spirit and sanctification — plus the church.

Of some dogmatics it is possible to say: this is first-, or second-, or third-article theologizing — based on clear-cut priorities, such that heavy emphasis on one article eclipses the significance of others. Liberalism, for example, tends in its own secularized way to be first-article theology (the universal fatherhood of God), Neoorthodoxy emphasizes second-article theology (Christomonism), and Pentecostalism drifts toward third-article theology (the gifts of the Spirit). Such trinitarian imbalance is hardly true of Calvin. He does hold that noetically the second article is the medium to the first, and that the third article enables both the first and second to come to their own. Ontically, however, as the right order for theoretical reflection, he follows the standard order of the Apostles' Creed, which is also the given order of the Scriptures — beginning with creation as the original and ongoing work of the Creator God.

It is perhaps not surprising that the Heidelberg Catechism, as a profoundly personal confession, leans strongly toward a highly noetic approach. It touches only lightly on the biblical doctrine of creation. In its three parts, it begins with sin (the fall), moving on from there to salvation and service. This is understandable in light of the sixteenth-century situation. All of Christendom, whatever its differences on other points of doctrine, was still basically united in its historic belief in the work of God as Creator. No "Darwinians" had yet arisen to challenge this universal conviction. Only later would modern science and historical-critical methods of biblical interpretation call into question the classic Christian reading of the Genesis narratives. In the context of the Reformation struggles, therefore, while questions of our guilt and misery, our deliverance through Christ, and our call to grateful service were indeed burning issues, creation did not seem to call for a very strong and explicit confessional restatement. It receives what seems to us today to be only passing attention. This is so even when the Heidelberger asks directly the question concerning the meaning of the apostolic testimony, "I believe in God the Father, Almighty, Maker of heaven and earth." Its confession on creation is there located, almost parenthetically, within the setting of the section on "Deliverance," tucked away within its affirmations on the way of salvation. Listen to its answer:

> . . . the eternal Father of our Lord Jesus Christ, who out of nothing made heaven and earth with all that is in them, who likewise upholds and governs the same by His eternal counsel and providence, is for the sake of Christ His Son my God and my Father. . . . (Q. & A. 26)

The Catechism thus adopts a noetic, experiential orientation in its creedal expression on creation. As a confessional approach this is wholly appropriate, as Calvin already intimates (*Institutes,* I,1,3). But, as he also

146

indicates, the "order of right teaching" calls for following the ontic order of things. Along these lines we shall chart our course.

I. 4. "In the beginning GOD. . . !"

The Bible is a very brusque book, at least by certain standards of polite discourse. It opens on an absolutely abrupt note. Without so much as a "How do you do," with profound simplicity it thrusts open the door and confronts us forthrightly with the wholly unembellished announcement: "In the beginning God. . . !" There are no introductions, no apologies for its blunt beginning, no attempt at justification or verification, no "Once upon a time" attention-getter, least of all any proofs for God's existence. In Scripture God is simply there as the "great presuppositional Person" (recall the root word *pre-sub-ponere,* "that which is posited underneath in advance").

This opening line offers a decisive cue for a biblically attuned dogmatics. It reminds us once again to start where the Bible starts, with God, and then move out from there. Otherwise we are unable to get started at all, or we get off on the wrong foot. In Scripture the existence, reality, and presence of God are assumed to be utterly self-evident. Accordingly it arrests us at the very beginning with its most fundamental affirmation: God is the absolutely Prior, the wholly Other, the Source and Origin of all that is.

What, then, must we think about the classic rational proofs for the existence of God? It might well be argued, on the basis of Scripture, that we should probably say nothing about them at all, that we should simply pass them by in silence. This attitude is certainly plausible, tenable, even defensible. The more so since in modern times these rational arguments have been largely discredited. One can never forget, however, that since the days of Lombard, Anselm, and Thomas a mind-set has dominated medieval and modern scholastic traditions which attaches great significance to them. That school of thought still claims a loyal following today. We can therefore hardly avoid taking these evidences seriously, not because the Bible does, but because Christians often do. They are part of our historical legacy. They therefore help us understand in part how we got to be the way we are.

Generally five such rational proofs have been advanced for the existence of God: the ontological, cosmological, teleological, moral, and historical arguments. Taken together, they are embedded in a dualist view of the relationship between reason and revelation. Their underlying assumption is that human reason, based on universal laws of logic common to all thinking men of goodwill, unaided by divine revelation, can establish firmly and indubitably certain elemental truths about God. Foremost among them is the idea that "God is." Without detailing each argument, all of them seek to move syllogistically from a certain set of allegedly self-evident givens in our world of experience upward to fixed conclusions concerning the reality of God's existence.

What judgment shall we pass on these venerable arguments? Impressive as they are misleading, they are notable examples of "Christian heresies." They come down to us as by-products of the Western Christian tradition. For centuries their credibility was held in high esteem. Actually, however, these arguments assume at the beginning what presumably they set out to prove. "Christian" conclusions are already built into their "Christian" assumptions. In the aftermath of the Enlightenment, therefore, once their assumptions (concerning the ontic status, order, goal, morality, and religious nature of human life and the world) were no longer commonly held to be true, the conclusions drawn from them were also repudiated. In an historical sense they are "Christian" — in the sense that they are thinkable only as the residue of a Western Christian tradition. Yet at heart they are "heretical" — in the sense that they represent something right gone wrong. Right was their well-grounded notion of belief in God. Wrong was their pretentious overestimation of the potentials of an unaided and autonomous human reason. Equally wrong was their underestimation of the needful role of revelation and the radical effects of sin on human rationality.

Therefore, when all is said and done, we must return to the Bible's opening thesis: God does not stand at the end of a syllogism. Rather, "In the beginning God. . . !" In addressing the Athenian philosophers on Mars Hill, Paul echoes a similarly blunt, confrontational approach: "What therefore you worship as unknown, this I proclaim to you: the God who made the world and everything in it, being Lord of heaven and earth . . ." (Acts 17:23-24).

I. 5. "Beginning" Means Definite Beginning

The "beginning," whenever it took place, was a real and decisively new event. It was God's primordial miracle, bringing into existence something totally new as an act of divine condescension. The creation has no preexistence. God, as it were, stooped to call forth out of nothing a reality wholly other than himself. Bending over and reaching down, God covenanted the world into existence, introducing something brand-new. God is "from everlasting to everlasting" (Psalm 90:2), but not creation.

Creation is "to everlasting," but not "from everlasting." It has a definite beginning.

For God this beginning meant ("humanly speaking," which is of course the only way we can speak) a radical change in his triune activity. He launched a completely new venture, which has no antecedents. It was no mere rerun of some earlier decretal drama. In creating, God established unprecedented relationships. He created otherness. Over against himself he set a world to image his glory, and within it he placed us, his crowning imager, his junior partner in covenant, his kingdom servant. Nothing like this had ever happened "before." Nor will it ever be repeated. The stakes were high, the risks great, and while, given Christmas and Easter, the outcome is no longer in doubt, its awesome potentials still await their final consummation. For God all this meant that things would never be the same again.

What language shall we borrow to stammer out our thoughts on this colossal act of innovation? The traditional idea of "immutability" seems wholly inappropriate to describe this momentous transition in divine activity. It is burdened with too much dubious freight of Greek origin. All too often it connotes the idea of dispassionate changelessness, static aseity, and immobility. Truer to the biblical narrative is an emphasis on the faithfulness of God. In all these unfathomable changes from precreational intratrinitarian fellowship (John 1:1; 17:5) to God moving out through his Word to fashion the world (John 1:3; Hebrews 11:3) and then in the fullness of the times the Word becoming flesh and dwelling among us (John 1:14) — in all these dramatically changing scenes in God's interaction with the cosmos, he remains ever faithful to himself. He remains unalterably true to his Word. This lends an assured sense of steadiness to God's covenantal embrace of his creation and a confident outlook on the final and full realization of his kingdom. Thus we are blessed with the breathing space and elbow room we need to live out fully our life together in his world.

God knows all about this beginning, for it is his doing. And he alone knows "the end from the beginning." For us, however, not only the end, but the beginning as well, is cloaked in mystery which only revelation can reveal. Though undateable, it stands firm as a fixed and unmovable sovereign act of inauguration. It is the definitive alpha-point for all creaturely existence. There is no way for us to slip around it in order to probe behind it. We can only approach it by hearing the Word which was its initial impetus. This ultimate point of departure establishes the temporal-spatial horizon of all created reality. It erects an impassable boundary line which circumscribes the range of our theoretical reflections. Every attempt to overstep it simply transgresses our rational potentials. There are no tools at hand adequate to delve into some retrojected arena of pre-beginnings. This point of ultimate origination is a standing reminder of our creaturely finitude, our utter dependence on our Creator God's revelation, and the relativity of all our human endeavors.

This barrier issues a constant warning against every form of philosophical (prolegomena) and theological (dogmatics) speculation about the preexistence of some sinister Demiurge who fashioned the world contrary to God's better intentions, about the possibility of primeval materials on which God drew to form the universe, about creation as an emanational overflow of divine being, about archetypal forms residing eternally in the mind of God of which this world is but a shadowy reflection, about the conceivability of "other possible worlds," about any prior effective cause whatever (apart from the will and good pleasure of God), about the world as the product of spontaneous emergence, and about some notion of an overarching category of being or time or rationality or language which is common to both the Creator and his creation. Nor is the world mere appearance, a mirage, or an illusion, emerging mysteriously from the hidden recesses of some dark and ominous mythological prehistory. Borrowing Luther's crass but apt utterance, the biblical idea of "beginning" muzzles the mouth of the curious who ask, "And what was God doing before he began to create the world?", by responding: "He was creating a hell for people who ask such questions!"

For theological reflection this decisive and emphatic "genesis" provides a much needed reassurance. For without it our minds can find no rest. Human reason, if it goes its own way in addressing the question of origins, unsubmissive to revelation, locks itself into a enervating pattern of infinite regressions. Plunging itself on a reverse course from where we are, it moves obsessively ever more deeply into the dim recesses of the past, with no place to stop. A firm "beginning" then becomes an ever receding, increasingly more elusive ideal. Contrastingly, "faith seeking understanding" takes its stand responsively within the parameters of the Genesis account. Revelation is not only its last, but also its first Word. A Reformed dogmatics, willing to rest its case "within the bounds of [biblical] religion alone," seeks to make progress in its pilgrimage by beginning where the Bible begins. This is the irreversible starting point for every learning impulse.

The thrust of these reflections is not to stifle intellectual inquiry, but to bring it into conformity with the norms of biblical revelation. Here as everywhere else, human reason plays an important and legitimate, though limited role. The point is this, that rationality finds its proper context within the overarching normativity of creational revelation. Revelation and rationality are therefore not antithetical nor mutually exclusive. Rather, they go hand in hand — the former being the very condition for the latter. Revelation is norm. Rationality is response. For rationality, too, is a creature. As such it is subject to the creation order. Accordingly, only on the basis of its pretended autonomy can human reason transcend the bounds of its creaturely limitations. The biblical doctrine of creation, on the other hand, accords rationality, whether in theology or the other sciences, its rightful servant role. Right thinking about the origins of our world is therefore at home only within the secure environment of the creation order.

I. 6. The Time Factor in Creation

If only we could break the deadlock in that unending round of conflicts between creationism and evolutionism. This raging controversy has consumed far too much valuable energy. What if all the resources poured into waging this battle were devoted instead to fostering justice, peace, prosperity, and compassion among the world's beleaguered populations! The opposing camps in this adversarial situation seem no closer to a common understanding today than when William Jennings Bryan faced Charles Darrow in the notorious 1925 "Monkey Trial." Could it be that from both sides we have locked ourselves into a set of dubious assumptions, false dilemmas, and methodological decisions which offer no promise of a happy outcome? For the way questions are framed is terribly important, so much so that wrong questions never yield right answers. As Susanne K. Langer puts it,

> a question is really an ambiguous proposition; the answer is its determination. . . . Therefore a philosophy is characterized more by the formulation of its problems than by its solutions of them. . . . In our questions lie our principles of analysis, and our answers may express whatever those principles are able to yield. (*Philosophy in a New Key*, pp. 1-2)

In the preceding section we set our sights on that ultimate act of "beginning" (in the singular) recorded in the opening verse of the Genesis account. Call it *creatio prima* (primary creation). Moving along now, we turn our attention to the follow-up drama of "beginnings" (in the plural) as it unfolds in the remainder of the first two chapters of Genesis. Call it *creatio secunda* (secondary creation). The biblical account of these "six days" continues to draw heavy fire in the seemingly endless running encounters between creationists and evolutionists.

This fierce debate over origins is, of course, not a trivial matter. Much more is at stake than calculating the age of the earth or the length of the "days" in Genesis; much more also than looking for "missing links," reconstructing a fossil record, weighing evidence pro and con, and refining scientific methods. The standoff between evolutionism and creationism (bypassing for now the shades of difference within each school of thought) involves deeply religious choices concerning world-views and life-visions, concerning God and man, concerning the destiny of the cosmos as well as viewpoints on its dim and distant past. What, for example, shall we say: "The earth is the Lord's"? or "the earth is the lord"? How shall we account for the world's (dis)order? What does being human mean? How did things get to be the way they are? The biblical doctrine of creation enlightens us not only about beginnings, but also about the present status and future hope of all things. If we get "first things" wrong, "last things" will also turn out wrong, together with everything else along the way. In addressing such fundamental issues, evolutionism proclaims another gospel, which is not the gospel.

Bible-believing Christians find their sympathies coming down quite naturally on the side of creationism. Yet a deeply disturbing feature of the creationist/evolutionist controversy is a frequent manhandling of the biblical text on both sides of the argument. Among evolutionists who still reckon with Scripture this usually takes the form of accommodating the Genesis record to the so-called "assured results of the scientific method" — though of late the once undaunted confidence in these find-ings is being severely tested. Its popularizers may continue to mouth evolutionary dogmas with nearly evangelical fervor. Many of its more knowledgeable proponents, however, feel the ground underfoot getting shaky. It is equally disconcerting to find many defenders of the creationist position adopting similar tactics. In the name of "scientific creationism" they fall into the trap of combating the opposition with its own weapons. One misrepresentation of the Genesis account gets offset by another. And so the stage is set again and again for ceaseless rounds of confrontation between science and counterscience, evidence and counterevidence, theory and countertheory. However well intentioned, creationists often employ methods of biblical interpretation as questionable as those of their antagonists. In the end we are left with the enigma of two opposing parties, holding sharply conflicting views, yet each in its own way seeking to bend Scripture to its own advantage — creationists appealing to it, evolutionists suppressing it. One unavoidable conclusion therefore forces itself on us: We must deal anew with the hermeneutic question of how to read, understand, and interpret aright the Genesis narratives.

Suppose we now pronounce a plague on both these houses. Is there an authentic third way to go? One which is not a mere blending of these two conflicting positions, but a genuine alternative? One which offers promise of relief and healing in the midst of this enervating dilemma?

And one which does greater justice to the hermeneutic demands of the biblical doctrine of origins?

To these several questions one can give an affirmative answer by working out the implications of a confessional hermeneutic (cf. Part One, V. 21). It calls for a new departure involving a rethinking of the biblical idea of time. On this view, time functions as an integral element in the emerging creation order as recorded in the "six-day" Genesis narrative. Each new "day" marks an advance in this series of creative beginnings. This unfolding development of the cosmos arises not from an autonomous process of evolution, nor by a natural flow of events intercepted periodically by divine interventions. These beginnings represent rather an ordered succession of sustained miraculous acts by the Creator. Running through this moving drama is a steady line of continuity, revealing divine workmanship. Yet repeatedly there are also new forward-looking impulses and innovative advances. Each new "day" marks the initiation of more fully opened-up sets of normatively structured relationships for life in God's world. Every later potential for historical development is given with and embedded in the preceding mighty acts of God. As J. Heinrich Diemer puts it: "Whatever appears in the course of time always appears with certain structures; potentially it already lies enclosed within these [earlier] structures and cannot go beyond the boundaries they set" (*Nature and Miracle,* p. 5). Accordingly, this series of "six-day" beginnings is not an index to spans of time by which to calculate the age of the earth. These daily beginnings point rather to orchestrated sets of developing life relationships within the emerging creation order. Time, like every other creature, participates in this creative process.

This linear view of the movement of time, as embodied in the Hebraic-Christian tradition, stands in sharp contrast to its cyclical counterpart among other ancient peoples. Among them the world was regarded as always there. It has no beginning and no end, and there are no new beginnings along the way. History is a ceaseless cycle of ever recurring events, an infinity of repetitions, thus reflecting something of the immutability of the gods. In this way Israel's neighbors sought to posit a certain constancy in the menacing temporal flux and flow of daily experience. The biblical view of time is emphatically different. Time is itself a creature of God's making. It is an integral dimension of all created reality. Its onward movement has a definite beginning, and a goal, with new beginnings and stopping-off points along the way. Time is linear, sequential, and teleological. One moment anticipates another. There are befores and afters. Each segment of time embraces something uniquely important and unrepeatable. It is prospective as well as retrospective. In the words of Langdon Gilkey:

God, who is eternal, has created time with a beginning and an end. Time is thus finite, giving to each moment the possibility of being unique and unrepeatable. Time is, moreover, "going somewhere": from its beginning in creation it moves toward its end or goal, and its moments are meaningful because they lead to this eternal goal. (*Maker of Heaven and Earth,* p. 249)

The ultimate origin of creation lies in its "beginning" (Genesis 1:1). But its condition then was still "waste and void." From that point on it underwent a process of "beginnings" (Genesis 1–2). The world as we know it emerged for the first at the close of this creative process of "beginnings." Then for the first, at the close of the "six days," it appeared as a finished product, ready to receive the divine benediction, "Very good!" Time is an integral concomitant of this creating process. So what holds for the rest of created reality also holds for time. Its origin, too, lies in the "beginning." It, too, underwent a process of "beginnings." Concurrent with all the rest, it, too, is part and parcel of this unfolding movement. It did not explode on the scene ready-made at the "beginning." Rather, time as we experience it, well ordered and fully synchronized, also came forth for the first at the close of the "six days."

In this way Genesis focuses confessionally on God as the Initiator of the cosmos. His sovereign will is the source and origin of all creaturely existence. By his outgoing and mediating Word he calls the world to order. By his Spirit he causes life to abound.

From this point of view, the crucial transition in the Genesis account from "day six" to "day seven" serves to indicate the crucial transition from time in the making to historical time. Thus time, too, has its preliminary history. Time as we know it, as we mete it out on calendars, clock time, is of a qualitatively different order than that time in the making which emerged during the era of "beginnings." What language shall we borrow to express this distinction? Perhaps this will do: Let us call that primeval time *creating* time and our present time *creational* time. The former suggests how time got to be the way it is. The latter describes time as it now is.

Creating time belongs to the world's preludial history. Its movements are measurable only by the six working days on the divine agenda of "beginnings." It reflects the ordered fashioning of the earth from its early "waste and void" state to its climactic appearance as a finished product, meriting the divine stamp of approval. Time matured steadily across that "six-day" span, concurrent with the full range of God's creating activity. During this phase of "beginnings" it was still creating time, not yet the kind of calendar time by which we now schedule our appointments and number our years. It therefore eludes all scientific and historical standards of measurement. It cannot be reconstructed into segments of creational time, whether long or short. For cosmic time, temporal history as we now reckon it, emerged fully with the "seventh day" as a kind of ongoing sabbath continuing onward into the new creation. Creating time anticipates that creational time which now constitutes the framework for our daily lives and scientific enterprises. But it operated on a succession of different wavelengths.

Augustine already wrestled with this mystery. Time, he says, is *concreatum:* it is given along with God's creating acts. The cosmos came into being not *in tempore* (in time), but *cum tempore* (along with time). We are not to think of time as instantaneously created as the very first and fully developed reality into which God then brought forth successively all subsequent creatures. It was not an all-at-once and once-for-all-time ultra-original act, serving as a ready-made temporal container into which God then proceeded to deposit one new spatial creature after another. Creating time is time in the making. Like every other creature, it participated in the ordering process of "beginnings." Listen again to Diemer:

> . . . The days cannot be measured by any standard. Each day is the beginning of the basic structure of a new realm of creatures. . . . Thus in the six days the creation order, without which a world history is impossible, is placed in time. In the account of creation this future history is anticipated. (*Nature and Miracle,* p. 13)

The implications of this view on time are clear, though perhaps unsettling. Those accustomed to conventional methods of conducting the creationist/evolutionist debate may even find them intimidating, if not downright revolutionary. For just as in the primary act of creating, at that ultimate point of "beginning," we encounter our first "Stop" sign, so now at the climax of this series of secondary "beginnings" we encounter a second "Stop" sign. The idea of creating time means that for our understanding of "beginnings" we are wholly dependent on revelation. The Genesis record is then our sole source of knowledge concerning the creating acts of God. For we have no scientific tools of analysis capable of reaching back that far. The "sixth day" marks a cut-off point for theoretical inquiry. Note once more what Diemer says:

> The miracle of creation reveals itself in the spontaneity with which new types of creatures appear. We can speak of a miracle here because something new arises time and again; new structures appear which cannot be reduced to what came earlier. Scripture is our guide here. It speaks of the miraculous works of God, the great things which human thought cannot fathom. (*Nature and Miracle,* p. 11)

Accordingly, historical and scientific methods apply only to creational time. They cannot handle creating time. Cosmogony (understood as a study of the "beginnings" of the world) must then be judged a futile undertaking. But this is no great loss. We are then freed up to concentrate on cosmology (understood as a study of the cosmos within the framework of creational time). That gives us more than enough to go on, to live by, and to work with.

The impossibility of giving a scientific account of these "beginnings" is further reinforced by recognizing that the record of God's creating acts is not couched in scientifically qualified language. This, it seems, is often overlooked by creationists (appealing to it as though it were) as well as evolutionists (discrediting it as though it were). Genesis is indeed a wholly trustworthy witness to real events, cast into practical, commonsense concepts familiar to its first recipients, the people of Israel. It recounts the primordial mighty acts of God, acts, however, which lie outside our presently qualified time zone. It therefore precludes the possibility of reaching firm scientific conclusions concerning how things fell into place. For there are no unbroken logical (including theological) lines of analytical continuity leading back to these "beginnings," let alone to the "beginning." The line of demarcation between the "six days" of creating time and the "seventh day" of ongoing creational time stands as an unbridgeable barrier. There the principle of uniformitarianism meets its dead end. No scientific method can circumvent this historical point of departure. What lies beyond is accessible only by revelation. Ultimate temporal retrogression is therefore impossible.

On this view, moreover, all our probings into "the first five seconds" can only be billed as a speculative enterprise. This perspective also has the effect of casting a heavy cloud of doubt over the "big bang" theory of origins. For every science, theology too, must learn to live within the fixed horizon of creational time.

The account of "beginnings" in Genesis confronts us thus with a picture of an orderly developing creation. Assertions of temporal and spatial invariance traceable to the "beginning," assertions which are actually assumptions, are thereby called into question. For if all things underwent a process of orderly development, by what reason can space and time, as properties of all created reality, be excluded?

This view of origins is not a devious maneuver concocted to escape knotty problems. Nor does it undercut the scientific enterprise. But it does call for shifting some basic priorities from the past to the present and the future. This need not be experienced as a restriction. It can in fact have a liberating effect, relieving us of the burden of an endless, obsessive pursuit of "beginnings" all the way back, as if that were possible, to the very "beginning." On these questions of ultimate and penultimate origins this view elicits a deeper reliance on revelation, coupled with a kind of prudent ignorance akin to the biblical idea of wisdom. Instead of depleting our resources restlessly and incessantly on retrospective research, we can then channel them more beneficially into avenues of present more constructive service.

I. 7. Structure and Function

A basic issue dividing creationists and evolutionists is that of structure and function, of order and process. Each of these "isms" absolutizes one of these aspects of creation at the expense of the other.

God brought forth a "cosmos," a normatively structured, orderly world, not a "chaos." In the beginning, therefore, the structures *of* creation answered fully to the divinely ordained structures *for* creation. But this was not the end of the story. This well-structured creation was also given a history, which involved active functioning, a dynamic opening up of the well-ordered potentials built into the creation. Creationism tends to overlook this creative process, emphasizing instead a static view of reality. Evolutionism tends to go in precisely the opposite direction. Its bywords are flux, mutation, adaptation, contingency, and random selection.

Both positions appeal to some ultimate standard. For the creationist there is a transcendent norm, for the evolutionist some immanent force operative intrinsically from within the world process. However one-sided in its emphasis, creationism arises out of historic Christianity. It may suffer from blind spots on the reality of process in creation. But it is not wrong in recognizing lawfulness as an essential principle in a Christian worldview. Evolutionism is a brainchild of the Enlightenment. Its proponents hypothesize billions of years of process in natural selection. If these staggering claims were compressed into a much shorter time space, they might qualify as "miracles." Stretched out over unthinkably long aeons of time and space, they fall into a category called "evolution." Is evolution, then, merely a slowed-down miracle, a stretched-out misreading of the wonder which the world really is? Perhaps it is then, after all, basically a "Christian heresy" in a radically pernicious form. For in this sense it feeds parasitically on the biblical worldview which includes linear development, but without embracing a definitive starting point with repeated new "beginnings" and a teleologically directed history.

Yet fundamentally these two views are radically divergent. The evolutionist thesis is that function precedes and determines structure. No ordered pattern of reality stands at the beginning. There was only a fluid mass of functions. Over protracted eras of evolutionary development these random functions fell into place. Our present sense of an ordered and structured reality is the product of process, evolving along the lines of phyla, genera, species, plant and animal kingdoms, the human race, and the institutions of society.

Biblical creationists adopt an opposite approach. All things act "according to their kind" (Genesis 1:12, 21, 25). The God-given orders and structures of creation precede and define their respective functions. What a creature does is dependent on what is. Identity circumscribes activity. Against the backdrop of a finished creation, and with "nothing new under the sun," the divinely appointed structures of the creation order delineate the boundaries as well as the potentials for every creaturely enterprise. Accordingly marriage is not the emerging end product of cultural evolution, but an ordinance given from the beginning in, with, and for our life in God's world (Matthew 19:3-12; Mark 10:2-12; Genesis 2:24). God did not, of course, create little red schoolhouses. Nor did he establish the institutional church on the corner. But he did constitute man a learning and worshiping creature. In time the potentials resident in these well-ordered tasks could take on liturgical and educational shape in churches and schools. The same holds for other structures of society. The way we give contemporary form to these nuclear tasks is always open to revision. But there is an abidingly normative order which defines the tasks themselves. If a culturally formed institution no longer functions well, if it fails to answer to its appointed task, then it is time for reformation. Thus, structure and function may not be played off against each other. They are mutually interacting aspects of our life in the creation.

I. 8. Creation "out of Nothing"

My childhood catechism book posed the question, "What does it mean to create?" It then taught us this answer: "To create means to bring forth something out of nothing by the act of an omnipotent will." That was quite a mouthful for a seven-year-old. Bad pedagogy, today's developmental psychologists would say. I readily admit that, as a young catechumen, I failed to grasp what I was reciting. I still cannot fathom it. Yet that confession remains indelibly inscribed on my memory. Even now I can hardly improve on it. It has stood the test of time. For it rings true to the pervasive message of the Scriptures.

Nowhere in Scripture do we find an explicit, verbal reference to the idea of *creatio ex nihilo*. Yet its truth is everywhere present. It is woven integrally into the entire fabric of the Bible's witness to the Creator. It captures the sustained teaching of Scripture on how the world came into existence. Note Hebrews 11:3: "By faith we understand that the world was created by the Word of God, so that what is seen was made out of things which do not appear." This confession sets our feet firmly on the path of the prophets and apostles and reflects the solid conviction of the historic Christian faith.

The opening words of the Genesis account (1:1) mark an absolute starting point. But in echoing these words, what are we really saying? The very thought of *creatio ex nihilo* stretches human vocabulary to beyond its breaking point. The thought of something totally new is utterly baffling. It blows our minds. We simply cannot grasp the idea of something absolutely new — a reality without precursors. The more so if we presume to conceive of something absolutely new initiating absolutely its own existence. We are closer to the truth if in the light of Scripture we say that creation has, not an absolute, but a relative beginning. That is, from its inception and ongoingly it is wholly God-related. It therefore has a relatively independent beginning and present status.

However stammeringly, we are obliged to say that this beginning has no "before." For "before" and "after" are time-conditioned creaturely categories of thought and speech. God's creating acts have no antecedents which our minds can ferret out. Creation out of nothing is a limiting concept. The Creator's fiat (his "Let there be . . .") sets the limits. Behind this ultimate origin lies only the willing Word of God, given in, with, and for the creation. There is no other word which either complements or cooperates with, let alone contradicts, his creating Word. His Word is the initiating decree for all life. There is no set of eternal decrees in the mind of God, over and beyond his Word, which theology is called to probe as a more ultimate topic of research. To do so is to indulge in "idle speculation" (Calvin). The eternal decree is knowable only through God's Word for creation. That Word marks the parameter for all human knowledge. There we encounter a firmly implanted "Stop" sign. Beyond it lies "no-man's-land," clearly marked with a "No Trespassing" sign. Commenting on this "intellectual crux," Hendrikus Berkhof says: "Here we stand before a wall. Existence cannot be traced back further. . . . We cannot penetrate this mystery; we can only make it our starting point. . . . Out of nothing simply means: not out of anything" (*Christian Faith*, pp. 152, 153, 154).

God's good pleasure is the only content we can give to this *creatio ex nihilo*. This "nothing," for example, does not allow for the idea of a certain "Nothingness" viewed as a negative "Something" standing over against God. Nor does it point to the idea of "Darkness" or "Abyss," conceived of as an intracosmic force which, during the course of his creating acts, God overcomes by his repeated affirmation of "Light" and "Being." To build such bipolar dialectical tensions into the Genesis account calls into question the good work of the Creator God as well as the integrity of creation itself. Some older theologies sought therefore to reinforce the idea of *ex nihilo* doubly by referring to it enigmatically as "negative nothing."

Looking ahead for a moment, on this score redemption is analogous to creation. Each in its own way is a work of God *ex nihilo*. The sole motivation of both is the sovereign goodwill of God manifest in the holding and healing power of his Word. In creation as well as redemption the only impetus and objective is the declarative glory of God. In this "out of nothing" idea, therefore, Christian theology stresses the absolute independence and self-sufficiency and unconditional freedom of the Creator-Redeemer in his covenant faithfulness toward his creation. He lends his creatures an existence distinct from his own, yet never autonomous. He grants them a relative independence, yet always fully dependent on his Word. Through his mediating Word God establishes covenantal interaction with his creation, yet without infringing on the otherness of the Creator/creature relationship. No analogy of being between God and man is possible. Creation out of nothing is a forceful reminder of this. For it stands in sharp contrast to the only kind of creativity we know, namely, creating something secondary out of that which is primordially there.

At the ultimate point of primordial beginnings we can only fall back on the language of analogy (word pictures, imagery). Otherwise we are confined to saying nothing. Yet, even then, at some point the most apt analogies themselves break down. For the fundamental relationship between the infinite Creator and his finite creatures bursts the bounds of human rationality and language. Theology and the other sciences are indeed free to study the history of our life together in God's world and the processes presently at work in it, but they cannot delve into that ultimate event by which it all came into being. At that point we must take Someone's Word for it.

The basic meaning of creation out of nothing can be summarized in these lines from Langdon Gilkey:

> The Christian doctrine of creation, therefore, expresses in theoretical language those positive religious affirmations which biblical faith in God makes in response to the mystery of the meaning and destiny of our creaturely finitude. These affirmations are: 1) That the world has come to be from the transcendent holiness and power of God, who because He is the ultimate origin is the ultimate Ruler of all created things. 2) That because of God's creative and ruling power our finite life and the events

160

in which we live have, despite their bewildering mystery and their frequently tragic character, a meaning, a purpose, and a destiny beyond any immediate and apparent futility. 3) That man's life, and therefore *my* life, is not my own to "do with" merely as I please, but is claimed for — because it is upheld and guided by a power and a will beyond my will. This is what the Christian means when he says, "I believe in God the Father Almighty, Maker of heaven and earth." This is what the idea of *creatio ex nihilo* is essentially "about." (*Maker of Heaven and Earth,* pp. 30-31)

I. 9. God and the gods

From beginning to end Scripture arises out of the unfolding drama of redemption. It participates in it and contributes to it. This, therefore, holds for the creation account too. Its narratives date from the early history of Israel. In its lingual forms, style, imagery, and concepts it echoes that stage in the history of redemptive revelation.

Standing within the mainstream of covenant history, the author of Genesis (as it were) casts his glances back across his shoulder to the dawn of cosmic history. Assuming the role of a firsthand witness, like an on-the-scene reporter, he is allowed to drop in on a kind of repeat performance of the original mighty acts of God. In rapid succession and with swift strokes he sketches the "signs of divinity" (Calvin) as they are being hung out prominently for "the morning stars" and "all the sons of God" to applaud (Job 38:7). For from the beginning this "cosmic theatre" (Calvin) bears witness to the "eternal power and deity" of its Maker (Acts 14:15-17; Romans 1:19-20). Drawing on oral and/or written traditions, the writer is transported revelationally to the dawn of world history. With pen in hand he is poised to witness a reenactment of the original spectacular display of divine handiworks. We are now allowed to look over his shoulder as he describes these breathtaking events from the vantage point of the messianically directed life of the ancient people of God. The Genesis story therefore carries with it the benchmarks of its author's age.

One striking evidence of this is the polemical thrust built into the pattern of the creation account. To sense this we must picture Israel living in a highly polytheistic world. Surrounding them on all sides are neighboring peoples enslaved to the veneration of a host of gods. Ensnared in pagan superstitions, they "exchanged the truth about God for a lie and worshiped and served the creature rather than the Creator," trading in "the glory of the immortal God for images resembling mortal man or birds or animals or reptiles" (Romans 1:22, 25). The seductive power of such idolatrous practices took its toll throughout Israel's history. Not until after the return from Babylonian captivity, it seems, did Israel develop a spiritual immunity to the lure of these false religions. Keenly aware therefore of these besetting sins, the author weaves into his account subtle but strong warnings against such apostasy. These antithetical elements were not actually present in the original good order of creation. They arose in the aftermath of the fall, posing real dangers to true religion at the time that Genesis was composed. Recognizing these dangers, the author punctuates the creation story with a number of alarm signals.

Note the following polemical thrusts. There we meet first the "waste and void" state of primeval creation. This is not an ominous abyss, however, which threatens to engulf the emerging creation. It is rather the raw material waiting to be shaped into a finished product, not deformed, but as yet unformed, preformed. So also, "night" is not a dark and sinister side of creation, but a restful intermezzo in the unfolding acts of this great drama. The "waters" above and below the firmament are not frightening floods threatening to swamp the earth, but an environment-in-the-making for "swarms of living creatures." The "greater light" is not a sun-god, nor is the "lesser light" a moon-god, nor do the stars shine as lower deities. None of them is a menacing force hovering overhead. They are all creatures of the Lord, suspended in the heavens at his command, appointed to illumine the earth. Similarly, the writer sets the record straight with respect to the "great sea monsters," "creeping things," and "flying birds." None of these creatures is to be feared as a pseudodeity who competes with God's rule or as a demonic power menacing his creation. For repeatedly we read, "and God saw that it was good."

The Genesis picture is clear: God does not create junk. Later, in the postlapsarian world, which is the world of the author, a radical change takes place. All sorts of fascinating creatures are alternately ascribed either divine or demonic qualities. Such irreligious fantasies come under attack in the Genesis account. The author reminds his readers that there is no need to cringe in fear before such symbols of supposed supernatural power, nor to placate the ill temper of these non-gods, nor to cling to the myths so highly esteemed among the Egyptians, Canaanites, Philistines, and other peoples who entered Israel's life. Yet Israel was slow to learn. These pointed warnings therefore reemerge in later stages of the history of revelation as oft-repeated themes in the writings of the prophets. Again and again Israel is admonished not to "fear what they fear." Fear the Lord your God alone! It is, after all, he alone who by his mighty Word of power holds the waters in check, saying, "Thus far shall you come, and no farther, and here shall your proud waters be stayed" (Job 38:11). God's people are not to fear the billowing waters, but to ascribe glory to the Lord who "sits enthroned over the flood" (Psalm 29). The godly can walk with a firm step, for the "the sun [god] shall not smite you by day," nor the "the moon [god] by night" (Psalm 121).

The author of Genesis takes these idols seriously, not because they are real rivals to God's rule, nor because God is intimidated by them (he who sits in the heavens laughs!), but because Israel repeatedly drifts into spiritual idolatry. Therefore he interlaces the creation story with these unobtrusive yet sharply barbed polemics. It is a faulty hermeneutic, however, to read the later sin-ridden condition of world history back into the original state of righteousness. We may not allow the dark shadows of human iniquity to becloud the shalom of God's good creation. For then good and evil forces become primordial realities standing in dialectical tension within the very structures of creation. Such a method of interpretation completely obscures the biblical story line of the good creation, fallen, now being redeemed, and one day to be consummated. Sin then loses its radically disruptive earnestness. Grace is robbed of its triumph. Creation is deprived of its goodness. The world is rendered unredeemable.

The biblical doctrine of creation, by contrast, highlights the sovereign goodness of God and the uncompromised goodness of his creation as a principle of first-order importance. God made all things good, and in the end they will be made good again. Even now that original goodness is in principle restored so that we can already enjoy a foretaste of its eschatological fulfillment. For, as Paul says, "everything created by God is good, and nothing is to be rejected if it is received with thanksgiving; for then it is consecrated by the Word of God and prayer" (1 Timothy 4:4-5).

I. 10. The Time of Day in Genesis

Few single words have aroused as much intense debate as the little Hebrew word *yom* ("day") in the Genesis account. This lively dispute extends from the early Christian era to the present. How are we to understand these seven "days"? Literal twenty-four-hour segments of time? Long periods of time? A literary device? An historical framework? A liturgical format? A saga or myth? In common parlance, millennia ago as well as now, the word "day" clearly had to do with calendar time. But how does *yom* function in the Genesis narrative? Does it simply measure temporal duration? Is it merely clock time?

Earlier (I.6) we argued that *creating* time (the "six days") is of a qualitatively different dimension than *creational* time (the "seventh day" and onward). Between them there is clearly a certain continuity, for creating time ushers in creational time. But there is also a real discontinuity. This recognition of both continuity and discontinuity doubtless contributes to the problem of interpreting the meaning of *yom*. But a recognition of the "seventh day" as the transition point in cosmic history can also help bring relief to this hermeneutic problem. Current instruments for measuring creational time break down in the face of creating time. Therefore, what we presently call "day" cannot be simply equated with "day" *(yom)* during the era of God's creating activity.

We are thus led to pursue a different hermeneutic route in seeking an understanding of the "time of day" in the creation account. The author of Genesis is familiar experientially with the weekly rhythm of six laboring days and a seventh day of rest. By revelation he accepts this sevenfold pattern in life's routine as a creation ordinance. It finds its prototype in the activities of the Creator himself (Genesis 2:1-3), which is to serve as a paradigm for our life-style, as clearly indicated in the decalogue (Exodus 20:8-11). The writer of Genesis then takes this weekly round of six working days (followed by a day of rest, which marks the inception of creational time) and employs it reflexively as his ordering principle in depicting sequentially the mighty creating acts of God. In the onward flow of biblical revelation the idea of *yom* (as "day of the Lord") takes on a surprisingly full meaning: it refers to Israel's impending captivity, its return to the homeland, the coming of Messiah, the consummation of all things. Thus *yom* connotes not only a succession of temporal moments in history *(chronos),* but also some momentously laden opportune moments to be eagerly grasped *(kairos).* So in Genesis we hear echoes of great creating moments of orderly development in divine activity as well as a revelation of their cosmically formative significance.

Perhaps we can picture it this way. The creation story as recorded in Genesis 2 is oriented to the earthly scene. Creation is given its finishing touches, climaxed in the appearance of humankind, Adam and Eve. They are appointed — and in them we, too — as stewards, caretakers, and administrators of this bounteous visible kingdom of God, called to serve as the Creator's representatives among his other creatures. It is a very down-to-earth narrative. Genesis 1 introduces this very earthy drama from a different perspective. There we are exposed to its deeper dimension. In this story of beginnings, as it were, we are led behind the earthly scenes to catch a glimpse of that motivating will and power within the heavenly realm which made it all happen. We are allowed to listen in on the minutes and proceedings of an original council meeting of the triune God: "Let us make man in our own image, after our likeness" (Genesis 1:26). Breaking forth from the transcendent chambers of divine decision making we hear the Word resounding again and again: "Let there be. . . !

164

Let there be. . . !" — and so it was. In so commanding, God also blesses. His imperatives descend as benedictions on the creation. Thus the focus varies in these two creation accounts. While Genesis 2 accentuates the condescending goodness of God ("It is not good that man should be alone. . . ," Genesis 2:18), Genesis 1 accentuates his sovereign greatness.

Genesis 1 is not a casual piece of writing. Attentive reading leads us to recognize a well-planned structure and style, almost rhapsodic in mood and tone. There are striking symmetries, the repetition of central emphases, a progressively unfolding parallel development, an alternating accent on God speaking and acting, and a close interaction between divine initiative and creaturely response. There is an unmistakable correlation between what took place on the first three days and the next three. It is a correlation, however, which moves beyond mere duplication and overlap to clearly marked advances. Day one — light breaking forth — finds its progressive parallel in day four — the appearance of the sun, moon, and stars. On day two the firmament is established, dividing the waters above from the waters below. It finds its progressive parallel, correspondingly, during the fifth day in flocks of birds winging their way across the skies and swarms of fish moving through the deeps. On day three dry land appears, separated from the waters, providing an environment for plant life. It finds its appropriate progressive parallel on the sixth day in the creation of animal life, and then climactically in the creation of human life — both forms of life to be sustained by "every green plant for food."

In recounting these creating acts, we are more than passive spectators leaning back in our seats and simply taking in the dramatic events transpiring within this cosmic theatre. Through our first parents, Adam and Eve, the great Director eventually draws us into the act as his covenant partners and citizens in his earthly kingdom. We are a deeply involved audience. Our only appropriate response is to rise to our feet spontaneously in a lifetime of standing ovations translated into works of obedience. For what is going on in the creation narratives is more than play-acting. Our artistic representations of it may not be allowed to obscure the down-to-earth reality of these primordial events in their impact on our lives.

Allowing, nevertheless, for a bit of poetic license, perhaps we can reconstruct this dramatic story of beginnings along these lines:

> The Theme: a proclamation of the comprehensive message of the creation narratives — "In the beginning God created the heavens and the earth" (Genesis 1:1).

> The Interlude: setting the scenes and preparing the props — "The earth was without form and void, and darkness was upon the

face of the deep; and the Spirit of God was moving over the face of the waters" (Genesis 1:2).

The Drama Reenacted: the successive creating acts of God covering six days (Genesis 1:3–2:1).

The Climax: the restful conclusion to a grand and finished production, which then marks a new beginning, the beginning of creational time — "And on the seventh day God finished his work which he had done, and he rested on the seventh day from all his work which he had done. So God blessed the seventh day and hallowed it, because on it God rested from all his work which he had done in creation" (Genesis 2:2-3).

In the end the drama of creation comes full circle. It closes as it opens, highlighting God as its Author, Director, and chief Actor. In every act he sustains his lead role. Then near the end, as the curtain falls on his creating acts and rises on his creational work of providence, God ushers us onto center stage and assigns us our roles. And so the days and weeks and years of our life story begin to unfold.

I. 11. Anthropomorphism

If only we could uncomplicate our theological jargon. But no, some concepts, if lost, would result in substantial impoverishment. Here is a case in point. The idea of anthropomorphism has gained a settled place in "the language of Canaan." It need not repel us. By exposing its etymological roots we can readily uncover its meaning. The word "anthropomorphism" is a combination of two underlying terms: *anthrōpos,* meaning "man," and *morphē,* meaning "form." Literally, therefore, it means "in the form of man."

Our point of reference here is, of course, Scripture as a whole, and more specifically the Genesis narratives. From start to finish, biblical revelation is anthropomorphic. God's self-disclosure is inscripturated in very human forms, in concepts suited to our creaturely level of understanding. It is God's Word in the words of men — couched in down-to-earth literary forms, word pictures, and imagery. In the original documents *(autographa)* and early manuscripts it was cast into the Hebrew, Aramaic, and Greek parlance familiar to the ancient people of God.

In Scripture God accommodates the revelation of his will to our creaturely and sinful status. We may speak therefore of a double conde-scension: God stoops first to meet us in our creatureliness, then in our sinfulness. The biblical message is clothed not in some divine or heavenly vocabulary, but in very human and earthy forms of speech. It is accom-modated to the cultural context of its original recipients — the largely agrarian and pastoral life-style of Israel and the more cosmopolitan setting of the early Christian community. While thus Scripture comes to us *in* the words of *men,* at the same time it also comes to us pervasively *as* the Word of *God.* It is canonical, self-authenticating, and normative. As such its message is transhistorical and transcultural in scope.

The Scriptures therefore are able to address people in every age with undiminished authority — our twentieth-century technological society no less than the first-century citizens of the Roman empire. Indeed, a confessional opening up of the Scriptures often puts our best hermeneutic skills to the test. Yet we may expect rewards on such diligent labors precisely because the Bible speaks anthropomorphically. In it God stoops to conquer us. Calvin holds, on the one hand, that we must regard the Scriptures "as having sprung from heaven, as if there the living words of God were heard" (*Institutes,* I,7,1). Yet at the same time he gives eloquent expression to the anthropomorphically condescending tenor of Scripture when he says:

> For who even of slight intelligence does not understand that, as nurses commonly do with infants, so God is wont in a measure to "lisp" in speaking to us? Thus such forms of speaking do not so much express clearly what God is like as accommodate the knowledge of him to our slight capacity. To do this he must descend far beneath his loftiness. (*Institutes,* I,13,1)

We are therefore well advised to reckon seriously with the intensely human-historical tone of biblical revelation — the personality, experi-ence, training, and idiosyncrasies of its authors, together with the time, place, and setting of its original readers. These anthropomorphic traits are clearly discernible in the Genesis text and in its echoes throughout Scripture. They must therefore enter into our interpretation of the biblical doctrine of creation.

All of Scripture, in its total extent and in all its parts, is anthro-pomorphic. But there are also those very concentrated anthro-pomorphisms in the biblical revelation of the mighty acts of God. It speaks very concretely of the "eyes" of the Lord which see all things, his "ears" which are open to the prayers of his people, his "mouth" from which his Word proceeds, his "arm" which is not shortened, and his "hand" which is not weakened. Such anthropomorphic expressions are not to be read univocally, as though they apply to God in the same way as they apply to us. Calvin already disputes this view in his critique of the "anthropomorphites" (*Institutes,* I,13,1). Nor should such anthropomorphisms be understood equivocally, as though they were mere figures of speech, empty symbols, words without a meaningful reference to the way God really is. It is best to interpret them analogically. Accordingly, the way "eyes," "ears," "mouth," "arm," and "hand" function in our daily experience is analogous to their meaning in divine revelation. When, for example, Scripture tells us repeatedly that the "nostrils" of the Lord are open to the sweet odors of Israel's sacrifices, then we are not to imagine that God is adorned with a nose such as ours, but that he is receptive to these Old Testament acts of atonement. Such sensitivity to the idea of revelational analogy should therefore also shape our understanding of the "saying," "seeing," and "resting" activity of God in the Genesis narratives. It is this sensitivity which colors the discussions carried on in the preceding sections.

Bethlehem cradled the ultimate in anthropomorphic revelation. There "the Word became flesh and dwelt among us" (John 1:14). There God identified himself completely with us. There the Son of God took on the "form *(morphē)* of man *(anthrōpos)*" so fully and truly as to become "like us in all things" (Galatians 4:4; Philippians 2:7). But wait — we are now running ahead of the story.

I. 12. General Revelation? Yes. Natural Theology? No

Most of the mainline theologies in the Western Christian tradition are dominated by dualist motifs. As a working principle they presuppose a worldview divided sharply along the lines of two realms of reality. On the one level they posit natural (general) revelation, issuing in natural law, which constitutes the basis for a natural theology. At a higher level they hold to a supernatural (special) revelation, the locus for divine law, which creates the possibility for sacred theology. God is of course regarded the author of both revelations. But he reveals himself in these two ways — which view is in itself true to the historic Christian faith. Despite its good intentions, however, when cast into the framework of dual orders of reality, enormous problems emerge. Creational revelation then comes to be viewed as a relatively independent and autonomous source of knowledge. It only lacks completeness and must therefore be complemented by a second and higher kind of knowledge. Yet, so the argument goes, in and of itself general revelation and natural law is universally accessible as a common fund to all right-thinking people. Its givens, appropriated by unaided human reason, provide an adequate rationale for constructing a natural theology.

On this view creational givens lose their revelational impact. They are reduced to religiously neutral phenomena. Natural law then becomes a secularized form of divine law. "Nature" takes on deist overtones. The meaning of reality can be grasped by common sense apart from reliance on revelation. The need for revelation is then reserved for acquiring knowledge at the level of sacred truths. Thus revelation is equated with the imparting of supernatural insight. It is viewed as exclusively soteriological in character. Only in such matters is biblical faith called for. But this leaves us with a natural theology, whether in a scholastic or liberal mold, a theology shorn of the need for a revelational base or a faith response.

Christian theology has been long plagued by this conundrum of natural theology. Little wonder that eventually someone should arise in strong revolt against it. A notable case in point is Karl Barth. Given these radical misconceptions of general (creational) revelation and its radically distorted reconstruction in a cluster of natural theologies, we can only applaud Barth's vigorous assault on it. His reactionary corrective, however, like all reactions, fails to yield a lasting and satisfying answer to the problem. For the Barthian tradition, too, lapses into a serious misreading of the real issue. It severely restricts the viable options in arriving at a biblically directed view of revelation. It throws out the baby with the bath water. In his passionate denunciation of wrong (natural) theology grounded in a wrong view of (natural) revelation, Barth pushes the pendulum over to an equally wrong extreme — a rejection of natural (general) revelation itself for the sake of rejecting natural theology. But two wrongs never make a right.

Barthians redefined revelation in exclusively soteriological terms. It is embodied solely in God's once-for-all personal act of reconciling grace in Jesus Christ. Creation is at most a witness and pointer to this Christomonist encounter of God with man. In the process the biblical testimony to God's handiwork in the creation is emptied of its revelational content. The result is a flight from creation as revelation. This christological remedy is hardly an improvement over the naturalist, rationalist, humanist, and secularist maladies it was intended to cure.

The biblical worldview, rooted in the witness of the Scriptures (Psalms 19, 24, 104; Romans 1; Acts 14, 17), calls for an uncompromising affirmation of creational (general, "natural") revelation without allowing ourselves to get crowded into the untenable corner of natural theology. This worldview also belongs to a time-tested tradition. It leads us to recognize the prime importance of distinguishing between divine revelation and human response, in creation as well as in redemption.

Revelation is always normative, response never is. Human responses, including theological responses, whether obedient or disobedient, can often be very instructive. But they never carry binding authority. This is the error of both scholastics and liberals, who grant natural religion and natural theology a normative status. In reaction, however, many evangelicals as well as Barthians are equally mistaken in rejecting general revelation in the name of rejecting natural theology.

Traditional natural theologies were right in acknowledging signs of God's handiwork in creation which impinge themselves inescapably on all men. They were wrong, however, in overestimating the potentials of human rationality and underestimating the effects of sin. In so doing they opened the door to the mistaken notion of a universally valid, naturally accessible, and commonly shared fund of true knowledge of God as Creator. This heresy literally begged for Barth's devastating critique. For natural theology minimizes the radical spiritual brokenness of our world with its cacophony of confessional visions, resulting in deeply divergent religious responses to God's Word for creation. Indeed, that Word still holds for one and all alike. Only by donning the spectacles of Scripture, however, in submission to the Christ of the Scriptures, and illumined by his Spirit, can we answer faithfully to creation's call. Otherwise, hearing we hear not, and seeing we see not. The recurring dangers of natural theology may not drive us, however, to a diminished appreciation of the continuing reality and unretracted fullness, forcefulness, and clarity of creational (general) revelation, as in Barth's theology. For God "did not leave himself without a witness . . ." (Acts 14:17). He is forever the Maker and Sustainer of all things for all seasons.

So, general revelation? Yes. Natural theology? No. As G. C. Berkouwer puts it cogently, ". . . the identification of general revelation and natural theology is an untenable position." For "in principle [natural theology] has no need of the idea of revelation. . . ," since "one can acquire a natural theology or knowledge of God in another way, namely, from nature by means of human reason" (*General Revelation*, pp. 47, 67).

I. 13. "Two Books"

Much of the vigorous debate surrounding the validity, scope, and effects of God's (general) revelation in creation centers sooner or later on Article II of the Belgic Confession (1561). In it many churches standing in the Calvinian tradition confess that "we know [God] by two means":

First, by the creation, preservation, and government of the universe, since that universe is before our eyes like a beautiful book in which all creatures, great and small, are as letters to make us ponder the invisible things of God: his eternal power and his divinity, as the apostle Paul says in Romans 1:20. All these things are enough to convict men and leave them without excuse. Second, he makes himself known to us more openly by his holy and divine Word, as much as we need in this life, for his glory and for the salvation of his own.

This confession was written by Guido de Brès, a Reformed preacher in the southern part of The Netherlands, now known as Belgium, during an era of severe Counter-Reformational persecution. A few short years later de Brès sealed his confession with a martyr's death. His work lives on, however, adopted as a creedal standard by many Reformed churches. Though it was drafted during Calvin's lifetime, there is no evidence that he had a direct hand in its composition. Yet de Brès's work does seem to rely heavily on the Gallican Confession (1559), of which Calvin, it seems, was a chief architect. Calvinist thought is certainly the most relevant background for understanding this "two-book" confession.

Calvin holds that it is not "for us to attempt with bold curiosity to penetrate to the investigation of [God's] essence, which we ought more to adore than meticulously to search out, but for us to contemplate him in his works whereby he renders himself near and familiar to us, and in some manner communicates himself" (*Institutes*, I,5,9). This knowledge of God as Creator is a matter of revelation, not of rational achievement. For the "skillful ordering of the universe is for us a sort of mirror in which we can contemplate God, who is otherwise invisible" (*Institutes*, I,5,1). Thus confronted with the "signs of divinity" and "sparks of his glory" everywhere on display in this "dazzling theatre" of creation, and with the "seed of religion" and "sense of divinity" engraven indelibly on our very way of being human, "men cannot open their eyes without being compelled to see him" (*Institutes*, I,5,1).

Calvin calls creational revelation the "alphabet of theology." Appealing to it, he concludes that knowledge of the Creator God "is not a doctrine that must first be learned in school, but one of which each of us is a master from his mother's womb and which nature itself permits no one to forget, although many strive with every nerve to that end" (*Institutes*, I,4,3). This is "the primal and simple knowledge to which the very order of nature would have led us if Adam had remained upright" (*Institutes*, I,2,1). Apart from sin creational revelation would be sufficient. Even now God has not withdrawn his Word for creation nor diminished his revealing presence in the world. Therefore no one can assume a religiously neutral stance over against creation. Accordingly "all excuse is cut off, because the fault of our dullness lies within us" (*Institutes,* I,5,15). For we are all like "a traveler passing through a field at night, who in a momentary lightning flash sees far and near, but the sight vanishes so swiftly that he is plunged again into the darkness of the night before he can take even a step — let alone be directed on his way with its help" (*Institutes,* II,2,18).

This is our universal human predicament. It emphasizes the dire necessity of that "second book" — the "spectacles" of Scripture. For, as Calvin puts it:

> Just as old or bleary-eyed men and those with weak vision, if you thrust before them a most beautiful volume, even if they recognize it to be some sort of writing, yet can scarcely construe two words, but with the aid of spectacles will begin to read distinctly; so Scripture, gathering up the otherwise confused knowledge of God in our minds, having dispersed our dullness, clearly shows us the true God. (*Institutes,* I,6,1)

"It is needful," therefore, "that another and better help be added to direct us aright to the very Creator of the universe" (*Institutes,* I,6,1).

This train of thought is background to de Brès's confession that "we know [God] by two means." For a right understanding of this statement of faith it is important to recognize that the "we" spoken of here in Article II harks back to the "we" of Article I. In both articles, and in all that follow, it is the Christian community within the Reformed tradition which is here confessing its faith. Its common faith is the context for reflecting on this twofold revelation. Accordingly, the relationship between these "two books," rightly understood, calls for a recognition of the *noetic* effects of sin on our minds and our need for the saving knowledge disclosed in Scripture. This is clearly the context intended by de Brès in his confession — "to His glory and our salvation." If it is understood *ontically,* however, this article allows anew for driving dualist wedges between these "two books." Then worldviews reemerge which divide these two forms of revelation along the lines of two realms of being and two orders of knowing — a higher and a lower level. When this happens, as it often has, then we can appreciate Barth's frontal attack on the confession embodied in this article, to which we now return.

I. 14. Barth's Counteroffensive

Karl Barth continues to stand tall as the twentieth-century's bellwether theologian. He spearheaded a strong counteroffensive on a theology of creation which had degenerated into a cluster of natural theologies. Any critical assessment of his thought must begin with a recognition of the validity of his attack on age-old deformations of the biblical doctrine of creation. Barth pointed an indicting finger at standard medieval theologies, the entire semi-Pelagian tradition, modern Roman Catholicism as defined by the decrees of Vatican I, both Lutheran and Reformed scholasticism, as well as the liberalist, rationalist, humanist theologies spawned by the Enlightenment and personified in Kant, Hegel, Schleiermacher, Ritschl, Troeltsch, and Harnack. In all these developments Barth sees a destructive form of "double bookkeeping" — an attempt to accommodate the two sources of revelation, creation and redemption. Its horrendous results became painfully evident in the "German Christianity" of the 1930s. And we brought it on ourselves, Barth argues.

For centuries Western Christianity had been sowing the winds of heresy, and then at last we reaped the whirlwind harvest of apostasy. Beside God's single revelation in Christ, great thinkers of the past, according to Barth, had appealed erroneously to a second source of knowledge — call it nature, history, reason, culture, conscience, or feeling. Whenever this happens, the "book of nature" inevitably subdues the "book of grace." "Nature *and* grace" becomes "nature *alone*." The end product of this pernicious process is the National Socialism of Hitler's Germany.

God spoke anew in 1933! so the Nazi theologians claimed. That decisive moment in German history marked the new moment of divine reawakening. The Fatherland embraced its mission. Divine destiny was on the side of this new Führer and his Third Reich. It was bound to usher in the long awaited millennium, directed providentially by Hitler's "higher intuitions." The Deliverer from the South (Jesus) was making way for the Deliverer from the North (Adolf). This new "revelation" was not only published in government propaganda, but was also proclaimed from pulpits, in lecture halls, and through editorials. An anti-Christian Trojan horse was smuggled into the City of God.

According to Barth, orthodoxy offered only feeble resistance. Roman Catholics countered by appealing to the magisterial authority of its supreme teaching office. The basic rejoinder of Protestantism was an appeal to its "paper pope," the Scriptures. It locked up the living Lord within a closed canon — as if God could speak only Hebrew, Greek, and Latin!

One must applaud Barth's sharply worded exposé of "German Christianity." The natural theologies of the past had issued in a monstrous distortion of creational revelation. The result was a thinly disguised paganism. These departures from the Reformation heritage completely blurred the antithesis between Christianity and an apostate

173

ideology. Natural theology betrayed the gospel of free sovereign grace. It led Christians into a flirtatious and seductive courtship with a deadly enemy. As a reactionary corrective, therefore, Barth was right in calling the church away from the enticing notions of natural theology as urgently as a mountain climber is well advised to avoid the slippery back of a deep and steep ravine. These strongly negative conclusions regarding natural theology, however, are then mistakenly applied to creational (general) revelation itself. If Barth's reactionary method were applied consistently across the board, we could then close the books completely on Christian dogmatics. For which doctrines have not been badly mishandled? But malpractice is never sufficient grounds for discarding biblical teachings. Barth answers bad theology with one of his own.

Barth holds, nevertheless, that his views are true to Calvin and the Reformation. He concedes that there are traces of a theology of creation in their writings. But this reflects only a failure on their part to draw out consistently the consequences of their unique position. This shortcoming comes to very unfortunate expression, he holds, in the second article of the Belgic Confession.

In paradise perhaps there was some form of revelation in creation. But that is now both "objectively" and "subjectively" lost. God now reveals himself solely through the Word made flesh in Jesus Christ. The Reformers, Barth argues, can perhaps be excused for their ambiguity on this matter. But Brunner ought to know better! For the historical evidence is plain to see: What was marginal in the Reformers eventually became a major theme in their successors. "Nature" was hailed as king. Queenly "grace" crowned it with a kind of religious halo. By allowing for some point of contact for the revelation of grace within the domain of creation Brunner was returning to the fleshpots of Egypt which he and Barth had together abandoned when they launched the neoorthodox movement and jointly entered the promised land. To Brunner's "betrayal" of their rediscovered gospel Barth issued his resounding "No!" Creation offers no open receptivity for the revelation of God's grace in Christ. Rather, sovereign grace creates its own state of readiness in "nature." This sharp clash over the possibility of general revelation, and an apologetic based on it, led to three decades of estrangement between "the elephant" and "the whale."

Barth held that he and his colleagues had rearticulated the true import of Reformation thought in the first thesis of the Barmen Declaration: "Jesus Christ, as He is attested to us in Holy Scripture, is the one Word of God which we must hear and obey both in life and in death." In a situation of mounting German crisis this testimony resounded with a clear ring of defiance. It openly challenged popular appeals to a dual standard of authority — the gospel unequally yoked with a national leadership imbued with a fanatic ideological sense of divine foreordination, providence, and destiny. It affirmed that God's Word in Christ alone is revelation. Jesus Christ is the undisputed Lord, who calls for a loyalty uncompromised by the competing claims of a new "messiah" who was out to seduce believers into the service of "another god."

Barth had a heavy hand in drafting this Barmen confession. Almost before the ink on the paper was dry, his efforts were rewarded by an enforced expulsion from Bonn to his native Basel. The Barmen Declaration stands nonetheless as a heroic witness against a radically distorted Christianity. This evil political ethic, rightly denounced at Barmen, does not in any sense follow, however, from the biblical idea of creation order or the Christian doctrine of creational revelation. At the same time, Barmen's singular emphasis on Jesus Christ as Word of God, understood in an exclusively redemptive sense, also undercuts the integrity of God's twofold revelation.

In support of his case Barth does not avoid those biblical passages which are traditionally cited as grounds for the doctrine of creational revelation (Psalms 19, 104; Romans 1). What emerges, however, in masterful fashion is a highly dogmatized exegesis, bending scriptural data to fit the structures of his systematic theology. The result is a reductionist representation of the biblical teaching on creation.

Barth leaves us with a strictly second-article theology (redemption in Christ). The first article of the Apostles' Creed (God the Father and creation) and the third article (the Holy Spirit and sanctification) suffer serious eclipse. Article II stands as our sole source of knowledge concerning creation. The Barthian tradition therefore fails to acknowledge creation as a continuing revelation of God, prior to and relatively independent of God's redemptive revelation in Christ. It obscures the role of Christ as Mediator of creation, assimilating it into the doctrine of Christ as Reconciler. Creation is made subservient to and finds its meaning in redemption. Soteriology takes over center stage, and the biblical doctrine of an originally good creation, despite extensive treatment, recedes into the background. Barth's christological epistemology dictates a christological ontology. Methodologically, therefore, creation is rendered nonoperative in his theology. It serves only as a relatively autonomous, religiously neutral domain, a nonrevelational given. "Grace *and* nature" makes way for "grace *against* nature."

In Barth the nineteenth-century liberalist brand of Article I anthropocentrism is replaced by a new anthropocentric theology based on Article II. For his theology implies giving priority to epistemology at the expense of ontology, to the possibilities of human knowledge rather than the actuality of God's creational work as revelation in the world. Despite Barth's heavy accent on "objectivity," it is human "subjectivity" which ultimately serves as the norm for true knowledge. Decisive is not the ontic order of God's acts in creation (as in Calvin), but the noetic order of human receptivity. Though Barth objected vehemently to the anthropocentrism of modern liberalism, yet his theology of creation betrays a method which is no less acutely anthropocentric, though in a uniquely Christomonistic way.

I. 15. The Eclipse of Creation

For nearly two thousand years the biblical doctrine of creation went nearly uncontested as a nonnegotiable article of the historic Christian faith. Only during the past couple of centuries has this unanimity been challenged. Even natural law theories testify obliquely at least to the reality of the creation order. In contemporary thought, however, both the historical reality and the revelational significance of the creation narratives are being called into question from various quarters. Let us take a brief look at five theological schools of thought which are contributing to a widespread eclipse of the doctrine of creation.

a) In many wings of *evangelical Christianity* a heavy emphasis on second-article theology tends to crowd out serious reflection on the first article. In its passionate concern to proclaim Jesus Christ as Savior, it sidelines a fundamental concern with the work of God the Father in creation. It gives the impression of bypassing creation in a hasty move to take a shortcut to the cross. Evangelicals do indeed make regular polemical excursions into the realm of creation to combat the evolutionist menace. Methodologically, however, creation is downplayed in mainline evangelical theologies. Special revelation eclipses general revelation. Coming to terms with the latter remains a matter of unfinished and largely untouched business on its theological agenda. This is a faulty and shortsighted approach. For the full biblical import of our sinful predicament, of the call to conversion and sanctification, and of our future hope comes to its own only against the backdrop of a solidly based commitment to the work of God in creation.

b) Dark shadows also fall over the doctrine of creation from the side of many twentieth-century *charismatic movements*. Like many evangelicals, pentecostal Christians discount the abiding validity of creational revelation. It is now so thoroughly obscured by the overwhelming impact of evil in the world, they argue, that there is no longer any possibility of reading aright God's handiwork in the world of his making. What is important is therefore not attachment to the "natural family" but membership in the "family of God." By turning aside from the first article of the Apostles' Creed (God the Father and creation), and drawing strength from the second article (God the Son and salvation), they seek to exploit as fully as possible the third article (the gifts of the Spirit). The goal of such hyperspiritualist odysseys is world flight. Such otherworldliness remains, of course, an unachievable prospect, since the creation order holds for all men, including charismatics. The very possibility of entertaining such illusions of escape from earthly realities is dependent on and therefore reflects indirectly the holding power of the creation order.

c) Another vigorous assault on the idea of a divinely ordained world order has been launched by modern *existentialism*. Overwhelmed by what they sense as the horrendous anomalies and ambiguities of world history, existentialists opt for a nihilist ethos. Life is unredeemable. Disorder is the order of the day. Capricious and chaotic powers, or its alternative, dull and deadening routine — this is our common fate. We are trapped in a theatre of the absurd, with no exit. Optimists in the existential camp may seek to screw up their courage and nurture the hope of a "brave new world." Realists among them, however, recognize no options but resignation and despair, or for the stouthearted, protest and rebellion. Life is a dead end. The world is a stubborn adversary. Meaninglessness is the only reliable norm.

d) A further challenge is posed by contemporary forms of *process theology*. They represent the dominant moving force in the intellectual world of our times. Propelling them onward is a monist view of reality in which all things, earthly and heavenly, are collapsed into a single spiraling historical movement heading toward an open-ended future. The origin of all things is not a created order, but an indefinable alpha-point of pure potentiality. A normative order for life in the world is not something given with creation from the beginning, but something continuously in the process of realization. Through the unfolding stages of evolutionary development the world is moving toward its goal, a goal which is strangely also its beginning. Insofar as that future is already now, life has meaning and direction. We must therefore live by hope, open to God's future, led by his Spirit. These theologies of hope fall, if anywhere, into the category of third-article thinking. They appeal to a kind of open-ended leading of the Spirit (or, among secularists, a "worldspirit") in which not only the idea of redemption but also the idea of creation is no longer discernible. What is left is a waffling existential hope which beckons us onward toward the horizons of an unknown future, when at last a normed order for life will be realized.

e) Finally, and perhaps most significantly, continuing reaction to theological developments in Hitler's Germany has also contributed heavily to an eclipse of the biblical doctrine of creation. Many "German Christians," imbued with the spirit of National Socialism, seized on the biblical idea of creation ordinances *(Schöpfungsordnungen)* and distorted it horrendously to undergird the pagan ideology of the ruling party. The Aryan race (the *Übermensch*), the German nation *(Volkstum)*, the destiny of this chosen land *(Blut und Boden)*, guided by divine decree *(Vorsehung)* — this visionary prospect of the Third Reich was viewed as foreordained to usher in the miracle of a new millennium. The outcome was the horror of the Holocaust. In reaction, Barth, Bonhoeffer, Niemöller, and others protested the very notion of a creation order. This reaction is understandable. And it has not yet run its full course. Many are still so permanently scarred by these hideous distortions that they find it impossible to view the idea of the creation order positively. As a reaction, however, these sentiments may not be granted normative status. For the demonic political ethic which cast its spell over the Germany of the 1930s must remain forever a gruesome caricature of the biblical doctrine of creation.

I. 16. The Creation Order:

I. 16. 1. Universal Normativity

By his Word God established a well-ordered creation. By that same Word he continually calls it to order. His Word is our life. For by it he put in place the permanently normative environment for our life together in his world. This network of structures and functions, governed by creational law, manifests his loving care for all creatures. Every creature, each in its own unique way, is subject to this constant yet dynamic ecosystem of creational laws. Compliance with it is not an odious burden. For it was not imposed by some alien force. The creation order is evidence of the caring hand of the Creator reaching out to secure the well-being of his creatures, of a Father extending a universe full of blessings to his children. Willing obedience to this life-enveloping, love-impelling, shalom-enhancing framework of law and order brings with it freedom, righteousness, and joy. It enables us to become all we are meant to be.

This good order for creation holds for all our life relationships. It defines our manifold callings. Christian thinkers seek to capture its meaning in the idea of the cultural mandate, given with creation, first inscripturated in Genesis 1:26-31, then further elaborated throughout Scripture. This cultural mandate lays its claim on us both as a benediction and a command *(datum* and *mandatum)*. It delineates in a typically biblical way the potentials for every human enterprise as well as the limitations on it. Therein lies the firm and abiding foundation for a myriad of practical vocations. Viewed in this light, every calling is a religious calling. In academics this holds for dogmatics and ethics, which few would contest; but it holds no less for philosophy and the other sciences. Every science is a revelationally normed discipline, anchored in deeply religious presuppositions, answerable to God's Word, and called to make its work serviceable to the good intentions of the Creator for his creatures.

No science, not even theology, can establish the meaning of things. That is given with creation. We live in a predefined world. The meaning of reality is funded by God's good order for creation. All scientific endeavor, including dogmatics, is therefore a discovery process. In acquiring knowledge, whether theoretical or practical, we are always and only responding creatures, set within the ordered surroundings of a stable (but not static) and unfolding (but not evolving) cosmos. Scientific inquiry is therefore a limited, humble, subservient, and tentative undertaking. It can only describe by empirical analysis the data and phenomena at hand. Its tools cannot penetrate to an original and fundamental explanation of the meaning of things. For this we are dependent on revelation, reflexively present in creation and noetically disclosed in Scripture. What are customarily called scientific laws (the law of gravitation, the laws of genetics, the law of diminishing returns, the rules of hermeneutics) are but fallible human attempts to account for the way we understand God's Word as it holds for the ordered life of his creatures. Insight into the depth dimensional meaning of reality calls for an understanding of the creation order. We are therefore guilty of a reductionist superficiality if in the name of the scientific method we seek to eliminate from consideration the revelational, and thus also the religious meaning of things which is embedded in the creation order. Creation does not merely *have* such meaning, which we are at liberty to reckon with or not. Nor does it await our attempts to lend it meaning. Creation *is* meaning. It is therefore meaningful, full of meaning. Christian scholarship is obliged accordingly to offer serviceable insight for meaningful living in God's world.

The creation order therefore holds for Christians and non-Christians alike — for non-Christians who live from it unconsciously and parasitically as well as for Christians who gladly acknowledge it. God thereby maintains his claim on all his creatures. For while this perspective is uniquely Christian, the reality to which it points is universal. God's Word is the dynamic holding power for all creatures. Christ is the Mediator of all creation. Christology is therefore more than soteriology. All men have to do with the Christ. For in him "all things hold together" (Colossians 1:15-20). Here we sense the universal claim of biblical religion. Creation belongs not only to the church, but to the whole world. The biblical doctrine of creation witnesses to the sovereignty of God over all. It is not a religious fantasy indulged in by some. It is an ordered reality that holds for all. Christian faith is bound inseparably to the world of God's making. The creation order provides the ontic anchor point for a distinctively biblical life-style. Yet the God who confronts unbelievers does not come to them as a strange and unknown God. For the givenness of God's relationship to the world means that, "knowing him not," they nevertheless "know him" (Romans 1:18-25). The norms which hold for the life of the world are immediately present to the consciousness of all men. Thus the creation order establishes a certain ontic commonality and solidarity among all peoples, even in the midst of the radical noetic polarities among differing faith communities. Based on creation, Christian affirmations are not wholly foreign to others. For the cultural mandate lays its claim on all as a divine imperative, whether recognized as such or not.

What God called to order in the beginning, what he ceaselessly sustains by the holding power of his Word, whose rebellious outbursts he continuously restrains by his preserving grace, what he is out to redeem by the healing power of that Word, is not a chaos but a cosmos — which throughout Scripture signifies a harmoniously multifaceted world order. This cosmic order is the very locus, context, and pattern for redemption. The renewing impact of the cross and resurrection enters into the very fabric of creation. The redirecting "order of redemption" is fully conformed to the structured "order of creation." For "God so loved the cosmos . . ." (John 3:16).

Our calling is to bring the order *of* our life in God's world, whether in the pulpit or in politics, in our halls of learning or in our marketplaces, into conformity with God's good order *for* our life in his world. Accordingly, we must recognize that the structures *of* creation find their touchstone beyond themselves in God's order *for* creation. Pursuing such conformity to the will of God calls for lifelong sanctification. We can face up to it only in prayer: Lord, teach us so to order our lives that our words may answer to your Word, our works to yours. Such prayer covers every part of life. We now turn to a further elaboration of that Word-and-work perspective.

I. 16. 2. Nuclear Tasks

God speaks, and speaking, creates. The God who speaks is also the God who acts. There is no disparity between his Word(s) and his work(s). His imperative ("Let there be . . .") issued in the indicative ("and it was so . . ."). The result was *shalom* — everything in its proper place, perfectly at home, and wholly at ease. From where we stand, we cannot, of course, transport ourselves back into that prelapsarian situation. That original state of rectitude lies beyond our reach. But the primordial Word for a well-ordered life in creation still holds. Scripture refocuses our sights so that we can begin anew to sense the constant and dynamic holding and healing power of God's Word as it calls us to an obedient response. By the light of Scripture, therefore, we are summoned to discern the abiding norms of the creation order.

Our world of experience is not describable as either sacred or secular, nor as partly the one and partly the other. It is rather wholly sacred in the sense that we pursue all our varied walks of life uninter-ruptedly "before the face of the Lord." It is at the same time wholly secular (from *saeculum,* meaning "this present age") in the sense that there is only one place to do so, namely, in this present world, this present age. Let us then eavesdrop on the Genesis narratives, listening in as along the way and between its lines we discern from this biblical rearticulation of our original nuclear tasks what our cultural callings are in the world today.

God's Word establishing order for the world may be likened to a prism. As a single shaft of light, passing through a prism, gets refracted into a rainbowlike spectrum of multicolored rays, so God's unitary Word (and its synonyms, law, will, decree, ordinance, command) gets refracted into a series of equally authoritative words covering the full range of our life activities. In this way God concretizes his claim on us in all the varied relationships and offices which shape our personal and communal lives. For just as there are on the response side many ways to walk the one Way, so on the revelational side these several mandates lay their claim on us in the form of very down-to-earth specifications of the single Mandate.

Let us listen to how these biblical pointers come to expression in the Genesis account. We hear a Word of God for marriage: God brings Adam and Eve together and instructs them to become what they are made to be, namely, bi-unitary parenting creatures. He then adds an imperative to his indicative creative act in saying, "Be fruitful and mul-tiply." With this is given the familial task of fostering the growth of children and nurturing them. There is also a Word of God for daily labor: "Till the soil." We also catch the intimation of a governing task: "Oversee the garden" — alluding perhaps to the presence of an evil power, lurking along the outskirts of Eden, seeking an occasion to intrude on man's peaceable habitat. In subtle tones Genesis also suggests what may be construed as a learning task: Adam is instructed to name the animals, each after its kind and in keeping with its nature. This sorting out process obviously falls short of scientific classification into genus and species. Yet some sort of elementary analysis and grouping procedure seems to

181

be going on there. Finally we hear God's Word for worship, the call to cultic fellowship, in what appears to have been Adam and Eve's practice of walking with God in the cool of the day.

This sketchy delineation of man's original nuclear tasks offers a concentrated preview of the greater vocational diversity which would in time emerge on the scene. Moreover, as with all Scripture, they are spelled out in very practical, naive, commonsense terms. We need not assume, furthermore, that Genesis intends to offer an exhaustive listing of all our cultural assignments. These are rather crosscut samples of a fuller range of callings which would eventually unfold as history moves along. But certain "kinds" of cultural activity are recorded as normatively structured "estates" of human existence within which mankind was to chart the course of future societal development.

Paradise was a sinless state. But it was not yet perfect in the sense that creation had already reached its full potential. Progress was possible and anticipated. For example, man as coworker was made to image God, the great Worker. Given with this core task was a potential for the later organization of labor unions and the very mixed blessings of a modern assembly line. If God's primordial act of calling forth something out of nothing may be called primary creation, and if the ordering process of the six days of Genesis may be called secondary creation, then at a different, responsive level man's fulfillment of these nuclear cultural mandates may be called a kind of tertiary creation *(creatio tertia)*.

All these blessings, expressed as commands, are couched in imagery and concepts familiar to the original recipients of this revelation, Israel, a nation made up largely of farmers and shepherds. Yet they speak no less normatively to us as scientifically conditioned twentieth-century people living in a highly secularized industrial society. That is the kind of book the Bible is. While the *forms* of our response to these creationally given, biblically illumined nuclear tasks may and must change to suit changing times, nevertheless in their core meaning, as *norms,* they are ever binding in their claim on us.

The central thrust of this truth is formulated by the fathers of the Reformation in Article XII of the Belgic Confession:

> We believe that the Father by the Word, that is, by His Son, has created out of nothing the heaven, the earth, and all creatures, when it seemed good unto Him, giving unto every creature its being, shape, form, and several offices to serve its creator; that He also still upholds and governs them by His eternal providence and infinite power for the service of mankind, to the end that man may serve his God.

182

I. 16. 3. Norm for Marriage

The continuing normativity of the creation order is reinforced by the comprehensive biblical witness on the question of marriage and divorce. The biblical pointers on this subject stand in judgment on modern individualist thought which regards marriage as a "social contract" in which two free and sovereign individuals negotiate a marital arrangement. On this contemporary view, marriage is treated as a secondary environment, artificially created by two consenting parties, not as an estate given with creation into which two people enter. Its status is dependent on the will of the partners. Another modern view sees marriage as an advanced stage in the cultural evolution of mankind. It is the product of many wide-ranging marital experiments coming up out of the past. Monogamous bisexual marriage, so the argument goes, is now becoming increasingly obsolete. Traditional patterns of lifelong commitment are being superseded by new, more promiscuous relationships. And this process is considered a normal stage in our cultural evolution.

Sharply contradicting these contemporary misrepresentations is the biblical affirmation of marriage as a relationship securely anchored from the beginning in the creation order. This is stressed emphatically in Jesus' dramatic encounter with the testy Pharisees of his day (Matthew 19:3-9). God's Word makes room for "a certificate of divorce," but only as a concession to our hardness of heart, as a second-best solution to unholy and untenable relationships which wreak havoc on marital and family living. In antinormative situations we may have to resort to antinormative measures in order to avoid even worse calamities. But don't declare the abnormal normal. Jesus then returns to his ultimate appeal: "From the beginning it was not so." Originally and abidingly marriage is meant to be an exclusive bi-unitary covenant between husband and wife. This is the Will of God. Marriage is for good and for keeps. This is the norm, rooted in the creation order.

I. 16. 4. Foundations for State Life

Take another concrete case — the state. The question of a basic rationale for political life continues to divide Christians. Where are we to locate the origin, basis, and norm for civil government? Across the centuries the Christian community has been haunted by three fundamentally divergent viewpoints. These three positions are oriented to the unfolding drama of biblical revelation. Each makes its fundamental appeal to one of the central themes in the biblical story line of creation, fall, and redemption. Is state life rooted in creation? Or in the fall? Or in redemption? Let us look briefly at these three positions in reverse order.

One view, which has come to the fore very prominently in modern times, lays the foundation for state life in redemption. Political activity is rooted in the cross and the resurrection. The redeeming grace of God for the world is manifest in Jesus Christ. It is embodied primarily in the church. But the righteousness, peace, and goodness of God, of which the church is a primary witness, model, and agent, must also find its analogy in the state. Christocracy is the form of God's rule in the world. The Light of the world in Jesus Christ, which shines fully in the church, must therefore also be reflected in the state. As the moon is to the sun, so the state is to the church. On this view state life is made dependent on the life of the church, with no divinely ordained legitimacy of its own. "Nature" loses out to "grace." Lurking within the shadows of this political theory is a theological school of thought which collapses redemption back into creation. The light side and the shadow side of creation, namely worship and politics, are juxtaposed as dialectical counterparts woven into the very fabric of the world order. Service in the state is relegated to a secondary and reflexive position. How different is the view of Calvin that "civil authority is a calling, not only holy and lawful before God, but also the most sacred and by far the most honorable of all callings in the whole life of mortal man" (*Institutes,* IV,20,4).

A second position, long present in the Western Christian tradition, and currently dominant in many evangelical circles, traces the origins of state life back to the fall. On this view civil government was introduced in the aftermath of original sin as a divine agency for counteracting the effects of man's inhumanity to man. As the church is the fruit of God's special saving grace, so the state's calling to settle disputes, to regulate commerce, to enforce justice, to punish criminals, and to defend the nation is an operation of God's common grace. The church lives by love, the state by power. To the church is entrusted the "sword of the Spirit," to the state the sword of temporal authority. Government is the providential means for restraining evil in society. On this view, therefore, from its very inception state life lies under the dark cloud of sinfulness. It lacks positive grounding. Given this pervasively negative view, Christians are well advised as much as possible to avoid involvement in political affairs.

The third view reflects the basic line of reasoning being pursued throughout this work. It holds that the origin, basis, and norm for state life are anchored in the creation order. The governing task, presently exercised by the state, is a divinely ordained aspect of man's original cultural mandate. This view sets political service on a positive footing. It enjoys a creationally legitimate status comparable to that of social work, business, education, artistry, even church ministry. This view accents the reality and abiding relevance of an orderly, developed creation. The fall into sin is indeed very real. But it does not result in the destruction of any originally given creational structures. Nor does redemption add to them. Our political task is therefore as old as the hills and as native to humankind as confessing our faith and caring for our bodies. We must, of course, distinguish between the state as it was meant to be and the state as we too often experience it today. But this is true of all other institutions in society as well, including family and church. For sin's disruptive forces are everywhere active. But God's preserving and redeeming grace is also a present reality. So the basic question we face is this: How well do the structures and functions *of* our governments answer obediently to the divinely normed structures and functions *for* government? Honest reflection yields a very mixed result. The antithesis cuts across all societal institutions, state life included. This truth echoes and reechoes across the pages of both biblical Testaments. Take, for instance, two classic New Testament passages — Romans 13 and Revelation 13. The former (state as "a minister of God") presents a normative picture of government, the state at its best, the state as it is meant to be. The latter (government as "the Babylonian whore") pictures an antinormative state, the state at its worse, the state enslaved to demonic powers, the state as it often confronts us in the morning headlines. In itself the state is right and good, even though, like all creation, it can go bad and wrong. And it has. But, again like all creation, state life is redeemable. Civil injustice is neither the first word nor the last word. God's first word for the world is political shalom, and his last word is a "new earth" in which uncontested righteousness dwells.

I. 16. 5. Framework for Community

The God-createdness of our ordered life together in the world sets the stage for true community. After sin, the holding and healing power of God's Word keeps societal life intact for the redemptive possibility of a "new beginning," both as a present reality and as an eschatological hope. But through it all the divinely preserved creation order remains the abiding context for communally shared shalom. Perhaps we can think of the Genesis scenario as the original construction site. God is there busy building a house. Step by step the project moves toward its completion. First the footings appear, then the foundations, floor boards, studs, rafters, windows, doors, siding, bricking, and roof. The Architect and Builder then becomes the Interior Decorator, moving in the furniture and other furnishings, until at last all is in a state of readiness, including the carpeting, curtains, paintings on the wall, even a piano, and as an added touch the household plants and pets, each "after its kind." Only then does the Creator, now turned Landlord, take his tenants, Adam and Eve, his family, the human community, and usher them across the threshold, leasing to them his estate to serve as housekeepers and caretakers. Thus, imaginatively, God set his house in order and made it our home.

The earthly home God established has its various rooms. Think of it this way: in it are the many rooms which correspond to our various cultural tasks, all conveniently located and easily accessible, arranged with an eye to smoothly flowing traffic patterns. Each room is attractively designed and well equipped for carrying out our diverse callings in life. There is a dining room for enjoying the fruit of the Garden, a living room for social entertainment, a family room for little coffee-break sabbaths and leisurely companionship, a kitchen and workshop for carrying out our daily chores, a tool shed equipped for tilling the soil, an inner closet for meditation and prayer, and the bedroom for restful sleep at the close of a delightfully busy day. Too idyllic? Perhaps, but conceding the imagery, that is roughly the way it was and the way it is meant to be. If only it could be so again! Come, Lord Jesus, come quickly — as You promised.

This picturesque reconstruction of the creation order is prompted largely by Calvin's commentary on 1 Peter 2:13-17, centering on the pastoral injunction, "Be subject for the Lord's sake to every human ordinance." This is the way Calvin puts it:

> The verb *ktizein* in Greek, from which *ktisis* comes, means to form or construct a building. It corresponds to the word "ordinance," by which Peter reminds us that God the Maker of the world has not left the human race in a state of confusion, so that we live after the manner of beasts, but has given them, as it were, a building regularly formed and divided into several compartments. It is called a human ordinance, not because it has been invented by man, but because it is a mode of living well-arranged and clearly ordered, appropriate to man.

The Genesis account discloses both the coherent unity and the rich diversity of the creation order. This pattern of diversified unity and unified diversity colors the entire story. As an unfolding drama it opens with the undifferentiated mass of Genesis 1:2 and then moves along through successive steps in the six-day process of increasing differentiation. There is a wholeness written into this account, but there are also clearly delineated boundaries. Genesis distinguishes between heaven and earth, plants and animals, male and female, tilling the soil and mothering. As Abraham Kuyper reminds us in his booklet "De Verflauwing der Grenzen," we must be careful not to blur the boundary lines which God has established in the creation. Just as the oneness of God's Word is revealed in a spectrum of divine Words, so on the response side the life of the human community is also called to display unity in diversity and diversity in unity. Neither uniformity nor fragmentation is normative. Absolutizing unity leads to a form of monism. Absolutizing diversity leads to internal tensions and polarization. A biblically balanced emphasis on unity and diversity in their proper interrelatedness is reflected in Calvin's commentary on Exodus 18:13-27, where he says:

> For as one ray of sun does not illumine the whole world, but all combine their operations as it were in one; so God, so that he may retain men by a sacred and indissoluble bond in mutual society and goodwill, unites one to another by variously dispensing his gifts, and not raising any one up out of measure by its entire perfection.

The well-ordered contours of the creation order establish the normative framework for human community. In Ephesians 5:21–6:9 Paul addresses various life relationships within the early Christian church — the network of relationships between husbands and wives, parents and children, masters and servants. Commenting on this passage, Calvin again highlights the variegated mutuality which is to characterize obedient living.

> Paul comes now to the various groups; for besides the universal bond of subjection, some are more closely bound to each other, according to their respective callings. Society consists of groups, which are like yokes, in which there is a mutual obligation of different parties.

It is these basic creational patterns, illumined by the Scriptures, which undergird that pluralist view of society which has come to be associated with the two-sided principle of sphere sovereignty and sphere universality. The former seeks to honor the identity and integrity of our various life relationships as they take shape within the several sectors of society. The latter seeks to capture the norm of integrated wholeness in life — the coexisting and proexisting partnerships which give the various life zones a unifying direction, making community possible. Drawing heavily as always on imagery, Kuyper appeals to the analogy of clockwork to clarify the picture. Each cogwheel in the timepiece performs its own unique function. Yet taken together these intermeshing cogwheels cooperate to produce a synchronized movement. Kuyper puts it this way:

> Human life, with its material foreground, which is visible, and its spiritual background, which is invisible, appears to be neither simple nor uniform,

but represents an infinitely composite organism. It is so constituted that the individual can exist only within the group and can come to full expression only in community. Call the parts of this great instrument cogwheels, each driven around its own axle by its own power; or call them spheres, each filled with its own exciting life-spirit — the concept or imagery does not matter — as long as you acknowledge that there are all kinds of spheres in life, as many as the starry hosts in the firmament, whose boundaries are drawn with firm lines, each having its own principle as a focal point. Just as we usually speak of "the world of morality," "the world of science," "the world of commerce," "the world of art," so we may speak more precisely of "the sphere of morality," "the sphere of home life," "the sphere of societal life," each with its own domain. And because each has its own domain, within the boundaries of that domain each has its own sovereignty. (*Sphere-Sovereignty*, pp. 13-14)

In his own inimitable way Bavinck, the seasoned and irenic dogmatician of the neo-Calvinist movement, paints the following kaleidoscopic picture of the creation order:

Everything was created with its own nature and is based on ordinances appointed by God for it. Sun and moon and stars have their own peculiar tasks; plants and animals and man have their own distinct natures. There is a rich diversity. But in this diversity there is also a supreme unity. The ground of both lies in God. It is he who created all things according to his incomparable wisdom, who continually sustains them in their distinct natures, who guides and governs them according to the potentials and laws created in them, and as the highest good and goal is desired and emulated by all things in keeping with their measure and manners. Here is a unity which does not destroy but maintains diversity, and a diversity which does not depreciate unity but unfolds it in its richness. By virtue of this unity the world can metaphorically be called an organism in which all the parts are related to the other parts and mutually influence each other. Heaven and earth, man and animals, soul and body, doctrine and life, art and science, religion and morality, state and church, family and society, etc. — they are distinct but not divided. There are all kinds of connections among them; an organic, or, if you will, a moral bond holds them together. (*Gereformeerde Dogmatiek*, Vol. II, pp. 399-400)

Bavinck lends added emphasis to the normed and lawful nature of the creation order in its significance for communal living in these words:

The Christian worldview opposes autonomy and anarchy with all its power. It holds that man is not autonomous, but is always and everywhere bound by laws not invented by man, but set forth by God as the rule for life. In religion and morality, in the family, society, and the state, everywhere there are ideas, norms which stand above man. They form a unity among themselves and find their origin and continuation in the Creator and Lawgiver of the universe. These norms are the most precious treasures entrusted to mankind, the basis for all societal institutions. (*Christelijke Wereldbeschouwing*, p. 90)

This development of a Christian worldview, based on the biblical doctrine of the creation order, did not stop with Kuyper and Bavinck. The theological insights of Kuyper and Bavinck, drawing on the Calvinian tradition, cleared the way for the philosophical work of Vollenhoven and Dooyeweerd. Like Reformed theology, this Christian philosophy grows out of disciplined reflection on the creation order understood in the light of Scripture. Accordingly, it also stresses concomitantly the "temporal diversity" and "coherence of meaning" which is given with creation. This interrelated emphasis on sphere sovereignty and sphere universality is clearly expressed in the following passage from Dooyeweerd:

The totality of meaning of our whole temporal cosmos is to be found in Christ, with respect to his human nature, as the root of the reborn human race. In Him the heart, out of which are the issues of life, confesses the sovereignty of God, the Creator, over everything created. . . . Our temporal world, in its temporal diversity and coherence of meaning, is in the order of God's creation bound to the religious root of mankind. Apart from this religious root it has no meaning and so no reality. . . . To the transcendental question: What is the mutual relation between the modal aspects of reality? [our philosophy] answers: sphere-sovereignty, that is to say: mutual irreducibility, yet in the all-sided cosmic coherence of the different aspects of meaning, as this is regulated in God's temporal order of the world, in a cosmic order of time. (*A New Critique of Theoretical Thought*, I,1,9, pp. 99-101)

Many nineteenth- and twentieth-century Christian thinkers came under the spell of modern historicism. These influences led them to interpret this reemergent pluralist view of community as the product of historical-cultural developments. Among them was Groen van Prinsterer. The very ideas worked out more fully by later neo-Calvinist thinkers were pioneered by him. He grounded them, however, in the momentous realignments taking place in society during the early centuries of the modern era. Kuyper, Bavinck, Dooyeweerd, and others, while building on Groen's groundwork, deepened his insights into "sphere independence" (Groen's term) by basing their view of community on an appeal to the creation order. Their insights have rubbed off on many contemporary thinkers within Reformed circles.

Among them is Hendrikus Berkhof. In his section on "The World as Createdness" he sets forth the following points.

1. The createdness of this world implies that it and everything in it is structurally good and important. Nothing is evil, nothing is mere appearance, nothing is inferior. . . .

2. Createdness not only means that everything is good, but also and for that reason that nothing is absolute. Nothing is less than a creature of God, but no more either.

3. The createdness of the world implies the fundamental unity of the world. More basic than the diversity of nations, races, and cultures is their unity. . . . The cultural consequences of this insight are far-reaching and clear, certainly in an age in which a strong desire for global unity is intersected by the formation of power blocs and by the contrasts between races and between rich and poor countries. But this faith also means taking a strong stand against the dualism in Western thinking since Descartes and Kant. . . .

4. Createdness implies parts, plurality, and variety. And that variety is real. If the world had its ground in itself, the variations, being only surface phenomena, could be reduced to that ground. But creation means that all phenomena are irreducible, because the world has its ground outside itself in its Creator. Everything forms a unity, but within it everything also has its own place and character: spirit is not "really" matter, a plant is not an animal, and an animal is not a plant. The variety is just as real as the unity, and the unity exists precisely as the composite of the diverse parts. . . . The belief in creation can stand the tension between unity and diversity. Now the one element, now the other requires emphasis against derailments in human ideas and practices. In our time each is alternately needed, . . . [since] a widespread misunderstanding with respect to the popularized idea of evolution often leads to the worldview which has been called "nothing but": man is actually "nothing but" a higher animal, thinking "nothing but" a movement of brain cells. . . .

5. Createdness by the God of holy love, who is faithful amid his changeableness, means that the world is dependable. It is not a haunted house or a bizarre fairy tale. We can depend on it. We can orient ourselves in it, feel secure in it, and make plans for its and our future. Its habitability depends on its knowability, and this knowability is that of a universe governed by law.

6. Createdness by the God of holy love, who is changeable in his faithfulness and who works toward his goal along ever new ways, means that our dependable world is at the same time open to surprises and changes. It is not a haunted house, but not a bunker either . . . [it leaves] room for miracle. . . . Biblical miracles can only be recognized by faith.

That does not, however, make them subjective, for what faith recognizes is a reality which precedes faith.

7. Createdness by the God of revelation also decides the purpose of existence. . . . It tells us that the world was purposefully made. It is not a chance result of a blind process of accidental evolutionary happenings. That belief is a return to the passive resignation of the nature religions which regard the chaos as the final secret of the cosmos. . . . Putting all these successive points of view on one denominator, we can say that the purpose of the world is the Kingdom of God, as the full realization of human existence through fellowship with God. (*Christian Faith*, pp. 160-65)

I. 17. Sabbath

The bottom line of the apostolic faith is "life everlasting" in the renewed creation. Its top line is creation: "God the Father, Almighty, Maker of heaven and earth." Creation and re-creation — these two momentous events are like bookends which hold the whole story together. If we lose our firm grip on this Alpha-to-Omega confession, everything in between collapses like a house of cards. For at countless crucial junctures along the way of salvation the Redeemer God confronts us as the Creator. Hear the words of the prophet:

Have you not known? Have you not heard?
The LORD is the everlasting God,
the Creator of the ends of the earth.

Thus says the LORD, your Redeemer,
who formed you from the womb:
I am the LORD, who made all things,
who stretched out the heavens alone,
who spread out the earth —
Who was with me? (Isaiah 40:28; 44:24)

Creation remains the unmovable foundation undergirding all ongoing revelation, together with the entire faith-life, confession, and theology of the church. It lends concrete significance and meaning to every other affirmation about God, the world, mankind, and history. Literally everything is totally dependent on the creative work of God. Without it the gospel of reconciliation evaporates into ethereal platitudes. For creation makes redemption viable, inexplicably important, and sets the

191

framework for its realization. The work of redemption is geared to the order of creation.

The biblical idea of creation is therefore not limited to that once-for-all series of creating acts of God in the beginning. It has a present relevance as well as a past reality. It reaches out to cover and embrace God's ongoing covenantal relationship to the cosmos of his making. The point of transition from the original creating work of God to his unending creational care is located in the seventh day in the Genesis narratives. The Creator designates this climactic day as the sabbath. We read that

> . . . on the seventh day God finished his work which he had done, and he rested on the seventh day from all his work which he had done. So God blessed the seventh day and hallowed it, because on it God rested from all his work which he had done in creation. (Genesis 2:2-3)

Six working days were rounded out with a sabbath rest. Not that God just quit from sheer exhaustion. His creative mission was accomplished. It stood forth as a finished product, a glorious cosmonomic theatre. The world was all it was meant to be. Then a day dawned for sabbath keeping. Having bent low for days putting the finishing touches on his masterpiece, God now leans back, as it were, to survey his handiwork and to revel in it with a deep sense of divine satisfaction. This initial sabbath marks the first in another ongoing series of new beginnings on God's part. Not that, now unemployed, God retires as an absentee landlord to his celestial retreat to let his creatures fend for themselves. Nor that, in deist fashion, the great Clockmaker, having assembled, tuned, and set in motion his timepiece, now allows it to run its course on its own inner momentum. Sabbath does not mean idleness. It ushers in a new phase in divine activity. God never withdraws from his world. Nor does he relax his superintending care. Not only in its origins but also in its continuity the cosmos is wholly dependent on the holding power of God's Word. In the later setting of an alleged sabbath violation Jesus declared, "My Father is working still, and I am working" (John 5:17).

The original sabbath stands as a creation ordinance with an abiding significance. By divine example it establishes a healthy rhythm of work and rest for the life of God's people in his world (Exodus 20:8-11). Workaholics, beware! For by design God leaves ample space for relaxation, reflection, and leisure. But work is also there as a blessing. In this respect, too, the great Worker leads the way. His sabbath forms a bridge from the original six days of creating history to that creational history which still governs the march of time. Thus the sabbath closes the door on *creatio prima* (creation out of nothing) and *creatio secunda* (the six-day formation of God's finished handiwork). In so doing it opens wide the door to *creatio tertia* (a tertiary form of creative activity: our mandate to serve as God's coworkers in the cultural development of creation's potentials).

The biblical idea of sabbath as a creation ordinance sounds hopelessly antiquated to many modern ears. It was not so with Christian thinkers of former generations. They were often guilty of an opposite error, overtaxing the call to keep the sabbath. Elaborate legalistic sabbatarian theologies were developed which imposed a concentration-camp style of life on the Christian community. Our times are slipping into an opposite, libertarian reaction. It is likely, however, that something more than sabbath keeping is at stake. The very reality of a creation order, in which the sabbath is rooted, is being called into question. Such wholesale reinterpretations of the Genesis record lead to a disavowal of the covenantal character of God's original relationship to the creation as well as the presence of the kingdom in world history from the beginning. What is left, then, is an indefinable relationship between God and the cosmos. Such impoverishment, if conceded, will of necessity exact its heavy toll on the preaching and teaching ministries of the church, on the faith-life of the Christian community, to say nothing of Reformed dogmatics.

By embracing the sabbath as one aspect of the creation order in its abiding normativity, it is possible to develop the rough contours of a "theology of the sabbath." Scripture calls the sabbath a "hallowed" day. This suggests the idea of holiness, that is, worship which opens the door to dedicating and sanctifying all of life to its God-intended purpose. Genesis clearly draws a picture of all God's creating acts as teleologically directed. That *telos* (end, goal, objective) is reached in the sabbath — the "hallowing" of our life together in God's world for its "chief end," namely, "to glorify God and enjoy him forever" (Westminster Confession). Sabbath is accordingly more than a single passing day located near the dawn of history. It is also, and more lastingly, the sign and seal and symbol of a sabbatical life-style. It lifts the curtain on that divinely ordained way of life to which all men are called, namely, "holy worldliness."

To the question, "Why did God create the world and man?", one way of arriving at a biblical answer is to say, "For sabbath keeping," that is, for celebrating our involvement in the work of the world with a sabbatical spirit. Such a "theology of sabbath" has little to do with the heavy sanctions of puritanical sabbatarianism, all concentrated into Sunday. It has as much to do with a way of life as with a day of the week. Such a sabbatical perspective is echoed in the words of the Heidelberg Catechism, Lord's Day 38. What does the fourth commandment require? This, ". . . that all the days of my life I rest from my evil works, let the Lord work in me by His Holy Spirit, and thus begin in this life the eternal Sabbath." We see thus that the sabbath, anchored in creation, also opens up an eschatological vision (Isaiah 65:13-14; Hebrews 4:8-10). Keeping sabbath means joining our Creator God in restful and delightful participation in the wonders of his world. It means the enjoyment of holiness — holiness understood as a life of covenantal fellowship and obedience directed to the glory of God. Even the pots and pans in the kitchen and the bells on our beasts of burden are to be inscribed with the confession, "Holy to the Lord."

As Herbert Richardson puts it, "God's establishment of the Sabbath reveals his ultimate purpose for his creation: namely, the sanctification of all things." In keeping with the biblical story line, the sabbath command as recorded in Exodus 20, which roots it in creation, takes revelational priority over its parallel statement in Deuteronomy 5, which bases it on Israel's redemption from Egypt. For, as Richardson goes on to say,

> According to the canon of Scripture, the creation interpretation is affirmed to be theologically prior to the redemption interpretation! This means, therefore, that the Sabbath commandment is always binding upon all men — whether they obey it or not! In the redemption of Israel from Egypt, the Sabbath is not established for the first time, but is re-established; the moral law is not first published at Sinai, but is republished there. Hence . . . the law of the Sabbath is grounded in the order of creation itself and pertains to all creatures. . . . (*Toward an American Theology*, pp. 112-15)

In the Genesis narratives, therefore, man is assigned a penultimate status. Ultimacy belongs to the God who declares a sabbath. The creation story ends with divine rest, as a paradigm for ours. The last as well as the first word in creation belongs to the sabbath-keeping God, who, anticipating the unfolding history of his handiwork, glories and delights in it — and calls us to do the same.

Chapter II

Anthropology

II. 1. Vantage Point

We turn now to the opening act in human history. At this point, too, we chart our course by the biblical story line of creation, fall, and redemption, on the way to the consummation. Originally we occupied that high ground known as "the state of integrity." This theological starting point stands as a hallmark of the historic Christian faith. It is truly catholic in the fullest sense of the word. Its catholicity is honored in the Reformation creeds, among them the Belgic Confession, Article XIV, which states it in these words: "We believe that God created man out of the dust of the earth, and made and formed him after His own image and likeness, good, righteous, and holy, capable in all things to will agreeably to the will of God."

So, too, with the Heidelberg Catechism, which, after acknowledging that we are now "prone by nature to hate God and [our] neighbor," goes on in Lord's Day III to ask the question: "Did God, then, create man so wicked and perverse?" Its answer is unambiguous: "By no means; but God created man good, and after His own image; that is, in true righteousness and holiness, that he might rightly know God his Creator, heartily love Him, and live with Him in eternal blessedness to praise and glorify Him."

To be biblically and confessionally faithful, then, a Reformed view of man must begin where the Bible begins. Mankind was endowed with an originally upright existence prior to and apart from our fall into sin and God's redeeming grace. It is important to take a good, long, hard look at ourselves as creatures if we are to appreciate our status as sinners and saints. For our creatureliness is an abiding reality. We never were, nor can we ever become, anything but what we are — crown creatures of God's making. We are "essentially" creatures. Fallenness and renewal

195

are "accidental" features of our being. They represent the misdirection and redirection of our creaturely status. To be duly impressed by this truth we must start where the Bible starts: "In the beginning . . . God said, 'Let us make man in our image, after our likeness'" (Genesis 1:1, 26).

This deeply held religious conviction, the virtually unanimous view of all Christendom over the past two millennia, is now being shattered. Under the impact of existentialist, monist, and process systems of thought, a fundamental revision is under way in the mainstream theologies of our day. Otto Weber, drawing on the Barthian tradition, states the case in the following dialectical fashion:

> There is no theological anthropology which could begin with any other thesis than this, that man is a creature. . . . [Yet] a temporal succession of these two states [of integrity and fallenness] is closed. For God is also the Creator of fallen man. (*Foundations of Dogmatics,* Vol. I, pp. 550, 553)

A "new hermeneutic" has emerged which no longer reads the biblical story line in sequential order. Sinfulness is viewed instead as a dialectical factor given with man's first breath. A kind of abnormal normalcy clings to our world of experience from the very beginning. We are involved in a ceaseless, tension-laden struggle to achieve the good purposes of the creation by overcoming the powerful stranglehold of sin on it. Righteousness is a creational potentiality. It is not a given but a goal. It applies to the last Adam but not to the first. It is not the starting point of history but its ending point. Godliness is man's destiny, an eschatological hope, realizable only in Christ. These current trends in mainline contemporary theologies are reflected in the following intensely dialectical excerpt from Hendrikus Berkhof:

> In the study of the faith, man as creature and man as sinner are usually dealt with in two separate chapters. That hangs together with the manner in which for centuries Genesis 2 and 3 were separated from each other. Genesis 2 was read as containing information about a shorter or longer period of human perfection and bliss in Paradise; the fall into sin in Genesis 3 rudely disturbed this idyllic situation, resulting in a radical change in man and his environment. Yet neither the purport of the Yahwist's narratives of the origin of man and the world, nor our knowledge of man's primeval history gives us grounds to assume two such successive phases in the history of mankind. Concretely we know no other man than the one who is a sinner. Therefore [our study of man as creature] does not refer to a past condition of mankind, but it describes the structure which God as creator has given to man. . . . The *humanum* as potentiality demands

196

actualization. And we know no other man than the one who mysteriously goes against the purpose of his existence. . . . Thereby we say that sin was not just a regrettable wrong step of our remotest parents, but is deeply rooted in the creaturely structure of the risky being called man. . . . [Yet] creation and sin do not coincide. Between them lies the leap of (misused) freedom. Sin is no incident — therefore it is discussed in the same chapter as man. Sin is not a creative given — therefore it is discussed separately after man. . . . The writer [of Genesis] wants to say two things: sin is as old as humanity, and yet it is not inherently part of the creation. . . . (*Christian Faith*, pp. 188-89)

Hendrikus Berkhof offers us here a dialectically mixed model of man. Our present reality, *simul justus et peccator,* is projected back on the original creation order. Thus not only noetically, but also ontically, anthropology is based on Christology, resulting in a reversal of Calvin's "right order of teaching," namely that ontically creational integrity takes priority over the realities of sin and grace. "Sin is not our nature, but its derangement" (*Institutes,* II,1,10). Accordingly, Calvin speaks of the " 'natural' corruption of the 'nature' created by God" (*Institutes,* I,1,11). It is therefore wrong to say, "To err is human." Error is not intrinsic to humanity, but belongs to sinful humanity. Human life was not always flawed, and someday it will be flawless again. Precisely because we are not originally and inherently corrupt, we are redeemable.

Berkouwer is nonetheless right in holding that we may not deal with pre-fallen mankind in a remote and abstract way. Our original state of integrity is not merely "a remembrance of something which was once existent but has now been lost," a reality which "now lives only in memory." Our primordial createdness still defines who we are. Sin can and did and still does distort our humanness, but it cannot destroy it. Implied in this viewpoint is the recognition of a rightful distinction between who we are structurally and directionally by virtue of creation, and who we now are as misdirected sinners. Berkouwer is therefore right in raising "the question of the relation between *homo creatus* and *homo peccator,* man before and after the fall." Can the idea of image of God still be applied to mankind even after the fall, he asks, or can it be "meaningfully employed only in relation to man as originally created, and to man after the restoration of the original image through grace?" (*Man: the Image of God,* p. 37). These questions clearly imply a distinction between a prelapsarian and postlapsarian view of man. Once again the creation, fall, and redemption motifs loom large as normative considerations in shaping a biblically Reformed doctrine of man.

II. 2. Anthropocentrism or Theocentrism?

How shall we develop our dogmatics: from a man-centered or a God-centered point of view? This age-old God/man problem drives us back to the question: How are the knowledge of God and self-knowledge related? Are they contradictory? Or complementary? Are God and man related as competitors or cooperators? Reviewing briefly the history of this tension-laden issue, we can identify at least three stages in its development. Until the eighteenth century an overwhelming consensus prevailed. The reality of a knowledge of God evoked a nearly unproblematic affirmation. Whatever uncertainties haunted earlier Christian thinkers, they were directed not toward God, but toward man. Modernity, however, brought about a radical reversal. It spoke confidently of the nearly unlimited potentials of modern science to expand man's knowledge of himself and his world. As it stood armed with this utopian mirage and exuding almost unbounded cultural optimism concerning human destiny, the long-standing felt need for a divine presence in life evaporated steadily in the face of a rapidly growing secular-humanist worldview. Man: most assuredly yes! God: maybe! hardly! perhaps even no! But once God is declared "dead," the "dust of death" (Os Guinness) soon settles over mankind. This leads, then, to the current predicament: Question marks are inserted not only behind the reality and knowability of God, but also of man. This identity crisis is a very modern problem. The anthropocentric concerns of the post-Enlightenment era, instead of creating clarity, have only added to man's confusion concerning himself. Is man the answer to the world's problems? Or is he himself the problem? Is life a meaningful pilgrimage or a theatre of the absurd? The agnosticism and pessimism of this century stand in sharp contrast to the assurance and optimism of the recent past. Neither, of course, offers a normative image of man. For both assume that man is able to define himself.

How, then, shall we approach the matter of self-knowledge, our identity and integrity as human beings, personally as well as communally and cosmically? And how shall we do this in a way which respects the methodology of a biblically Reformed dogmatics? Shall we adopt a theology "from below" or a theology "from above"? Or is this perhaps a misleading statement of the problem?

Calvin shatters this false dilemma in the opening lines of *The Institutes,* where he says that "nearly all the wisdom we possess, that is to say, true and sound wisdom, consists of two parts: the knowledge of God and of ourselves" (I,1,1). The footnote to that passage adds the following comment:

This statement, thrice revised, stands at the beginning of every edition of the *Institutes*. The French version of 1560 expresses even more strongly the association of the two aspects of sound knowledge: "In knowing God, each of us also knows himself." These decisive words set the limits of Calvin's theology and condition every subsequent statement. (John T. McNeill, ed., *Institutes*, I,1,1, footnote 1, p. 36)

Calvin refuses to get locked into the fruitless dilemma of anthropocentric versus theocentric theology. He vigorously attacks scholastic thinkers who begin their theologies by asking, Who is God "in himself"? He would doubtless have been equally critical of later humanists who pose the question in upside-down fashion, Who is man "in himself"? Calvin thereby rejects both a self-contained knowledge of God and a self-contained knowledge of ourselves. Directed toward self-knowledge, such vain efforts lead to "pride" instead of "humility." Directed toward God-knowledge, such speculation, in the words of Pascal, leads to "the God of the philosophers," but not to "the God of Abraham, Isaac, and Jacob."

Calvin views these two aspects of true knowledge as inextricably intertwined. The idea of "knowledge" is roughly equivalent to that of "revelation." As the editor of *The Institutes* puts it, "The word 'knowledge' in the title, chosen rather than 'being' or 'essence,' emphasizes the centrality of revelation in both the structure and the content of Calvin's theology" (p. 35). Accordingly, the link which binds together our knowledge of God and of ourselves in an inseparably interrelated, covenantally compacted, unbroken series of religious encounters between the revealing God and a responding mankind is the mediating Word of God in creation as well as in the Scriptures (*Institutes*, I,1-10, especially 6). This twofold knowledge is like the two sides of a single coin. It is always relational: God coming out to us *(ad extra)* in his Word to meet us where we are, and we being drawn irresistibly into a living confrontation with him.

This twofold knowledge may be likened to a two-way street. Traffic flows in both directions, but with a difference. Viewed from the Godward side, the flow of traffic is describable by the concept "comparison." Only by comparing ourselves with God can we come to truly know who we are. In the words of Calvin, "It is certain that man never achieves a clear knowledge of himself unless he has first looked upon God's face, and then descends from contemplating him to scrutinize himself" (*Institutes*, I,1,2). Viewed from our side, this movement is describable as "stimulus." True self-knowledge stimulates us to a knowledge of God. Again, as Calvin puts it, "The knowledge of ourselves not only arouses us to seek God, but also, as it were, leads us by the hand to find him" (*Institutes*, I,1,1). Thus, every theological affirmation has an anthropological correlate, and every anthropological affirmation has a theological correlate. This correlation is actually not a *co*-relation, however, since it is always qualified by the ineradicable Creator-creature distinction. Yet God bridges his "otherness" revelationally by the mediating, impinging, faith-eliciting power of his Word. Every theology, therefore, carries with it an anthropology, either explicitly or implicitly.

On the God/man problem, therefore, Calvin defies attempts to impale him on the horns of an either/or dilemma. Reformational theology follows in his footsteps. It, too, resists the false dilemma, theocentrism or anthropocentrism, as though it were a mutually exclusive choice. Within the structures of creation as illumined by the Scriptures, true self-knowledge is never autonomous (self-normed) but always heterono-mous (normed by another), and thus in fact theonomous (divinely normed). True knowledge of God, based on Calvin's idea of the *duplex cognitio Dei* (the "twofold knowledge of God" — as Creator as well as Redeemer), is accordingly always *pro nobis* ("for us"). The question, therefore, is not, "Who is God in himself, in his inner being *(ad intra)*?", but rather, "Who is God for us *(ad extra)*?" Revelation is always refer-ential. It always addresses us as responding creatures. This simultaneity in the revelation/response relationship between God and man is neverthe-less nondialectical. It is better described as dialogical, that is, a running dialogue between God the Revealer and man the responder which is simultaneously theocentric and anthropocentric in a way which respects the deeply religious otherness of the two partners in this covenantal relationship. The modern God/man dilemma is a misleading way of stating the case. Accepting it ends either in a Godless view of man or a nonhuman view of God. Our God-relatedness is, moreover, not a super-naturally added layer of grace superimposed on natural reality. It is intrinsic to our very way of being human, whether we are consciously aware of it or not.

This idea of full relationality creates the possibility of a Christo-centric worldview with this concomitant, concurrent emphasis on God and man as held together in covenant partnership. For Christ is the Word by which this *relatio* between these two *relata* (God and man) was first established and later restored. Both creationally and redemptively he is the one Mediator between the Creator and his creatures.

These perspectives, traceable to Calvin and more fully developed in the Calvinist tradition, represent a marked advance over the thought of Calvin's favorite ancient theologian, Augustine. In his *Soliloquies* (I,7) the Bishop of Hippo formulates the God/man relationship in the follow-ing truncated terms: "God and the soul, that is what I desire to know. Nothing more? Nothing whatever." Besides assuming two-factor theolo-gizing, the Christian message is here also squeezed into the mold of neo-Platonic thought. The soul is viewed as the "real" man. Bodily existence is eclipsed, leaving us with a docetic anthropology. Human life is "spiritualized."

Similar charges are also frequently laid at the feet of the most endearing and enduringly ecumenical creed of the Reformation era, the Heidelberg Catechism. Is its pedagogy not basically anthropocentric at the expense of that theocentric emphasis which is a hallmark of the Reformed tradition? After all, the Heidelberger never tires of pressing its claims in a very personalized way: "What must *I* know?" "What is *your* only comfort?" "What does it profit *you?*" Clearly the Heidelberger allows for no religiously detached self-knowledge. Revelation always demands a decisive answer to the question, Who am I personally? and, Who are we communally? God's Word never comes as an additive to natural self-awareness. It confronts us with a radical and sweeping definition of who we are, primarily before God, and, in light of this primordial relationship, who we are in the company of our fellowmen and within the full-orbed context of creation.

Repeatedly and forcefully the Catechism drives home this set of truths in its own unique way. But in doing so, does it not, as is often alleged, tip the scales toward a one-sided accent on man-centered concerns at the expense of the God- and Christ-centered message which is the very heartbeat of the gospel? This is not a self-evident conclusion. The charge of anthropological imbalance is defensible only if one plays the Heidelberger's call to *sola fide* on man's part off against its proclamation of the divine *sola gratia*. Echoing the Scriptures, the Catechism restates the Word of the personal God in his address to believers in a highly personal way. By means of the question and answer format, it brings the theo- and Christocentric truth of the gospel to bear on Christian faith-life in a pedagogically masterful way through its incisively anthropocentric thrust. Thus it displays a happy balance between revelation as norm and our normed response. As Hendrikus Berkhof puts it,

> No abstract God, no objectivistic truth is the starting point of Christian discipleship. But neither is this point to be sought in an abstract man, in subjectivistic religion, or in a presupposed conception of existence. The starting point is the union of a real God and a real man in an encounter which is real and relevant because it is an encounter of dissimilar persons. It is my comfort that I belong to my faithful Savior, Jesus Christ. (*Essays on the Heidelberg Catechism*, p. 94)

To be human is to be a creature, and to be a creature is to be a servant of one's Maker. Within these creationally established contours of human existence true knowledge of God and of ourselves go hand in hand. You cannot have the one without the other. To center on the one does not exclude but rather includes the other. In his study *The Knowledge of God in Calvin's Theology,* Edward Dowey elaborates this theme of relationality along the following lines. First, there is "the accommodated character of all knowledge of God." In Calvin's words, "God accommodates [*attemperat*] himself to our capacity in addressing us" (*Institutes,* I,13,1). As Dowey explains, this involves a twofold accommodation: God reckons first with our finite creaturely understanding, and then further with our human sinfulness. Next Dowey discusses "the correlative character of the knowledge of God and man." For

> God is never an abstraction to be related to an abstractly conceived humanity, but the God of man, whose face is turned "toward us" and whose person and will are known. And correspondingly, man is always described in terms of his relation to this known God: as created by God, separated from God, or redeemed by him.

There is also "the existential character of all our knowledge of God." By this Dowey means "knowledge that determines the existence of the knower." He describes this as "a practical knowledge, engaging the whole human personality, soliciting all the energies of the conscience and heart, putting in motion all the spiritual faculties" (pp. 3-40).

There is accordingly no conflict, contradiction, or even dialectical tension, but rather a truly dialogical relationship between the knowledge of God and of ourselves. Dowey elucidates this thesis on its Godward side. Thomas Torrance, on the other hand, does so on its manward side. Both, however, tend to read Calvin through twentieth-century Barthian glasses. Yet in Torrance as well as Dowey our major thesis concerning the simultaneity and relationality of knowing God and knowing self stands unassailed. Note the following statement from Torrance:

> This is the basic fact about all true knowledge of God: it is essentially an acknowledgment, not an excogitation. It is the sin of men that they will try to ground their knowledge of God upon the exercise of their own imagination, upon analogies which the human mind itself can manipulate, and so measure God by its own capacity, but all this, says Calvin, only leads to a feigned and new God. Acknowledgment, on the other hand, is the act of knowing in which men yield their minds to the imprint of the divine Truth, and submit themselves to the accommodating activity of the Word. Instead of bringing God within the measure of their own minds, they admit that "there is a certain measure within which men ought to keep themselves, since it is God who applies to our capacity whatever He testifies of Himself." "Therefore it is not for us to attribute anything to God, but it belongs to Him to utter Himself, and we must only receive

what He reveals to us, and hold ourselves to it." (*Calvin's Doctrine of Man*, pp. 148-49)

We conclude, then, that to construe theocentrism and anthropocentrism as dialectical polarities is to erect a false antithesis.

II. 3. "What Is Man. . . ?"

This provocative question (Psalm 8:4) lies at the very heart of all biblically directed anthropological reflection. With these words the Psalmist leaves us not with an open question, but with an exclamation of wonderment. He is overwhelmed by the grandeur of God's majestic handiwork brilliantly displayed throughout the vast expanses of the universe. O God, by comparison, where then do we stand, puny human beings, that You pay so much careful attention to us?! You have placed us but a step removed from the glories of the heavenly realm. You have crowned us with dominion over all the creatures of your hand. Under God and over creation — this is the high and holy position of stewardship assigned to us in the world. What a magnificently contextualized status is ours! The Psalmist defines both our comparative smallness and our comparative greatness by reference to our Maker, by opening and closing the psalm with this doxology: "O LORD, our Lord, how majestic is thy name in all the earth!" Francis Schaeffer captures this paradoxical biblical view of man in arguing that

> . . . man is wonderful: he can really influence significant history. Since God made man in his own image, man is not caught in the wheels of determinism. Rather man is so great that he can influence history for himself and others, for this life and the life to come. . . . One of the great weaknesses in evangelical preaching in the last few years is that we have lost sight of the biblical fact that man is wonderful. . . . Man is indeed lost, but that does not mean he is nothing. . . . [For] even though he is now a sinner, he can do those things that are tremendous. . . . In short, man is not a cog in a machine; he is not a piece of theatre; he really can influence history. From the biblical viewpoint, man is lost, but great. (*Death in the City*, pp. 80-81)

Directionally we now experience both our lostness in Adam and our renewal in Christ. Yet through it all we are structurally still the wonderful crowning creatures of God's making.

Scripture therefore allows for no disinterested, coolly dispassionate reflection on human existence. We must always approach self-knowledge with a profound sense of awe and reverence for the sanctity of human life. For "What is man?" is a deeply moving religious issue which touches our life at its very core and in all its ramifications. God himself has situated us at center stage and assigned us our crucial roles in the unfolding drama of world history.

But is it possible thoughtfully to clarify our identity within creation? There is, after all, a mysterious depth dimension to human life which we can never fully plumb. As the Psalmist says, we are "fearfully and wonderfully" made (Psalm 139:13-16). How are we to see ourselves? Adapting a familiar remark by Augustine: "When no one asks me who I am, I know full well; but when I am asked to explain it, words fail me." As persons we can never get outside ourselves, as it were, to hold ourselves at arm's length for "objective" scrutiny. How often we are mistaken about ourselves. It always seems easier to get other people and other creatures into clear focus. Anthropological reflection seems easier, moreover, when it comes to considering man in general. There we meet a more generic person. And we recognize him more readily. Arriving at true knowledge of our concrete selfhood, however, always remains a mysterious undertaking. For we always take ourselves along in the process. We are epistemologically limited to the horizon of our own world of experience.

Yet, very unique creatures that we are, it does seem possible consciously to think ourselves apart from our particular existence, to project ourselves, as it were, onto an imaginary screen for a closer look. Recall the episode of King David confronted by the prophet Nathan. The impact of the prophetic Word ("Thou art the man!") drove David to the point of honest self-recognition (2 Samuel 12:1-15). At a very practical, everyday, commonsense level of discernment we all have a measure of intuitive, immediate self-knowledge. For the impinging power of God's Word constantly gets through to us. It confronts us with a firsthand answer to the question of self-identity. This first-order knowledge of our selfhood serves as the basis for its extension into our second-order theoretical reflections on human nature. Our primary view of man funds our secondary methods of self-analysis, those which function in anthropological studies, as, for example, in dogmatics. At every level of self-knowledge, however, human life is never self-explanatory or self-justifying. The most profound clues to the meaning of our life lie beyond ourselves. For an authentic answer to the question, "What is man?", we are dependent on a Word from beyond. In the words of Dooyeweerd, "How, then, can we arrive at real self-knowledge? This question: Who is man? contains a mystery that cannot be explained by man himself." It cannot be resolved by rational inquiry. Yet we are not left in the dark. For the question of self-identity has been answered by God's Word-revelation, which uncovers the religious root and center of human nature in its creation, fall into sin, and redemption by Jesus Christ. . . . It is the Word alone, which by its radical grip can bring about a real reformation of our view of man and of our view of the temporal world. . . . (*In the Twilight of Western Thought*, pp. 179, 195)

II. 4. Theological Anthropology

The Bible is not a handbook on anthropology, whether philosophical or cultural or theological. We should therefore also refrain from speaking of a "Johannine anthropology" or a "Pauline anthropology." That is not the kind of book the Bible is. It does not supply us with theoretical data. That is not its intent and purpose. It addresses us religiously, not theologically; empirically, not abstractly; in a commonsense, everyday, practical way, not theoretically; in our wholeness as human beings, not in all our highly diversified modes of being human.

Accordingly, Scripture confronts us with a *view* of man, but not a *theory* of man. It offers no scientific doctrine of man (or of God, the earth, or the church, for that matter). But it does clearly stake out the revelational pointers which define who we are. Moreover, what the Bible says about us is open to theological reflection, and its light must direct and illumine our anthropological studies. It addresses us as social, economic, and political creatures, but it does not do so in politically, economically, or socially qualified terms. Rather, it focuses confessionally on these and all other aspects of human life. Without even suggesting a ready-made theological anthropology, it lays its claim on the "whole man" in a deeply religious, integrally unified, confessionally focused way. Only by donning the "spectacles" of Scripture are we as Christians equipped to enter the field of theological anthropology. In this dogmatic study of man we must therefore respect the limitations which are common to every theoretical enterprise. For, like every science, theology is not able to deal with man in the totality of his being. It focuses instead on the faith-aspect of his life. As other scholars investigate what it means to be human biotically, or psychically, or lingually, so theological anthropology investigates man confessionally. These limitations are forcefully reflected in the most personal and crucial of all our life experiences, birth and death. Both of these personal borderline events are inaccessible to critical self-reflection. We can only examine these mysteries vicariously. Theological analysis of personal self-knowledge must therefore confine itself to a disciplined look at human life between birth and death.

Thus self-knowledge in its profoundest sense is not dependent on scientific insights, not even those of theologians. "After all," as Berkouwer says,

> . . . theology as a science does not command some sort of special methodology which can reach that which other sciences, dealing with aspects of man's nature, cannot reach. Nor can its aim be merely to repeat what philosophy and the special sciences have already discovered about man. Nor can we say that theology, as queen of the sciences, deals with some kind of arcane knowledge about man, or with the key to this knowledge. (*Man: The Image of God*, pp. 29-30)

To construct a Christian model of man, therefore, we must turn to the structures and functions of human behavior as normed and upheld by the creation order. Cognizant, however, of the creationally disruptive and noetically distorting effects of sin, a Christian anthropology must allow the light of Scripture to flood this enterprise.

Scripture, then, is indispensable in putting human self-knowledge back into proper perspective. It addresses us in the totality of our many ways of being human, and it does so before the face of the Lord. Its central concern is not to inform us about the inner and outer workings of the various facets of human conduct. For such data we must turn to a study of our creaturely habits. What Scripture does is expose us to the searching eye of God in the religious wholeness of our existence. In that covenantal relationship we can begin to discern the undergirding principles by which to shape the basic presuppositions, methodologies, and theories for engaging in theological anthropology. Citing Berkouwer once again: "It is clear enough from Scripture that its concern is with the whole man, the full man, the actual man as he stands in God's sight, in the religious bond between the totality of his being and God" (*Man: The Image of God*, p. 31). In anthropology no less than in cosmology a clear understanding of the interrelatedness of creational and redemptive revelation is of utmost importance.

Theological anthropology can help deepen and enrich true self-knowledge, but cannot generate it. Otherwise the scribes, Pharisees, and lawyers, the theological experts of Jesus' day, should have led the way. Instead, true self-knowledge, which turns our hearts to the Lord, dawned on the poor and humble. To rely on theology for this is misleading. As Dooyeweerd states it,

> . . . as a dogmatical science of the articles of the Christian faith, theology is no more able to lead us to real knowledge of ourselves and of God than philosophy or the special sciences which are concerned with the study of man. This central knowledge can only be the result of the Word-revelation

of God operating in the heart, the religious center of our existence, by the
power of the Holy Spirit. (*In the Twilight of Western Thought,* pp. 184-85)

Anthropological reflection draws on that heartfelt self-knowledge which
is the fruit of the captivating power of God's Word, accompanied by the
convicting power of his Spirit. Religious knowledge is foundational to
theological knowledge. For God's Word addresses us primarily as the
common human creatures that we are, and then secondarily as people
engaged in theoretical reflection. Religion funds theology. Being human
takes priority over being a theologian. The way we respond to God's
Word sets the tone for doing theology. Quoting once again from Dooyeweerd:

> In this central and radical sense, God's Word, penetrating to the root of
> our being, has to become the central motive-power of the whole of the
> Christian life within the temporal order with its rich diversity of aspects,
> occupational spheres, and tasks. As such, the central theme of creation,
> fall into sin, and redemption should also be the central starting point and
> motive-power of our theological and philosophical thought. (*In the Twi-
> light of Western Thought*, p. 187)

In his own way Gilkey emphasizes these same ideas. He argues that
"the world for the Christian is a realm of definable structures and real
relations, and so it is a possible object both for scientific and philosophical
study." Such study involves "pre-philosophical intuitions," however, "decisions which are the foundations rather than the conclusions" of Christian
thought. In light of this the Christian "confesses that he is the recipient of
revelation, rather than the originator of insight." He therefore "knows that
both his own total being and the being of the finite things he encounters
are real and yet dependent beyond themselves on a transcendent power."
Accordingly, "he knows now that while there is an inherent order to his
life, it is an order that points beyond itself to a deeper meaning. His own
life's coherence [proves] not to be self-sufficient. . . . Thus, when he looks
at the world, he knows that while he can find order there, nevertheless the
final source of meaning transcends both his science and his philosophy"
(*Maker of Heaven and Earth*, pp. 117, 135, 137).

II. 5. Identity Crisis

The focus here is on our common humanity within the context of creation. Yet, in the light of our fall into sin and redemption in Christ,

spiritual antithesis is also a big-as-life reality. To get things straight, therefore, we must put on the "spectacles" of Scripture. But what of those who decide to discard these corrective lenses? One result is the contemporary proliferation of clashing and confusing anthropologies, spelling identity crisis for modern man.

The contemporary marketplace of ideas is cluttered with a host of random yet very real models of man. A few examples will suffice. 1) Man is a political creature, a pawn of the state. 2) Man is an economic commodity in the industrial complex, a producer and consumer, a prime target for media manipulation. 3) Man is a mathematical digit, a serial number stored in the memory bank of a computer center. 4) Man is a biochemical organism whose chief end is bodily gratification: watch your diet, therefore, since "You are what you eat!"

Such notions of what it means to be human are largely praxis oriented. Reinforcing these popular views are a cluster of more theoretical models of man. With a few fast strokes let us paint a picture of their competing claims on our loyalty.

a) Liberalist View of Man

Classic nineteenth-century liberalism drew heavily on anthropologies emerging from the Renaissance and the Enlightenment. Standing in that tradition, it proclaimed the "social gospel" with its utopian view of man. Relying on historical-critical methods of biblical interpretation, liberalism displaced the traditional Hebraic-Christian view of man with a reconstructed Pelagian-Arminian view of human history and destiny. It proudly announced the doctrine of man's inherent goodness. Our basic problem is not sin, but shortcomings yet to be overcome. Appealing to Darwinian ideas, it held that humanity has already made great progress. Man is steadily coming of age. Given a little more time and a fair chance, we are capable of reaching our full potential. Ever onward and upward! For by dint of sheer determination on the part of all reasonable people of goodwill the kingdom of heaven is achievable here on earth. Many confidently waved the banner, "the kingdom of God in America within this generation." Such an enculturated Christianity was waiting to be exported to the benighted regions of the world with a kind of messianic, evangelistic fervor. The church's mission in the world is social rehabilitation.

On this view, man is the measure of all things. In Europe this cultural optimism died a suffocating death in the gas-filled trenches of the Siegfried and Maginot lines between 1914 and 1918. The outbreak of this Great War marked the real close of the nineteenth century, and with it the demise of liberal anthropologies. But optimism dies harder in North America. World War I was indeed a very bitter pill for liberals to swallow. Yet the dream lived on — for a while at least. For at bottom, it was argued, the evolutionary advance of mankind is irresistible. The human spirit is invincible. The onward march of history, with its dialectical tension between setbacks and advances, may at times sorely test man's faith in the future. But hope springs eternal in the human breast. Armed with this ideology, liberals viewed even the Great War as "the war to end all wars."

b) Humanist View of Man

Our troubled world has not dealt kindly with humanist manifestos which proclaim the glories of man. Even the most undaunted humanists are compelled to concede man's failures, the tragic brokenness of his life, his demonic conduct. The human drama is often a source of great disappointment and embarrassment. Yet, even chastened humanists cling religiously to their faith in the ultimate value of being human. For behind the darkened visage of everyday appearances, in the secret depths of man's inner being, there we discover the real man, the ideal man. Even against overwhelming odds, mankind possesses a reservoir of inalienable goodness and inviolable greatness. These wellsprings of hope must be tapped. We must bring out the best in every man. Let mankind come to its own by coming of age. It is not easy, however, to be a devoted humanist in our times.

c) Existentialist View of Man

As this century enters its final stages, a radically altered scenario confronts us. The historical upheavals which marked the course of events during the twentieth century have left their deep scars on the self-image of modern man. In the wake of the Great Depression, the Holocaust, World War II, Hiroshima, Kuwait, countless Viet Nams, Sowetos, and Beiruts — in short, in the aftermath of more wars than years in this century, the liberalist and humanist illusions of man as a paragon of virtue are now thoroughly discredited. Their dream world, resembling ethereal castles-in-the-sky, lies shattered in a thousand irreparable pieces at our feet. These idols of our time have failed us. Man is not on the way to deification. He is far from saintly, let alone angelic. Man is a demon with an unpredictable and incalculable capacity for bestial, even satanic, atrocities. Daily headlines and newscasts memorialize man's inhumanity to man. The surrealistic anthropologies of contemporary existentialist and nihilist commentators paint a picture of human nature starker than the grimmest old-fashioned sermons on total depravity. The future of man is not utopian peace and prosperity, but a nuclear doomsday. Human rights, so boldly proclaimed by liberalist and humanist visionaries, are daily trampled in the dust. The most universal thing about universal human rights is their almost universal violation.

Indeed, a veritable anthropological revolution has overtaken our world. Mankind is no longer viewed as the crown of God's creation, nor as an emerging wonder of the historical process, much less as the hope for a better world. Being human is a liability, not an asset. We can no longer look to man for answers, for he is himself the problem. He is a threat to his own existence and the likely annihilator of the cosmos. In the very depths of his being man is afflicted with a sickness unto death, for which there is no known cure. What a difference a century can bring! A more drastic reversal in anthropological perspectives is hardly conceivable.

d) Evolutionary View of Man

Cutting across this cluster of anthropologies, and in large measure supplying their basic ideological underpinnings, is the modern fascination with evolutionary theories. These developments are symptomatic of the historicist mind-set which gathered momentum in the nineteenth century and now lays its almost undisputed claim on modern man. Whatever norms there are for human life must be sought in the relativities of the historical process. This is the matrix out of which evolutionary anthropologies emerged.

Since the publication of Darwin's *Origin of the Species* in 1859, the view of man he projected has conquered the minds of more and more people. At first only modest claims were made for these ideas. Evolution is merely a theory, enjoying only hypothetical status. Now, however, a century and a half later, these early disclaimers are largely forgotten. Evolutionism has come to be embraced in ever widening circles as undisputed dogma. With this came an uncritical acceptance of the idea that the human race has evolved over aeons of time from primitive forms of inanimate and animate existence to its present stage of development. This complex process is explained in terms of genetic mutations, environmental adaptation, and natural selection, resulting in a survival of the fittest.

Evolutionism is not an isolated movement. It is an outgrowth of the radical and sweeping overhaul of Western Christianity ushered in by the Enlightenment. With it came a secularized worldview, together with a dialectical view of history, issuing in naturalistic anthropologies. Both liberalism and existentialism grounded their views of man in the dogma of evolution. The former appealed to it in support of its optimistic view of human progress. The latter drew very opposite conclusions from the same evolutionist premises. Human advance has stagnated at the level of a highly developed animal existence. We prove it daily by our brutal behavior. Our evolutionary odyssey is, therefore, more a cause for sober reflection than happy expectation.

During recent decades these evolutionist dogmas have been incorporated into many of the monist worldviews which have come to dominate contemporary theology. Monist thinkers posit an original indefinable alpha-point as the primordial source of the evolutionary process which now spirals onward toward its open-ended future. Both God and man are viewed as caught up in this dialectical evolutionary movement. Our brightest prospect is God, the future of man. In the end, man may come out on top. But he could also go under. One's outlook on such evolutionist eschatologies depends on whether one is inclined pessimistically toward an existentialist-nihilist view of man or optimistically toward a liberalist-humanist view.

e) Technological View of Man

Our century has given birth to a new breed of human beings, the technological man. He was conceived during the scientific revolution, nurtured through the labor pangs of the Industrial Revolution, and finally brought to maturity by the technological revolution of our times. This very modern man is willing to entrust his fortunes to the proven results of science and technology. Technological genius is the motor of progress, and continuing scientific exploration is the fuel which fires this machine. This technocratic man relies heavily on systems analysis. The computer is the versatile tool to control our forward movement into an ever more efficiently programmed future. Man functions as one factor in this universal system. The goal is a planned society where human error, unpredictable variants, and uncontrollable interventions are kept to a bare minimum. Cybernetics enables man to reform himself, remold society, and, by forecasting the results of current trends, to reconstruct our presently splintered global village into a unified world order. Shades of Huxley's "brave new world" and Orwell's "1984"!

Such futurologies reduce man to an impersonal standardized cog in the larger wheel of progress. Human input and output are governed by statistical probability. By extrapolating the lines of human development coming up out of the past into the present, and then projecting

211

them into the future, a predetermined totalitarian technocracy can be lifted from the drafting boards and put in place. The devising of such master plans must be entrusted to the expertise of the scientifically and technologically skilled leadership of an elite company of planners who alone are competent to calculate a number of viable plans, sort them out, choose the most workable ones, and then implement them. Perhaps this can be accomplished by voluntary participation rather than by bureaucratic imposition. But democratic participation is not essential to its realization. The end justifies whatever means are needed. The eschatological goal is a well-ordered society, free of outside intervention, where people-roles are made subservient to an efficiently engineered world order.

f) Revolutionary View of Man

Strongly opposed to the technocratic view of man is a revolutionary school of anthropologists. Both embrace certain utopian expectations. Yet the utopias they envision are radically different. In yet another respect they are also formally similar. Both technocrats and revolutionaries embrace their chosen social philosophy as the standard by which to define their view of man. With this, however, all similarities cease.

Revolutionaries adamantly reject the idea of a scientifically planned society, with man locked into a tightly organized system under the control of an elite technocratic leadership. Their anthropology allows no room for a well-ordered transition from the past, through the present, and onward into the future. For them man is a creature in constant revolt. They stress the need for radical breaks and discontinuities in the historical course of events. Only by new, surprising, uncontrollable, unpredictable developments can man be emancipated to achieve his potentials. They therefore call for protest, conflict, struggle. The dialectical process of confrontation, resolution, and renewed confrontation is the only way for man to come of age. Ongoing revolution is therefore the locomotive of history, and the fuel which fires it is a utopian dream of liberation. The future depends not on logical analysis, but on the heroic power of imagination. Oppressed peoples must take a radical leap from present reality into the realm of future possibility. True humanity can never be at home in the establishment or in attempts to erect a new world on it. For man is inherently caught up in conflict. Revolutionary aspirations must therefore replace the existing order.

g) The Freudian View of Man

"Sorry — that was a Freudian slip!" This very casual coverup remark has worked its way into our daily conversations. It indicates how deeply Freudian ideas have infiltrated the contemporary mind. The results of Freud's lifelong work in experimental psychology have in fact revolutionized modern man's self-understanding, bringing with them a radical distortion of the biblical view of personhood. It is indeed so, as Scripture says, that all the issues of life arise from our very heart of hearts (Proverbs 4:23). Moreover, under sin, "the heart is deceitful above all things, and desperately corrupt" (Jeremiah 17:9). Again, as our Lord says, "from within, out of the heart of man, come evil thoughts . . ." (Mark 7:21). In the Freudian ideology, however, this biblical insight into the depth dimension of human experience is radically perverted. What emerges is a dark and murky, highly psychologized doctrine of "human depravity," and that with a vengeance.

Since he is an avowed atheist, Freud's ideas on human behavior presuppose a thoroughly secularized, determinist view of what it means to be human. In step with a Darwinian worldview, all reality is reduced to the emerging product of natural evolution. Our most basic attitudes and patterns of behavior arise, on this view, from deep-seated animalic instincts. Rigorous introspection, penetrating to the hidden depths of our innermost being, is therefore the key to unlock the meaning of life. It calls for the relentless application of methods known as psychoanalysis. Such probings alone can uncover the underlying, long-suppressed impulses which explain our present moods and conduct. Many in our time have anointed such practicing psychiatrists as the high priests of modern society. Hovering over their proverbial couches, these gurus induce their clients to retrieve from their long-forgotten subconscious past the traumas which allegedly account for their present disorders. Self-analysis is thus the appointed "revelational" route to self-understanding.

In Freudian terms, human beings are comparable to an iceberg. Seven-eighths of our troubled makeup is traceable to deeply submerged, aggressive sexual drives. A direct cause-and-effect connection links the inhibitions of these childhood experiences to the personality problems of adulthood. This is a universal human condition. It may very well be true, therefore, that society as a whole is also afflicted with this neurosis. Lodged deeply in the foreboding nether regions of our collective consciousness is an oedipus complex which may conceal the ultimate source of the world's problems — a predicament from which there is no escape. For its wellspring and its outpourings are beyond our control. This ominous condition cannot be judged as either good or bad, right or wrong. It is value free. It just is. And there is no liberating Word from beyond. By a kind of mechanist necessity we are locked into our own self-contained universe of experiences.

The only hope for "deliverance" is to expose these subterranean habits and to deal openly with the dreams which bring them to the surface. Religion can offer no help, for the Hebraic-Christian faith is merely an illusion rooted in our father/mother complexes. What believers call the forgiving and healing voice of God is nothing but the subliminal echo of parental influences. There are no transcendent norms that hold for human life, no revealed reasons for charting our course, no control beliefs, no moral choices that make a real difference. Man is the psychological victim of his hereditary fate.

b) The Behaviorist View of Man

Like Freudians, behaviorists view the human race as a product of evolutionary processes. They agree, too, in utilizing the scientific methods of the natural sciences, drawing heavily on animal research, in creating their models of man. With that, however, the similarities cease. Though rooted in heredity, Freudian anthropology is cast into a profoundly and pervasively "spiritualist" mold. In sharp contrast, behaviorist anthropology is thoroughly "materialist" in its view of man. It links human conduct inexorably to the conditioning effects of our cultural environment. Not inner drives, but external factors are the coercive forces which determine human behavior. Self-understanding comes, therefore, not through the introspective methods of psychoanalysis but through a rigorously controlled analysis of environmental pressures. For psychic states of mind have no real, independent existence. They are but side effects of physiological functions. Human beings are basically biochemical organisms interacting with the external stimuli of our cultural environment. Man is a complex machine conditioned and controlled by his past and present history. People are therefore to be treated not as persons, but as products of their changing environment.

Clearly then, behaviorism, too, leads to a total eclipse of the biblical view of personhood. The Hebraic-Christian faith, indeed any religious faith, is reduced to a myth which must be relegated to a bygone prescientific age. The church must therefore also be discarded as an outdated cultural mechanism. In the past it exerted its misguided environmental controls on the masses, manipulating them to cling to ancient myths. But that time is now forever past.

This radically secularized view of man goes hand in hand with an equally secularized worldview. Absolute determinism defines the meaning of all life. We have no choice but to give up our illusions about personal or communal freedom, dignity, lived and shared memories by which to shape our future hopes, and a sense of responsibility for our actions. Virtues such as religion, morality, neighborly love, and loyalty to traditions are vanishing by-products of that ironclad logic which governs the evolutionary process. New, scientifically formulated values must take their place.

This mechanist view of reality poses a host of questions. What set of newly evolved values can answer to the crying needs of modern society? Who defines them? Since human behavior is thoroughly conditioned by our cultural environment, which cultures should be preserved? Or must new environments be created? Who decides such crucial issues? And by what standards? Are the available norms good or bad, or are they all amoral? If survival of the species is the ultimate concern, why should this be considered important?

On this view, the only way to solve humanity's problems, to reform an obsolete society, to create a more utopian culture, is by the rigorous application of scientific methods. The aim of the behavioral sciences is therefore to recondition all existing social, economic, educational, and political institutions. For human behavior can be changed only by changing the culture which conditions it. This calls for a resolutely planned economy, imposing firm controls on the conditioning effects of the environment, thus making for more predictable outcomes. Such reforms demand a technology of human behavior. By a system of reinforcements, rewards, and manipulative techniques, it is possible to modify human behavior. People can then be induced to act in "more socially acceptable ways." But who decides what is "acceptable" behavior? And what controls are needed to achieve this end? Who appoints the controllers? And are their decisions not also culturally conditioned? In the end it therefore appears that we are locked into a vicious cycle with no way of escape.

*   *   *

This checkerboard collage of contemporary models of man highlights the identity crisis of our modern Western societies. Together they represent a sometimes self-conscious, sometimes unconscious abandonment of the biblical view of man. Since the Enlightenment declared its independence from historic Christianity, modern anthropologies have staked their case on the assumption that ". . . it is man's self-awareness that constitutes man as man, and it is this self-conscious man who both makes and constitutes the reality of history" (Ronald G. Smith, *The Whole Man: Studies in Christian Anthropology,* p. 25).

The contemporary quests for self-identity degenerate into the many faces of modern man's self-deception. He re-creates himself into the

215

likeness of his own multimasked image. Yet this restless search also betrays some notable areas of overlap. This should come as no surprise. For, though the models of man are legion, there is but a single mankind. By virtue of creation, constitutionally we all share certain common features. And the impinging power of God's Word still holds for all his creatures. By it he upholds human nature, keeping it intact, so that certain commonalities force themselves on the attention of all thinking people, cutting across even the most conflicting views of man.

Running through all these highly divergent anthropologies is the bipolar dialectic which has plagued our Western world over the past few centuries — the Kantian dualism between the ironclad rationality of the scientific mind, on the one hand, and morality with its urge for freedom, on the other. Accordingly, some views exploit the science ideal of the rationality pole, while others appeal to the personality ideal of the morality and freedom pole. Modern man finds his life caught up in a tension-laden tug of war between the competing claims of these two magnetically powerful forces. How are we to reconcile this bipolar commitment? We put our trust in science to create a well-ordered way of life, guaranteed growth, and uninterrupted prosperity through the blessings of technology. We like the security of rationally planned societal structures, very predictable and free of uncontrollable factors. At the same time, however, the irrepressible urge arises to "escape from reason" (Schaeffer) and take the liberating leap into the realm of surprising and exhilarating experiences where our personalities can soar to new heights.

Both visions offer the promise of a "better world," but along very different routes. The science ideal tends to canonize the establishment. It urges people to hold the course, building on past and present scientific achievements and projecting them into the future as the utopian dream of mankind. This view of the human prospect silences the much needed healing power of God's Word with its summons to inner renewal and religious redirection. The personality ideal calls for a radical reconstruction of the established order so that the human spirit can enjoy its more intuitive, aesthetic, culturally uplifting impulses. This outlook on the human odyssey has little eye for the holding power of God's Word, reminding us that no situation is ever utterly unredeemable. Since both of these ideals remain firmly entrenched in the human consciousness, modern man is locked into being a creature of "eternal conflict" (Bonhoeffer).

The contemporary pantheon of self-images confirms the biblical teaching that "those who make [idols] become like them" (Psalm 115:8). All these self-portraits, however apostate, arise from a deeply ingrained though radically distorted sense of the reality of God and man and their relationship. For man is never free of God, even when he bows to another god. These are presuppositional givens, embedded in the creation order. They therefore lie beyond verification or falsification. For behind every practically held or scientifically formulated anthropology lies an intuitively held, profoundly religious view of our common humanity. Man's contemporary identity crisis therefore reflects the fundamental religious crisis of our times.

As Christians we are not immune to these contrary winds of doctrine. The pastoral admonition has therefore lost none of its relevance: "Beloved, do not believe every spirit, but test the spirits to see whether they are of God . . ." (1 John 4:1). With discerning, discriminating minds, we must therefore "test all things, [and] hold fast to what is good" (1 Thessalonians 5:21). For to some extent all of us are guilty of synthesis. We compromise our professed biblical view of man by allowing unbiblical anthropological motifs to intrude on our patterns of thought and action. Consciously or unconsciously we all tolerate and sometimes even cherish ideas about ourselves which are alien to the gospel. Absorbed as we are in the mainstreams of Western culture, we can never fully escape such accommodating tendencies. We must therefore be critically aware of the misdirected religious spirits which permeate traditional and contemporary models of man, while at the same time remaining sensitive to the right insights, however blurred, of other thinkers. For the holding power of God's Word, the impinging presence of the creation order, commands even the resistant attention of non-Christian thinkers.

II. 6. "Heart" as Religious Unity

Recent decades have witnessed a careful reassessment of the way many key concepts function in the Scriptures. Among them is the idea of heart. Across the pages of biblical revelation the word "heart" refers consistently to the whole man. During the early and medieval eras of Western Christianity, however, under the influence of Hellenist anthropologies, this holist view was largely lost. Heart was generally reduced to some part of human response to revelation. With the Reformation, in Luther as well as in Calvin, came a rediscovery of its original biblical meaning. Perhaps this is epitomized best in the visual symbol of Calvin's thought, the flaming heart in the outstretched hand, with its familiar commentary: *Cor meum tibi offero, Domine, prompte et sincere* ("My heart I offer to you, Lord, eagerly and earnestly"), or its less familiar variant, *Cor meum quasi immolatum tibi offero, Domine* ("My heart as a flaming sacrifice I offer to you, Lord"). Such expressions are not absent from the writings of pre-Reformation thinkers such as Aquinas, ". . . but the parallels are

217

often more verbal than substantial" (cf. J. T. McNeill, ed., *Institutes,* III,1,3; footnote 6).

With the resurgence of Protestant scholastic theology in the modern period, the reformational rearticulation of a holist concept of heart was again largely eclipsed. Recently, however, renewed biblical studies confirm the more holist approach of the reformational tradition in contrast to the more rationalist idea of heart in scholastic traditions. As Calvin puts it, we are called to a knowledge of God which is not "content with empty speculation," which "merely flits in the brain," but that which will be "sound and fruitful if we duly perceive it, and if it takes root in the heart" (*Institutes,* I,5,9). The editor of Calvin's work then adds this comment: "Calvin here distinguishes between *cerebrum* and *cor,* brain and heart, in relation to the knowledge of God, characteristically giving importance to the latter" (*Institutes,* I,5,9; footnote 29). Calvin makes the same point in arguing that assent to the gospel "is more of the heart than of the brain, and more of the disposition than of the understanding" (*Institutes,* III,2,8). Calvin's emphasis on the centrality of the heart is not completely free of certain ambiguities. But he is clearly moving in the direction of a holist view. Recent studies have updated his insights. Note the following oft-repeated line from Barth's *Church Dogmatics:* The heart represents "man in a nutshell, the whole man — not only the seat of his activity, but its summary" (III/2). Regin Prenter makes the same point in saying that, as soul is "a synonym for person" (cf. Romans 13:1), so "the heart is the center of the soul, the point from which the soul's life issues" (*Creation and Redemption,* pp. 273-74).

More than 800 references to heart are woven into the fabric of biblical revelation. An overview of these passages reflects a clear pattern. They all point consistently toward a single and simple truth: The heart represents the unifying center of man's entire existence, the spiritual concentration point of our total selfhood, the inner reflective core which sets the direction for all of our life relationships. It is the wellspring of all our willing, thinking, feeling, acting, and every other life utterance. It is the fountainhead from which flows every movement of man's intellect, emotions, and will, as well as any other "faculty" or mode of our existence. In short, the heart is the mini-me. He who has my heart has me, not just part of me, but me wholly. Hence the urgency of the divine summons, "My son, [my daughter], give me thy heart!" (Proverbs 23:26). The Word of God, in addressing us, speaks directly to the heart, setting the spiritual direction of all our bodily activities. The heart is, therefore, the focal point of religion, that is, of life. For life is religion. Religion, rooted in the heart, is not a certain talent possessed by some but not by others. Nor is it a quality of life which may be lost and regained. In the words of Gilkey:

218

Whether he wishes it or not, man as a free creature must pattern his life according to some chosen ultimate end, must center his life on some chosen ultimate loyalty, and must commit his security to some trusted power. Man is thus essentially, not accidentally, religious, because his basic structure, as dependent and yet free, inevitably roots his life in something ultimate. (*Maker of Heaven and Earth,* p. 193)

Religion, centered in the heart, is the response side of our covenantal relationship with God. Accordingly, heartfelt religion engages every aspect of the whole man from his innermost being to his remotest extremities. For "out of the heart are [all] the issues of life" (Proverbs 4:23). The heart accordingly refers to man as a whole. This holist perspective also holds for other anthropological ideas in Scripture, such as "soul," "spirit," "mind," "inner man," and also "body." All are holist concepts. Each in its own unique way refers to the whole man. That reflects the kind of book the Bible is. As Word of God it always confronts us as whole persons, looked at now from one point of view, then from another.

This biblically grounded holist view of man comes through with unmistakable clarity in the following random sampling of the hundreds of biblical references to "heart."

a) Samuel the prophet is instructed to go to Bethlehem to anoint a successor to the antitheocratic King Saul from among the sons of Jesse. One by one the young men put in an appearance. Samuel sets his sights on Eliab. Judged by his stature and demeanor, he has royalty written all over him. But no, "the LORD sees not as man sees; man looks on the outward appearance, but the LORD looks on the heart" (1 Samuel 16:1-7). The heart is the key to who a person really is before the face of God. Seven sons of Jesse failed to pass the test. Just when Samuel's mission seemed doomed to failure, the least likely candidate of all was called in from the fields. "Arise, anoint him!" comes the command. For David is a "man after God's own heart" (1 Samuel 13:14). So God has a "heart" too! From that time onward, throughout Israelite history, David is held up as a paradigm of theocratic kingship. Future kings are judged by their heart commitment. We read of one king after another, "But his heart was not right with the LORD his God, as was David his father." Not military prowess or diplomatic genius, but right-heartedness is the measure of divine approval.

b) Turn now to the latter prophets. Repeatedly, through them, God complains about Israel's hard-heartedness. Israel's obstinacy offers evidence abundant that "the heart is deceitful above all things . . ." (Jeremiah 17:9). Yet in his mercy God announces, "And I will give you shepherds after my own heart, who will feed you with knowledge and understanding" (Jeremiah 3:15). In the midst of well-deserved judgment God still offers a message of hope: "A new heart I will give you, and a new spirit I will put within you; and I will take out of your flesh the heart of stone and give you a heart of flesh" — a pliable and docile disposition (Ezekiel 36:26). Yet Israel did not abandon its duplicity. Though my people "honor me with their lips," cries God, "their hearts are far from me" (Isaiah 29:13). In the fullness of the times Christ reiterated this prophetic protest: "You hypocrites! Well did Isaiah prophesy of you, when he said: 'This people honors me with their lips, but their heart is far from me'" (Matthew 15:7-8).

c) With this fulfilling Word of Jesus we move on into the New Testament. Its writings also witness pervasively to God's dealings with us in our wholeness as human beings. In Christ God speaks to us in the language of the heart, whose allegiances disclose the ultimate concerns of our lives. Our Lord accents this truth when he says, "For where your treasure is, there will your heart be also" (Matthew 6:21). As a good tree bears good fruit, and a bad tree bad fruit, so it is with the heart of man. It is decisive in setting the course of action for life as a whole. Christ puts it this way: "The good man out of the good treasure of his heart produces good, and the evil man out his evil treasure produces evil; for out of the abundance of the heart the mouth speaks" (Luke 6:45; Matthew 12:34).

The heart, then, is the pivotal point around which all of life revolves. It is the hub where all the spokes which hold the wheel of life together converge. There life in all its richly diverse manifestations finds its anchor point of religious unity. It is the wellspring from which all the streams of life issue forth, for good — "Out of [the] heart [of the believer] shall flow rivers of living water" (John 7:38) — or for evil — "For from within, out of the heart of man, come evil thoughts . . ." (Mark 7:21). Faith as the spiritual act of full-bodied commitment of the whole man to God and his ways is embedded in the heart, as Paul says: "For man believes with his heart and so is justified, and he confesses with his lips and so is saved" (Romans 10:10).

Challenged by his critics to set forth the chief commandment, Jesus reached back to the law of Moses (Deuteronomy 6:5) and summarized it in these words: "You shall love the Lord your God with all your heart, and with all your soul, and with all your mind, and with all your strength" (Mark 12:30). What are we to make of this fourfold accent? On the biblical view of man are we then to conclude that we are composed, not of two parts (the dichotomist position — "body" and "soul"), nor merely of three parts (the trichotomist position — "body" and "soul" and "spirit"), but of four parts ("heart" and "soul" and "mind" and "strength")? All such interpretations misread the intent and purpose of the biblical message. "Heart," together with these other avenues of human response, reflects the whole man looked at from different points of view.

Scripture is praxis oriented. It speaks of man in confessional language. On the basis of these revelational pointers Christian thinkers develop an anthropological model as the theoretical elaboration of certain fundamental beliefs concerning what being human means. Such basic convictions lie beyond rational verification or falsification. They function as the ultimate validation of all anthropological theories. A fundamental shift in one's anthropology therefore involves a kind of "conversion." If we fix our hearts on some aspect of created reality rather than on the Creator, then we have sold out to an idol. In its operative view of man, a community gives expression to the deepest loyalty of its collective heart.

In light of these biblical perspectives, it is high time to lay aside some anthropological caricatures which are very popular in Christian circles. We must remember that God's work of redemption does not violate his work of creation. His way of saving man honors the unified way he made man. Redemption "fits" creation. Therefore some very appealing misconceptions should be banished from our Christian vocabulary. In preaching and teaching it is commonplace to discuss Christian living in terms of the "head," the "heart," and the "hand." These categories are a popularized version of the views of faculty psychology, which divides being human along the lines of intellect, emotions, and will. These three faculties are regarded as the three parts which together make up the whole man. On this theory, the "head" is identified with intellect, the "heart" with emotions, and the "hand" with volition. Repeatedly, then, the cry goes up: What we need is less "head" knowledge and more "heart" knowledge — meaning less doctrinal and more inspirational preaching and teaching. It is then often argued that, while some Christians emphasize the "head" (intellectualism), and others the "heart" (emotionalism), and still others the "hand" (activism), we Calvinists distinguish ourselves by a balanced emphasis on all three. It all sounds so neat and clean and clear! In the process, however, we have effectively undercut Scripture's unifying view of the whole man. By playing these three "parts" off against each other we manhandle in scholastic fashion the biblical address to man in his oneness, fullness, and totality before the face of God. The "heart" then stands for a part, not for the whole of our existence. When this happens it is high time to recall the Psalmist's prayer, "O LORD, . . . unite my heart to fear thy name" (Psalm 86:11).

Berkouwer summarizes well the biblical idea of heart. In his chapter on "the whole man," he argues that all the richly diversified structures and functions of human nature come to their religiously focused unity in the heart. Referring to Proverbs 4:23 — "Keep thy heart with all diligence, for out of it are the issues of life" — Berkouwer comments as follows:

> Such words have as their purpose not the shedding of light on the compositional structure of man, but rather to deal with the whole man in all his complex functions; not to deal with a part of man in distinction from other parts, but to deal with man in his total existence, which lies open before the examining eye of God. . . . [For] in the heart man's whole life is open before God, who is the knower of hearts, of all hearts. . . . The heart [therefore] shows forth the deepest aspect of the whole humanness of man, not some functional localization in a part which is supposedly the most important. The term "heart" deals with the total orientation, direction, concentration of man, his depth dimension, from which his full human existence is directed and formed. He who gives his heart to the Lord gives his full life (cf. Proverbs 23:26). (*Man: The Image of God*, pp. 202-3)

This holist viewpoint is similarly expressed in the most ecumenical of all Reformation creeds. In the words of Howard Hageman,

> . . . It is an indication of the true greatness of the Heidelberg Catechism that it recognizes the totality of human need from start to finish. The point is made in the very first question, though so quietly we may never have seen it. "I belong — *body* and soul — to Jesus Christ." Here is no pietistic abdication of part of human existence to other powers, as later evangelical religion has so often done. Here is no narrowing of concern to matters of the soul, something characteristic of contemporary popular piety. Here in the opening words of the Catechism is the frank acknowledgment that all of human life belongs to Jesus Christ, that in the deepest sense of the word what a man eats, his sexual relationships, the way he earns his living and pays his bills are as important to Jesus Christ as the way he says his prayers or listens to the "domine" preach a sermon. . . . [Therefore] the Catechism is not addressing that religious abstraction called my *soul*, but is addressing *me*, a whole person. (In D. Bruggink, ed., *Guilt, Grace, and Gratitude*, pp. 14-15)

In the spirit and style of the baroque period, Bach immortalized the biblical idea of heart musically in the following chorale from his "Christmas Oratorio":

Ah! Dearest Jesus, Holy Child,
Make Thee a bed, soft, undefiled,

Within my heart, and there recline,
And keep that chamber ever Thine.

II. 7. Man — the Image of God

The Christian confession concerning the image of God captures the very heartbeat of the biblical view of man. Understandably, therefore, all theologians in the Christian tradition, past and present, have been induced by the biblical witness to deal with this crucial idea. The resulting anthropological literature is voluminous. Interpretations of the *imago Dei* are, moreover, as diverse as the wide-ranging schools of theology which produce them. For views of man are integrally related to the worldviews they represent, and are just as varied.

Despite such intense and sustained attention to the question of man's creation in the image of God, its full and precise meaning still remains cloaked in the very mystery which constitutes our being human (cf. Psalm 139:13-18). Perhaps this concerted reflection on the idea of the *imago Dei* is prompted by the relatively few direct references to it in Scripture. Apart from New Testament teachings on the restoration of the image of God in Christ (Romans 8:29; 1 Corinthians 15:49; Colossians 1:15; 3:10), basically the only references to man's being created in the image of God are found in the opening chapters of Genesis (1:26-27; 5:1; 9:6; cf. James 3:9). Yet clear pointers are pervasively present throughout Scripture (cf. Psalm 8). True to its revelational intent and purpose, however, Scripture nowhere offers a systematic theory of man. This leads Bavinck to say that "nowhere [in Scripture] is the full content of the image of God unfolded" (*Gereformeerde Dogmatiek*, Vol. II, p. 494). Yet the Bible does not fail in existential ways to shed its light on what it means that we are created as imagers of God. "We are God's *poiēma,*" says Paul, "God's poem, created in Christ Jesus for good works . . ." (Ephesians 2:10).

The Bible, in fact, wastes no time in clarifying the question of human identity. As a climactic act in God's creating work we read, "Then God said, 'Let us make man in our image, after our likeness. . . .' So God created man in his own image, in the image of God created he him; male and female he created them" (Genesis 1:26-27). The "book of the generations of Adam" opens with a reiteration of this truth: "When God created man, he made him in the likeness of God" (Genesis 5:1). When later God pronounced his just judgment on murder, he grounded his declaration of the sanctity of human life on the fundamental creational reality, "For God made man in his own image" (Genesis 9:6).

223

Across the centuries Christian thinkers have been tempted repeatedly to introduce a disjunction between the biblical concepts "image" and "likeness." They often argue that "image" refers to man's divinely endowed status *(datum)*, while "likeness" points to a higher goal of holiness which man is to pursue *(mandatum)*. This results in a kind of dual image — the greater and the lesser. Such interpretations are well suited to a dualist anthropology — natural gifts and supernatural aspirations. But they cannot stand the test of biblical usage. In Scripture these two concepts carry a roughly equivalent meaning. Accordingly, this distinction, tending toward a dualist reconstruction of the biblical view of man, though present in such thinkers as Augustine and Aquinas, was largely abandoned by the Reformers. As Calvin puts it: "There is also no slight quarrel over 'image' and 'likeness' when interpreters seek a non-existent difference between these two words, except that 'likeness' has been added by way of explanation" *(Institutes,* I,15,3). Along the same line, Bavinck holds that while "image" and "likeness" are "certainly not identical, nevertheless one cannot point to an essential, substantial difference between them. They are used promiscuously and interchangeably without any apparent reason" *(Gereformeerde Dogmatiek,* Vol. II, p. 492).

This divine image/likeness is integral to our very way of being human. Man is not first a unique creature to which these imaging, mirroring, echoing qualities are then added for good measure. The image of God is not a *donum superadditum* — a supernatural gift which supplements or complements our otherwise purely natural state. It is not an afterthought appended to an already existing human nature. Rather, to be human is to be the image of God. *Imago Dei* therefore describes our normal state. It points not to something in us or about us, but to our very humanity. Stated pointedly, it may be said that God imaged man into existence. It is therefore misleading to say that we *have* the divine image. Nor are we merely image-*bearers*. This conventional way of speaking carries connotations too external to our way of being human. It suggests the possibility of choice — as in cross-bearing, whether to bear the image or not. Imaging is not a choice but a given. We *are* imagers of God. Imaging God represents our very makeup, our constitution, our glory, and at the same time our high and holy calling in God's world.

These fundamental insights pertain to the whole man, nothing excluded. The idea of *imago Dei* covers human nature in its total extent and in all its parts. It embraces everything we are and have and do. In the emphatic words of Bavinck,

> . . . the whole man is the image of the full Godhead. . . . And he is that completely, soul and body, in all his capacities and powers, in every situa-

tion and relationship. Man is the image of God because and in so far as he is true man; and he is man, true and essential man, because and in the very measure that he is the image of God. . . . Therefore the whole man is the image and likeness of God. He is that in soul and body, in accord with all his abilities, strengths, and gifts. Nothing in man is excluded from the image of God. It reaches as far as our humanity itself. It is the humanness in our humanity. (*Gereformeerde Dogmatiek*, Vol. II, pp. 493, 516, 523).

With unmistakable clarity Bavinck contradicts the recurring tendency to limit the *imago Dei* to some larger or smaller aspect of human nature, to locate it in one primal faculty of our being at the expense of others. In this sense there is no "seat" of the image of God in man, as though one facet of human nature is elevated above, takes precedence over, and controls the other facets. The biblical view of man resists all such reductionisms. It is holist. We are pervasively imagers of God. This anthropological perspective leads Berkouwer to say:

Scripture's emphasis on the whole man as the image of God has triumphed time and again over all objections and opposing principles. Scripture never makes a distinction between man's spiritual and bodily attributes in order to limit the image of God to the spiritual, as furnishing the only possible analogy between man and God. (*Man: The Image of God*, p. 77)

An enormous amount of anthropological speculation has nevertheless been expended on the question: Where within the human constitution are we to locate the so-called "seat" of the image of God. On which aspect of human nature is the image enthroned so as to overrule all the other aspects? This reductionist approach generally assumes that there are certain ontic qualities in man which correspond to similar, though superior ontic qualities in God. One of these ontic qualities — be it rationality, lingual ability, creativity, or some other virtue — is then regarded as central to and definitive of the other lesser qualities. Then the debate gets heated: Which has the leading role? Which of these attributes are "communicable" (properties which God shares with man) and which are "incommunicable" (properties which God alone possesses)? This scholastic method has proven to be a thoroughly fruitless venture — a treasure hunt without biblical clues. For it presupposes an erroneous worldview, an "analogy of being" *(analogia entis)* between God and man. Thus it eclipses or at least seriously blurs the essential and qualitative distinction between the Creator and his creation, including his human creature. It loses sight of the mediating Word of God as the fixed boundary, which is simultaneously also the communicating bridge between these two partners in covenantal fellowship. For man is not an ontic "copy" of God, nor a substantial "duplicate," nor in essence a divine "alter ego." Rather, as imagers of God we are called at a creaturely level to reflect, mirror, and echo the will of God in our life together in God's world. We learn what imaging God means best by looking to the Word incarnate in Jesus Christ, who became like us in all things, who came to do the will of the Father, and who through his Spirit lends an eschatological perspective to all who seek to be faithful imagers of God. We are therefore unique creatures — "other" than God and "other" than the rest of creation. Other creatures are made "after their kind," but God created man "in his image and likeness." This vertical orientation is direction setting for all other life relationships, contrary to the horizontalist view of evolutionary theories. Human life is God-defined and primarily God-related.

Countless Christians have nevertheless been seduced by views of man which blur the nearness as well as the otherness of God, thus reducing the image of God to some allegedly chief part of man. Such notions cannot stand the test of Scripture nor of daily experience. Yet they continue to exercise a magnetically attractive power over the way people think and speak and write and otherwise act in both practical and theoretical affairs. It is commonplace, for example, to define man as a rational and moral being. Presumably then, on the basis of a correspondence theory of reality, human rationality and morality correspond in some way to similar qualities, attributes, or properties in God. Within this misguided worldview, the question then arises: Where are we to locate the "seat" of the image of God in man? In our rationality? After all, is not God the great Thinker? And are we not called to "think his thoughts after him"? One can then hardly escape the dogma of the primacy of the intellect. Such intellectualism, however, does not satisfy the deepest yearnings of the human heart. People then seek an "escape from reason" (Schaeffer) with its dead orthodoxy. Thus, once having defined man as a rational-moral creature, if rationality fails us, there is nowhere to turn but to morality. That must then be the ultimate meaning of life — the "seat" of the divine image in us. After all, God is the Author of morality, the world is a moral order, and man is a moral agent. Scripture "proves" it, as they say, and the classic moral argument for the existence of God confirms it. But what happens when modern man — overwhelmed by the immoralities of the Holocaust, subway brutalities, racial strife, and an impending apocalypse — no longer shares the traditional conviction concerning the reality of a moral order in the universe?

And so the reductionist search for the "seat" of the image of God in man goes on. Perhaps it lies in the lofty spirit of man, as the humanists hold. Or perhaps, aping the hedonist, in bodily gratification. Again, if not in the intellect, man's rational soul (the view of the scholastics), shall we seek it then in his deepest feelings (Schleiermacher's followers) or in his willpower (social activists)? In more orthodox Christian circles we meet the distinction between the image in its "narrower" and "broader" sense. All these misdirected anthropological ponderings obscure the biblical teaching that the *imago Dei* embraces our entire selfhood in all its variegated functions, centered and unified in the heart. We must therefore learn very concretely "to see eating and drinking as a way of expressing our love for God, not by means of accompanying words of grace, but by the act of eating and drinking itself; to know how a commercial career can be as rich an experience of serving God as a career in theology; to experience a visit to the toilet as an act as holy as prayer" (Stuart Fowler, *On Being Human,* p. 7).

Etymologically, it seems, the concept *imago Dei* is derived from the way coins functioned in ancient societies. Coins were stamped with the image and likeness of the ruling monarch (an idea not entirely foreign to modern practice). Thus the image of a king on a coin represented his presence, his authority, and his concerns throughout his domain. (Recall the incident concerning paying tribute in the gospel narrative, where Jesus answers his critics on the matter of imperial taxes with the question: "Whose image and inscription is this?" — Matthew 22:15-22. Where the coin goes, Caesar goes.) So also with man as image of God: Wherever man moves about in God's creation, there he is to represent the presence, the sovereignty, the care of his Maker in and for his world. Imaging means that we "represent God, like an ambassador from a foreign country, . . . [representing] the authority of God, . . . [seeking to] advance God's program for the world . . . [and to] promote what God promotes" (Anthony Hoekema, *Created in God's Image,* pp. 67-68).

Precisely because we, humans, are uniquely the image of God, God so strenuously forbids the making of other images (Exodus 20:4-6). The prerogative of establishing an image of himself belongs exclusively to God. And he has exercised that prerogative once for all in creating mankind. Every attempt to "play God" by imaging him in any other way than he has willed must be adamantly resisted. For he is filled with holy jealousy over his image-making project, and frowns on every attempt to arbitrarily control or manipulate his presence, his rule, his purposes in his world. In the words of Berkouwer:

> The second commandment deals with a prohibition against the arbitrariness with which man tries to have God at his beck and call. . . . [For] there lies, in every human attempt to make an image of God, an attempt to control Him, to bring Him close by. And it is this which is prohibited in the second commandment. . . . [To attempt this] is in its very origin an act

of unmistakable alienation from God. And it is, simultaneously, an act of extreme self-alienation, since man thereby seeks to construct an "image of God," although he himself, in communion with God, should be that image in all of his being. . . . It is only when man's communion with God is broken that there can arise such confused and aimless attempts to find the "image" by filling the vacuum with an artificially constructed divine "presence." (*Man: The Image of God*, pp. 79-82)

The biblical idea of *imago Dei* is therefore a relational, referential concept. It is not to be sought in some ontic quality within us. It has rather a dynamic, active, functional meaning. "God has created us in his image so that we may carry out a task, fulfill a mission, pursue a calling" (Anthony Hoekema, *Created in God's Image*, p. 73). As with God, so also with man, the Bible's definition is not *ad intra*, but *ad extra*. We discover the significance of being imagers of God not by looking within ourselves or searching out our inner being. Instead, the meaning of imaging God is discovered by looking outside ourselves. The *imago Dei* does not create introverts but extroverts. It is not a structural but a directional idea. It refers to that network of religious relationships which constitutes the framework for covenantal obedience — our relationship to God which is decisive for the normed relationships which hold for our personal lives, for our life together in human communities, and also for our dealings with God's other creatures great and small within the cosmos as a whole. The idea of image refers to our status and task: We are not divine, but we are sacred. Human life is wholly sacred, because it is lived before the face of God. It is also wholly secular in the sense that it is lived nowhere but in the midst of this age *(saeculum)*. The creational given of being the image of God and its concomitant call to be imagers of God coincide with the call to covenant obedience and kingdom service. Imaging God is doing his will. It is a matter of our hearing and heeding God's Word — our task and calling. It is "not static but dynamic"; we should therefore think of it "not as a noun, but as a verb" (Hoekema, *Created in God's Image*, p. 28). In the words of Weber, "As the being who is like God, we are supposed to do something" (*Foundations of Theology*, Vol. I, p. 560). For life is religion; religion is service; and imaging God is serving him and our fellowmen. The call to conversion is therefore a call to renewed service, so that "man who was using his God-imaging powers in wrong ways [may] now again [be] enabled to use these powers in right ways" (Hoekema, *Created in God's Image*, p. 86).

II. 8. Man in Office

As the message of redemption, Scripture assumes and builds anew on the givens of creation. Accordingly it presupposes both the idea of man as image of God and man in office. It points, moreover, to a close connection between these two ways of describing and prescribing our single comprehensive calling as human beings: We are to image God in the very way we exercise our office(s).

The classic Christian idea of man in office has fallen on hard times. It suffers from disuse, abuse, and misuse under the impact of contemporary humanist and secular usages. The results are upon us: Who still thinks of everyday human life as the exercise of a God-given office? Very few, and for that we are all the losers. To recover this lost ground it is important to reclaim and rehabilitate this soundly biblical concept by taking a renewed look at an old idea.

The term "office," referring to man's place and task in the creation, is largely absent from Scripture. Yet the idea of office is implicitly present in the full sweep of biblical revelation. It is woven integrally into the total fabric of its unfolding drama of salvation. Think, for example, of the official designation of priests, kings, and prophets in the Old Testament, and of apostles, deacons, elders, ministers, and evangelists in the New Testament. Undergirding these special offices is the official designation of the entire company of Christ-believers as "a chosen race, a royal priesthood, a holy nation, God's own people" (1 Peter 2:9).

Until Reformation times, however, the Christian church failed to take full advantage of this biblical idea of man in office. As leadership roles in the early church were gradually recast into the patterns of medieval Christianity, the full-orbed biblical meaning of office was increasingly displaced by an elitist notion of officialdom. The body of Christ-confessors as a whole was disenfranchised. Common believers were deprived of the fundamental sense of holding a universal office. Instead, the idea of exercising a Christian office was reserved mainly for authorities in the church and the state. Office was identified with the bureaucratic status of princes in the realm of nature and priests in the realm of grace. Secular rulers could thus plead exemption from political accountability with an appeal to "the divine right of kings," while spiritual leaders asserted even bolder pretenses to supreme authority, claiming that ultimately "both swords [temporal as well as sacred authority] rest in a single hand" — that is, they are housed in the hierarchy.

In light of these severely reductionist tendencies, deeply entrenched in Western Christianity, one must be deeply appreciative of the dramatic contribution of sixteenth-century Reformers to a recovery of the biblical idea of office. Luther, as pioneer in this reformational movement, set in bold relief the truth of the universal priesthood of all believers. As a second-generation Reformer, Calvin developed even more fully a theology of office. He related Christ's threefold office as Mediator to the corresponding threefold office of his body, the church. Christ exercises his kingly office with a view to empowering his people for perseverance. For "such is the nature of his rule, that he shares with us all that he has received from the Father" (*Institutes*, II,15,4).

> Therefore, whenever we hear of Christ as armed with eternal power, let us remember that the perpetuity of the church is secure in this protection. Hence, amid the violent agitation with which it is continually troubled, amid the grievous and frightful storms that threaten it with unnumbered calamities, it still remains safe. (*Institutes*, II,15,3)

Calvin sounds a similar accent in his treatment of the prophetic office of Christ. For

> . . . He received anointing, not only for himself that he might carry out the office of teaching, but for his whole body that the power of the Spirit might be present in the continuing preaching of the gospel. (*Institutes*, II,15,2)

Consistent with this line of thought, Calvin concludes his discussion of Christ's mediatorial office by saying that

> . . . Christ plays the priestly role, not only to render the Father favorable and propitious toward us by an eternal law of reconciliation, but also to receive us as his companions in this great office (Rev. 1:6). For we who are defiled in ourselves, yet are priests in him, offer ourselves and our all to God, and freely enter the heavenly sanctuary that the sacrifices of prayers and praise that we bring may be acceptable and sweet-smelling before God. (*Institutes*, II,15,6)

As Calvin makes clear in an entire chapter (*Institutes*, II,12) devoted to the question, *Cur Deus homo?* ("Why did God become man?"), Christ appeared as the "last Adam" solely "to take Adam's place." In holding thus that Christ restores man to his threefold office, Calvin attests reflexively to man's original status as officer in God's world.

This theology of office inaugurated by Calvin was further developed in the neo-Calvinist movement around the turn of this century. In his Princeton lectures of 1898 Kuyper opens up the worldview perspectives of our universal office by discussing "the three fundamental relations of all human life." According to Kuyper office entails relationality. The three basic relationships which lend structure and context to our creationally endowed (now fallen and redeemed) office as human beings are definable theologically, sociologically, and cosmologically. We are, first of all, servants of God; second, we are guardians of our joint humanity (including our own lives); finally, we are also stewards of the manifold riches of the rest of the cosmos. Theologically, therefore, office implies servanthood; sociologically it implies guardianship; and cosmologically it implies stewardship (*Lectures on Calvinism*, pp. 19ff.).

The Scriptures offer a wide variety of roughly interchangeable terms which, taken together, form the basis for the biblical idea of office. Among them perhaps *oikonomos* ("steward," literally "one in charge of the household") offers the best summation of the various equivalent usages in Hebrew and Greek (cf. Luke 16:2, where the "unrighteous steward" is commanded, "Turn in an account of your stewardship," literally "your housekeeping" — see also Luke 12:42). As Paul Schrotenboer puts it,

> In the broadest sense the idea of office refers to man's administration of the entire world which God has given him to manage. The creation account in Genesis clearly states that God placed man over the world to rule it in obedience to his Maker. That man as vicegerent of God is the administrator of the world was not the mere notion of the earliest and most primitive peoples; it was the heartbeat of the faith of the Hebrew people of God who got the idea by divine revelation. (*Man in God's World*, p. 4)

Standing in office is intrinsic to being human. It is more than a mere function. It is a matter of personal and communal identity. Office is not a matter of choice. It is a given which defines our very humanity. Being an officer in God's world is intrinsically ours. When it comes to the differentiation of this generic office into a variety of vocational offices, then obviously decisions are involved (for example, whether to exercise the office of "keeper of sheep," as in the case of Abel, or of "tiller of the soil," as in the case of Cain). Moreover, a certain differentiation of tasks is also built into the very ontic order of creation (for example, motherhood and fatherhood respectively, as in the case of Eve and Adam). But beneath such differentiations in calling there is a fundamental solidarity in office which holds generically for all humankind. For corporately we are all placed under the obligation of servanthood, guardianship, and stewardship.

Structurally our common human officership (given in Adam, restored in Christ) involves a mediating role. Standing in office means occupying an in-between position, a position in relationship. We stand both *under* and *over* — under God and over the rest of creation. We are accordingly both responsible *to* and accountable *for* — responsible to God and accountable for the things entrusted to our care. As officers we are vicars and representatives of our Maker, called to earthkeeping and caretaking, embracing our cultural mandate, and managing the affairs of God's world on his behalf.

Stated differently, the biblical idea of office opens our eyes to the following three basic perspectives on life. First, all exercise of office rests on divinely delegated authority. This holds for our common, generic office as human beings. It holds no less for the full range of differentiated avenues of service by which our corporate office comes to a host of concrete expressions — such as in parenting, farming, homemaking, doing business, studying, legislating, journalizing, and all the rest. In no office may we act on our own. For office is not a right but a trust, an endowment. We are not to act autonomously, but as representatives of the Giver of every official task. Here as everywhere it is true that "nought have we gotten but what we've received." What Jesus said to Pilate holds for every office in life: You would have no authority at all if it were not given from above (John 19:10-11). Accordingly, every earthly office wields only limited authority, limited first by the overarching sovereignty of God, and limited also by the coexisting and proexisting jurisdiction of other offices in society.

Second, the biblical idea of office involves accountability. As responding creatures, we are responsible for the way we administer our office(s). To whom is this responsibility due? There are, of course, earthly authorities to whom we are answerable in certain circumscribed ways; but ultimate answerability is to the King of kings and Lord of lords. Third, office is for service. To use office for personal prestige or promotion, for self-gratification or self-aggrandizement, is a distortion of the biblical idea of office. Such malpractice is an affront to our fellowmen as imagers of God. It disrupts the divinely established fabric of human relationships. Those vested with authority must therefore demonstrate their qualifications for exercising office. Such trust must be earned. When, however, office results in disservice, the officer in charge forfeits his right to exercise authority. Then the time is ripe for impeachment, deposition, or dismissal. For rendering obedient service — parents on behalf of their children, pastors on behalf of their parishioners, rulers on behalf of their citizens — this is essential to the exercise of office.

This biblical view of office serves as the source of countless blessings. It also helps to avert serious disruptions in society. On the one hand, it acts as a deterrent to totalitarian tendencies, whether political, economic, or ecclesiastical. The biblical message of authority, liberty, and service challenges every tyrannical power which seeks to crush the free expression of other legitimate human offices. On the other hand, it also helps to avoid egalitarian tendencies. Over against modern democratizing movements which seek to wipe out divinely ordained patterns of rank and order in human communities (such as parents and children, teachers and students), the biblical view of office honors the diversity of gifts and callings which God has distributed among men, while still affirming the fundamental equality of all men before the face of the Lord.

II. 9. The Whole Man: Body/Soul

How were we constituted by the hand of our Creator? What is our makeup? Sooner or later, it seems, every serious discussion of human nature gravitates toward this crucial issue. Basically the choice we face is between a holist and a dualist view of man. Are we body and soul? Or body, soul, and spirit? Or is there a better way of understanding the unity in diversity which makes us who we are? Is there an essential unity to our lives? And if so, is the whole simply equal to the sum of its parts or is it somehow greater than all its parts?

For nearly 2,000 years these problems have plagued the Christian community, with very unsettling consequences. Nowhere have the deforming influences of Greek philosophy on the Christian religion and its theology taken their toll more heavily than in the area of anthropology. Since the fateful Greco-Christian synthesis of the second century, dichotomous theories have dominated Christian thought and practice, with trichotomy emerging as a more refined version of dichotomy. With Fowler we must recognize that "the two component theory of the human person is an unbiblical idea that has been read into Scripture in the Christian tradition. . . . It is a corrupting intrusion of pagan philosophy into Christian thought and a serious hindrance to experiencing the full richness of the gospel" (*On Being Human*, pp. 3-4).

A melodramatic rendition of such bipartite anthropologies comes down to us in a story told by Thomas Mann in his book *Joseph the Provider*. In the beginning, so his mythological account goes, God created two distinct kinds of creaturely existence — spiritual beings, the angels, and the material realm of nonhuman creation. And all was well. For the spiritual and the material enjoyed a peaceful coexistence in a separate, unmixed, and undiluted state of affairs. But then, according to Mann's legend, God decided to create a third kind of being, man. He was to be the combination of a spiritual soul and a material body. The angels looked on in dismay. Dumbfounded by this freakish project, they expressed their vigorous disapproval. Such a hybrid of soul and body is doomed to disaster. It is unworkable. It constitutes an unstable mixture. But, so the drama unfolds, God always knows best. So he resolutely proceeded with this absurd plan. Man appeared on the scene, a divine protégé, partly body and partly soul. Like a self-fulfilling prophecy, just as the angels had predicted, before long inevitable calamity struck. Man failed to pass the test. His hybrid nature fell into disarray. At this the angels turned on God with a "We told you so" attitude. Even then, however, God stubbornly refused to abandon this impossible experiment. He set out to restore this fallen monstrosity called man. Indignant at such divine obstinacy, the angels at last rebelled, and thus sin and evil descended on the world.

Mann's story is, of course, an incredible bit of metahistorical fiction. Perhaps more than we would care to admit, however, it embodies dubious motifs which quite accurately expose the dualist views of humanity so prevalent in Western Christianity. Christian thinkers borrowed from their Greek forebears the notion of the superiority of the spiritual over the physical, of mind over matter. Bodily functions belong to a lower order of reality, inferior to the pious exercises of the soul. Many Christian thinkers (among them Calvin) succumbed to the Hellenist idea that the body is "the prisonhouse" of the soul. In keeping with this schizoid model of man, conscientious Christians were exhorted to subdue the body, rejecting nourishment, marriage, shelter, and the normal amenities of societal life in favor of the spiritual disciplines of ascetic self-denial, celibacy, and the privations of the monastic order and the hermitage. Not only were anthropologies based on such dualist views of reality, but the ranking of institutions and vocations within the Christian community as well. The church, devoted to the spiritual care and eternal destiny of souls, excels the state, which deals only with the earthly and temporal concerns of bodily existence. Within the church itself, the clergy represent the soul and the laity the body of believers. A call to the seminary is holier than pursuing a career in politics. Bible colleges hold a spiritual edge over Christian liberal arts universities. Evangelism is clearly a Christian mandate, while Christian social action is at best optional. Even those two sworn enemies, Fundamentalism and Liberalism, agreed in accepting this body-soul dualism as a point of departure, though they then moved out from there in diametrically opposed directions. Indeed, has any Christian tradition remained immune to such unbiblical views of man?

As a child of his times, trained in the humanist tradition of his day, Calvin, like his contemporaries, was unable to extricate himself completely from the stranglehold of prevailing medieval anthropologies. Plato was too much part of his thought world. Calvin's view of man therefore stands as the least reformed element in his theology. He does indeed break with the medieval notion of a partial fall and therefore also a partial redemption. He holds instead that the whole man is created good, that the whole man

234

is overturned by sin, and accordingly that the whole man is also redeemed in Christ. Directionally, therefore, his anthropology is reformed, but structurally it remains unreformed. For, in addressing the questions of body and soul and of the faculties of the soul, Calvin betrays his dependence on Hellenist philosophies, borrowing their concepts of man as a "microcosm" of the world, with the body as "the prisonhouse" of the soul. Such dichotomous constructs were then accepted as dogma in the theologies of the modern Protestant scholastic tradition. In combating a resurgent Thomism, post-Reformation thinkers chose to attack the enemy with its own weapons — with concepts and categories of analysis drawn from the Greco-Christian arsenal so familiar to medieval Christianity. Methodologically, therefore, such anthropologies represent attempts to pour Protestant wine into Roman Catholic wineskins.

In contemporary Reformed circles Louis Berkhof stands out as a well-seasoned exponent of this venerable tradition in Protestant orthodoxy. His anthropology clearly reflects this scholastic tradition. In it he wrestles with the problem, How are we to do justice to both the unity and the dichotomy which define man? Berkhof holds that Scripture, "while indicating that there are two elements in man, yet stresses the organic unity of man." Moreover, "this is recognized throughout the Bible." Emphasizing again the unity of human nature, he states:

> While recognizing the complex nature of man, [Scripture] never represents this as resulting in a twofold subject in man. Every act of man is seen as an act of the whole man. It is not the soul, but man that sins; it is not the body, but man that dies; and it is not merely the soul, but man, body and soul, that is redeemed in Christ.

At the same time Berkhof argues that "the prevailing representation of the nature of man in Scripture is dichotomic." Commenting on the relation between soul and spirit, he rejects the trichotomous distinction between the two, since "a careful study of Scripture clearly shows that it uses the words interchangeably. Both terms denote the higher or spiritual element in man, but contemplate it from different points of view." Berkhof therefore concludes that "it may be said that man *has* spirit, but *is* soul. The Bible therefore points to two, and only two, constitutional elements in the nature of man, namely, body and spirit or soul. This Scriptural representation is also in harmony with the self-consciousness of man" (*Systematic Theology,* pp. 191-96).

This very traditional yet highly ambivalent anthropological analysis is no longer accepted as self-evident. For since around mid-century a new consensus has been emerging. Basing their views on renewed biblical studies as well as on work being done in Christian philosophy and the human sciences, Christian thinkers began to focus as never before on the idea of the wholeness of man. Steadily the recognition grew that the Scriptures do not present us with a dualist (or trichotomist) view of man. Rather, we see ourselves mirrored there as whole human beings. This insight is corroborated by the findings of anthropological studies in various branches of learning. Human consciousness, daily experience, and many other reflections on our created nature testify to the fundamental unity which pervades all our ways of being human. Gradually holist views replaced the older dualist views.

The conventional terms, long used to designate the supposedly higher and lower parts of man, though drawn from the Scriptures, were nevertheless shaped by Hellenist thought. They fail, moreover, to demonstrate convincingly that man consists of two parts. For this entire range of biblical concepts — "body," "soul," "inner man," "outer man," "flesh," "heart," "mind," "spirit" — points to the whole man looked at from different points of view. This recognition of the heart-centered unity of the whole man in all the rich diversity of his many life relationships is not completely absent from the more traditional anthropologies. For no man in any age can rest content with a dualist self-image or a theory of split personality. All men strive for some sense of wholeness, integrity, and coherence in life. Generally, as in Louis Berkhof, this leads to an affirmation of unity-in-duality. Merely saying so, however, does not make it so. For dualist starting points (body and soul) resist unified conclusions (human wholeness).

Despite its good intentions, the result is what Berkouwer calls a "fictitious unity." This is how he states the case:

> The most controversial form of dichotomy in theology is that which pictures man as a composite of two substances, body and soul. This idea, for which support is claimed in Scripture, does not in the least intend to imply a dualism, a polar tension. The attempt is rather made to show the unity of man despite — or, rather, in — this duality, by calling attention to some relation which, in whatever way it is more closely described and defined, unites soul and body. But merely posing such a duality-in-unity does not mean that we actually have a real unity. The question always remains whether this duality-in-unity is not so construed that the tension between the two terms, the impossibility of joining them, becomes unmistakably clear; and whether, actually, the two terms which are first separated in a dualism are not illegitimately joined in a fictitious unity. (*Man: The Image of God,* p. 212)

To those of us who by virtue of lifelong training have grown accustomed to live our lives in terms of the traditional dichotomous view of man, this rearticulated biblical view of the whole man may at first sound disconcerting. It seems so indisputably natural to understand biblical references to soul as meaning the higher, spiritual part of us, and body as the lower, more mundane part. How else could they possibly be read? Such a reading does, of course, make sense on a dualist worldview. But is this the only or best way to read Scripture? Does a dichotomous model of man really do justice to the best in biblical hermeneutics within the Reformed tradition? Perhaps we have been reading Scripture with bifocal glasses. Such malpractice is bound to create visual images of the dualist sort. Such distorted impressions reside, however, in the eye of the beholder, not in the text. Once we realize this, we can leave those conventional dualist views of man behind as optical illusions. We are then free to replace these worn-out bifocal glasses with unifocal ones. Scripture is certainly open to this possibility.

Herman Ridderbos helps greatly in breaking this new ground through his careful study of the Pauline epistles. He concludes that "man in the whole of his existence is 'body.'" In dealing with the relationship between "body" and "flesh," he holds that, though "one should not lose sight of the different points of view from which both descriptions regard man in his earthly mode of existence," yet they "are used synonymously in describing the whole man in his temporal bodily existence." "Body," in a usage parallel to that of "soul" and "spirit," refers to man's "concrete mode of existence, coextensive with man himself." Further emphasizing this unitary anthropological perspective, Ridderbos argues that a close examination of Pauline usage reveals that "body" and "flesh" are not thought of as "the external 'constituent part' of man, as the material casing of the real, inner man, but rather denote man himself according to a certain mode of his existence." Moreover, "man does not only 'have' an outward and inward side, but is as man both 'outward' and 'inward'; [man] exists both in the one way and in the other." It is clear, then, that "body" is "not to be thought of detached from man himself, as though it were only the material-sensory organ: man not only 'has' a body, but is a body" (*Paul: An Outline of His Theology*, pp. 115-18).

Accenting the same holist view of man from another point of view, F. H. von Meyenfeldt says,

> Man is every inch "soul"; and "soul" is every inch man. That is to say, the "soul" is not a vague and shadowy something, but the "soul" is the blood and needs the breathing-space of our good earth. It denotes our concrete and emotional earthly existence. ("The Old Testament Meaning of Heart and Soul," in *Toward a Biblical View of Man*, eds. Arnold De Graaff and James H. Olthuis, p. 74)

A dichotomist view of man is accordingly at odds with our life experience set in the light of Scripture. "Body" is not some "animal baggage" carried over from a primitive past. We are not merely "embodied souls" nor "animated corpses." Human nature is not composed of a mundane body, somehow linked with a higher spirit. Rather, all our ways of being human are thoroughly corporeal and at the same time thoroughly spiritual. It is impossible to say where bodily life leaves off and spiritual life starts. For not only driving an automobile and typing a letter are bodily expressions, but dreaming, rational reflections, and creative imaginations also involve bodily impulses. A good belly laugh erupts from inner joy. Salty tears well up from an anguished soul. Lustful thoughts can defile a person as certainly as acts of fornication (Matthew 5:28). Hateful attitudes can kill as surely as bullets and methane gas (Matthew 5:22). A secular-humanist education can destroy life with a finality as real as a hit-and-run driver. All human behavior, in its profoundest depths as well as in the full range of its external manifestations, is everywhere and always fully corporeal and fully spiritual. In the words of Bavinck,

> the nature of the union of soul and body is incomprehensible; but it is more integral than is supposed by the theories of occasionalism, preestablished harmony, or systemic interpretations; it is not moral but substantive; it is so intimate that a single nature, a single I, is the subject of both in all their activities. (*Gereformeerde Dogmatiek*, Vol. II, p. 521)

Gilkey also stresses the integrality of human nature within the Christian perspective, contrasting this with both modern naturalist-secularist views of man and the classic pagan views of the ancient world. This is how he states his case: In the biblical religion

> . . . existence is not seen as split down the middle between a meaningful ordering principle and a meaningless dynamic and material principle. Rather, according to the Christian idea of creation, each finite being in all its aspects was called into existence by God's purposive will. Thus every facet of an entity and every significant factor in man's life is potentially creative, and involved essentially in any real human fulfillment. The divine is no longer related to *one* of the elements of existence, thus reducing the others in value. Rather the divine is the source of *all* aspects of being so that all share in value. . . . Thus, as opposed to the contemporary pagan writers, Christians insisted that the whole man includes body as well as soul, and would be "saved" only within the body and not by its loss. . . . The basic problem of life, therefore, was no longer the achievement of the victory of one factor of man's nature over another. . . . As a result of this

reinterpretation of existence, the unity, the reality, and the meaning of each individual existence is for the first time fully and powerfully affirmed. (*Maker of Heaven and Earth,* pp. 168-69)

Man accordingly is not "partly this" and "partly that" — that is, partly body and partly spirit, as held by dichotomists. Trichotomy only compounds the problem by inserting a third factor, in this case the soul, in order to establish a measure of harmony between the two other hostile factors, spirit and body. No part/part analysis of our humanness rings true to daily experience. Homesickness, which is at bottom an inner disorientation, can have devastating bodily repercussions. Likewise, a toothache can trigger a nagging depression. None of the joys and sorrows of life are ever purely spiritual or purely bodily sensations. This creational reality is being recognized increasingly in the practice of holist medicine. Nor does a part/part analysis of human nature comport with a biblically directed view of man.

Such insights can help in laying to rest once and for all the fruitless dilemmas imposed on us by dichotomous and trichotomous anthropologies. For man is a unity in diversity, not an assemblage of parts. There is an integral wholeness to being human which runs deeper than the sum of our few or many parts. As George E. Ladd says, body, soul, and spirit are "different ways of viewing the whole man" (*A Theology of the New Testament,* p. 457). Traditional bipartite and tripartite anthropologies violate this fundamental oneness of human nature, just as they also fail to do justice to our richly diversified ways of being human. We function in more than two or three, or even four ("heart and soul and mind and strength") ways. Such biblical concepts do not provide categories for partitioning human nature off into compartments. They are rather life-enriching, mysteriously variegated points of view on the whole man.

Whenever this unified perspective gets eclipsed, the life of Christian community suffers deep and lasting scars. Such is the case with the theory of the immortality of the soul. This doctrine contradicts the biblical view of the whole man in his relationship to God, fellowmen, and the cosmos. It is more Greek than Christian. For it presupposes once again an essential antinomy between soul and body. This Hellenist theory, imported into Christian theology, represents an assault on the integrity of our Maker's work in creating the whole man, bodily as well as spiritually, good and upright in his image. For it involves a denigration of the body while suggesting a semideified state for the soul. It advocates the natural mortality of the body and the spiritual immortality of the soul. At stake is not the continuation of human life, but how to account for it. The biblical approach is radically different. For Scripture speaks of eternal life for the whole man, not the survival of an everlasting soul. And it speaks, not of a mortal body and an immortal soul, but of an eschatological restoration of the whole man to resurrected glory. Oscar Cullmann puts it well:

> . . . The Greek doctrine of immortality and the Christian hope in the resurrection differ so radically because Greek thought has such an entirely different interpretation of creation. The Jewish and Christian interpretation of creation excludes the whole Greek dualism of body and soul. . . . For the concepts of body, soul, flesh, and spirit (to name only these), the New Testament does indeed use the same words as the Greek philosophers. But they mean something quite different. . . . The New Testament certainly knows the difference between body and soul, or more precisely, between the inner and outer man. This distinction does not, however, imply opposition, as if one were by nature good, the other by nature bad. Both belong together, both are created by God. The inner man without the outer has no proper, full existence. . . . [Thus] body and soul are both originally good in so far as they are created by God; they are both bad in so far as the deadly power of the flesh has hold of them. ("Immortality of the Soul or Resurrection of the Body? The Witness of the New Testament," in *Christ and Time*, pp. 66-71)

Regin Prenter lends added support to this holist anthropology in his summary statement that "the Biblical words 'soul' (spirit) and 'body' together and separately cover everything which we have described as man's nature." Along the way he states the case as follows:

> Soul is a form for man's whole being, including his body, in fact, one might almost say especially his body. Man's appearance and actions constitute above all else the picture of his soul. The soul is not a formal faculty in man, for instance, the ability to know, to feel, to will. But the soul is man's concrete content, his factual being which expresses itself in everything that he is and says and does. . . . The body therefore is not another part or area in man in addition to the soul. The body or corporality is the peculiar nature of the human soul. The human soul manifests itself in the body.

In referring to the New Testament usage of key anthropological terms, Prenter goes on to say that "Paul is so much of an Israelite in his pattern of thought that the several expressions which he uses for man — body, soul, spirit — do not designate so many parts or substances in man, but the whole man seen from different viewpoints" (*Creation and Redemption*, pp. 272-74).

This integrally coherent view on the unity within diversity which is man can also serve to put an end to the long-standing controversy regarding the origin of the soul. From ancient times onward Christian thinkers were practically unanimous in rejecting the Greek theory of preexistentism. On this view, as adopted by Christians, God in the beginning created, as it were, a storehouse of souls. Throughout history, then, from generation to generation, with the procreation of each new person, God would summon from this preexisting supply of souls one well suited to each newly forming human being and implant it in this body in the making. This view is so highly speculative, so crassly dualist, so foreign to Christian sensitivities, that it never gained a serious following. The conflict centered therefore on two other views, presumably more compatible with the Christian faith. On the one hand, there is the theory known as traducianism. According to traducianists souls as well as bodies are passed on from parents to children in the process of procreation by a kind of division of substances. On this horizontalist, hereditary view of human history, parents impart both soul and body to their children — lending credence to the ancient adage, "like father, like son." Over against this view stands the creationist theory which seeks to explain the origin of the soul by an appeal to an ongoing series of creative acts of God. According to this verticalist view, at some point in the process between conception and birth God intervenes to create a new soul for each new person and implants this soul into the body in the making.

From the second century onward Christian thinkers lined up on both sides of this running controversy. Even in our times the debate continues — until recently, at least, with little prospect of settlement. Traducianism is viewed as man oriented, creationism as God oriented. Traditionally, Lutheranism has leaned toward the former, Catholicism and Calvinism toward the latter. Louis Berkhof, for instance, engages in a lengthy discussion of the many intricate arguments for and against both positions. He concludes that though "the arguments on both sides are well balanced," and many have therefore found it "hard to choose between the two" since scriptural evidence "can hardly be called conclusive on either side," thus making it "necessary to speak with caution on the subject," yet "it seems to us that Creationism deserves the preference . . ." (*Systematic Theology*, pp. 200-201).

Looking back over centuries of heated debate on this issue, perhaps now is an appropriate time to stand back and ask whether indeed there actually are compelling reasons for joining the fray at all, or even for accepting this inherited problem as a legitimate statement on the body-soul issue. As Berkouwer puts it, "must a critique of the older creationism necessarily lead to an acceptance of traducianism? Is the dilemma so stated a real dilemma? Must we choose for one or the other standpoint, with no third possibility open before us?" He with others holds that there is an authentic alternative — a biblically directed holist view of man, in light of which "rejection of the [above] dilemma is not loss but gain." For "given the dualistic conceptions both shared, it was impossible for either to convince the other" — least of all with appeals to Scripture. For there we read of a constitutional wholeness which marks both our origin and our continuing existence, a wholeness which finds its source in the deeply religious relationship of total dependence on the God by whom we are "fearfully and wonderfully made" (Psalm 139:14). "There is no science, and no theology," Berkouwer continues, "which can unveil for us this mystery of man." We must learn to think more bibliologically about who we are. On this score both creationists and traducianists fall short. For together they fail to honor the body-soul unity which marks human life from conception through birth, and onward from the cradle to the grave. A close examination of traducianism reveals that it actually starts from the same presuppositions as creationism. This is apparent from the fact that traducianism, as well as creationism, concentrated on the origin of the soul as a separate entity and thus presupposed, as did its opponent, an ontic duality of body and soul. For in reality, says Berkouwer,

> . . . creationism and traducianism indeed stood in many respects closer together than was once thought. Perhaps it was for just that reason that each found it so difficult to convince the other. They could not find the way to each other's position because they both viewed the problem of the origin of the soul from the same point of view: the origin of the soul as a spiritual substance — which somehow co-exists with the body as an independent material substance. (*Man: The Image of God*, pp. 305, 307)

Dualist views of human nature also create insuperable dilemmas, not to mention needless complications, in addressing the urgent contemporary question of abortion. If one posits a separation of some sort between body and soul, and if furthermore human personality is regarded as unthinkable apart from spiritual existence, then the problem arises, When does the fetus become a person? When is the soul united with the body? During the first trimester, or the second, or the third? We are then left with irresolvable anthropological dilemmas. What is worse, we then stand horrendously guilty before the Giver of human life for wanton violations of the birthright of the unborn. For on a biblical view of man, human life in the integrally coherent unity of its bodily-spiritual wholeness begins embryonically at conception. All rationalizations of abortion on demand, supported by appeals to a disjunction of body (fetus) and soul (personhood), stand condemned as ruthless assaults on a biblically illumined view of human creatureliness. For a divinely bestowed sanctity is insinuated into the total fabric of human life from its sunset years all the way back to its inception.

A key passage in these anthropological discussions is Romans 12:1-2. Reading such passages with bifocal glasses leads to dualist distortions. Donning unifocal glasses, on the other hand, opens up the possibility of a more unified interpretation. Paul speaks there of being "transformed by the renewal of your mind" (that is, soul, spirit), conjoined with the call to "present your bodies as a living sacrifice." This Pauline injunction should not be understood, dualist fashion, as saying that our "soul part" must be transformed and our "body part" sacrificially offered in service to God. Both concepts, "mind" and "body," are holist in their thrust. Body is the outer existential form of the soul, and soul is the inner mode of existence of the body. A better reading of this Romans passage is therefore this: By the inner transformation of our whole personhood let all our bodily expressions be dedicated to such "spiritual worship" as is "holy and acceptable to God." Thus Scripture calls for an inner renewal of the whole man such that it translates into the full-bodied reformation of all our historical activities.

So far our discussion has been confined to our cradle-to-the-grave life span in God's world. This holist view of man offers a liberating lease on life. But how shall we deal with "the last enemy" whom we all face at "threescore years and ten," or sooner, or later? The dualist outlook on temporal death is familiar. On this part/part view one is led to say that our body part dies and is buried, while the soul part departs to be with the Lord. The result is a kind of "escapist" theology. Scripture teaches that "the wages of sin is death" (Romans 6:23). On the dualist view, however, the body ends up bearing the full brunt of this divine death penalty, while the soul escapes the payment of this awesome debt. The lesser part of us dies, while the "real man" is received into glory. This view is clearly burdened with enormous problems and anomalies.

A holist view of man opens up dramatically and distinctively different though not less mysterious perspectives on the meaning of death and dying. Take, for example, the words of Jesus that "he who believes in me, though he die, yet shall he live" (John 11:25). A dualist reading of this passage constrains us to say that we die in part (the body) and continue to live in part (the soul). But this is to impose a preconceived body-soul dichotomy on the text. Jesus, however, says here of the singular "he" (the whole person) that "he" both dies and lives. In light of the *analogia Scripturae,* therefore, with its consistent address to the whole man, these words may be understood as saying that, though a man dies bodily, yet spiritually shall he live. From the viewpoint of bodily life, the whole man dies. All his bodily expressions expire. All his modes of historical existence cease to function. Man no longer sees, feels, thinks, speaks, laughs, or cries. Yet in the very same breath our Lord emphasizes this central point, that spiritually the whole man continues to be alive and well with the Lord.

Such a bibliologically mysterious way of reflecting on our pilgrimage calls for a radical readjustment of our way of thinking about our exodus from this life to the life hereafter. This shift may seem at first blush so shocking as to elicit stiff resistance. After all, the traditional dualist view seems so natural, much easier to grasp, and more rationally explicable. It fits quite neatly into a mathematical formula: One-half body (which dies) and one-half soul (which lives on) equals the whole man. In contrast, the holist view involves mysterious depths and dimensions which defy our powers of rational analysis. Bodily the whole man dies. Spiritually the whole man lives. Thus, stated mathematically, one whole man plus one whole man equals a coterminous one whole man! This bibliological mystery is enough to baffle the best of minds. Yet in the end this holist view can endure the light of Scripture and can stand up to the test of the impinging power of God's Word for creational life better than its alternative. Is it perhaps always so that the truer position is seldom the easier one to grasp and clarify?

Accounting for life experience is one thing. A holist view of man offers more rewarding prospects for biblically attuned, creationally responsible reflections on human life than its dualist counterpart. Death, however, is another story. It remains a conundrum. With the arrival of this alien intruder the anthropological plot thickens. For death literally defies every attempt at a satisfying theoretical analysis. But perhaps this breakdown in rational comprehension should not strike us as strange or unexpected. It should not surprise us that we are so hard-pressed to draw normative conclusions from such an antinormative state of affairs as death. Death is an awful enigma, so much so that, given the deeply entrenched idea of a disjunction between body and soul, reflection on it can lead to radical distortions even by those who use holist language. Take, on the one hand, the materialist who holds that man is nothing but body. His graveside epitaph might be, "This person is *all* dead. . . . There is *nothing* left. . . . Life is *completely* gone. . . . This is the end of *everything*. . . . For the body is *all* there is." Notice that this materialist is using holist language. He is nonetheless dead wrong. For his commentary repudiates the other biblical point of view on the whole story of man. The spiritualist, on the other hand, is guilty of a similar though opposite error in holding that man is basically nothing but soul. His eulogy would go something like this: "The real person lives on. . . . *Nothing* essential has happened. . . . Fundamentally *everything* remains unchanged. . . . *Only* a shell has been left behind. . . . For corporeality has *nothing* to do with who we really are. . . . It is of *no* real value."

Notice that the spiritualist also employs holist terms. But his one-sidedness is equally flawed, for it casts a shadow over the full and real meaning of the resurrection of the body. Both of these commentators are miserable comforters. The biblical language of faith is strikingly different: "Whether *we* live, or whether *we* die, *we* are the Lord's" (Romans 14:7-9). "We" refers here to the wholeness of our many human ways of being. Now "we" live bodily and spiritually; eventually "we" die bodily yet live on spiritually; in the resurrection "we" experience the total renewal of life bodily and spiritually.

II. 10. Man in Community

Human beings are not an aggregate of individuals (the dominant view in the West); nor are we a collective mass (the dominant view in the East). These two social philosophies, individualism and collectivism, with their respective individualist and collectivist anthropologies, represent the two leading ideologies contending for the hearts and lives of people today. Both reflect radical departures from the Judeo-Christian tradition as rooted in the biblical witness to man's place and role in the creation order. For Scripture pictures mankind as a peoplehood. We live as communities in community. By virtue of creation we find the meaning of our lives in a plurality of associations. We participate in a divinely ordained network of life relationships.

Individualist anthropologies proceed on the assumption that human beings are essentially discreet, atomistic, independent personal entities. Individuals are the basic units and building blocks of society. Such a view cannot do justice to the solidarity of the human race, nor to the idea of an organic peoplehood. Societal structures such as marriage, family, nationhood, church, and school are then reduced to secondary and artificial environments which free and sovereign individuals will to create by means of social contracts. Collectivist anthropologies, on the other hand, reduce people to mere cogs in a larger societal mechanism. Human life then has meaning only insofar as it is subsumed under some societal megastructure, such as the Greek polis, the medieval church, or the modern absolutist state. Such superinstitutions as big government, big business, or big labor provide the ordering principles for establishing and maintaining organizational unity within human communities.

As Kuyper already argued so perceptively around the turn of the century, at bottom individualism no less than collectivism displays a decidedly anti-Christian spirit. He therefore vigorously rejected both of these prevailing theories. For both betray the unbiblical stance of the

Enlightenment and the French Revolution. And both thereby defy the good order of creation for our life together in God's world. This led Kuyper to reject both constructs, "that of Popular-sovereignty, as it has been atheistically proclaimed in Paris in 1789; and that of State-sovereignty as it has of late been developed by the historico-pantheistic school of Germany. Both of these theories," he held, "are at heart identical," since both replace the sovereign will of the Creator with some form of human autonomy. In opposing rugged individualism, Kuyper argued that "God might have created men as disconnected individuals; . . . but that was not the case. Man is created from man, and by virtue of his birth he is organically united with the whole race" (*Lectures on Calvinism,* pp. 85, 79). Reflecting on the radical rebellion against historic Christianity which erupted in the eighteenth and nineteenth centuries, Kuyper holds that its "root-principle is its God-provoking 'No God, no master,' or, if you will, humanity emancipated from God and his established order. From this principle there develops not one line, but two." The one violates the creation order by "letting nothing remain but the individual with his own free will and imaginary supremacy." In contradicting this ideology within the context of his native country, Kuyper maintains that

> . . . our national society is, as De Costa said, "not a heap of souls on a piece of ground," but rather a God-willed community, a living, human organism. Not a mechanism put together from separate parts; not a mosaic, as Beets says, inlaid with pieces like a floor; but a body with members, subject to the law of life; that we are members of each other, and thus the eye cannot get along without the foot, nor the foot without the eye. It is this human, this Christian truth which by the French Revolution was most deeply misjudged, most stoutly denied, and most grievously assailed. (*Christianity and the Class Struggle,* pp. 47, 41)

Reinforcing this critique, Dooyeweerd writes:

> According to the divine creation ordinances our temporal social order is not built up from atomistically constructed autonomous individuals. The very birth of every child from the union of a set of parents is incompatible with an individualistic theory. (*Christelijke Perspectief,* no. 1, p. 211)

Kuyper is equally critical of collectivism and its supporting anthropology. In counteracting individualist views of man, collectivism is right in its contention that human communities are not "the sum total of individuals"; for "it has correctly seen that a people is no aggregate, but an organic whole." Yet this second line of Enlightenment development is also destructive of a Christian way of life. For in pursuing it, man is "tempted to push aside not only God and His order, but also, now deifying [himself], to go and sit on God's throne, as the prophet said, and create a new order of things out of [his] own brain" (*Christianity and the Class Struggle*, p. 47).

The biblical alternative to both individualism and collectivism is a pluralist view of communal living. No man is an island. But neither are people mere components in a totalitarian societal system. By virtue of God's good order for creation, human life is integrated into a coherent web of familial, social, political, economic, academic, cultic, and other relationships. We belong to each other in myriads of ways. For "man cannot be truly human apart from others" (Hoekema, *Created in God's Image,* p. 77). In a plurality of "associations in consociation" (Johannes Althusius) we are called to be our "brother's keeper" through neighborly love and service. Our commonly created identity as imagers of God lays an abiding foundation for that human solidarity which undergirds even the brokenness arising from the spiritual antitheses among men. For God himself "gives to all men life and breath and everything," since "He made from one every nation of men to live on all the face of the earth" (Acts 17:25-26). Our universally shared humanity, rooted in creation, constitutes the basis for God's abiding claim on us all. From the beginning we are all his. This divine claim on a created peoplehood also constitutes the abiding basis for the gospel appeal. For in the end God envisions a renewed humanity on a renewed earth. The meaning of personal identity is inextricably linked to the communal relationships which bind us to others. As Dooyeweerd puts it,

> I cannot know myself without taking into account that my ego is related to the ego of my fellowmen. And I cannot really have a personal meeting with another ego without love. It is only by such a meeting in love that I can arrive at true self-knowledge and knowledge of my fellowmen. (*In the Twilight of Western Thought,* p. 178)

Such an understanding of our cohumanity is the biblically animated antidote to all individualist notions of human rights as well as to every form of racial ideology, ethnic arrogance, and national superiority complex. The right of both Someone (God) and someone else (the unborn) is also radically negated by a legal system which defines abortion in individualist terms, as in the case of a teenager's right to be "boss of one's own belly," divorced from familial and communal concerns. The biblical sense of communal responsibility also lays a heavy burden of corporate guilt on communities that assume an attitude of indifference in the face of holocausts and genocides. True solidarity is rooted in God's creation of the original man, the first Adam, and all of us in him. The renewed humanity is rooted furthermore in the last Adam, Jesus Christ. This redemptive perspective on community is reflected in the words of Berkouwer, when he says that . . .

> so deep is this community that it does not arise from men who, having been individually renewed, now seek each other out; it is a peace which is proclaimed and which is actuality in Christ, through the Cross. In this newness, barriers are taken away, as two are made into one. In this community and this peace, the wonderful newness of man's humanness is manifested. . . . [Then] man comes to his true nature, his nature as God intended it to be, a nature in which true community is no longer threatened, in which one man is no longer a danger for the other. (*Man: The Image of God*, pp. 98-99)

Thus, as history moves along, God affirms human community, judges it for its brokenness, and restores it in Christ.

The origins of this creationally given solidarity of the human race go back to the nuclear community established with Adam and Eve. At first Adam was alone ("loneliness" even in Paradise!). The animal kingdom enjoyed its form of communality. But for the man there was no helper and partner. God then put an end to man's individual existence: "It is not good that the man should be alone . . ." (Genesis 2:18). In seminal form all life relationships are embedded in this primal human community. In time these God-given potentialities for differentiated forms of communal life would unfold and come to their own more fully. Barth is right in highlighting the original nuclear human community embodied in the Adam-and-Eve relationship as the prototype of all further communal developments. Commenting on the *imago Dei*, he says that

> . . . by the divine likeness in Genesis 1:27ff there is understood the fact that God created them male and female, corresponding to the fact that God himself exists in relationship *(Deus triunius,* not *Deus solitarius),* not in isolation. . . . The first and typical sphere of fellow-humanity, the first and typical differentiation and relationship between man and man, is [therefore] that between male and female. . . . [For] man never exists as such, but always as the human male and human female. Hence in humanity, and therefore in fellow-humanity, the decisive, fundamental, and typical question, normative for all other relationships, is that of the relationship in this distinction. (*Church Dogmatics,* III/4, no. 54, pp. 116-17)

It is unwarranted on Barth's part, however, to limit the *imago Dei* to such "horizontal," communal relationships, apart from its primary, "vertical" dimension. Kuyper is nearer the truth in holding that our relationships to each other and to the cosmos find their

> . . . starting point in a special interpretation of our relation to God. . . . How we stand toward God is the first, and how we stand toward man is the second principal question which decides the tendency and construction of our life. . . . First looking to God, and then to one's neighbor was the impulse, the mind, and the spiritual custom to which Calvinism gave entrance. . . . [Thus] if Calvinism places our entire human life immediately before God, then it follows that all men and women, rich or poor, weak or strong, dull or talented, as creatures of God, and as lost sinners, have no claim whatsoever to lord it over one another, and that we stand as equals before God, and consequently equal as man to man. Hence we cannot recognize any distinction among men, save such as has been imposed by God himself, in that He gave one authority over the other, or enriched one with more talents than the other, in order that the man of more talents should serve the man with less, and in him serve God. (*Lectures on Calvinism,* pp. 20, 28)

The biblical idea of human community rests on the confession that all peoples live corporately *coram Deo*. Every attempt to forge a plan of organic, organizational solidarity among the inhabitants of our "global village" or "secular city" which is based on strictly horizontal, historical givens carries within itself the seeds of its own destruction. A transcendent openness to the unifying power of God's Word is essential to true human community. As Weber puts it,

> . . . the unity of mankind is rooted in the unity of God as the living, triune unity in which God discloses himself to man. . . . [Therefore] the implementation of the proclamation intended to make "all nations" into disciples (Matthew 28:19) is a declaration of war against all national polytheisms and international pantheisms. The nations receive their honor and dignity, but also their relativization and the abnegation of their religious self-importance through the proclamation of the Son of God, who is the king of Israel. (*Foundations of Dogmatics,* Vol. I, p. 537)

II. 11. Human Freedom as Responsibility and Service

Being a creature means being a servant in God's world. As the Psalmist puts it, "All things are thy servants" (Psalm 119:91). This holds for every creature "after its kind." Responding to God's Word, each plays its unique servant role in the cosmic drama. No creature is mute. Each adds its "joyful noise" to this symphony of praise.

> Let the sea roar, and all that fills it;
> The world and those who dwell in it!
> Let the floods clap their hands,
> Let the hills sing for joy together. . . . (Psalm 98:7-8)

All creatures, great and small, are gifted — whether belonging to the kingdom of plants, animals, or things — each true to its own nature: the lily as a lily, the lion as a lion; likewise the stars, the moon, and the sun ("which in its circuit its Maker obeys"). Those creatures also serve which can only stand and wait, willy-nilly, on the fixed laws of creation, complying without freedom of choice: falling rocks, shooting stars, budding trees, migrating birds, and hibernating animals. These creatures have been entrusted to our care to help make us, as earthkeepers, better servants of our Lord (Genesis 1:29-31; 9:1-3). We, as responsible stewards, are free to domesticate their instincts, cultivate their use, and harness their powers, but always with tender, loving care. For their serving roles are integral to our being and well-being.

Excelling all others, we humans loom large as the most highly endowed of all creatures. We stand in a class by ourselves. A very special service is ours. To us much is given, from us much is also expected. With all our potentials — our rationality, imagination, feeling, culture-forming activity — we are called to play our servant roles in creation. This holds, too, for our structured tasks in society: friendship, marriage, family nurture, education, worship, and governance. They also contribute to the good order of creation. Within that context we are to serve God, our fellowmen, and the cosmos as a whole as free and responsible agents. That is our office. That is what imaging our Maker means and that sets us apart from all other creatures. They do not possess such decision-making freedom. They do not bear responsibility for other creatures. They have no such responsive choice in how to act and react. They behave involuntarily, instinctively, intuitively. Atoms, raindrops, sparks, solar systems, minnows, and polar bears are bound to the ordered laws of creation, the so-called "laws of nature," which dictate their conduct.

How different it is with the norms for human conduct! We are confronted with the issue of normative and antinormative behavior. We are free, even obliged, to make choices. And we are held responsible for them. We are decision-making creatures, for better or for worse (recall Genesis 3! also Joshua 24:15 — ". . . choose this day whom you will serve . . ."). Such freedom of choice reflects the enormous divine "risk" involved in the creation of man. As popular parlance has it, "The bigger they are, the harder they fall." Only a creature of such great proportions could tumble so low. The tremendous weight of human responsibility is further evident in this, that our original choice (in Adam) and our subsequent choices (for example, in ecology) affect all other creatures. By God's covenantal arrangement, we act for them, destructively in the first Adam (Genesis 3:14-19). Yet, happily, in the last Adam "the glorious liberty of the children of God" will signal the renewal of all creatures (cf. Romans 8:19-23).

Ours is not an initiating but a responsive and responsible freedom. We are responsible *to* God and responsible *for* his other creatures, accountable *to* our Maker *for* his cosmos. This understanding of human freedom, grounded in creation and illumined by the Scriptures, is far removed from the modern secularized version of freedom, the pretended autonomy of human reason. For true freedom rests on willing submission to the Word of God, not emancipation from it. Within the lawful and normed context of creation we are free, able, and called to utilize the rich creational resources at our disposal — to discover, but not to destroy them; to employ, but not to exploit them. We are at liberty to fulfill our cultural mandate in architecture and farming, in mechanics and journalism, in family nurture and statesmanship, in personal relationships and in communal associations. The abiding framework for human freedom is faith in God, love toward our neighbors, and care for the earth. This biblical perspective excludes the so-called freedom of contrary choice, as though man is fully free only when he is equally disposed toward good and evil, as though he possesses an open choice between right and wrong. Such freedom has never existed, not even in Adam, and certainly not since then. A presumed freedom of contrary choice is foreign to God's good creation. For to choose evil is not freedom but bondage. By divine design we are never free to disobey. Obedience to God's Word is the only open door to a liberated and liberating life.

II. 12. Human Rights

The biblical doctrine of creation stands as the original and abiding charter of human rights. One searches the Scriptures in vain, of course, for an explicit address to human rights issues in the complex ways we face them today in our highly industrialized, technological societies. This recognition reminds us once again of the kind of book the Bible is. It is a redemptive republication in lingual form of God's original and abiding revelation in creation. Despite our terribly mixed responses to it, that fundamental revelation has lost none of its reality. It is still fully in force.

In deciding on the meaning of human rights it holds for us today as authoritatively and normatively as for all past and future generations. To counteract the effects of sin, however, and to reopen for us the true meaning of that creational Word, we must now don the "spectacles" of Scripture. For its message is the liberating rearticulation of God's original and abiding Word on human rights. Though its disclosure of God's will for righteousness, justice, and peace in human affairs is set within the historical-redemptive framework of Israel's pilgrimage and the emergence of the early church, though its norms are couched in the various literary forms of sixty-six books composed over many centuries, and though this "library of books" comes down to us from two thousand years ago and (for many of us) half a world away, nevertheless its directives continue to lay their transhistorical, transcultural claim on us with undiminished urgency in addressing the perennial problem of human rights.

In light of past and current history, the thesis appears incontestable that the most universal thing about the so-called universal human rights (as formulated, for example, in the "Universal Declaration of Human Rights" by the United Nations in 1948) is their almost universal violation. How fundamental is the right to life? The right to work? The right to peaceable family life? The right to just treatment under law? The right to participate equitably in the political process? The right to a fair share in the bounties of creation? The right to voluntary association? The right to freedom of worship? The right to religious liberty in the public arena? These are not primarily social-economic-political issues. They raise very profound anthropological questions. At bottom the biblical view of man is at stake. Human rights issues touch on the life of the whole person and on the livelihood of entire human communities. They are as holist as the biblical ideas of man as image of God, man in office, and man as heart and body and soul. A biblically directed anthropology calls into question the ideology of dominance and dependence in which one "world" is subjected to the greater power of another "world." It stands in judgment on Roman Catholic inquisitions, Protestant power plays, Black slavery, anti-Semitism, racial discrimination, ethnic arrogance, capitalist imperialism, communist aggression, terrorist activities, and gangland warfare. The biblical view of man, grounded in the the creation order, is the divine standard for weighing these and other human rights issues.

That is the standard by which we are called to honor the universal claims of God's Word on us to "do justice, and to love mercy, and to walk humbly with your God" (Micah 6:8). Our ("vertical") relationship of response to God is ultimate and all-encompassing. It is definitive of all our ("horizontal") relationships to our fellowmen. Loving God above all and wholeheartedly, which is "the first and great commandment," gives meaning and direction to "the second commandment, like it," which is to "love your neighbor as yourself" (Matthew 22:39). But who are our neighbors? To that question Jesus gives an unambiguous answer (Luke 10:27-37) — all who in God's providence cross our paths and need our help. Every human-historical ("horizontal") moment in our lives is laden with a divine ("vertical") mandate. Accordingly, every human rights issue is inseparably bound up with our responsibility to our Maker. God's covenantal Word is the constant normative reference point for gaining insight into what our duty toward our fellowmen means, and what claims they may rightfully make on us. Thus Scripture lifts our sights far above humanist appeals to "the brotherhood of all men" and secular appeals to the destiny of the historical process. God's law is the norm for safeguarding human rights. In renewing, deepening, and enriching our sensitivities to rightful relationships among people, Scripture opens up a three-dimensional perspective, namely: 1) our responsibility toward others, 2) their responsibility toward us, and 3) both of these relationships subsumed under our joint responsibility to God. Stated differently, Scripture reinforces 1) the rightful claims of others on us, 2) our rightful claims on them, with 3) all human rights claims subservient to God's comprehensive claim on us all. In this light we see that human rights are always qualified by human duties, responsibilities, obligations, and mandates, no less than by human freedoms and mutual claims. Within this perspective, all men have the creationally funded right to be imagers of God, to exercise their God-given offices, to pursue the cultural mandate, and to share equitably as good stewards in the rich resources of God's good earth.

This three-dimensional biblical worldview deflates the arrogant notion that to practice righteousness in human relationships is a work of charity deserving of meritorious acclaim. Advocacy of human rights is not an act of goodwill or generosity. It is a matter of simple justice which others may unapologetically lay at our doorstep, and we at theirs. For, having done "all that is commanded," we are still "unworthy servants" who have "only done what was our duty" (Luke 17:7-10). Moreover, the biblical injunction to deal rightly with our fellowmen is not grounded on some natural and inalienable humanitarian quality of dignity and nobility which supposedly resides inherently in mankind. This modern humanist theory of human rights secularizes the biblical view of man by eclipsing the fundamental Godward ("vertical") dimension of all creaturely existence. Divine imperative alone constitutes the firm foundation for the implementation of human rights. Indeed, "the poor and the needy" are always with us (Matthew 26:11). This statement by our Lord is, however, a description, not a prescription. It is therefore not an excuse for quietism but a call for societal reformation. "I command you," says the Lord, that "you shall open wide your hand to your brother, to the needy and to the poor in the land" (Deuteronomy 15:11). This is a matter of righteousness, not charity. It is based not on some alleged human goodness but on a divine command.

Furthermore, the promotion of human rights is not dependent on an assessment of what some people deserve compared to others, but once again on the demands of God's Word. For such comparisons are usually hypocritical, often badly misdirected, and almost always injurious of others. When Scripture declares that God "maintains the right" of the oppressed, it is not passing judgment on their superior moral worth or value. God is rather defending their "cause." Whatever their state, doing righteousness to others is based, not on human merit, but on God's revealed Will. Nor may we, finally, exonerate ourselves from the call to help right the hurts of wronged people by disclaiming guilt for their plight. Human rights appeals are not rooted in an implied blame which some bear for their condition. Was, for example, the Good Samaritan any more at fault for the calamity which befell the Jericho traveler than the priest or Levite? The abiding basis for the God-given rights of human beings lies not in the subjective judgment of some people about others, but in the abiding claim of God's comprehensive love command on us all.

Human rights cannot be projected into the future as teleological goals toward which creation is moving, whose realization is the anticipated climax of an eschatological process — as held by futurist theologians. Jürgen Moltmann, for example, affirms repeatedly that "being created in the image of God is the basis of human rights." Yet, this biblical idea is consistently referred to, not as man's original *state*, but as his "original *destiny*." On this view, man's createdness and his sinfulness function as original, existential givens. The real story of the recovery of "the image of God as destiny," on which human rights is based, begins with "the liberation of Israel from slavery in Egypt, the covenant of the liberating God with the liberated community. . . ." Moltmann's theology of human rights clearly incorporates the basic elements of the biblical story line (creation, sin, redemption, consummation). They all get convoluted, however, into the dialectical mold of a process theology emerging from an indefinable past and moving toward a future norm. As Moltmann states it:

> The universal purpose of Israel's and Christianity's particular experience of God is found in the reality that the God who liberates and redeems them is the *fulfiller* of the history of the world, who will bring his claim upon his creation to realization in his kingdom. Thus his liberating and redeeming action in history reveals the true future of human beings; the image of God

is their true future. In all their relationships in life [human beings] have a "right" to a future. . . . [Thus] the political recognition and pursuit of human rights ultimately gain their significance in this perspective of the future. Human beings become free and affirm their rights and duties as their true and eternal future gains power over them in hope, and conditions their present. ("Theological Basis of Human Rights," pp. 8-13)

At this point a host of questions arise. Before God, and in good conscience, can we ask the suffering millions in our world to wait for the arrival of that open-ended future? Does not God's claim to rightful dealings among men rest on us abidingly from the beginning? And if we eclipse the normed righteousness of that beginning, is there any hope of recovering it in the end? Losing sight of the creation order, are we then not also condemned to losing our hold on a rightly ordered eschatological hope? Does not Scripture represent the consummation of all things as the restoration of the full potentials of what God declared "very good" in the beginning? May we expect the future to add anything essentially new over and beyond what was originally given with the right order of creation? Does not the paradigm of world history delineated by futurist theologians such as Moltmann involve a radical inversion of the biblical worldview?

If a dialectical tension between good and evil is collapsed back into the original framework of creation, how then shall we come to terms with the biblical teaching of sin as freely enacted defiance of the Word of God? If the creation was fundamentally flawed from the very beginning, is the call to personal societal reformation still credible? If sin is a necessary and essential ingredient in our creatureliness, can we still be held accountable for human rights violations? Are we then not compelled to embrace oppression as an inevitable ally rather than as an enemy to be overcome? Does this view not lead to a fatalistic resignation to injustice, rather than a deeply biblical commitment to reformation? Can such a process theology offer more than an ever receding utopian dream?

In response to this flood of questions, Scripture points to norms for human rights securely anchored in the good order of creation. They cannot be shifted with impunity to an open-ended eschatological future arching back on the present. The historic Christian view on human rights is therefore shaped by the biblical story line of creation, fall, and redemption, on the way to the consummation. While these rights are now christologically directed toward their final fulfillment on the new earth "in which righteousness dwells," their norms function here and now already as divine claims which from the beginning rest abidingly on us all. This demands a passionate advocacy of human rights, a "hungering and thirsting for righteousness" (Matthew 5:6). We must work to make our societal orders answer obediently to the creational order for rightfully structured human relationships. In the measure that we begin to catch this vision, the right of one becomes the duty of another, and the duty of one becomes the right of another (cf. *Reformed Ecumenical Synod Testimony on Human Rights,* pp. 94-125, esp. pp. 96-101).

II. 13. Cultural Mandate

The first recorded Word of God addressed to mankind (Genesis 1:28-30) has come to be known as the cultural mandate. Within the unfolding drama of the Genesis narratives it assumes the form of a *creatio tertia*. *Creatio prima* refers to God's primordial act of creating the universe out of nothing. This is followed by God's ordering process, called *creatio secunda*. Then, as a tertiary, ongoing phase in the life of creation, God mandates mankind, as his "junior partners," to join him as coworkers in carrying on the work of the world. The original creation was good, but not yet perfect. It stood poised at the threshold of its historical development. God's creating work was finished. Nothing good was lacking. Both structurally and directionally, everything was in a state of readiness, laden with potentiality. All these very promising potentials were eagerly awaiting their intended realization. To this end God enlists the services of his imagers, male and female, as his coworkers. Made in the divine likeness, we are called to exercise our office by continuing his work in the midst of his world. This original mandate still stands as a direction-setting cultural signpost along the roadway of world history.

Clearly the God of Genesis is not like the gods of Greek mythology who, dwelling in ethereal aloofness, jealously guarded their self-serving remoteness from earthly affairs. The God of Scripture is the "great Worker." He is more than willing to "get his hands dirty" with mundane things. But he also stands ready to delegate responsibility. This is where our cultural mandate comes in — the call to image God's work for the world by taking up our work in the world. By sovereign design, the Garden was destined to become a City. To this end our Maker issues mandates designed to elicit the talents of all God's richly gifted people. In Genesis this cultural mandate, refracted into a resplendent array of mandates, is described in agrarian, pastoral terms appropriate to the culture of its original readers. But it is no less normative for a highly scientific, industrialized, technological, computerized society such as ours. Such a hermeneutic reflects the unique book the Bible is. In our obedient responses to this cultural mandate — therein lies our blessing, our delight, our deep sense of satisfaction and service. In elucidating this cultural mandate, Scripture speaks of exercising "dominion" over the earth and "subduing" it. Too often these words have been cited as excuses for wantonly plundering the creational resources of land and sky and sea. Wrongly so, however, for ours is a subservient authority, to be expressed in earthkeeping and caretaking. We are not to be greedy potentates, but faithful stewards of God's good earth, treating other creatures with tender concern as we seek to meet our appointed needs.

We are thus creatures made to whistle spontaneously while we work — free of the curse of sin, of chronic unemployment, of environmental exploitation, of workaholic enslavement, and of an obsessive craving for retirement. Free to image God in our daily tasks. Freed, too, from that false piety which seeks to negate the world for the sake of a higher spiritual experience. Free to delight in our cultural mandate. Would to God it were still so! It can be so now already! And one day it will be so again, perfectly!

II. 14. Covenant/Kingdom

There are many entryways into that house called Reformed dogmatics — front doors, back doors, side doors. Each doorway gives access to the many rooms inside. At the moment we are spending time in that room called anthropology. We have already examined the contents of this room from several points of view. We turn now to its very centerpiece, the biblical teachings on covenant/kingdom. The dual idea of covenant/kingdom is not an occasional theme scattered randomly across the pages of Scripture. It pulsates with the very heartbeat of all biblical revelation. It is the very matrix and enduring context of our life in God's world. By his royal/covenantal Word for creation the triune God makes us his covenant partners and citizens of his kingdom. Though the ideas of covenant and kingdom are distinguishable for purposes of theological analysis, they are never actually distinct. We can perhaps think them apart for the sake of greater clarity. But we never experience them separately. Before dealing with covenant/kingdom as distinguishable realities, let us consider them first in their unity.

A. The Bi-unity of Covenant-and-Kingdom

The biblical idea of covenant-and-kingdom is a bi-unitary index to the meaning of creation. In this two-in-one approach God comes out to us, sovereignly and engagingly, relating himself concretely to our life in the world. Covenant-and-kingdom are therefore not two independent themes. They are more like the two sides of a single coin. What holds for the one also holds for the other. They share the same starting point. They are alike in their depth of meaning and coterminous in their cosmic scope. They pursue a concurrent course through world history. Together they are moving forward toward a common eschatological goal. We therefore note with Ridderbos "how closely the ideas of covenant and kingdom are related." For "in the coming of the kingdom God reveals himself primarily as Creator and King, who does not abandon the world to the powers of destruction, and as Preserver and Guarantor of his people, to whom he has solemnly bound himself unto salvation" (*The Coming of the Kingdom,* pp. 38-39). In the covenant the Creator reveals himself primarily as Father, in the kingdom as Lord. This bi-unitary theme also comes to clear expression in the following lines from Meredith Kline:

> God's covenant with man may be defined as an administration of God's lordship, consecrating a people to himself under sanctions of divine law. In more general terms, it is a sovereign administration of the kingdom of God. Covenant administration is kingdom administration. The [covenant] treaties are the legal instruments by which God's kingship is exercised over his creatures. (*By Oath Consigned,* p. 36)

Given this unbreakable coherence between covenant-and-kingdom, how shall we distinguish them as two confluent ways of understanding the Creator-creature relationship? Perhaps we can put it this way: Covenant suggests the idea of an abiding *charter,* while kingdom suggests the idea of an ongoing *program.* Covenant is more *foundation* oriented; kingdom is more *goal* oriented. Covenant may thus be conceived of as kingdom looking back to its origins, but with abiding significance. Kingdom may then be conceived of as covenant looking forward with gathering momentum toward its final fulfillment. Thus nuanced, covenant and kingdom are interchangeable realities. They have a common Origin. They cover the same ground. They involve the same people, whether viewed as covenant people or kingdom citizens. Accordingly, all history may be defined as either covenant history or kingdom history. In the Old Testament God binds himself to his people both as *Yahweh* (the faithful, covenant-keeping God) and as *Adonai* (the sovereign Lord). Likewise in the New Testament God reveals himself in Christ both as *Pater* (Father) and as *Kyrios* (Lord). This bi-unity is so intimate that we may say, In the beginning God covenanted his kingdom into existence. Conversely, we may also say, With royal authority God proclaims his covenantal claim on his creatures.

Covenant and kingdom are accordingly not *structural* realities standing over against or beyond or alongside the structured realities of creation. They are *direction*-setting realities. They point the direction for childlike faithfulness and obedient servanthood within the good orders of creation. Given our fall into sin, they now serve as the *redirecting* power which operates redeemingly within the structures of the fallen creature — just as the qualifier "Christian" indicates a renewed directional orientation in family living, education, doing politics, or running a business. What Ridderbos says about the "kingdom of heaven" being "at hand" also applies to the covenant. The kingdom should not be thought of as "a spatial or static entity, which is descending from heaven; but rather as the divine kingly rule actually and effectively starting its operation, . . . as the divine action of the king" (*The Coming of the Kingdom*, p. 25). The covenant is similarly a dynamic reality.

B. The Everlasting Covenant

Theological reflection on the biblical idea of covenant yields a rich harvest of helpful insights. Note the following six theses.

1. All God's dealings with creation are covenantal in character. Our life in God's world is set within a pervasively covenantal context. To be a creature is to have a covenantally defined place to be and role to play within the cosmos. At the heart of covenant is the divine promise *(Wort)* and the appropriate human response *(Antwort)*: I am your God, you be my people. The entire created order is anchored securely in God's mediating covenantal Word, by which he called the world into existence, by which he also continually calls it (back) to order. This lends a solid constancy, even a certain predictability, to the affairs of daily experience:

> While the earth remains, seedtime and harvest, cold and heat, summer and winter, day and night, shall not cease. . . . [For] I establish my covenant with you . . . [so that] when the bow is in the clouds, I will look upon it and remember the everlasting covenant between God and every living creature of all flesh that is upon the earth. (Genesis 8:22; 9:11, 16)

In a different setting Paul adds this stern reminder of the covenantal constancy of God's way with the world: "Do not be deceived; God is not mocked, for whatever a man sows, that he will also reap" (Galatians 6:7). There are therefore realities in life on which we can count with certainty, and for which we can also give an account. We are not delivered over to arbitrary surprises. The biblical worldview is not governed by capricious voluntarism. So we can go our way in the sure knowledge that God holds himself to his covenant Word and holds us to it as well.

Fundamentally, therefore, we all get out of life what we want most from it — covenant-keeping blessing or the curse of covenant breaking. This alternative is given already with God's primeval covenanting declaration: Serve me, or else . . . (Genesis 2:15-17). We know now what the universal outcome was: "But like Adam they [Israel] transgressed the covenant . . ." (Hosea 6:7).

2. The covenant is rooted in God's work of creation. God covenanted his world into existence. Covenantal relationships are given in, with, and for all created reality. From the beginning creation is unthinkable apart from its covenantal relationship of dependence and responsiveness *coram Deo*. Though the word "covenant" *(berith)* does not appear in the creation account (Genesis 1, 2), the basic elements of classic covenant making are clearly present. They are evident in (a) the preamble with its prologue, introducing the Sovereign in his relationship to the second party, (b) the promises and obligations which define the community established by the covenantal pact, and (c) the blessing-and-curse formula, with its stated condition for fidelity and its stated penalty for infidelity (cf. D. J. McCarthy, *Old Testament Covenant,* pp. 1-10). This creationally based understanding of covenant reflects the traditional Reformed outlook.

Of late, however, this view is being challenged. The beginnings of covenant are being shifted from Adam as the original covenant head of the human race to the time of Noah and/or Abraham. Proponents of this latter-day view of covenant making acknowledge that from the beginning God did sustain a special relationship to his creation. This relationship is left largely undefined, however, which then raises the questions: If Adam was not the covenant head of mankind, what then was the nature of his headship? And if it was not a covenant he broke, how then shall we describe the relationship which he broke? Support for such late-dating views on the beginning of covenant making relies largely on an argument from silence — the absence of an explicit reference to the Hebrew word for "covenant" *(berith)* in the early Genesis narratives. Critics point instead to its initial usage in the text of the Noah (Genesis 6–9) and Abraham (Genesis 12ff.) accounts. Meredith Kline touches on this argument by quoting Eichrodt to the effect that "the crucial point is not — as an all too naive criticism sometimes seems to think — the occurrence or absence of the Hebrew word *berith,*" since "the latter is 'only the code-word' for something more far-reaching than the word itself" *(By Oath Consigned,* p. 27).

Advocates of the newer view hold that "oath-bound swearing," a feature of later covenant making, is an essential aspect of all covenants. They then point to its absence in the creation context as a decisive argument. But is this not a case of reading a more explicit feature of later redemptive covenant renewals back into the preredemptive covenant given with creation? This covenantal deconstruction of Genesis 1–3 appears, moreover, to undermine Paul's teaching concerning the "two Adams" in Romans 5. It runs the risk, moreover, of shifting the norm for biblical interpretation from the *analogia Scripturae* to an exaggerated reliance on extrabiblical archeological sources (for example, the Hittite "suzerainty treaties"). It also disrupts the close biblical connection between creation and redemption by reducing the idea of covenant to an exclusively salvific reality. One is then hard-pressed to avoid a dualist worldview, structured along nature-creation/grace-covenant lines. This approach also lends support to the current tendency to find in the early Genesis record increasingly fewer matters of substantial importance for the faith-life and theology of the Christian community (for example, aversion to the idea of creation out of nothing, creation order, sabbath, and now covenant). It seriously interrupts the flow of covenant-kingdom continuity as a unifying theme running throughout biblical revelation. Contrastingly, therefore, Scripture still warrants the conclusion that God's "new beginnings" with Noah, Abraham, Moses, and David represent successive renewals of the single covenant, reclaimed after the fall, but given originally and once for all time with creation.

In a very telling passage the prophet Jeremiah reassures the captive Hebrews of God's covenant faithfulness by appealing to the creation order. He draws a parallel between the creational and redemptive perspectives on the covenant. The trustworthiness of the latter is confirmed by that of the former. This is his message:

> Thus says the LORD: If you can break my covenant with the day and my covenant with the night, so that day and night will not come at their appointed time, then also my covenant with David my servant may be broken. . . . If I have not established my covenant with day and night and the ordinances of heaven and earth, then I will reject the descendants of Jacob and David my servant. . . . (33:20-21, 25-26)

Commenting on this passage, Calvin notes that the prophet here introduces a "similitude."

> For he shows that God's covenant with the people of Israel would not be less firm than the settled order of nature, . . . no less fixed and unchangeable than what it is with mankind with regard to the government of the world. . . . For I am the same God who created the heaven and the earth, who fixed the laws of nature which remain unchangeable, and who have also made a covenant with my church. (*Commentary on Jeremiah*, pp. 261, 266)

The clear thrust of this Jeremiah passage is further echoed in the comments of G. C. Aalders. He states that God's faithfulness to the Davidic kingship and the Levitical priesthood is

> . . . here confirmed by pointing to the order of nature: both are as certain of their continuity as the succession of day and night. . . . By pointing to the constancy of day and night as God's *covenant* with the day and the night, [the prophet] accentuates the inviolability of this divine arrangement. There is, as it were, a binding agreement made by God with the day and with the night. (*Jeremia,* Vol. II, in "Korte Verklaring," pp. 118-19)

We may therefore conclude with Kline that

> The mere absence of the word "covenant" from Genesis 1 and 2 does not hinder a systematic formulation of the material of these chapters in covenantal terms, just as the absence of the word "covenant" from the redemptive revelation in the latter part of Genesis 3 does not prevent systematic theology from analyzing that passage as the earliest disclosure of the "Covenant of Grace." Obviously the reality denoted by a word may be found in biblical contexts from which that word is absent. So it is in the present case. For the divine administration to Adam at the beginning corresponds fully with the law type of covenant as it appears in the later history. In fact, the biblical theologian discovers that the standard features of ancient law-covenant treaties and administration make most satisfactory categories for the comprehensive analysis of the pertinent data of Genesis 1 and 2. . . . There are other biblical perspectives favorable to the formulation of the creation order as covenantal. The postdiluvian ordering of the world revealed in the divine disclosures to Noah (Gen. 8:21–9:17) was in effect a reinstituting of original creation arrangements, and it is designated a "covenant." . . . The close, broad, and basic correspondence between this later order, specifically called a "covenant," and the original order founded by God's work of creation favors a covenantal construction of the latter. . . . Evidently Isaiah (in ch. 43) regarded the Creator's establishment of his kingship over man at the beginning as a prototype of his later covenant making with Israel. Certainly the major elements of the law-covenant structure are present in God's administration of his sovereignty over Adam in Eden. . . . Failure to develop the concept of the preredemptive covenant as the foundation for redemptive covenant administration will, it may be added, deprive dogmatics of the conceptual apparatus required for a satisfactory synthesis of the work of Christ and the redemptive covenant. (*By Oath Consigned,* pp. 26-29)

In further support of this classic Reformed covenantal theology,

O. Palmer Robertson argues that "by the very act of creating man in his own likeness and image, God established a unique relationship between himself and creation." This special relationship is based not only on his "sovereign creation-act," but also on the fact that "God spoke to men." Thus, "through this creating/speaking relationship, God established sovereignly a life-and-death bond. This original bond between God and man may be called the covenant of creation." In the measure that we diminish this original and abiding covenantal reality, we incur serious loss. For "by thinking too narrowly about the covenant of creation, the Christian church has come to cultivate a deficiency in its entire world-and-life view. Instead of being kingdom-oriented, as was Christ, we become exclusively church-oriented" (*The Christ of the Covenants*, pp. 67-68).

The view of Kline, Robertson, and others echoes the position taken earlier in this century by the ever timely theology of Bavinck, who comments as follows:

> Even though the word "covenant" may never appear in Scripture to describe the religious relationship of Adam to God, not even in Hosea 6:7, nevertheless the religious life of man before the fall still bears the marks of a covenant. Reformed people were never so narrow-minded as to insist on the word, if only the matter itself stood firm. . . . Usually, however, resistance to the word disguised resistance to the idea itself. But we neither can nor may abandon this point, since covenant is the essence of true religion. . . . [For] when religion is called a covenant, then it is thereby designated as true and real religion. No other religion has ever understood this: all peoples either pull God down pantheistically into created reality or elevate him deistically high above creation. In neither case does it result in true fellowship, true covenant, true religion. Scripture, however, maintains both truths: God is infinitely great and condescendingly good. He is the Sovereign, but also Father. He is Creator, but also archetype. In a word, he is the God of the covenant. . . . This characterizes religion before as well as after the fall. For religion is singular, just as the moral law and the destiny of man. The covenant of works and of grace do not differ in their final goal, but only in the way which leads to it. In both there is but one mediator, then for communion, now for reconciliation. . . . [True] religion is always essentially the same; it only differs in form. (*Gereformeerde Dogmatiek*, Vol. II, pp. 530-32)

True religion therefore centers covenantally on the mediating Word of God, spoken in creation, inscripturated in the Bible, and incarnate in Jesus Christ.

3. The covenant is one-sided (monopleuric, unilateral) in its origin, and two-sided (dipleuric, bilateral) in its continuation. The Creator God

acted out of sovereign initiative in establishing his covenant with his creatures. It is therefore not a fifty-fifty arrangement, a contract between equal partners, with each coming halfway, meeting in the middle, and negotiating mutually agreeable terms. Rather, God came out to us con-creationally in his covenant Word to meet us where we are and to draw us into a bond of fellowship with himself. He made the first move, and continues to do so. That is how it all began. God spoke the first Word. And he reserves the last Word too.

Along the way, however, once the covenant is inaugurated, from then on it functions bilaterally. We as human beings are now called irresistibly to play our decisive roles. We are summoned to responsible partnership, with God as "Senior Partner" and we as "junior partners." The covenant serves as a two-way street, with movement in the traffic of covenantal communion and communication flowing freely in both directions. God "carries the contract," not we, for it is his doing. But we are to "keep in contact" with him. In the beginning that is how it was, that is how it is still meant to be, and that is the way it will one day again become.

4. From beginning to end covenant history reveals a basic continuity. God remains ever true to his good beginnings. He never withdraws his covenantal claim on his creatures. From his side the covenant remains unbroken. Repeatedly God steps in to counteract the perennial effects of sin on the world. In grace he comes back again and again to renew the covenant. The biblical story line discloses a series of "new beginnings," the unfolding phases in the single plan of God's covenantal dealings with mankind. We meet God announcing the *protevangelium* to our first parents, cleansing the earth in the days of Noah, calling forth a chosen people in Abraham, creating a new nation under Moses, reclaiming the promised land under Joshua, founding the monarchy under David, keeping alive a Messianic line through the tangled histories of Israel and Judah, and leading back a remnant from captivity. Then in the fullness of the times Christ appeared as the last Adam, the Head of the renewed covenant community, proclaiming the "new covenant in my blood." This long series of "new" covenants spanning the ages is at bottom a single covenant repeatedly "renewed."

5. All men are either covenant keepers or covenant breakers. In Adam we died under the curse of the broken covenant. In Christ we are restored to covenant partnership and fellowship. This is "already" so in principle. It is "not yet" so in perfection. For the reality of the covenant promise still beckons us onward as an eschatological hope. Yet even in its future consummation the covenant is still a reaching back to reaffirm its very beginning, to gather up its movement through history, and thus to restore us and our world to that covenant fellowship which God originally ordained for the creation.

6. Covenant is a full-bodied way of life which we are called to live before the face of God and in the midst of his world. Already in the Garden it was sacramentally sealed in the sign of that very special tree of life. But it pointed beyond the observance of that symbol. It involved more, too, than "walking with God in the cool of the day." It encompassed the full scope of man's cultural mandate. The prophets declared tirelessly that covenantal living involved more than adherence to the cultic rites. Doing justice, loving mercy, caring for the poor and needy, and remembering jubilee were all ways of walking humbly with the God of the covenant. So, too, in our New Testament era, covenant keeping extends beyond commemorating the sacramental signs and seals of baptism and the Lord's Supper. It envisions covenant partnerships, with God and with others, in business, farming, politics, and labor, as well as covenantal nurture in home, church, and school. For keeping covenant is a full-fledged way of life. Illumined by Scripture, rooted in creation, it encompasses the full range of our life relationships and activities.

C. *The Coming Kingdom*

In the beginning God created . . . his kingdom! He covenanted his kingdom into place. The concept "the heavens and the earth" encompasses the whole of creation. It is universal in scope, embracing creatures great and small. It takes such cosmic dimensions to circumscribe the parameters of the kingdom of God. For the kingdom is the entire realm over which God rules — with the Father as Initiator, the Son as Mediator, and the life-giving dynamic of the Spirit moving across the face of creation. Thus the biblical idea of kingdom sets our sights on the Creator as the good and wise Ruler of all things, on the loving nature of his reign, and on the realm over which his kingly authority extends. All creatures are God's regal servants.

This royal vision challenges us on at least two counts. First, as modern people, we find such totalitarian claims intimidating, even menacing. Nothing could be more undemocratic. We pride ourselves in belonging to a "free world." We live under republican forms of government. We elect our own rulers. Every egalitarian impulse within us reacts violently against the biblical idea of divine monarchy. So how do we handle it? Often we adopt a hermeneutic of accommodation, domesticating the doctrine of divine sovereignty to suit our notions of popular sovereignty. Just as contemporary kings and queens "reign" but do not "rule," just as they serve as traditional, nostalgic symbols of the past, as mere figureheads of national life but not as chiefs of state — so, too, with God. We try to cut his omnipotence down to manageable size. The

ngdom of God is, of course, an anthropomorphic and
pt: it speaks of a transhistorical reality in very down-to-
terms. Nevertheless it carries with it more transcendent weight and
substance than many of our modern democratic notions can tolerate.

Second, the biblical idea of the kingdom of God challenges the
tendency of many evangelical Christians to reduce his reign to very
personal proportions. Many confine the rule of God to "the hearts and
lives" of believers. Such truncated notions of the kingdom also fail the
test of Scripture. The Psalms, like all Scripture, are replete with unambiguous references to God's sovereign rule over all created reality. "The
mighty One, God the LORD, speaks and summons the earth from the
rising of the sun to its setting. . . . For every beast of the forest is mine,"
he says, "the cattle on a thousand hills" (Psalm 50:1, 10). Turning to
another sphere of life, a similar note is struck in Proverbs 8:15-16: "By
me kings reign, and rulers decree what is just; by me princes rule, and
nobles govern the earth." Little wonder that Handel's "Messiah" should
rise to a mighty crescendo in extolling God as "Lord of lords, and King
of kings forever and ever." The kingdom of God is on public display.
This should put an end to whatever privatizing inclinations are left in
us. Kingdom commitment settles not only questions of personal devo-
tions, church attendance, and favorite hymns, but also questions of
life-style, educational choices, career decisions, organizations we join,
and causes we support. Kingdom business is never an after-hours avoca-
tion. It is a total agenda. The distinction between full-time and part-time
kingdom workers is therefore utterly fallacious. Our entire life in God's
world is called to be kingdom service. The kingdom is indeed "not of
this world." That was true when Jesus spoke these words (John 18:36).
It is still true today, and it has been true from the beginning. The world
could no more establish itself as the kingdom of God than it could create
itself. The kingdom is "from above." It is nonetheless "in" the world,
integral to our life in the world. It can therefore be said that nothing
matters but the kingdom, but because of the kingdom everything matters.

Kingdom defines our place and task in the world. This is clearly
reflected in the kingly aspect of our threefold office. We are servants (Old
Testament) and citizens (New Testament) in the kingdom of God.
Throughout Scripture kingdom ideas are familiar household terms among
the people of God. They also find their echo in the thought and life of
the Christian community down through the centuries, though not always
as prominently as in Scripture. Other motifs, such as the salvation of
souls, the church, mission, and personal piety, sometimes eclipse the
kingdom perspective. This has also happened in the Reformed tradition.
As Ridderbos puts it,

As far as the tradition of Reformed theology is concerned, one may observe that in it the church has occupied a more central position than the kingdom of God. In the Reformed confessions the kingdom of God is not treated with great comprehensiveness; nor can we say that it occupies a dominating place in the structure of these confessions. . . . The central significance which the kingdom of God has, for example, in the preaching of Jesus is [not] shown to full advantage here and in the Catechism as a whole. Other motifs govern the structure of these Reformed confessions.

But with the neo-Calvinist resurgence around the turn of this century, a change set in. For "in the revival of Reformed theology, particularly in such authors as Kuyper and Bavinck, the idea of the kingdom of God occupies a more central position." Counteracting the liberalist supremacy of the nineteenth century, Ridderbos continues by saying that

. . . with the intuition of genius and a mighty faith [Kuyper] grasped for the idea of the kingdom of God, and so came to the famous declaration that "there is not an inch in the whole of the broad terrain of human life to which Christ does not lay claim." As far as the heart of the matter is concerned, Kuyper could find affiliation with Calvin, for whom also surely not only the soul, nor only the church, but public life as well is the place where the kingship of Christ must be brought to recognition. ("The Church and the Kingdom of God," *International Reformed Bulletin*, no. 27, p. 9)

Chapter III

History

III. 1. Time, History, and Culture

The idea of history is unthinkable apart from the idea of time. These two realities are not simply identical, though they are closely intertwined. Clear definitions elude us. What Augustine is reputed to have said about time also holds for history: When no one asks, I know what it is; but when asked, words fail me. God's creating time qualifies the happenings described in the first six days of the Genesis narrative. With the dawn of the seventh day, creational time sets in. Then for the first we can speak of cosmic time as we experience it. Time then reaches its full measure. It, too, evokes God's benediction, "Very good!" With the completed creation the transition takes place from creating time to creational time, to time as we know it today. This story of time is also the story of history. For history presupposes time. The transition from day six to day seven, from "pretime" to "calendar time," also marks the transition from "prehistory" to "world history," to dateable history which can be documented and researched, history as it from then onward and everlastingly contextualizes our life together in God's creation, even into the new creation.

Accordingly, the ongoing course of history is securely anchored in the march of time. As with space and all other created realities, so both time and history, in their essential confluence, are creatures of God. They are therefore his servants, called into existence and continuously upheld by his Word (which holds also for the very rationality which enables us to reflect, feebly at least, on these things). There is thus a Word of God for temporality, establishing and maintaining time as an irreducible dimension of all created reality, qualifying all historical experience. This time factor is formatively involved in our perception of beginnings, duration, and endings.* It decisively

---

*For a succinct comparative analysis of the concepts "past," "present," and "future" as keys to understanding history in the Western secular, native American, and biblical perspectives, see B. J. Van Der Walt, *Being Human: A Gift and a Duty*, pp. 40-42.

shapes the succession of moments in our lives, the ordered sequence of events and epochs in world history, the very story line of biblical revelation, as well as pauses in a musical score and developmental stages in human life.

As we realize all too well, it is possible to transgress the good temporal order of creation. This is reflected in conventional jargon, such as "killing time," "time is a-wasting," or failing to "take time," say, for proper rest. Such shortcomings prompt the earnest biblical injunction to heed God's law for temporal obedience by "numbering our days" and "redeeming the times."

The history of creation, integrally linked to the temporal order of things, implies and explicates the drama of human culture. The historical dimension of all created reality involves human communities in dynamically unfolding processes set within creationally normed patterns of development. It encompasses "befores," "afters," and "midway points." It highlights the "rise" and "fall" of civilizations. It opens our eyes to the temporal horizons of "already" and "not yet." In this respect the biblical view of time (as a qualification of history and culture) stands in sharp contrast to the cyclical, treadmill conception of time prevalent in many ancient societies. Major pagan thinkers viewed the fluctuations of time spent on earth as an endless series of repetitions over against their conception of eternity as immutable. Time and history locked people into a chronological predicament to which they could only resign themselves fatalistically, submitting their cultural activities dispassionately to its inexorable lot. Mundane affairs offered little meaning, held out only meager hope of a better future, and pointed to no higher goal than eventual escape.

As these pagan notions, in semievangelized forms, entered mainstream Christian traditions, they generated a spirit of otherworldly piety. Temporality and historicity became identified with ceaseless flux and flow, characterized by uncertainty and relativity, by inherent imperfection and ever besetting corruptibility. This led the church fathers and later Christian thinkers to conjure up a sharp antinomy between the inescapable ambivalences of the present life and the sure and changeless perfections of eternity. Earthly existence is natural and accordingly transient; heavenly existence is supernatural and eternal. This view ignores the biblical testimony that heaven too, in its various senses, belongs to created reality, and that it is therefore also temporal and has its own unique history. The traditional bipolar conception of life in terms of two starkly contrasting orders of existence is foreign to God's Word for creation as illumined by the written Word. It reflects the dualist construct of long-standing nature/grace speculations. Scripture discloses no such depreciation of history, earthly life, or cultural engagement, and no such antithesis between the here and the hereafter. It reflects a dynamically normed view of time as a creational condition for historically significant and culturally formative human activity within the divinely ordained

269

cosmic order. History follows a linear course. It comes from somewhere and is going somewhere. It is not a haphazard concatenation of random data, nor a theatre of the absurd, nor a hapless puppet in the hands of an ironclad fate, nor the mere outworkings of natural law. History has a past, present, and future normatively grounded in the creation order, an integral aspect of God's covenant with his world, purposefully directed toward the coming of the kingdom.

Time, history, and culture are as all-encompassing as creation itself. Obviously, then, historical research and reflection cannot possibly recount all that has happened in the past, nor can it address all that is happening now. The study of history therefore concentrates on persons, places, events, and movements in time which make a culturally formative impact on our life in God's world. A redemptively qualified principle of selectively focused historical narration is also evident in the time-lined message of Scripture which is aimed at the restoration of human culture.

As time and history are thus closely related, so too are history and culture. Culture refers to that which is historically significant, just as historical reflection dwells on that which is culturally formative. The history-making forces which shape culture involve the ongoing interaction between divine revelation and human response. Cultural history is therefore subservient to the sovereign Word of God. This overarching, normative reference point does not, however, lessen human accountability for the course of events in our life and in our world. Rather, it heightens it. Precisely because God is sovereign, we are the more responsible. It is therefore a basic misnomer, or at least potentially misleading, to speak of history as *"His-story."* We may not that easily exonerate ourselves and indict God for the world's calamities. Creation is exclusively God's good work; that mixed blessing which we call culture is ours. Closer to the truth is therefore the affirmation that, under the sovereign rule of God's holding and healing Word, history is *"our* story." We remain responsive recipients of revelation and responsible agents in using the time God gives us in shaping history and in forming culture. History is accordingly the record of obedient and/or disobedient responses to the cultural mandate on the part of various human communities down through the ages.

III. 2. The Providence of God

These three creational realities — time, history, and culture — all converge theologically in the biblical doctrine of divine providence. The idea of providence is pervasively presupposed as well as explicitly taught throughout the Scriptures. Scripture itself is a verbal product of God's providential care for the redemption of his creatures. Yet the word "providence" is absent from the Bible. It was introduced into the Hebraic-Christian tradition through the influence of the Apocrypha and the Septuagint, which came into existence during the intertestamentary period. Later the concept "providence" was given a settled place in Christian theology through the works of early church fathers who borrowed it from the writings of ancient philosophers. Christian thinkers, however, gave it a significantly and substantially different meaning. Among the classical authors in the Greco-Roman tradition it referred variously to cosmic forces thought of as "fate" or "fortune" or "chance." Christians, however, ascribed to providence a personal address as "that act of God whereby he from moment to moment upholds and governs all things" (Bavinck, *Gereformeerde Dogmatiek,* Vol. II, p. 556). These considerations lead Weber to comment on its current usage as follows:

> The concept of "providence," which in its usual application is quite alien to biblical language, possesses in its usage outside of the Christian faith such power that Christian theology can make use of it only with the exercise of the greatest care. [Think of its radical distortion at the hands of the "German Christians" — G. J. S.]. This special care must consist, first, of its being conceived of as actual governing activity, and secondly of considering simultaneously the subject of the activity meant by it, namely, the triune God. It is quite clear that today "providence" is often the coded designation of a god which is not the God proclaimed by the Church, and this is also true of the term "fate." Both of these refer to an ultimate, unknown, silent, and abstract Beyond — this is seen, for instance, in the fact that one cannot pray either to "providence" or "fate." (*Foundations of Dogmatics,* Vol. I, pp. 512-13)

Perhaps nowhere is the integrally biblical and profoundly religious heartbeat of divine providence expressed with such soul-stirring eloquence as in the Heidelberg Catechism (Q. & A. 27). There we read that the providence of God is

> the almighty and everywhere present power of God, whereby, as it were by his hand, He still upholds heaven, earth, and all creatures, and so governs them that herbs and grass, rain and drought, fruitful and barren years, food and drink, health and sickness, riches and poverty, yea, all things, come not by chance but by his fatherly hand.

In answer to the question, "What does it profit us to know that God has created, and by His providence still upholds, all things?", the Heidelberger goes on to say (Q. & A. 28), that we may be patient in adversity, thankful in prosperity, and with a view to the future may have good confidence in our faithful God and Father that no creature shall separate us from His love, since all creatures are so in His hand that without His will they cannot so much as move.

Where God's creating activity leaves off, there his providential care takes over. These two phases in the mighty acts of God are inextricably connected. Providence presupposes creation. And creation moves on naturally and directly into providence, with no gap in between. In Scripture God's creating activity is described metaphorically as "work," and his providential care as "rest" (Genesis 2:3). Reflecting on these biblical ideas, Bavinck says that "for God creating is not 'work,' nor is preservation 'rest.' Divine rest simply means that God finished bringing forth new things (Ecclesiastes 1:9-10); that the work of creation in the proper and strict sense of producing things out of nothing was ended; and that God then reveled with divine good-pleasure in his completed work" (*Gereformeerde Dogmatiek,* Vol. II, p. 551).

In our theological reflections the line of demarcation between God's creating and providing activities may be exceedingly thin. It is nevertheless very real. We are therefore obliged to respect fully this point of transition. For to erase or obscure this distinction is an open invitation to serious distortions of the Creator-creature relationship. This is evident in theories of evolution in which God's creative and providential work are conflated into a single prolonged process. Such blurring of biblically sanctioned boundaries is also apparent in the idea of "continuing creation" *(creatio continua).* On this view God is forever actively engaged in creating the world anew, calling it back into existence moment by moment from an ever impending state of nothingness. The advocates of this view may intend thereby to stress the world's constant and absolute dependence on its Maker. In reality, however, this view leaves us with a highly dialectical view of reality in which creation teeters ceaselessly on the brink of nullity. The "in the beginning"-ness of God's creating handiwork gets eclipsed and the radically definitive character of the *creatio ex nihilo* gets redistributed over aeons of time.

On the biblical view, once God launched his primary act of creation, nothingness was henceforth forever excluded. The Creator's handiwork, once begun, would forever endure until fully done. Providence is the divine follow-up work to creation, not its perpetual repetition. Only creation is "out of nothing," not providence. God's providential care is rather the dynamic way he continuously operates by his Word in sustaining and directing the existing creation. There is thus both continuity and discontinuity between the creating and providing activity of God: continuity in the sense that both are works of God acting on the same created reality, and discontinuity in the sense that they are differentiated acts of God. In the words of Berkouwer,

> . . . he who would fully appreciate this constant flow of the power of God must at the same time always recognize the once-for-all-ness of God's creative work. Our confession does this when it speaks of the good God, who "after he had created all things did not abandon them." . . . [Thus] the unity of God's work must be acknowledged and, at the same time, the Scriptural distinction between beginning and continuation maintained. . . . There was once a call out of nothing; now there is a call to continuation. (*The Providence of God,* pp. 72-73)

On the idea of *creatio continua,* Berkouwer holds further that, "though Reformed theologians use the term 'continuous creation' in order to emphasize the greatness and divinity of the work of sustaining, they nevertheless reject the idea in the sense of renewed acts of creation out of nothing" (*The Providence of God,* p. 70). Diemer elaborates this same point as follows:

> The creating Word through which all things were made in six days was in no way silenced when this work was finished. This Word can be heard to the end of time as it supports all things by its power and wisdom. From ancient times this providential care has been called the *creatio continua,* the continuing creation. However, this term must not be understood to mean that completely new things originated beside those already created. Rather, it must be taken to mean that the Spirit of God continues to cause new things to appear within the framework of the created order wherein they were potentially enclosed. (*Nature and Miracle,* p. 13)

To affirm God's providence is to confess — even in the face of all appearances to the contrary — that he is Lord of all forever. This confession implies an open repudiation of the ultimacy, autonomy, and omnipotence of all "principalities and powers." It implies further a condemnation of the contemporary as well as ancient pseudogods of "fate," "chance," "the law of averages," "probability," or the horoscope. It also calls into question scientific reliance on "natural law," exposing it as a secularized version of holding the power of God's providential Word. Our life processes are as dependent on God's ordering Word in their continuation as in their origin. Let God withdraw his Word for even a moment, and the world would cease to be what it is, without hope of becoming what it is meant to be. Providence not only relates to the creative beginning of all things, but also points teleologically to the goal of creation in the final coming of the kingdom. It links God's *alpha* as beginning with his *omega* as realization. In the words of Hendrikus Berkhof, by providence

> . . . we want to indicate that activity of God by which he does not abandon the world which he creatively called into existence, but takes care of it in such a way that it is and remains on the way to the goal which he has in mind. (*Christian Faith*, p. 210)

Such convictions prompted Christian thinkers to ward off various other distorted versions of the doctrine of providence. On the one hand, they sidestepped the pitfall of pantheism both in its classic forms and as now updated in the form of panentheism. As with all heresies, this heresy lives parasitically off some element of the truth. Pantheists and panentheists wish rightly to honor God's involvement with the affairs of the world. In the process, however, they sacrifice divine transcendence, the integrity of the world, and human responsibility. History then becomes an expression of divine "panergism," with human decisions and actions assimilated into divine immanence and destiny. At issue is not the question: Is God present and active in his world. It is rather a question of the nature of such divine engagement — is it mediate or immediate? Affirming the former, Reformed theology confesses that God governs the world by his Word and Spirit.

Christian thinkers are equally resolute in rejecting another extremist view on God's dealings with the world, namely, deism. As a heresy, it, too, represents a distortion of some element of the truth — in this case, a false emphasis on the transcendence of God. As pantheism's chief concern is with God's present involvement with history, so deism stresses mainly his original initiation of a largely self-perpetuating world process (note the familiar clockmaker imagery). Both are misleading. In both, apparent virtue is in actuality default. In pantheism, divine reality overwhelms human activity, inducing mystical quiescence. In deism, history unfolds under the dictates of "natural law," except for the occasional interventions of a *Deus ex machina*.

In contrast to the one-sidedness of both these caricatures of divine providence, whether born of ancient Greek philosophy or of modern secular theology, Reformed dogmatics seeks to do full justice to an integrally coherent view, however mysterious, and however unfathomable, of God's sovereignty and man's responsibility. These are neither mutually exclusive nor mutually limiting realities. In God's providential way with his world our complete dependence on God and at the same time our relative and responsible independence go hand in hand. Within the framework of his very provocative contemporary Roman Catholic theology, Karl Rahner describes this Creator-creature relationship as follows:

Basically creation "out of nothing" means to say: creation totally from God, but in such a way that the world is radically dependent on God in his creation. . . . By the very fact that God establishes the creature and its difference from himself, the creature is a genuine reality different from God, and not a mere appearance behind which God and his own reality hide. . . . It is clear that here genuine reality and radical dependence are simply just two sides of one and the same reality. . . . Not until one experiences himself as a free subject responsible before God and accepts this responsibility does he understand what autonomy is, and understand that it does not decrease, but increases in the same proportion as dependence on God. On this point the only thing that concerns us is that man is at once independent and, in view of what his ground is, also dependent. (*Foundations of Christian Faith*, pp. 78-79)

Providence is therefore more than an academic issue suited to theoretical inquiry. It is a profoundly vital, urgently existential issue in our day-to-day experience, the more so now that sin and its attendant evils have invaded our world. Many serious-minded Christians today find that belief in the providential hand of an all-wise God who is both able and willing in all things to work for our good creates pressing problems, even a crisis in faith. How are we to account for the agonies of terminal illness, for tragic accidents, for genocide, for natural catastrophes, for horrendous injustices, for famine, for the ravages of war? In the face of such calamities and more, it is infinitely more than a cheap platitude to embrace with heart and mouth and life the confession of the Heidelberg Catechism (Q. & A. 29) concerning "the almighty and everywhere present power of God. . . ." This is a costly faith. It requires not only that we acknowledge the will of God, but that we resolve to do it; that we live out the implications of our daily prayer, "Thy will be done on earth . . ." — standing as we often do at the very epicenter of countless terrible ambiguities. What is the meaning of it all? The daily newscasts are not self-explanatory. The idea of divine providence, as an "explanation" of world history, is under heavy fire. Those who reject it are nevertheless impelled to seek other "explanations." The suppression motif (Romans 1:18-23) is very much alive. Providence remains, perhaps as never before, a daring article of faith. As Hendrikus Berkhof puts it, "The confession of the preservation of the world by *this* God is the confession of people who do not see and yet believe" (*Christian Faith*, p. 213). The acknowledgment of such an eschatological "not-yetness" does not end in historical agnosticism, though this is strongly suggested by Weber in saying that "it is impossible to make a Christian interpretation of the course of history. To be a Christian means rather to be able to endure the uninterpretability of events" (*Foundations of Dogmatics*,

Vol. I, p. 510). Providence also involves assurance. For the creation order remains its abiding anchor point. Its laws and norms continue to hold for our life in God's world. They offer guidelines in seeking to come to terms, however humbly and tentatively, with the momentous events of our day and with our calling to help shape a more obedient, just, and peaceable culture.

In Christian theology the doctrine of divine providence is generally approached from three points of view. First, there is that aspect called *preservation*. This refers to the ongoing activity of God who by his Word continues to uphold his creation ordinances. By maintaining his creation order God preserves the structures of life and sets bounds to the rampaging power of evil. Built into the normed functioning of creation are certain restraints, certain self-correcting and self-healing potentials which are expressive of the impinging power of God's Word. By them he urges men to faithful obedience or otherwise prompts them to perfunctory compliance. Divine preservation accordingly does not entail human passivity, as though "God does it all." Precisely the opposite is true: It creates the very possibility for responsible living.

The second element in divine providence is *concurrence*. This idea indicates that

> the same deed is in its entirety both a deed of God and a deed of the creature. It is a deed of God insofar as it is determined from moment to moment by the will of God. And it is a deed of man insofar as God realizes it through the self-activity of the creature. There is interpenetration here, but no mutual limitation. (Louis Berkhof, *Systematic Theology,* p. 149)

Concurrence is another way of elucidating the Creator-creature relationship. It excludes all notions of competition, fifty-fifty cooperation, half-and-half complementation, or mere supplementation. God by his Word works in, with, and through the currents of history to prompt the elicited yet uncompelled responses of human communities.

Government is a third way of understanding providence. Our world is not a speck of matter lost in the vast expanse of the universe, cut loose from its orbit, drifting aimlessly through space. Life has purpose. Nihilism is not the answer. God so directs the life of his creation that its final felicitous outcome is assured. Divine government therefore speaks of orientation to a goal. That goal is the "new creation."

A careful reading of Calvin's *Institutes,* I,16 and 27, indicates how well he already addresses the fundamental issues which arise perennially in connection with providence. He speaks of it as God's "secret plan" for the world. Let the following excerpts suffice in reflecting the abiding relevance of his insights.

> ... To make God a momentary Creator, who once for all finished his work, would be cold and barren, ... [for] we see the presence of divine power shining as much in the continuing state of the universe as in its inception. ... For unless we pass on to his providence ... we do not yet properly grasp what it means to say: "God is Creator," ... [since] nobody seriously believes the universe was made by God without being persuaded that he also takes care of his works. ...

Calvin rejects the ideas of "fortune," "chance," "fate," unconditioned "necessity," "natural law," and logical "causality" as perversions of the biblical doctrine of providence. Yet he does not argue for the rational transparency of the often tragic and absurd happenings in the course of history. He in fact holds that "the true causes of events are hidden to us." In seeming anticipation of contemporary nihilist outlooks on life, Calvin goes on to say that

> ... however all things may be ordained by God's purpose and sure distribution, for us they are fortuitous. Not that we think that fortune rules the world and men, tumbling all things at random up and down; for it is fitting that this folly be absent from the Christian's breast! But since the order, reason, end, and necessity of those things which happen for the most part lie hidden in God's purpose, and are not apprehended by human opinion, those things, which it is certain take place by God's will, are in a sense fortuitous. For they bear on the face of them no other appearance, ... [since] as far as the capacity of our mind is concerned, all things therein seem fortuitous. ... [Yet we are not to doubt] that God's providence exercises authority over fortune in directing its end. ... [Therefore] what for us seems a contingency, faith recognizes as a secret impulse from God.

Calvin is thus led to define providence as "... not that by which God idly observes from heaven what takes place on earth, but that by which, as keeper of the keys, he governs all events. Thus it pertains no less to his hands than to his eyes" (*Institutes*, I,16,1-9).

III. 3. Taking History Seriously

The original creation was not chaos but cosmos, a well-ordered world. Human life was contextualized by a coherent network of nuclear tasks. Originally, it appears, these nuclear tasks were clustered in the family circle. Within the setting of home life we can discern the genetic origin of later societal developments. Therein lies the original locus of mankind's variegated mandate — the nurturing task, but also the working, governing, learning, and worshiping tasks. All our present-day God-given callings were potentially present there at the dawn of human history. As the petals of a flower are all enveloped within the bud, so our nuclear tasks were present in that primal community, ready to unfold. In ongoing response to the cultural mandate and under the superintendency of divine providence, the increasingly structured realization of the potentials resident in these primordial life relationships was to be achieved through a centuries-long process called historical differentiation. Biblically directed Christian thought is therefore obliged to take history seriously. For we are bound to honor history as God's way with his world. History is his way of directing the unfolding potentialities of his creation toward the final coming of his kingdom. History adds nothing ontically new to creation. Rather, it moves seedtime and firstfruits along toward the ripened products of harvesttime. What from the beginning was seminally and germinally present is brought to fruition. A certain brand of salt, for example, advertises itself under the slogan: "Nature puts the flavor in, it takes salt to bring it out." In some such way creation funds all human enterprises; but it takes history, like salt, to bring them gradually to fuller realization. This long tradition of historical differentiation, coming up out of the past, molds the present and makes it possible to shape the future. Our lives can make a difference.

III. 4. Historical Differentiation

III. 4. 1. In the Old Testament

The Bible does not set forth a philosophy of history. But it does offer pointers on the meaning of history. It does this largely in narrative form, revealing the history of salvation. Along the way it sheds its redemptive light on universal history, even as it concentrates on the course of events in Israel and the early church. As we listen in on this biblical commentary, eavesdropping (as it were) on its message, scanning its lines, but also reading between the lines, it is possible to retrace and reconstruct some of the broad lines in the process of historical differentiation.

In the early chapters of Genesis we meet Adam simply as God's general handyman in the creation, equipped for every task, a man for all seasons and trades. Shortly thereafter, however, a measure of vocational specialization sets in: Cain takes up farming, and Abel tends the herd. Moving along, a further division of labors is evident: Nimrod is the hunter, Tubal-Cain the metalworker, and Jubal the musician. This

historical opening-up process does not appear to have followed an unbroken and steady course, however. Abraham arrives on the scene as a
versatile figure whose colorful career reflects an as yet largely undifferentiated stage of vocational development. In his movements through the
land he assumes the role of husband, father, leading educator, chief
liturgete, land developer, migrant citizen, managerial herdsman, well
digger, patriarchal head of his political community, and commander in
chief of a military task force. All these functions were embodied in this
single person. Moses, too, stands out as a generalist. Practically the total
burden of Israelite leadership during the exodus era rests on his shoulders,
until finally he is persuaded to delegate certain responsibilities to a team
of subordinates.

A similarly undifferentiated picture emerges in the case of Samuel
during the tumultuous transition period in Israel from judgeship to
monarchy. The law of Moses provided for the threefold office of prophet,
priest, and king. Samuel, however, is clothed with all three offices, reflecting again an as yet largely undifferentiated distribution of authority.
He speaks prophetically as God's spokesman to his people; standing in
the priestly lineage of the house of Levi he leads in the sacrificial rites;
and as judge he renders kingly service in adjudicating legal disputes
during his annual circuits throughout the land. But signs of change were
in the air. Movement in the direction of a more normative delineation
of tasks was appearing on the horizon. King Saul was dethroned for
usurping the prerogatives of the priesthood, for "to obey is better than
sacrifice" (1 Samuel 15:22) — suggesting that the transgression of one's
proper sphere of jurisdiction stands condemned as a violation of divinely
prescribed ordinances. The later King Uzzah was also severely punished
for a similarly presumptuous act (2 Chronicles 26:16-21).

With the founding of the kingdom under David a more stable and
enduring differentiation of tasks takes shape in the structures of Israelite
society. The offices of prophet, priest, and king assume a firmly institutionalized place. Thus King David is rebuked by the prophet Nathan,
and both submit in turn to the liturgical leadership of the high priest
Abiathar. This long historical process of differentiation comes to a head
in Israel's three major institutions: the schools of the prophets, the royal
palace as the seat of public justice, and the temple as the cultic center.
Despite the criticism of modern historical scholarship, the comprehensive
testimony of the Scriptures points toward a positive assessment of these
developments. These prophetic, priestly, and kingly institutions reflect
their divinely ordained right of existence and reason for existence. Standing in coexisting and proexisting interrelatedness to one another, they
were to function in unison as channels of blessing to God's people. In
this differentiation of societal structure it is possible to catch at least

a faint glimpse of that idea which was later captured in the theory of sphere sovereignty/sphere universality.

The binding character of this differentiation principle is further evident from the era of the divided kingdom in the dramatic encounter between King Jeroboam I and the unnamed prophet from Judah (1 Kings 13:1-10). The king, arrogating to himself a priestly function, burns false incense before an unauthorized altar. The paralyzing judgment which descends on him for this display of self-willed worship reflects divine disapproval on such reversions to pagan despotism. It represents an antinormative mixing of two distinct offices in Israel. A similar transgression of limits of authority, perpetrated by the later Israelite king Jeroboam II, and defended by the false priest of Bethel, Amaziah, is sternly condemned by the prophet Amos (Amos 7:10-17). Amaziah arrogantly declares the shrine at Bethel a legitmate place of worship, basing this claim on a royal edict: ". . . It is the king's sanctuary, and it is a temple of the kingdom." This violation of the principle of differentiation of institutions also elicits a strongly worded divine judgment. Commenting on this passage, Calvin levels a sharp critique on this haughty appeal of Amaziah to an assumed royal prerogative to regulate worship by imperial decree. "Hence," says Calvin, "he ascribes to the king a twofold office, — that it was in his power to change religion in any way he pleased, — and then, that Amos disturbed the peace of the community, and thus did wrong to the king by derogating from his authority." He goes on to say that "they are inconsiderate men who give [rulers] too much power in spiritual things." Looking about him, Calvin then expresses his concern over similar church-state coalitions in the Germany and England of his day. ". . . This evil is everywhere dominant in Germany, and in these regions it prevails too much." The fruits of such distorted patterns of authority are evident in this,

> . . . that princes, and those who are in power, think themselves so spiritual, that there is no longer any church discipline; and this sacrilege greatly prevails among us; for they limit not their office by fixed and legitimate boundaries, but think they cannot rule, except they abolish every authority in the Church, and become chief judges as well in doctrine as in all spiritual government. . . . Amaziah wished here to prove by the king's authority that the received worship at Bethel was legitimate. How so? "The king has established it; it is then not lawful for anyone to say a word to the contrary; the king could do this by his own right; for his majesty is sacred."

The English reformation manifested a similar disregard for the principle of differentiation in offices. For, says Calvin, "they who at first extolled Henry, King of England, were certainly inconsiderate men; they gave him the supreme power in all things; and this vexed me grievously; for they were guilty of blasphemy when they called him the chief Head of the Church under Christ. This certainly was too much . . ." *(Commentary on Amos, passim)*.

III. 4. 2. Between the Testaments

To label the Intertestamental Period "the silent 400 years" is clearly a misnomer. These roughly four centuries between the close of the Old and the opening of the New Testament eras (Malachi to Matthew) are, of course, "silent" in terms of biblical revelation. Recorded prophecy ceased, awaiting the apostolic witness. These bridging years were, however, anything but "silent" in the life of the Jewish people. In the aftermath of the Assyrian and Babylonian captivities Israel lost its national independence, its monarchy, and its religio-cultural unity. A large majority of the exiled Jews became dispersed among the nations (the diaspora). A remnant returned to resettle the promised land, now reduced largely to Judea. There they were reconstituted as a priestly community under the political-military control of a succession of foreign powers. The temple was rebuilt, though in lackluster fashion, and its services were restored. As a continuing legacy arising from the exigencies of the captivity years, synagogues were established in every sizeable Jewish community. Among the repatriated as well as the dispersed Jews the synagogue served its adherents not only as a center for sabbath worship and the religious education of the young, but also as a focal point in Jewish social life. In Palestine a confusing array of sects and parties emerged, contributing to the seething unrest and inner turmoil of its beleaguered inhabitants. All in all it was an intensely turbulent epoch in Jewish history. Eventually nearly every traditional aspiration of the covenant people was crushed, leaving only the Messianic expectation as a spark of hope kept alive among a faithful few. That Israel survived at all may be counted among the great wonders of world history, leading to Barth's cryptic comment that the only proof for the existence of God is the continuing existence of the Hebrew people. What was happening *in* and *to* Israel is one thing; what God was nevertheless working *through* Israel is another. As Jesus would later say, "Salvation is from the Jews" (John 4:22).

In tracing the history of the differentiation principle let us focus now on a single extended episode from this period. From the year 198 B.C. onward the Jewish people endured ruthless persecution at the hands of Syrian occupation forces, especially during the reign of Antiochus IV (called Epiphanes, "the Illustrious," by his followers; but renamed Epimanes, "the Madman," by the Jews). The Seleucids, rulers from Syria, were out to exterminate the heritage of the Hebrew people. Their harshly enforced policy of oppression resulted in a veritable reign of terror, matched only by the Holocaust of our century. In the year 167 B.C. violent reaction erupted, touching off the Maccabean Rebellion. This revolt was spearheaded by the Hasmoneans, a priestly family. Initiated by the father, Mattathias, it was carried forward successively by his sons, Judas "the hammerer," Jonathan "the clever," and Simon "the jewel." After over two decades of underground resistance and guerrilla warfare the revolution came to a successful conclusion. Israel was liberated. In 142 B.C., as a crowning event, and in recognition of the militant leadership of these Hasmonean priests, the third member of this clan, Simon, was installed as governor of the land. By this act the priestly and kingly offices were merged into a single authority. Civil and ecclesiastical institutions converged in a kind of church-state coalition — in violation of the Old Testament legacy calling for "the separation of church and state."

If this were the end of the matter, it would by itself already make an interesting case study. But there is more to it. It has far-reaching implications, intruding on the very crowded climax of the New Testament gospel witness. Approaching Good Friday, at a crucial stage in his trial, Jesus is hailed before the tribunal of Annas and Caiaphas, high priests in Israel. This courtroom scenario, with cultic leaders sitting in judgment on trumped-up civil charges, is a belated outcome of the coronation of Simon as priest-governor nearly two centuries earlier. It represents a travesty on justice rooted in the antinormative fusion of two distinct life callings. In violating the principle of vocational differentiation, it undermines the identity as well as the integrity of both priestly (ecclesiastical) and kingly (civil) offices. In such a "conflict of interest" both spheres in life lose their relative independence under the rule of God. Of course, the case of Jesus Christ involved a "higher justice." An absolutely unique judgment of divine grace was actively present in, under, through, and with this human judgment, incorporating it into the plan of redemption. In the normal affairs of men and nations, however, such deformations of societal structures lead to countless miscarriages of justice. Differentiated responsibility is the norm.

III. 4. 3. In the New Testament

After the retrogressive impact of Jewish history during the Intertestamental era, the New Testament writings reflect some renewed advances in the unfolding process of vocational differentiation. In the Gospels there is, first of all, that classic case of confrontation between Jesus and the critics of his day. In their recurring efforts "to entangle him in his talk," the leaders of the opposition, opening the conversation with a poorly disguised compliment, seek to corner this unsettling Rabbi from Nazareth with the loaded question, "Is it lawful to give tribute to Caesar?" Now at last, gloatingly, they think they have this disturber of the peace caught on the horns of a self-incriminating dilemma. Whichever way he turns, he is in trouble — either with Jewish loyalists, if he answers affirmatively, or with the Roman authorities, if he responds negatively. These "hypocrites" obviously underestimated the infinite resources of their rival. Jesus, asking for a coin and holding it up for all to see, turns the tables on this conspiracy with his counterquestion, "Whose image and inscription is this?" The answer is clear: "Caesar's." Driving the crucial point home, Jesus then sent his dumbfounded inquisitors on their way by affirming the principle, "Render therefore to Caesar the things that are Caesar's, and to God the things that are God's" (Matthew 22:15-22).

Unfortunately, far too often Christians have interpreted this utterance of Jesus along dualist lines: One part of life belongs to civil government, another part to the service of God. Such a hermeneutic clearly implies a dichotomous sacred/secular worldview. If this is actually the intent of Jesus' teaching, then indeed his opponents succeeded in trapping him in his words by pitting him against the pervasive message of all Scripture. Honoring contextual reflection as the basic norm for biblical interpretation, however, we may say that Jesus' response comes down to this: Give to God what is rightfully his, namely, total and undivided allegiance. Then, under the sovereign claim of God's Word, give to Caesar what is justly his — no more, no less. By extension Christ's words lead us to conclude: Give also to parents, to church officers, to educators, to administrators in every sphere of life the respect which is rightfully theirs — remembering that all earthly offices and institutions have but a limited authority. God's authority alone is absolute and all-encompassing. Thus understood, Christ's rejoinder stands as a reaffirmation of that abiding norm which calls for differentiated tasks within communal relationships.

Turning to the Acts of the Apostles, this idea of an opening-up process in our life callings is reinforced by developments in the life of the early church. Initially, it appears, authority in the Christian community was vested exclusively in the apostolic office. As the apostles became overburdened, however, and as the church's ministry became more diversified, a division of labors emerged. As the church expanded, this redistribution of tasks led to the appointment of the three familiar offices of deacon, elder, and minister within local congregational settings.

The epistles, too, address Christian responsibility within multiple spheres of societal activity. Each sphere has its own distinctive norm, yet altogether coordinated in a unified pattern of communal life. Paul stresses such partnership when, in writing to the Ephesian Christians, he says, "Be subject to one another out of reverence for Christ" (5:21). In addressing believers in Colossae Paul's emphasis falls on their involvement in several distinctive callings: "Whatever your task, work heartily, as serving the Lord and not men" (3:23). Both Pauline injunctions are accompanied by specific guidelines for various arenas of communal interaction — husbands and wives, parents and children, masters and servants (cf. 1 Timothy 6:1-2). Commenting on the Ephesians passage, Calvin says:

> Paul comes now to the various groups; for besides the universal bond of subjection, some are more closely bound to each other, according to their respective callings. Society consists of groups, which are like yokes, in which there is a mutual obligation of parties. . . . So in society there are six different classes, for each of which Paul lays down its peculiar duties. (*Commentary on Ephesians: 5:21–6:9*)

Furthermore, we find directives for shaping the relationship between church officers and members of the congregation spelled out in 1 Timothy 3. And in his monumental message on civil life Paul in Romans 13:1-7 enunciates the fundamental principles governing the conduct of rulers and citizens. These ideas are reiterated in 1 Peter 2:12-17, on which Calvin comments as follows:

> The verb *kitizein* in Greek, from which *ktisis* comes, means to form or construct a building. It corresponds to the word "ordinance," by which Peter reminds us that God the Maker of the world has not left the human race in a state of confusion, so that we live after the manner of beasts, but has given them, as it were, a building regularly formed, and divided into several compartments. It is called a human ordinance, not because it has been invented by man, but because it is a mode of living well-arranged and clearly ordered, appropriate to man. (*Commentary on I Peter*, esp. 2:13)

As a final New Testament instance of putting the principle of vocational and institutional differentiation into practice, consider one of the many knotty problems which plagued the Corinthian church. Disputes arose over goods and property. Christians resorted to bringing charges against fellow Christians before pagan judges. This is not a proper forum for settling differences, Paul argues. Why bring your cases before those "least esteemed by the church"? Can you expect to get a Christian hearing in a pagan court? Are you not empowered as a believing community to pass judgment on such matters? Is there not a better way? Why not appoint a wise and trusted person from among you to adjudicate such issues? Paul seems to be advocating a Christian ombudsman, a court of appeals within the Christian community (1 Corinthians 6:1-7). It is significant to note that Paul does not advise bringing such civil suits before the church council. For such matters do not belong properly to the domain of church officers. Paul is thus appealing implicitly to an established norm which honors the differentiated nature of ecclesiastical and civil jurisdictions.

III. 4. 4. In the *Western Christian Tradition*

With the closing of the New Testament canon and the end of the apostolic age, the door of history swings open to the patristic, medieval, Reformation, and modern eras in Western Christianity. Throughout these past nineteen centuries the question of a well-normed differentiation of offices and institutions has continually haunted the life of the Christian community. This unfolding story takes some very strange twists and turns — a mixture of both relatively normative and highly antinormative developments, reflecting both progression and retrogression. Let us look briefly at two major institutional issues arising from this our common history which continue to shape our lives today — namely, church/state relations and the development of the university.

a) Perennial Church/State Struggles

With the Edict of Milan in A.D. 313 Christianity was established as the official religion of the empire. Within one generation persecution had ceased and Christians moved out of the catacombs and onto the throne. The result was an unholy wedlock between church and state. With it the pagan empire became the Holy Roman Empire. Thus the Constantinian era was ushered in, based on a confusion of political and ecclesiastical jurisdictions. This convergence of imperial power and papal authority set the scenes for both cooperative ventures and fierce power struggles which lasted down to very recent times. Princes appointed and deposed priests. Priests manipulated and excommunicated princes. In the best of times a policy of shared dominion prevailed. The entire arrangement was predicated, however, on a dubious nature/grace dogma, inherited from Greek thinkers and propagated by leading Christian thinkers. This interlocking, tension-laden concord stands as an unmistakable departure from the normed contours of the creation order. For centuries it stifled the productive unfolding of a diversified spectrum of nonecclesiastical and nonpolitical vocations, retarding the development not only of healthy differentiation (sphere sovereignty) but also of a healthy and mature sense of community (sphere universality).

The Reformation effected a partial and temporary restoration of a more creationally and biblically normed pattern of differentiation-within-unity in the societal order. In Calvin's Geneva, for example, the relationships between the consistory, the town council, the schools, industry, and the academy reflected a renewed movement in the right direction. The good initiative of the Reformers — Luther, Calvin, and others — failed, however, to make a consistent and enduring impact on the Western world. It was soon offset by a resurgent scholasticism. Instead of building on the social philosophy of reformational thinkers such as Johannes Althusius (1557-1638), Protestant scholastics, like their Roman Catholic counterparts, reverted to Constantinian, Augustinian, and Thomist models of societal life. With the gradual breakdown of Western Christianity and the steady ascendency of secular humanism in the wake of the Renaissance and the Enlightenment movements, the medieval ideal of a dominant church, based on a collectivist view of community, was dislodged by modern individualist or collectivist ideologies. In its place came the bureaucratic power of modern secular states. The annals of Western Christian history are replete with frustrated yearnings for a truly pluralist society — communities normed by the abiding principle of differentiated societal structures functioning as partners within a unified perspective.

b) The Development of the University

For about half a millennium, since the closing of the Greek academies in A.D. 529, the "lamp of learning" remained nearly extinguished in the Western world. Only the work of Boethius and certain monastic orders helped to keep it alive, rejuvenated later by the rise of Mohammedan scholarship. Then, around the tenth and eleventh centuries, serious revival set in. This marks the earliest beginnings of what we today call the university, emerging in such towns as Salamanca, Jana, Heidelberg, Paris, and Oxford. They were "free universities," free associations of peripatetic scholars and students. These new learning centers were clearly differentiated from other existing structures in society. They lived neither by a grant from the state nor by the grace of the church. They stood on their own merits, and therefore regularly suffered from poverty. Before long, however, they lost their independent status. By the high medieval period, as society became increasingly ecclesiasticized, most universities came under church control. The dogmas of churchmen, which represented a synthesis of Aristotelian logic and the Christian gospel, dictated the principles and parameters of academic pursuits.

Under the initial impulse of the Reformation, Protestant universities were released from the authoritarian tutelage of the ecclesiastical *magis-*

terium and redirected according to the *sola Scriptura* principle. Such renewal took root especially in theology. But philosophy and the other sciences were left largely untouched by inner reformation. In these fields of inquiry a scholastic mind-set was perpetuated. This contributed significantly and enduringly to the secularization of learning centers within nearly every Protestant tradition.

In the modern era, under the influence of Renaissance and Enlightenment thought, this secularization process gained steady momentum. Both medieval church dogma and the Reformation faith were systematically banished from the university. The secular state replaced the church as the dominant force in society. Thus the university, too, fell under the control of civil government.

Free universities, church universities, and community-based universities — nearly all of them were displaced by state universities. The state's ideological commitment (usually secular humanism) was generally imposed on its institutions of higher education. This is our predicament today. Throughout its history, therefore, whether by ecclesiastical or political annexation, the university has suffered a steady loss of its differentiated status in society. With it came the loss of its unique sense of identity and integrity. Along the way there were indeed a few exceptions to this trend; but their number is so small as to simply prove the rule. One notable case was the dramatic act of Kuyper and his cohorts in 1880 in founding the Free Reformed University in Amsterdam. In light of Scripture Kuyper appealed to the principle of responsible differentiation embedded in the creation order. By divine ordinance, he held, learning centers such as the university have a rightful place of their own within society. Their task is not dependent on either church or state. Such Christian institutions of higher education are the appointed place for the inner reformation of scholarship. In our times this vision has been severely blurred. Yet the fundamental principle of a differentiated community continues to confront us as an urgent call to societal reformation.

III. 5. Miracles

For more than a millennium biblical teachings on the mystery of miracles have been seriously beclouded by the scholastic distinction between God's "ordained power" (*potentia ordinata* — providence) and his "absolute power" (*potentia absoluta* — miracles). Among thinkers who stress the *will* of God, the idea of the "absolute power" of God often ended in pure voluntarism. On this view God's hand reaches out directly and immediately into the affairs of our world. God can do anything he wills to do — a caricature of the biblical teaching that "with God all things are possible." The ongoing acts of divine providence are conceived of in a crassly arbitrary, even capricious way. Such voluntarist notions of "absolute power" negate biblical teachings on God's covenantal constancy in his dealings with the world, securely anchored in his mediating Word for creation. Other thinkers, emphasizing divine *rationality*, appeal to the idea of "absolute power" to argue that God is able to do whatever is consistent with the laws of logic. Only such divine acts are logically conceivable which do not involve a violation of the rule of noncontradiction (even the sacramental miracle of the mysterious transubstantiation of bread and wine in the eucharist was held to be logically defensible). The case for such rational demonstrations of the absolute power of God to perform miracles relies heavily on Aristotelian methods of reasoning, introduced into Western Christianity by Boethius, canonized in the *Sentences* of Lombard, and elaborated by the great thinkers of the medieval church. Such thinking was largely repudiated by the Reformers, but was soon revived in Protestant scholasticism through the influence of Beza and Melanchthon. The lingering effects of this tradition are present, though ambiguously, in the following definition of the sovereign power of God by Louis Berkhof:

> Power in God may be called the effective energy of his nature, or that perfection of His being by which He is the absolute and highest causality. . . . The *potentia ordinata* can be defined as that perfection of God whereby He, through the mere exercise of His will, can realize whatsoever is present in His will or counsel. (*Systematic Theology*, pp. 79-80)

On traditional scholastic assumptions, the mighty acts of God in history are reduced to rational problems to be analytically solved by the human intellect. Divine decrees are accommodated to the laws of causality, resulting in the tyranny of logical probability. God himself is reduced to the major premise undergirding an extended process of deductive argumentations. Thus the active, holy, covenant-keeping God of Abraham, Isaac, and Jacob, the Father of our Lord Jesus Christ, disappears behind the arguments of philosophers and theologians (Pascal). The deeply spiritual tenor of the biblical message is largely silenced. The idea of "the analogy of being" *(analogia entis)*, with its correspondence theory of knowledge, dominates the discussion, encompassing God and man in a shared network of logical intricacies. The autonomy of human reason rivals divine revelation as an operative principle. Christian thinkers become blind to the fact that rationality is itself a created function subject to creaturely norms and limitations. Thus the Creator-creature distinction suffers nearly total eclipse.

This scholastic tradition in theology results in a number of dubious approaches to the question of miracles. Some argue that miracles are *contra naturam:* they operate contrary to the established norms for the creation order. Others characterize them as *supra naturam:* from time to time and place to place God momentarily and locally suspends his "natural law" which normally governs the orderly course of events in order to make room for supernatural interventions. Both positions rest on dialectical-dualist worldviews. As Diemer points out, when modern man seeks to explain miracles by an appeal to the supernatural, the miraculous is itself actually denied.

> I fear that a number of contemporary Christians, with their concept of miracles as supernatural, and with their knowledge of present-day medicine and psychology, would doubt the miraculous character of the cures told about in Scripture if they occurred in Europe today. Supernatural events neither occurred in Palestine then, nor do they occur in Europe today. . . . [For] the supernatural was, is, and always will be an *asylum ignorantiae* into which one can push anything and everything which cannot be explained. . . . I am [therefore] convinced that it is not at all necessary to posit supernatural interventions as an explanation for the miracles that Scripture relates. Anyone who uses the supernatural as an explanation cuts himself off from gaining insight into the real nature of those events. (*Nature and Miracle,* pp. 21-23)

On a biblically directed, holist worldview, God and the world are not competing forces. Accordingly, in what we call miracles God does not eliminate the instrumental agency of his creatures. They remain his servants responding to the commanding power of his Word. These mighty acts of God, therefore, neither contravene nor supersede his dynamic yet stable order for creation. The potential for miraculous deeds is given from the beginning in and with God's abiding Word for our life in his world. Miracles are therefore not supernatural "breakthroughs" over and beyond the creation ordinances. In his wonder-working power God does not withdraw his providential care, or set it aside, or bypass it, or hold it in abeyance, or cancel its impact. The will of God revealed in such awesome signs and wonders resides in the very impinging power of his Word itself. There is nothing arbitrary or capricious about them. From our perspective they may appear as surprising, unexpected, extraordinary interventions of God's hand in history. For God, however, miracles are not miracles as we perceive them. They are rather the outworkings of his will in other ways, ways which to us appear unusual and exceptional, ways which are, however, consistently at God's command. For, citing Diemer once again, "with the signs and miracles of

God's providence in the history of mankind no laws or fixed relationships are circumvented. But under other than the ordinary, well-known conditions, other powers are opened up. This happens when man lives and acts out of faith and prayer. The potentials and powers of nature are thus harnessed in the service of the coming of God's kingdom on earth" (*Nature and Miracle,* p. 16). In the biblical view, therefore,

> a miracle is not a sign that a God who is usually absent is, for a moment, present, . . . [but rather] a signal that God is, for a moment and for a special purpose, walking down paths He does not usually walk, . . . a sign that God who is always present in creative power is working here and now in an unfamiliar way. (Lewis Smedes, *Ministry and the Miraculous,* pp. 48-49)

All creational possibilities are God's servants. Miracles therefore do not contradict, but rather open up in dramatic ways the holding and healing power of God's Word for creation. That Word includes stunning potentials of which we are barely aware, which often escape our attention, and to which we are largely insensitive. In the words of Berkouwer,

> It is not that in miracles a greater power is revealed than is present in the ordinary course of things. Everything that God brings into being is a work of His singular omnipotence. But in miracles God takes another way than that which had come to be expected of him in the usual course of events. This "otherwise" of God's working is often discernible in Scripture and it lays the foundation for the witness character of miracles. This accounts for the arousal of amazement. (*The Providence of God,* p. 231)

We must therefore be sensitive to God's providential care not only in our "mountain top experiences" and in our "narrow escapes" from threatening disaster, but also in our "daily routines." God's provision of manna in the wilderness is hardly more miraculous than casting seed into the ground, where it dies, bringing forth new grain in the field. His answer to fervent prayer can be as real in medical therapy as in the dramatic healings performed by Jesus and his apostles. In the words of Bavinck,

> [Providence] manifests itself not only and not primarily in extraordinary events and miracles, but just as much in the stable order of nature and in the common occurrences of daily life. (*Gereformeerde Dogmatiek,* Vol. II, p. 580)

The deepest and fullest meaning of God's special providence, which we call miracles, is indeed shrouded in mystery. But this is true of his general providence, too. No aspect of created reality, no event in history, is rationally transparent. Rationalism is proud pretense. The mysterious depth-dimensional meaning of miracles is, accordingly, more to be reverentially adored than intellectually fathomed. Such humility "spares us from both a superficial optimism, which fails to sense the riddles of life, and from a proud pessimism, which despairs of the world and our destiny" (Bavinck, *Gereformeerde Dogmatiek,* Vol. II, p. 580).

It is difficult to draw a clear line of demarcation between regular providence and miracles as God's "other way" of dealing with creation. Calvin posits a close relationship between these two aspects of divine providence in commenting on two "miracles," the sun standing still in Joshua's day and its moving backward on the sundial in response to Hezekiah's request. These are his words:

> God has witnessed by those few miracles that the sun does not daily rise and set by a blind instinct of nature, but that he himself, to renew our remembrance of his fatherly favor toward us, governs its course. Nothing is more natural than for spring to follow winter; summer, spring; and winter, fall — each in turn. Yet in this series one sees such great and uneven diversity that it really appears each year, month, and day is governed by a new, a special providence of God. (*Institutes,* I,16,2)

All God's acts have a mysteriously miraculous depth-meaning. Belief in the historical reality of miracles is accordingly an enduring aspect of the historic Christian faith. The biblical doctrine of providence and a Christian view of history are unthinkable apart from such mighty acts of God as creation, the exodus, and the resurrection, integrally woven as they are into the total fabric of biblical revelation.

With the arrival of modernity, however, a radical shift set in. Enlightenment thinkers relegated miracles to the mythological worldview of ancient times. This prescientific worldview was declared obsolete. A new worldview was aborning. Modern man, now at last come of age, rules out any need for the "hypothesis" of divine providence, let alone such "variables" and "deviations" as miracles. The "god of the gaps" is dead. For we live in a self-contained universe, a closed continuum of uniform cause-and-effect relationships, a world hermetically sealed in by the law of analogy, which excludes such scientifically uncontrollable factors as providence, miracles, or a "higher hand" in history. Contemporary criticism of the biblical witness to signs and wonders and miracles is pointedly exposed by Helmut Thielicke in the following lines, where he echoes the mind of modern man:

. . . Certainty is possible only if the truth that claims me is analogous to what my structure of consciousness contains within it as the consciousness of truth. Since I am a rational being who is aware of being enlightened and mature, any truth-claim that reaches me can be received and appropriated by me only if it contains a rational truth. This means, however, that a truth which is only historically attested and not validated by reason is a mere scrap. If, on the other hand, it is so validated, it can be detached from the history that attests it, once it has been perceived. For religion is not true because the evangelists and apostles taught it; they taught it because it is true. I thus have my own autonomous access to truth. Perhaps in the dull and immature stages of my development the truth will first come to me by way of history. But when I perceive it and have myself appropriated it, I am independent of the one who transmits it and stand on my own feet. When the historical education of the race ends, there will be only the pure and eternal gospel of reason. (*The Evangelical Faith*, Vol. I, p. 42)

The bold, self-confident presumption undergirding this nineteenth-century rationalist view of man and the world has been severely chastened by the revolutionary events of the twentieth century. Contemporary thinkers speak with greater caution and tentativity concerning the so-called "assured results of the scientific method." They are less absolute in their statements about the fixed "laws of nature." They concede that things appear to be more complex than formerly assumed. Notions of contingency, indeterminacy, relativity, even irrationality are common expressions in scholarly circles today. A "paradigm revolution" is upon us. Christians are sometimes tempted to rejoice in such signs of softening and retraction in the modern mechanist-determinist worldview. They may be inclined to think that this shift offers at least some slight hope of carving out anew a little room for acts of divine providence and miracle. As though miracles exist by the fortuitous shortcomings of science! Those who succumb to this negative mentality, allowing modern science to write the decisive agenda, and being content to pick up the meager bits of faith which fall from its table, can then await further scientific explorations with little else than a sense of fear and trepidation. As Berkouwer puts it,

He who rediscovers room for the activity of God in the crisis of natural science . . . has already implicitly relativized this [divine] activity and has posited it over against a natural order seen as a self-existing reality. In this way the question of miracles will always be entangled in the problems of natural science. And for the most part the Biblical manner of speaking about the activity of God in this world will have been abandoned. (*The Providence of God*, pp. 219-20).

In our century, however ambiguously, Barth, Bonhoeffer, and others launched a heavy counterattack on the historical-critical hermeneutic of modern liberalism, rooted in a naturalist-secularist worldview, which stripped biblical revelation of the reality of miracles. This led Barth to take issue with the radical demythologizing method of Bultmann. Well known is also Barth's "Yes" over against Brunner's "No" on the miracle of the virgin birth. As with every consistent hermeneutic, however, Barth's method of interpreting miracles finds its context of meaning in his peculiar worldview. In it he draws a sharp line of demarcation between "history" and "suprahistory." Accordingly, he distinguishes between "miracle" (the historical event) and "mystery" (its suprahistorical meaning). Miracles, such as the virgin birth, really happen, Barth insists, in opposition to his modernist teachers. To grasp their real significance, however, we must look beyond their historical event-character to their transhistorical meaning, the mystery of the free and sovereign act of God in Jesus Christ. In dealing with the "miracle of Pentecost," Barth therefore distinguishes this miraculous event itself from its mysterious meaning. In his words,

> The miracle is the form of the mystery. It cannot be separated from it. But it must be distinguished and considered apart. The account of it is related to that of the mystery as is the account of the Virgin Birth of Jesus to that of the incarnation enacted in this birth, or that of the empty tomb to that of His life as the Resurrected, or that of the miracles of Jesus to his Messianic utterances expressed in them. Here as everywhere miracle has the particular and indispensable function of indicating and at the same time characterizing the mystery, of giving its definite and distinctive sense and interpreting it as it is to be understood. Here as everywhere the form cannot be separated from the matter, nor the matter from the form. Here too, however, there can be no doubt that the miracle is in this sense the form of the mystery, of the divine act and revelation attested.

What, then, is the specific meaning of the miracle of Pentecost? ". . . It is the absolutely divine mystery of the freedom of these men to be messengers of the risen Jesus to Israel and the world." The crucial and decisive test of faith lies, however, according to Barth, not in the miraculous signs of the Pentecost event as such, but in the mysterious meaning of these dramatic happenings as expounded in Peter's sermon. Nevertheless,

> Luke's account of this miracle was indispensable, not to explain this miracle, which speaks for itself, nor to enhance or establish its historicity, but to limit and define it. Its message is that in the ensuing acts of the

apostles we really have to do with the wonderful works of God and not the works of men, and that these works consist in the fact that they will overcome the gulf between near and distant neighbors with their word. (*Church Dogmatics*, III/4, no. 54, pp. 320-23).

Barth's distinction between miracle and mystery, interpreted as form and matter, betrays the marks of an existentially oriented reversion to the dualist tendencies of Protestant scholasticism. A new nature/grace scheme then emerges. Such dichotomist views, leaning toward a deist conception of the Creator/creature relationship, have long plagued our understanding of miracles. In the words of Bavinck:

> The major objection to deism is certainly this, that by divorcing God and the world, the infinite and the finite, and setting them dualistically alongside each other, it turns them into competing powers, locked in ceaseless struggle, disputing each other's dominion. What is given to God is taken away from the world. The more God's providence is extended, the more the creature loses its independence and freedom. And conversely, the creature can maintain its self-activity only by repelling God and robbing him of his sovereignty. (*Gereformeerde Dogmatiek,* Vol. II, p. 563)

Such worldviews proceed on the assumption that created reality operates basically in accord with natural law. Sporadically, however, we experience supernatural intrusions from beyond into the established regularities of the natural order for the purpose of demonstrating a very special grace or providential care. Behind such an interpretation of miracles lies the only slightly hidden assumption of a dualist worldview in which natural causality functions independently of the Word of God, with only occasional corrective interference by a *Deus ex machina*.

Such perspectives stand diametrically opposed to the biblical worldview, which confronts us with God providentially active at every point along the way, ceaselessly sustaining and governing all his creatures by the holding and healing power of his Word. We do well therefore to discard many of the commonplace categories regularly employed to distinguish miracle from ordinary history. Among them are the following: (a) the distinction between natural and supernatural, since everything in creation is "natural" in the sense of possessing its own unique creaturely identity, yet "supernatural" in the sense of being subject constantly to divine ordinance; (b) the distinction between mediate and immediate acts of God, since in every life relationship God deals with his creatures covenantally through the mediating power of his Word — contrary to Calvin's comment that God's providence is "the determinative principle of all things in such a way that sometimes it works through an intermediary, sometimes without an intermediary, sometimes contrary to every intermediary" (*Institutes,* I,17,1); (c) the distinction between normal and abnormal, since these categories also represent a highly pejorative way of differentiating among God's providential works. This view assumes that God's activity sometimes departs from the normed order of creation.

That method is also very suspect which (d) distinguishes miracles from God's constant superintendency of history by resorting to the Aristotelian distinction between primary and secondary logical causes in order to emphasize the supernatural and unmediated *(contra media)* nature of miraculous occurrences (cf. Louis Berkhof, *Systematic Theology,* pp. 176-77). (e) Finally, that view of miracles which distinguishes them from ordinary historical events by declaring them unexplainable or incomprehensible is also very dubious, since it implies that the meaning of most events is transparent. Actually we are unable to fathom in depth even the most commonplace happenings in our daily experience. In the words of Herman Hoeksema, therefore,

> It is true that we cannot understand how the Lord can multiply the few loaves of bread in His divine hands, so that a veritable multitude can be fed thereby. But no more does it lie within the limits of my conception how a seed can fall in the earth and die, in order to bring forth fruit a hundred fold. It is certainly true that my mind is amazed when the Savior calls Lazarus out of the grave after he has been four days asleep in the dust; but no less does the birth of a little child transcend my boldest comprehension. How the Lord Jesus at the wedding of Cana could change water into wine is certainly a mystery for us; but it is no less incomprehensible for us how the vine can produce grapes and in that way change different elements into wine. In other words, it does not make any difference for my understanding whether God by His almighty power operates in the common and known way upon the vine and causes it to bring forth grapes, or whether by the same almighty power He works upon water to change that into wine. When the sun and the moon stand still upon the word of Joshua, we confess that we cannot comprehend this phenomenon; but when the Lord every morning anew causes the sun to rise on the eastern horizon, that work of God also transcends my comprehension. . . . [M]iracle causes us to stand amazed and draws our special attention. But the cause of this must not be found in the fact that we comprehend the common events and acts of God's providence, while the wonders transcend our comprehension; but it must much rather be found in this, that we become so accustomed to the daily works of God's omnipresent power that we usually pay no attention to them. In the miracle God certainly performs something special which exactly through its special character draws the attention. Nevertheless, neither in the so-called supernatural, nor in the immediate character, nor

in the incomprehensible character of a wonder can the proper idea of a miracle be found. (*Reformed Dogmatics,* pp. 242-43)

The biblical accent falls not on miracles as a problem to be solved, nor on puzzling over their possibility or probability, but on their matter-of-fact reality. Naturally miracles happen! What else should we expect? Concerning the resurrection, critics may exclaim: Impossible! Scripture, however, speaks a wholly different language: It was impossible for death to keep Christ down (Acts 2:24-28). Miracles are confirmations of the invincible truth of God's Word. They are not raw displays of power. Their purpose is not to impress people with overwhelming demonstrations of divine omnipotence. Nor are they given to satisfy our curiosity. Miracles are laden with a revelational intent, purpose, and meaning.

Scripture accordingly posits a close relationship between miracles and faith. Faith has an eye for the wondrous works of God, being itself a wonder of divine grace. In the Gospels, where unbelief struck people blind, we read that "[Jesus] could do no mighty work there . . ." (Mark 6:5). Perhaps our frequent spiritual impotency is related to lack of faith in the "greater works" (John 14:12-14) which our Lord promised. There is no good biblical reason, therefore, to restrict God's wonder-working power to certain (past) times and (faraway) places — such as during the biblical era. To reject out of hand the reality or even the possibility of miracles in our times betrays our surrender to the secular spirit of our day. Life is as open to miracles today as it ever was. To capitulate to a closed worldview is to impoverish the power of prayer. On the other hand, an obsessive fascination with miraculous signs easily blinds us to God's providential care in the common occurrences of everyday living. Miracles are not out-of-this-world sensations. They are integral to our down-to-earth experience. More things are wrought by miracles, in response to prayer, than most of us ever dream possible. In them God acts not *contra naturam,* but *contra peccatum* — counteracting the sinful misdirection, distortion, and perversion of life in the world, not contravening his creational handiwork.

Miracles are therefore not abnormal or unnatural happenings. Such notions presupposes the normalcy of "natural law." Rather, they are reaffirmations of the normativity of the good creation order, of God's abiding faithfulness to his covenant promises. Miracles are signs and wonders of God's intended shalom, now shattered, but restored in Christ, a shalom whose final restoration is held up before us as an eschatological hope. They represent manifestations of the future kingdom within present reality. They are forceful reminders of the "already" dimension of the coming kingdom. As Jesus declared, "If I by the finger of God cast out demons, then has the kingdom of God come upon you" (Luke

11:20). But he amazement they conjure up among us is also an emphatic reminder of the "not yet" dimension of the kingdom. Nevertheless, their seemingly exceptional occurrence should not mislead us into thinking that they are "detours," excursions into some "never, never land." Miracles are rather kingdom signposts, firmly planted along that christologically reopened way which ushers in the renewal of that good earth in which perfect righteousness dwells.

PART THREE
SIN AND EVIL

Introduction: The Good Creation . . . Fallen

A very tight-lipped president, returning from church on a Sunday morning, was asked by his wife, "What did the minister preach on?"

"Sin," he replied.

"And what did he say about it?"

"He was against it."

So far, so good, as we turn our attention now to the sinfulness that infests our lives. In dealing with the fallen creation, however, we cannot simply leave behind the doctrine of the good creation. The mighty creating acts of God do indeed belong to the past. That chapter in world history is now closed. "Primary creation" *(ex nihilo)* and "secondary creation" (the six days) represent once-for-all events. In that sense there is "nothing new under the sun."

It is different, however, with "tertiary creation" (our roles in the work of God's world). Creation understood as createdness, the ongoing creaturely status and function of all things, is the permanent setting for responding to God's Word. Apart from this Creator-creature relationship we cannot even begin to shape a biblically directed doctrine of our original sin, our sinful condition, our actual sins, and the overwhelming presence of evil in and around us. Only a high view of creation can clear the way for exposing the radical depths of the universal curse which hangs heavy on our life together in God's world. It is precisely the witness of Scripture to sin and its effects that confronts us with the awful reality of a fallen creation.

Sin belongs to the biblical story line of creation-fall-redemption-restoration only as a total "misfit." In its beginnings, but also as a present existential reality, sin stands out as an unremovable link which Scripture forges into that unbreakable chain of historical moments which makes us what we are. Yet it does not really "belong" there. It is an antinormative disruption. It defies all attempts to weave it smoothly into the fabric of the good order of creation. Sin is ever an alien force, an enemy to be overcome. It just does not "fit," except like a square peg in a round hole.

Sensitive Christians experience this in daily living. But the dissonant, clashing sounds of sin are also present in every attempt to orchestrate our theological reflections. Sin is simply nowhere at home. It does not deserve a "locus" of its own. Yet its radical and sweeping impact, misdirecting all things, will not allow us to bypass it. Where then shall we place the doctrine of sin? This question of location is not unimportant. For where a topic is dealt with is a significant index to one's overall theological perspective. In a Reformed dogmatics it is best to allow the doctrine of sin a bridging role, no more and no less. It serves an antinormative transitional function in moving from a consideration of the norms of creation to the renewed normativities of the gospel of redemption. It represents a violation of the creation order, and as such it sets the stage for God's way of salvation in Christ Jesus.

This point of view is reflected in the flow of thought in Calvin's *Institutes*. In Book I he deals with the knowledge of God as Creator. He then moves on directly into Book II: the knowledge of God as Redeemer — thus from creation to redemption without an intervening "book" on sin. Calvin refuses to give "equal time" to the question of sin. Instead, he subsumes it under the topic of redemption (Book II, 1-6). The doctrine of sin and its effects serves as the occasion for discussing law and gospel, followed by the person and work of Christ. It is an offbeat note, played in a minor key between the major movements of creation and redemption.

In thus downplaying sin as a "locus" in his theology, without minimizing its serious and devastating impact, Calvin in his *Institutes* structures his thinking along the fairly traditional lines of the trinitarian pattern of the Apostles' Creed. In this ecumenical creed the reality of sin certainly colors Article II (on Christ), Article III (on the Holy Spirit), and also the final article on the church. But sin is not accorded the honor of a separate article. It would indeed be abhorrent to the Christian community to "believe (in) sin." Instead, sin is subsumed under the rubric of the church, where the saints in communion confess, "(I believe) . . . the forgiveness of sins."

A similar restraint is typical of Scripture. For in its total extent and in all its parts the Bible is the saving revelation of God in Jesus Christ. Accordingly, the record of our fall into sin is compressed into the brief span of a few verses — Genesis 3:1-7. The rest of this chapter, together with Scripture as a whole, is the unfolding story of God's intervention to counteract the effects of that calamitous event. Yet the Genesis 3 narrative is not an isolated episode. Its message of human failure (dis)colors every page in the unfolding biblical drama and is verified by every chapter in human history. The biblical focus nonetheless falls on the Messianic promises and their fulfillment. Therefore the Scriptures view even that original act of sin from the vantage point of the unfolding plan of redemption.

It is imperative, then, that we take our stance where the Bible writers stand. For we are so deeply enmeshed in the webs of iniquity that, apart from this revelation, we fail to see our sinful condition and our actual sins for what they really are. Seeing evil, we see it not. We pin a thousand false labels on it. Therefore, as with creation, so with sin, we must begin where the Bible begins.

Chapter I

Exposing the Roots

I. 1. The Origin of Sin and Evil

When it comes to sin, it takes a Christian with Bible in hand and heart to "call a spade a spade." Yet any thinking person recognizes that there is something persistently and pervasively wrong with our world. There is a universal awareness of mankind's "sickness unto death." Its haunting reality has exercised the best of minds in every time and place. But what went wrong? When did it happen? How did it originate? On these baffling questions there is little consensus.

Across the centuries Christian thinkers, and others, have wrestled with this knotty complex of problems. How are we to account for the origin of our sinful condition, our actual sins, and the concomitant evil powers at work in our world? In light of the good creation, is it possible to come to terms with these alien forces? Where shall we turn for answers? Even the most dogged attempts to uncover the root cause of the evil behind our sin must finally come to rest in the reformational byword — *sola Scriptura*. The biblical witness is decisive in setting the agenda and establishing the parameters for our theologizing on this as on every issue. For we have no access to any word over and beyond this Word of God. Every quest for some deeper insight or more ultimate answer leads inescapably into dead-end speculations.

What light, then, does Scripture shed on these restless probings to discover some original evil lurking behind our original sin? How are we to "explain" it? In its own unique way the Bible issues a much needed, stern reminder of the friendly limits which the Creator has imposed on our human rationality. However frustrating to our speculative inclinations, it speaks only of the *beginning* of sin, not its *origin*. Just as it safeguards whatever mysteries may lie behind the beginnings of creation, so too with the beginnings of the fallenness of creation. At this point,

303

too, we must start where the Bible starts. And its starting point, as formulated in the Heidelberg Catechism, is this: "the fall and disobedience of our first parents in Paradise."

With this very sober account we must make our peace. Every pursuit of a more original and ultimate "explanation" is bound to come up empty. The origin of evil remains forever that ultimately inexplicable "mystery of ungodliness." Calvin therefore advocates approaching this issue in the spirit of humble and pious ignorance. Seeking to break the bounds of Scripture is "a kind of madness." Accordingly, he says, "we should contemplate the evident cause of condemnation in the corrupt nature of humanity — which is closer to us — rather than seek a hidden and utterly incomprehensible cause in God's predestination" (*Institutes*, III,23,8). Bavinck sounds a similar cautionary note:

> Whoever tries to comprehend or to explain our sin, or attempts to show that it must follow necessarily from what has gone before, does injustice to sin's very nature. He obscures the boundaries of good and evil and derives our evil from something that is good. (*Gereformeerde Dogmatiek*, Vol. III, p. 47)

This point is further reinforced by Weber, who says that . . .

> this mystery is made manifest in that sin is beyond all explanation. We cannot say how it came into the world. Even the biblical statements which revolve around Genesis 3 do not explain, but recount what is inexplicable. (*Foundations of Dogmatics*, Vol. I, p. 607)

In its inception as well as in its ongoing overwhelming power, sin-and-evil remains an unfathomable reality. Only such words as enigma, puzzle, riddle, folly, and stupidity come close to describing its bastard status. There is no legitimacy in this illegitimate intruder, no sense in its senseless stranglehold on us. As Berkouwer puts it, all arguments that seek to clarify the origin of evil "shrivel into nothingness." We cannot explain it; we can only confess it. For . . .

> in the act of confession we do not, and we cannot, yearn for an "explanation" of our sins. We [can only] recognize our sins as our very own. . . . If [there is any] . . . pointing of our fingers, it should be only to that ugly self-guilt which stands directly and irrefutably before our very eyes. "For I know my transgressions, and my sin is ever before me" (Psalm 51:3). (*Sin*, p. 19)

Hendrikus Berkhof concedes that "perhaps there is no answer" to the question "why God permitted sin, and still puts up with it." Yet he holds that "it must be possible, nonetheless, to consider this question without the hidden motive of minimizing sin and of justifying self" (*Christian Faith,* p. 197).

Methodologically Berkouwer agrees that the many theories on the origin of sin and evil must be critically examined, stating that "the driving force in these efforts is so strong that we can hardly afford to ignore them." In doing so, however, "we wish only to be better warned" against speculation (*Sin,* p. 26). With this rationale, we turn now to the major theories which seek to trace mankind's original sin back to some deeper and more ultimate cause.

I. 1. 1. A Double Presupposition

In weighing these theories we must bear in mind the two fundamental principles which have traditionally circumscribed the boundaries for Christian reflection on this question. One concerns the creation, the other the Creator. The first presupposition is this: the goodness of creation. Sin can claim no creaturely status. Evil is not an ontic reality present from the beginning. As Calvin says, we are "corrupted by natural vitiation," but this sinfulness "did not flow from nature" — that is, we are sinners "by (our corrupted) nature," but not "by (our created) nature" (*Institutes,* II,1,11). For the seal of divine approval rests originally on every creature. Repeatedly God declares the emerging orders of creation "(very) good." There were no hidden flaws. The Maker's creative handiwork was all it was meant to be — completely "in order," sacred, holy.

That brings us then to the second nonnegotiable tenet of the historic Christian faith. If original sin is not traceable to some defect in creation, what alternative is left? Is God then somehow its "Prime Mover"? Did evil then in some transcendent way originate in him? Perish the very thought! It is this anathema which hedges in the other side of the problem. For "God is light, and in him is no darkness at all" (1 John 1:5). Classic Christian theology flatly refuses even to entertain the notion that the Creator himself is in some sense the Author, Source, or Cause of sin and evil. This option is repudiated in the strongest possible terms in the confessions of the Reformation era. "God is neither the Author of nor can He be charged with the sins which are committed" (Belgic Confession, Article 13). A similar disavowal is expressed in the Canons of Dordt: "The cause or guilt of this unbelief as well as of all other sins is no wise in God, but in man himself" (I.5). Moreover, even the decree of reprobation "by no means makes God the Author of sin (the very thought of which is blasphemy) . . ." (I.15).

With the a priori exclusion of these two "explanations" as unacceptable options, the speculative impulse of Christian thinkers found itself caught between "a rock and a hard place." Yet restless minds were not deterred by these two biblically attuned presuppositions. Countless quests were launched in search of a "solution." Out of these laborious efforts three main theories were born.

I. 1. 2. Monist "Explanations"

In the closing doxology to his classic passage on God's way with Israel, Paul writes: "For from [God] and through him and to him are *all* things . . ." (Romans 11:36). Is it possible that this reference to "all things" also includes that "thing" called sin? In some supremely sovereign sense does evil originate in the divine decree? It is questions such as these that have long agitated the minds of supralapsarian thinkers inclined toward a decretal theology. After all, nothing happens apart from the will of God. All things, adversity as well as prosperity, are in his hand. The entire checkered mosaic of world history is under his command — the light that shines, but also the dark shadows. Reasoning along these lines, monist thinkers seek to incorporate good and evil alike into a logically symmetrical system.

Some monist theologians do not hesitate to project the mystery of ungodliness back on God himself. It is he who hardens Pharaoh's heart (Exodus 4:21) and incites David to call for a census (2 Samuel 24:1). Even in the sixth petition of the Lord's Prayer, "and lead us not into temptation," are we not implicitly acknowledging that God opens the door to temptation? Such thinking often takes refuge in the distinction between God's *revealed* will, his norm for obedient living, and his *secret* will. The latter is then regarded as the real and efficacious will of God, the deciding factor in all that takes place. Sometimes an "explanation" is sought in an appeal to the dialectical tension between *Deus revelatus* and *Deus absconditus* — the "two faces" of God. The one discloses "right handedly" the good side of God's work, the other reflects "left handedly" his involvement in the works of darkness.

One cannot escape the stresses and strains which such theologizing imposes on God's self-revelation in Scripture. For he is not "a God of disorder, but of peace" (1 Corinthians 14:33). How then can the utterly disorderly power of evil be harmonized with the God of "decency and good order" (verse 40)? Alert to this problem, some theologians define God's willing of sin in terms of *permission*: He does not overtly will it, but he does permit it. The plot thickens when we focus on specific sinful acts. It is sometimes argued that God wills sin in general, but not particular sins. In other cases the argument is reversed. Sin, however, is never a vague abstraction, but always overwhelms us as a concrete reality. When therefore we turn to gross acts of concrete sinfulness — premeditated murder, fatal accidents, the drug culture, wanton slaughter of the unborn, terrorist bombings — biblical sensitivity resists all our dogged attempts to relate such devastating experiences to God in some cause-and-effect way.

Such painstaking efforts to incorporate an "explanation" of sin and evil into a closed system of thought centering on God's decrees is certainly understandable. It is a by-product of our long legacy of scholastic theology with its misleading results. In one respect at least such theologizing is even commendable. It adamantly refuses to grant wickedness an independent, autonomous status. Reading Scripture as some decretal theologians do, certain texts even appear to lend validity to these "solutions." Nevertheless, the troublesome idea of causality, so roundly rejected by the Reformation creeds, remains a nearly inescapable pitfall in every monist attempt to reduce good and evil alike to a single principle.

Evil has no divine origin, not even "in a certain sense." God is "in no sense" the Cause that "explains" our original sin. To espouse the opposite is sheer speculation. It leads us away from the heartbeat of the gospel. Luther's word still stands: "Let God be God!" He is omnipotent, even in the face of sin's devastations. Evil itself is in "good hands." God can intercept evil, bending it to good ends (Genesis 50:20). He can "draw a straight line with a crooked stick." But precisely because God is God, his relationship to sin and evil is marked exclusively by righteous indignation, just judgment, reconciliation, and in the end perfect redemption. In the meantime, however, as Bavinck puts it, the power of evil is "the greatest contradiction tolerated by God in his creation, and is used by him in the way of righteousness and justice as an instrument for his glory" (*Gereformeerde Dogmatiek*, Vol. III, p. 126). Berkouwer strikes a similar note: "God intercepts man's sin — in the revelation of that profound mystery He both condemns and expiates his sin" (*Sin*, p. 62).

At stake in monist attempts to "explain" the origin of sin and evil is Calvin's hermeneutic: try to say no less than Scripture, for that means impoverishment; but try also to say no more, for that leads to speculation. The liberating message of Scripture offers the possibilities for, but also imposes limitations on, our understanding of how spiritual darkness began. We have no word over, beyond, or behind this Word.

I. 1. 3. Dualist "Explanations"

If then, on biblical and confessional grounds, it is illegitimate to relate our sinfulness causally to our Creator, and if moreover the power of evil is not resident as an ontic reality in the creation, what is left for those who seek by speculation to account for these origins? Faced with this dilemma, some Christians have flirted with dualist "explanations." To relieve God of this terrible responsibility, they posit the coexistence of a second deity. The God of Christian faith is the Source of light; the other is an antigod, who casts a dark spell over the world. These two deities are poles apart, but nonetheless coequal and coeternal. All world history is a manifestation of the inexorable power struggle between them. Life is a battleground, pitting two opposing forces against each other. We are caught inextricably in this crossfire of conflict, with no assurance of a happy outcome, the tragic victims of an ultimate and fearful fate.

On this view the evil which led to our downfall has a pseudodivine origin. Sin and evil are ontic realities, as real and ultimate as goodness and peace. They represent an autonomous power, acting independently of and contrary to the God of Scripture. The result is an absolute dualism, a primordial antithesis between two cooriginating principles irreconcilably opposed to each other.

Some thinkers, impressed by the way Scripture highlights the idea of "God above all the gods," propose a qualified dualism. They reduce the second deity to an unequal power, seeking thus to safeguard the eventual triumph of good over evil. Others advocate the idea of a more proximate dualism — not an antithesis between two hostile divine powers, but the struggle between two earthly realms of reality, the one superior, the other inferior. This idea opens the floodgates to the widespread notion of an antinomy between the higher spiritual and the lower bodily functions in human life.

In our times it is commonplace to read the biblical account of beginnings as a titanic struggle between two competing cosmic powers. "Waste" and "void" and "darkness" (Genesis 1:2) are then interpreted as chaotic forces which God must subdue in his work of creation. These primordial elements are conceived of as a menacing abyss lurking along the fringes of a world in the making, threatening moment by moment to plunge it back into a state of nonbeing. They constitute a contrary force acting aggressively at cross-purposes with God's affirmation of being. Though defeated, this negative counterforce casts its dark shadows over creation.

We see, then, that these various dualist "answers" to the problem of the origin of evil take many fascinating twists and turns. In the final analysis, however, they interject "a dualism which is profoundly foreign to Genesis; the text contains not the slightest hint of any battle whatsoever" (Henri Blocher, *In The Beginning*, p. 64). In a similar vein, Berkouwer, appealing to Bavinck, concludes that biblical revelation "tells us nothing about a chaotic force which existed independently of or before God's creative activity" (*Sin*, p. 83).

Throughout the Christian era "hard dualisms" never really gained a solid foothold in the life of the believing community. They were vigorously resisted as an assault on the exclusively sovereign prerogatives of the One whom Scripture reveals as Lord of all. Translated into "soft dualisms," however, these intriguing ideas have left their mark on the church. As Weber points out, "evil as an independent and anti-divine power — that is certainly a tempting explanation for the puzzle posed to man in all generations by evil and the wickedness which it has produced" (*Foundations of Dogmatics,* Vol. I, p. 582). It helps "explain" the yawning chasm between good and evil, the seductive attractions of pride and greed, the conflict between oppressors and oppressed. To transfer the cause of evil to some suprahuman reality alleviates the urgency of our sinful condition, helps to excuse it, and relieves our sense of guilt both personally and collectively. For man "bears proportionately less responsibility the more transcendent and absolute this opposition is conceived to be" (Weber, *Foundations of Dogmatics,* Vol. I, p. 583).

These heretical tendencies entered the Christian tradition through the influence of the Manichees and Marcionites. Their ideas posed the greatest threat to the early church in the form of Gnosticism, a widely diffusive movement which offered a synthesis of Christian faith with ideas from neo-Platonic philosophy and elements borrowed from the mystic religions of the day. Well known is the experience of Augustine. On his turbulent pilgrimage along the way toward becoming the Bishop of Hippo, for a full decade he came under the enticing spell of Manichean mysticism. Later in life, looking back, he pours out his soul in true confession.

> I believed Evil also to be some such kind of substance, and to have its own foul and hideous bulk; whether gross, which they called earth, or thin and subtle, (like the body of the air), which they imagine to be some malignant mind, creeping through the earth. And because a piety, such as it was, constrained me to believe that the good God never created an evil nature, I conceived two masses, contrary to one another, both unbounded, but the evil narrower, the good more expansive. And from this pestilent beginning, the other sacrilegious conceits followed on me. . . . (*Confessions,* V.20)

Augustine then tortured his mind in search of answers:

> Where is evil then, and whence, and how crept it in hither? What is its root, and what its seed? Or hath it no being? And why then fear we and avoid what is not? Or if we fear idly, then is that very fear evil, whereby the soul is thus idly goaded and racked. . . . Or was there some evil matter

309

from which He made, and formed, and ordered [a lesser good], yet left something in it which He did not convert into good? (*Confessions*, VII,7)

Finally, during the fourth decade of his life, Augustine made a clean break with his Manichean past. Historic Christianity then followed his lead in rejecting dualist "explanations" for the origin of evil. As Thielicke puts it, "two things have to be avoided." Not only must we resist "the error which robs evil of its antithetical character and makes it simply the dialectical counterpart of the good," but also "the Gnostic and Manichean error which sets evil over against God in an abstract dualism so that finally there are two opposing gods" (*The Evangelical Faith*, Vol. I, p. 263). The Creator God has no arch rival, no primordial sinister antagonist. Creation came into existence "out of nothing" — nothing but the beneficent will of God. Accordingly, the basic thrust of the Genesis narrative, in the words of Berkouwer, is "to illumine the majestic character of God's creative activity in contrast to everything that could possibly threaten or render impossible a structured cosmos" (*Sin*, p. 85).

I. 1. 4. Demonic "Explanations"

This third "solution" sidesteps both monist and dualist "explanations" of the origin of evil. It points an accusing finger instead at the devil and his demonic cohorts. The source of human sin is the "evil one." Those holding this view posit a fall behind our fall, a prior rebellion in the angelic realm. Appeal is often made to two passages from Scripture — 2 Peter 2:4 and Jude 6 — which refer to angels who "sinned" by not "remaining in their positions of authority but abandoned their proper dwelling." At their head is "the father of lies" who deceived, tempted, and overpowered our first parents. We are thus the hapless victims of a fateful demonic conspiracy.

This view is sometimes called "the happy doctrine of the devil." It offers a ready excuse for our sinfulness and relieves our sense of guilt. The devil becomes our "scapegoat"! Yet this is not the way the story of our downfall unfolds in Genesis 3. Eve and Adam appear there as active participants in this diabolical dialogue. We cannot simply shake off our responsibility. On the one hand, "the serpent deceived Eve by his cunning" (2 Corinthians 11:3). Still, it is also true that "sin came into the world through one man" (Romans 5:12). Mankind is not a passive, innocent victim of demonic intrigue. Yet in a strangely baffling way we were lured into this satanic plot, all the while cooperating willingly. This leaves us, in the words of Hendrikus Berkhof, with "a tension which we can barely endure in our life and mind" (*Christian Faith*, p. 202).

Arguing along similar lines, Brunner holds that human sinfulness "presupposes a tempting power" which seduces us from the outside. For if we were capable of originating sin on our own, then the dark shadows of a demonic disposition would fall over our very creatureliness. Simultaneously, therefore, original sin and all subsequent sins represent a confluence of both "an act of satan" and "spontaneous ignition." For "man is not ingenious enough to invent sin by himself" (*Dogmatics,* Vol. II, p. 108).

Against the impenetrable backdrop of this demonic intrusion into the good creation, Scripture strips us of all excuses. The tempter plays his beguiling role. But we are not conquered by some irresistible power which forces our hand. There is blame enough to go all around — the serpent, Eve, Adam, all of us. We cannot dislodge the burden of guilt from our own doorstep.

Scripture paints a truly grim picture of the awful effects of that original sin. Its pages abound with warnings against "the power of darkness," against "principalities and powers," "the world rulers of the present darkness," "spiritual hosts of wickedness in heavenly places," "the god of this world," "the evil one" who "deceives the nations." All this is terribly real. Apart from Christ, moreover, we are helpless to resist this overwhelming power. Yet the compelling reality of this "kingdom of darkness" in no way exonerates us of our responsibility and guilt. We must simply conclude that "it is impossible for us to say how temptation could find a point of contact in a holy person. And it is even more difficult to explain the origin of sin in the angelic world" (Louis Berkhof, *Systematic Theology,* p. 224). This theory of the demonic origin of evil is therefore also a dead-end street. As Hendrikus Berkhof puts it, "it explains nothing, but only shifts the problem partly into a suprahuman sphere" (*Christian Faith,* p. 202).

*　　　*　　　*

All three "solutions" abandon us to the slippery slopes of speculation. As "explanations" they are "all equally untenable" (Berkouwer, *Sin,* p. 128). As rationalist inquiries, however desperately pursued, they yield little more than exercises in futility. For they seek "answers" to questions that the Bible leaves unanswered. A "theodicy of sin" is out of the question. We simply cannot probe whatever hidden depths may lie behind the narrative of Genesis 3. The confession, "in Adam's fall, we sinned all," is the bottom line. This conclusion is not the flight of a defeated mind seeking refuge in the asylum of ignorance. It is rather a demonstration of respect for the biblical starting point. Scripture sheds no light on the many attempts to ferret out a more ultimate "explanation." The *origin* of evil remains an inexplicable mystery. But its *beginning* is a matter of biblical record. We must therefore start where the Bible starts on the story of sin and evil.

I. 2. Original Sin

Scripture draws the curtain on all behind-the-scenes speculation into the origin of evil. Instead, in Genesis 3 it sets at center stage the down-to-earth scenario of our fall into sin, commonly called the original sin. This devastating event represents the second crucial turning point in the biblical story line. There, in a few brief verses (3:1-7), followed by scattered reflections on it throughout Scripture (Psalm 51:1-5; Romans 5:12-21; 1 Corinthians 15:22), we stand face-to-face with the originating sin which lies behind all our sins. This is Scripture's most ultimate and profound way of accounting for the avalanche of evil which has descended on the human race.

At first glance this narrative of sin's entry on the stage of history may seem like such a trivial affair. After all, what is so bad about eating an apple, or peach, or fig, or whatever it was? The fruit of this "tree of knowledge of good and evil" was probably not much different from that of the surrounding trees. And a healthy appetite is a blessing bestowed on us by our Creator. What we see, then, in this violation of the probationary command is good desire gone wrong. The prohibition was a test of creaturely obedience, pure and simple. For by divine arrangement this forbidden fruit served as the decisive proving ground for covenant faithfulness. God's Word in the form of the probationary command was clear: "Obey me, or else. . . ." At stake was the total relationship between man and his Maker. For this command was a friendly protective hedge, safeguarding our place and task in the creation. It was a test of our willingness to let God be God and to live within our creaturely limitations in full dependence on the will of our Creator. Would we accept God's Word as the norm for life, or seek it in something creaturely? That was and is the basic choice (Romans 1:25). By our willful disobedience we unleashed the "or else" side of God's Word on ourselves and our world. The warning Word of impending curse became reality. Now, therefore, "not only the creation, but we ourselves, groan inwardly as we wait for our . . . redemption . . ." (Romans 8:23).

With this act of "man in revolt" (Brunner) the most radical and sweeping changes take place. In one sense, structurally, nothing changes. God is still God, his Word still holds, human beings retain their identity, creation is still intact. God's preserving grace maintains a lawful order for life. At the same time, however, everything changes. Abruptly and drastically, our very existence becomes completely misdirected. This becomes painfully evident when the next divinely appointed "sabbath rest" comes around. The communion between Creator and creature lay in disarray. Lines of communication were badly tangled. Yet God refused to turn his back on the guilty pair. Returning to the garden, apparently in theophany, the Creator launches his first act of redemption. He goes out looking for the hidden culprits. Their sin is exposed by the searching eye of the Judge. But even God's judgment signals the dawn of a new day of grace. With the fall into sin all hell breaks loose; but then all heaven moves in to turn the tide. From then on *sola gratia* would become the only hopeful rule of life.

That first encounter in a fallen world reveals the depths of our human predicament and our dire need for restoration. Husband and wife now blush in shame. They sew fig leaves to cover their unprecedented sense of complete nakedness. This act is already an ominous sign for the human race of a future punctuated by countless cover-ups. They hide amid the foliage, foreshadowing our chronic disposition to circumvent the truth. A gracious Father calls out to the prodigal son, "Adam, where are you?!" The heir has deserted his rightful place in the creation. Everything is out of joint. When at last "the Hound of heaven" (Francis Thompson) overtakes his errant crown creatures, they fabricate excuses, pointing accusing fingers outward: "the woman you gave me," "the serpent beguiled me." Only as a last resort does the presence of the great Inquisitor evoke a true confession, "I ate" (Genesis 3:12-13). In their evasive maneuvers, desperately seeking excuses, they recapitulate the seductive steps which led to their downfall. Bit by bit the craftiness of the tempter broke down their resistance: sowing seeds of doubt about the reality of the divine command, suggesting that this prohibition was an infringement on their rights and freedoms, calling into question the consequences of breaking the agreement, appealing to the proud prospect of "being like God," and finally arousing the lust of the eye. Our first parents fell for this satanic line. They tried then to rationalize their acts. Sharing in their deceit, we their children have learned to devise even more sophisticated ways of "passing the buck." We blame our misbehavior on traumatic effects of faulty parental upbringing, on getting up on the wrong side of the bed, on a virus invading our computers.

In his ballad entitled "Reverse Creation," Bernard Blackman sings eschatologically about the impact of human rebellion.

And man said, let there be darkness, and there was darkness. Man said the darkness was good and he called the darkness — security. And there was no evening and no morning on the seventh day before the end. . . .

313

And then man said, let us create God in our own image lest some other god compete with us. . . . And there was no morning on the day before the end.

Divine judgment is fully present in these strained and broken relationships. Each guilty party is judged "after his/her/its kind." God metes out penalties suited to the peculiar nature and task of each actor in this terrible comedy of errors — the man in his daily vocation, the woman in childbearing, and the serpent (who alone is given no opportunity to answer for himself on his satanic role in the drama) in his despicable place in the animal kingdom. Just as redemption "fits" creation, so too there is a perfect "match" between the variations discernible in the divinely imposed judgment and the diversities present in the divinely wrought creation.

Fortunately, in the end a stern but merciful Hand reaches out to unmask us until, driven to our knees, we pray, "Against thee, thee only, have I sinned . . ." (Psalm 51:4). The Black spiritual poses the question, "Were you there when they crucified my Lord?" To which the Christian replies, Yes, I was there — my sins nailed him to the cross. So, by a parallel but reverse analogy, the question can be paraphrased: Were you there when our first parents fell into sin? The answer comes back, Yes, I participated in their guilt (Romans 5:12). Above our cries of repentance a reassuring Voice then sounds, "Blessed is he . . . whose sin is covered" (Psalm 32:1). This way of escape is securely anchored in God's original annunciation of the Good News (Genesis 3:15). We hear in this *protevangelium,* however dimly and from a distance, the promise that the divinely interposed "enmity" would one day be reconciled through the coming Messiah.

Chapter II

Bearing Bitter Fruit

II. 1. Sin "by Any Other Name . . ."

"A rose by any other name," wrote Shakespeare, "would smell as sweet." Laying aside its nominalist overtones, and by way of paraphrase, this well-known adage may be adapted contrastingly to the question at hand: Sin by any other name is no less repugnant. How then shall we identify it? People in every age, but especially we moderns, have devised an endless list of euphemisms to escape its full force. We call it a momentary lapse of good judgment, a Freudian slip, a little white lie, acting out of sorts — almost anything to avoid "calling a spade a spade." This collage of misnomers reflects the wide range of self-images and worldviews present in our pluralist societies.

Scripture, however, is an unabashedly honest book — honest to God and honest with ourselves. It confronts us squarely with the reality of sin as an all-pervasive blight which is inescapably ours. Sin touches our entire personhood. It bends all our life relationships out of shape. "Small wonder, then," as Hoeksema puts it, "that we find in Holy Writ many different words for sin; for sin is as many-sided as life itself" (*Reformed Dogmatics,* p. 245). It is centered in the heart, which is "deceitful above all things, and desperately corrupt; who can understand it?" (Jeremiah 17:9). Its rootage in the heart means that it envelopes the whole man, polluting all "the springs of life" (Proverbs 4:23). None of our highly diversified ways of being human is free of contamination.

Accordingly Scripture presents us with a lengthy catalogue of our unpaid bills (that is, apart from Christ), too long to tally. And it minces no words. Its checklist of our dirty laundry includes the following charges: covenant breaking, transgressing the law of life, rebellion within the kingdom, disobeying God's Word, falling short of the glory of God, missing the mark, self-centeredness, pride, unbelief, idolatry, the lusts of the flesh, half-heartedness, going astray like sheep, hypocrisy. Our sinfulness runs deeper than mere outward acts of discord. It is more than muddled thinking, cultic malpractice, neurosis, social misbehavior, economic greed, public injustice. At bottom sin is a matter of inner disposition. Our Lord drives this point home forcefully in his Sermon on the Mount: the norm for kingdom living condemns not only murder but also the hatred from which it springs; not merely the act of adultery but also the lust which arouses it. Sin is a reality more profound than capitulating to peer pressure. For, in the incisive words of Jesus,

> "What comes out of a man is what defiles a man. For from within, out of the heart of man, come evil thoughts, fornication, theft, murder, adultery, coveting, wickedness, deceit, licentiousness, envy, slander, pride, foolishness. All these evil things come from within, and they defile a man." (Mark 7:20-23)

But enough is enough. The point is unmistakably clear: "Wretched man that I am! Who shall deliver me from this body of death?" (Romans 7:24).

Sin carries as many names as the many-sidedness of life itself. It is that broken relationship with God which shatters all other created relationships — with self, with others, and with the cosmos as a whole. The multifaceted character of our life in God's world creates the possibility for countless reductionist views of sin. Among them we find the following. a) Sin is a *privation* of the good, a view which goes back as far as Augustine. All created reality is good. Evil is then the absence, the lack of the good. This view has a laudable intent: it seeks to avoid the idea that sin is an ontic counterreality. But it fails to do justice to the biblical teaching of sin as a "positive," aggressively real power which wreaks havoc in the world. Closely related is the more modern idea of sin as *negation* of the good. Being is good. Its negation, nonbeing, is evil. This highly speculative notion is subject to a similar critique.

b) Others have argued that evil is a *necessary condition* for the good to come to its own. It is a negative agent to stimulate the good. Just as there can be no light without darkness, so the argument goes, so there can be no good without evil. Evil is the shadow side of the good. Thus man had to eat the forbidden fruit from "the tree of knowledge of good and evil" as a necessary condition for achieving his true humanity. Otherwise he would be condemned to a brutish existence. On this view, contrary to the intent of the previous one, it is hardly possible to avoid the conclusion that wrongness belongs to created reality as fundamentally as rightness does.

c) "In praise of human freedom" was a central creed of the Enlight-

316

enment age. Accordingly, sin was equated with *"nature,"* the raw potentials of a resistant environment which were to be mastered by the free moral agency of human reason. "By nature" we are ensnared in the tentacles of primitive forces. But our indomitable spirit seeks liberation from these powers so that man may come of age. This false antithesis between nature and freedom represents an updated secularized restatement of the equally dubious medieval antithesis between nature and grace. Both are radical misreadings of the biblical antithesis between sin and grace.

d) The rise of Darwinian theories of evolution, now widely acclaimed as dogma, gave birth to what is doubtless the most prevalent contemporary view of "sin." It is a *lingering remnant* of our primitive, prescientific past, a transitional stage in our evolutionary development. These Darwinian ideas often go hand in hand with the dialectical philosophy of Hegel. Sin is then viewed as the antithesis standing in tension with the thesis, the good. Under the directing power of the "world spirit," the antithesis gets taken up again and again into the thesis to form a new synthesis. The stage is then set for the next evolving round in world history. Thus evil forms the ethical counterpole to the good. It is not yet good in itself, but belongs to the forward-moving process of history. Its goal is progress. This optimistic view is largely out of touch with the harsh realities of our day.

Basically, as Weber puts it, in all such speculative theories "a working compromise is reached with evil which is then integrated into the total system of reality." These ideas can arise only "if the God who made himself into the opponent of evil in Jesus Christ is unknown or no longer known." For "where this God is unknown, evil will not be recognized as sin" (*Foundations of Dogmatics,* Vol. I, p. 587). It takes Scripture, therefore, the knowledge of God as Redeemer, to call sin by its appropriate name(s).

II. 2. From One State into Another

The doctrine of "the two states" receives scant attention in most contemporary theologies. The reason for this is clear enough. This concept presupposes the biblical story line of a good creation which is now in a fallen state. Classic Christian theologies spoke of man's fall from "the state of righteousness/integrity" into "the state of condemnation/corruption." Most current Christian thought has broken with this biblical hermeneutic. In place of this historical(-redemptive) line of thought, an existentialist dialectical understanding of "original righteousness" and "present being-under-judgment" has arisen. Weber, for example, concedes that "it is justifiable to speak of two 'states' *(status)*, the original and that state which is in fact the destruction of the original." But, he adds, "we do not speak of these two states as historical conditions which follow upon each other. Instead we can speak of the one as not abrogated but as the origin which remains present in both the commandment and the promise, which does not weaken the other but is preserved as a state of man." The two states are and always were coexistent realities. Weber argues, however, that "this [line of thought] is not dialectical but is solely Christological . . ." (*Foundations of Dogmatics,* Vol. I, p. 580).

Hendrikus Berkhof argues similarly that there are no "grounds to assume two such successive phases in the history of mankind." Pointers to an upright state do not refer to "a past condition of mankind, but describe the structure which God as creator has given to man. . . . This structure is permanent and indestructible." Accordingly, this "*humanum* as potentiality demands actualization. And we know no other man than the one who mysteriously goes against the purpose of his existence." For sin "is deeply rooted in the creaturely structure of the risky being called man." Still, sin and creation should not be discussed in the same breath. "For sin does not belong to created reality and does not issue from it" (*Christian Faith,* p. 188).

These two citations are quite representative of mainline theological reflection in our day. The viewpoint they express assumes a dialectical tension which pervades all human relationships throughout world history. A corrupt nature is one side of our self-knowledge. Simultaneously we are also aware of a righteousness which is both our origin and our destiny. Is it ever possible on this view to escape such dialectical tensions? To be able to say, "Free at last!"? To exclaim with Paul, "If anyone is in Christ, he is a new creation; the old has passed away, the new has come" (2 Corinthians 5:17)? Is this unremitting dialectic the only, or even the best, way to understand existentially what *simul justus et peccator* means?

Classic reformational thought offers a better way. According to it the idea of "state" refers to one's legal position or status before the tribunal of divine justice. As a result of our original sin we no longer stand upright in God's presence. The Judge declares us guilty. His sentence rests heavy on us. We are under his just judgment, condemned to death, and our condemnation is well deserved. We have undergone a radical change in status. In our original state of integrity our Maker's resounding declaration, "Very good!," echoed all around us and within us. In our fallen state that relationship lies shattered, awaiting the life-renewing word of the gospel, "There is therefore now no condemnation for those who are in Christ Jesus" (Romans 8:1). In him the broken contact is restored.

Our legal status before God is now either "in Adam" or "in Christ." In ourselves we are still fallen, but in Christ we are "raised to newness of life." The "old man" in us still wages his vicious rearguard actions, but he is no longer in control. The "new man" in Christ has gained the upper hand. The covenant relationship, made and then broken, is now restored. Guilty in ourselves, we are declared righteous in Christ. That is our new status. This doctrine of "the two states" forms the theological background to the satisfaction doctrine of the atonement. But to fully appreciate the "high estate" to which God's grace and justice in the cross and resurrection of his Son restore us, we must never lose sight of the "low estate" from which we are delivered.

II. 3. "Far as the Curse Is Found . . ."

This line is taken from a favorite Christmas carol. In it the effects of our fall into sin are offset by God's act of lifting the curse through the coming of Christ.

> No more let sin and sorrow grow,
> Nor thorns infest the ground;
> He comes to make his blessing flow
> Far as the curse is found. . . .

In Genesis 3:14-19 the dark clouds of divine judgment descended on human life from the cradle to the grave. Nothing escapes its curse. Every creature great and small bears its brunt — the soil, plant life, animals, human relationships — not least of all, marriage and vocation. Like a drop of ink falling into a glass of water, our originating sin has a ripple effect on our entire environment. As Hoeksema puts it, "The tree of life is [now] corrupt and produces [only] corrupt fruit" (*Reformed Dogmatics*, p. 274). Ardent proponents of "hungering and thirsting for righteousness" in society sense keenly the frustrations that come from realizing how inextricably entangled we are in the inequities of our modern social, economic, and political structures.

The overwhelming impact of this disastrous turn of events early in human history goes by the name of "total depravity." Life is corrupt in its total extent and in all its parts. We have turned the tables on God's original intent and purpose with the creation. "The chief end of man" was and still is "to know God and enjoy him forever" (Westminster Confession). But original sin opened the floodgates to a tidal wave of corruption which knows no bounds. No aspect, faculty, or relationship — the most intimately personal as well as those openly publicized in the daily headlines — remains untouched.

This biblical teaching on the universal effects of sin is sometimes called the doctrine of absolute depravity. This concept is, however, certainly ambiguous, even misleading. Sin is perverse enough, without having to overdo it. Let us therefore be clear on this matter: the doctrine of total depravity does not mean that things have become as bad as bad can be. Such a condition is presently unthinkable. It is reserved for hell. Yet this is what the idea of absolute depravity implies, that things have reached a point of no return, that at least some of God's creatures lie beyond the pale of redemption. Such a grim fate holds for the fallen angels (2 Peter 2:4; Jude 6; Revelation 20:10), but not for fallen human beings, except apparently in those borderline cases which fall under the heading "the unpardonable sin" (Matthew 12:32; Mark 3:29; Hebrews 6:4-6; cf. Louis Berkhof, *Systematic Theology*, pp. 253-54; Berkouwer, *Sin*, pp. 323-53). Yet even in the midst of such radical distortions God maintains the structures of his creation. God's preserving, conserving grace — commonly called "common grace" — is an ever present reality. Life, though fallen, is still liveable. In this life we never experience the unrestrained outpouring of iniquity. The divinely interposed "enmity" is painfully real. The antithesis between our sin and God's grace is big as life itself. It takes shape in two opposing kingdoms. It is embodied in covenant-keeping and covenant-breaking. By virtue of God's "general grace," however, human corruption never comes to its ultimate and absolute expression in the here and now. That is reserved for the hereafter.

Meanwhile, a "mixed economy" marks world history. Thorns and thistles continue to restrict the growth of good crops. Reaping the benefits of our labor in "the sweat of our brows" is therefore the order of the day. Yet the "wheat" ripens, despite the "tares," until the appointed time of harvest (Matthew 13:24-30, 36-43). And God still causes his sun to shine and his rain to fall on both the good and the evil, the unjust and the just (Matthew 5:45).

How then shall we conceive of the relationship between our total depravity, God's preserving grace, and the antithesis? They are not mutually excluding or mutually limiting realities. All three extend "far as the curse is found." They are operative everywhere. We may not divide the field among them. No partly-this and partly-that analysis can do justice to the teachings of Scripture. No doctrine of the so-called "remnants" or "vestiges" of goodness which presumably survived the devastations of the fall may be allowed to blunt the reality of total depravity or take the edge off the antithesis. Only God's grace can restrain total depravity and soften the antithesis.

The idea of total depravity represents our attempt to capture in words the radical and sweeping misdirection and disorientation of our lives. The antithesis refers to the running encounter between two conflicting ways of life, pulling us in opposite directions. Both total depravity and the antithesis are therefore directional and orientational concepts. The same is true of God's preserving grace as it impacts the structures of life, upholding and governing them. By it he curbs and inhibits the forces of sin and evil, holds the creation order intact, and checks the outbursts of human depravity, thus allowing the historical drama of the antithesis to run its appointed course. Conservingly, therefore, as well as redeemingly, this is still "the day of grace." The totality of sin is the biblical flipside of the totality of grace. In summary, then, all three — total depravity, preserving grace, and the antithesis — go hand in hand as holist realities throughout this present dispensation.

This totality-oriented vision is a hallmark of the reformational worldview. Within this tradition all the key terms in the historic confessions of the church are understood "in a universal, all-encompassing sense." They "are held to be cosmic in scope." For

> nothing apart from God himself falls outside the range of [the] foundational realities of biblical religion. . . . What distinguishes a reformational worldview is its understanding of the radical and universal import of both sin and redemption. There is something totalitarian about the claims of both Satan and Christ; nothing in all of creation is neutral in the sense that it is untouched by the dispute between these two great adversaries. . . . The horizon of creation is at the same time the horizon of sin and salvation. . . . Everywhere the things of our experience begin to reveal themselves as *creaturely,* as under the curse of *sin,* and as longing for *redemption.* (Albert Wolters, *Creation Regained,* pp. 10, 60, 71, 72)

Perhaps the comprehensive sweep of sin can be further clarified by asking what it means to confess that we have "lost" the image of God (Heidelberg Catechism, Q. & A. 6). What kind of "loss" is this? A quantifiable loss? Is it (pardon the crass analogies) like losing weight or losing money? If Adam had stepped onto the scales in Genesis 2, and then after "losing" the image of God in Genesis 3, weighed himself again in Genesis 4 — would he have dropped, say, from 180 pounds to 140? If before the fall he possessed, say, 101 faculties, would these then be reduced to 51? No, it was not that kind of substantive, structural, functional "loss." Adam would still weigh 180 pounds. He would still function in all 101 capacities. Structurally nothing changed. For in a fallen world God maintains the structures of his creation by his preserving grace. Yet directionally everything changed. Instead of employing all 180 pounds in the service of his Maker, Adam began to throw all his weight around in serving idols.

Instead of dedicating all 101 aspects of our being to loving God and our neighbors, we, like Adam, turn them all to ends which defame God and defy our neighbors. We are still fully and truly human, but misdirected, disoriented humans. Perhaps the "lostness" of our ability to image God in all our creaturely callings can be compared to "getting lost" in an immense forest without a compass. Though "lost," we are still "all there." But we have "lost" our bearings and "lost" our way home. Disoriented and misdirected, we find ourselves wandering aimlessly. Total depravity means total misdirection, complete disorientation.

II. 4. Like Father, like Son

To be or not to be sinners — that is not for us to decide. That decision was made long ago. It was made for us, but not apart from us. Adam's decision was also ours. We were and are involved in it (Romans 5:12-21), just as we were and are also involved — though in the very opposite way — in God's counteracting decision in Jesus Christ (Romans 6:3-5). We share fully in that original sin, its act, its guilt, and its consequences. Scripture denies us the dubious luxury of standing like spectators along the sidelines, dispassionately observing that drama of human downfall. Nor are we merely hapless victims of a tragic fate which befell us. Our guilt is not an alien guilt, foreign to the stark realities of our life experience. In a very real sense we were present there vicariously as active participants in that original sin. In Scripture, therefore,

> man is not addressed as a victim, but as a doer. He is not pitied, but accused. Up to the present day this has had enormous consequences for every segment and aspect of societal and cultural life. Nothing does more for the humanization of man than addressing him as one who is fully accountable relative to God and his neighbor. (Hendrikus Berkhof, *Christian Faith*, p. 210)

Though the permanent damages resulting from that originating sin are overwhelmingly evident in the human condition called original guilt and corruption, still the haunting question continues to plague us: How did we, arriving on the scene so much later, get to be the way we are? Why should Adam's act of disobedience send me on a guilt trip? Impulsively, even belligerently, we vent our frustrations on the Author of the Book which unravels this tale of woe: It simply is not fair! And Adam, why in heaven's name did you do it?! I refuse to bear the blame! Yet the facts of life stare us stubbornly in the face: like son/daughter, like

322

father/mother, like grandfather/grandmother. . . . No matter how far into the distant past we track down our family trees, there is no break in this chain reaction. "All have sinned and fall short of the glory of God. . . . None is righteous, no, not one" (Romans 3:23, 10). There are no exceptions to the universal rule of sin — except, of course, the "first Adam" prior to the fall, and the "last Adam."

How are we to account for this unbroken line of rebellion running back from generation to generation? The history of Western thought has generated four major attempts to explain this problem of the transmission of original guilt and corruption. The first three were already well known in Calvin's day. One he rejects, another he quietly sets aside, while the third he strongly affirms. Since Calvin touches on all three quite adequately, we shall allow him to speak to this issue. The fourth view, an evolutionary theory, is a product of post-Reformation, eighteenth-century Enlightenment thought. We shall deal with it on its own terms.

a) There is, first, the doctrine of sin espoused by the British monk Pelagius (ca. A.D. 350-420). Though his views were condemned as heretical by the councils of Carthage in Augustine's native North Africa during his lifetime, significant aspects of his heresy lived on in the semi-Pelagian traditions of the medieval church, in the Arminian theologies of the post-Reformation era, and in modern liberalism.

Pelagius agreed with Augustine and the church of their day that all men without exception are sinners. How are we to account for this? By *imitation,* was his answer. Sin exists among us only in the form of concrete deeds. It does not take shape in a sinful human nature. By his act of disobedience Adam injured himself only, no one else. As Calvin puts it, in the typical polemical style of his times, Pelagius arose with "the profane fiction that Adam sinned only to his own loss without harming his posterity." When confronted with the biblical witness to the universality of sin (Romans 5:12), confirmed by human experience, "Pelagius quibbled that it was transmitted through imitation, not propagation" — the latter being, in part at least, Augustine's view.

According to Pelagius, all men enter the world innocent, as Adam did, free of sin with its guilt and pollution. As Augustine put it, Pelagius holds that "there is no congenital evil in us, and we are begotten without fault; and before the exercise of a man's own will there is nothing in him except what God created." However, our environment is contaminated by the actual sins of our forebears, who followed in Adam's footsteps. We are now surrounded by these bad examples. Thus we are led to emulate their bad habits. Pelagius did not claim that "anyone is to be found who has never in fact sinned throughout his whole life." Yet "man can be without sin, and can keep the commandments of God, if he so wills, . . . through his own effort and the grace of God" (Henry Bettenson, *The Later Christian Fathers,* pp. 193-94).

In refuting this optimistic view of human nature in Pelagius, says Calvin, "good men (and Augustine above the rest) labored to show us that we are corrupted not by derived wickedness, but that we bear inborn defect from our mother's womb." He then concludes that "with this we ought to be content: that the Lord entrusted to Adam those gifts which he willed to be conferred upon human nature. Hence Adam, when he lost the gifts received, lost them not only for himself but for us all." The concern of Calvin and other Augustinians was not simply to insist on orthodox views of man and the transmission of human sinfulness. At stake basically was the biblical truth of salvation by grace alone. For if "Adam's sin was propagated by imitation, . . . then does Christ's righteousness benefit us only as an example to imitate? Who can bear such sacrilege!" Through Pelagius's "subtlety Satan attempted to cover up the disease and thus render it incurable" (*Institutes,* II,1,5-7).

Despite the negative judgment of the historic Christian tradition on it, revised forms of Pelagianism continue to attract large followings. In our times, however unknowingly, Pelagian-like ideas offer the underpinnings for views of life which locate the root of societal evils not in the apostasy of the human heart but in cultural conditioning, adverse stimuli in the environment to which we respond in the form of misbehavior.

b) We turn secondly to the views of Augustine (A.D. 354-430), already alluded to in the discussion on Pelagius. The Augustinian position was endorsed not only by the councils convened during the lifetime of these two antagonists, but also later by the Council of Orange (A.D. 519). In the centuries which followed, however, it often appeared that, while Augustine had won the battles, Pelagius was winning the war. This theological drift helped set the scene for the sixteenth-century Reformation. There we find Calvin as well as Luther, a product of the Augustinian order, appealing above all to the theology of Augustine.

Augustine's views on the transmission of sin remain rather ambivalent, however. Certain strands in his thought clearly anticipate the central message of the Reformers. These are reinforced by the way he relates original sin to the ideas of representation and imputation. The Reformers joined Augustine in viewing Adam as representative head of the human race acting on our behalf. By divine arrangement, they held, the guilt and corruption of his original sin are now reckoned to our account. Such forensic theologizing comes to at least muted expression in Augustine's doctrine of sin. It is more clearly expressed when he deals with the way Christ's righteousness becomes ours. In this respect therefore his Christology can serve as a corrective on his anthropology.

In reacting to Pelagian denials of original sin, Augustine leaves us with a very realistic understanding of how guilt and pollution are passed on from Adam through all the generations of humankind. According to the Bishop of Hippo, all men are seminally present in Adam. His sin is ours "as it were by heredity." For "the life of the one man embraces all that was to be in his posterity." When Adam fell "the whole human race was 'in his loins.' Hence, in accordance with the mysterious and powerful natural laws of heredity, it followed that those who were in his loins and were to come into this world through the concupiscence of the flesh were condemned with him." This original sin is "transmitted to all his posterity by generation, and only to be purged by regeneration" (Henry Bettenson, *The Later Christian Fathers,* pp. 197-200). For Augustine the human race is not an aggregate of individuals, committing a series of isolated acts of sin, but an organic whole (Acts 17:26), now corporately steeped in sin. Sinfulness is accordingly passed on from parents to children by *propagation.*

Thus in Augustine's theology the idea of our condition as sin-infected heirs overshadows that of our legal status as guilty participants. The guilt of original sin rests on us not *immediately,* by virtue of our covenantal representation in Adam, but *mediately* — by way of our genetic unity in solidarity with the entire sinful human race.

c) Calvin refrains from open attack on the views of Augustine, his most honored church father. Sometimes his expressions even sound strikingly the same: "the beginning of corruption in Adam was such that it was conveyed in a perpetual stream from the ancestors into their descendants." Yet basically Calvin holds that sin's "contagion does not take its origin from the substance of the flesh or the soul. . . ." He wishes, in fact, to avoid all "anxious discussion" of the question of "derivation." Instead, he moves the discussion of the transmission of original sin to a quite different footing, one only implicitly present in Augustine. He bases this doctrine on the idea of a divine "ordinance," a covenant arrangement in which Adam acts as the representative head of humanity. Within this framework God then "communicates," that is, imputes his guilt to our account. For "it had been so ordained by God that the first man should at one and the same time have and lose for himself and his descendants, the gifts that God had bestowed upon him." In the words of Paul, "Death reigned . . . even over those whose sins were not like the transgression of Adam . . ." (Romans 5:14). This, then, is "the relationship between the two: Adam, implicating us in his ruin, destroyed us with himself; but Christ restores us to salvation by his grace." If, then, "it is beyond controversy that Christ's righteousness, and thereby life, are ours by communication, it immediately follows that both were lost in Adam, only to be recovered in Christ" (*Institutes,* I,1,6-7).

Accordingly, Calvin holds that we all "inherit" sin, but not by "heredity." Rather, the guilt and corruption that come to us from the "first Adam's" original sin are grounded in the biblical teaching of *imputation* based on covenant *representation*. So too, in a redemptively counteracting way, the righteousness of God in the "last Adam" is imputed to us on the ground of his representative role as Mediator of the renewed covenant community. Adam acted as head of the "old humanity," Christ as Head of the "new humanity." Following Calvin's lead, the reformational tradition unfolded this complex of fundamental truths as a distinctive hallmark of the Christian religion, the firm foundation undergirding its confession of the sovereignty of God's grace and our justification by faith alone.

d) The dominant contemporary view on sin has been shaped by the emerging evolutionary ideology of the past couple of centuries. At its root lies the historicism of the modern mind which reduces the meaning and/or meaninglessness of life to strictly historical processes. Its seeds were sown during the age of the Enlightenment. It was carefully nurtured under the tutelage of Hegelian philosophies and Darwinian theories dating from the previous century. This parasitic plant is now beginning to bear its ripened fruit, as is evident from the monist worldviews and process theologies of our times.

These evolutionary ideologies presuppose an ongoing, basically unbroken, linear pattern of development in world history. At bottom, therefore, this dogma is unable to accommodate the idea of that radically disruptive event which Scripture describes as our universal fall into sin. It excludes on principle the very idea of original sin as understood in the historic Christian tradition. The biblical teaching of a good creation which somewhere near the dawn of human history went awry with sweeping, abiding consequences, simply does not fit its view of reality. Evolutionist thinkers do not fail to recognize mankind's perpetual struggle to subdue the obstinate powers of evil within us and around us. But these obstacles to human freedom are generally regarded as residing in the very nature of things. The continuing encounter with these hostile forces which impede our historical movements toward emancipation are the negative side of what is hopefully a more positive process. Our true destiny is progress.

On this evolutionary model, sin and evil are *remnants* of our more primitive past. They represent the leftover baggage of an earlier pre-scientific and subethical stage of development. We must contend with evil as the dialectical counterpole of the good which is our future. This is the antithesis which moves along with us through history, always acting in tension with the thesis, our becoming all that we are meant to be. As the thesis assimilates and overcomes the antithesis, it lifts us to greater heights in a newly emerging synthesis. Such advances then clear the way for the next round in mankind's odyssey toward an open-ended future. Everything is in flux. And our lives are caught up in this perpetual cycle of oscillating processes. Sin and evil are a series of transitional stages along the way in "man's coming of age."

Or hopefully so. For in our times many of these cultural optimists find that the most they can do is cross their fingers and hope for the best. The ever recurring crises of our times, which refuse to recede into the past, are having a strong tempering effect on these futurist dreams. The grandiose hopes of past decades are turning out to be utopias — a utopia being literally a "no place."

II. 5. Reaping the Whirlwind

Sowing the wind, reaping the whirlwind. That adage aptly describes the close connection between original sin and actual sins. The seed of original sin, swept along on the winds of time, has taken deep root. Whirlwind harvests have come our way. Year after year we reap bumper crops of actual sins. As our Lord testifies, "From within, out of the heart of man, come evil thoughts, fornication, theft, murder, adultery, coveting, wickedness, deceit, licentiousness, envy, slander, pride, foolishness" (Mark 7:21). We can never relegate original sin to our dim and distant past. With dogged persistence it haunts us all our days. With dismaying regularity we hear, sense, and see it emerge in our words and thoughts and deeds. By the grace of God in Christ, as forgiven sinners, we can indeed put it behind us as completely "as if we had never known or committed any sin," as a Reformed liturgical formulary puts it. But this is no cheap grace. It calls for costly discipleship. We must still contend with the actual sins which daily beset us. We do what we do because we are who we are. Our existence defines our activity. It is important to keep clearly in mind this close connection between being sinners and committing sins. To place exclusive emphasis on sin as singular acts breeds legalism, moralism, anxiety. To view sin only as a condition, however, apart from actual sins, lulls us into quietism, indifference, false security.

The grace of God continues to wend its way through world history. This is the story of the Bible. We call it *Heilsgeschichte* — the history of redemption. But sin has its history too. The early chapters of the Bible paint a startling picture of the unfolding drama of sin. It takes time for the whirlwind to gather its full force. But it does happen, and with gathering momentum. When Adam's sin stares him in the face, he fumbles for an *excuse*: The blame lies with the woman You gave me (Genesis 3:12). When later Cain is confronted with his bloody crime, he seeks to

327

evade it: "Am I my brother's keeper?" (Genesis 4:9). The drama of sin then rises to a crescendo pitch with Lamech's infamous "sword song." He *exalts* in his atrocious deeds: "I have slain a man for wounding me, a young man for striking me. If Cain is avenged sevenfold, truly Lamech seventy-sevenfold" (Genesis 4:23-24). Sin then reaches unprecedented proportions in the days of Noah — "every imagination of the thoughts of [the human heart] was only evil continually" (Genesis 6:5). A more sweeping indictment is hardly conceivable. The whirlwind unleashed its full fury. The early world was ripe for judgment.

God, being God, cannot put up with sin. Yet he remains compassionate toward the sinner. He loves what he has made of us, even while he hates what we have made of ourselves. Combining grace with judgment, therefore, he rescues the creation from its watery grave and creates a new beginning. The sacramental proof is there in the sign of the rainbow.

Yet the whirlwind keeps on blowing. For water cannot wash the world clean of sin. It takes blood to do that. So with David we are compelled to acknowledge that "my sin is ever before me" (Psalm 57:3). Yet how often we seek refuge in the distinction between our sinfulness and our sins. We turn sinfulness into a generality. Such abstract talk we can easily endure. It leaves us as persons untouched. But when it comes to concrete sins — that is a very different story. For then the lightning strikes too close to home. The truth is, however, that neither sin nor sinfulness can be reduced to abstractions. Both the sinfulness which infests our very makeup and the besetting sins of our daily walk are down-to-earth realities. Both — the one as an evil root and the other as bitter fruit — are thoroughly contextual. They are geared to our time and place in history, related integrally to our cultural situation. This was true in the case of Adam, Cain, Lamech, and Noah's contemporaries. A similar culturally related concreteness echoes through David's prayer of repentance in response to the arrogance which moved him to take a census of his people: "I have sinned greatly in what I have done" (2 Samuel 24:10). The same is true of Isaiah's confession, "Woe is me! For I am lost; for I am a man of unclean lips, and I dwell in the midst of a people of unclean lips" (Isaiah 6:5). Jesus, too, exposes sin not abstractly as a generality, but with forthright concreteness: "An evil and adulterous generation seeks for a sign . . ." (Matthew 12:39). Paul is also utterly candid in enumerating "the works of the flesh" which threaten the life of the early Christian community: "immorality, impurity, licentiousness, idolatry, sorcery, enmity, strife, jealousy, anger, selfishness, and the like" (Galatians 5:19-21). The concrete reality of actual sin applies no less to us in our particular time and place in history. Our sins, too, are wholly at home precisely within the social fabric, the economic and political structures, the domestic and ecclesiastical and educational institutions of our modern societies. Need we be reminded of the evils of white-collar crime, AIDS, apartheid, abortion, Third World poverty, and all the rest?

Sin is indeed personal. As such it is nontransferable. But it is no less interpersonal. It finds us out within the intricate human relationships and institutions which mark our way of life. We all share in the global solidarity of actual human sinfulness. It is therefore possible, perhaps to some extent even inevitable, for people to lead each other astray.

Scripture frequently defines our human predicament in terms of "flesh." Humanity as a whole is "flesh." This concept has nothing to do with the popular dichotomy which sets "body" off against "soul." It applies to the whole man, in his spiritual as well as bodily existence. In very realistic ways, the biblical concept "flesh" opens up three distinguishable perspectives on our life together, depending on the context. It refers at times to people in general in their role as creatures of God. So, for example, we read in Psalm 145:21: "Let all flesh bless his holy name forever and ever." Again, "flesh" points to us as human beings carrying the scars of our fallen condition. "All flesh is grass" (Isaiah 40:6). Such passages reflect our frailty, weakness, transience, mortality. Third, "flesh" is a description of "the spirit that is now at work in the sons of disobedience" (Ephesians 2:2). In this sense "flesh" is that death-dealing power opposed to the life-giving Spirit of God. It is the principle of evil at work in us. Its vitiating power cannot be confined to our bodily functions. For "flesh" also has a mind of its own ("the mind of the flesh is enmity with God," Romans 8:7). It affects the very heart (Romans 1:24) and soul (Revelation 18:14) of man. The "flesh" is at war with the "Spirit," the principle of new life in Christ. We therefore face a crucial choice: "We must decide between death and life, that is, between flesh and spirit . . ." (Gustavo Gutiérrez, *We Drink from Our Own Wells,* p. 70).

We share one and all, without distinction, and equally, in original sin. When it comes to actual sinning, however, there are distinctions. We recognize this quite rightly in our courts of law, at least where a sense of equity prevails in the judicial system. The punishment should fit the crime, implying degrees in both. Scripture, too, points clearly toward degrees of culpability. We find our Lord rebuking "the cities where most of his mighty works were done, because they did not repent." The principle seems to be that "to whom much is given, from him much is also required." The Light of the world shone in all its fullness in the towns and villages of Judea and Galilee. The greater the light of revelation, therefore, the greater the accountability. Accordingly it will be "more tolerable on the day of judgment" for Tyre and Sidon and Sodom than for Chorazin, Bethsaida, and Capernaum (Matthew 11:20-24).

By our whirlwind harvest of actual sin we have brought God's judgments down on the earth. Tragedies, disasters, and calamities befall us. They are the self-inflicted burdens of life. They are at the same time God's judgments mediated through our corporate involvement in sin. In facing such suffering, however, we must avoid the logic of Christ's disciples, who asked, "Rabbi, who sinned, this man or his parents, that he was born blind?" (John 9:1-3). God's way with his world does not allow for such "one man, one sin, one judgment" speculation. Such judgmental attitudes, such individualizing of the sorrows of life, has no place in the biblical view of life. Our Lord makes this abundantly clear in commenting on "the Galileans whose blood Pilate had mingled with their sacrifices" and "the eighteen upon whom the tower in Siloam fell and killed them." Referring to these deaths, he posed the pointed question: Were these victims "worse sinners than all other Galileans"? And those crushed by the collapse of the tower, "Were they worse offenders than all others who dwelt in Jerusalem?" To these rhetorical questions the clearly implied answer, and the bottom line for us all, is this: "No, but unless you repent . . ." (Luke 13:1-5).

II. 6. Freedom/Bondage of the Will

Freedom of the will, along with the autonomy of human reason, was one of the widely acclaimed themes of the Enlightenment. A more tempered and biblically oriented notion of free will was already a bone of contention in the Arminian-Calvinist controversy surrounding the Synod of Dordt (1618-1619). The issue is still alive. In our day there are congregations which announce publicly, We are "a free will church." What are we to make of these age-old questions? What does free will mean? In what sense are our wills free? And are they also bound? What did Luther mean by "the bondage of the human will"? And Calvin in speaking of "a will enslaved to sin"?

In these utterances the Reformers were responding to the idea of free will prevalent in the medieval era. The view of the scholastics on freedom of the will was closely related to their view of human nature. Influenced heavily by Greek philosophy, they held generally to a tripartite anthropology. Calvin restates their case in the following words:

> . . . Man was commonly thought to be corrupted only in his sensual part and to have a perfectly unblemished reason and a will also largely unimpaired. . . . [Thus] they locate the will midway between reason and sense. That is, it possesses the right and freedom of itself to either obey reason or to prostitute itself to be ravished by sense — whichever it pleases. . . .

> [In summary,] reason which abides in human understanding is a sufficient guide for right conduct; the will, being subject to it, is indeed incited by the senses to do evil things; but since the will has free choice, it cannot be hindered from following reason as its leader in all things. (*Institutes*, II,2,4; II,2,2; II,2,3)

On this view of a partial fall into sin, the human will is like a neutral pendulum which swings freely between the positive pole of our rational soul and the negative pole of our bodily senses. The deciding factor is the presence or absence of divine grace. If we fall from the state of grace by committing mortal sin, the will gravitates toward "the lusts of the flesh." Our wills then act contrary to the revealed will of God. Once restored to the state of rectitude, however, which typically takes place through the infusion of sacramental grace, the will then swings back toward compliance with the dictates of reason.

Luther calls such freedom of contrary choice "an empty word. . . . It befits theologians, therefore, to refrain from using the term when they wish to speak of human ability, and leave it to be applied to God alone." For all such talk of "a power of freely turning in any direction, yielding to none and subject to none," serves only to "endanger and delude faithful people" ("Bondage of the Will," in *Martin Luther: Selections from His Writings*, ed. J. Dillenberger, pp. 188-89). In a similar vein Calvin refers to a "free choice equally of good and evil." Yet, as many medievalists conceded, man regularly makes the wrong choice. This leads Calvin to comment sarcastically: "A noble freedom indeed. . . . What purpose is served by labelling with such a proud name such a slight thing?" (*Institutes*, II,2,7). These responses by both Luther and Calvin are motivated by a deeply practical, pastoral concern. For them it was not an abstract argument over theological propositions. Basically it was a matter of the assurance of salvation. In the words of Luther,

> I frankly confess that, for myself, even if it could be so, I would not want "free will" to be given me, nor anything be left in my hands to make me endeavor after salvation. . . . [For] if I lived and worked to all eternity, my conscience would never reach comfortable certainty as to how much I must do to satisfy God. Whatever work I had done, there would still be a nagging doubt. . . . [So] by the power of "free will" none at all could be saved. . . . ("Bondage of the Will," p. 199)

Luther and Calvin were agreed in rejecting the mother church's teaching of a partial fall which supported the idea of free will. "The whole man is flesh," says Calvin. "Sin overturns the whole man" (*Institutes*, II,3,1; II,1,9). Similarly, in the first of his Ninety-Five Theses Luther states, "When our Lord and Master, Jesus Christ, said, 'Repent!', He called for the entire life of believers to be one of repentance." Our fall into sin affects the human will as much as any other faculty. For "the whole man is overwhelmed — as by a deluge — from head to foot, so that no part is immune from sin and all that proceeds from him is to be imputed to sin" (*Institutes*, II,1,9).

Luther similarly holds "that 'free will' without God's grace is not free at all, but is the permanent prisoner and bondslave of evil, since it cannot turn itself to the good." This evil bent of the will is not born of "necessity" or "compulsion." For these terms "cannot accurately be used of either man's will or God's." Rather, "the will, whether it be God's or man's, does what it does, good or bad, under no compulsion, but just as it wants or pleases, as if totally free." What this leads to in reality is "the immutable will of God on the one hand and the impotence of our corrupt will on the other" ("Bondage of the Will," pp. 187, 183). Calvin carries this line of reasoning a step further. "A man sins of necessity," he says, " but without compulsion. . . . The chief point of the distinction," he continues,

> must then be that man, as he was corrupted by the Fall, sins willingly, not unwillingly or by compulsion: by the most eager inclination of this heart, not by forced compulsion; by the prompting of his own lust, not by compulsion from without. Yet so depraved is his nature that he can be moved or impelled only to evil. But if this is true, then it is clearly expressed that man is surely subject to the necessity of sinning. (*Institutes*, II,3,5)

In this context Calvin cites the extremely compact line from Augustine, that "the will is indeed free but not freed." He takes Augustine to be using the concept "free will" as a term of ridicule — "he seems aptly to mock its empty name" (*Institutes*, II,2,8). Being no "wrangler over words," Calvin adds that

> if anyone, then, can use this word without understanding it in a bad sense, I shall not trouble him on this account. But I hold that because it cannot be retained without great peril, it will, on the contrary, be a great boon for the church if it be abolished. (*Institutes*, II,2,8)

The question now remains, Can the concept "free will" be used in a good sense? Taking Augustine's phrase more seriously than Calvin, does it hold out the possibility of a better understanding? Let us try to unpack its meaning. The human will is presently "free but not freed," says Augustine. It is moved by a voluntary kind of "must." How can this be? Calvin himself offers a helpful clue when he states:

332

> I say that the will is effaced; not in so far as it is will, for in man's conversion what belongs to his primal nature remains entire. I also say that it is created anew; not meaning that the will now begins to exist, but that it is changed from an evil to a good will. (*Institutes*, II,3,6)

Luther strikes a similar note:

> . . . if we meant by "the power of free will" the power which makes human beings fit subjects to be caught up by the Spirit and touched by God's grace, as creatures made for eternal life or eternal death, we should have a proper definition. ("Bondage of the Will," p. 187)

Implied in both these statements is a distinction developed later in the reformational tradition — the distinction between structure/function and direction. Structurally, as an aspect of man's constitution given with creation, the will is free to function as our Maker intended. We have the right and freedom, even the obligation, to make all kinds of choices. We can decide what to eat, when to sleep, what kind of work to do. Despite the effects of the fall, God by his preserving grace maintains this structural feature of the human makeup and its ability to function freely. This is part of what it means to be human. Even after the fall, human beings are still fully human, nothing more, nothing less, and nothing else. What then about the impact of sin on our will? It, too, became totally depraved, that is, radically misdirected and disoriented. Structurally and functionally we are what we always were; but directionally nothing is the same. Our wills, too, are now "so corrupt that we are wholly incapable of doing any good, and inclined to all evil" (Heidelberg Catechism, Q. & A. 8). If Adam once had and then lost the freedom of contrary choice, we no longer have that option. By our sinful nature, our wills are bent out of shape and thus turned in the wrong direction.

This happens not under "compulsion" but by "impulsion," by a strange and fearsome inner "necessity." We are inveterately inclined toward wrong choices, not "unwillingly" but "willingly." While structurally and functionally our wills are "free," yet directionally they are not "freed" from bondage to sin. We are burdened with an "enslaved freedom" — unless liberated and redirected by the life-renewing grace of God. Perhaps an analogy can help to clarify the point. Think of a hardened drug addict. He will do whatever he must do to get his daily fix. No one applies "compulsion." There is no outside pressure. In fact, his surroundings may offer restraints and inhibitions, or even positive incentives to offset his habit. Yet predictably, with a fateful kind of inner "necessity," the enslaved addict is freely driven to take action.

Lord Jesus, make us your servants, your slaves *(douloi)*, for then we shall be free. That is the point of Paul's self-answering question, "Do you not know that if you yield yourselves to anyone as obedient slaves, you are slaves to the one whom you obey, either of sin, which leads to death, or of obedience, which leads to righteousness?" (Romans 6:16). So then, Christ Jesus, by the power of your Spirit, be our Lord, for "where the Spirit of the Lord is, there is freedom" (2 Corinthians 3:17).

II. 7. The Wages of Sin

"The wages of sin is death," writes Paul, "but the free gift of God is eternal life . . ." (Romans 6:23). Life and death — the interface between these two extremes confronts us throughout Scripture. Death or life? — that is the to-be or not-to-be question we all face. It touches the very heartbeat of gospel proclamation: the death of the cross and resurrection life.

The ominous umbrella of death hovers over life from beginning to end. "Death reigned" from Adam to Moses, and ever since (Romans 5:14). All humanity is "dead in trespasses and sins." From our first gasp of fresh air, and even before, until we breathe our last, a deadly virus is at work within us. Death "entered the world through one man, . . . and in this way death came to all men, because all sinned . . ." (Romans 5:12). Scripture establishes a close link between sin and death. Death as we now know it all too well is both a consequence of sin and a divinely imposed penalty on it. It represents the well-earned wages on our sinful labors. Sin brings its own punishment. Every sin is, moreover, a mortal sin. For with God there is no hierarchy of sins: guilty of one, we are guilty of all. For sin, like the law which it violates, is of one piece.

When we in Adam chose the way of death instead of the way of life, God kept his Word. In the Word given with creation, by which God mediates the covenant partnership between himself and his creatures, his will was clearly revealed: "Obey me, . . . or else." In it we hear the friendly warning of a loving Father. It was like a caring mother sternly cautioning her child: Don't play with the matches. . . . Don't touch the hot stove, . . . or else you will get burned! In response to the fall the "or else . . ." side of God's Word went into effect. No new decree was needed. God's original Word had built into it from the beginning the potential for addressing a broken world as well. As its Author had predicted, incurring the "or else . . ." spells death. Then and there, and ever since, man died. He really died, in the full sense of the word. Very soon its meaning dawned on us: radical separation from the source of life. A sweeping alienation set in. Estrangement from God made us strangers in our own house, set us at odds with others, and put us out of tune with creation at large. We may try to tone down our predicament by distinguishing between physical, spiritual, and eternal death. But no matter how we slice the pie of human existence, nothing in us or around us escapes the death-dealing power of sin. It affects the whole person and every life relationship, dragging us down to defeat. We hear echoes of our own death knell in the monotonous funeral march of earlier generations: "And he died, . . . and he died . . ." (Genesis 5:3-31).

Nevertheless, life goes on! This happens not because God went back on his Word, nor because he settled for something less than the full enforcement of his "or else . . ." clause. Creation found its continuity not by moving into a halfway house between life and death. New generations arise and the seasons still come and go only because of the intervening grace of God. God's crown creatures forfeited their right of existence and reason for existence. But this is still the Father's world. Moved by holy jealousy for his prized possession, now fallen, he sets out on a new course of action. He grants his creatures a stay of execution. He holds the full force of the death penalty in abeyance. Thus he makes room for the renewal of life, for his unfolding plan of salvation, for Israel, for planting a cross on a hill outside Jerusalem, for the empty tomb, for the church, for the coming of the kingdom, and ultimately for a Paradise regained, where death will be forever banished and life in its fullness restored.

For the time being, however, death remains a living enigma. It is our archenemy. It stalks our path as an alien intruder. It does not really belong here. That is the riddle of our existence — the relentless grip of death in the midst of a divinely preserved life. And as we all know, death takes its heavy toll. The grim reaper wields a host of strangely forged sickles by which to claim his victims. Pornography — it can be more fatal than an onrushing automobile. A slanderous word — it can kill with greater finality than a "Saturday night special." A secular education — it can be more deadly than an overdose of sleeping pills. The disease is contagious. Death begets death. And it is no respecter of persons. It exposes the sham of our pretended human autonomy and our vaunted modern ideal of unending progress. All this should come as no surprise. For God's Word of "or else . . ." holds, and he holds us to it. He is simply taking us at our word. What we asked for in Adam, and in him continue to ask for, is what we are getting. Our Maker allows us to choose what we want most out of life, and then to do as we please. The choices we make in pleasing ourselves are, moreover, decisive. Choosing the way of sin and death, we find that these choices are finally ratified by a form of death which makes our choices final.

Here and now already there are people who embody a living death as they walk among us. Christ once said, referring to Lazarus in the tomb, "He who believes in me, though he die, yet shall he live" (John 11:25). The converse is also true, already now: Though they are counted among the living, some are already actually dead. Structurally and functionally they are alive, but directionally they are dead. For as God and life go together, so sin and death also go hand in hand. Such anomalies are not foreign to the experience of Christ-believers. We, too, suffer from sin as the "sting of death." But in Christ's resurrection "death is swallowed up in victory" (1 Corinthians 15:54-56). For on the cross God exacted from his Son the "wages of sin" in full. Then by his resurrection he broke the power of death. It has lost its inexorable hold on us.

What happens, then, at "three score years and ten"? At that point we face the "last enemy." All earthly ties are severed. Often that involves a very intense deathbed struggle. The serenity of a Socrates drinking the hemlock is certainly not a universal model. Yet dying can be accompanied by a deep sense of reassurance. Our Lord has been there before us. In him a life-renewing death is possible, even real. For it marks the transition to a fullness of life which is in principle already here. The "first Adam" was forcefully escorted away from the "Tree of Life," lest he should become subject to a perpetual state of living death. In this divinely imposed penalty there is at the same time a sign of grace. Then already God was creating an opening for the renewal of life. The door to a better future stood ajar. Now in Christ, the "last Adam," the door stands wide open. In the climactic words of a triumphant hymn, "He died eternal life to bring, and lives that death may die."

Chapter III

Knowing Our Sin —
On the Road to Recovery

III. 1. The Place of the Law within Redemption History

In the hand of the Spirit, the law of God "convince[s] the world of sin and righteousness and judgment" (John 16:8). Left to ourselves, however, we resort to camouflage instead of turning to confession. Such human response confirms Paul's highly charged message that "apart from the law sin lies dead"; but when confronted by the law, "sin revived and I died" (Romans 7:7-13). This is our predicament. But it was not always so. For the revealed will of God for our life in his world predates our fall into sin. It was given as a friendly guide with creation. Its Author is the triune God. All three Persons are pervasively involved in issuing and upholding the law. Yet each Person is engaged prevailingly in his own unique aspect of it. From the beginning God the Father is the Originator and the Son of God the Mediator. God the Holy Spirit is the Enabler — the One who dynamically implements the law of life within the creation. In the beginning all was well.

The law remains ever good and ever the same (Romans 7:7, 13, 14). With the entry of sin into our world, however, radical and sweeping changes set in. The joint operations of the triune God continue. But now on the response side the law-Word exposes our persistent failure and disobedience. It reveals the severity as well as the goodness of God. The threefold work of the triune God by which he from the beginning covenants with his creatures, namely, origination, mediation, and implementation, is now accommodated to the sin-infested condition of our life in the world. The command of the Father still stands, convicting us of sin. But it now addresses us as "the law of the Spirit of life." Its aim is to set us free from "the law of sin and death" (Romans 8:2). Thus

337

we come to recognize God's condemnation of sin and evil not only as an "objective" historical reality, but also "subjectively" as the re-awakened voice of conscience concurring in this judgment.

The law of God loses its meaning apart from the biblical story line. For when we lift it out of its context in the history of redemption, we play into the hands of the Pharisees, the critics of our Lord, and the Judaizers, Paul's antagonists. They converted the law into an independent and autonomous rule of conduct. Doing this breeds legalism, moralism, and rigorous attempts at self-justification. The entire perspective of Scripture, however, in both Testaments, is on Christ as "the end of the law." On the way from Adam to Christ, "law came in to increase the trespass." That is, the law of God in its written Mosiac form "was added because of transgressions" to intensify man's sense of guilt. ". . . But where sin increased, grace abounded all the more." For it envisioned "the offspring . . . to whom the promise had been made" (Romans 5:20; Galatians 3:19). "This is what I mean," says Paul, "the law [of Moses] which came four hundred and thirty years [after the covenant with Abraham] does not annul a covenant previously ratified by God, so as to make the promise void" (Galatians 3:17).

The covenant of grace is therefore the abiding framework for responding to the law. Based on his study of covenant structure in the Old Testament, Meredith Kline concludes that "the increased emphasis on the covenantal context of the law underscores the essential continuity in the function of the law in the Old and New Testaments" (*Treaty of the Great King*, p. 24). If therefore severed from God's electing love to Israel and the church, the law degenerates into an instrument for works-righteousness. Within the living flow of the biblical drama the law never appears as a "second source of revelation" or an "optional way of salvation." There is a single christologically focused way of salvation within which both law and gospel play their roles. Law within covenant — this truth is expressed in the preface to the decalogue, "I am the LORD your God, who brought you out of the house of bondage." This insight lies behind Augustine's prayer, "Lord, ask what You will, but first give what You ask." Calvin fleshes out more fully this historical-redemptive perspective in developing the idea that "the law was given . . . to foster hope of salvation in Christ, until his coming." The biblical witness is clear, he says. The law was "added"

> not . . . to lead the chosen people away from Christ; but rather to hold their minds in readiness until his coming; even to kindle a desire for him, and to strengthen their expectation, in order that they might not faint by too long delay, . . . and Moses was not made a lawgiver to wipe out the blessing promised to the race of Abraham. Rather, we see him repeatedly

338

reminding the Jews of that freely given covenant made with their fathers of which they were the heirs. It was as if he [that is, Moses] were sent to renew it. (*Institutes,* II,7,1)

Not only is Christ "the end of the law" and the covenant its context, but even in the elaborate rites of the Levitical priesthood and in the royal lineage of the house of David "Christ was set forth before the eyes of the ancient folk as in a double mirror" (*Institutes,* II,7,2). In the hypocrisy which Christ denounced and in the legalistic threat which Paul opposed in the early church "we see the increase of sin in direct connection with the misuse of God's law and the desire to justify oneself. . . . [Therefore] Paul was interested in the tremendous dynamic of redemption-history in which man's sin bursts forth as an open flame and reveals itself, and precisely in this way is made servile to God's purposes" (Berkouwer, *Sin,* pp. 179-80).

III. 2. Law and Gospel — Hand in Hand

Francis Schaeffer argues that "there is a time, and ours is such a time, when a negative message is needed before anything positive can begin." That is, people must be brought to a conviction of sin before they will listen to the good news of salvation. The heavy hand of the law must precede the liberating touch of the gospel. "People often say to me," Schaeffer continues, "What would you do if you met a really modern man on a train and you had just one hour to talk to him about the gospel?

> . . . I would spend forty-five or fifty minutes on the negative. . . . Then I would take ten or fifteen minutes to preach the gospel, . . . for often it takes a long time to bring a man to a place where he understands the negative. And unless he understands what's wrong, he will not be ready to listen to and understand the positive. . . . We are too anxious to get to the answer without having a man realize the real cause of his sickness. (*Death in the City,* pp. 70-71)

As a matter of strategy, perhaps Schaeffer has a point. At any rate, whatever the order, law and gospel are inseparable. The Heidelberg Catechism in Part One raises a similar issue in dealing with the knowledge of sin. It asks, "Whence do we know our sin and misery?" — and then answers the question, "Out of the law of God." Not until Part Two on "Deliverance" does the Heidelberger expound the doctrine of salvation.

Must we conclude, then, that this sequence is the normative strategy for biblical proclamation? Not necessarily, it seems, for already within the context of the knowledge of sin the Catechism anticipates the gospel message in the phrase, "unless we are regenerated by the Spirit of God" (Q. & A. 8). Law and gospel go hand in hand in Christian living. Law without gospel is legalism. The good news without the imperatives of God's will is "cheap grace."

True knowledge of sin comes to its own in moments of penitential confession. In the Christian community, therefore, as well as in Israel, the penitential psalms are staples in our daily spiritual diet. Inasmuch as the "old man" in Adam carries on persistently with his rearguard warfare within and among us, the heavy hand of divine judgment still rests on us. Like a penetrating X-ray the law exposes our "secret sins" and "hidden faults." The Lawgiver working through his law elicits that "broken spirit" which is to him an "acceptable sacrifice." For the promise stands, "a broken and contrite heart, O God, thou wilt not despise" (Psalm 51:17). For he dwells not only "in the high and holy place," but "also with him who is of a contrite and broken spirit, to revive the spirit of the humble, and to revive the heart of the contrite" (Isaiah 57:15).

Judgment and grace converge in the life of the believing community through the two-in-one blessing of law and gospel. Their close inter-relatedness must be kept clearly in mind, lest we drive a dualist wedge between Old Testament as law and New Testament as gospel, creating two ways of salvation. Scripture holds them together in a clear pattern of historical continuity. There is a single way of salvation for Israel as well as the church. The promised "good news" of a coming Messiah was foreshadowed under the veil of Old Testament ways of keeping the law. The patriarchs, lawgivers, prophets, and psalmists enjoyed a foretaste of the grace and glory which appeared in Christ. It was retroactively present among them. As Calvin puts it, the present full reality of the gospel "does not exclude the pious who died before Christ from the fellowship of the understanding and light that shine in the person of Christ." Yet, though law and gospel are two in one, converging in Christ, they are not one and the same. Between them there is also a certain discontinuity in focus similar to that between the two Testaments. For "the mysteries which they but glimpsed in shadowed outline are manifest to us" (*Institutes*, II,9,1).

Our whole life long we remain *simul justus et peccator* — concurrently sinful in ourselves and yet righteous in Christ. As long as this is true, law and gospel continue to blend their voices in a mixed refrain at every step along the way. We therefore confess that

> the knowledge of grace and the knowledge of sin go together; they presuppose and reinforce each other. Without repentance all the notes of the

Christian faith are off-key and fall silent. Then the gospel is changed from a marvelous message of liberation into a more or less self-evident ideology of cheap grace. If repentance falls away, the amazement and joy of God's free grace also fall away. For that reason repentance is not just a passing mood at the start of the road of renewal, but the abiding undertone of all the Christian life, a tone which is expressed in the churches, Sunday after Sunday, in a liturgical confession of guilt. (Hendrikus Berkhof, *Christian Faith,* p. 429)

Though lifelong repentance, induced by hearing the law, is the abiding undertone, the overtone is set by the freely given righteousness of Christ, who comes to us "clothed with the gospel" (Calvin). We are at one and the same time humbled by the law and exalted by the gospel, "just as the prodigal who returns home from the far country is both the alienated son and also the one to whom as such the right of return and the attributes of sonship are given" (Thielicke, *The Evangelical Faith,* Vol. II, p. 189). In the words of the Heidelberger, since daily conversion embraces mortification as well as vivification (Q. & A. 88), the law must be "strictly preached . . . our whole life long" (Q. & A. 115). Gripped by this inner tension, we are impelled with Paul to cry out, "O wretched man that I am!" Yet in the midst of this ongoing struggle we can also join in Paul's song of victory, "Thanks be to God through Jesus Christ our Lord!" (Romans 7:24-25). For the "Great Exchange" (Luther) has taken place. Christ has laid hold on us (Philippians 3:7-16). Within a courtroom setting, Thielicke personalizes the joint operation of law and gospel.

Always, then, I am the one I am for God. In my carnal existence I am the one He accuses in the law while my conscience defends me (God as prosecuting attorney and the heart as counsel for the defense). Then I am the one He defends while my conscience accuses me (the heart as prosecuting attorney and God as attorney for the defense). The change in identity finds expression in this alternation of accusations and defense. . . . Faith itself can only accept what it is by God's defense — a defense for which it can find no reason and which simply comes as a miracle. . . . (*The Evangelical Faith,* Vol. II, pp. 189-90)

What Calvin says about the "twofold knowledge of God" — God as Creator and as Redeemer — applies here too: "While joined by many bonds, which one precedes and brings forth the other is not easy to discern" (*Institutes,* I,1,1). Yet law and gospel are not identical. For "the law was given through Moses; grace and truth came through Jesus Christ" (John 1:17). In moving on, then, we can appeal with Calvin to "the order of right teaching," which in this case means the pedagogical order. Experientially law and gospel go hand in hand through life. It is possible, nevertheless, to think them apart for the sake of clearer analysis. With this in mind, therefore, we proceed to the following two-step discussion.

III. 3. The Law as "Tutor" to Christ

Commenting on this idea, Louis Berkhof says that the law serves the Christian as "his tutor to lead him to Christ, and thus becomes subservient to God's gracious purpose of redemption" (*Systematic Theology,* p. 614). This description of the law as our "tutor," "custodian," and "schoolmaster" goes back to Paul (Galatians 3:24). Pauline teaching on the role of the law in Christian living must be distinguished sharply from the views and practices of the Judaizers whom he opposes. "Almost the entire argument of the letter to the Galatians," says Calvin, "hinges upon this point" (*Institutes,* III,19,3).

"O foolish Galatians!" writes Paul, "who has bewitched you? . . ." (Galatians 3:1). He is deeply disturbed by their tendency to depart from the costly freedom they obtained in Christ. They are in danger of exchanging the reality of justification by faith alone for the mirage of works righteousness, and thus slipping back into their former enslavement to legalism. For "no man is justified before God by the law." Moreover, "all who rely on works of the law are under a curse" (Galatians 3:10, 11). Paul's quarrel, Calvin continues, is with "false apostles who were trying to reintroduce into the Christian church the old shadows of the law that were abolished by Christ's coming." This is no trivial matter, for "the clarity of the gospel was obscured by these Jewish shadows. . . ." Therefore, "because those imposters imbued the common people with the very wicked notion that this obedience obviously availed to deserve God's grace, Paul here strongly insists that believers should not suppose they can obtain righteousness before God by any works of the law, still less by those paltry rudiments." For "through the cross of Christ [we] are free from the condemnation of the law, which otherwise hangs over all men (Gal. 4:5), so that [we] may rest with full assurance in Christ alone. . . . He who thinks," therefore, "that in order to obtain righteousness he ought to bring some trifle of works is incapable of determining their measure and limit, but makes himself debtor to the whole law." So where does this leave us? "Is the law then against the promises of God?" Paul answers his own question with a resounding "Certainly not!" (Galatians 3:21). "In Christ" the law is not obsolete. For it was

Christ himself who said, "Think not that I have come to abolish the law and the prophets; I have come not to abolish them, but to fulfil them" (Matthew 5:17). These biblical pointers lead Calvin to say that no one should infer from Paul's dispute with the Judaizers "that the law is superfluous for believers." For "it does not stop teaching and exhorting and urging the good, even though before God's judgment seat it has no place in their consciences" (*Institutes,* III,19,2). The law is never a dead letter. In fact, "Except for the law," says Paul, "I should not have known sin" (Romans 7:7).

As long as the earth and the heavens endure, the law of God impinges itself with full normativity on all his creatures. By it our Maker maintains his authoritative claim on all men (Romans 2:12-16). People everywhere are aware of glaring discrepancies between what ought to be and what is. There is a religio-moral gap which needs to be bridged, an "enmity" which must be appeased. The law of God holds in such a way that some sense of being wrong and of wrongdoing, however blunted, blurred, or distorted, is present as a haunting reality to all men. In the words of Hendrikus Berkhof,

> There is no culture or language without some vocabulary to designate man's guilty failing. . . . But their idea of the what or the one before whom they are guilty varies immensely. . . . The substance of sin varies with the value systems against which one sins. For that reason one cannot appeal to an awareness of sin which is common to all men. (*Christian Faith,* p. 193)

True knowledge of sin is born only through encounter with the Lawgiver who issues his righteous commands in covenant with Israel (Galatians 3:17) and in the sending of his Son ("born under the law," Galatians 4:4).

The law has not lost a single jot or tittle of its significance. This is abundantly clear from the Sermon on the Mount. There our Lord deepens the meaning of the law but does not cancel or even relax it. Instead, he updates and restates it in the redemptive language of the New Testament era. Even within this christological context of fulfillment, the law still retains its sin-disclosing function. It has lost nothing of its negative impact. Its tutorial purpose is to "consign all things to sin" (Galatians 3:22). As "tutor," "custodian," "schoolmaster," and "pedagogue" the law leaves us empty-handed at the mercy of God. "Tutors" in Paul's day were not highly esteemed persons. They were generally slaves, hired "custodians," whose task it was as "schoolmasters" to discipline unruly youths and keep them in line with society's expectations. In its sin-disclosing function, therefore, "the law is not a peaceful preparation for faith, but it sets man under curse and death and servility" (Berkouwer,

Sin, p. 169). It radically undercuts every ground for self-justification. This explains Paul's indignation at those who seek to use the law for self-justifying ends. The good law of God works in us who are evil in such a way that "sin might be shown to be sin, and through the commandment might become sinful beyond measure" (Romans 7:13).

This is what we see (or at least should see) as we look into the mirror of God's law. Mirror gazing, however, does not lead automatically to honest self-analysis (James 1:23-24). So, too, the mere act of holding up this mirror does not necessarily result in true knowledge of sin. It may induce self-adulation, the very opposite of its intended use. Something very dramatic must happen to the one who "beholds his face" in this mirror. He must recognize this mirror for what it really is, the perfect law of God which lays its total claim on our lives. In this face-to-face encounter we then come to see ourselves for what we really are and see our sin for what it really is. A happy outcome is assured only when in the law we meet the Lawgiver, and when in his law we hear an echo of the gospel. As Berkouwer points out, we cannot derive "the knowledge of our sin from the law apart from the Lawgiver." That is, "the knowledge of the law," its "sense and purpose . . . can never be 'had' apart from the deepest intentions of the Lawgiver." Apart from its Author, the law is turned into "a legalistic ordinance." Therefore "the path of knowledge can only be trod in connection with, and in terms of, the Gospel" (*Sin,* pp. 180-82). Ultimately, then, the gospel must set our sights as we gaze intently upon the mirror. In the history of redemption Christ is indeed "the end of the law." But he is also experientially its "beginning." In him we come to a true knowledge of sin. As this liberating process of self-disclosure unfolds, "we can only state what has already happened when the law has done this work in us. . . . But how does that happen? How could it be that here man does not do what we always in fact do, that is, rebel?" There is only one answer:

> the law has encountered us as God's commanding and judging Word. . . . The law has truly revealed what the introductory sentence, so important to the Reformed catechisms, states in the biblical decalogue, "And God spoke all these words." The law has overpowered me. (Weber, *Foundations of Dogmatics,* Vol. I, p. 589)

Only by lowering the standard (". . . be perfect, as your heavenly Father is perfect," Matthew 5:48), or by exaggerating human achievement (". . . I thank thee that I am not like other men . . . ," Luke 18:11), is it possible to be soft on sin. And if we should try to escape the accusing finger of the law by pretending innocence with respect to this particular commandment or that one, we must then still contend with the sharply focused impact of the central love command: Love God with all you are and your neighbors as yourself. In this summary, the "Ten Words" and the many other "decrees," "statutes," and "ordinances" of the Lord are brought together and unified in that single, all-encompassing, concentrated command. For "love is the fulfilling of the law" (Romans 13:10). Before it we stand naked, unmasked, totally exposed, and stripped of all our self-justifying maneuvers. Therefore, "when the law of God is dissected into many commands" in a desperate attempt to salvage a bit of self-righteousness, then "the meaning of God's single command to have fellowship and love is no longer understood" (Berkouwer, *Sin,* p. 183). For basically the law of God is of one piece.

III. 4. The Gospel as "End of the Law"

In the words of Calvin, ". . . under the law Christ was always set before the holy fathers as the end to which they should direct their faith." For "the gospel did not so supplant the entire law as to bring forward a different way of salvation. Rather, it confirmed and satisfied whatever the law promised, and gave substance to the shadows" (*Institutes,* II,6,3; II,9,4). The law comes to its own in the gospel. For "the gospel is not a critique of the law, but its fulfillment" (Otto Weber, *Groundplan of the Bible,* p. 49). By faith alone we learn to agree with God's judgment on us and to internalize it. By faith alone we realize that his searching eye sees through all our devious charades, and yet amazingly that he still loves us. Ultimately then "knowledge of sin is faith knowledge" (Hendrikus Berkhof, *Christian Faith,* p. 194).

Knowledge of sin through the law and knowledge of grace through the gospel are not precisely the same. But neither can we have the one without the other. They walk hand in hand throughout a life of repentance and faith. We should keep this in mind in working our way through the Heidelberg Catechism. Its three parts — "sin, salvation, and service" — are not successive stages in Christian growth, as though one must first spend time enduring the chastisements of divine judgment in the valley of sin and misery before ascending to the higher ground of salvation and service. Rather, all three moments go together and grow together in Christian living. The law is therefore not a prior stage of preparation on the way to receiving the gospel. Repentance is not a vestibule leading into the house of faith. Calvin stresses this point in stating that "when we refer the origin of repentance to faith we do not imagine some space of time during which it brings it to birth; but

345

we mean to show that a man cannot apply himself seriously to repentance without knowing himself to belong to God" (*Institutes,* III,3,2).

These reflections on sin and grace, law and gospel, touch on the well-known doctrine of "the three uses of the law," which Calvin discusses in *The Institutes,* II,7,6-12. Taking them in reverse order, he holds that "the third and principal use, which pertains more closely to the proper purpose of the law, finds its place among believers in whose hearts the Spirit of God already lives and reigns." As its "second function . . . the law restrains malefactors and those who are not yet believers." The first use of the law is that it "shows the righteousness of God, . . . that is, the righteousness alone acceptable to God, [since] it warns, informs, convicts, and lastly condemns every man of his own unrighteousness. . . . The law is like a mirror" in that it "discloses our sinfulness, leading us to implore divine help." Its aim is that, justified by faith alone (*Institutes,* III,11), we may enjoy Christian freedom (*Institutes,* III,19), and thus "rest with full assurance in Christ alone." Returning to Calvin's order, the third and principal function of the law, which is "dependent upon the first," is that "consciences observe the law, not as if constrained by the necessity of the law, but that freed from the law's yoke they willingly obey God's will."

Clearly the pedagogical (first) and normative (third) functions of the law are inextricably interrelated. Thus, according to Berkouwer, "when we bear in mind the relation between sin and the Gospel we can also appreciate why the unity of the law and the Gospel is of decisive import for the knowledge of sin." The "tutorial" function of the law "may therefore never be divorced from the meaning of the law or the preaching of the Gospel in which the end of the law is set forth. . . . For the law, in exercising both these functions, exercises them simultaneously and conjoins them in the single commandment of God." Therein "the sin of man is announced and renounced, and the way of obedience is once again pointed out." Thus God's law confronts us "as a single commandment that both condemns and directs. It negatively prohibits and positively enjoins" (*Sin,* pp. 186, 185, 165). Yet, in its "principal use," the law offers guidelines for life within the Christian community. The Heidelberg Catechism highlights this point by expounding the meaning of the law in its third part on our service of gratitude.

Our brothers and sisters in the Two Thirds World need no lengthy discourses to convince them of the horrendous realities of sin and evil. We, however, who live in "the over-developed West" (Bob Goudzwaard) are so mesmerized by our humanist, secularist progress ideologies that it often takes a hard-hitting Catechism sermon to realize "how great our sin and misery is." The life situation of the fathers of the Heidelberger was more akin to that of Third World Christians than to the comfort and complacency which often afflict us. Yet even they, in those troubled times, called for a "strict preaching" of the law if we are "to be renewed more and more after the image of God . . ." (Q. & A. 115). It is therefore incumbent on us as surfeited Westerners to allow the words of Hendrikus Berkhof to sink deeply into our consciousness. The acts of God in Israel and in Christ . . .

> presuppose our existence as humans, and in these acts we are unmasked as lost sons, rebels against the order of his holy love, enemies of his kingdom. That is a terrible and entirely unexpected discovery. We would not know of it without the representatively radical place of Israel in the encounter with this God, and without the cross of Christ in which this history is climaxed. For whatever else the cross may tell us, it certainly proves that we cannot stand God and that He must be eliminated if He comes too close to us. . . . For one who sees God acting in Jesus, this is precisely the evidence of our radical and total alienation from God. Since the cross it is no longer possible to think optimistically about man and to expect salvation to come from his own good potential and abilities. (*Christian Faith*, p. 193)

For the cross is at one and the same time both God's greatest compliment extended to us and his greatest condemnation heaped on us. His greatest compliment — for it demonstrates the value he places on us as creatures of his hand. His greatest condemnation — for it also demonstrates the enormous sacrifice it took to win us back.

PART FOUR

THE WAY OF SALVATION

Transitional Comments

The plan of salvation represents God's way of restoring the fallen creation
to all it was and is meant to be. To that end God in Christ intervened
redemptively in the affairs of our alienated world to win it back. That
mighty act of reconciliation is still going on. The decisive battle has
indeed been fought and won at the cross and in the resurrection. In
principle the war is over. The outcome is settled. But very intense rearguard skirmishes continue. In this campaign of conquest God chose Israel
as his beachhead. As "end-time" believers moving along on the road of
redemption, we now cast our glances back across our shoulders to that
earlier stretch in our common pilgrimage — God's way with Israel.

Chapter I

"One Way"

Law and gospel, as we have seen, converge in the one way of salvation. The two Testaments, the Old together with the New, all 66 books, composed by roughly forty authors across a time span of nearly 1,500 years, record a single unfolding drama of redemption moving along eschatologically, act after act, through all its ups and downs toward the final consummation of all things. We rend asunder what God has thus joined together only to our own hurt. For those who play the New off against the Old end up losing both. The annals of Western Christianity offer ample evidence of movements which violated the unity of the biblical narrative in this way. There were the followers of Marcion (ca. A.D. 150) who ascribed the entire Old Testament and even large sections of the New Testament to the inferior, vengeful God of Jewry. There were the Gnostics in the early church who extolled the "spiritual" virtues of Christianity at the expense of the barren "carnal" elements of the Hebrew faith. There are contemporary Dispensationalists who fragment the biblical story line into sharply contrasting eras, each with a different way of salvation. Calvin also takes on such "pestilent fellows" in his day (*Institutes,* II,10-11). In the Lutheran tradition, too, the unity of biblical revelation is often seriously disturbed by a sharp distinction between the Old Testament as "law" and the New Testament as "gospel."

Scripture itself resists such dissecting of its message. It is all of one piece. Its striking pattern of cross-referencing one part with another reflects the central Story which runs through its many stories. There is a single-mindedness to God's way with his world. This unifying note is echoed repeatedly in the words of the Old Testament: "Hear, O Israel, the LORD your God is one . . . ," "I am the LORD, and there is none beside me . . . ," therefore "Turn aside, neither to the right nor to the left." Consistent with the organically progressive relationship between the two Testaments, this motif of unity comes to even clearer and fuller expression in the New Testament: Paul speaks of "one body," "one spirit," and "one hope," climaxed in the words, "one Lord, one faith, one baptism, one God and Father of us all, who is above all, through all, and in all" (Ephesians 4:4-6). In this vision the household of faith includes descendants of Abraham as well as followers of Christ, for Abraham is the father of all believers. In Christ the blessings of Abraham now also come on the Gentiles (Galatians 3:14).

The early church father Irenaeus (ca. A.D. 130-200) strongly opposed Marcionite and Gnostic theologies which drove deep wedges between so-called "heavenly" and "earthly" parts of biblical revelation. He expressed the unity of the two Testaments very pointedly in these words:

> The Word of God, present with his handiwork from the beginning, reveals the Father to all whom He wills, when the Father wills and how He wills. Thus in all and through all there is one God the Father and one Word, one Son, and one Spirit, and one salvation to all who believe in him. . . . [For] one and the same householder produced both covenants, the Word of God, our Lord Jesus Christ, who spoke with both Abraham and Moses. (*Against Heresies,* IV,6,6; IV,9,1)

"Because of its thoroughness," says Hendrikus Berkhof, "Calvin's discussion of this problem is of lasting importance" (*Christian Faith,* p. 223). Calvin holds that Old Testament believers inherited "a common salvation with us by the grace of the same Mediator" (*Institutes,* II,10,1). "It is important to make this point," he says. For though he goes on to "freely admit the differences" between the two Testaments, this should be done "in such a way as not to detract from [Scripture's] established unity" (*Institutes,* II,11,1). Calvin's major thesis is, therefore, that "the covenant made with all the patriarchs is so much like ours in substance and reality that the two are actually one and the same" (*Institutes,* II,10,2).

In the introduction to his magnificent work on covenant history, S. G. De Graaf emphasizes this same point in offering helpful pointers on how to tell the Bible stories. Speaking to teachers, he says,

> . . . Your stories should tell about [Christ], whether you tell the history of the Old Testament or of the New Testament. . . . The Old Testament is the book of the Christ who is to come, while the New Testament tells us of the Christ who has come. . . . [Therefore,] every story in Scripture reveals something of the counsel of God for our redemption, even though every story tells it differently. And in every story God is the prime agent, revealing himself through his acts as the Redeemer. . . . The redemption in the Mediator is revealed to us in every story. But this is not to say that the

whole sweep of redemption is visible in every story. . . . [Yet] the seed of redemption is present in every story in the Old Testament. Our job is to use the light of the New Testament to uncover it. (*Promise and Deliverance*, Vol. I, pp. 18-21)

This central focus on the Messiah as the unifying theme of all Scripture is summarized well in the following statement:

As the history of redemption the Bible speaks of beginnings and ends. The Bible is not a record of unrelated actions and sayings of God, but is a record in which the various events, sayings, and responses bear a fundamental relationship to each other. There is a single plan of redemption and the whole of revelation points in that direction. Hence the history of redemption as recorded in the Bible can be characterized as the saving revelation of God in Jesus Christ. From its beginning to its end, from the beginning of history to the final coming of the kingdom, the history of redemption moves toward and flows from Jesus Christ. Thus the only correct understanding of the tremendous variety contained within Scripture is that which interprets it in its relationship to Jesus Christ. He is its unifying theme. ("The Nature and Extent of Biblical Authority," pp. 24-25)

Chapter II

God's Way with Israel

As God's way with Christ and his followers is the central thread which runs through New Testament revelation, so proleptically his way with Israel is the heartbeat of redemption history in the Old Testament. That unfolding plan of salvation includes at least the following aspects: the universal background to God's new initiative in the call of Abraham, Israel's mission as a chosen people, the line which runs from Israel to the church, the Old Testament as covenant history, and the place and role of the Hebrew Scriptures as abiding canon within the Christian community.

II. 1. Israel's "Prehistory"

Israel's history as a chosen people begins with the call of Abraham (Genesis 12) early in the second millennium B.C. This seemingly insignificant yet very momentous transition point in biblical revelation does not, however, mark the beginning of salvation history. To recover that we must reach back to the "mother promise" (Genesis 3:15) as given in the Paradise lost. Between the "new beginning" in Adam and God's "new beginning" in Abraham lies yet another "new beginning" — God's preservation of the human race from its watery grave in the days of Noah. All this belongs to the universal history of mankind. With a few swift strokes the author covers more than half of our human lineage, stringing countless generations together in an unbroken line of genealogical connections which link Adam to Noah to Abraham. The fast pace of the narrative suggests that the writer is in a hurry to get to the patriarchs. Genesis 1–11 can therefore be viewed as Israel's "prehistory." This universal perspective which forms the backdrop to Abraham's call is nonetheless of lasting importance. It serves as a standing reminder that Israel is not God's last word for the world. Though for nearly

355

two millennia God's Messianic concerns remain focused on this chosen people, it is not this Hebrew particularism but the more original universal perspective which reflects God's ultimate purpose in redemption. This larger horizon is clearly depicted in the "registry of the nations" in Genesis 10–11. The multitude of strange names there duly recorded expresses the biblical principle that these non-Israelite peoples are not permanently dismissed from the plan of salvation. For along the way already as the Lord "registers his people" — including even outsiders from Babylon, Philistia, Tyre, and Ethiopia — he records, "This one was born [in Zion]" (Psalm 87). Then finally at Pentecost the original universal perspective re-emerges when these other peoples, waiting long in the wings, move back onto center stage (Acts 2:8-11).

II. 2. A Chosen People

". . . You are a chosen race, a royal priesthood, a holy nation, God's own people . . ." (1 Peter 2:9). These words are reminiscent of Israel. Yet the reference is to the church. The truth they convey bridges both Old and New Testaments. For the church as well as for Israel, God's electing love comes as a wholly unmerited favor. It is a gift, not an achievement. It therefore radically excludes every notion of self-aggrandizing privilege. It leaves no room for superiority complexes. God's free sovereign grace is rather an urgent call to service, even sacrifice and suffering, certainly a summons to share these riches with others. For as Peter goes on to remind early Christians, they are chosen so that they may "declare the wonderful deeds of him who called [them] out of darkness into his marvelous light."

The church is a chosen people. Within the full sweep of salvation history, however, Christ-believers are not God's first elect community. That honor belongs to Israel. Christians are latter-day children adopted into God's earlier family of faith, a point expounded at great length by Paul in Romans 9–11. The words of Peter cited above echo God's earlier choice of Israel during their journey of return from the house of bondage to the promised land. "You are a people holy to the LORD your God," says Moses. ". . . [He] has chosen you to be a people for his own possession. . . ." What are the grounds for God's choice of this haggard band of ex-slaves? "It was not because you were more in number than other peoples that the LORD set his love upon you and chose you, for you were the fewest of all peoples. . . ." Why then this divine initiative? It is simply "because the LORD loves you, and is keeping his oath which he swore to your fathers" (Deuteronomy 7:6-8).

This reassuring word of undeserved blessing takes us back to "square one" in Israel's long pilgrimage — God's call of Abraham and his promises to the patriarchs. As Pascal put it, "He is the God of Abraham, Isaac, and Jacob, not the god of the philosophers and scholars." When that "wandering Aramean," that nomadic nobody renamed Abraham, heard and answered God's call to pull up stakes and set his sights on an unknown promised land where he would possess nothing but a tomb, by all ordinary standards of historical valuation that act of sheer obedience should have earned him the reward of everlasting oblivion. Except, of course, as Paul says, that "the gifts and the call of God are irrevocable" (Romans 11:29). The election of this "father of believers" was then reaffirmed in that second memorable date, the exodus event. These two dramatic moments of divine intervention are the master key which unlocks the meaning of the entire Old Testament legacy. It opens the door to a future which is even now an ongoing present. For in choosing Abraham God was choosing Israel, and in choosing Israel he was choosing Christ, and in choosing Christ he is choosing a renewed people today. To Abraham God promised, "I will bless you." That was the top line. And the bottom line was this, "And by you shall all the families of the earth bless themselves" (Genesis 12:2-3). This leads then, as Louis Berkhof states, to "the election of Israel as a people for special privilege and for special service" (*Systematic Theology,* p. 114). Abraham was thus the twice-called pioneer of Israel's destiny — called from out of the pagan world of his day with a view to his calling to and for the world at large. By this chain of events Israel was created as "the people to whom God speaks and by whom He speaks to the rest of the world" (S. de Dietrich, *God's Unfolding Purpose,* p. 51). Thus God's people of old became "the port of entry which the living God has freely chosen in order to draw near to all nations. But He chose a way which leads through history" (H. J. Kraus, *The People of God in the Old Testament,* p. 70).

Nothing but the persistent electing love of God was able to sustain Abraham's descendants along the way of their historic mission. Accordingly, "the whole Old Testament message is based on the first call and on the first promise. . . . But the sound of this call does not die away. Abraham is not left alone" (Kraus, *The People of God in the Old Testament,* p. 27). Vicariously Israel represents all mankind. In her proxy role she is obliged to bear testimony among the nations to God's sovereign rule and gracious purpose for the world. " 'You are my witnesses,' says the LORD, 'and my servant whom I have chosen, that you may know and believe me and understand that I am He. . . . I, I am the LORD, and besides me there is no savior' " (Isaiah 43:10-11). Like humanity as a whole, however, Israel repeatedly spurned her calling and turned a cold shoulder to God's electing love. God's word of judgment then descended through his servants the prophets, "You only have I known of all the families of the earth; therefore

I will punish you for all your iniquities" (Amos 3:2). The human heart is an "idol factory" (Calvin) working overtime to produce its pseudogods. Life in Israel was no exception, with all its awesome consequences. As a chosen people the great honor was hers, as was the heavy burden of being more sternly judged than others. As Israel arrogated the blessings of election to herself and acted presumptuously, God reveals his sovereign lordship over all history, and yet through it also his redemptive purposes, by moving the surrounding nations to carry out his judgments. The story of Israel's steady, steep, and almost unbroken descent into captivity offers not a shred of evidence in support of the theory of moral and cultural evolution. ". . . There is no upward line of progress; . . . there is [only] a steady recurrence of failure and transgression" (Kraus, *The People of God in the Old Testament*, p. 61).

The full impact of God's righteousness comes to rest finally on the Messiah. Along the way, through acts of judgment tempered by an overriding grace, the call of Abraham stands as "the first link in the long succession of divine interventions that we call 'salvation history'. At the end of the chain stands a hill" — first Moriah (Genesis 22), then Golgotha" (de Dietrich, *God's Unfolding Purpose*, p. 50). In all these demonstrations of a divinely resolute electing love we see that "a profound mystery controls the history of this chosen people Israel. In its midst God has wrought those mighty works which point forward to the coming of Jesus Christ . . ." (Kraus, *The People of God in the Old Testament*, p. 9). For "when faithless Israel fails in its task, God, who is always faithful to himself, raises up One who, incarnating all Israel in his own person, attacks heaven, hell, and all mankind, and emerges the Victor" (de Dietrich, *God's Unfolding Purpose*, p. 57). Thus, in contrast to those who denigrate the Old Testament, Reformed theology accentuates the positive, enduring aspect of God's chosen way with Israel, the "good news" in its Old Testament form. It regards the recurring negative elements, the expressions of divine judgment on Israel's recalcitrance, as impediments which retard but cannot decisively obstruct the steadfast, electing love of God. Election is the firm assurance that the holy jealousy of Israel's God is bound to prevail until his redemptive purposes are achieved in "the fulness of the times."

II. 3. Covenant History

"I will be your God — you shall be my people." This two-in-one divine declaration is the very heartbeat of the covenant relationship. It reverberates with the two-sidedness of the one eternal mediating Word of God, promise and obligation. God holds himself to that Word, and holds his people to it as well. It is the dynamic interaction of these two partners down through the centuries to the present time that we call covenant history.

> And at the center of this history stands a cross. This cross is the great paradox of the Bible and of all human history, for it shows us that God, in order to save the world, chose a way of doing so that meant being nailed to a cross. From the first page of Genesis to the last page of Revelation, everything that happens points toward this cross, and likewise everything arises from it. For since it was firmly fixed in the center of the world, the world has been understandable only in terms of it and by means of it. (de Dietrich, *God's Unfolding Purpose,* pp. 20-21)

This covenant history, ultimately centered in Christ, takes its point of departure in the finished work of creation which its Maker declared "very good." Covenant is the very foundation and framework for all biblical religion. Covenantal religion defines the fundamental structures undergirding all human relationships and every societal calling. It is not limited to a few highly "spiritual" moments in life — the birth of a covenant child, the sacramental signs and seals of the covenant, covenant training, or the covenant community at worship. It embraces every earthly institution — marriage, schooling, labor, social service, science, art, even politics. Even when we in Adam betrayed our calling, God did not abandon the covenant. Instead, he intervened in grace to keep it alive, setting out on the long road of salvation history to revive the bond of fellowship. Covenant history is a story without an ending. It covers not only God's way with Israel but also that of the Christian community today and on into the future. Its charted course is punctuated by a series of renewal movements — not the establishment repeatedly of new covenants, for there is a single covenant to which God remains forever true, but covenant reenactments. We witness the unfolding phases in the history of covenant renewal in representative "mediators" such as Noah, Abraham, Moses, David. This forward thrust in God's covenant-keeping agenda is clearly expressed by Jeremiah:

> Behold, the days are coming, says the LORD, when I will make a new covenant with the house of Israel and the house of Judah, not like the covenant which I made with their fathers when I took them by the hand to bring them out of the land of Egypt, my covenant which they broke, though I was their husband, says the LORD. But this is the covenant which I will make with the house of Israel after those days, says the LORD: I will put my law within them, and I will write it upon their hearts; and I will be their God, and they shall be my people. (31:31-33)

359

These promises were kept in the Messiah who proclaimed "the new covenant in my blood" (1 Corinthians 11:25).

> It is God alone who is the guarantor of the covenant. His honor is pledged. And although Abraham's descendants break the covenant, God himself comes in Jesus Christ and offers himself in place of the defaulting partner, and pays the price of his faithlessness. (de Dietrich, *God's Unfolding Purpose,* p. 56)

Covenant making was a common practice in Old Testament times, much like going to a notary public today to sign and seal a contract. It involved a binding agreement between two parties, with specified rights and duties. Yet there are strikingly unique features in God's covenant with his people. Covenant renewals in Scripture are not fifty/fifty deals arranged by the mutual consent of two equally responsible parties. In fact, the two partners are very unequal — the One unfailingly faithful, the other persistently unfaithful. God seizes the initiative and never surrenders it. He comes as the Revealer, and his people are drawn into the covenant relationship as respondents. As the "Senior Partner" he sets the terms for himself and for his "junior partner." In its origins, therefore, the covenant is unilateral. Both Israel and the church are called first of all to "wait upon the Lord." But the other side of covenant making and keeping is also real. In its outworkings the covenant relationship is bilateral. We are called to "walk with the Lord." The covenant is therefore of enormous abiding importance. For,

> Without covenant, there is no religion, no conscious fellowship between man and God, no exchange of love and faithfulness. Without the covenant, man would be just an instrument in God's hand. When God created man He had more than an instrument in mind: He made a creature that could respond to him. Only if man is capable of responding would he be able to assume his position as partner in the covenant. Without a covenant, God would have only claims and man only obligations. But as soon as God gave man a promise, man also had a claim on God, namely, to hold God to that promise.... Once the promise is given, we can speak of a covenant, for a covenant, after all, is an agreement between two parties in which the claims and obligations are spelled out. (De Graaf, *Promise and Deliverance,* Vol. I, p. 36)

The biblical covenant involves a lifelong, exclusive relationship between God and his people which knows no bounds of time or space. It cannot tolerate "rival lovers" or divided allegiances. Away with the Baals, therefore, and pagan fertility rites, together with the idols of the nations, their nature gods, self-help religions, and Mammon! As Maker and Keeper of the covenant God regards his people with the holy jealousy of a husband toward his wife, a father toward his child, a master toward his servant, the owner of all toward his steward. The promised land itself served as a holy habitat for God's presence among his people. On Israel's pilgrimage, moreover, circumcision served as a sacramental sign of entrance into the covenant community, and its enduring blessings were sealed in the sacrament of the Passover. In all these varied relationships God continually reveals himself to his people by his personal covenant name "Yahweh," rooted in the Hebrew word "to be." This is not to be understood as "abstract being," but as "being there for someone," "being in relation to his people." He is the God who ever was, is, and will be for his people. If then "God is for us, who can be against us?" (Romans 8:31). He keeps covenant with us and for us not as discrete and isolated individuals, but as believing communities in which every member shares in the life of the body as a whole.

Covenant fellowship among God's people is indeed a unique way of life. Yet the covenant renewals narrated in the Old Testament, especially those going back to the early stages in Israel's history, reflect some very remarkable structural parallels with the suzerainty treaties of the surrounding nations. This is especially evident in the covenant code of Exodus 19–24 and the renewal of the covenant in Deuteronomy. God's covenant relationship with Israel is there described in terms which formally resemble certain features of the then prevailing pacts between rulers and their subjects. In content God's covenantal way with Israel differs markedly from his way with other nations. Yet it takes place within the give-and-take of their interacting histories. Meredith Kline offers the following commentary on these analogies:

> The Near Eastern vassal treaties were . . . law covenants, declarations of a great king imposing his authority upon a subject king and servant people. Normally they were ratified by an oath of the vassal. . . . To enter into the oath meant for the vassal to come under the dual sanctions of the covenant, the blessing and the curse. The lordship of the great king might be exercised in the form of protection or of destruction. . . . Now since in certain notable instances it pleased the Lord of Israel to describe his covenant relationship to his people according to the pattern of those vassal treaties, no other conclusion is warranted than that the "covenant" in those instances denoted at the formal level the same kind of relationship as did the vassal covenants on which they were modelled. That is, "covenant" in the divine-human transactions denoted a law covenant and hence was expressive of a lordship that could satisfy the terms of the covenant by stretching forth its sceptre in either blessing or curse. (*By Oath Consigned*, pp. 21-22)

". . . It would seem indisputable," says Kline, "that the book of Deuteronomy . . . exhibits the structure of the ancient suzerainty treaties in the unity and completeness of their classic pattern. . . . What is remarkable is the detailed extent to which God has utilized this legal instrument of human kingdoms for the definition and administration of his own redemptive reign over his people" (*Treaty of the Great King,* pp. 41-42).

The intermingling of grace and judgment is precisely what marks covenant history in Israel. In this Israel was a paradigm of God's way with the world. Its international relations at their best were governed by a *centripedal* effect: Come in unto us and we will show you what the Lord has done for us. The heirs of Abraham were to be a blessing to the nations, but in keeping with the principle of *particularism.* A steady, though uneven narrowing down process is operative in God's redemptive concerns, so that even in Israel the Messianic hope is kept alive only in a faithful remnant. Finally it comes down, as Paul says, not to many "offsprings," but to the single "Offspring," Christ Jesus (Galatians 3:16). The centuries-long concentration of covenant history in Israel was therefore not God's last word for the world. God's last Word for the world was Christ. The goal of covenant history is therefore *universalism.* The Old Testament already offers some breakthroughs toward a universal perspective, though only sporadically — as in Rahab, Ruth, and the Ninevites. Isaiah, too, points in this direction: ". . . my house shall be called a house of prayer for all peoples" (56:7). In his prophecy concerning the suffering servant of Yahweh, he says, "I will give you as a light to the nations, that my salvation may reach to the end of the earth" (49:6). Accordingly, Old Testament particularism "was not intended to be permanent, but to disappear after it had served its purpose. . . . [For] when Christ brought his sacrifice, the blessing of Abraham flowed out to the nations — those who were afar off were brought near" (Louis Berkhof, *Systematic Theology,* p. 300). In fulfillment of this promised opening up of covenant history, our Lord's word is now our command: "Go therefore into all the world . . ." (Matthew 28:19). The good news of the covenant now has an outgoing, *centrifugal* impetus: from Jerusalem, through Judea and Samaria, and to the ends of the earth (Acts 1:8). The whole world, at our doorstep and beyond, is now our parish. Still, in every age the terms of the covenant remain the same: "I will be your God — you shall be my people." The anticipated response is captured in the words of the familiar hymn: "Trust and obey, for there is no other way. . . ."

II. 4. The Old and the New: "Concealed . . . Revealed"

Israel and the Old Testament, the people and the canon, go hand in hand through salvation history. But it is not an easy, comfortable relationship.

On the one hand, these writings are deeply embedded in and arise directly out of the legacy and destiny of this ancient people of God. At the same time, as a Word which comes to them from beyond and stands over against them, it is the measure by which Israel is weighed and found wanting. The Old Testament therefore speaks then and there as well as here and now both descriptively and prescriptively. It is the weal-and-woe story of God's chosen nation. But it is also canonical, the rule for faith and life in every generation. Reading it as the descriptive account of Israel's history, we are left with the checkered career of a people who owe their very existence to God's electing love and gracious acts of deliverance, yet who from start to finish are guilty of covenant breaking and promises unkept. Nonetheless, through all its twists and turns the Old Testament writings also speak prescriptively with full authority. In their progressive unfolding, as law, prophecy, and wisdom literature, they are the norm and standard by which God continually judges his people, calls them to repentance, urges renewal of life, holds out the hope of salvation, and keeps the Messianic expectations alive. We must therefore distinguish between what is happening *in* Israel — almost uninterrupted unfaithfulness — and what is happening *through* Israel — God's faithfulness to the covenant, pushing forward the program of the coming kingdom. In Israel we meet a people, much like ourselves, unwilling and unable to live up to its covenant calling. The future hinges, however, on God's overriding commitment to promises to be fulfilled in the coming Messiah. The New Testament draws together these broken pieces of the past in a double focus: Israel's futile attempts to make its own way in the world and the mounting pressure for that unmerited yet sorely needed deliverance which called for yet another "new beginning," God's climactic, decisive initiative in Christ Jesus.

Clearly, then, our understanding of the gospel message stands and falls with our view of the interrelatedness of the "older" and "newer" covenant, of the two parts of the single canon, of Israel and the church. In the measure that we loosen these ties we seriously shortchange Christian faith and life. Not only is the Old Testament by far the larger part of the Bible, which we neglect only to our own hurt. But more importantly, detached from its subsoil in the Old Testament, the New Testament is like a cut flower which, severed from its roots, soon withers in our hands. For much of its very household language and its key concepts are borrowed from its Hebrew heritage. If we remember this, we spare ourselves the unrewarding trouble of seeking the basic meaning of central New Testament ideas (such as *logos, metanoia,* body, soul) in Greco-Roman culture and philosophical thought. The benchmarks of the Old remain indelibly impressed on the New. Jesus himself is not an isolated person carrying out a solo mission. As Christ, the "anointed One," he is the incarnation of the Messianic, "anointed" hopes of the fathers. The entire history of redemption coming up from the past culminates in him. In his "corporate personality" he represents all Israel, old and new. Thus the evangelist can appeal to Hosea 11:1, "Out of Egypt have I called my son," referring to the exodus of Israel, and apply it to Jesus (Matthew 2:15). In light of Christ's resurrection and the outpouring of the Spirit, Paul declares that the church is built on the foundation not only of the apostles but also of the prophets (Ephesians 2:20).

It is hardly possible to overestimate the fundamental importance of God's way with Israel in the Old Testament for the Christian life of faith — except perhaps when dealing with the very intriguing views of A. A. Van Ruler. In his theology the canonical center of gravity shifts heavily from the New Testament to the Old. Essentially, he holds, the Old Testament is the real Bible. Closing out a lengthy exploration of the many fascinating interrelationships between the two Testaments, Van Ruler asks, ". . . If there is only one canon, has the New Testament simply been taken up and integrated into the Old?" That is, ". . . Is there only one canon in the sense that the Old Testament alone is the canon and the New Testament has just been added at the end as an explanatory glossary?" (*The Christian Church and the Old Testament,* p. 94). In *Religie en Politiek* he offers an affirmative answer to these questions. He there defends the thesis that "the New Testament, so to speak, is no more than an appendix further clarifying some strange concepts" (p. 123) left over from the Old. Stated even more strongly, the New Testament is "the definitive proclamation of the Old Testament as the only real Word of God in the world" (p. 142). The New lends no additional meaning to the Old. It signifies rather that, far from being discarded, the Old is now finalized. Thus the New Testament is like "an index at the back of the Book, announcing that the Old Testament is now complete. . . . In a very unique way the New Testament closes the canon, just as the Lord himself closed the door of the ark behind Noah" (p. 142). What then shall we say about Jesus Christ? He represents "the compilation and summary of God's promises which lie more or less scattered throughout the Old Testament, so that one can now sort them out more easily and more easily dispose of some of them" (p. 143). No depreciation of the New Testament is intended here, only a very substantial shift in focus. But clearly Van Ruler's views do have a direct bearing on the question of a "closed canon." Was the biblical canon essentially closed with Malachi rather than with Revelation? Was the core of the message of salvation already proclaimed by about the fourth century B.C.? Is then the coming of Christ an "anticlimax"? Do the Gospels leave us with a "letdown" feeling?

As an antidote to practical dispensationalism, Van Ruler's views can serve as a much needed corrective. For retiring the Old Testament is a greater threat to the life of the church today than his dramatic shift in the biblical center of gravity. But there is a better way: the organic unity of the two Testaments viewed as promise and fulfillment — what is *latent* ("concealed") in the Old becoming *patent* ("fully revealed") in the New, as the old adage has it. This is closer to the heart of the matter. Far from fostering a neglect of the Old Testament, this view stresses its indispensability for a right understanding of the New. Hendrikus Berkhof's comment is therefore to the point: "Reformed theology is particularly interested in emphasizing that for a correct understanding of the New Testament we are entirely dependent upon the experiences and concepts of the Old Testament" (*Christian Faith*, pp. 224-25).

II. 5. The Old Testament Canon: Book of the Covenant

Israel's history is part of a continuing story. Its writings, the Old Testament, come down to us as Part One, and the New Testament as Part Two, in the Book of the Covenant which covers the Bible as a whole. They are, on the one hand, products of covenant history. At the same time they shape that history. Even from a Christian viewpoint, perhaps especially so, the Old Testament is never "old" in the sense of being outdated. It remains rather the "older" phase in a permanently relevant body of revelation of which the New Testament is the "newer" phase. Within this eschatologically directed movement of revelation, Israel occupies a crucial position between the original creation, now fallen, and the gospel with its vision of the renewed creation.

Common practice today leads us to divide the canonical writings of the Old Testament into four main segments: law, history, writings, and prophecy. The Hebrew tradition, however, views this matter differently. It identifies three major divisions: the law, the prophets, and the writings (Luke 24:44). The books that we tend to call historical the Hebrew Bible regards as the "earlier prophets," acknowledging thereby that they proclaim "prophetic history." That is, they do more than chronicle historical events in God's way with his people. More importantly, they convey a message. They are running commentaries on the ups and downs in covenant history. The books that we usually call the "major" and "minor" prophets are regarded as the "latter prophets" in the canonical order of the Hebrew Bible. In dealing briefly now with this "older" phase in the single unfolding drama of covenant history which encompasses both Testaments, we shall follow the order of the Hebrew Bible. For, as Hendrikus Berkhof puts it, "Israel's real covenant history runs from the law to the prophets [cf. Luke 24:27]. But every man who participates in this history will always [also] recognize in these writings, then here and then there, his own questions and experiences" (*Christian Faith*, p. 235).

II. 5. 1. The Law

The law as "Torah" is generally viewed as covering the first five books of Moses. It is best understood not as a rigorous legal code of rules and regulations with rewards and penalties attached, but as instructional guidelines for covenant living. Of central significance is the fact that the law addresses life in its diversified yet coherent unity. It touches on the full range of human relationships. Perhaps nowhere is the comprehensive scope of its urgent call to covenant obedience, accompanied by appropriate blessings and judgments, more challengingly expressed than in the divine provisions for sabbatical and jubilee years (Leviticus 25) — though there is no evidence that Israel was ever able to muster the courage to observe these special times of rest and renewal.

The mind-set and praxis of our modern world tends to split life very deliberately and self-consciously into two compartments, private religiosity and public affairs. In Old Testament law, however, "there is no [such] distinction between 'secular' and 'sacred'; for even in its [so-called] secular existence the people is still the covenant people of Yahweh" (Otto Weber, *The Groundplan of the Bible,* p. 48). Israel was called to a theocratic life-style. That is, whatever its form of government, the beneficent sovereign rule of God by his Word was to serve as the touchstone for the whole life of his people in the promised land. Note the strong emphasis on this point by de Dietrich: "The law shows clearly that all of life must be placed under God's commands, for it has to do not only with the relationship of man to God and with his neighbor, but with every aspect of religious and civil life." Though de Dietrich's comment may suggest it, there are no incipient dualisms in God's Word for our life together in his world. For, as de Dietrich goes on to say, though . . .

> the modern world tends to separate the "sacred" and the "secular," this does not happen in Biblical revelation. Civil and religious laws cannot be separated, for they both originate in the will of God and their purpose is to glorify God. It is because the earth is the Lord's that the first fruits of the harvest and the first-born of the flocks are to be offered to him. This is also the reason why each person must treat his neighbor's ox and ass with due respect and be sure that everyone is treated justly. It is because God reveals himself as the Savior-God at a decisive point in its history that Israel must always celebrate the Passover of the Lord. It is because Israel remains a sinful people that it must offer sacrifices of expiation for its sins. From this time on, the law really covers the *whole life* of the people of God. It is Israel's charter, not a "bill of human rights," but a charter of God's claim upon men. For the real guardian of human law and liberty is God. The law represents the commands that men and nations may not

ignore without bringing about their own destruction. (*God's Unfolding Purpose,* pp. 75, 80)

The reign of God in the "older" covenant, often called theocracy, is now redemptively updated in the regal claims of the Messiah. The Land of Canaan was an interim paradigm of the coming kingdom of God, sketched on the canvas of ancient history as a geographically limited reality. That kingdom is now a present universal reality in Jesus Christ. All authority belongs to him in heaven and on earth (Matthew 28:18). Since he is the "End" of the law, we are now called to "lead every thought captive in obedience" to him (2 Corinthians 10:5). The law of God is now also the law of Christ. In him we find its abiding meaning. He is its "principle" of interpretation for both the "older" and "newer" Testaments.

II. 5. 2. The Prophets

The law is the vital pulsebeat of covenant living. In the next section of the Hebrew canon we meet the earlier and latter prophets. They present us with a critical review of how these instructional guidelines actually fared among God's chosen people. Scanning the horizons of their day, these "seers" not only point to the future but in doing so also draw on the past and impact the present. In their prophecies we hear "the story of what happened to the covenant in history, a story of judgment and grace, of apostasy and accusation, of human faithlessness and faithfulness, and new promises from the side of God" (Hendrikus Berkhof, *Christian Faith,* p. 229). The prophets were divine "mouthpieces," those who "speak forth" on behalf of their Sender, who calls them "my servants."

Tirelessly (or almost so — recall the despondency of Elijah the refugee prophet, 1 Kings 19:9-10) they denounce the evils rampant in the nation. They summon God's people to renewal of their personal and communal lives and the reformation of their societal institutions. They lash out especially at the judges, deliverers, priests, kings, and false prophets — those assigned "mediatorial" roles in the covenant community. These leaders were to serve as living links, representatives, ambassadors, and intercessors between God and his people. To them much was entrusted. From them much was expected. Their heresies, therefore, in misleading the common folk, attracted the special attention of these "watchmen on the walls of Zion." For those in high places are supremely accountable for the exercise of their offices — including greedy land barons and unscrupulous merchants. No privileged status was immune to divine judgment. The indicting finger of these divine "defenders" pointed in every direction, without fear or favor.

The motivation behind these ultimatums is clear. Israel was called to maintain its identity by living in radical separation from the evils around them. Issuing such urgent reminders was the heavy burden resting on the hearts of those whom God raised up as his "delegates." Israel must honor its heritage as an "unassimilated and unassimilatable people" (de Dietrich). Initially the prophets bring a conditional message: Repent or else. . . . As increasingly Israel defaults on its covenant vows, however, the prophetic word becomes an unconditional pronouncement: The purging fires of exile are coming. God becomes an adversary of his own cherished people. Yet his judgment is tempered with hope: I will deliver, says the Lord, but solely "for my own name's sake." Thus a window remains ever open to the Messianic promise. Repeatedly the prophets draw on that future expectation to meet head-on the crying needs of the moment. Yet the meaning of that vision of the coming "day of the Lord" remains vague and ambiguous throughout Israel's history, awaiting its clarification in "the fulness of the times."

Judgment and redemption — this is the dual theme which pervades the message of the prophets. Judgment is clearly a matter of sight. It becomes painfully evident in the destruction of Jerusalem and the captivity of its inhabitants. The promised salvation is evident, however, only to the eye of faith. To see God anew as the Keeper of the covenant, Israel had to be stripped of literally everything on which it set its misplaced trust. Nothing was left but the Messianic promise. This was the single surviving ray of hope. It was in this light that the prophets were able to see what the others failed to see. In view of God's sanctifying grace, things are never so good as to need no renewal. But by virtue of that same grace, things are never so bad as to be utterly hopeless. Paradoxically, therefore,

> When everyone is optimistic and the word is "All is well!" the prophet speaks of doom. But when Israel is at the bottom of the pit, when there is nothing but desolation and ruin, the solitary voice of the prophet is lifted up afresh, this time to proclaim the God of all comfort. . . . The prophet smells death in the air where others are dazzled by the brilliance of a civilization still at the heights of its glory. And on the other hand, just when life seems buried and condemned, he perceives the secret work of God and receives the promise that resurrection lies ahead. (de Dietrich, *God's Unfolding Purpose,* p. 112)

This surprising prospect is embodied in the "suffering servant of the LORD" (Isaiah 53:1-6). Who is this mysterious figure? One of the prophets? A rehabilitated Israel? Looking ahead we learn from the Gospels that "there is only one servant who has really borne the sins of his people, only one who, being righteous, has suffered for the unrighteous. . . . This one servant is Jesus Christ, the Son of God" (de Dietrich, *God's Unfolding Purpose,* p. 123). Illumined by the presence of his spirit among us, we now learn to discern in Israel's history the earliest history of the church, indeed, our own life story. The words of the prophets draw us back vicariously, yet with an irresistibly magnetic attraction into this earlier phase in covenant history.

II. 5. 3. The Writings

These books, straddling the middle of our Bibles, Job, Psalms, Proverbs, Ecclesiastes, and Song of Songs, constitute a third rubric in the canonical structure of the Hebrew Scriptures, which are now also Christian Scriptures. This collection of writings embraces a tremendous variety of literary types — drama, dialogue, poetry, wise sayings, instruction, and more. It is clearly impossible to deal adequately with this fascinating diversity in overview fashion. The best we can hope for is to locate these writings within the biblical canon and get a feel for their contribution to its unfolding covenant/kingdom history. ". . . In the writings, the core of which are the psalms, we hear the voice of man as he relates himself to the God of the covenant in confession of guilt and thanksgiving, in doubt and exultation, in meditation and lament" (Hendrikus Berkhof, *Christian Faith,* p. 229). They are rich in imagery, word pictures, parallel expressions, clever plays on words, similes, and metaphors. These poets, thinkers, dramatists, and song writers allow us to sense keenly their innermost moods — bitter grief in the face of suffering in Job, fatherly concern in Proverbs, bewilderment over the mysteries of divine providence in Ecclesiastes, passionate fidelity in the Song of Songs. It is often not altogether clear how these writings fit into the mainstream of salvation history.

With the Psalms, however, we are on firmer footing. In large part at least they are much more closely related to God's way with Israel. We hear in them deeply religious reflections on God's covenant relationship with his people and his sovereign rule in their lives. Covenantal obedience means life and peace, disobedience leads to death and futility. Willing submission to God's gracious rule is the key to joyful servanthood; a rebellious spirit is self-destructive. The Psalmists are strong advocates of loyalty to the law of God. In lyrical fashion they also reinforce the message of the prophets. They write as gifted individuals, yet they speak as members of the community — to their contemporaries and for them. This is what Israel ought to believe and confess, they say, and how they ought to live. The call to true piety arises in rhapsodic strains from their hearts in intensely experiential ways. Pride is the ultimate vice, and humility the undergirding virtue of a God-fearing life. In responding to this fundamental choice, the Psalmists strike a wide range of notes — repentance, trust, anxiety, gratitude, justice, love, complaint, joy, hope.

Where then shall we locate this psalter within the Old Testament canon? Responsiveness is its basic feature. With the law as the transcendent norm for our life together in God's world, and prophecy as a critical commentary on how these claims actually function in the history of God's people, in the Psalms we are exposed to profoundly religious responses to both the law and the prophets.

Luther sees in the Psalms a summary of basic themes which are present in the rest of Scripture. He therefore calls the Book of the Psalms "the Bible in miniature, . . . in a nutshell." A central unifying motif which binds the 150 Psalms and the other writings together is the recurring theme, "the fear of the LORD" as "the beginning of wisdom" (Psalm 111:10; Proverbs 1:7; 9:10). This highly concentrated set of the heart involves such attitudes as reverence, surrender, and trust.

Given the expressions of solid piety which overflow in the Psalms, there is little reason to wonder at the dominant role they played in Israel's temple service and in the liturgy of their festivals. This tradition of using the Psalms in worship lived on in later history as faithful Hebrews gathered for worship in their synagogues. Within the redemptively updated context of the New Testament era the psalter also won a settled place in the life of the early Christian community. Encouraging this practice among Christ-believers, Paul says, "Let the word of Christ dwell in you richly, as you teach and admonish one another in all wisdom, and as you sing psalms and hymns and spiritual songs in your hearts to God" (Colossians 3:16). This long tradition of communal psalm singing was lent renewed impetus by the Reformers of the sixteenth century. Since then the Psalms have served as the book of praise and prayer in many Christian circles. Borrowing a comment from Karl Barth, "Blessed are those churches that still honor this tradition today."

II. 6. Israel, the Messiah, and the Church

According to Barth, the only proof for the existence of God is the continuing existence of the Jewish people. But what about the future? What prospects does Scripture hold out for the ancient people of God during these "end times"? Has God washed his hands of them? Or do they still have a special place in ongoing covenant history? For centuries those questions have persisted as matters of unfinished business on Christian and Jewish agendas. A new urgency surrounds them in our times, however, as we take stock of the countless episodes of anti-Semitism which darken the pages of Western history, especially in recent decades as our world agonizes over the lingering horrors of the Holocaust era. Can we as Christians still in good conscience extend to the Jewish community the gospel call to conversion?

Looming large at the very center of these contentious issues is the sovereignly solitary person of the Messiah himself. He is the righteous Judge of the nations, of the church as well as of Israel. Who crucified the Son of Man? Was it the Roman soldiers? Was it the Jewish leaders? Or were we present, too, when they nailed him to the cross? Scripture points beyond these historical factors to an overriding divine justice and mercy which converged on Golgotha. Paul therefore leads us to say that we were "united with him in a death like his" so that we may also be united with him in "a resurrection like his" (Romans 5:5). This is the biblical mystery of our contemporaneity with Christ through the work of the Spirit. It was humanity's sin, the collective guilt of all the sons and daughters of Adam and Eve, and that alone, which accounts for the death of the Son of God.

Such a deepening sense of our corporate guilt led the fathers of Vatican II to retract the long-standing indictment of the Jews as the "deicide race," the "God killers." In its declaration on "Non-Christians," the council "deplores the hatred, persecutions, and displays of anti-Semitism directed against the Jews at any time and from any source." It recalls "the spiritual bond linking the people of the New Covenant with Abraham's stock." Although it was the Jewish mob which "pressed for the death of Christ, . . . his passion cannot be blamed on all Jews then living, without distinction, nor upon the Jews of today" (W. M. Abbott and J. Gallagher, *The Documents of Vatican II*, pp. 664-67). While correct as an historical judgment, this concession misses the truly profound point that God was there dealing not simply with some Jews, nor with some Gentiles, but that he was there "in Christ reconciling the world to himself" (2 Corinthians 5:19). The cross and empty tomb now stand as that moment of crisis in redemption history by which we must seek to account for both the gathering together of Israel and the church and the parting of the ways between them. Israel therefore has "a qualified future which derives from the same free grace of God from which its past emerged and out of which the present Jewish-Gentile community of salvation lives" (Otto Weber, *Foundations of Dogmatics*, Vol. II, p. 487).

This dual effect arises from sharply conflicting views on the continuity and/or discontinuity in covenant history coming up from the Old Testament era into the New. Holding to the idea of a radical discontinuity, Judaism goes its own way, while the Christian community, with hearts attuned to the New Testament, lives out of a deep sense of continuity with the law, the prophets, and the writings. "Salvation is from the Jews," as the Lord himself affirmed (John 4:22). And the mighty acts of salvation centered in him were accomplished "according to the Scriptures" of the Old Testament (1 Corinthians 15:3-4). It is not the idea of "dual covenants," one for Jews and another for Christians, emerging from recent Jewish-Christian dialogues, but the organic unity of the two Testaments which is crucial to a fully biblical understanding of the person and work of Jesus the Messiah. For

> the election of Jesus Christ is the sole reason for the authority of the Old Testament in the [Christian] community. Without it, it would be just the "letter" (II Corinthians 3:7ff.). Without it, the Old Testament would have neither a center nor a purpose. The Old Testament has no validity in and of itself, apart from Jesus Christ. (Weber, *Foundations of Dogmatics,* Vol. II, p. 485)

Detached from the concrete realities of creation and covenant history in the "older" covenant, therefore, New Testament Christianity degenerates into abstract individualism, a purely personal notion of soul salvation, a mystical spirituality, pietism, cheap grace, otherworldliness.

The bridging figure, straddling the boundary line between the "older" and "newer" stages in covenant history, is John the Baptist (Luke 3:1-22). In a single vision he fuses these two horizons and focuses them on "the one who is mightier than I." In his highly confrontational preaching John sums up God's entire way with Israel and brings it to bear on "the Lamb of God who takes away the sin of the world" (John 1:29). John is the herald of the Messiah, preparing the way for him who would draw all men to himself (John 12:32). In his baptism at the hands of John, Jesus plunges himself vicariously into the sin- and guilt-laden stream of both Jewish and Gentile iniquity. Thus, in his transitional mission John serves as the last of the prophets and the first of the evangelists.

The wide assortment of names given to Jesus by the writers of the New Testament link him unmistakably, through John, with the past: He is the Son of Man, the Son of David, the true Melchizedek, the Bread from heaven, the suffering servant of the Lord, the great High Priest — in short, the Messiah of prophecy. As such he seeks out "the lost sheep of the house of Israel" (Matthew 10:6). Yet when "He came to his own home, . . . his own people received him not" (John 1:11). This note of rejection also forms the climax to Stephen's sermon at his stoning (Acts 7:51-53). Jesus himself explained his repudiation by the Jews as a re-enactment of past history in his parable of the treacherous tenants (Mark 12:1-10) and in his lamentation over Jerusalem (Matthew 23:29-39). Thus the Old Testament ends with "To be continued. . . ," and the New picks up on this unfinished theme.

Jesus was clearly recognizable from the Messianic legacy of the fathers by those whose eyes were open to its forward-looking promises. For, as he declares, "it is they that bear witness to me" (John 5:39). In his coming, he takes the cup of Israel's blessing, which over the long centuries had been gradually filling up but was never quite full, and fills it full to overflowing. In him a "greater" than all the Solomons and Jonahs (Luke 11:31-32) appeared. In the words of Herman Ridderbos:

> The birth of Jesus is the great crown and conclusion of that sacred history of Israel, which God himself has directed. . . . [For] He is the hidden root of Israel, the One in whom all is summed up, in whom in the end it all becomes visible. He accounts for Abraham's election; he is also the seed of Abraham, in whom all the nations of the world are to be blessed. He is the everlasting King of David's house, under whose government God will bless Israel and the nations. He is also the ending of the fourteen generations of the Exile, since in him alone can Israel find forgiveness of his sins, and resurrection from his destruction. (*Matthew's Witness to Jesus Christ,* pp. 19-20)

Rejection of the Messianic way of life is a darkening cloud which hangs heavy over our Western secular societies, including Jewish communities. As a result, the gospel now seeks embodiment within a basically triangular situation: it must be related to Israel, the church, and other world religions. In this setting the parting of the ways between Israel and the church remains an especially painful reality. For this "is not according to Scripture. Israel is the church, and the church is Israel, gathered from Jews and Gentiles. Mount Zion, Jerusalem, temple and altar, sacrifices and shadows are all fulfilled in Christ . . ." (Hoeksema, *Reformed Dogmatics,* p. 818).

As Messiah, Jesus ushered in the "last days," the "end times" of covenant history. In him the kingdom was breaking through as a present reality. Isaiah had foretold that "the LORD God who gathers the outcasts of Israel [would] gather yet others to him besides those already gathered" (56:8). That prophecy, together with the wide-embracing words of Psalm 87, was coming true. New branches were being ingrafted into the old vine. Israel as a whole refused, however, to join in the celebration of this "new age" movement (Matthew 11:16-19). Nevertheless, "God's promise attains its fulfillment in spite of the rejection elicited by Israel, through that very rejection, and ultimately over and beyond that rejection" (Weber, *Foundations of Dogmatics,* Vol. II, p. 483).

Accordingly, first-generation disciples were busy discovering "three basic elements" in their Old Testament Scriptures: "the faithfulness of God, the unfaithfulness of man, and the expectation that some day the former would triumph over the latter" (Hendrikus Berkhof, *Christian Faith,* p. 258). That day, long in coming, was now dawning. Jesus the

Messiah appeared as the great reunifier of factious peoples. But his appearance also occasioned the great divide. Israel and the church set out on separate ways. The church confesses that the mighty saving acts of God which came to their crowded climax at this crucial crossroads mark the decisive turning point in world history. In principle all things are "already" new, though their "not yet" dimension is also still distressingly real. Whether God has spoken and acted definitively in Christ Jesus — it is conflicting answers to this question that creates the yawning chasm separating Israel and the church. Israel's chosen route through history is lined with signposts bearing a single marking, "not yet," as though nothing has really changed. This parting of the ways remains one of the church's most poignant reminders of the haunting reality of its own "not yet." Hendrikus Berkhof comments as follows on the agony of this separation:

> Because the great majority in Israel withdrew from [the prophetic vision], the appearance of Jesus, contrary to the intent, has led to two forms and two ways of the people of God. The first form, Israel, continues the old covenant dialectic, and waits for its solution, as if Jesus Christ had made no change in this respect. The second form, the church, which has never lacked a "remnant" out of Israel as a sign of hope, lives from the new covenant, the accomplished work of salvation, and experiences the working of the Spirit everywhere among the nations of the world. Those who are on the one way cannot understand those on the other; and vice versa. That from faith in the same God one could move in two such different directions has occasioned great bitterness and hostility, first of Israel toward the church, but after that, for centuries, everywhere in the world, even more of the (dominant) church toward the Jews in the dispersion. (*Christian Faith,* p. 261)

This is the troublesome rift in covenant history which leads Paul to unburden his innermost yearnings in Romans 9–11. In this weighty passage he "reduces the fall of Israel to the same impenetrable and sovereign decree as that which at one time lifted the patriarchs and the nation [of Israel] from paganism." Without attempting a further analysis of these chapters, let the following summary statement suffice:

> 1. This decree is not arbitrary; it corresponds with Israel's unwillingness to walk God's way of salvation. 2. Due to this decree the Gentiles have been drawn to the light. 3. Israel is not completely forsaken by God; the "remnant" which the prophets saw enter into the Messianic age through this crisis became a reality in the Jewish-Christian Church. Paul had in mind the great crisis of the Messiah's appearance, death, and resurrection.

The remnant which lives through this crisis and recognizes Jesus as the Messiah is the real Israel. (Hendrikus Berkhof, *Christ the Meaning of History*, p. 141)

As the painful story of alienation continues to unfold, Israel's besetting sin is what Paul calls its "blindness" (2 Corinthians 3:14), and that of the church its spiritual arrogance (Romans 11:20). The gospel continues to challenge Judaism to "both lose and find itself, transcend and fulfill its own uniqueness, in the 'body of Christ' as the realized achievement of its Old Testament destiny" (Richard De Ridder, *My Heart's Desire for Israel*, p. 11). In response to Rabbi Abraham Heschel's question whether, from the Christian point of view, it would really be to the greater glory of God to have a world without Jews, De Ridder answers with a firm negative.

We so respond because, first of all, God is not finished with His people. Second, it is only together with Israel that the people of God will find completion. And third, because the very presence of Israel speaks loudly to both the church and the world. We may not forget that Christianity arose as the result of a very profound crisis within Israel. This crisis concerned the universalizing of the covenant as well as Israel's election; it was a crisis of law and righteousness (justification), of expectation and fulfillment. (*My Heart's Desire for Israel*, p. 108)

How then shall we approach our Jewish neighbors? De Ridder offers the following guidelines:

The church must recognize, contrary to a widespread Christian opinion, that the Jews are still the Israel of the Old Testament covenants and promises, and that God continues to have a saving purpose with Israel until all "the children of promise" within Israel shall be saved. . . . The church must recognize that now is the day of Israel's salvation; that the salvation of "all Israel" does not await a new epoch in the history of salvation. . . . The church must recognize that . . . Jew as well as Gentile is called by the gospel to faith in Jesus Christ as the only salvatory response to God's redemptive works. . . . Both the motive and the attitude of the church's mission to the Jews must take account of Israel's priority of privilege with respect to the gospel which is hers by virtue of the promises and covenants of God in the history of salvation. . . . The church's attitude toward the Jews must conform to God's continued yearning after Israel. . . . (*God Has Not Rejected His People*, pp. 81-82)

Chapter III

God's Way in Christ

God's way with the creation, his way with the nations of the world, his way with Israel, and now his way with the church all find their deepest meaning in his way in Christ. For in him all creation "holds together." He is "a light to the nations." He is "the hope of Israel." He is the "Head of his body," the church. The cosmic scope of biblical revelation and the full sweep of redemption history reach their point of concentration in the mighty acts of God embodied in his Son. Paul captures this breathtaking vision in two highly focused concepts which rise to the surface repeatedly in his letters: "All things" *(ta panta)* . . . "in Christ" *(en Christō)* (cf. Colossians 1:15-20). The full measure of God's being there for his world, in both "older" and "newer" covenant history, centers on Christ. "He is the [very] image of the invisible God, . . . for in him the fulness of God was pleased to dwell." God's way of coming out to us in Christ the Mediator reaches back to the creation — and even beyond, for he is "before all things." Then, in the beginning, with time and in time, "all things were created . . . in him . . . through him . . . and for him." The upshot of this all-encompassing perspective is that "in all things he may be preeminent."

The preeminence of Christ Jesus comes to its fully-filled-up manifestation in the writings of the New Testament. Their message stands in an unbroken line of continuity with salvation history coming up from the past and opening up into the future. It aims at changing the lives of those who hear it. Its validity, however, is not limited by human response, whether acceptance or rejection. For "in salvation history . . . more takes place in heaven and outside me than in the *nous* that constitutes self-understanding." This calls for "my adoption into Christ's history by implantation into the continuity of salvation history" (Thielicke, *The Evangelical Faith,* Vol. I, p. 63). The *alpha* and *omega* of all history, God's beginning and his ending, converge in the person of Christ as God's ever present reality among us as the great "I am," the One who is and was and will be. As Thielicke puts it, "He is the Truth in bodily form present among us. He is thus characterized by 'am' and 'is' judgments which articulate being and not just doing" (*The Evangelical Faith,* Vol. I, p. 205). In Christ all covenant history and the length and breadth and height and depth of the coming kingdom are grounded securely and abidingly. With this the credibility of the New Testament canon stands or falls. For in it God's Word of reconciliation, its claim to authority, and its crucial role in the ongoing history of redemption are all woven together as in a seamless garment.

The pivotal significance of Christ is accentuated in three inter-related motifs: witness *(martyria),* proclamation *(kērygma),* and teaching *(didachē).* The interacting combination of these three accent points serves well to disclose the comprehensive message of the full body of New Testament literature (cf. Herman Ridderbos, *The Authority of the New Testament Scriptures,* pp. 52-80).

III. 1. A Threefold Motif

A survey of these three motifs makes clear that the New Testament resists all efforts to divide the field among them, as though its writings were partly witness, partly proclamation, and partly teaching. In interlacing ways each motif appears and reappears, now here, now there, throughout the canon. Each is comprehensive in scope. Yet each brings with it certain unique insights, though never in isolation from the others. They reinforce each other, with each point of view enriching the message as a whole.

III. 1. 1. Witness (Martyria)

Christ charged the apostles to be his *martyres,* his witnesses (Acts 1:8). In current parlance a "martyr" (derived from *martyria*) is one who seals his witness with his blood. In the New Testament we find a more original usage. There witnesses are people appointed to stand up before men and nations to certify the historical reality and truthfulness of what happened in Jesus Christ. The Lord himself commissioned them to bear this testimony concerning his life, death, and resurrection. It is this that qualifies them to pass on to succeeding generations a reliable account of these events. A courtroom scenario comes to mind, where witnesses are obliged to verify the facts of the case and set the record straight against all falsifications. Before the tribunal of justice truth rests on trustworthy evidence. Viewed in this light, the apostolic writings address us as the firsthand testimony of eye- and earwitnesses submitting their well-attested recollections of what they personally experienced during those three memorable years. Thus grounded, their words carry the weight of apostolic authority. They were therefore empowered to assert boldly, "We did not follow cleverly devised myths. . . , but were eyewitness of [Christ's] majesty" (2 Peter 1:16). Thus they embarked on their mission declaring, We were on-the-spot observers: Hear us! For "we beheld his glory . . ." (John 1:14). John elaborates this point emphatically in his first letter (1:1-3):

> That which was from the beginning, which we have heard, which we have seen with our eyes, which we have looked upon and touched with our hands, concerning the word of life — the life was made manifest, and we saw it, and testify to it, and proclaim to you the eternal life which was with the Father and was made manifest to us — that which we have seen and heard we proclaim also to you, so that you may have fellowship with us; and our fellowship is with the Father and with his Son Jesus Christ. And we are writing this that our [your?] joy may be complete.

Repeatedly the authors of the New Testament cite the hard facts of their collective experience to vouch for the veracity of their message. These are their credentials. Their mission was endorsed by the Sender himself: "You are my witnesses, because you have been with me from the beginning" (John 15:27). "You are witnesses of these things" (Luke 24:48). Their testimony was as unique as the absolutely once-for-all events to which they bore witness. Led by the Spirit, they are the living links between Christ the Head and the church his body. The authenticity of their message rests on these claims to direct and regular contact with its source. These close associations with the Master defined the disciples' new calling in life: "This is the disciple," says John, "who is bearing witness to these things, and who has written these things, and we know that his witness is true" (21:24).

This witnessing motif stands out most prominently in the Gospels. They are the primary, historically based, visibly and audibly verified record of what God was doing in Jesus Christ. But this is not confined to the Gospels. It carries over into and sets the tone for the other New Testament writings as well. In a larger canonical sense, therefore, Paul, too, stands as a witness to the cross and resurrection, though he was not bodily present there (1 Corinthians 15). He is a witness even to Christ's presence among God's people in the wilderness (1 Corinthians 10:1-5). Witness *(martyria)* lays the foundation for both proclamation *(kērygma)* and teaching *(didachē)*. But it is at the same time qualified by the other motifs. Gospel witness is accordingly not just a lesson in ancient history, not just a case study for cool and dispassionate research. It is kerygmatic and didactic history. It makes no pretense to reporting "brute facts," but facts suffused with meaning, laden with a message, a witness which carries in it a Spirit-moved power to communicate, translate, and interpret who Christ is and what he has done and still does for the world. These authors do not merely chronicle Jesus' death. Their passion narratives also proclaim that he endured this suffering "to give his life a ransom for many" (Matthew 20:28), and they teach similarly that he was "raised for our justification" (Romans 4:25).

This contextualized witnessing motif remains basic to Christian faith and calling. For, as Paul argues, "If Christ has not been raised, then our preaching is in vain and your faith is in vain. . . . But in fact Christ has been raised from the dead" (1 Corinthians 15:14, 20). Gospel witness aims at arousing and sustaining faith. It is especially John's gospel that stresses the note of "belief." In reporting on the crucifixion he says, "He who saw it has borne witness — his testimony is true, and he knows that he tells the truth — that you also may believe" (19:35). Luke too, "having followed all things closely for some time," sets out to recount "the things of which you have been informed" in order to establish Theophilus in the certainty of his faith (Luke 1:1-4). Thus authorized by Christ, and directed by the Spirit, this witness to Christ is now also his witness to the world.

III. 1. 2. Proclamation (Kērygma)

The gospel message is cast into the mold of proclamation/preaching hardly less than witness. As a noun *(kērygma)* this motif appears only sporadically in the New Testament writings. It sometimes designates the act of preaching (Titus 1:3), at other times the content of preaching (1 Corinthians 1:21), and yet again the office of preaching (2 Timothy 4:17). In its verbal form *(kēryssein),* however, we meet it nearly everywhere. It is used with reference to John the Baptist (Mark 1:4), Jesus (Luke 4:18-19), and the apostles (Acts 10:42). This active kerygmatic motif is perhaps the most typical feature of the gospel message. Like the witnessing motif, it too gives a distinctive slant to every segment of the New Testament writings. It stands out prominently in the Gospels. We catch it as we listen in on the apostolic sermons summarized in Acts. It also lends a note of urgency to the instructional guidelines for living in the epistles.

As followers of Christ, then and there, but also here and now, we are therefore entrusted with a three-dimensional task: witnessing, proclaiming, and teaching the truth. These three ways of expressing the faith have a single focus: announcing in Christ the fulfilling of the covenant and the coming of the kingdom as the decisive turning point in redemption history (Acts 28:31).

In the New Testament, therefore, historical reality *(martyria)* and its proclamatory meaning *(kērygma)* are inseparably interconnected. For "the *kerygma* stands or falls with the factuality of the historical events of which it is the proclamation." It is therefore "concerned with what happened once and for all, with what happened on our behalf." For it can retain "its absolute meaning only when it is based upon the factuality of the historical redemptive event proclaimed in this *kerygma*" (Ridderbos, *The Authority of the New Testament Scriptures,* pp. 59-60). Proclamation devoid of historical foundations would yield only "cleverly devised myths"; an historical record shorn of its kerygmatic meaning would leave us with just another ancient document. By holding *martyria* and *kērygma* together, the New Testament comes to us as more than the repository of a fund of information imparted for its own sake. "It is not their goal to communicate a quantity of historical data. . . . Nor are the epistles of Paul theological treatises. . . ." As Ridderbos goes on to say:

> The New Testament does not direct itself to the "historian" or the "theologian" in man. It has a much more practical and existential intention, understood in this sense that it grips or makes a claim upon man in his deepest being, in his heart, in the center of his self-determination, and thus places him before a radical decision, or to say it in a word, places him before the demand of faith. (*The Authority of the New Testament Scriptures,* pp. 58-59)

The coherent unity of the New Testament writings resists reading into it dialectical tensions between the "pure religion" of Jesus and the "heavy theology" of Paul, or between the "Jesus of history" and the "Christ of faith," or between the "Jesus who was" (the "real historical man of Nazareth") and the "Jesus who is" (the "deified Being of latter-day saints"). For the message which the New Testament calls us to embrace cannot be uprooted from its witness to the undergirding reality of those great redemptive events which took place in Jesus Christ. Its kerygmatic claim is therefore as cosmic as the Christ at its center. It is "totalitarian," for "it touches every sphere of human life and knowledge; for the redemption of which it speaks is totalitarian. . . . It illumines man, the world, history, and the future; church and nation, state and society, science and art, from a single perspective, namely, from the standpoint of the coming, the death, the resurrection, and the second coming of Christ" (Ridderbos, *The Authority of the New Testament Scriptures,* pp. 61-62).

III. 1. 3. Teaching (Didachē)

The didactic passages of the New Testament are concentrated largely in the epistles. Wherever they are found, however, they are not theological treatises but pastoral messages, oriented to practical issues facing the early Christian community. As proclamation is related to witness, so instruction in the faith is related to both. Doctrine builds on the foundations laid by the apostles in their kerygmatic witness to Christ Jesus, explicating its significance for daily living, drawing out its implications for both orthodoxy and orthopraxy. This is especially evident in the numerous "therefore" passages of the New Testament. Take Romans 12:1: following through on his soaring hymn of praise to the sovereign grace of God, Paul "therefore" urges complete dedication to the good, acceptable, and perfect will of God. Or again, 1 Corinthians 15:58: in view of his witness to and proclamation of Christ's resurrection victory, Paul "therefore" exhorts believers onward toward active perseverance in works of faith.

Witness and proclamation take on a variety of pedagogical forms. But whether couched in terms of doctrine, precepts, admonitions, warnings, encouragement, or calls to exemplary living, *didachē* is an integral aspect of the entire analogy of Scripture. Its insights and urgings echo the full sweep of salvation history in the Old as well as New Testament. As Paul writes, "All Scripture is inspired by God" and is therefore "profitable for teaching, for reproof, for correction, and for training in righteousness, that the man of God may be complete, equipped for every good work" (2 Timothy 3:16-17). In view of the unity of the church with Israel, it is not surprising that New Testament teachings regularly assume a Hebraic, rabbinic style. True to this venerable tradition, they stress "knowledge" (1 Timothy 2:4), "wisdom" (James 1:5), and "truth" (Ephesians 4:25). There is a very definite cognitive side to these doctrines, but also an affective aspect; they are in fact holist. For such faith-knowledge is rooted in the heart; as such it is comprehensive, involving our entire personhood and all our life relationships. Nothing in all creation is in principle excluded from the didactic thrust of the gospel. The authority of the New Testament therefore pertains not only to its witness and proclamation, but also to the many issues covered in its teaching. Doctrine geared to practice aims at building up the body of

Christ, training the Christian community in the ways of justice, love, and peace, nurturing the young in covenant living, and thus equipping the church as a whole for kingdom service.

III. 2. Jesus: History and Kerygma

At bottom every theological issue turns out to be a problem of hermeneutics. The question of what to say about Jesus is no exception. In some very basic ways the early church already confronted this challenge in its running encounter along two fronts. On one side the church faced a lingering Judaism. These contacts occasioned disputes between Christian and Jewish thinkers on how to interpret the Old Testament in light of the appearance of Jesus Christ. On the other hand, the church fathers were drawn into the risky enterprise of maintaining the integrity of the biblical message while clothing it in "pagan rags" (Harnack) borrowed from Greco-Roman culture. How the early church handled these hermeneutic issues in forging its confession of faith — this is in large measure the story of the trinitarian and christological controversies. Three centuries of heated debate led to the confessional consensus of the Council of Chalcedon (A.D. 451). Jesus Christ is fully and truly divine, the fathers declared, as well as fully and truly human. In him "the Word" (God's ultimate *kērygma*) "became flesh" (the embodiment of historical reality).

The orthodoxy of the Chalcedonian creed prevailed throughout the medieval and Reformation eras. With the advent of the Renaissance, however, which signaled the beginnings of modernity, the long-standing christological consensus began to break down. This loss of unanimity reached crisis proportions in the wake of the Enlightenment movement. The christological problem reasserted itself then with a vengeance in a radically reversed order. For centuries the doctrine of Christ had been approached "from above," seeking to understand what it means that the Son of God condescended to become like us and live among us as the Son of Man. Anselm expressed the traditional "top down" hermeneutic in the question with which he entitled his work, *Cur Deus Homo?* — Why (did) God (become) Man? The modern mind turned the tables on this method. It replaced the older theocentric approach with a new anthropocentric logic. Christology became "Jesusology," approaching the prophet of Nazareth "from below." What can we conclude about him? With this, a host of modern quests for the historical Jesus was under way.

This hermeneutical reversal has been gathering momentum steadily over the past two centuries. As a result the question of the relationship between the gospel's witness to the historicity of Jesus and its kerygma has usurped a place of high priority on our theological agendas. Factuality and meaning, and their interrelatedness, these have emerged as dominant categories in contemporary biblical-theological reflection. As Carl Braaten puts it, "The problem of the relation between Jesus and the kerygma has become the crucial question in current New Testament study." And the stakes are high. For as Braaten goes on to say, "A kerygma without [a real historical] Jesus is a verbal vacuum, and Jesus without the [apostolic] kerygma is a meaningless surd" (*History and Hermeneutics*, p. 62). At a most profound level the sweeping changes in hermeneutics ushered in by modern liberalism are indicative of a radical shift in worldview. The revolutionary impact of these realignments is evident in the succession of quests for the historical Jesus which has been launched over the past two centuries. Running through all these intriguing pursuits is a common theme, as persistent as it is destructive, namely, the idea of playing history and kerygma off against each other. We turn now to a hasty survey of these quests and re-quests.

III. 2. 1. The Old Quest

The "old questers," as they are jovially known, breathed the heady atmosphere of the Enlightenment. Their views came to the fore during the latter decades of the eighteenth century. Philosophically they reshaped the biblical kerygma to fit the humanist idealism of Descartes, Spinoza, and Leibniz. This kerygmatic side of their theologies was held in sharp tension with a newly emergent view of history as defined by the empiricism of Locke, Berkeley, and Hume. By taking these two philosophical traditions, the one exploiting the *phenomena,* the other the *noumena,* redefining them as "pure reason" (science) and "practical reason" (religion/morality), and fusing them into a dialectical synthesis, Kant established himself as "the maker of the modern mind." The convergence of these two philosophical movements, then further influenced greatly by the historicism of Hegel, ushered in a profound change in the course of Western thought. This complex set of Enlightenment ideologies was translated into the theology of modern liberalism by such thinkers as Reimarus, Strauss, Baur, Schleiermacher, Ritschl, Harnack, Troeltsch, Herrmann, Wellhausen, and Schweitzer. These developments mark the beginnings of the historical-critical method, opening the door in turn to a long series of modern quests for the historical Jesus. From the start this venture was beset by the problem: Are the historical data capable of sustaining the weight of these latter-day christological theories?

The working assumption of the old questers was clear. They approached the New Testament as an ancient, purely historical document. It is therefore subject to forms of critical analysis essentially no different than those which apply to other significant writings from the past. Its authors were not infallible. Their memories were often faulty, and their testimony often conflicting; therefore their witness is not necessarily reliable. As zealous disciples of their Master, moreover, they often embellished the facts, leaving us with eulogized, mythologized, even divinized accounts of who Jesus was and what he did. Our task as latter-day historians and theologians is, therefore, to free ourselves of these traditional biases, reexamine the texts objectively by means of contemporary tools of analysis, and thus rediscover and reconstruct the real Jesus of history. Revelation as affirmed by historic Christianity now had to pass the test of rational inquiry. This project is not only possible, so the argument goes, but urgently important for the survival of faith in our times. For man is now at last coming of age. The childlike faith of the fathers died with the birth of this new era. Its fate was sealed by the widely acclaimed dogma of the autonomy of human reason. There is no turning back.

These "assured results" of the scientific method in biblical studies left the old questers with the other side of the problem of history: What about the kerygma? — the preacher's problem, the Sunday sermon. What can the church proclaim as good news for modern man? Is it still possible to salvage a meaningful message from a radically historicized Jesus? Undaunted by the magnitude of the challenge, liberals rose to the occasion. True to their dogmas, and by resorting to ingenious methods of interpretation, they managed to distil allegedly eternal truths from events which belong supposedly to a strictly temporal order of reality. Take the gospel narratives concerning Jesus multiplying the loaves. In real life such miracles simply do not happen. They defy the inexorable logic of cause-and-effect relations. Yet this impossible story illustrates a parabolic truth: the virtue of sharing what we have with others, which can work wonders. Similarly, the stilling of the storm at sea points to man's emerging power to control the chaotic forces of nature. The well-attested witness to Jesus' resurrection posed almost insurmountable obstacles to the hermeneutic wizardry of the historical-critical method. In Bible times already this stunning event was a stumbling block to Jews and foolishness to Greeks. The more so for children of the Enlightenment with their adherence to the law of analogy. For, while such myths may fit quite comfortably into the prescientific worldviews of ancient people, they are no longer at home in this age of reason. Yet not all is lost. Jesus did arise to newness of life, not from the tomb, but in the believing consciousness of his followers. So we, too, may cling to the abiding truth: hope springs eternal in the human breast.

All old quest theologies carry a single basic tune. But there are numerous variations on it. In this blend of voices some accentuate the historical motif, others the rational, moral, existential, or eschatological motifs. Some honor Jesus as the most distinguished teacher of eternal truths, others as the world's noblest example of moral virtue, a social reformer who was ahead of his times, a political revolutionary, a romantic hero, the visionary of a new world order, a great crusader for peace who even in defeat enriched us with a utopian dream, the tragic victim of a cruel populace not yet come of age. Some ill-tempered old questers went even further, projecting highly negative images of Jesus: He was a fraudulent imposter who deceived his gullible followers into embracing him as a messiah, knowing all the while that he was not. Or he was a deranged personality, suffering from illusions of grandeur, imagining himself a messiah, though, as we know, such transcendent beings do not exist. Within the prevailing framework of Kant's philosophy, all these laborious efforts to rescue some sort of kerygmatic reconfiguration of the real Jesus of history from what was left after the historical-critical method had done its work can claim only an "as if" status. For a monumental study of the many images of Jesus concocted by this school of thought, see Albert Schweitzer's *The Quest of the Historical Jesus,* which covers over fifty representatives of this theology.

Looking back over this panoply of liberal views of Jesus, we may conclude that "their claim to be objective and without presupposition was itself a myth" (Fred Klooster, *Quests for the Historical Jesus,* p. 26). Their new "findings" were already deeply embedded in their commonly held starting points. For "much of what was dished out as historically 'assured results' was only the product of one's own choice or bias, or the reflection of one's own cultural situation and ideals" (Hendrikus Berkhof, *Christian Faith,* p. 269). Restated in the words of Braaten,

> Between the lines of the great biographies of Jesus we can read the personal religious viewpoints of their authors. The nineteenth century biographers of Jesus were like plastic surgeons making over the face of their patient in their own image. . . . (*History and Hermeneutics,* p. 55)

From the old questers we inherited a Jesus stripped of his divinity, with a radically domesticated humanity, deconstructed history, and a kerygma revised almost beyond recognition. The Jesus who confronts us in the witness, proclamation, and teachings of the New Testament writings recedes ever more deeply, like a mirage, into a boundless never-never land. Eventually even many advocates of the old quest were left in a state of disillusionment with only unkept promises to show for their efforts, but no good news. "For man's salvation lies in what has actually happened through and with Jesus. Salvation depends on the historicity of these events" (Hendrikus Berkhof, *Christian Faith,* p. 270). As a result, "The field of modern gospel research is strewn with the debris of broken hypotheses. . . ." Thus, by the turn of the century,

> the historical approach to the Jesus of the gospels was nearing exhaustion. Schweitzer's study was signalling the end of an era. . . . The mood had shifted from bold confidence and naive optimism in the earlier period to an unsettling malaise, a sense of frustration. One could point to no sum of assured results, no clear directions; and scholars were falling into opposing camps. The stage was being set for a new breakthrough. (Braaten, *History and Hermeneutics,* pp. 53, 58)

III. 2. 2. Neoorthodox Interlude

Repeatedly "the unsolved problem of one theological generation becomes the starting point of the next" (Klooster, *Quests for the Historical Jesus,* p. 63). This judgment is confirmed by a dramatic turn of events early in this century. The disintegration of the "old quest" left Western Christianity with an aching void. Then out of the ruins of World War I a stunningly robust alternative theology fell like a time bomb into the playground of the theologians, exploding and sending shock waves in every direction. Swiftly this newcomer rushed in to occupy the ground abandoned by a badly deflated liberalism, now in full retreat. This vigorous counteroffensive, known as neoorthodoxy, was spearheaded by an aggressive contingent of "no questers," as they came to be called — Brunner, Gogarten, Thurneysen, and Tillich, but especially Barth and Bultmann.

This new generation of theologians had received its early education sitting at the feet of their old liberal mentors. Now, however, chastened by the agonizing crises of their times, the sobering realization crept over them: the prevailing historical-critical methods had been weighed in the balances of the world's crying needs and found wanting. Liberalism's bold pursuit of the real historical Jesus ended in chasing fantasies. Its hermeneutics left the church with a kerygma which was spiritually bankrupt. The old quest was dead. So call off the search. Like his partners, Barth concluded that "liberal theology had reached a state of aporia, even though liberal theologians would not admit it." When a critic charged him with being a "declared enemy of historical criticism," Barth responded that "the historical-critical school must become more critical in order to suit me" (Eberhard Jüngel, *Karl Barth: A Theological Legacy,* p. 70).

Washing their hands of the old quest for Jesus "from below," Barth and his cohorts advocated a vigorous new Christology, one that moves in on us "from above." In strong reaction "they turned with a vengeance on history and began to talk so much about the 'Word of God' (Barth) or the 'kerygma' (Bultmann) or 'personal encounter' (Brunner) or 'I-thou relationships' (Gogarten) that historical concerns were submerged beneath the avalanche of theological rhetoric" (Braaten, *History and Hermeneutics,* p. 25). History was sacrificed on the altar of kērygma. In repudiating the old quest, neoorthodoxy was negating, or at least denigrating, the very element of truth which made possible the heresies of the old quest, namely, the historical reality of God's mighty acts in Jesus Christ. Revelation does indeed come *to* real historical people at real times and places, according to Barth, but it can never take up residence *in* history.

With Barth leading the way, neoorthodoxy showed a willingness to accommodate itself to a severely modified use of the historical-critical method. In the hands of the old questers its highly touted "assured results" proved to be a fiasco, and rightly, even inevitably so. In the very nature of the case, neoorthodoxy argued, it was doomed from the start to come up empty-handed. For history is inherently dubious. The historical events narrated in the Gospels are therefore also very problematic. Brunner states the case strongly in these words:

> Even the bare fact of the existence of Christ as an historical person is not assured. . . . It belongs to the nature of the Christian religion to have a Christ whose historical existence can be doubted by nonbelievers, and even denied by them, without being able to offer any convincing proof of his historicity. (*The Mediator,* pp. 186-87)

Commenting on the dialectic so typical of neoorthodoxy, Paul Jewett explains that according to Brunner

> . . . even to call the Jesus event an event *(Vorgang)* reflects inadequacy of expression, since it is that which "does not happen" *(nicht passiert),* yet "does happen" *(geschieht)* in a unique sense of the word. It is "an 'eschatological' event, primal-eschatological history" *(ur-Endgeschichte).* Recognizing the inadequacy of all analogy, Brunner does, nonetheless, make some suggestions. He sometimes uses the figure of lightning. While we do not see the bolt strike, yet we see the after-effects as a tree is rent asunder. Again, it is like an echo in a canyon; or the ripples agitated by a pebble tossed into the water. Though we do not see the actual piercing of the water, yet the rings constitute a visible evidence that the event really happened. (*Emil Brunner's Concept of Revelation,* pp. 40-41)

Such absence of direct historical evidence, it was held, represents no great loss. For what matters basically is the kerygma pointing to Christ, which is not dependent on historical findings. Historical-critical methods can indeed analyze the way recipients of revelation responded to God's Word in Christ, their witness to it and proclamation of it. But such studies cannot touch revelation itself. No matter what such research uncovers, the kerygma and faith in it remain unassailed. For they are not anchored in *Historie* (the ordinary flow of events), but *Geschichte* (God's transcendent act of revelation in Jesus Christ which intercepts our life story). Barth was therefore led to wonder out loud about the liberals, "Are these historians, whom I truly respect as scholars, quite unaware that there is a content [in Scripture], a cardinal question, a Word in the words?" (Jüngel, *Karl Barth: A Theological Legacy*, p. 76).

The narrative events in the Gospels may well have happened, and happened as they are recorded. But ultimately they serve simply as a pointer *(Hinweis)* to the real Event, the personal revelation of the free, once-for-all act of God's sovereign grace in Christ. The Jesus of history is an index to the suprahistorical Christ, but the two are not identical. For revelation cannot be extended into history. The finite cannot contain the Infinite. This view allows for no history of redemption, only redemptive breakthroughs into history which, however, leave no tracks behind. Comparing Barth and the liberals, Jüngel concludes paradoxically that "although they based their arguments on diametrically opposite premises, they accused each other of the same thing: making historical understanding impossible" (*Karl Barth: A Theological Legacy*, p. 75).

From a neoorthodox viewpoint, both the opening and closing acts in the gospel narratives demonstrate convincingly that the original kerygma as *Geschichte* supersedes *Historie*. The virgin birth as well as the resurrection defies historical analysis. They are pure acts of *Geschichte* with no grounding in *Historie*, thus severing the kerygma from the factualities of history. This neoorthodox hermeneutic reflects a worldview reminiscent of Kierkegaard's infinite qualitative distance between eternity and time. For Barth, accordingly, God is "the wholly Other" and the world is "the far country." Only God can bridge this gap, and he has done so dialectically in his Son, Jesus *(Historie)* Christ *(Geschichte)*. In thus resolving the problem of the preceding generation of theologians, history at the expense of kerygma, Barth creates a new one, kerygma detached from history. In critiquing this legacy, Braaten affirms that

> The category of history is undoubtedly indispensable for a theology based on God's reconciling activity in Christ. The act of reconciliation is a climactic historical event, with definite historical presuppositions in

Yahweh's covenant with Israel and equally definite historical results in the election of the church. (*History and Hermeneutics,* pp. 16-17)

Bultmann is even more skeptical of critical research on the Jesus of history than Brunner and Barth, and even more radical in rejecting its results. It is impossible to recover and reconstruct a factual picture of the historical Jesus. This is no cause for regret, however, for the kerygma needs no historical base. Well known is Bultmann's argument that "since the early Christian sources show no interest" in such matters and "are moreover fragmentary and often legendary, . . . we can now know almost nothing concerning the life and personality of Jesus . . ." (*Jesus and the Word,* pp. 8-9). Not only are the gospel accounts too meager and often contradictory, but from start to finish they present a mythologized image of Jesus.

Bultmann develops this idea extensively in his *Jesus Christ and Mythology.* Referring to the kingdom as a central theme in the Gospels, he holds that since "Jesus' conception of the kingdom of God is an eschatological one," it "transcends the historical order." Being mythological, it is "impossible to make use of this conception in dogmatics" (pp. 12-13). In fact, "the whole conception of the world which is presupposed in the preaching of Jesus, as in the New Testament generally, is mythological." This was so "from the very beginning of earliest Christianity." Bultmann calls the worldview of Bible times mythological because "it is different from the conception of the world which has been formed and developed by science since its inception in early Greece and which has been accepted by all modern men." In the modern worldview "the cause-and-effect nexus is fundamental." The modern mind refuses to "take into account any intervention of God or the devil or of demons [or of angels] in the course of history. Instead the course of history is considered to be an unbroken whole, complete in itself" (pp. 15-16). Today, therefore, "the mythological conception of the world, the conception of eschatology, of redeemer and redemption, are over and done with." Yet a kerygma remains. The hermeneutic task of contemporary theology is therefore not to abandon the New Testament, nor to reduce it to the social gospel of the liberals, but to discover "a still deeper meaning which is concealed under the cover of mythology." This method Bultmann calls "de-mythologizing" the Bible (pp. 17-18). He concedes that "de-mythologizing takes the modern world-view as a criterion" (p. 35). This pre-understanding *(Vorverständnis)* demands that we "interpret Scripture, asking for the deeper meaning of the mythological conceptions and freeing the Word of God from bygone world-views" (p. 43).

Bultmann acknowledges readily his indebtedness to the existentialist philosophy of Heidegger. In his theology, therefore, the center of gravity shifts from the gospel narratives to the personal existential encounter of the recipient with the kerygma as that takes place today in the moment of proclamation. The historicity of Jesus makes way for the historicity of the individual hearer. Thus "the eschatological event which is Jesus Christ happens here and now as the Word is being preached, . . . regardless of whether the Word is accepted or rejected" (p. 81). The biblical message is validated "as an event which happens here and now" (p. 71). For "only such statements about God are legitimate as express the existential relation between man and God. Statements which speak of God's actions as cosmic events are illegitimate" — as, for example, "that God is creator" (p. 69).

Bultmann's kerygma, dehistoricized and demythologized, is hardly distinguishable from the mystical and romantic platitudes of certain old liberals. At its deepest level the incarnation means the emergence of self-awareness in faithful hearers today. What then shall we say about the householder who awakens to find that at an unexpected hour his home was ransacked by a thief (Luke 12:39-40)? To interpret this as a summons to readiness in expectation of Christ's promised return is to remain enmeshed in an outdated eschatological form of mythologizing. Its deeper meaning for today is to keep us alert to happenings which may take us by surprise as we move along toward God's open-ended future. In a similar vein, the accounts of Jesus' resurrection point to the rebirth of a glad hope among his followers.

Despite his adamant critique on the historicity of the gospel narratives, at the heart of Bultmann's theology lies an unresolved dilemma, which Braaten probes by asking:

> Why has the kerygma so little historical content in Bultmann's way of thinking? Bultmann realizes that if all the historical content is eliminated, the kerygma loses its attachment to Jesus and balloons into a celestial myth. On the other hand, if much of the historical content is retained, then it appears that the kerygma becomes vulnerable to historical research, and faith, contrary to its nature as an existential act of decision, is bound up with assent to historical facts. To insure faith's independence of historical research, the cost of the premium is the dismissal of all historical elements in the kerygma. Bultmann, however, makes a single exception: the bare fact of Jesus' historicity and his death on the cross. (*History and Hermeneutics*, p. 64)

This "single exception" turned out to be the Achilles' heel in Bultmann's theology. It suggests strongly his inability to press his radical hermeneutic to its consistent conclusion. He then passed this dilemma on to his followers as an unresolved problem. They in turn were left to struggle with this "glaring inconsistency," as it is commonly called. Thus the stage was being set for the next act in the ongoing quest for the historical Jesus.

III. 2. 3. The New Quest

The beginning of a new quest for the historical Jesus occurred within the Bultmann school. By the publication of his essay "The Problem of the Historical Jesus," Ernst Käsemann rolled away the stone that blocked the passageway behind the kerygma. That was in 1954. Since then the rest of the leading disciples of Bultmann took off in pursuit of a closer connection between the kerygma of the primitive church and the historical Jesus, . . . trying to establish more precisely the sort of continuity that really does and must exist between Jesus and the kerygma. A common concern of the new questers is to reassert the constitutive significance of Jesus for Christian faith. (Braaten, *History and Hermeneutics*, p. 68)

The new questers set out therefore to chart a course between the Scylla of the old questers and the Charybdis of their mentor's no-quest theology. They resolved thus, on the one hand, not to return to "the fleshpots of Egypt" — liberalism's fatal fascination with writing new biographies of the real historical Jesus based on evidence uncovered by historical research. Yet, on the other hand, they were convinced that a tenable Christology and a meaningful kerygma require a more substantial base in history than neoorthodoxy allows. The result was a rather precarious tight-rope act. Nonetheless, the quest was launched in the belief that within the New Testament kerygma itself we can find sufficiently clear clues as to who Jesus was and what he did.

Bultmann's "glaring inconsistency" had left the doorway to history standing slightly ajar. Seizing on this opening, Käsemann and his fellow new questers made a case for going beyond their master. They posited a closer connection between the Jesus of history and the Christ of proclamation. Direct continuity, however, would be an overstatement, they believed. For the gospel writers were not slavish scribes. Their witness to Jesus is creatively shaped to accentuate the kerygma. Their reports are therefore a step or two removed from the events themselves. The distance is not so great, however, as to justify the conclusions of either the old questers or the no questers. There is in the New Testament narratives a nucleus of historical factuality firm enough to support its kerygma and the church's proclamation of it.

Accepting the self-imposed limits of this perspective — not too much historical reality but still enough — the "old Marburgers" sought to forge a fusion of horizons between the intentionality of the New Testament writers then and there and believing receptivity in the pulpit and pew here and now. To bridge this hermeneutic gap they appeal to an existentialist view of history. Biblical historiography is not to be approached "objectively." It presupposes, rather, a vital bond between these ancient voices and their hearers today, an I-thou person-to-person affinity. Thus, as with their mentor, theologizing among the members of the "Bultmann Circle" reflects the continuing influence of existentialist philosophy. They, too, were unable to cope with the great stumbling block of modern theology, the resurrection. As Klooster puts it,

> The results of their renewed historical investigations lead them all to conclude that the resurrection was basic to the kerygma for the early Christians, but the New Questers share Bultmann's presupposition that resurrections do not happen. (*Quests for the Historical Jesus,* p. 63)

This great exception among leaders of the new quest then becomes the very starting point for yet another phase in the ongoing pursuit of the historical Jesus.

III. 2. 4. The Future Is Now

The past quarter century has witnessed the appearance of a "theology of history," led by Wolfhart Pannenberg. With it we have now entered the latest phase of this centuries-old history/kerygma odyssey. Not to be outdone by its predecessors, this current school of thought has been christened the "now quest." Its hermeneutic signals the resurgence of a self-consciously historical method of biblical studies, appealing strongly to rational, philosophical forms of argumentation. Like the old questers, the now questers also approach Christology "from below." As Pannenberg puts it, "The judgment about whether an event, however unfamiliar, has happened or not is in the final analysis a matter for the historian. . . ." Yet this new theology is definitely not a return to the old liberalism. For as Pannenberg adds, the question of the event-character of biblical narratives "cannot be prejudged by the knowledge of natural science" — as the old questers assumed (*Jesus — Man and God,* p. 98). The now questers therefore reject liberalism's capitulation to an ironclad cause-and-effect logic and the law of analogy. They also take leave of the neoorthodox no questers' attempt to subvert history for the sake of the kerygma. Rather, "their battle cry is that kerygma without history is a meaningless noise. The preaching of the 'Word of God' is an empty assertion if it is severed from what truly happened in history" (Braaten, *History and Hermeneutics,* p. 26). Accordingly the Pannenberg school stresses revelation, not merely *in* history or *through* history, but *as* history. In doing so they are also moving beyond the tenuous rescue mission of the new questers with their balancing act between enough history but not too much. Instead the Pannenbergers focus precisely on the interpenetration of the two prime factors. They pin the kerygma and everything else on the historical reality of the gospel's witness to Jesus Christ. The windows of history stand wide open to the light of revelation. Thus, instead of Jesus' resurrection being the great stumbling block, it is the very centerpiece of their theology. It really happened as the most centrally significant time-and-space event in all human experience.

The historical dimension is therefore utterly crucial to a right understanding of man's relationship to God, the mission of Jesus Christ, and indeed the future of all creation. As Pannenberg says,

> History is the most comprehensive horizon of Christian theology. All theological questions and answers are meaningful only within the framework of the history which God has with humanity and through humanity with the whole creation — the history moving forward toward a future still hidden from the world but already revealed in Jesus Christ. (*Basic Questions in Theology,* Vol. I, p. 15)

The resurrection of Jesus stands as the very pivotal point of all world history. In it God declares his ultimate intentions for the cosmos. The end of all things is already present in this momentous turning point as a preview of things to come. Thus "Pannenberg's revised historical method enables him to regard the resurrection as a real event of history, . . . as the cornerstone of his theology." It is in fact "an event of such great significance that his entire theology is built upon it" (Klooster, *Quests for the Historical Jesus,* pp. 71, 83).

Quite understandably, this theology of history is also called a theology of hope. Its forward-looking perspective is captured existentially in the byword, "the future is now." Out of the empty tomb a divine impetus and momentum arises which thrusts world history forward toward its eschatological goal. At the same time that future also reaches back with a magnetically attractive power to impinge itself on our present lives and to draw us onward. History is therefore bracketed, as it were, by the pushing power of the resurrection behind us and the pulling power of the eschaton ahead of us. As a homey illustration, the movement of history is like a window shade. It takes two power sources to make it work — the spring-loaded tension packed into the fulcrum at the top, and the strength of a human hand at the bottom. Acting together, these two power sources allow the shade to be pulled down toward us, but also to return upward to its resting position. So the resurrection and the eschaton as its final realization combine to define each successive present moment along the way.

According to Pannenberg, not only salvation history but universal history as well is revelatory. For there are not two histories, but a single comprehensive world history. In every age, however, God reveals himself not directly but indirectly, ambiguously, in acts which are not self-evident as acts of God. In the measure that their meaning is discernible, however, all men have access to it. Accordingly, revelation as history comes not only to those who live by faith, but to all who act in accord with reason. For "since theology is a public affair, faith cannot be allowed to retreat into a private world of personal experience" — as in Barth and Bultmann. Moreover, "although faith is primary for salvation, reason provides the foundation of that faith. . . . Reason is the logical foundation of faith" (Don Olive, *Wolfhart Pannenberg,* in "Makers of the Modern Theological Mind," pp. 36, 39). As Pannenberg puts it, truth is "open to general reasonableness" (*Revelation as History,* p. 137). Otherwise "faith would be blind gullibility, credulity, or even superstition" ("The Revelation of God in Jesus of Nazareth," *New Frontiers in Theology,* Vol. III, p. 131). It would then succumb to "the danger of distorting the historical revelation into a gnostic knowledge of secrets" (*Revelation as History,* p. 137).

Pannenberg's theology of history and hope, together with the work of Jürgen Moltmann, has made significant contributions in recent decades to the emergence of a large number of political and liberation theologies.

*   *   *

In looking back for a moment at the dominant theological trends of the past two centuries, the rise and fall of successive quests for the historical Jesus, certain common features stand out. In one way or another all adherents of the historical-critical method attempt to define what is "specifically Christian" in the New Testament writings. This leads to the idea of a canon within, or behind, or above the accepted canon. All such ventures end in failure, however, as Gerhardt Maier argues, because

> . . . no one is in the position of convincingly and meaningfully defining a canon in the canon. Since each theologian conceives of the canon differently, and since this is done on the basis of an assumption no longer questioned (i.e. by free choice), uncontrolled subjectivity has the last word concerning what should have divine authority. (*The End of the Historical-Critical Method,* p. 47)

One's chosen principle of selection serves as the decisive norm of canonicity. The basic flaw in this approach is its arbitrary presuppositions and preconceived notions. "Man," Maier continues, "who began critically to analyze revelation and to discover for himself what is normative, found at the end of the road: himself!" (p. 35).

This modern project was bound to fail because "it was not suited to the subject" (p. 49). For "the correlative or counterpart to revelation is not critique but obedience; it is not correction, . . . [but] let-me-be-corrected" (p. 23).

> Thus the use of the higher-critical method has put us into a monstrous hole. . . . What the real Word of God is became more and more nebulous. . . . The subtle net woven by the higher-critical method resulted in a new Babylonian captivity of the church. It became more and more isolated from the living stream of proclamation, and therefore more and more uncertain and blind both as to its own course and also in relation to its influence toward the outside. (P. 48)

Maier's quotation from Hans Küng is very much to the point:

> The bold program of finding a "canon in the canon" demands nothing else than this: to be more Biblical than the Bible, more New Testamently than the New Testament, more evangelical than the Gospel, and even more Pauline than Paul. Radical earnestness is the intention, radical dissolution is the result. . . . [For] the true Paul is the entire Paul, and the true New Testament is the entire New Testament. (*The End of the Historical-Critical Method*, p. 45)

III. 3. "The Christ of God"

From every direction the way of salvation reaches its point of high concentration in Jesus Christ. There a christological convergence takes place which brings together a plurality of approaches. Each of these approaches enters fully, not partially into the total picture of "the Christ of God" (Luke 9:20). Intersecting in him, they combine to reinforce Scripture's comprehensive answer to the pivotal question: "What do you think of the Christ?" (Matthew 22:42). . . . "Who do men say that the Son of Man is? . . . But who do you say that I am?" To which Peter responds, as spokesman for the original circle of disciples and for the church of all ages, "You are the Christ, the Son of the living God" (Matthew 16:13-16).

That question and its answer cannot be compressed into a single mold. In categories supplied by Hendrikus Berkhof (*Christian Faith,* pp. 267-68), a full answer discloses four distinguishable approaches. There is first the approach "from behind" — Christ Jesus as the fulfillment of that legacy of promises carried along with growing intensity throughout God's way with Israel. The second approach is "from below" — the gospel witness to the historical reality of God's presence in Jesus of Nazareth. He is fully and truly human. This is the pervasive testimony of the entire New Testament. All these writings honor Jesus' most typical way of identifying himself as "the Son of Man," emphasizing the integrity of his human nature. Contradicting all Gnostic and other docetic tendencies, Scripture affirms his authentic creatureliness. He experienced the normal stages of human development with its limitations, feelings, sufferings, and death itself (Galatians 4:4; Philippians 2:5-8; Hebrews 4:15; 5:8).

We come now in this section to the third approach, "from above." Jesus is the Christ, the eternal Son of God, the Word by whom all things were created, who for us and our salvation became flesh and dwelt among us (John 1:1-14). His mediatorial, reconciling work hinges on the unabridged testimony to the integrity of both natures, human and divine, in the single person of our Savior and Lord. This full-orbed witness of the New Testament writings opens the door then to a fourth approach, which Hendrikus Berkhof somewhat ambiguously calls "from before" us. This perspective points to "what [Jesus Christ] works through the centuries in human hearts and in the peoples of the world" (*Christian Faith,* p. 267). This "up ahead" viewpoint will be addressed in later sections.

III. 3. 1. Immanuel — "God with Us"

Matthew (16:16) gives us the fullest account of Peter's decisive answer (cited above) to the central question concerning the Messiah's identity, with Mark (8:29) and Luke (9:20) giving more abbreviated versions. Jesus points to the radically vertical "from above" dimension of Peter's confession when he says, ". . . flesh and blood has not revealed this to you. . . ." Peter's affirmation transcends all human, historical possibilities. It is prompted by "my Father who is in heaven" (Matthew 16:17). On the "rock" *(petra)* of Peter's *(Petros)* confession Jesus then promises, "I will build my church" (16:18). Here Jesus clearly declares his divine Sonship. Though the Synoptics accentuate the "from behind" (Jesus' historicity) and the "from below" (his humanity) approaches — his hidden Messiahship, his bloody agony in the Garden, his cry of dereliction from the cross — their message is also punctuated pervasively with references

396

to the "from above" aspect of his mission — his Messianic titles, his claims to divine prerogatives, his supratemporal insights, his miracles, his bold assertions of the wide-embracing effects of his life, death, and resurrection. John and Paul, however, stress most strongly these transcendent aspects.

Christian faith embraces "the picture in its totality," says Hendrikus Berkhof. "No one, however, is equally motivated by all the parts of the picture." Nevertheless, "when one is gripped by one aspect, it leads to a recognition of the other aspects" (*Christian Faith,* pp. 280-81).

The "from above" perspective reveals Jesus Christ as *Immanuel,* "God with us" (Isaiah 7:14; Matthew 1:23). He is the one in whom "all the fulness of God was pleased to dwell" (Colossians 1:19). "He who has seen me," Jesus therefore declares, "has seen the Father" (John 14:9). For "when the time had fully come, God sent his Son, born of a woman, born under the law . . ." (Galatians 4:4; cf. Matthew 11:27; Mark 1:11; John 3:16; Hebrews 5:5; 1 John 4:9). This idea of "divine Sonship" is not entirely new to the New Testament. It has a "from behind" lineage, rooted in the Old Testament history of redemption, where kings, judges, other leaders of the people, heavenly angels, and even Israel itself are sometimes called "sons of God" (Psalm 82; Job 38:7; John 10:33-38; Hosea 11:1). Christ Jesus as Son of God is the culmination of this covenant tradition. He thus lays the groundwork for also calling New Testament believers "sons of God" (Romans 8:19-23; 1 John 3:2). Between "Sonship" and "sonship" there is, however, an essential difference. We are sons and daughters in the family of God by adoption, whereas he is "the only begotten Son of the Father," God's "one and only" Son in a sovereignly unique and preeminent way. Many modern theologies blur this distinction between Christ's Sonship and ours, domesticating the Lord of glory. This prompts William Temple to comment pointedly, "Why anyone should have troubled to crucify the Christ of Liberal Protestantism has always been a mystery" (*Readings in St. John's Gospel,* p. 24). The historic Christian faith, however, holds that Christ's filial relationship to the Father is original and ours a gift. His Sonship, moreover, has cosmic significance, touching "all things" *(ta panta)* with life-renewing power (1 Corinthians 8:6; Ephesians 1:10; Colossians 1:15-20; Hebrews 1:1-4). This redeeming work continues until finally, with "all things in subjection under his feet, . . . he delivers the kingdom to God the Father. . . ; then the Son himself will also be subjected to him who put all things under him, that God may be everything to every one" (1 Corinthians 15:24-28).

III. 3. 2. *Christological Controversies*

During the lifetime of the apostles already, before the close of the first century, christological heresies were beginning to infiltrate the church. Some clear hints of this are present in various New Testament writings, especially the pastoral epistles. There were, on the one hand, Judaizing tendencies. Among some Christians, notably those affected by the Ebionite movement, the insistent monotheism of the Old Testament was viewed as an obstacle to embracing Jesus as a "second deity." The testimony of the law, the prophets, and the writings was unmistakably clear: "Hear, O Israel, the LORD your God is *one* God. . . ." For those clinging to this basic article in the faith of the fathers, and eschewing compromise, the confession of Christ as Son of God seemed tantamount to blasphemy. On the other hand, early Christians were also exposed to Hellenizing influences which cast dark shadows over our bodily existence. These docetic tendencies led some in the Christian community to call into question the full and true humanity of Christ. Such christological cross-currents led eventually to the ecumenical councils of the fourth and fifth centuries.

III. 3. 2. 1. Preliminary Encounters

Early Christian thinkers struggled to gain some measure of clarity on the question, What does it mean that "the Word became flesh"? In their reflections on the mystery of the incarnation the central issue was the person of Jesus Christ in relation to the established belief in God the Father and the concomitant biblical witness concerning the Holy Spirit. Thus it came about that "the trinitarian and Christological dogmas together make up the basic content of normative church doctrine as it developed in the course of the emergence of the catholic tradition" (Jaroslav Pelikan, *The Emergence of the Catholic Tradition — 100-600*, p. 278). The early church fathers had no long and deep creedal tradition to draw on. They were exploring virgin territory. The canon of the New Testament was, moreover, still in its formative stages of finalization. Out of this highly fluid situation critical voices arose, both inside and outside the church, challenging the Christian faith. The earliest defenders of orthodoxy were the apostolic fathers, successors to the inner circle of Christ's followers. Their writings are largely catechetical and pastoral. They were, it seems, too preoccupied with trying faithfully to transmit the gospel handed down by the original witnesses to engage in extended theological disputation. To them the Master was quite simply truly God, truly man, the sinless One, their Savior and Lord, whom they worshiped and served. As Hebrew and Greco-Roman congregations sprang up around the Mediterranean world, however, early Christian thinkers were compelled to contend with infringements on both the deity and humanity of Christ Jesus.

a. Serious violations of the deity of Christ first arose among Ebionite believers, for whom the emphatic monotheism of the Old Testament proved to be an insuperable obstacle. Within this wing of early Christianity, Jesus was viewed as purely human, the son of Joseph and Mary, whose virtuous life qualified him to serve as the Messiah. This group included early Zionists, who looked to Jesus as the founder of a new Jewish society. Going a step further, others taught that at his baptism Jesus was adopted by God the Father to the subordinate status of quasi-divine "sonship." This early version of a "Christology from below to above" is predictive of many current theological views which emphasize "humanity transcending itself" (Weber, *Foundations of Dogmatics,* Vol. II, pp. 108-9).

b. In Greco-Roman circles deviations from orthodox Christology took the form of a Christianized monotheism called monarchianism (meaning literally "a single principle"). Two types of monarchianism emerged to trouble early Christian communities. The one, known as dynamic monarchianism, closely parallels the monotheist ideas of Ebionite Christians. On this view, Christ was not eternally Son of God but achieved divinity, though never in more than a subordinate sense. At his baptism by John at the Jordan River his godly conduct was crowned with divine blessing when the voice from heaven declared, "This is my beloved Son, with whom I am well pleased" (Matthew 3:13-17). Dynamic monarchians interpreted this account to mean that then and there Jesus' human spirit *(logos)* was preempted by an infusion of the divine Spirit *(Logos)*. In this movement the church was confronted by a subordinationist, adoptionist view of the person of Christ, coupled with strong moralist overtones. The result was a Christology which compromised the true and full humanity of Jesus as well as his deity.

c. A second form of monarchianism also arose, known as modalism — a view which, couched in more contemporary concepts, has experienced a strong resurgence in recent times (cf. Hendrikus Berkhof, *Christian Faith,* pp. 330-37). In its earliest expressions modalist monarchianism is closely associated with the names of Praxeas and Sabellius. They advocated a basically unitarian view of God. According to them the conventional distinction of persons — Father, Son, and Holy Spirit — does not refer to a real differentiation of persons, but to three modes or "masks" or manifestations in which the one God comes to us. Jesus Christ is one such mode of divine self-revelation.

These three schools of thought within early Christianity all emphasize the unity of the Godhead at the expense of the genuine duality of natures in Christ, failing particularly to do justice to his full and true deity. Rising up to confront those challenges were Christian apologists such as Irenaeus and Tertullian. While affirming Christ's humanity, they stress his deity. Their writings are lacking, however, in a clear and profound delineation of the troublesome issues involved. They were concerned basically to honor as fully as possible the mystery that is Jesus Christ — the identity and integrity of his two natures within the unity of his person.

d. From a very opposite quarter orthodox Christology came under attack by the most formidable and pernicious heresy to invade the life of the early church — Gnosticism. Gnostic influences (denoting an esoteric type of "knowing") sprang from ideas deeply embedded in Greek philosophy — the superiority of spiritual, divine reality over the unreality, or at least lesser reality, of physical, human, bodily things. Such dualisms allow for no personal integration of the divine and the human. Christ was therefore viewed as the divine Spirit *(Logos)* who indwelled, "took up residence in," the man Jesus, but short of personal union. Humanity simply "housed" deity. At the crucifixion, therefore, some held that the divine nature, which is immune to suffering, abandoned the man Jesus, leaving Satan with only a body. In the Gnostic menace the church became entangled in the most insidious forms of docetism (from *dokeō,* meaning "to seem to be," a mere "semblance"). Docetic tendencies led many to think of Christ's humanity as an apparition, an optical illusion. The real Christ was purely divine. His bodily presence was a phantom; or he had a celestial, not earthly body, one which he took with him from heaven.

In these confessional struggles the early church came to realize keenly that salvation depends on Christ's true and full humanity as well as his full and true deity. Rising up in defense of orthodox Christology were the anti-Gnostic fathers. Their writings betray certain reactionary leanings, however, tending toward subordinationist views — that he is indeed divine, but of a lower order than the Father. These preliminary doctrinal encounters, followed by more refined articulations of these heresies, occasioned the convocation of a series of ecumenical councils during the fourth and fifth centuries. In these conciliar developments there was a strong tendency, under pressure from the then current ways of thinking, to make "the person [of Christ] an independent and almost isolated theme in separation from [his] work." Yet we should never lose sight of the underlying question, "whether this or that definition might truncate or distort the work of salvation. To this extent there is never an absolute separation between person and work" (Thielicke, *The Evangelical Faith,* Vol. II, p. 344).

III. 3. 2. 2. The Ecumenical Councils

The age of persecution was now past. During the first three centuries various Christian communities had endured wave after wave of reprisals by the Roman state against the church. Some were regional, others empire-wide, and they were of varying intensity. With the imperial Edict of Milan, A.D. 313, these threats came to an end. The Holy Roman Empire was born. The emperors themselves were now Christians, and Christianity became the officially prescribed religion of both the East and the West. In the meantime, a more highly institutionalized church took its place alongside a highly organized state. Within the framework of this emerging political-ecclesiastical coalition, bishops and civil rulers often collaborated in convening a series of ecumenical councils (in the sense of "worldwide"). Political factors often loomed as large as confessional factors in setting the agendas and determining the outcomes. Despite their drawbacks, the lasting importance of these conciliar decisions lies in the developing dogmas, trinitarian and christological, which they bequeathed to the church past, present, and future.

a. On the Council of Nicea, Berkouwer says,

> The year 325 will always remain a milepost in the development of Christological reflection in the church. [There] the simple faith of the church successfully resisted one of the most serious attacks it ever faced. . . . [For] the religion of Nicea harks back to the witness of the Scriptures and is an echo, loaded terms notwithstanding, of the adoration with which the New Testament is imbued. (*The Person of Christ,* pp. 60, 63)

The central actors in the drama were Arius and Athanasius. Arius was a strong proponent of a subordinationist Christology. Christ is *homoiousios* with the Father, he held, of "similar substance," God-like, but not fully and truly divine. God is one, he argued, and he is eternal. Besides him there is only created reality, all of which originates in God's will, not his essence. Christ is "the first-born of all creation" (Colossians 1:15). He is therefore not eternal, nor "consubstantial" with God the Father. As Son of God he has a beginning — that is, God was once not a Father, and had no Son. In begetting Christ as his primordial act of creation, God became Father. Christ is therefore the "only begotten," but not the "eternally begotten" Son of God. Because Christ enjoys this very special relation to God the Father, Arius was prepared to call him the Son of God — not according to essence, however, but according to the divine will. "The net result of his teaching was to reduce the Word to a demi-god" (J. N. D. Kelly, *Early Christian Doctrine,* p. 230).

The champion of christological orthodoxy at Nicea was Athanasius.

He maintained that Christ is *homoousios* with God the Father, "consubstantial" in the sense of being coeternal and codivine. Many ambiguities beset the work of the council. A number of contending parties arose. The fathers of Nicea wished to rely solely on the simple testimony of Scripture. Yet the desire for confessional clarity drove them to employ some highly charged philosophical concepts. The emperor's involvement, politically motivated, was a further complicating factor: he wished to preserve one faith throughout the empire by avoiding a schism between East and West. In the end, however, Athanasius won the day, and his views later found their way into the Nicene Creed. By means of this creed, in emphatic and repetitious phrases, the church confesses its faith ". . . in the one Lord Jesus Christ, the only-begotten Son of God, begotten of the Father before all worlds; God of God, Light of Light, very God of very God, not made, being of one substance with the Father." By rejecting the *homoiousios* of Arius and adopting the *homoousios* ("of one substance") of Athanasius, "the expositors of the Nicene doctrine attempted to safeguard the soteriological and liturgical concerns of the church, for which it was mandatory that Christ be divine" (Pelikan, *The Emergence of the Catholic Tradition — 100-600,* p. 206).

It seemed for a time that, while Athanasius had won the battle at Nicea, Arius was winning the war. Athanasius was repeatedly driven into exile. Meanwhile, though condemned, Arian Christianity continued to attract a sizeable following in some sectors of the church. In strikingly analogous ways it returned with a vengeance in nineteenth-century liberalism. Taking a reverse look at history, Abraham Kuyper comments that "one merely has to write other names and other dates into the history of the Arian heresy, and, provided one takes it in broad outline, the course of Modernism is repeated" (cf. Berkouwer, *The Person of Christ,* p. 10). Eventually, however, from Nicea until the age of the Enlightenment, Arianism failed to gain a permanent foothold in the Western Church. It was Nicene Christology that prevailed.

b. Soon after the Nicene settlement disputes came to the fore concerning the other aspect of the christological issue: Jesus' full and true humanity.

This led to the convening of the Council of Constantinople in A.D. 381. The central figure there was Apollinaris, a great admirer of Athanasius and a strong supporter of the Nicene decisions. His attempts to understand John 1:14, "the Word became flesh. . . ," led him, however, to compromise the humanity of Christ. It is impossible, he held, for the divine *Logos* to be fully united with the man Jesus, since this would result in a *tertium quid,* a third kind of being, neither completely divine nor completely human, but a mixture of the two. Apollinaris tried to resolve this problem by resorting to a trichotomous view of man. He saw human nature as composed of three parts — body, soul, and spirit. In Jesus the divine *Logos* (Spirit) replaced the human *logos* (spirit), thus severely reducing his full humanity. For since the *logos* in man, and supremely so in Christ, is the active principle of rationality and self-determination, the humanity of Jesus Christ was severely suppressed and reduced to passivity. Moreover, since, according to Apollinaris, the human spirit is the wellspring of sin, his view made it possible to stress the sinlessness of Christ. The result, however, was a form of docetism, a nearly total eclipse of his humanity. Jesus is no longer "like us in all things." His humanity is sacrificed to deity, is in fact assimilated into it, leaving Christ essentially with a single nature, the divine. Thus Apollinaris represents a revival of monarchianism, paving the way for two later christological heresies, monophysitism (a single nature) and monothelitism (a single will).

The Council of Constantinople condemned the views of Apollinaris. After reaffirming the Nicene decisions on the full and true deity of Christ, it went on to affirm his full and true humanity. With this the stage was set for the next round in these ongoing christological controversies. The question arose: Given agreement with both Nicea and Constantinople, how is the church to understand the interrelatedness of Christ's two natures? Two quite opposite answers were offered, one by Nestorius, the other by Eutychus. These conflicting views occasioned the convening of the next two councils on the way to the climactic Council of Chalcedon.

c. The Council of Ephesus in A.D. 431 addressed the Nestorian error. Nestorius reasoned from two natures, the one human, the other divine, to two persons, the one human, the other divine. Duality of natures implies a split personality, a double ego, thus driving a deep wedge between the divine and the human in Christ. Yet, according to Nestorius, the two natures are one in spirit. They are joined by a moral union of two wills in perfect fellowship, but short of the integral personal union of God and man. Ephesus rejected this dichotomous way of resolving the mystery.

d. In A.D. 448 another council was convened in Constantinople to address the views of Eutychus, who argued the very opposite of Nestorius. He held that a single person implies a single nature. The result was another *tertium quid* proposal. The pre-incarnate Christ, Eutychus held, was a purely divine person. His nativity in Bethlehem, however, resulted in a comingling of the divine and human. The Christ of faith is therefore a single person with a single nature, no longer either fully and truly divine nor fully and truly human, but a confluent mixture of the two. The fathers of Constantinople rejected this confusion of natures as proposed by Eutychus. The "Robber Synod" the next year, however, vindicated Eutychus, thus creating the chaotic situation which the Council of Chalcedon was called to settle.

e. The "Chalcedonian settlement" (Kelly), sometimes regarded as "a Roman victory" over Alexandria and Constantinople in the East (Weber), marks the watershed event to three centuries of heated dispute on the doctrine of Christ. Its classic formulations have stood the test of time. They proved to be "fundamental ever since to the Christological development of all the Latin West, much of the Greek East, and some of the Syrian East" (Pelikan, *The Emergence of the Catholic Tradition — 100-600*, p. 263). Building on earlier foundations, Chalcedon counteracted in summary form the heretical views dealt with by previous councils. It affirmed the duality of natures in Christ coexisting in personal union. In setting parameters to the mystery, Chalcedon declared that Christ's two natures coexist 1) "unconfused" — against Eutychus, 2) "unchanged" — against the subordinationist-adoptionist views of Arius, 3) "undivided" within each nature — against Apollinaris, and 4) "unseparated" — against Nestorius. The fathers of Chalcedon were content thus to safeguard the mystery — the identity and integrity of the two natures within unity of person, to circumscribe it, and thus to ward off misrepresentations. This confessional consensus shaped the future — heresies to be avoided, truths to be affirmed, the mystery to be honored. Its decisive stance leads Berkouwer to say that "There is a 'halt!' at Chalcedon which will indeed continue to sound against every form of speculation which attempts to penetrate the mystery farther than is warranted by revelation" (*The Person of Christ*, p. 88).

The charge of "bald negativism" has often been leveled against Chalcedonian orthodoxy. Yet an essentially different approach is hardly conceivable. Chalcedon said what needed saying without going beyond what Scripture warrants. Even its negative statements carry a positive thrust. In the face of its mystery "our language collapses" and we are reduced to "stammering." For Chalcedon "says those things which leave men 'speechless.' Its terms are not a means for grasping, but rather for making known that we have been grasped" (Weber, *Foundations of Dogmatics*, Vol. II, p. 116). As a capstone declaration,

> Chalcedonian Christology set the terms for theology and devotion of the Latin church at least until the time of the Reformation, and even then the various contending doctrines on the person of Christ vied with one another in their protestations of loyalty to Chalcedon. (Pelikan, *The Emergence of the Catholic Tradition — 100-600*, p. 266)

This changed radically, however, with the advent of modernity. Chalcedon's "from above" approach to Christology made way for the "from below" hermeneutic of the Enlightenment mind. Liberal theology, therefore, not only refused to call a halt at Chalcedon, but went on to break with it.

f. The Chalcedonian formula covered all the basic terms in the christological equation. Later developments did little more than reveal some intriguing twists and turns on this dogma. Eastern Christianity focused ontologically on the *person* of Christ, the West soteriologically on his *work*. In the Reformation era Socinians, as forerunners of modern liberalism, pushed the Arian heresy to its ultimate conclusion. The Reformers responded by reiterating the faith of the ecumenical councils: Jesus Christ is "the only begotten Son of God, begotten from eternity, not made, . . . but co-essential and co-eternal with the Father. . . . He is the Son of God, not only from the time that He assumed our nature, but from all eternity . . ." (Belgic Confession, Article X). As an opposite extreme, certain "stepchildren of the Reformation" downgraded the true humanity of Christ. Therefore, "in opposition to the heresy of the Anabaptists, who deny that Christ assumed human flesh of his mother," the fathers of the Reformation confessed that he took on himself "true human nature with all its infirmities, sin excepted" (Belgic Confession, Article XVIII). Calvin, whose thinking lies behind these creedal statements, "adheres strictly to the line of Chalcedonian orthodoxy" (John T. McNeill, ed., *Institutes*, Vol. I, p. 482, footnote 1). "Away with the error of Nestorius," he says. He speaks also of "that impious fabrication whose author is Eutychus," holding that both were "justly condemned" by the ecumenical councils (*Institutes*, II,14,4 and 8). Calvin resists attempts, however, to canonize the often dubious philosophical terminology employed by the early church fathers. Such concepts may be "necessary to unmask false teachers," he argues. But he then adds, "I could wish they were buried" if only believers could agree on the simplicity of the biblical testimony (*Institutes*, I,13,4 and 5). Calvin's Christology is most at home in the context of redemption history. In light of both Old and New Testaments he presents Christ as Mediator of the covenant. In his threefold office Christ is our Teacher, Intercessor, and King (*Institutes*, II,14,3; 15).

The Chalcedonian settlement came back to haunt the Reformers in a heated dispute between followers of Calvin and Luther. Because Calvinists confess that "in his human nature Christ is not now on earth," while in his divinity "He is not absent from us for a moment," and since "Christ's divinity is surely beyond the bounds of the humanity he has taken on," Lutherans therefore accused them of the dualist error of Nestorius. This so-called "extra-Calvinisticum" (*Institutes*, II,13,4), Lutherans argued, forces a separation of the two natures, even though Calvinists confess at the same time that "his divinity is and remains personally united to his humanity" (Heidelberg Catechism, Q. & A. 47 and 48). In their countercharge Calvinists accused Lutherans of reviving the error of Eutychus. According to Lutheran tradition Christ's ascension to glory involved a radical change. His glorified body took on the divine quality of omnipresence. At this point Lutheran Christology has a direct bearing on its view of the real presence of Christ in the Lord's Supper — that the body of Christ is everywhere present "in, under, and with" the bread, as heat is in a white-hot iron (Luther). This idea, according to Calvinists, is reminiscent of the Eutychian confusion of the two natures.

At this point the plot thickens even more. For out of this doctrinal encounter arose the question of the *communicatio idiomata* — the idea of the interchange of properties between the two natures (*Institutes*, II,14,1). Lutherans held that the divine property of omnipresence was conferred on Christ's humanity — as a "mixture," not by "confusion." Calvinists maintained that there is no exchange of properties between the two natures. Each nature retains fully its own unique identity and integrity. Rather, the "communication of properties" means that all human and all divine qualities are conferred on the single person of Christ Jesus. It is clear from this doctrinal confrontation that these two Reformation traditions were both pressing Chalcedonian Christology to its limits. Summarizing Calvin's views, Berkouwer says:

> In Christ there is only one acting subject, but in it lies the distinction between properties — the mystery of Chalcedon. . . . [Accordingly Calvin was] on guard against any crossing of creaturely boundary-lines — also in Christ. . . . The Son of God assumed human nature in an act of love and reconciliation, and this human nature is in all things like us . . . — even in the humanity which Christ has after his glorification. . . . We must be concerned to maintain that all the deeds of Christ were performed by his *one* person and that in the sufferings of Christ the human nature was indissolubly united with the divine. The communion of natures therefore comes to expression in a communion of actions. (*The Person of Christ*, pp. 282, 293)

III. 3. 3. The Mediator's Presence among Us

Redemption as the restoration of the fallen creation to what it was and still is intended to be and become — this is the basic biblical story line which shapes Reformed thinking. As Mediator of redemption (2 Corinthians 5:18-19; Colossians 1:20; Ephesians 2:16), Christ builds anew on the foundations he laid as God's mediating Word for creation (John 1:3; Colossians 1:16-17). That original work is now badly mis-aligned. God's reconciling way with his world in Christ presupposes nonetheless an unbreakable bond between creation and redemption.

406

Thus, far from drawing us away from the world, salvation history relocates us in it with a life-renewing vision.

Turning now to Christ's presence among us in his threefold office as Mediator of redemption, we must therefore bear in mind that there is a close connection between this doctrine and the earlier creational doctrine of "Man in Office." For Christ, the "last Adam," came to take the place of the "first Adam" and his fallen race. His mission therefore has universal, purposeful significance. Accordingly, "the concept of 'office' [removes] the activity of Christ from the sphere of the private, the arbitrary, and the capricious" (Weber, *Foundations of Dogmatics,* Vol. II, p. 170). This doctrine of the threefold office, given originally with the creation of mankind, and now vicariously renewed in Christ, owes its first clear formulation to the Reformers. Not that it is wholly absent in medieval thinkers. But, as Calvin comments, they treat it "coldly and rather ineffectually" (*Institutes,* II,15,1). Luther, therefore, with his views on the priesthood of all believers, and Calvin more fully, led the way in its development. Appealing to the strong biblical emphasis on the single Mediator between God and man (1 Timothy 2:5; "no other name," Acts 4:12), and accordingly on the oneness of the way of salvation (John 14:6), reformational thinkers held that Christ's mediating office is indivisibly singular. Yet it is possible within this single office to distinguish three aspects — the prophetic, priestly, and kingly — without, however, drawing sharp lines of demarcation between them. For they act in unison. Christ's person and work as Mediator colors all three. This leads Berkouwer to say, "Christ's kingship in inseparable connection with his prophecy and priesthood is a blessing to the world" (*The Work of Christ,* p. 76).

Calvin's treatment of this doctrine (*Institutes,* II,15) draws heavily on Old Testament analogies. There ordination to office is regularly described as being "anointed by the Lord" through his appointed agents, and being thus "commissioned" to serve as "chosen instruments of the Lord." Kings, priests, and prophets all occupy creaturely offices. Accordingly, they always serve under and are accountable to a higher authority. Office is a holy vocation. "One does not call himself to an office, but is called to a task" (Berkouwer, *The Work of Christ,* p. 64). The various elements which define the biblical meaning of office all reach their concentration point in Christ the Mediator. In this sense "only Christ, and no one else, can be the locus of this work and hence the bearer of these offices" (Thielicke, *The Evangelical Faith,* Vol. II, p. 342). He is the promised "Messiah," the "Christ" of God — both of these names meaning the "anointed One" (compare Isaiah 61:1 with Luke 4:18; Acts 4:27). As our Substitute, vicariously living our life, dying our death, and pre-assuring our resurrection, his atoning work infuses all three aspects of his mediatorial office, which, though quite sharply delineated among the officers of God's people in the Old Testament, are integrally united in Christ. Thus, "the doctrine of the 'threefold office' is an appropriate tool for the prevention of every one-sidedness and for the full interpretation of the oneness and totality of the work of this one person in all its fullness" (Weber, *Foundations of Dogmatics,* Vol. II, p. 176).

III. 3. 3. 1. Christ as Prophet

In his prophetic office Christ Jesus is the incarnate Word, speaking as God and for God to a lost humanity. He identifies his message with that of the Old Testament prophets (Matthew 21:33-46). But he also represents "something greater" (Luke 11:32). There is more than a simple line of continuity between himself and the old prophets. His mission is the fulfillment of theirs and gives ultimate meaning to their message. He is therefore now our "chief Prophet" (Heidelberg Catechism, Q. & A. 31). In the total scope of his mediatorial office, the prophetic aspect included, Christ reveals both an active and passive obedience to his Father's will. "I have given them thy word," he says (John 17:14). He is fully submissive to his heavenly mandate. "My teaching is not mine," he adds, "but his who sent me" (John 7:16). This perfect submission is at the same time the free expression of his own resolute will. For he also speaks on his own: ". . . Before Abraham was, I am" (John 8:58). Not only does he witness to the truth he received from on high, but he also claims personally to be "the Truth." The crowds were therefore often astonished at his bold prophetic utterances, "for he taught them, not as their scribes, but as one who had authority" (Matthew 7:29).

Throughout his earthly ministry Jesus was keenly conscious of his prophetic office. At twelve years of age already, while dialoging with the rabbis in the temple, there are clear intimations of this deep awareness: "Did you not know," he later asks his inquiring parents, "that I must be in my Father's house?" (Luke 2:49). When rejected by his hometown people, he responds, "No prophet is acceptable in his own country" (Luke 4:24). Lamenting over Jerusalem's hard-heartedness, he comments wryly, "It cannot be that a prophet should perish away from Jerusalem!" (Luke 13:33). He never backed off from this profound sense of prophetic calling, not even in the face of the most severe forms of suffering and shame. His heart bled most deeply during the trial, when members of the Sanhedrin taunted him with despicable mockery: "Prophesy to us, you Christ! Who is it that struck you?" (Matthew 26:68). In his fascinating exposition of this passage Klaas Schilder says that Christ, "the chief Prophet," is here mocked as "He stands upon the mountain of prophecy." The worst abuse was not the beatings and spitting, but that his own people — and we with them — "mocked the most awesome and profound function in his life: They converted his [prophetic] office into a joke." There on "the mountain of the prophets. . . . He tasted of the hellish terror which exists in the deep abyss of all dismissed prophets" (*Christ on Trial,* pp. 173-94).

As prophet Christ Jesus proclaims consistently the meaning of both his priestly task and kingly claims. For all three aspects of his mediatorial office are one. This oneness finds its continuation in the work of the Holy Spirit. With prophetic urgency the Spirit now calls Christ's followers to self-sacrificing service and royal obedience. For his importance as prophet can hardly be overestimated. But it can be badly distorted. That is the sad spectacle of modern liberalism, which extols his prophetic gifts at the expense of his priesthood and kingship, enshrining him as the rabbi from Nazareth in their "hall of fame" as one of history's most distinguished teachers of morality. As with all ideas, these, too, have their consequences, in this case dire and tragic ones. For to separate one aspect of Christ's office from the others is to lose them all. Christ himself affirms their interrelated-ness when confronted with Pilate's question, "So you are a king?" In reply he says in effect, "You said it!" — and then links his kingly and prophetic offices in adding, "For this I was born, and for this I have come into the world, to bear witness to the truth" (John 18:37-38). According to Berkouwer, therefore, Bavinck is correct in saying that "Christ does not just perform prophetic, priestly, and kingly activities, but his whole person is prophet, priest, and king, and . . . everything He is, does, and speaks reveals his threefold dignity" (*The Work of Christ,* p. 70). We are thus cautioned against viewing Christ's person abstractly or his work in isolation from his person. The two go hand in hand.

III. 3. 3. 2. Christ as Priest

Christ's priestly office, too, is closely connected with the office of priest-hood as it functioned in the Old Testament history of redemption. Implicit throughout the New Testament, this connection is developed most ex-plicitly, as might be expected, in the letter to the Hebrews, addressed as it is to Christians with a strong Jewish background. In 5:1-10 the un-known author describes the task of "every high priest" as it applies to Christ. He is "chosen from among men"; he "does not take the honor upon himself, but is called by God, just as Aaron was"; he is "appointed to act on behalf of men in relation to God"; his task is to "offer gifts and sacrifices for sins." This was true of the Levitical priesthood. In Christ a greater than Aaron and his sons has appeared (Hebrews 7:26-

28). For he is "a high priest forever after the [enduring] order of Melchizedek" (Hebrews 6:20). In him "a shadow of the good things to come" is fulfilled in "the true form of these realities" (Hebrews 10:1).

In thus reestablishing the older covenant in its newness and finality, Christ as our "only High Priest" (Heidelberg Catechism, Q. & A. 31) demonstrates both active and passive obedience to his Father's will. He "came not to be served, but to serve, and to give his life a ransom for many" (Mark 10:45). Far from being the tragic victim of an unfortunate conspiracy, he is the active, leading participant in God's plan of salvation. "For this reason," he says, "the Father loves me, because I lay down my life, that I may take it again. No one takes it from me, but I lay it down of my own accord. I have power to lay it down, and I have power to take it again; this charge I have received from my Father" (John 10:17-18).

Christ not only actively pursues his priestly task "to fulfill all righteousness" (Matthew 3:15; 5:17-18; John 15:10) but also suffers passively as the sacrificial Lamb. This is the heart of John the Baptist's testimony, "Behold, the Lamb of God who takes away the sin of the world!" (John 1:29), echoing Isaiah's prophecy concerning "a lamb that is led to the slaughter" (53:7). Paul reinforces this point, relating the Mediator's obedience unto death (Philippians 2:8) to the central event of Old Testament history, the exodus, when he says that "Christ, our paschal lamb, has been sacrificed" (1 Corinthians 5:7). Scripture opens up an even more profound perspective on Christ's sacrificial suffering and death in its pastoral teaching that believers are ransomed "with the precious blood of Christ, like that of a lamb without blemish or spot." While this was "made manifest at the end of the times," it was so "destined before the foundation of the world" (1 Peter 1:18-20). Christ is therefore both priest and sacrifice simultaneously.

These two interwoven themes inform Christ's priestly ministry from start to finish: not only his once-for-all atonement then and there, but also his ongoing intercession here and now. The former is unrepeatable, bracketed completely by those three momentous decades in the first century, and climaxed decisively by the cry from the cross, "It is finished!" (John 19:30). Sovereignly, exclusively alone, Christ our Substitute was driven increasingly into absolute isolation. "The great Shepherd of the sheep, left completely isolated in his calling, performed the supreme act of care for his sheep, the act which had to explain and make valid every other act" (Schilder, *Christ in his Suffering*, p. 456). The otherwise unbearable burden of the world's guilt was never lifted from his shoulders. No one could share it or lighten its load. For Christ endured it all *pro nobis* — "for us." As the prophet foretold, "the LORD has laid on him the iniquity of us all" (Isaiah 53:6). Christ embodied the mysteriously unique blend of his innocence and our guilt: personally no one was able

410

to answer his challenging question, "Who of you convicts me of sin?" (John 8:46); yet forensically he was the world's greatest sinner. As Paul says, "For our sake [God] made him to be sin who knew no sin, so that in him we might become the righteousness of God" (1 Corinthians 5:21). The "great exchange" (Luther) has taken place. Unwittingly even Caiaphas the high priest testified to this truth, rationalizing that "it is expedient for you that one should die for the people." John interprets these wretchedly motivated yet profoundly apt words to mean that through his vicarious death Christ would "gather into one the children of God who are scattered abroad" (11:49-52).

That is the way it had to be, and that is the way Christ himself willed it to be. Therein lies a holy "must." As the incognito Christ explained to the travelers to Emmaus, "Was it not necessary that the Christ should suffer these things and enter into his glory?" (Luke 24:26; for "everything written about me . . . must be fulfilled," verse 44). This necessity arises out of the biblical story line: the desperately needed restoration of a sin-riddled creation. In this once-for-all, unrepeatable act of atonement, the Jewish leaders acted unjustly, shedding innocent blood. Concurrently supervising it all, however, was a far greater justice. For though Jesus was "crucified and killed by the hands of lawless men," it was "according to the definite plan and foreknowledge of God" (Acts 2:23). Therefore as Berkouwer comments, "Through the mesh of human arbitrariness runs the thread of God's plan and action" (*The Work of Christ,* p. 146). The occasional calls in our day to reopen the trial of Jesus therefore miss the fundamental point. For at the cross, in an absolutely unique way, divine justice and love met to embrace each other. This called for blood. For "without the shedding of [this] blood there is no forgiveness of sins" (Hebrews 9:22). Modern liberals may call this "butcher shop theology." Those faithful to the historic Christian faith, however, will continue in good conscience to drink the sacramental cup in commemoration of the words of the Lord, "Drink of it, all of you, for this is my blood of the covenant, which is poured out for many for the forgiveness of sins" (Matthew 26:28).

A second phase in Christ's priestly service is his ongoing intercession. He now "always lives to make intercession" for those who "draw near to God through him" (Hebrews 7:25). As our Advocate with the Father, he pleads our cause. This is not a new undertaking, a mere appendix to his work of reconciliation. It is follow-up work. The once-for-all atoning work which Christ began and "finished!" on earth, he now brings to fruition from his heavenly vantage point. Therefore, we must not allow the "already" to get lost in the mists of ancient history. His "ministry of intercession should not be dissociated from the atonement, since they are but two aspects of the same redemptive work of Christ, and the two may be said to merge into one" (Louis Berkhof, *Systematic Theology*, p. 402). We must not think of our prayers, and his prayers for us, as attempts to bring a faraway cross closer by. For in Christ a fusion of horizons takes place.

We meet the praying Christ already during his days on earth. He utters a prayer of lamentation over Jerusalem (Matthew 23:37). As Peter stands at the brink of betrayal, Jesus keeps him from total collapse: "I have prayed for you that your faith may not fail" (Luke 22:32). In his high-priestly prayer in the upper room he implores the Father for his disciples, "that they may be one, even as we are one" (John 17:11). Looking beyond them, he also prays for "those who believe in me through their word" (John 17:20), envisioning the "other sheep" who must enter his fold (John 10:16). Christ's intercessory work as Mediator now continues throughout these "end times" with the ring of authority merited by the One who suffered, died, arose, ascended, and reigns forever in glory. He takes our prayers and makes them his own, sanctifying them through the work of the Holy Spirit, our "second Advocate," who "intercedes for us with sighs too deep for words" (Romans 8:26). Who then shall "bring any charge against God's elect"? For Christ Jesus "intercedes for us" (Romans 8:33-34). When therefore the "accuser of our brethren" brings his barbed indictments "day and night before God" (Revelation 12:10), Christ becomes our "attorney for the defense." The devil is at his fiendish worst, says Luther, when he whispers doubt in our ears, undermining our assurance of salvation and unsettling our conscience. But Christ is greater than our conscience. In him we have a high priest "who in every respect has been tempted as we are, yet without sinning. Let us then with confidence draw near to the throne of grace, that we may receive mercy and find grace to help in time of need" (Hebrews 6:15-16).

III. 3. 3. 3. Christ as King

Like the other two aspects of Christ's office as Mediator, the kingly aspect brings together the various lines of biblical revelation as they converge on his person and work. There is first the historical line "from before": "The Lord will give him the throne of his father David" (Luke 1:32). There is the "from below" approach: Mary's "Magnificat" reflects on "the low estate" of his nativity (Luke 1:48). There is also the "from above" intervention: "I have set my king on Zion" (Psalm 2:6). There is finally the "from ahead" perspective: "The kingdom of the world has become the kingdom of our Lord and of his Christ, and he shall reign forever and ever" (Revelation 11:15). All four viewpoints, covering the past, present, and future, merge into the unified picture of Christ's all-embracing kingship. Its cosmic scope is reflected in the successive articles of the Apostles' Creed. The birth announcement of Jesus served notice on the proud that in Christ God has "put down the mighty from their thrones" (Luke 1:52). In launching his public ministry, one of Jesus' earliest recruits was Nathanael, whose instinctive response was "You are the King of Israel" (John 1:49). Atop the cross Pilate posted the contentious death sentence, "Jesus of Nazareth, the King of the Jews" (John 19:19). After his resurrection, nearing his ascension to glory, Christ declared, "All authority is mine in heaven and on earth" (Matthew 28:20).

In these biblical testimonies we meet Christ as king (as well as prophet and priest) in both of his "states," as commonly defined — the state of humiliation and the state of exaltation. Actually, in light of the full sweep of biblical revelation, this christological sequence involves three steps: from exaltation ("the glory which I had with you before the world was," John 17:5), through humiliation ("the man of sorrows," Isaiah 53:3), and then, based on his mission fully accomplished, Christ's return to glory ("Therefore God has highly exalted him. . . ," Philippians 2:9). This series of transitions points to the element of truth in the ancient "recapitulation" doctrine (Irenaeus): as the "last Adam" Christ retraced the steps of the "first Adam" from the state of integrity, into his fallen state, in order thus to restore Adam and his children to a state of righteousness. As Berkouwer puts it, this distinction in states

> . . . is meant to do justice to the testimony of Scripture concerning the historical progression in Christ's life from humiliation to exaltation, through suffering to glory. . . . The confession of the two states of Christ's life means to express the value of history, of this history. (*The Work of Christ,* pp. 36, 51)

The cross and the crown — this central biblical motif reflects the two stages in Christ's exercise of his kingly office: at first thoroughly concealed, then fully manifest. These two royal paths intersect to form the decisive crossroads in redemption history. Bethlehem's stable shelters a barely recognizable king, "wrapped in swaddling cloths and lying in a manger" (Luke 2:12). Scripture consistently relates the King's humble birth inextricably to our desperate need for reconciliation with God, and thus also with ourselves, our fellows, and the cosmos as a whole. This is the single, all-inclusive motivation behind the incarnation. This biblical rationale is not self-evident to all, however. In Reformation times it became a matter of heated dispute between Calvin and a contemporary

413

thinker, Osiander. "On the pretext that it is nowhere specifically refuted in Scripture," Osiander — spokesman for a long-standing voluntarist tradition — argued that even "if Adam had never fallen from his original and upright condition, Christ would still have become man," since this was predetermined by God. In response Calvin maintains that the one and only reason for the incarnation is our need for redemption. Christ took on Adam's nature in order to "bridge the gulf [of sin] between God and ourselves," thus to be "obedient in our stead" (*Institutes,* II,12,1 and 3 and 5).

Osiander's ideas did not die with him. Various versions of them live on in modern liberalism, often developed along adoptionist and modalist lines. The divine became human in Christ, so current reasoning often goes, in order that all reasonable people of goodwill may achieve their divine destiny. Scripture, however, says Berkouwer, "preaches not the *elevatio* of human nature, but its deliverance and restoration. . . . From the very beginning it is evident that Immanuel's coming is historically decreed, and that it does not merely have a 'general' meaning which can be described as a 'unity between God and man'" (*The Work of Christ,* p. 29). For "the Word became flesh and dwelt among us, full of grace and truth; and we have beheld his glory, glory as of the only Son from the Father" (John 1:14). This is the heartbeat of the biblical witness to the incarnation. This is the mystery of Christmas — "the manger of Bethlehem cradles a king." The profundity of this momentous event comes to expression in the miracle of the virgin birth. "The eternal Son of God, He through whom the universe was made, did not despise the virgin's womb! What a wonder is there!" (J. Gresham Machen, *The Virgin Birth of Christ,* p. 394). This first step in Christ's humiliation, as narrated by Matthew and Luke, held an undisputed place of honor in the church's confession until modern times. The age of the Enlightenment, however, with its historical-critical investigations, brought on a radical change.

> As long as the Holy Scriptures were accepted as the trustworthy Word of God. . . , the virgin birth of Christ was accepted and confessed without any crisis of conscience. Ever since the attack on the authority of Scripture, however, the door was opened for far-reaching criticism. (Berkouwer, *The Work of Christ,* p. 97)

In recent decades this crucial issue touched off a sharp confrontation between Barth and Brunner. Because on this point "the New Testament tradition is rather precarious," Brunner raises the question whether we are "obliged to represent to ourselves the divine miracle of the Incarnation of the Son of God as a Virgin Birth?" No, he answers, for the virgin birth accounts represent an attempt by the postapostolic church to rationalize the miracle by means of a "biological explanation" derived from the antisexual biases of Greek thought. We can, therefore, according to Brunner, confess "that" God became man, but not "how" (*The Mediator,* pp. 322-25). To Brunner's "Nein" Barth responded with a resounding "Ja!" "Brunner's denial of the virgin birth is a bad business" (*Church Dogmatics,* I/2, p. 184). For at the level of natural reality *(Historie),* says Barth, the virgin birth did indeed happen. This is the "miracle." This miraculous event is, however, only a "sign," a "pointer" *(Hinweis)* to what is ultimately important, the "mystery." It represents the "penetration and new beginning" by an absolutely free, sovereign, and exclusively divine act of self-revelation in the person of the Son (understood as *Geschichte,* supranatural, eschatological history). Barth then concludes, "The mystery does not rest upon the miracle. The miracle rests upon the mystery. The miracle bears witness to the mystery, and the mystery is attested by the miracle" (*Church Dogmatics,* I/2, p. 202). This is the triumph of God's sovereign grace: that Christ's exaltation is revealed precisely in the depths of his humiliation (Berkouwer, *The Triumph of Grace in the Theology of Karl Barth,* pp. 132-35).

In the gospel record Christ's exalted kingship long remains hidden. It is veiled under the cloak of servanthood — feeding the hungry, opening the eyes of the blind, healing the sick, raising the dead, ministering to the poor. Such regal demonstrations of compassion, rather than of judgment, prompted John the Baptist's frustrating inquiry: "Are you he that is to come, or shall we look for another?" (Matthew 11:3). Jesus' response is captured in effect in these words, "But if it is by the finger of God that I cast out demons, then the kingdom of God has come upon you" (Luke 11:20). The result was kingdoms in conflict. For the Jewish population was imbued with false messianic expectations of an earthly kingdom. Even Jesus' closest disciples were infected with these misguided notions (Matthew 20:20-28), clinging to them almost to the very end (Acts 1:6). It took Pentecost to change their outlook. Through the illumining power of the Spirit the meaning of Christ's words dawned on them: the kingdom is not *of* this world. It is *of* God. But it is surely *in* this world and *for* it. For where the King is, there is the kingdom (Luke 17:21).

The transition from the cross to the empty tomb marks the great turning point in Christ's kingly ministry from humiliation to exaltation. In the crucifixion people played their bloodthirsty roles — the Jewish leaders, the mob, the Roman soldiers. But most decisive was Christ's self-sacrificing surrender to the Father's way of salvation. For even in this ganglion of wild human emotions, God's involvement is "like an invisible, mysterious hand which rules and guides all human actions from beginning to end" (Berkouwer, *The Work of Christ,* p. 142). Finally, in the cry of dereliction, the King bows his head and dies. As if this were not suffering enough, the humiliated King sinks to even greater depths: "He descended into hell" — the final article to be included in the Apostles' Creed. Early church fathers disagreed on whether this act represents the last step in Christ's humiliation or the first step in his exaltation — descending to hell to proclaim his victory. They agreed, however, that this actually happened to him in his human nature. Centuries later, however, Calvin and his cohorts concluded that this idea has no biblical warrant. So the question arose, Should this article then be dropped from the creed? But this would mean breaking with a venerable tradition. Instead, therefore, the fathers of the Reformation chose to revise the original meaning of this article along more biblical lines: Christ did not descend to hell, but hell, as it were, leaped up to engulf him. In the words of the Heidelberg Catechism, "by his inexpressible anguish, pain, terrors, and hellish agony in which He was plunged during all his sufferings, but especially on the cross, [Christ] has delivered me from the anguish and torment of hell" (Q. & A. 44).

In the events which mark the transition from the agonies of Good Friday to the ecstatic joy of Easter Sunday, humiliation ended, and exaltation began in earnest. The time of Christ's hidden kingship receded into the past. The kingdom was ushered in as an "already" present reality, awaiting the filling out of its "not yet" dimension. From the moment of Christ's resurrection victory onward, "the royal power of the Son of Man given him by the Father, a power and authority embracing heaven and earth (Matthew 28:20), is placed first of all in the service of the preaching of the gospel" (Ridderbos, *The Coming of the Kingdom*, p. 174). In the words of Berkouwer, stressing once again the unity of Christ's threefold office, "The prophetic office is wholly directed to the coming of the kingdom, which in turn is closely connected with the priestly office" (*The Work of Christ*, p. 67).

III. 4. The Coming of the Spirit

The church year calendar is constructed around a series of Christian holidays ("holy days"). All are Christ-centered, focusing on one crucial event in his earthly mission after another: Christmas (his birth); Epiphany (the visit of the Magi); Ash Wednesday, Maundy Thursday, and Good Friday (his sufferings and death); Easter Sunday (his resurrection); and nearly forgotten in most Christian circles, Ascension Day (his exaltation into glory). This chain of events at the crossroads of redemption history reveals "all that Jesus began to do and teach" (Acts 1:1) while present

416

among us. But this is not the end of the story. Christ's mediatorial ministry, his work as prophet, priest, and king, did not cease with his triumphant "homecoming." Luke's opening verse in the Acts of the Apostles implies that the narratives which follow are a record of what the resurrected, ascended, and glorified Lord continued to do through the acts of the apostles and other early disciples. Through these transcendent acts of the Lord (Acts 3:12-16) the Christian church was born and experienced its initial stunning growth (Acts 2:41). The world of that day was touched by the "upside down" (Acts 17:6) rightside up power of the gospel. The pivotal event on which all this turns is Pentecost — the climactic yet also frequently overlooked red-letter day on the Christian calendar, which opens the door to this "new age" and keeps the windows open to the final Rendezvous.

III. 4. 1. The Pentecost Event

On that "festival day (Sunday, May 28, A.D. 30)" (F. F. Bruce, *The Spreading Flame*, p. 58) the international crowd gathered in Jerusalem to celebrate the ancient Jewish feast of harvest was astounded by what they saw and heard — signs and wonders and an unprecedented sermon. How are we to account for this bewildering display of newly unleashed power? All 120 disciples were suddenly "filled with the Holy Spirit" (Acts 2:4). As their leading spokesman Peter explained, Joel's prophecy was coming true: "In those days I will pour out my spirit . . ." (Joel 2:28-32). This outpouring of Holy Spirit-ed boldness in witnessing to the risen Lord was reinforced by strong winds, flaming tongues, and transcultural communication. In the Pentecost event the alienating impact of Babel's chaos was being overcome.

> But perhaps the most astonishing thing of all was the fact that this body of men . . . consisted of those disciples of Jesus who had forsaken him at his arrest, while the man who acted as their spokesman was Peter, the disciple whose nerve had failed so ignominiously in the high priest's courtyard. Their nerve had certainly returned. (Bruce, *The Spreading Flame*, p. 59)

What had happened during those preceding days to generate this dramatic change? Peter's sermon leaves no doubt. It was their renewed encounter with Jesus as the risen Lord. This revolutionary turn of events left its indelible, unforgettable mark on the disciples: ". . . We have been born anew to a living hope by the resurrection of Jesus Christ from the dead" (1 Peter 1:3). The Pentecostal outpouring of the Spirit, who

417

"proceeds from the Father and the Son" (Nicene Creed), stands therefore in an unbroken line of continuity with the gospel's witness to the life, death, and resurrection of Christ. As Hendrikus Berkhof puts it,

> It is only due to the appearances of the risen Lord that despair gave way to a new and unusually strong faith. Therefore the resurrection may be called the decisive redemptive event. . . . Without [it] all we have left is the late Jesus of Nazareth, one of the many martyrs who died for their convictions. . . . Therefore the Christian faith stands or falls with the resurrection. (*The Christian Faith*, p. 307)

That ultimate miracle is the validation of all that went before. Without it, nothing would have changed; then it would be true that "[our] faith is futile and [we] are still in [our] sins" (1 Corinthians 15:17). But the resurrection is not only God's stamp of approval on the past; it is also the firm foundation for all that follows, beginning explosively with Pentecost.

III. 4. 1. 1. Christ and His Spirit

The Scriptures affirm a close connection between the Holy Spirit and Christ — as close as that between the resurrection and Pentecost. There are two ways of approaching this issue: from the viewpoint of the preincarnate Son of God and the incarnate Christ. The former involves the historic Christian confession of the triune God. The Christology of the ecumenical councils fell short of gaining a clear consensus on the relation of the Spirit to the Son and the Father. Throughout the century following Nicea (A.D. 325) and Chalcedon (A.D. 451), therefore, this question continued to agitate the early church fathers. A confessional settlement was finally reached in the West at the Synod of Toledo in A.D. 589 with its confirmation of the *filioque* statement. The Holy Spirit is "consubstantial" with the other two persons of the Trinity, Toledo stated, and proceeds from both the Father *"and the Son."* This was "the rock on which the East and the West split" (Louis Berkhof, *The History of Christian Doctrines*, p. 96) — intensifying a growing rift which led eventually to a complete rupture in A.D. 1052, which has never been fully breached. The Eastern Orthodox churches, rejecting the *filioque* clause, continued to hold that, as with the Son, so the Spirit proceeds from the Father alone. This position resulted in a very tenuous view of the relationship between the incarnate Word and the Spirit, allowing for the development of a rather independent role for the Spirit in Christian living. This loose connection between Word (orthodoxy) and Spirit ("spiritual" praxis) fostered a highly experiential Christianity epitomized in rapturous liturgies. Such "pentecostal" tendencies also arose in the West. They were generally balanced, however, by the disciplining effects of a closer connection between the Word (doctrine) and the Spirit (ecstatic experience). In contrast with the East, however, this often degenerated into the "dead orthodoxy" of scholastic theology.

Sound and healthy Christian living rests in large part on a right understanding of the relationship between Christ (the Word) and the Spirit. For this we turn to the second approach, the historical redemptive testimony of the Scriptures. This biblical witness must serve in turn as the ultimate ground for a right understanding of the first, more "ontological" approach. Accordingly, Jesus Christ is "conceived by the Holy Spirit" (Apostles' Creed, Luke 1:35). The Spirit descends on him at his baptism (Mark 1:10) and then immediately leads him into the wilderness to face temptation (Mark 1:12; Luke 4:1). The Spirit equips Christ for his healing ministries (Acts 10:38), fills him without measure (John 3:34), braces him for his sacrificial death (Hebrews 9:14), and sustains him in his resurrection (Romans 1:4). In short, Christ was "vindicated by the Spirit" (1 Timothy 3:16). Thus the Spirit empowers Christ actively, dynamically for his mediatorial tasks. But the relationship is also reciprocal: Christ is also actively and dynamically involved in the coming of the Spirit. "And I will pray the Father," he says, "and he will give you another Counselor, to be with you forever" (John 14:15). Moreover, "If I go, I will send him to you" (John 16:7). These two passages in tandem lay the basis for the Western confession of the *filioque* — the Spirit "proceeds from the Father *and the Son.*"

The Spirit does not initiate new works. He honors the finished work of Christ. It is typical of his person and work not to draw attention to himself, but to fix our attention fully on the risen Lord. As Jesus foretold in his parting words to the apostles:

> I have many things to say to you, but you cannot bear them now. When the Spirit of truth comes, he will guide you into all the truth; for he will not speak on his own authority, but whatever he hears he will speak, and he will declare to you the things that are to come. He will glorify me, for he will take what is mine and declare it to you. All that the Father has is mine; therefore I said that he will take what is mine and declare it to you. (John 16:12-15)

Appealing to such biblical testimonies, Calvin introduces the Spirit as "the bond that unites us to Christ." He is poured out on the church in order "to share with us what [Christ] received from the Father." The Spirit is our "second Mediator," our "second Advocate," pleading our cause (Romans 8:26-27), thus "taking Christ's [merits] and imparting them to us." He is the great Implementer, indwelling God's people, quickening our response to revelation, so that "we come to enjoy Christ and all his benefits" (*Institutes,* III,1,1). He is our "inner Teacher," our "inner Schoolmaster" (*Institutes,* III,1,4). "To sum up, the Holy Spirit is the bond by whom Christ effectually unites us to himself" (*Institutes,* III,1,1). We are therefore called into "the fellowship of the Holy Spirit" (2 Corinthians 13:14), for without such participation "no one can taste either the fatherly favor of God or the beneficence of Christ" (*Institutes,* III,1,2). We therefore conclude that as the Father is the Initiator in both creation and redemption, so the Son is the Mediator and the Spirit the Enabler. In contrast to Hendrikus Berkhof's modalist view of the Spirit as "God's active presence" in Christ, the church, and the world (*Christian Faith,* pp. 331-32), Louis Berkhof affirms the traditional Christian view: There is a certain mutually interacting division of labors among the three persons of the triune God, so that we may speak "of the Father and our creation, of the Son and our redemption, and of the Holy Spirit and our sanctification" (*Systematic Theology,* p. 424). Weber offers very helpful insights in pointing to the work of the Spirit as the continuation of Christ's work in his threefold office. Thus "the witness of Jesus Christ (the 'prophetic office') is attested by the Spirit, . . . the reconciliation Jesus has wrought for us (the 'priestly office') is made effective in us in the Spirit, . . . [and] Jesus Christ's royal kingship (the 'royal office of Christ') is realized in us in the Spirit" (*Foundations of Dogmatics,* Vol. II, p. 244).

III. 4. 1. 2. The Spirit before Pentecost

The long road leading to Pentecost, as charted in the Old Testament and the Gospels, is lined with many interim signposts pointing the way. They carry some highly paradoxical, even dialectical, markings, however. On the one hand, the coming of the Spirit is often viewed as an entirely new future event. Attending a feast in Jerusalem, for example, Jesus compares faith in him to "rivers of living water" flowing from the heart of believers. The gospel writer takes this promised outpouring and refers it to the Spirit "which those who believed in him were to receive; for as yet the Spirit had not been given, because Jesus was not yet glorified" (John 7:39). At his ascension Jesus instructed the apostles to remain in Jerusalem "to wait for the promise of the Father," since "before many days you shall be baptized with the Holy Spirit" (Acts 1:5). On the other hand, the New Testament also presupposes clearly the presence and activity of the Spirit during the era of the older covenant. At his stoning

Stephen forces a crisis by charging his audience with joining their fore-bears in always resisting the Spirit. "As your fathers did, so do you." For "which of the prophets did not your fathers persecute?" (Acts 7:51). Looking back to these prophets, Peter says, "They inquired what person or time was indicated by the Spirit of Christ within them when predicting the sufferings of Christ and the subsequent glory" (1 Peter 1:11). Re-flecting on their writings, he says, "No prophecy ever came by the impulse of men, but men moved by the Holy Spirit spoke from God" (2 Peter 1:21).

Clearly, then, the Spirit was at work in Old Testament prophecy. But Scripture opens up still larger, even cosmic vistas. In the beginning we find the Spirit hovering over creation in the making (Genesis 1:2). In passing judgment on Noah's generation God says, "My Spirit will not contend with men forever" (Genesis 6:3, NIV). Confronted with the inescapable divine presence, the Psalmist presses the question, "Whither shall I go from thy Spirit?" (Psalm 139:7). Every creature is dependent on the life-infusing power of the Spirit (Psalm 104:30). Thus Louis Berkhof concludes rightly that "it is evident from the Old Testament that the origin of life, its maintenance, and its development depend on the operation of the Holy Spirit" (*Systematic Theology,* p. 425). Moreover, the Spirit endows certain people with special culture-enriching skills (Exodus 31:1-5; 35:30–36:1). He also qualifies certain people for leader-ship tasks and offices: Joshua (Numbers 27:18), Samson (Judges 15:14), Saul (1 Samuel 10:6), and David (1 Samuel 16:13). These references to the presence and activity of the Spirit are indeed still vague and ambigu-ous, reflecting the shadowy cast of the Old Testament phase in redemp-tion history. But there is a growing clarity, especially in the prophets, as confirmed by the New Testament appeal to their writings.

As with the covenant and kingdom ideas, and no less with the Messianic predictions, so, too, with these earlier activities of the Spirit. They also bear both an "already" and a "not yet" character. They, too, participate in an overall eschatologically directed movement. Pentecost therefore stands in continuity with the past. At the same time it bursts on the scene with a dramatic newness. Many Christian thinkers have struggled to clarify this paradoxical tension — usually with unsatisfying results. The Old Testament, according to Kuyper, reveals "the work of the Holy Spirit upon individuals," whereas after Pentecost it "consists in the extending of his operation to a company of men organically united" (*The Work of the Holy Spirit,* p. 120). With Pentecost "the Christian community was in principle liberated from Israel's existence as a nation," says Bavinck, "from the priests and the law, from the temple and the altar; as the new people of God it took the place of the Israel of old and stood on its own as an independent religious community" (*Gerefor-*

meerde Dogmatiek, Vol. IV, pp. 262-63). Hendrikus Berkhof sees the contrast in "the fact that the covenant, though present [in the Old Testament], was present more in offices and structures than in the hearts and lives of men" (*Christian Faith,* p. 321).

More helpful is the analysis of Harry Boer. "In the O.T. and in the gospels," he says, "the Spirit is treated as one who already is and as one who is yet to come. . . . The difference is one of presence in principle and of coming in full realization." Just as "the basis for the outpouring and work of the Spirit in the New Testament is the work of Christ in cross, resurrection, and ascension," he continues, so "the soteric operations of the Spirit in the Old Testament" are based on "the work of Christ." Thus

> the Spirit that was poured out at Pentecost worked under the old covenant, albeit differently, less clearly, less powerfully than under the new covenant. On the basis of the scriptural data we can only affirm *that* this happened, we cannot explain how this happened. . . . [Nevertheless,] we must conceive of the operations of the Spirit before Pentecost, then, as an arching backward, a retrocipation of the historical reality that did not exist until Pentecost.

This happened in a way appropriate to the Spirit's "retrospective activity." His involvement in "the redemptive process of the old dispensation" is comparable to "a moon that had no light of itself but received and reflected light from the sun that had not yet appeared on the horizon" (*Pentecost and the Missionary Witness of the Church,* pp. 67-77).

III. 4. 1. 3. The Rebirth of the Church

With the outpouring of the Spirit, the *qahal,* the consolidated people of God in the Old Testament, became the *ekklēsia,* the "called out" body of believers in the New Testament. This historical redemptive transition reflects both continuity and discontinuity with the past. At Pentecost the church was not born but reborn. An updating took place. The renewed humanity began to come of age. The story of the church as people of God reaches back, however, to the beginning, to the calling of that first human community to "walk with God in the cool of the day" and to be his stewards in the midst of creation. As a result of the fall we as God's imagers became "unchurched." In grace God then intervened to "re-church" fallen mankind through the believing line of Seth, Enoch, and Noah. With the call of Abraham the Israelite phase of the Old Testament church came into existence as a chosen people to prepare the way for the coming Messiah. Israel is therefore God's original olive tree. Though some of its branches are lost, the root is still alive. Into that root the New Testament church is grafted as a wild olive shoot, and from that root it draws its life (Romans 11:17-21). With Pentecost Gentiles now share in the riches of "the commonwealth of Israel." For Christ destroyed "the dividing wall of hostility" between Jews and others, thus creating "one new man in place of the two." All now have "access in one Spirit to the Father" and are jointly "members of the household of God," a "holy temple in the Lord." This grand reunion rests on foundations anchored in the joint witness of apostles and prophets (Ephesians 2:11-22). Stephen could therefore speak of Christ's presence in "the church in the wilderness" (Acts 7:38). That wilderness church drank from "the spiritual Rock . . . and the Rock was Christ" (1 Corinthians 10:4).

The movement from *qahal* toward *ekklēsia,* however, was not always, perhaps never, smooth and untroubled. Again and again Israel "stumbled." A "hardening has come upon part of Israel," says Paul. The faithful were once reduced to a mere "seven thousand." Not all who are "from Israel belong to Israel" (Romans 9–11). In fact, " 'Israel' shrank into a remnant; it became a normative and after that an eschatological concept" (Hendrikus Berkhof, *Christian Faith,* p. 339). At one low point, when Israel's outlook was utterly bleak, Ezekiel cries out, "Ah Lord GOD! wilt thou make a full end of the remnant of Israel?" (11:13). Christ himself adds these threatening words, "The kingdom of God will be taken away from you and given to a nation producing the fruits of it" (Matthew 21:43).

Only God's steadfast promise carried Israel through to the "fulness of the times," when at Pentecost the shadows made way for the reality. The Old Testament temple with its feasts, sacrifices, and rituals was fulfilled in Christ, so that now his body, the Christian community, has emerged in its place as "the temple of the living God" (2 Corinthians 6:16). Through the Pentecostal transition the altar was replaced with a pulpit, and priests with ministers, evangelists, elders, and deacons. There was a dramatic reshuffling of furniture as well as dramatic changes in life-style; but membership in the household of faith remained intact, open to Old Testament saints as well as New Testament believers. For

the lines runs through. . . . [Therefore] the church may not be separated from Israel. [For] there are not two sets of promises — one for Israel, the other for the church. . . . [There is] but one flock under one Shepherd, . . . one God and Father of all and in all, one Lord Jesus Christ rich over all who call upon him, one Spirit of that one Lord dwelling in all, one body of Christ, one kingdom of God, one people of God, gathered throughout the ages — the one holy, catholic, church. (Hoeksema, *Reformed Dogmatics,* pp. 588-95)

Even in our times the continuity between Israel and the church remains so strong that "in countries that leave no room for Israel to be herself (Hitler's Germany, Russia), the church does not have a chance to be herself either" (Hendrikus Berkhof, *Christian Faith*, p. 340).

III. 4. 2. *The Spirit's Abiding Presence*

To the nucleus of the early church, and through that inner circle of disciples to the church of all ages, Christ gave the promise that his Father would send "another Comforter, to be with you forever, even the Spirit of truth" (John 14:15). He added, moreover, that "when the Spirit of truth comes, he will guide you into all the truth" (John 16:13). These promises came true with Pentecost. The continuing work of the Spirit unites us to the Father. For "God sent the Spirit of his Son into our hearts, crying, 'Abba! Father!'" (Galatians 4:6). Through the bonding power of the same Spirit we are also united to Christ. For "by this we know that he abides in us, by the Spirit which he has given us" (1 John 3:24). By "the grace of the Lord Jesus Christ," therefore, "and the love of God, and the fellowship of the Holy Spirit" (2 Corinthians 13:14) the church is empowered to serve as a witness, model, and agent in the coming of the kingdom. The kingdom is cosmic in scope, embracing not only the church but our entire life together in God's world. Such global parameters also define the work of the Spirit.

III. 4. 2. 1. Movements of the Spirit in the World

The actions of the Spirit are like the movements of the wind — mysterious and sovereignly free. They cross the boundaries of both Israel and the church. The Spirit of the Lord enlisted the foreign ruler Cyrus as his anointed servant to rescue his chosen people from captivity (Isaiah 45:1-6). Throughout history, by his "general operations," the Holy Spirit

> restrains for the present the deteriorating and devastating influence of sin in the lives of men and of society, and enables men to maintain a certain order and decorum in their communal life, to do what is outwardly good and right in their relations to each other, and to develop the talents with which they were endowed at creation. (Louis Berkhof, *Systematic Theology*, p. 426)

Calvin, with his strong background in humanist studies, relates the work of the Spirit to the brilliant insights of ancient thinkers in science and art. "We ought not to forget those most excellent benefits of the divine Spirit," he says, "which He distributes to whomever He wills," not as self-adulatory privileges, but "for the common good of mankind." The Spirit does not act contrary to "nature" but in accord with it, unfolding its good potentials, even in a fallen world. For when God "fills, moves, and quickens all things by the power of the Spirit," he "does so according to the character that he bestowed upon each kind by the law of creation." Therefore "we cannot read the writings of the ancients on these subjects [of art and science] without great admiration" — that is, great admiration for what God's restraining and preserving grace through the work of the Spirit is able to accomplish even in pagan cultures "to preserve all that is." For "shall we count anything praiseworthy or noble without recognizing at the same time that it comes from God?" Yet, however impressive humanity's capacity for cultural grandeur, it remains "an unstable and transitory thing in God's sight, when a solid foundation of truth does not underlie it" (*Institutes,* II,2,14-16; II,3,3).

These universal gifts of the Spirit, often attributed to "common grace," do not cure the root problem of human sinfulness, but only temper its effects. When, then, some of his contemporaries made bolder claims, seeking to "Christianize" the ancients, Calvin raised his voice in protest. Responding to ideas advanced by Zwingli and especially Erasmus — *Sancte Socrates, ora pro nobis* ("Holy Socrates, pray for us") — Calvin sternly rebukes "the stupidity of those persons who open heaven to all the impious and unbelieving without the grace of him whom the Scripture commonly teaches to be the only door whereby we enter salvation" (*Institutes,* II,6,1; cf. footnote 8). Such universalizing tendencies, exceptional in Calvin's day, are commonplace in modern ecumenical circles. They are often encapsulated in the phrase "anonymous Christianity." Christians and non-Christians have much in common, so the argument goes. They can therefore make significant contributions to each other's faith-life. In such syncretist thinking we sense the lasting impact of the nineteenth-century schools of "comparative religion." Followers of the world's great religions, it is often argued, are all engaged in a common quest for God/god/the good. There is, as it were, a single holy mountain, and all earnest seekers are climbing it — from different angles, to be sure, some further along toward the top than others, some with an easier climb than others, some with better mountain gear than others. But all religious people are united in this common spiritual venture. Our Christian mission in the world is therefore not to call others away from their misguided quests and lead them to Mt. Zion, but to lend others a helping hand along the way in our joint pilgrimage.

In his intriguing book *Eternity in their Hearts,* Don Richardson marshals a host of case studies in support of his complementary thesis:

"a world prepared for the gospel" and "the gospel prepared for the world" (p. 213). Biblical religion, he holds, is uniquely true. Yet there are remarkable points of contact between Christianity and many non-Christian religions. While "shunning all alliance with the Sodom factor," uncritical syncretism, Richardson holds that "as Jahweh's special revelation — the Abraham factor — has continued to reach out into the world through both the Old and New Testament eras, it has continually found that Jahweh's general revelation — the Melchizedek factor — is already on the scene, bringing out the bread, the wine, and the blessing of welcome" (p. 32).

In reflecting on this issue, the distinction between structure and direction offers a helpful tool for critical analysis. Since every societal issue is at bottom a human issue, and since all human life is religion; since, moreover, all men are "incurably religious" (Calvin), possessed of a "universal religious consciousness" (J. H. Bavinck), it should therefore not surprise us to discover certain structural, functional similarities among the world's religious communities. All people worship at some altar, all cling to "myths" about beginnings, an original "golden age," the intrusion of evil into the world, and a way of escape to a better life, together with cultic practices to restore peace of mind and harmony in society. Yet, considering the direction and orientation of life, religious antithesis is no less real. The distinction between "common" and "special" grace is a conventional way of accounting for these structural and functional commonalities, on the one hand, and the equally real conflict of spirits on the other. Are there then "two different kinds of grace"? But then we are burdened once again by the dualist mind-set of scholastic theology.

A better approach is to follow the biblical pointers to the single grace of the one God who through his Spirit works preservingly, restrainingly in the unbelieving world and redeemingly where the gospel is embraced. In the words of J. H. Bavinck, "whenever we consider non-Christian religions carefully, we are soon confronted by a host of striking analogies among them." Contrary to first impressions, there is "a uniformity and interrelatedness among them. There appears to be a kind of universal consciousness of the divine, which remains intact despite all differences in race, time, and climate." From this we should not conclude, however, that "all these religions arose from a normal and natural religion." Such a common original religion does not exist, "only a universal religious sense which spontaneously produces all these analogies." For "all these religions, however noble and seemingly perfect, are distorted by sin." At bottom they remain "a flight from God" (*De Boodschap van Christus en de Niet-Christelijke Religies*, p. 26). Yet, when a Christian

426

"comes into contact with a non-Christian and speaks to him about the gospel, he can be sure that God has concerned himself with this person long before" (J. H. Bavinck, *The Church between Temple and Mosque,* p. 126). The possibility of a fruitful encounter growing out of this "point of contact" appears, however, to be increasingly dubious in our rapidly secularizing modern neopagan societies. Our only certainty lies in this, that

> God was concerning himself with these ["others"] before we came to them. We do not open the discussion, but need only to make it clear that the God who has already revealed his eternal power and Godhead to them now addresses them in a new way, through our words. It is always God who takes the initiative. (J. H. Bavinck, *The Impact of Christianity on the Non-Christian World,* p. 109)

III. 4. 2. 2. The Spirit's Activity in the Church

All the sections which follow elaborate this theme. At this point we shall restrict our discussion to a single current issue. The New Testament speaks of both the "fruits of the Spirit" and the "gifts of the Spirit." What is the relationship between them? The resurgence of Pentecostal movements in our day has forced the church to face up to this question. Many charismatic Christians advocate a stereotyped two-stage spiritual experience. What unites all Christians, they say, is their repudiation of the "works of the flesh" (fifteen listed, Galatians 5:19-21) and their demonstration of the "fruits of the Spirit" (nine listed, Galatians 5:22-23). In addition, however, some Christians, "filled with the Spirit," experience a "second blessing." Through this "baptism of the Spirit" such believers receive the special gifts *(charismata)* of the Spirit. These represent a more advanced stage in spiritual maturity. Ranking high among the extraordinary gifts are speaking in tongues, prophecy, and healing.

In the New Testament we find a listing of many gifts (Romans 12:6-8; 1 Corinthians 12:8-10, 28; Ephesians 4:11; 1 Peter 4:10-11 — a total of about twenty). There is apparently no fixed catalog. Rather, the Spirit bestows his gifts abundantly in keeping with the needs of various times and places. The only basic distinction is between the gift of the Spirit and his many differentiated gifts variously bestowed. As Richard Gaffin puts it, "All believers without exception share in the [singular] gift of the Spirit. . . . The gifts [plural] are workings of the Spirit variously distributed within the church." The "special gifts," among them prophecy and tongues, are "provisional and sub-eschatological" (1 Corinthians

13:8-9). Once mastered by the Spirit, we receive his works and fruits —
faith, hope, and love. They are more enduring. They have an "eschatological 'reach'" ("Life in the Spirit," in *The Holy Spirit: Renewing and
Empowering Presence,* p. 53).

In seeking to "help overcome the problems of the nature-grace
scheme in connection with the charismata," Jan Veenhof addresses the
question: "How is the charismatic work of the Holy Spirit related to our
humanity. . . ?" On his view, "grace adds nothing to human nature, but
instead restores the covenant relation which is disturbed and disrupted
by sin." Citing the refreshing exegesis of Jan Versteeg with approval,
Veenhof holds that "the ability to be helpful and to administer are for
Paul just as charismatic as, for example, glossolalia." We must therefore
abandon "a miraculous conception of the charismata." For "God does
not use certain gifts because they are so special; rather . . . they are
'special' because God uses them." They are means, not ends ("Charismata
— Supernatural or Natural?," in *The Holy Spirit: Renewing and Empowering Presence,* pp. 83-90).

Since the Holy Spirit is given to all who believe, the body of believers
as a whole shares in Spirit-baptism (1 Corinthians 12:12-13) and thus
in both his fruits and his gifts. For "no believer exists who has not been
baptized in the Holy Spirit. All believers have entered the new age, and
the sign and reality of that new age is the Holy Spirit," whose gifts are
bestowed "for the enrichment and the empowering of the body of
Christ." This demonstration of the Spirit's presence belongs not just to
individual believers here and now, but to "the people of God of all ages,
and it comes to us only as members of the body of Christ" (David
Holwerda, *Neo-Pentecostalism Hits the Church,* pp. 13, 15, 36).

"Within the overall working of the Spirit," moreover, "the New
Testament distinguishes between the gift and the gifts of the Spirit. All
believers without exception share the gift of the Spirit by virtue of their
union with Christ, the life-giving Spirit, and their incorporation into the
Spirit-baptized body, the church." This Gaffin calls the principle of
"universal donation." At the same time, "the gifts (plural) of the Spirit
. . . are workings of the Spirit variously distributed within the church.
No one gift, in this sense, is intended for every believer." They are
bestowed on the principle of 'differential distribution'" ("Life in the
Spirit," in *The Holy Spirit: Renewing and Empowering Presence,* p. 53).

Reaffirming this point, Veenhof holds that "charismata [plural] are
concrete and particular manifestations of the single *charis,* grace, that is
given [to all believers] in Christ." The gifts of the Spirit therefore are not
suprahuman in the sense of radically new, previously unknown personal
powers, added to our human nature, rising over and beyond it. They
must rather be viewed in "the perspective of creation," endowments

rooted in "created reality" which are then "charged, . . . animated and enlivened by the Spirit to an unusual degree." For the Holy Spirit "manifests himself in and through our humanity" (J. Veenhof, "Charismata — Supernatural or Natural?", in *The Holy Spirit: Renewing and Empowering Presence,* pp. 75, 76, 80, 83).

The gift of prophecy is no exception. While in the life of the church "the prophetic office is pivotal, the lubricant on the pivot could be the recovery of the special gift of prophecy given to some." These two — gift and office — go hand in hand. Accordingly, "a community of prophets calls for the exercise of the special gift of prophecy," but conversely "the special gift of prophecy calls for a community of prophets" (George Vander Velde, "The Gift of Prophecy and the Prophetic Church," in *The Holy Spirit: Renewing and Empowering Presence,* pp. 95, 118).

III. 5. The Church as Institute

The Old Testament employs two quite interchangeable concepts to describe the people of God, each with only a slightly different shade of meaning. The one, *qahal,* denotes "to call." It represents the assembly of the children of Israel. The other word, *'edah,* from the root "to appoint," refers to Israelite society at large as represented in its officially appointed heads, whether as a gathered congregation or as a peoplehood engaged in their daily callings. In the Septuagint both are generally translated as "synagogue" (*synagōgē,* a "coming together"). In later Judaism, with the dispersion of the Jews following the exile, synagogues emerged as centers of worship, instruction, and social life in all sizeable Jewish communities. These developments in covenant history carry over into the Christian era, so that "the New Testament church is essentially one with the church of the old dispensation" (Louis Berkhof, *Systematic Theology,* p. 571). For to speak of the church as people of God in the New Testament

> was to assert an enduring solidarity with that Israel of whose story the Law and the Prophets provide the authoritative account. The early Christians did not date the beginning of God's people from Jesus' birth or ministry, from the Eucharistic feast or resurrection, or even from the descent of the Spirit at Pentecost, but from the covenant making activity of God in the times of Abraham and Moses. (Paul Minear, *Images of the Church in the New Testament,* pp. 70-71)

Thus the Hebrew tradition of a "gathered people" embodied in the concepts *qahal, 'edah,* and *synagōgē* comes to redemptively updated expression in the *ekklēsia,* the New Testament "church." This concept identifies those "called out" and knit together into the renewed people of God. This ecclesial community is founded on the witness of the prophets and apostles, reinstituted by Christ as its Head, and empowered by the Spirit. The church, therefore, "lives by the will of its Lord which essentially establishes it and determines its structure" (Weber, *Foundations of Dogmatics,* Vol. II, p. 513).

III. 5. 1. *"Church" and "church"*

In recent decades there is a growing awareness, not only in reformational circles, true to its own tradition, but also among Roman Catholics (cf. *The Documents of Vatican II,* "The Church," Ch. II: "The People of God," pp. 24-37), that being church means more than maintaining a societal institution. Christian life is not confined to participation in the ministries housed in a building on the corner with its pulpits and pews, its liturgies and collection plates. For basically the church is people, and secondarily structures. It is at bottom the people of God, the body of Christ-believers, in the full range of its multifaceted life relationships and vocations in the midst of God's world. Even if all the chapels, sanctuaries, and cathedrals on earth were destroyed, the church would still live on (Matthew 16:18). For the church is a renewed community "called out" of the world (John 15:19) with a view to being "sent forth" into the world (Matthew 10:16). Prompted by such biblical insights, Bavinck spoke of a "double conversion" — the Christian community is converted *"from* the world" of demonic powers and simultaneously converted "back *to* the world" of historical happenings as the appointed arena for Christian discipleship.

Being church therefore means more than "going to church" on Sunday. This recognition gives rise to the distinction between the church as institute (call it "church" with a small "c") and church as organism (call it "Church" with a big "C"). Though often resisted, some such distinction is inescapable. It is implicit already in the variously shaded meanings of *qahal* and *'edah* in the Old Testament. It is reflected much more explicitly and with greater profusion in the rich imagery used to describe the New Testament church (Minear, *Images of the Church in the New Testament,* pp. 268-69). The medieval era lost sight of this distinction, with long-lasting harmful consequences for the life of God's people. The cathedral was christened the "basilica" (from *basileia,* the New Testament word for "kingdom"). This nomenclature accords with the *corpus Christianum* notion of Western society, fostering an ecclesiasticizing of the entire life of the Christian community and impeding its growth in spiritual maturity. In the words of Ridderbos,

> In the tradition of Roman Catholic theology the church and the kingdom coincide: the church is the realm of Christ, and the Roman Catholic hierarchy is the means by which Christ exercises his dominion. The pope in that system is the vicar of Christ, in whom the kingdom of God on earth finds its highest representative. ("The Church and the Kingdom of God," *International Reformed Bulletin,* no. 27, October 1966, p. 8)

In the age of the Reformers the distinction between church as organism and church as institute, though never so worded, served nonetheless as a working principle of differentiation. This is evident from the sequence of ideas in Calvin's *Institutes.* Book Three focuses on "The Christian Life," the everyday life of the Church (big "C"). In Book Four Calvin discusses the church (small "c") with "its government, orders, . . . powers, . . . [and] sacraments." In the opening lines on "the necessity of the church" he says that since "we need outward helps to beget and increase faith within us, and advance it to its goal," God has added "the external means" of the church to "provide for our weakness" (IV, 1,1). This distinction reached its definitive formulation around the turn of this century in the works of Kuyper. According to him,

> the conception of the instituted church is much narrower than the church . . . when taken as the body of Christ, for [the latter] includes all the powers and workings that arise from re-creation. . . . The instituted church finds her province bounded by her offices, and these offices are limited to the ministry of the Word, the sacraments, benevolence, and church government. . . . All other expressions of the Christian life do not work by the organs of these special offices, but by the organs of the re-created natural life; the Christian family by the believing father and mother, Christian art by the believing artist, and Christian schools by the believing magister. . . . [Accordingly, personal faith-knowledge] has as its circle the life-sphere of the individual, [confessional knowledge] the sphere of the instituted church, and [scientific knowledge] the sphere of the church taken as an organism. (*Principles of Sacred Theology,* pp. 587-88, 590)

With the resurrection of Christ a dramatic shift took place in our weekly rhythm. The seventh-day sabbath, looking back on the week gone by, made way for the Lord's Day, opening the door to a new week. In view of this transition, Sunday is now directed toward Monday, and worship toward service. So also the ministries of the church as institute are subservient to the "worldly" life of the church as organism. These two aspects of church are "coordinate in a sense, and yet there is a certain subordination of the one to the other." For, as Louis Berkhof goes on to say, "the church as an institution or organization *(mater fidelium)* is a means to an end, and this end is found in the church as organism, the community of believers" *(Systematic Theology,* p. 567). Accenting this point, Hendrikus Berkhof holds that the "institution is the means to bring about a community of renewed people." He then adds that

> the word "means" does not say enough. The institution is the womb and the fertile soil out of which this community must constantly be born anew and grow up. This community is what the institution is about. . . . Thus the church has two faces: she is institute and community, fertile soil and plant, mother and family. And these two are not related in an artificial equilibrium, but so that the first is the foundation and root of the second and the second is the purpose and fruit of the first. *(Christian Faith,* pp. 392-93)

Resorting for a moment to popular metaphors, the institutional church is a recruitment station to enlist "soldiers of the cross," a training center, equipping God's people for wielding "the sword of the Spirit" in a life of Christian discipleship. It is, once again, a refueling, recharging station along that highway of life known as the Christian pilgrimage. In order to make progress pilgrims must drop in regularly at these service centers, lest they "run out of gas" and their spiritual batteries go dead. Those, however, who regard the institutional as a delightful oasis in the otherwise desolate wilderness of life, a spiritual retreat which holds them permanently in its spell, will fail to advance in the journey of Christian living. To change the analogy, such Christians are like a football team that forms a huddle, and keeps on huddling — reflecting, praying, meditating — without ever breaking the huddle, getting on the line, and running another play. Eventually time runs out, and they will be penalized for delay of the game.

The gatherings of the institutional church (small "c") therefore play a vitally important instrumental role in the life of the Church (big "C"). For the proclamation of the gospel, which is the heartbeat of worship, is meant to equip God's people for implementing the "liturgy of life" all over creation (cf. Romans 12:1, where the word *liturgeia* is used to describe our full-bodied, life-transforming task in the world). On Sunday, then, the Church goes to church, that is, to its place of worship. But where is the Church on Monday morning? It then goes to work, or to school, is on vacation, and so on. A sign mounted on a building along the highway captures the right idea: "The Church of Christ worships here." That church is truest to its calling which best prepares the Church for living the kingdom life in the midst of the world. For the intentions we have concerning our life in the world are not realized within the inner circle of the kingdom, the church, but are rather taken up in the wider circle of the kingdom, the world. Therefore, while the life of believers is indeed nourished and stimulated in and through the church, [our life in society] does not have an ecclesiastical but a "worldly" character.

The task of ecclesiastical officebearers is therefore to "make the [Church] come of age in the world. . . . Hence believers must be prompted from out of the church, be made awake, be instructed with respect to their task in the world" (Ridderbos, "The Kingdom of God and Our Life in the World," *International Reformed Bulletin,* no. 28, January 1967, p. 11).

III. 5. 2. The Church as "Mother of Believers"

Calvin perpetuated the traditional imagery of the institutional ("visible") church as the "mother of believers." Among the early church fathers it was doubtless Cyprian who expressed most strongly the maternal role of the church in his classic statement: "He cannot have God for his Father who has not the Church for his Mother" (Henry Bettenson, *The Early Christian Fathers,* p. 265). Augustine upholds a similarly high view of the ("visible") church. His position is tempered, however, by his conflict with the purist claims of the Donatists, who promoted the idea of a church "without spot or blemish." Appealing to divine predestination, Augustine accordingly holds that "many who seem to be outside are within, [and] many who seem to be within are outside" (Bettenson, *The Later Christian Fathers,* p. 239). The idea of the mothering task of the church developed into a hardened dogma during the medieval era. Drawing on Cyprian's exclusivist thesis, high church theologians reasoned that just as destruction was inevitable "outside Noah's ark," so there is no salvation "outside the doors of the church." Thus the doctrine of *extra ecclesiam nulla salus* emerged: separation from the "mother church" leads to spiritual death.

Calvin, however, did not allow such ecclesiastical rigidity to rob him of a proper biblical idea of the church as the "mother of believers" (Galatians 4:26). Instead, he recast its meaning. The decisive consideration is not an authoritarian institution with its exclusivist claims, but the pedagogical role of the "visible" church in the life of the Christian community. Accommodating himself to our weakness, God instituted the church, says Calvin, so that we may "learn even from the simple title 'mother' how useful, indeed how necessary, it is that we should know her."

> For there is no other way to enter into life unless this mother conceive us in her womb, give us birth, nourish us at her breast, and lastly, unless she keep us under her care and guidance. . . . Our weakness does not allow us to be dismissed from her school until we have been pupils all our lives. Furthermore, away from her bosom one cannot hope for any forgiveness of sins or any salvation. (*Institutes,* IV,1,4)

Thus Calvin does not break with tradition but reforms it. This reforming insight made a strong impact on the young Kuyper. Reading the English novel *The Heir of Radcliffe* proved to be a crucial turning point in his life. There he caught the vision of an institutional church tenderly mothering her children. "O for such a church!" he responded. This moving experience lent additional impetus to his drive for reforming the church of his day.

The New Testament abounds in ecclesial word pictures. Among them, "the figure of upbuilding predominates," according to Ridderbos. This analogy of "the church as edifice" presupposes that "the New Testament church did not immediately reach its final goal and perfection." It remains "the abiding object of God's care" and is therefore "called to progress, extension, consolidation, in a word, to its own upbuilding." Running parallel to this image of the church as "temple" or "building" is a more "organic" concept — that of "the growth or increase of the church," of "planting," "watering," "cultivating," and "pruning" (*Paul: An Outline of His Theology,* pp. 429ff.).

As a societal institution the church takes its coexisting and proexisting place alongside other institutions within the community, such as home, school, political associations, labor organizations, the media, business establishments, and institutions for higher education — interacting in partnership with these other spheres of activity. To each belongs its own uniquely God-given task. Within this context the church as institute claims its own peculiar identity, integrity, and calling. To it belongs the official proclamation of the gospel. In faithfulness to this mandate it must open God's Word so clearly and convincingly that the people of God gathered in worship are moved to act obediently as a community of believers in the other areas of life. Every local congregation, in union with broader ecclesiastical assemblies, possesses its full share of all the ministries, fruits, and gifts of the Spirit. None is merely a subdivision which functions as part of a larger whole. Each is a full manifestation of "the one, holy, catholic, and apostolic church." Whether viewed metaphorically as "upbuilding" or as "growth," the church's calling is "extensive" (outreach) as well as "intensive" (edification). "There can scarcely be a question of any priority or preponderance in what is called the 'preserving' and the 'increasing' of the church," as Ridderbos puts it; "nor can one posit as a dilemma whether the nature and destiny of the church are situated in its missionary calling or in its inner consolidation. . . . [Together they lie] in its *pleroma,* in the extensive as well as the intensive sense of the word" (*Paul: An Outline of His Theology,* p. 435).

III. 5. 3. Ministries of the Church — in and for the World

Between the church as "communion of the saints" and the world which lives outside that fellowship stands the cross of Jesus Christ. That cross represents the great divide. For by it the world has been crucified to the church, and the church to the world (Galatians 6:14). But the cross is also the great unifier. For "God was in Christ reconciling the world to himself," entrusting to the Christian community this "ministry of reconciliation" (2 Corinthians 5:18-20).

This double impact of the cross thrusts the church into a dialectical tension in its stance toward the world. On the one hand, the antithesis is as painfully real as the conflict between the opposing kingdoms of light and darkness. Conformity is therefore a denial of the faith. On the other hand, the church is called to keep its doors and windows open to the world at its doorstep and at a distance. It must demonstrate its solidarity with and openness to those who still walk in darkness. It must actively promote the upbuilding and growth of its members as channels of blessing for carrying on its ministries in and for our neighbors near and far. For as a body of saved sinners we are not strangers to their predicament. Since we share in the common lot of all mankind, the mandate rests on us as "God's own people" to "declare the wonderful deeds of him who called [us] out of darkness into his marvelous light" (1 Peter 2:9). Having the "prophetic word made more sure," the church must pay attention to it "as to a lamp shining in a dark place" (2 Peter 1:19). With the world as its parish, the church in its varied ministries must be oriented to a compassionate and concerned engagement with those around us and with the structures of society which shape their lives for better and/or worse. Among these ministries Scripture highlights the following.

III. 5. 3. 1. Missions

Missions is one delightfully heavy mandate the Lord has entrusted to his church. The day of grace continues. The fields are still "white for harvest"

(John 4:35). Our field of labor is no longer just Jerusalem and Samaria, but the "ends of the earth." As doors open to the gospel, the church, in response to the mission mandate, must commission its qualified representatives to evangelize the world, both next door and in remote outposts. Increasingly our world is becoming a "global village." In its worldwide outreach the church may not fail to take full advantage of the appropriate technological advantages at its disposal in proclaiming the "good news," without, however, compromising the biblical message. For our methods must be in keeping with the apostolic message. With the enduring Word of life in heart and hand, the church must challenge that motley array of contemporary death-dealing idols which enslaves its adherents. In the name of Christ we must seek to cast out the demons of our times — superstition, indifference, the occult, greed, unbelief, oppression. We must work to hasten the day when that myriad of "-isms" which besets us and our fellowmen — humanism, secularism, selfism, hedonism, materialism, racism, nationalism, militarism — when all these "-isms" are reduced to "wasms." For a holist concern "in evangelizing people is not just to 'save souls,' but to restore the image of God to its proper functioning in all of life, to the greater glory of God" (Hoekema, *Created in God's Image,* p. 90).

III. 5. 3. 2. Intercession

A worshiping church must intercede for our world. Its liturgy must include prayers for the countless millions who have never learned to pray, who are "too busy" to pray, who have given up on prayer, whose prayers are wrongly addressed. It is called to pray on behalf of an unpraying world. For prayer is "the chief part" of Christian gratitude (Heidelberg Catechism, Q. & A. 116). In thankfulness for the blessings of creation, God's providential care, his salvation full and free, the church appeals to the "worldly" love of God (John 3:16). Since God has not turned his back on a broken and bleeding humanity, we have no right to do so either. Emboldened by the mediatorial work of Christ and the promised intercession of the Spirit, the church can approach the throne of grace as the voice of the voiceless, as prayer partner for those who have no advocate, pleading the cause of the poor and needy, of hurting and powerless peoples. There is so much that calls for fervent intercession: prayers for the advance of the gospel through word and deed, for peace and prosperity, freedom and justice for all, for an end to war and hostility and oppression, for tangible signs of the coming kingdom of righteousness, for the relief of persecuted Christians and non-Christians, for wisdom and self-effacing service on the part of social, economic, and political leaders whose decisions affect the lives of men and nations. Intercessory prayer by the church for the world is a matter of simple obedience to Paul's injunction, "I urge that supplications, prayers, intercessions, and thanksgivings be made for all men, for kings and all who are in high positions, that we may lead a quiet and peaceable life, godly and respectful in every way" (1 Timothy 2:1-2).

III. 5. 3. 3. Diaconal Service

The world as a whole is the open arena for the church's diaconal ministry *(diakonia)*. Though lending a helping hand to "the household of faith" is a first line of duty, yet over and beyond that, "as we have opportunity," we are to "do good to all men" (Galatians 6:10). For "faith by itself, if it has no works, is dead." The avenues of sanctified Christian service are paved with the cobblestones of justified and justifying works (James 2:14-26). Faith in action is a demonstration of whose we are and whom we seek to serve. In carrying out the church's diaconal ministry we are not to quibble over the questions, Who are our neighbors? Are they Jews or Samaritans? (Luke 10:25-37). The question is rather, To whom can we render neighborly service? Who needs the kind of disaster relief, health care, supplies of food and clothing, literacy programs, work skills, and agrarian reforms which the church is able to offer? This call to put biblical principles into practice by sharing with those in need the rich resources of God's creation is a rightful claim which others can bind on our hearts. It stems from the seeds of renewal planted by the Spirit within the bosom of the church. The harvest is not limited to church members, however. The world around us must also taste liberally of its fruit. Diaconal ministries are a witness to the longsuffering and lovingkindness of the God in whom we all live and move and have our being.

III. 5. 3. 4. Equipping the Saints

In support of its missionary, intercessory, and diaconal ministries, the church must faithfully carry on its proclamatory (kerygmatic) task in the life of its congregations. True to its ecumenical heritage ("one holy, catholic, and apostolic church"), and bearing honorably the marks of a true church ("pure preaching of the Word," "right administration of the sacraments," and "faithful exercise of discipline"), the church as institute must mobilize, equip, and train its members for their mission in and for the world. It must self-consciously and deliberately direct its ministries toward personal renewal, and thus also, through individual and communal efforts, toward the renewal of all our life relationships and the structures of society. As Klaas Runia puts it, its worship services are not to be

> a retreat from reality, but a rallying-point, a launching-pad, a spring-board which sends believers forth upon their way as "living letters known and read of all men." The . . . ministries of the church must shape and mold the Christian community to challenge the "principalities and powers" of this world as it carries out its reconciling mission in society. (Reformed Ecumenical Synod, *The Church and Its Social Calling*, pp. 21-24)

III. 5. 4. Contextualizing the Church

Where in the world is the church? Traditional answers to this question open up enormously wide and deep perspectives. In an unfolding series of converging distinctions the present reality of being church is set in a context as expansive as all creation, embracing both heaven and earth. The faith of the Christian community distinguishes, first, between the "church triumphant" and the "church militant." To the former belong those who now "rest from their labors, for their deeds follow them" (Revelation 14:13). Their warfare is over, the battle won. They now wave "palms of victory," having received from "the righteous Judge" the "crown of righteousness" which in the meantime still awaits all those "who have loved [Christ's] appearing" (2 Timothy 4:8). The "church militant" refers to the church within our world of experience, God's people called here and now to "fight the good fight," to "finish the course," and to "keep the faith" (2 Timothy 4:7).

Within the "church militant" a further distinction arises — that between the "visible" and "invisible" church. These interrelated concepts played a significant role in the sixteenth-century controversy between Rome and the Reformation. In resorting to this distinction the Reformers meant to say that there is more to the church than meets the naked eye, more than formal adherence to the visible, external, hierarchical structures of the medieval church. The meaning of church as people of God is not exhausted in such institutional visibility. It encompasses the "communion of the saints" wherever faith is present as "the conviction of things not seen" (Hebrews 11:1). The intention of the Reformers was not, however, to suggest that there are "two churches," nor "the desire to flee from visibility into invisibility, to a docetic, unearthly ecclesiology; it was to remind us of the church's essence as the congregation of the faithful in fellowship with Christ through the Spirit" (Berkouwer, *The Church*, p. 37).

This distinction served an understandably useful purpose in the religious struggles of that day. Yet it carries with it very ambiguous and even troublesome connotations (cf. Louis Berkhof, *Systematic Theology*, pp. 565-67). It smacks of the Platonic notion of an "ideal" church over against the "real" church, the superiority of spiritual over corporeal realities. Lutherans were inclined accordingly to view the "invisible" church as an ideal for which to strive, while Calvinists tended to view it as the body of the elect, the inner core of the church, its essence. This "visible/invisible" distinction was also employed to account for the church as a "mixed assembly," including hypocrites as "visible" members along with true believers. Sometimes these concepts simply slipped over into the distinction between the church as institute, viewed as "visible," and the church as organism, the body of believers in their daily lives, viewed as "invisible."

These persistent ambiguities therefore beg the question, Is this a valid distinction? And is it still helpful today? For, after all is said and done, it belongs to the very genius of the Christian church, both as institute and as organism, to "declare," that is, to verbally and visibly manifest "the wonderful deeds of him who called [us] out of darkness [invisibility] into his marvelous light [visibility]" (1 Peter 2:9). As Hendrikus Berkhof puts it, "an 'invisible' church is a contradiction in terms" (*Christian Faith*, p. 398). For the church "participates fully in the character of an earthly body, with all that this earthiness means. It is not an ideal, but a real, living, earthly community" (Fowler, *The Church and the Renewal of Society*, p. 16). As Hans Küng puts it, "The church is essentially a people and therefore visible. Precisely because it is a building in the Spirit it is truly a building and therefore visible" (*The Church*, p. 342).

Clinging to the idea of an "invisible" church easily fosters the seductive tendency to privatize the Christian religion. It downplays our calling to stand up and be openly counted as people of God in the public square. Some appeal to it, moreover, to minimize the importance of bringing healing to a badly broken church in a badly bleeding world. They argue that, though the Christian community is visibly rent asunder by countless schisms, this is not a serious problem. For this visible disunity is offset by our invisible oneness in Christ.

At its best this distinction between the church "visible" and "invisible" can serve to remind us of the difference between the church "as we see it" and "as God sees it." It can prompt us to recognize that, though the church is "*in* the world" and therefore "visible," it is not "*of* the world" — that is, it draws its life from an "invisible" source, the transcendent power of God's Word and Spirit. In this light, the church in all its historically concrete reality, as "the assembled, ordered, visible community, grounded on the Word addressed to it, may be certain that it is in truth the Community of Jesus Christ" (Weber, *Foundations of Dogmatics,* Vol. II, p. 547).

Moving along, we come now to the third set of distinctions relating to the biblical idea of church. In distinguishing between the church "triumphant" and "militant," our focus fell on the latter. Reflecting next on the church "militant," our thoughts converged on its "visible" character. Within the framework of the church "visible," conventional Christian wisdom distinguishes once again two aspects: the church as "organism" and as "institute." We are concentrating now on the latter. The church "triumphant" forms the deeper background and goal of the church as institute in its varied ministries. Its "invisible" dimension is also real. It is, however, the institutional church in its historically concrete "visible" reality, and within that setting its call to contend "militantly" for the faith, which is our present concern. We may think of it in terms of a concentric circle. The church as institute constitutes the inner circle of which the larger outer circle is the church as organism, the body of believers, called to daily kingdom living.

In Scripture the institutional church as worshiping community is illumined from several viewpoints. "The varying translations of *ekklesia,*" however, whether "as 'assembly', 'Community', or 'Church', are not to be regarded as in competition with each other, but as belonging together" (Weber, *Foundations of Dogmatics,* Vol. II, p. 531). Sometimes *ekklēsia* refers to a regional cluster of congregations (Galatians 1:2, 22), at other times to household gatherings (Romans 16:5; Colossians 4:15), but most generally to local congregations (Acts 8:1; 13:1; 1 Corinthians 1:2; 1 Thessalonians 1:1). When such a local church community "comes together at a specific time, it is a full manifestation of the 'Church'. The whole promise of the Word is given to it. Jesus Christ has given himself completely to it. It is called in its totality to witness in word and deed" (Weber, *Foundations of Dogmatics,* Vol. II, p. 532). Individualism is therefore a heresy. For the church is never an aggregate of individuals but an ecclesial body of persons who sustain a confessional relationship to each other. With all their ethnic, social, economic, and political differences, they are members of a body. This is what binds the church as institute together. At bottom believers belong to this community not by individual decision but by the magnetic power of divine election and calling.

III. 5. 5. The Attributes of the Church

From early in the Christian era, the words of the Apostles' Creed, "I believe one holy catholic [and apostolic] church," echo the settled conviction of Christians everywhere. These four attributes — *una, sancta, catholica,* and *apostolica* — were viewed as defining the church's very essence. Medieval thinkers appropriated them as exclusive properties of Rome as the one true church. As abiding, self-evidently present qualities, they served as static concepts accentuating the Mother Church's claim to an exclusive right of existence. These attributes inhere substantially in its very being and structures. This church is always and everywhere the single infallible and indefectible institution in human society. It is the sole source of salvation for all people. The Roman Catholic Church is therefore the one and only holy, catholic, and apostolic church.

Luther, Calvin, and the other Reformers openly challenged these pretentious claims. No church, they held, is self-authenticating. These four attributes are not automatic possessions of any church. A church's existence is never self-justifying. Every church which elevates itself above the judgment of God's Word thereby forfeits its status as a true church of Christ. With an appeal to Scripture the Reformers therefore introduced a new set of criteria by which to weigh the orthodoxy and orthopraxy of a church. These came to be known as the marks of a true church, namely, the "pure preaching of the Word" and the "right administration of the sacraments." By these marks the attributes of the church are to be judged. Thus a more dynamic approach emerged to the question of true and false churches. Only where these two marks of the church are faithfully observed can we speak of the one, holy, catholic, and apostolic church.

Rome resisted this testing process aimed at reforming the church. Its traditional theology did not allow for such a distinction between marks and attributes. The marks were viewed as so completely assimilated into the attributes that they cannot be employed as a standard by which to pass judgment on the Roman Catholic Church's exclusive claim to unity, holiness, catholicity, and apostolicity. For, as Bavinck puts it, according to Rome "it is precisely those attributes which are the index to a true church." Thus,

> the attributes must be conceived of as being so open to the senses, so tangible and external, that they apply only to the Roman Church. . . . Thus the first attribute, the unity of the church, means that the church has but one Lord, one faith, and one baptism; but according to Rome this comes to expression primarily in this, that the church instituted by Christ has a single head, the pope, and [therefore] can never recognize another church beside itself. The pope is thus the unique and definitive mark of the church. (*Gereformeerde Dogmatiek,* Vol. IV, pp. 304-5)

In response the Reformers raised the crucial question, What is the operative faith and actual practice of the church? With the marks as a biblical touchstone, every church must engage in critical self-examination to determine whether and to what extent the attributes are present as a vital force in its life. "The decisive point is this," according to Berkouwer, that "the church is and must remain subject to the authority of Christ, to the voice of its Lord. And in this subjection she is tested by Him." Therefore, "such concern for the marks of the church is and remains of decisive importance for the church as the Church of Jesus Christ" (*The Church*, pp. 15, 23). More on this later.

We turn now to a discussion of the attributes of the church. Both historically and theologically we have inherited a certain classic order in the development of these points of doctrine. We must remember, however, that "all [four] aspects are so closely connected that any priority [of the one over the other] is unthinkable" (Berkouwer, *The Church*, p. 25).

III. 5. 5. 1. Unity

"We are one in the Spirit. . . ." These lyrics cross the lips of Christians everywhere. Yet ecclesiastical reality speaks a different language: God's one church — our many churches. These are not two separate churches, the one "ideal," the other "real." For the only church we know is the concrete, historical community of believers here on earth — in Corinth and Rome during apostolic times, in Chicago and Toronto and London in our day. The church's oneness is certainly not a self-evident fact of life. We are struck rather by its all-too-obvious absence. Disunity among ecclesial bodies constitutes a crisis of major proportions in an age captivated by the ecumenical spirit. We sense keenly the tension-laden paradox: the brokenness of the Christian community, on the one hand, and the biblical affirmation of our oneness in Christ, on the other. This is the enigma of our sinful existence.

The closer we get to Christ, the closer we get to each other. This is a central biblical norm for church life, its antidote to a splintered Christianity. The unity of the church centers on Jesus Christ. As there is "one Lord," so we are called to "one faith, one baptism." The unity of the Christian community does not rest first of all in "the subjective states of the individuals who make it up," but in its Head, "the bearer of the unity within which the community lives" (Weber, *Foundations of Dogmatics*, Vol. II, pp. 553-54). For in Christ those who were "two" are made "one." He has broken down the barrier, "the dividing wall of hostility" (Ephesians 2:14). Whether Jew or Greek, therefore, whether slave or free, whether male or female, all now have full and open access to the riches of salvation. In Christ we are "all one" (Galatians 3:28).

But this oneness in the Lord must also come to expression in the world. For the church's unity is not only a gift of grace — "one body and one Spirit" — but also an urgent mandate — "called to one hope." The church must therefore be "eager to maintain the unity" which is presently alive and well and at the same time seek to recover lost ground. For unity is an imperative as well as an indicative. It is one of the articles of the Apostles' Creed, but of a different order than the others. For, as Calvin explains, we should say "I believe the church," not "*in* the church" (*Institutes,* IV,1,2). This oneness of the church is exclusively a fruit of divine initiative. It comes by grace alone, through faith. For "the community became community solely through the Gospel" (Weber, *Foundations of Dogmatics,* Vol. II, p. 554). Unity is therefore a very precious but at the same time a terribly vulnerable treasure.

Clearly, then, divisiveness and brokenness contradict what the church is meant to be. They are public declarations of our failure and guilt. A partisan spirit, "I am of Paul!" and "I belong to Apollos!", betrays a "fleshly" mind (1 Corinthians 3:1-4). Such dissension undercuts the church's credibility. Such polarizations defy Christ's high-priestly petition that "they may all be one, . . . so that the world may believe . . ." (John 17:21). Disrupted unity is therefore, as Berkouwer says, "a catastrophe for the world," even though "we are so accustomed to disunity that we are in danger of becoming immune to this warning" (*The Church,* p. 46). Calvin already argued strenuously that wherever the marks of the true church are authentically present no one may "desert it or break its unity." As long as a church "cherishes the true ministry of Word and sacraments, we may not abandon it, even if it otherwise swarms with many faults." For "the Lord esteems the communion of the church so highly that He counts as a traitor and apostate from Christianity anyone who arrogantly leaves any Christian society" (*Institutes,* IV,1,10, 12). All such fragmentation of the body of Christ must impel us to humble repentance, says Bavinck, for breaking the bond of unity is "sin against God, in conflict with the prayer of Christ, and caused by the darkness of our mind and the lack of love in our hearts" (*Gereformeerde Dogmatiek,* Vol. IV, p. 300).

Schism has but one source, says Louis Berkhof, "the influence of sin." It is due to "the darkening of the understanding, the power of error, or the stubbornness of man" (*Systematic Theology,* p. 573). All attempts to justify disunity are therefore contraband. This includes appealing to ecclesiastical "invisibility" as a way of escape into a docetic concept of the church. It is also wrong to elevate "pluriformity" to an attribute of the church, as though there were some "ideal" church which represents the "rainbow coalition" of many churches, each contributing its unique coloration to a larger whole, thus turning the vice of many competing churches into a virtue. Nor may we take refuge in the eschatological vision of a perfect church, resigning ourselves now to countless disruptions with the excuse that unity is assured "in the end." Biblical pointers to the hope of glory do indeed offer consolation amid our present trials. But, as Berkouwer puts it, "the eschatological outlook never weakens our concrete calling and evangelical admonition" to seek the peace of Jerusalem. Nor does it "leave room for any form of defeatism" (*The Church*, p. 36).

Unity does not imply uniformity. And it need not always lead to organizational unification. Where confessional unity prevails, church union is a legitimate goal, perhaps even an obligation. All attempts at unifying separated churches which are in accord with the biblical norms for genuine church unity must be motivated by a sense of spiritual strength, not weakness. There are, moreover, rich diversities within the human family, rooted in the creation order and unfolding under the providence of God, which merit a place of honor within the body of Christ without disrupting its unity — such as diversities in ethnic origin, locality, language, and culture. The redeeming work of Christ in and through the church does not wipe out such diversities, but sanctifies them by incorporating them into a more encompassing unity. When, for example, "a chorus of three hundred voices renders Handel's 'Messiah,' the whole choir is a unity. . . . The same is true of the church" (Hoeksema, *Reformed Dogmatics*, p. 605).

On the other side of the ledger, church history is punctuated with many painful reminders that, as a last resort, earnest efforts aimed at reforming a deformed church sometimes end in separation. Such action may not be undertaken, however, as an end in itself, but as the means to a better end: severing external ties for the sake of recovering true unity. When, for example, as Louis Berkhof says, "the Reformers broke with Rome, they did not deny the unity of the visible church, but maintained it" (*Systematic Theology*, p. 573). Well known is Calvin's stated willingness to cross seven seas if that would help to recover the lost unity of the church.

Reflecting on its pilgrimage, the church sings in a minor key, "by schisms rent asunder, by heresies distressed." But that is not the last word. For, as Bavinck reminds us, "What unites all true Christians is always more than what divides them." For though "there is no Christendom above or beneath differences in faith, there is a Christendom present even in these differences" (*Gereformeerde Dogmatiek*, Vol. IV, p. 305). Such is the mystery of Christ's all-sufficiency which preserves the church "in the unity of true faith" (Heidelberg Catechism, Q. & A. 54).

III. 5. 5. 2. Holiness

"One holy church" — these words from the Apostles' Creed sound utterly pretentious. Yet Paul and the other apostles regularly address the early Christian communities (even in Corinth!) as "saints" and as those "called to be saints." Echoing the epistles, the Apostles' Creed then adds this qualification, "the communion of the saints." Like the other attributes, therefore, holiness is both an affirmation and a challenge. As an article of faith, it, too, draws its credibility from the redeeming work of Christ. Covered by his righteousness, the church is reckoned holy before the tribunal of divine judgment. It is "sanctified in Christ" (1 Corinthians 1:2).

Holiness should not be understood as a display of super-piety. Saints are not a spiritually elite class of believers. Both saintliness and holiness are honest-to-God yet down-to-earth attributes of the church. Basically they mean dedication — the dedication of all life to the lordship of Jesus Christ. Holiness therefore calls for constant self-examination and mutual discipline. These elements must go hand in hand in the life of the church. For "discipline is not only directed to holiness, but also presupposes it." Together they summon Christians to a "testing not only of the lives of others, but also of one's own life" (Berkouwer, *The Church*, p. 377). In the measure that the church lives up to its confession of holiness it experiences freedom from the alien claims of other lordships. For "the community is 'holy,'" says Weber, "in that it does not belong to itself, but to God alone, and thus is free from any other intervention or claim" (*Foundations of Dogmatics*, Vol. II, p. 560). This radically liberating note resounds clearly in the Barmen Declaration:

> Jesus Christ, as He is attested to us in Holy Scripture, is the one Word of God, which we must listen to, whom we must trust and obey in life and in death. . . . Through him we experience joyous liberation from the godless bondages of this world unto the free and thankful service of all his creatures. We [therefore] reject the false doctrine according to which there are sectors of our life in which we need not have Jesus Christ, but other masters as our own. . . . (*Die Barmer Theologische Erklärung*, pp. 34-35)

Though ultimately the church's claim to holiness rests "in Christ," it must nonetheless, or better, it must therefore, bring it to public expression. The coming New Order will usher in undivided allegiance to the King, complete consecration of all things to him. Such holiness cannot be simply postponed to the Last Day, however. It is a gift of grace which even now defines the church's ongoing calling. In dedication to its calling, the institutional church must proclaim the Word of its Lord to the gathered congregation, so that the people of God may in turn bear witness to it in the world. Holiness involves the church's primary commitment to her Lord. ". . . This relationship is the inspirational source and the content as well as the standard for her directedness to the world." This order, moving from Christ to the world, may not be reversed. For

> if reflection on the church starts from her mission to the world, the danger is that [her attributes] are more or less taken for granted as postulates and as such are not really taken into account; while if reflection starts from the other end and takes its inception in God, Christ, and the covenant, we cannot stop there, but are inexorably sent on to the world. (Hendrikus Berkhof, *Christian Faith,* p. 414)

III. 5. 5. 3. Catholicity

Catholicity, too, is an imperative as well as indicative. The latter, the biblical affirmation of the church's wide horizons, is epitomized in Ephesians 1:23. There Paul speaks of the church as the body of Christ, "the fulness of him who fills all in all." Though throughout the New Testament the concept "catholic" is nowhere explicitly applied to the church, the idea of catholicity is embodied in the Pauline expression "fulness." The Father bestows on the church "power to comprehend with all the saints what is the breadth and length and height and depth" of the love of Christ, so that the church "may be filled with all the fulness of God" (Ephesians 3:18-19). Both gift and task are built into this attribute. As Berkouwer puts it, this "outlook on fullness overflows with promise and proclamation, prayer and admonition, and only in that framework can fullness be rightly understood" (*The Church,* p. 113).

Catholicity therefore implies mission. For the gospel of the kingdom is to be "preached throughout the whole world as a testimony to all nations" (Matthew 24:14). These global dimensions of the mission mandate are opened up clearly in the epilogue to Mark's gospel, where Jesus instructs his disciples, "Go into all the world and preach the gospel to the whole creation" (16:15).

> The key motif of [Paul's] missionary thought is the breakthrough of the proclamation of the gospel to all the nations (Rom. 1:16; 3:22ff.; 15:9ff.); with that the catholicity of the church has been given in principle (Gal. 3:28; Col. 3:11; I Cor. 12:13); there are no spatial boundaries set to the proclamation of the gospel and to the church; everything works toward the *pleroma,* the full number intended by God both of Jews and gentiles (Rom. 11:12, 25), a perspective with which for Paul also the end of history

coincides (Rom. 11:25, 26). (Ridderbos, *Paul: An Outline of his Theology,* p. 433)

The idea of catholicity therefore conjures up a big picture of the church's worldwide embrace, its international scope, its ecumenical outreach — in short, its universality. It crosses the fixed boundaries between peoples. It breaks through barriers of resistance. The church must seek a presence, lift its voice, and share its witness in every domain claimed by its Lord. For the Father has "put all things under his feet and has made him the head over all things for the church" (Ephesians 1:22). In principle this is "already" so. It is a present reality. But it remains an unfinished agenda. This "not yet" perspective points to its eschatological fulfillment, where John envisions "a great multitude which no man can number, from every nation, from all tribes and peoples and tongues, standing before the throne and before the Lamb" (Revelation 7:9). But now already "Christ is strictly catholic" (Hoeksema, *Reformed Dogmatics,* p. 608).

Catholicity implies the mutuality of Christian fellowship everywhere, reciprocal relations, and solidarity with all who belong to "the household of faith," in their cross-bearing as well as their crowning achievements. For "the expectations and needs of each community are fundamentally the concern of every other" (Weber, *Foundations of Dogmatics,* Vol. II, p. 561). A truly catholic church thrives not only on a sense of its present global vision, but also on its heritage handed down from the past. It confesses its faith in the God of Abraham, Isaac, and Jacob. It builds on the testimony of the prophets and apostles. It embraces in its living memory the church fathers, Augustine, Anselm, Luther, Calvin, and with them an enormous "cloud of witnesses." Sinking its foundations securely in this evangelical tradition, it flings its doors open wide to the present realities of our world far and near, and keeps its windows open to the future hope of a restored creation. Denominationalism is therefore a heresy. No church may absolutize its own existence. Catholicity banishes all parochialism and sectarian tendencies. As Küng puts it, "The catholicity of the church consists in the notion of entirety, based on identity and resulting in universality. From this it is clear that unity and catholicity go together; if a church is one, it must be universal; if it is universal, it must be one" (*The Church,* p. 392).

We see thus that catholicity and unity are closely related attributes of the church. Its unity implies catholicity viewed intensively, and catholicity implies unity viewed extensively. Accordingly, the church is "never bound to its spatial and temporal limitations. . . . Instead, the realm in which it thinks and acts is the world. . . . As the one church, the community as the community of Jesus Christ encompasses the world" (Weber,

Foundations of Dogmatics, Vol. II, p. 561). Helpful in illuminating the interrelated themes of unity and catholicity, viewed in both their intensive and extensive aspects, is the distinction between quantitative and qualitative catholicity. The former refers to scope; the latter is a depth concept. Throughout church history, and also in many ecumenical circles today, it appears that the quality of the church's catholicity has often been eclipsed by an inordinate concern with quantifiable results, with numbers and statistics, with the size and extent of a movement. To counteract this misplaced emphasis, the qualitative/quantitative distinction can serve a good purpose, since it "fixes our eyes upon both the spatial extension and the depth of the salvation preached to all." It is useful in avoiding "a cult of numbers." True catholicity brings with it "a perception of depth that also seeks breadth — the ends of the earth — in an irreversible order of succession." For the church's

> universality is founded in God's love for the world; and then space, extension, and quantitative catholicity automatically become meaningful. [The latter are] in themselves only a formal schematic, and whoever formalizes or quantifies catholicity misses the depth of the actual mystery. Only the relatedness of quantitative extension to qualitative catholicity can protect the church from externally striving for power and unity. (Berkouwer, *The Church,* pp. 107-11)

Catholicity is the biblical answer to all dualist worldviews and life-styles. For, in the words of Bavinck, Christianity is not "a quantitative entity" which "hovers transcendently" above our life in the world, but a religious power which "enters immanently" into it. It is opposed to nothing creaturely, but "banishes only what is impure." The Christian religion proclaims "the joyful news of the renewal of all creatures." For in it "the gospel comes fully into its own, comes to true catholicity." "There is nothing that cannot and ought not to be evangelized. Not only the church, but also the home, school, society, and state are placed under the principles of Christianity . . ." (*Katholiciteit,* pp. 30, 32).

III. 5. 5. 4. Apostolicity

This attribute, though left unmentioned in the Apostles' Creed, may nevertheless be viewed as the silent presupposition undergirding the church's confession of its unity, holiness, and catholicity. It affirms the church's commitment to the apostolic witness of the New Testament. With it comes a long and deep perspective on centuries of church history. Apostolicity suggests the faithful preservation of an authentic Christian tradition. It points to a vital continuity with its origins, and along the way opposition to heresy and contending for "the faith once for all delivered to the saints" (Jude 3). In claiming its apostolic heritage the church is obliged to "hold firm to the sure Word as taught" from the beginning, steadfastly imparting "instruction in sound doctrine" (Titus 1:9). Appealing to personal experience, Paul admonishes his readers not to "go beyond what is written" (1 Corinthians 4:6). The church is warned not to "run ahead" of "the doctrine of Christ," but to "abide" in it, lest it break fellowship with God (2 John 9).

These exhortations clearly inject an element of restraint into the preaching, teaching, and pastoral ministries of the church. They do not exclude, however, "growing in the grace and knowledge" of the truth. The apostolic legacy is not a call to rigid conservatism, a static adherence to the past, theological stagnation, or romanticized attempts to replicate first-century piety. Respect for tradition ("that which is handed down") does not obstruct advance. It is, in fact, indispensable for making progress. A good building depends on firm foundations. Under the promised leading of the Spirit, deepening, enriching, and widening insights into the apostolic message are both legitimate and realizable goals, even delightfully heavy mandates. Yet, as Berkouwer says, growth "can only occur in holding true to what has been attained (Phil. 3:16), in abiding in the doctrine *(didache)* of Christ (2 John 9), and in not abandoning what was received" (*The Church,* p. 226). As custodian of the gospel the church must also unfold it ever more fully.

With lusty voice generations of Christians have marched to the tune, "Onward, then, ye people, join our happy throng. . . ." Another line of this hymn, "marching as to war," may jar the sensitivities of an age yearning for peace. Yet the standing invitation captured in the joyous lines above expresses the church's well-meant offer of salvation, yesterday, today, and tomorrow. This is the mission of the church, present and future. This mission remains linked unbreakably to its past, its normative origin in the mission of the apostles. For "apostolicity reaches back incontestably to this beginning, the beginning of the gospel of Jesus Christ (Mark 1:1)" (Berkouwer, *The Church,* pp. 225-26).

Such ongoing continuity with the past, shaping the present and the future, is not a docetic, ethereal concept which hovers abstractly in the rarefied atmosphere of theological discussions. It is a matter of down-to-earth historical reality. It is never detached from a succession of persons, movements, and institutions. It involves bodies of believers, churchmen, Christian thinkers, ecclesiastical agencies. Apostolicity may never be identified, however, with a given person or magisterial office, as in the Roman Catholic tradition. Rome absolutized the apostolic legacy by institutionalizing it in the Vatican and investing the papacy with supreme authority. It canonized as infallible truth the doctrine of "the primacy of Peter." Thus the Vicar of Rome became the ultimate embodiment of apostolic succession. The Reformers broke with this highly personalized view. The apostolic continuity of the church rests not on "Peter" *(Petros)*, they held, but on the "rock" *(petra)* of his confession, "You are the Christ, the Son of the living God." On this confessional "rock," Christ declares, "I will build my church, and the gates of Hades shall not prevail against it" (Matthew 16:16-18). With this interpretation of Scripture the Reformers were not abandoning the doctrine of apostolic succession. They viewed it, instead, not as a continuing succession of episcopal persons, but as ongoing adherence to apostolic teaching. Donald Bloesch therefore concludes that

> the true apostolic succession is one of doctrine rather than ministry as such. It lies not in the office of the ministry but in the proclamation of the ministry, and this conception too has roots in the pre-Reformation tradition. Moltmann rightly declares: "The apostolic succession is, in fact and in truth, the evangelical succession, the continuing and unadulterated proclamation of the gospel of the risen Christ." (*Essentials of Evangelical Theology,* Vol. II, p. 279)

To this gospel a true church, its members, officers, and institutions, are called to pledge their hearty allegiance.

Speaking for the Reformers, Calvin says, "Nothing is given to Peter which was not also common to his colleagues." What, then, is "the difference between the apostles and their successors? . . ." Since the former were "sure and genuine scribes of the Holy Spirit," their writings are "oracles of God." But "the sole office of the others is to teach what is provided and sealed in the Holy Scriptures" (*Institutes,* IV,6,3; 8,9). For "no other word is to be held as the Word of God, and given place as such in the church, than what is contained in the Law and the Prophets, then in the writings of the apostles . . ." (*Institutes,* IV,8,8).

It is not enough to honor apostolic fidelity as a formal attribute of the church. It must function as a vital, dynamic force permeating all its ministries. Calvin emphasizes this point in saying that "the saints are gathered into the society of Jesus on the principle that whatever benefits God confers upon them, they should in turn share with one another" (*Institutes,* IV,1,3). For, "only in the context of the living church does [apostolicity] acquire its concrete meaning and significance" (Berkouwer, *The Church,* p. 276).

III. 5. 6. The Marks of a Church

The religious and ecclesiastical struggles of the sixteenth century gave birth to the doctrine of the marks of the church. In light of "the tragic necessity of the Reformation" (Jaroslav Pelikan, *The Riddle of Roman Catholicism,* pp. 45-57), a crisis made worse by widening rifts within Protestantism, a felt need arose for a standard by which to assess the faithfulness of coexisting ecclesial bodies. The Reformers endorsed the biblical norms of unity, holiness, catholicity, and apostolicity as attributes of a true church. Facing the unprecedented situation of a plurality of churches, the question then arose, How must these attributes be applied in concrete cases? How can it be determined whether and where they are actually present, alive and well? According to Berkouwer, therefore, the marks introduce "a new element into ecclesiology, . . . a different view of the church's reality, which sees her existence as inseparable from testing." Whatever a church claims to be or do, the marks serve to focus attention on "what actually happens in and with the church" (*The Church,* p. 15). Appealing to apostolic teaching, the Reformers developed the doctrine of the marks as the church's "means of grace." They are meant to function as biblical criteria for engaging in ecclesiastical self-examination, in order thus to assure the continuing relevance of the four classic attributes in the life of the church.

On this approach to church life the Reformers and their heirs demonstrate striking agreement. In defining which marks serve this purpose, however, a variety of viewpoints emerged. *Sola Scriptura* was a hallmark of the Reformation. True to this confession, the Reformers emphasized the centrality of God's Word and its faithful proclamation as the major mark of a true church. They charged their "mother church" with a persistent failure to proclaim fully and freely the gospel of justification by faith in response to the sovereign grace of God. They also called into question Rome's doctrine and practice of the sacraments, all seven, but especially the Mass. Out of this conflict the faithful administration of the sacraments arose as a second mark of the church. As is well known, clashes developed among the Reformers themselves concerning the meaning of the Lord's Supper, especially on the nature of Christ's presence in the bread and wine. Despite these sharp differences, however, a right administration of the sacraments, baptism and the eucharist, continued to serve as a second distinguishing mark of the church.

On the two major marks of the church, therefore, the Word and the sacraments, there was great unanimity. But is it possible to identify church discipline as a third mark of the church? Ambiguity surrounds this question. For Bullinger there are only two marks, Word and sacraments. This is basically Calvin's position as well, though at times church discipline also receives honorable mention. Ursinus grants full standing to this third mark. This is also the position of the Belgic Confession:

> The true church can be recognized if it has the following marks: the church engages in the pure preaching of the gospel; it makes use of the pure administration of the sacraments as Christ instituted them; it practices church discipline for correcting faults. (Article 29)

Generally, however, this third mark was viewed as an outgrowth of the two major marks, as a means of supporting and implementing faithful preaching and a right administration of the sacraments. Around the turn of this century Kuyper applied the principle of sphere sovereignty to this position. He held that official proclamation of the Word and administration of the sacraments were the two marks which apply uniquely and exclusively to the church. This does not hold true, he continued, for discipline. For every institution in society, not only the church but also the home, school, and state, exercises a form of discipline in keeping with its own task.

The Belgic Confession takes the question of the marks of a true church a step further. It includes not only the official exercise of the three marks but also faithful response on the part of the congregation. Accordingly, it identifies "the distinguishing marks of Christians" as "faith," "pursuing righteousness," "loving God and their neighbors," and a readiness to "crucify the flesh and its works." In this way the ministries of the church as institute must equip God's people to carry out their Christian callings in daily living.

Discussion concerning the number of the marks, whether two or more, should not obscure the fact that the reformational tradition recognized among the various aspects of church life a central point of concentration. Not all marks are of equal weight and consequence. The proclamation of the gospel is crucial to all the others. It is the fundamental touchstone for all doctrine and life. Even the Belgic Confession, with its threefold delineation of the marks, forges a unity among them in a summary statement: "In short, if all things are managed according to the pure Word of God." A similar concentration is evident in Bavinck. The power of God's Word, he holds, is not limited to its official proclamation by the church. Yet, by apostolic ordinance, this mark, verified in the sacraments, represents the official "means of grace." Since, however, the Word can stand apart from the sacraments, but not the reverse, "the first and foremost means of grace is the Word of God" (*Gereformeerde Dogmatiek,* Vol. IV, p. 427). Along the same line, Louis Berkhof says that gospel proclamation is "the most important mark of the church."

In fact, "strictly speaking, it may be said that the true preaching of the Word, and its recognition as the standard of doctrine and life, is the one mark of the church" (*Systematic Theology*, p. 577). Herman Hoeksema adds that

> the church is where Christ is, and Christ is where the Word is preached and maintained in all its purity. . . . The one all-important distinguishing mark of the true church is the pure preaching of the Word of God. Where the Word of God is preached and heard, there the church is present. Where that Word is not preached, there the church is not present. And where that Word is adulterated, the church must either repent or die. (*Reformed Dogmatics*, pp. 620-21).

Given the broadening horizons of our ecumenical age, concentration on only one or two marks has made way for more diffused understandings of the "marks" of the church. Hendrikus Berkhof, for example, arrives at "nine elements that are essential to the church as a transmission institute." He then proceeds to discuss as "institutional elements" the following: "instruction, baptism, sermon, discussion, Lord's Supper, diaconate, worship service, office, and church order" (*Christian Faith*, pp. 345ff.).

III. 5. 6. 1. The Sermon

Appealing to Calvin (*Institutes,* IV,2-4), Berkouwer affirms that "the mark of the church that is unmistakable is listening to the voice of the good Shepherd. Nothing else than that can correctly indicate the church" (*The Church,* p. 65). But listening implies preaching. As Paul says, "How are they to hear without a preacher?" For "faith comes from what is heard, and what is heard comes by the preaching of Christ" (Romans 10:14, 17). The apostles, as "ambassadors for Christ, God making his appeal through us" (2 Corinthians 5:20), were simply acting in obedience to their Lord's command, "Go into all the world and preach the gospel to the whole creation" (Mark 16:15). Thus impelled, Paul exhorts Timothy to "attend to the public reading of Scripture, to preaching, to teaching" (1 Timothy 4:13). Stressing this point, he adds, "Preach the word, be urgent in season and out of season . . ." (2 Timothy 4:2).

In our day as always the various ministries of the church stand or fall with faithful proclamation of the gospel. The confessions call boldly for "the pure preaching of the Word." What church, what preacher is equal to such "purity"! In the ministry of the Word, as in every other Christian calling, "even the holiest has but a small beginning of perfect obedience." Perfection eludes even the greatest pulpiteers. Yet, before God and his people, the sermon must always be appellable to the witness of the prophets and apostles. For "in the sermon the Spirit seeks to bridge the gap between the world of the prophets and apostles and our world" (Hendrikus Berkhof, *Christian Faith,* p. 357). Various discontinuities remain between the then and there and the here and now. Yet

> God's word addressed to Israel is [still] meaningful for the church today because recipients then as well as now are people of the same covenant of grace. In a very real sense we are the same people, created and redeemed by the same God, sharing the same faith, living in the same hope, seeking to demonstrate the same love. . . . Moreover, since the ultimate narrative of God's coming kingdom reaches beyond the Old Testament and beyond the New Testament into the future new creation, relating [a biblical] narrative to this ultimate narrative will link it directly to modern times, for the past as well as the present forms part of that one history. (Sidney Greidanus, *The Modern Preacher and the Ancient Text,* pp. 171, 215)

This perspective calls for the kind of earnest and lively exposition of a passage which opens the door to its meaningful implementation in the daily experience of the Christian community. The sermon as monologue is then no obstacle to true worship if it opens up arenas for ongoing applications in covenant living and kingdom service, coupled with an urgent call to participate in these ventures. At bottom preaching is a proclamation of God's abiding claim on us. As Bavinck puts it, "as disclosure of God's will" preaching "addresses all men and is of universal significance," serving "to arouse faith where it is lacking," but especially "to strengthen believers in the faith as they gather in worship" (*Gereformeerde Dogmatiek,* Vol. IV, p. 428). For God's Word, in all its various forms, is our life.

III. 5. 6. 2. The Sacraments

Word and sacraments go together. Detached from the Word, the sacraments become empty rituals. Rightly administered and received, they are a visible proclamation of the gospel. As "means of grace" mediated through the ministry of the church, they confirm in concrete forms the message of salvation centered in Jesus Christ. Calvin calls the sacraments "another aid to our faith related to the preaching of the gospel." God, as it were, goes a second and third mile with us, putting an end to all our contradictions and doubts through the tangible elements of water, bread, and wine. This leads Calvin to a "proper definition" of a sacrament as

454

an outward sign by which the Lord seals on our consciences the promises
of his good will toward us in order to sustain the weakness of our faith;
and we in turn attest our piety toward him in the presence of the Lord and
of his angels and before men. (*Institutes,* IV,14,1)

With this theology of the sacraments the Reformers were following
the lead of Augustine, who distinguished between the sacramental sign
and the redemptive reality represented by it. Thus in baptism and the
Lord's Supper we are blessed with "a visible form of an invisible grace."
These visible, tangible manifestations of God's condescending love are
not "new creations," but draw on realities and customs — the practice
of circumcision, sharing a common meal, cleansing by water, the nour-
ishing quality of bread and wine — which were commonplace in ancient
cultures. "Just as God made use of conventional practices among other
peoples in establishing the temple and its priesthood, the altar with its
sacrifices, and his laws and statutes in Israel," so, too, according to
Bavinck, the signs and seals of sacraments have a very earthy quality
about them (*Gereformeerde Dogmatiek,* Vol. IV, p. 474). They are accommodated very directly to our various ways of being human. In the
words of Berkouwer, "The sacramental approach to God . . . is deeply
rooted in man's religious and social psychology" (*The Sacraments,* p. 18).

In the unfolding plan of salvation the New Testament sacraments
are linked redemptively with their counterparts in the Old Testament.
Passover is fulfilled in the Lord's Supper, and circumcision in baptism.
Within the context of this covenant history there is, for the rest, "no
essential difference between the sacraments of the Old and those of the
New Testament" (Louis Berkhof, *Systematic Theology,* p. 619). Together
they belong to all of us as members of the single household of faith.

III. 5. 6. 3. Baptism

The water of baptism signifies and seals our initiation into the Christian
community. It opens the door to membership and eventually to full
participation in the life of God's people — at home, in church, at school,
and all the rest. "For by one Spirit we were all baptized into one body
— Jews or Greeks, slaves or free — and all were made to drink of the
one Spirit" (1 Corinthians 12:13). The signs and seals, therefore, "cannot
be detached from the power of God and the working of the Spirit"
(Berkouwer, *De Sacramenten,* p. 175). So from earliest times the church
baptized believers and their children in obedience to the Lord's commission to "go and make disciples of all nations, baptizing them in the name
of the Father and of the Son and of the Holy Spirit" (Matthew 28:19).

A deep appreciation of this sacrament springs from the unified witness of all Scripture. Its roots are sunk deeply in the full sweep of redemptive history. The practice of baptism is part and parcel of the biblical story line coming up out of the Old Testament and reaching its fulfillment in the New. In Israel circumcision served as the rite of entry into the covenant community. As the corporate personification of God's chosen people, our Lord himself was circumcised on the eighth day (Luke 2:21). In thus fulfilling the righteousness of the law, Christ was rounding out the Old and ushering in the New. Circumcision was being redemptively updated in baptism (Philippians 3:3; 1 Corinthians 7:19; Galatians 5:6; Colossians 2:11). This transition was heralded already by John the Baptizer, who came preparing the way for the Messiah by "preaching a baptism of repentance for the forgiveness of sins" (Luke 3:1-17; Mark 1:1-8). Water cleansings as purification rites were already observed in certain Jewish circles around the dawning of the New Testament era. But John's baptism had a more radical and sweeping once-for-all character, announcing that "the kingdom of God is at hand."

Following through on John's Word-and-sacrament mission, even in the face of John's objections, Jesus allowed himself to be plunged beneath the waters of the Jordan as a sacramental act of inauguration to launch his public ministry (Matthew 3:13-17). In fitting response the church now prays that Christ, "who went down into the Jordan and came up to receive the Spirit, who sank deep into death and was raised up Lord of life, will always keep us and our little ones in the grip of his hand" ("Service for Baptism"). The Jordan marks Jesus' decisive baptism — as our substitute. This baptism, though once for all, was nevertheless also a harbinger of yet another and even more decisively bitter "baptism" to come — the cross, followed by the empty tomb. Along the way Christ, "the great divider," issues the startling announcement as a prophecy of things to come, "I have a baptism to be baptized with; and how am I constrained until it is accomplished!" (Luke 12:49-53). In the end, therefore, baptismal water was the symbol, the blood of the cross the reality — thus paradoxically bringing about decisively the transition from circumcision (cleansing by blood) to baptism (cleansing by water).

This analogy is a basic theme running through the Scriptures. Think of Noah's flood. Water symbolizes judgment as well as cleansing. It is a sign and seal both of our descending into death and our rising to newness of life. This is clear from Paul's pointed question:

> Do you not know that all of us who have been baptized into Christ Jesus were baptized into his death? We were buried therefore with him by baptism into death, so that as Christ was raised from the dead by the glory of the Father, so we too might walk in newness of life. (Romans 6:3-4)

456

The final ground of baptism, then, is the cross and the resurrection (1 Peter 3:18-22). But its original ground lies in the order of creation. God created mankind in community. From the beginning our lives were set in a network of relationships which bind us together as families, friends, neighbors, and in the fellowship of worshiping communities. In his work of salvation God honors the structures of his original handiwork. Redemption is the restoration of creation to what it was and is intended to be. Re-creation "fits" creation. In Israel, therefore, circumcision was a family affair involving parents and children and members of the extended family. It had communal dimensions. This is evident, too, in the circumcision of Jesus, as also in the parental act of presenting him officially in the temple (Luke 2:21-40). In that liturgical setting Jesus was surrounded by Joseph and Mary, together with Simeon and Anna representing a faithful remnant of God's ancient people. Their anthems of praise, moreover, placed this rite of dedication within the larger context of "all peoples," "a light for revelation to the Gentiles," "the glory of thy people Israel," "the fall and rising of many in Israel," and "the redemption of Jerusalem." The sacrament of entry into the new humanity is not an individual act, but familial and communal. The appropriation of salvation in baptism is "the incorporation and entry into a solidaric relationship that is not first constituted by baptism, but is grounded in the antecedent good pleasure of God and forms the secret of the all-encompassing significance of Christ's death and resurrection" (Ridderbos, *Paul: An Outline of His Theology,* p. 410). The norm for baptism in the covenant community is therefore, "here are we, and the children you have given us." Thus the congregation as a whole shares in the joys of this festive commemoration and also commits itself to nurturing the younger generation in the life of faith. For "precisely along the [sacramental] pathway of [God's] promise and [our] responsibility we come to recognize that we can speak of God's unconditional assurance without minimizing in any way our covenantal calling" (Berkouwer, *De Sacramenten,* p. 207).

Luther emphasizes the idea of *regressus ad baptismum* — reaching back again and again to our baptism as the sure ground of God's promises and of hope for us and our children. Thus, according to Hendrikus Berkhof,

> it is not for nothing that the images of creation and birth have again and again been used for this washing. It does not express the fullness of the Christian's path of faith, but only the beginning, which is entirely from God and which consists in the salvation that is prepared for us and without us. But it is a beginning which we can never leave fully behind. All the time we must fall back on it as the ground, the center, and the source of

our whole life as believers. The water event at the beginning tells us that we live from a redemptive and creative act of God, from imputation and justification. (*Christian Faith*, p. 351)

III. 5. 6. 4. The Lord's Supper

The word "sacrament" does not appear in Scripture. It is derived from the Vulgate translation of the Greek word "mystery" *(mystērion)* as found in the New Testament. While this sacramental "mystery" applies to baptism as well as to the Lord's Supper, it is associated most closely with the latter. Our rapidly secularizing world with its commitment to a scientific worldview is not very hospitable to such mysterious realities. This is one very pressing aspect of our contemporary crisis of faith. It is all the more important, therefore, to keep clearly in mind that "remembering the death of Christ, until he comes again, is the most essential and urgent communion motif," and that "its significance increases in the measure that the meaning of Christ's suffering and death in our world are called into question" (Berkouwer, *De Sacramenten*, pp. 394-95).

The New Testament illumines the meaning of this sacramental meal with a rich variety of word pictures. Not only is it called "the Lord's Supper" (1 Corinthians 11:20), but also "the table of the Lord" (1 Corinthians 10:21), the eucharist (from "giving thanks," Matthew 26:27), "the breaking of bread" (Acts 20:7), and "the cup of blessing" (1 Corinthians 10:16). Together these metaphors hark back to the night of Jesus' betrayal. The three Synoptics all record what happened. Though these "gospel narratives are not alike in every detail, taken together they nevertheless point to a single important and decisive event, the institution of the Lord's Supper." This event is also recounted by Paul, accompanied by the call to self-examination and exhortations concerning worthy participation (1 Corinthians 11:23-34). "This is not an ordinary meal," but one that carries with it "a clear indication of the meaning of such eating and drinking, the meaning of these actions: . . . [namely] 'This is my blood of the new covenant, which is poured out for many for the forgiveness of sins'" (Berkouwer, *De Sacramenten*, p. 255).

The Upper Room gathering where this took place stands at the crossroads of the Old and the New, forms the link between them, and is the transition from the one to the other. In Bible times shared meals were treasured experiences. That is still true today. Mealtimes can be festive occasions, moments made for relaxing fellowship, earnest and happy communication, places where reconciliation, reunion, and recommitment can take place. There, in the circle of his disciples, Jesus converted this evening rendezvous into a meal to be remembered. The words he spoke echoed the language of the Old Testament. The Passover was being updated redemptively into an abiding Supper, looking backward to God's way with Israel and forward to "the marriage supper of the Lamb" (Revelation 19:9). Its centerpiece was the impending cross on a hill, crowned with a mutilated body and shed blood, all of which was being visibly and tangibly represented in the broken bread and poured out wine.

In addressing the early church, and through them also us, Paul can therefore affirm that the cup and the loaf bring us into fellowship *(koinōnia)* with the body and blood of Christ (1 Corinthians 10:16). The entire way of salvation reaches its crowded climax in that "Last Supper." It is the concentration point of our entire Christian pilgrimage. There we recall Christ's sacrifice in the light of his resurrection, while at the same time looking ahead with anticipation to the eschatological banquet, looking up in worship to our exalted Lord, and looking around us within the company of believers. "From now on," therefore, "the way of Christ's church goes from meal to meal" (Hendrikus Berkhof, *Christian Faith*, p. 363). Even Christ's parting words — "I shall not drink again of this fruit of the vine until that day when I drink it anew with you in my Father's kingdom" (Matthew 26:29) — these very words of farewell open wide the door to a continuing commemoration and celebration of this memorial Supper. For "the eschatological perspective imparts the character of a farewell to the last meal which Jesus had together with his disciples. And this fact should lead to our understanding of the permanent meaning of the Eucharist" (Ridderbos, *The Coming of the Kingdom*, p. 416).

The heated debates in Reformation times concerning the manner of Christ's presence in the elements of bread and wine seem strangely out of place in the life of the church today. In the ecumenical dialogues of our day attention has shifted to forging a greater sacramental consensus among the various branches in Western Christianity. Very few take the old traditional questions very seriously anymore. As Hendrikus Berkhof puts it, "The 'that' is infinitely more important than the 'how'." He therefore ventures the opinion that "the practice is going to be more important than the theology" (*Christian Faith*, p. 368). Still, today's doctrinal convergences are understandable only in terms of yesterday's differences. We must therefore take note briefly of these differences. The Roman Catholic view of Christ's presence in the sacrament is called "transubstantiation." Though the elements retain their accidental features of sight and touch and taste, the true essence *(substantia)* of the bread and wine is transformed into the real body and blood of Christ when blessed by the priest. Lutheran theology holds to "consubstantiation." This view is based on the belief that at his ascension Christ's body became everywhere present. Accordingly Lutherans have traditionally taught that his body is now sacramentally present in, under, and with the bread and the wine. The Calvinist tradition emphasizes the "real spiritual presence" of Christ — that "by his Word and Spirit He is never absent from us." Zwinglians viewed the Supper as a memorial feast which believers erect as a testimony to our faith. With their negative attitude toward "mundane elements," the Anabaptist movement often tended to downgrade the importance of the sacrament. That Christian communities should split over such points of theological dispute seems incongruous to the spirit of our times. Views on the Supper today appear to be drifting in the direction of being "softer" regarding Christ's presence among us at his Table. Roman Catholics speak of "trans-signification." Lutherans seem to be leaning toward a Calvinist position. Calvinists in turn seem to be downplaying the sacrament as a "means of grace" and accentuating its role as a memorial feast.

Calvin himself stressed the close connection between Word and sacrament in worship services. He therefore advocated very frequent celebration of the Lord's Supper. The pressures of the Geneva town council, however, forced him to compromise his position. Yet in all these developments the issue of "worthy" administration and "worthy" participation remained urgently relevant. For at bottom it poses the question of a radical antithesis. In the words of Berkouwer, "If anything is clear, then it is this, that our remembrance of the death of Christ can offer a clear and unambiguous witness to the world only when the boundary lines between the Lord's Supper and the many other 'signs' [of the anti-Christ] coincide with those between worthiness and unworthiness" (*De Sacramenten,* p. 394). Where the people of God live by faith,

> the Supper is the continuing proclamation of the redemptive significance of Christ's death; it is spiritual food and spiritual drink for the time between the times, as manna and water from the rock after the exodus and before the entrance into Canaan; in its constant repetition it spans life in the present world, until He comes. (Ridderbos, *Paul: An Outline of His Theology,* p. 425)

III. 5. 7. False and True Churches

Within the Reformation tradition the two marks, Word and sacraments, served as criteria for distinguishing true and false churches. The dawn of modernity, however, brought with it an increasing reluctance to apply these marks rigorously to sister churches. Generally Baptist communions were not excluded, despite their nonconforming practice of believers' baptism. Contrasting views on the commemoration of the Lord's Supper, moreover, were not regarded as sufficient grounds for banning other churches. This outlook on church life changed dramatically, however, during the nineteenth century. The widespread "free church" movements of that era led wave after wave of evangelical Christians to sever ties with established churches. The radical liberalism of these state churches evoked charges of being "false churches." The gospel was silenced in their pulpits. Humanist ideas shaped baptismal rites and participation in the Lord's Supper. Biblical religion was barely able to survive. Typical of these developments is what happened in Reformed circles in the province of Niedersachsen in western Germany. The liberalist mind-set of these dominant churches has been captured in these words:

> Man and reason occupied center-stage. All life was viewed as scientifically explainable. Miracle and mystery disappeared. Human virtue was proclaimed as the ultimate moral goal for citizens and pastors alike. Pious Christians found it impossible to survive on such a spiritual diet. It left them out in the cold and before long also outside the official church. (G. J. Beuker, *Umkehr und Erneuerung*, p. 57)

During our century these "free churches" achieved a settled place in their societies. Given the rather static theology of Protestant scholasticism, they often appealed to the "false church/true church" distinction to rank churches into permanent categories. Some were "true," others "false." Sometimes a sliding scale was applied: neighboring churches were classified as either more or less "true" or more or less "false." Each group tended to have its own rather clearly delineated orders of orthodoxy. All too often the place assigned to a given church was regarded as a fixed ranking.

Implicit and often explicit in such judgments is the conviction that one's own denomination stands as the "purist" manifestation of the body of Christ. The dangers inherent in this outlook are obvious. Wherever a church insists on its own right of existence or is inordinately concerned with its self-preservation, wherever institutional security prevails over confessional submission to the Word and sacraments, and wherever adherence to ecclesiastical structures and regulations takes precedence over the spiritual well-being and pastoral care of the congregations — there the threat of hierarchical tyranny and the binding of consciences rears its ugly head. Such a church loses sight of the reformational principle, *ecclesia reformata semper reformanda est* — "the church once reformed must be continually reforming."

A static view of "pure" and "false" churches contradicts the dynamic power of God's Word to break through in even highly resistant situations. The work of the Spirit cannot be bound. Like the wind he blows where he wills. As Luther puts it, the gospel is like a local shower: it moves freely from place to place. It can cross denominational boundaries. Wherever and whenever the gospel is faithfully proclaimed in Word and sacrament, there we find a "true church." For "apart from God's Word there is no church." But "where God's Word is rightly preached, there the sacraments are also faithfully administered" — and where this happens, there the church is truly present (Bavinck, *Gereformeerde Dogmatiek,* Vol. III, p. 339).

The marks of the church are therefore not permanent possessions. They can be lost and regained. Such changes can open and close gaps from congregation to congregation. Such "true/false" shifts can even take place within a given congregation from Sunday to Sunday. Returning from a worship service, we can say, "We really experienced church today!" or "It wasn't much like church today!" That church is truest to its calling where the preacher in the pulpit and the elders at the Table act as faithful ministers of God's Word, and thus as ministers to all God's ministers in the pew. A "true church" is one which equips God's people to fulfill their covenant vows and tend to their kingdom callings.

III. 5. 8. Church Leadership

Office is for leadership. To this end every association has its officebearers — home, school, the state, a business, bowling leagues, social clubs. In each case, the nature and purpose of the institution define the powers and tasks of its officers. The church is no exception. Every Christian community regulates its life by certain biblical and confessional norms which shape its expectations for those who hold special office in the church as institute. Within each Christian tradition the prevailing church order — whether episcopal, presbyterial, or independentist — shapes the context for defining the official mandates and ministries of the church. Let us look briefly at these two formative aspects of church life, its special offices and its governing orders.

III. 5. 8. 1. Special Offices

Already in Israel "church life" discloses a certain differentiation of responsibilities for nurturing the life of God's people. There we meet priests, Levites, elders of the people, prophets, and scribes. This principle of a division of labors comes to growing expression in the New Testament church. Christ is its supreme Lord. Through the outpouring of the Spirit he entrusted leadership in the early church to his chosen band of apostles. They were the living links between Christ the Head and the members of his body, the church. To meet emerging needs within the early church, the original apostolic office opened itself up into a cluster of more specialized offices — deacons, elders, and ministers. Their labors of love were in turn strengthened by the auxiliary services of evangelists, teachers, helpers, administrators, prophets, miracle workers, and interpreters (Ephesians 4:11; 1 Corinthians 12:27-30). Like a flowering bud in springtime, gradually unfurling its petals, so near the dawn of the Christian era the apostolic office branched out into a rich array of more specialized serving roles with differentiated callings. All Christians are gifted people. There are accordingly many avenues of service.

Reading through the Acts of the Apostles and the New Testament epistles, we observe special offices in the church springing up from their common root in the apostolic office as instituted by Christ. Those holding these offices therefore enjoy a basic parity in honor and authority. There is no hierarchy. Offices differ only in their assigned tasks, each having its own focused mandate. This fundamental unity of ecclesiastical offices predates the rebirth of the church in the New Testament. It even predates God's way with Israel. For, as with every office in the human community, ecclesiastical offices are rooted in the universal office of all mankind given in the beginning with the creation order. As the last Adam, Christ restored the fallen office of the first Adam and his posterity. Through the work of the Spirit he now restores his followers to rightful service in the general office of all believers through the exercise of the special offices.

In his mediatorial office Christ came not to be served, but to serve (Mark 10:42-45). So those who now hold special office in his name are also called to exercise their authority for the good of the congregation. They are "first among equals." The authority of the special offices therefore stands in the service of the universal office of all believers. Service and authority go hand in hand. Taken together, these two aspects, qualifying each other and functioning in tandem, define the meaning of ecclesiastical office. Only when officeholders are duly authorized are they able to render acceptable service. Thus endowed with serviceable authority, they are to "tend the flock of God that is under [their] charge, not by constraint but willingly, not for shameful gain but eagerly, not as domineering over those in [their] charge but being examples to the flock" (1 Peter 5:2-3).

In the church, as in other human agencies, there is indeed rank and order. No one may seize a leadership role, however, as a personal privilege or prerogative, nor as an inherent right. It is rather a vocational authority, delegated by the Lord, and conferred on qualified members of the congregation by the active involvement of fellow members. Servanthood in relationship is the key. For officeholders occupy an in-between position.

They are to serve "under" Christ while ruling "over" his people. Being responsible and accountable *for* the faith-life of the church, they are at the same time responsible and accountable *to* our common Lord. In pursuing this calling, officers are to play an enabling role in the church's mission — in its preaching and teaching ministries, in administering the sacraments, in promoting evangelism and missionary outreach, in diaconal service, pastoral care, and fellowship.

Being open to the directives of God's Word, demonstrating a loving solidarity with his people, and honoring the mature input of the congregation — these are marks of faithful officeholders. Alert to the needs of the day, they must echo the voice of the Good Shepherd. What "the church at the end of the twentieth century" (Schaeffer) needs most is not more and better public relations people, managerial experts, high-powered executives, or tycoons of televangelism, but self-effacing servants who speak and act humbly with a "Thus saith the Lord" ring of authority. Of deacons Calvin accordingly says that originally "it was not secular management that they were undertaking, but a spiritual function dedicated to God"; and of a bishop/elder, that his primary duties were "to feed his people with the Word of God, or to build up the church publicly and privately with sound doctrine" (*Institutes,* IV,4,4-5).

In extreme cases of waywardness, and as a last resort, this may call for stern measures. Discipline and even excommunication may be needed. But such steps must be taken in a spirit of mutual exhortation and with an eye to reconciliation (Matthew 18:15-20; 1 Corinthians 5:1-5). Serviceable authority excludes all selfish ambition or thirst for "worldly" power. "Greatness" and "first place" undergo a radical transformation within the Christian community (Mark 10:42-45). All partisanship and special pleading are contraband. For being "one in Christ Jesus," there is "neither Jew nor Greek, there is neither slave nor free, there is neither male nor female" (Galatians 3:28). Rather, taking to heart Paul's apostolic urging,

> Put on then, as God's chosen ones, holy and beloved, compassion, kindness, lowliness, meekness, and patience, forbearing one another and, if one has a complaint against another, forgiving each other; as the Lord has forgiven you, so you also must forgive. And above all these put on love, which binds everything together in perfect harmony. And let the peace of Christ rule in your hearts, to which indeed you were called in the one body. And be thankful. Let the word of Christ dwell in you richly, teach and admonish one another in all wisdom, and sing psalms and hymns and spiritual songs with thankfulness in your hearts to God. And whatever you do, in word or deed, do everything in the name of the Lord Jesus, giving thanks to God the Father through him. (Colossians 3:12-17)

III. 5. 8. 2. Church Order

The church in Corinth was Paul's problem child. In addressing the troubled situation in that congregation, Paul lays down the following abiding principle: "Let all things be done for edification; . . . for God is not a God of confusion but of peace; . . . [therefore] all things should be done decently and in order" (1 Corinthians 14:26, 33, 40). Commenting on this biblical injunction (as a theologian with a background in law), Calvin says that

> as no city or township can function without magistrate and polity, so the church of God . . . needs a spiritual polity. . . . This ought especially to be observed in churches, which are best sustained when all things are under a well-ordered constitution. . . . Therefore, if we wish to provide for the safety of the church, we must attend with all diligence to Paul's command that "all things be done decently and in order." (*Institutes*, IV,11,1; 10,27)

As we page through the New Testament writings we discover that they offer no fully developed theoretical model of church government. As Bavinck puts it, "Scripture is not a legal code-book, which goes into great detail, but leaves much to the freedom of the churches" (*Gereformeerde Dogmatiek,* Vol. IV, p. 370). We are not left wholly in the dark, however. There are a number of biblical pointers indicating that important decisions call for active participation by the body of believers under the supervision of the special offices. This pattern of cooperative interaction, from "below" as well as from "above," emerges clearly in the selection of the first deacons. "Brethren," so the apostles announced, "pick out from among you seven men of good repute, full of the Spirit and of wisdom, whom we may appoint to this duty." So seven were chosen. As deacons-elect they were then "set before the apostles," who "prayed and laid their hands upon them" (Acts 6:1-6). Though the body of believers plays an active role, Bavinck holds that "the communion of the saints is not autonomous," and therefore "its offices are not derivable from the congregation but from their institution by Christ" (*Gereformeerde Dogmatick,* Vol. IV, p. 369). Thus "the community can produce only the bearers of office, but not the office itself"; yet "all governance of the community is a matter of fraternal cooperation" (Weber, *Foundations of Dogmatics,* Vol. II, p. 570).

Concerning preferred forms of government, the force of Calvin's argument leads him to recognize certain structural similarities between state and church. Not that Scripture offers any theoretical prescriptions for either of these two spheres of life. Accordingly, "apart from circumstances," Calvin holds, "it is not easy to distinguish which one of them excels in usefulness, for they contend on such equal terms" (*Institutes*, IV,20,8). It is therefore not surprising to find a variety of church orders arising within Western Christianity. In Lutheran and Anglican lands nationally or regionally established models were created. Such coalitions involve serious compromises, Weber argues. For because the church has "its own responsibility," it can never rest content with being "the churchly side of city or state functions" (*Foundations of Dogmatics*, Vol. II, p. 581). These high church traditions developed episcopal, hierarchical structures. Meanwhile, in low church circles democratic practices set the tone for decision-making among loosely affiliated independent congregations. The former accentuate collective unity at the expense of local identity and clerical rule at the expense of congregational involvement, while the latter move in the very opposite direction. To avoid these extremes, Calvin appeals to "the Scriptural archetype" in opting for an alternate church polity. He seeks to balance grass-roots participation with the supervisory roles of duly ordained officeholders. While "pastors ought to preside over [ecclesiastical affairs] in order that the multitude may not go wrong . . . through disorder," decisions should nonetheless be taken "by the consent and approval of the people." Even of Paul and Titus he says that "they were over the rest only to give good and salutory advice to the people, not that they alone, in disregard of all the rest, might do as they pleased!" (*Institutes*, IV,3,15).

It is therefore arguable that a Reformed-Presbyterial church polity, which honors "the principle of representation" (Louis Berkhof, *Systematic Theology*, p. 591) with elected officeholders acting on behalf of the body as a whole, answers best to the biblical pattern of "fraternal cooperation." Bavinck holds accordingly that the presbyterial system, based on the ruling office of elders, "captures the thought of Scripture most purely and honors the rights of the congregation most vigorously." For Christ's lordship in the church is "neither democratic, nor monarchical, nor oligarchical, but [a combination of] aristocratic-presbyterial." By his Word and Spirit, he rules the church through "the prophetic, priestly, and kingly activities" of its officeholders (*Gereformeerde Dogmatiek*, Vol. IV, p. 371). Such a polity offers the strongest possible assurance that ecclesiastical gatherings shall abide by their prescribed mandate, conducting only churchly business, and that in a churchly way — in and by and for the church.

Calvin's views on state hold by analogy also for the church. The question of the best form of civil government "admits of no simple solution but requires deliberation," he says, since its outcome "depends largely upon circumstances." Yet "a system compounded of aristocracy and democracy far excels all others." He concedes, however, that in church as well as state, all three major forms of government are subject to gross abuse. For "the fall from kingdom to tyranny is easy; but it is not much more difficult to fall from the rule of the best men to the faction of a few; yet it is easiest of all to fall from popular rule to sedition." All in all, Calvin concludes that it is "safer and more bearable for a number to exercise government" (*Institutes*, IV,20,8).

The rather delicate balance inherent in a Reformed-Presbyterial form of church government makes it susceptible to a peculiar set of tensions. Some greet questionable practices with the cry, "synodocracy," "bureaucracy," and "boardism"! Others raise the countercharge, "independentism" and "congregationalism"! A healthy measure of "fraternal cooperation" is required to strike a happy balance between the rights and responsibilities of local congregations, which are fundamental to all church life, and the organic unity of the church as a whole as that comes to expression in its broader assemblies. There is, moreover, the ongoing question of maintaining a strong sense of ecclesiastical stability based on biblical and confessional norms while at the same time demonstrating creative adaptability in meeting the demands of changing situations and differing cultures. Advocates of a representative type of church order "assert that its fundamental principles are derived directly from Scripture," but are also "quite ready to admit that many of its particulars are determined by expediency and human wisdom" (Louis Berkhof, *Systematic Theology*, p. 581). Given these complexities, Hendrikus Berkhof concludes that "church orders — certainly in our times — should be loose-leaf!" (*Christian Faith*, p. 384).

III. 5. 9. Transition

From a discussion of the church as institute (small "c") we turn our attention now to the Church as organism (big "C"). To build a bridge from the one to the other, we note briefly three transitional aspects of church life. Together they open the doors and windows of the institutional church to the Church as people of God, as they seek to live their lives and demonstrate their discipleship in the midst of the world.

a) The church/Church as Witness

Everybody is somebody's witness. For human life is referential. It points beyond itself. This is no less true of communities. The ministries of the church and the Church's other callings must therefore offer ringing testimonies to God's way with Israel, his way in Christ, and the promptings of the Spirit along the way of salvation which shapes the future.

b) The church/Church as Model

For nurturing people in the Christian faith nothing plays a more formative role than modeling that faith in action. Christians must therefore cooperate in creating model communities in every sphere of life. Our world desperately needs to see concrete signs of an alternative life-style. Together we are called to recapture God's original intent for human relationships by modeling more authentically the renewed human solidarity which Christ called into existence, thus also modeling in eager anticipation that New Order of righteousness and peace which is our future hope of glory.

c) The church/Church as Agent

"He who believes in me will also do the works that I do," says our Lord, "and greater works shall he do . . ." (John 14:12). That is a benediction and mandate which we can never fully fathom. But this much at least is clear: Christ enlists us as his representatives, his agents, his emissaries in carrying on his work in the midst of his Father's world. If the world is to witness a model community in operation, it will have to be through agencies maintained by the people of God serving as salt, light, and leaven in society.

III. 6. The Church as Organism

"Is Christ divided?" (1 Corinthians 1:13). The clearly implied answer is "No." There is a single body of believers, not two. Nor is such a duality suggested by the distinction between "church" (as institute) and "Church" (as organism). Both concepts refer to the one people of God, but in two identifiably different modes of existence. Accordingly, the distinction "church/Church" reflects two ways of viewing the "family of God" — as a worshiping community with its various ministries, on the one hand, and, on the other hand, as Christ-believers engaged in their daily callings in the various nonecclesiastical spheres of life. Though these two points of view are never wholly distinct, they are nonetheless distinguishable. For in obedient response to the all-encompassing claims of God's Word, the "Church" demonstrates its discipleship in more ways than "going to church" on Sunday. Otherwise Christianity degenerates into "churchianity." These two aspects of Christian communal living are as closely related as Sunday is to Monday, as worship is to service. It is therefore the task of the "church" to equip the "Church" for daily kingdom living in the midst of the world.

III. 6. 1. *"In the World, but Not of It"*

This well-known adage summarizes well the place of the Christian community in a secular culture. Wrapped up in it, however, is an intriguing shift in the meaning of the concept "world." Christians are indeed not "of the world." They are "of Christ" and "in Christ," as Paul reminds us repeatedly (cf. Colossians 2:1-5). And they are clearly also "in the world." But what is meant by "world"? The New Testament writings betray some subtle nuances in the way they use this concept. Sometimes it indicates *how* we are to live, how we are to relate and not to relate to our environment. We are to shun "worldliness" and emphasize in its place the spiritual redirection and reorientation of our lives. But Scripture also defines *where* we are to take our stand — "in the world." This rather elusive interplay of words is woven into the fabric of Christ's high-priestly prayer as he anticipates his departure:

> "and now I am no more in the world, but they [the disciples] are in the world; . . . and the world has hated them because they are not of the world, even as I am not of the world. I do not pray that thou shouldst take them out of the world, . . . [for] as thou didst send me into the world, so I have sent them into the world." (John 17:9-19)

A similar ambivalent usage comes through in Bavinck's familiar call to conversion. Christians, he says, must experience a twofold conversion: they must first be converted "from the world" (in one sense), and then converted "to the world" (in another sense).

Across the pages of the New Testament we encounter again and again this skillful intermingling of ideas in the way the concept "world" functions (cf. 2 Corinthians 10:3-4). In each case its meaning must be gleaned from the context. It is of far-reaching importance to discern this shifting pattern of meanings. For at stake is a right understanding of the biblical worldview and the Christian way of life.

Searching the Scriptures, we discover that the concept "world" carries with it three basic connotations. Two of them are positive in their thrust. They refer to "world" as the structures of created reality and as the arenas of human relationships — the contexts and places where we are to make our presence felt. The third usage is strongly negative in its impact. It is couched in the language of stern warnings, alerting us to false religious drifts in our lives. Failure to weigh carefully these multiple meanings opens the door to very misleading responses to the principle, "in the world, but not of it." Reading a positive meaning into every usage of the concept "world" can lead to an enculturated Christianity. The opposite reading prompts fearful Christians to retreat from reality. Let us then survey the three basic meanings of "world."

a) In some passages "world" *(cosmos)* refers to God's created handiwork (Hebrews 11:3). Though fallen, this is still "our Father's world." In Christ he set out to restore his masterpiece. If, then, God has not turned his back on his creation, neither may we. In fact, every attempt to flee the world in this sense is tantamount to a death wish. It is therefore very misleading to sing along with that catchy gospel hymn: "This world is not my home, I'm just a-passin' through. . . ." For the time being at least, this world, and none other, is our God-appointed habitat. Of all people, Christians have every right to feel at home in this world of God's making — at home, but not at ease, for the challenges of earthkeeping and caretaking are enormous. Polluted air and water, depleted soil, the extinction of creatures great and small, assaults on the quality of human life, the spiraling potential for a global holocaust — for the sake of their Maker, these concerns demand a place of high priority on our Christian agendas. For after all is said and done, what kind of world do we wish to present to our Lord when he returns?

b) *Cosmos* can also refer to the world of people, the structures of society with their complex patterns of human behavior. It envisions the various crossroads of civilization, the marketplace, the halls of justice, the academies. Scripture presents a world-affirming, -judging, and -redeeming picture of this mingling mass of humanity. Think of John 3:16: "For God so loved the world that he gave his only Son, that whoever believes. . . ." Our Lord echoes this outlook in his mission mandate: "Go therefore [into this world] and make disciples of all nations . . ." (Matthew 28:19). For what good is salt stored on the shelf, or light hidden under a basket, or leaven kept by itself? In our world-penetrating strategies we aim at bringing the life-changing impact of the gospel to bear on the people who cross our paths. But who they are, what they do, and how they act and react are influenced strongly by the social, economic, and political context which surrounds them. These structures need the healing touch of the gospel as well.

The Christian community must therefore develop a creative and effective presence at those crucial crossroads of culture where momentous decisions are made which affect the lives of hundreds of thousands of people for better or for worse. We must act with a sense of urgency, "making the most of the times, because the days are evil" (Ephesians 5:16). Rocky marriages, broken homes, industrial strife, ethnic and racial tensions, social inequities, child abuse, abortion, political corruption — the list goes on. These pressing problems belong to that inescapable world which lies at our doorstep. To respond, "But I don't want to get involved," is unbecoming of Christians. For beyond personal witness, basic as that is to being Christian, are those large-scale challenges which call on the Christian community to join forces along various fronts. Admittedly, the gospel offers no quick and easy fixes. Christ is the Answer, but that decisive Answer must be worked out in concrete, contemporary ways. This is never easy. As Henry Zylstra says, in addressing our challenge in the field of education,

> It is hard work to be in the world, really in it, I mean, fully aware, that is, of the religious and prophetic tensions and pressures of it, the ultimate loyalties and allegiances of the various cultures in it, the religio-moral choices of men in the past that make the cultural challenge of the present what it is; I say, it is hard work to be in the world that way, and then not to be of it. Yet this proving or testing or trying of the spirits whether they be of God, this being in the world and yet not of it, this, precisely this, is almost the whole business of liberal education in our schools. (*Testament of Vision,* p. 146)

c) In sharp contrast to the first two senses of "world," understood as the structures of created reality and as societal relationships and functions, the third usage has a radically anti-Christian religious meaning. It refers to the demonic forces of the kingdom of darkness which invade the very existence of all creatures and every human relationship, misdirecting, distorting, and enslaving them, and thus bringing them under divine judgment. Paul warns repeatedly against these hostile "principalities" and "powers" (Romans 8:38; 1 Corinthians 15:24). Originally they were part of God's good creation in Christ (Colossians 1:16). But they turned against their Maker. Though Christ the Redeemer has now "disarmed" them and "triumphed" over them (Colossians 2:15), like diehards they continue to wreak havoc on our life in God's world. These "anti-Christs" (1 John 2:18) become incarnate in group actions, movements, and organizations which align themselves against God's reconciling work in Christ Jesus.

"World" in this sense is "a description of the totality of unredeemed life dominated by sin, . . . the powers of evil, misery, and death that hold sway in this world." In such strongly negative, antithetical forms

> Paul speaks repeatedly in summary fashion of the life-context before and outside of Christ and of the human mode of existence in that life-context . . . as a self-contained life-context [which] stands over against God and his kingdom, and can therefore appear in a personified sense as the singular subject of human sin and depravity: . . . indeed the "*pneuma* of the world" is even spoken of as a power determinative for all the thinking and doing of men, which places itself over against the Spirit who is of God (I Corinthians 2:12). (Ridderbos, *Paul: An Outline of His Theology,* pp. 91-92)

471

In passing judgment upon the sinfulness rampant in our world Scripture indicts all of us. Personally and collectively we are all responsible agents. But there are also alien "principalities" and "powers" which act on us. "In approaching the Pauline doctrine of sin," therefore, "we must not orient ourselves in the first place to the individual and personal, but to the redemptive-historical and collective points of view," since for Paul "sin is not in the first place an individual act or condition to be considered by itself, but rather a supra-individual mode of existence in which one shares, . . . and from which one can be redeemed only by being taken up into the new life-context revealed in Christ (Colossians 2:13)" (Ridderbos, *Paul: An Outline of His Theology,* pp. 91, 93).

Alerting his spiritual children to worldly seductions, the apostle writes:

> Do not love the world or the things in the world. If any one loves the world, love for the Father is not in him. For all that is in the world, the lust of the flesh and the lust of the eyes and the pride of life, is not of the Father but is of the world. And the world passes away, and the lust of it; but he who does the will of God abides for ever. (1 John 2:15-17)

Playing once again on the subtly nuanced meaning of "world," Paul reminds us that "though we live in the world, we are not carrying on a worldly war, for the weapons of our warfare are not worldly but have a divine power to destroy strongholds" (2 Corinthians 10:3-4). Facing the "world" in this evil sense, we can only pray as Christians in Germany did concerning Hitler, "O Lord, either convert him or take him away!"

III. 6. 2. Mission Unlimited

In the beginning already our Creator conferred on us a "mission unlimited." Traditional theology has a name for it: the "cultural mandate." It involves a cluster of God-given tasks, including marriage, family nurture, daily labor, governance, learning, and worship. By our willful disobedience we reneged on this original "great commission." The tortured history of Israel and the Gentile nations, but hardly less that of the church past and present, testifies to our persistent failure to live up to our Maker's expectations. In the fullness of the times God countered our broken covenant vows by sending his Son to live for us and among us, restoring the blessings of an obedient response. The gospel writers echo his call to renewal in the "commissions" which Jesus repeatedly issued during his earthly ministry. "If you love me," he said, "keep my commandments," "wash one another's feet," "be peacemakers," "hunger and thirst for righteousness," "be a neighbor to others," "work while it is day," "give unto Caesar what is his," "love your enemies." This sampling of the many Messianic mandates comes to concentrated expression in the closing episode of Matthew's gospel.

Addressing the inner circle of his disciples as the nucleus of the body of all future Christ-believers, Jesus draws on the many "commissions" revealed in the Old Testament as well as those recorded in the Gospels, and pulls them together into what has come to be called the "great commission."

> "All authority in heaven and on earth has been given to me, [Jesus said]. Go therefore and make disciples of all nations, baptizing them in the name of the Father and of the Son and of the Holy Spirit, teaching them to observe all that I have commanded you; and lo, I am with you always, to the close of the age." (Matthew 28:18-20)

In this parting message Christ takes the "great commission," enunciated by his Father at the dawn of creation, and restates it in the language of redemption for the New Testament era. As "the horizon widens," our Lord "speaks of his own unlimited authority (all power); He commits to [his disciples] an unlimited task (all nations); he assures them of an unlimited companionship (all the days)" (Ridderbos, *Matthew's Witness to Jesus Christ,* p. 94). Let us reflect briefly on these three points.

a) Unlimited authority. This cosmic claim answers the question of the highest court of appeal in the Christian community. Where is the authority center in life? The early disciples were compelled to resolve this issue. Is it Peter, the chief of the apostles? Or the synagogue, the pivotal point in Jewish society? Or the Sanhedrin, a Palestinian legal forum exercising a limited measure of self-rule within the empire? Or Pilate? Or Herod? Or Rome, the seat of the Caesars? The Reformers faced this question anew in their day. Who holds the scepter? The emperor? Or the pope? Or church councils? Or the traditions of the fathers? Christ breaks through all these and other false dilemmas, these worldly power struggles, these forms of misplaced trust when he declares, "All authority is mine!" He is Lord of lords and King of kings. His is "the kingdom, the power, and the glory forever." On the basis of this unlimited claim, he then issues . . .

b) An unlimited task — "go into all the world," "make disciples of all nations," "teach people to observe all that I have commanded." To his followers, therefore, Christ entrusts an "all"-embracing mandate. Its sweep includes the mission station but also the gas station. Our Lord does not call every fisherman to become a preacher like Peter, nor every tentmaker to become a missionary like Paul, nor every doctor to become an evangelist like Luke. Within the Christian community there is ample room for fishermen, tentmakers, and doctors — and for secretaries, artists, lawyers, farmers, machinists, merchants, and journalists as well. In the unforgettable words of Kuyper, "There is not a single square inch of the entire universe of which Christ the sovereign Lord of all does not say, 'This is mine!'" It is our obligation to honor this claim and to press it whenever and wherever possible. This calls for political discipleship, academic discipleship — in short, for all sorts of cultural discipleships. This constitutes a truly staggering agenda. In pursuing it, however, we are never alone. For Christ backs up this assignment of an unlimited task with his promise of . . .

c) An unlimited presence — "I am with you always, to the very end." As church and as Church we are fortified by the conviction that "with respect to his Godhead, majesty, grace, and Spirit, [Christ] is at no time absent from us" (Heidelberg Catechism, Q. & A. 47). This assurance is the might of a Christian minority in every generation.

III. 6. 3. Marks of Christian Communal Living

Being "of Christ" while living "in the world" clears the way for a "mission unlimited." Christian pilgrims can make progress in this venturesome undertaking, not by disavowing the world of God's creation and human culture, but by taking the refined "treasures of the nations" with them on their journey to "the city which has foundations." Such a way of life calls for "walking circumspectly," weighing the issues, "[testing] everything, [holding] fast what is good" (1 Thessalonians 5:21). The route we travel is not an uncharted course through a trackless wilderness. We take our bearings from the landmarks of creation. A large "cloud of witnesses" has gone before to show the way, with varying results. And Scripture offers indispensable guidance. It erects two clearly marked signposts along the way, pointing the direction of the coming kingdom. Around these two major reference points the Christian community must orient both its personal and the communal life. These two points are freedom and holiness.

III. 6. 3. 1. Christian Freedom

According to Calvin, "He who proposes to summarize gospel teaching ought by no means to omit an explanation of this topic." For "freedom is especially an appendage of justification": being justified not by works, but by faith alone, we experience the liberating power of the gospel. Christian liberty is therefore "a thing of prime necessity." For apart from it "consciences dare undertake almost nothing without doubting; . . . they constantly waver and are afraid" (*Institutes,* III,19,1). Calvin proceeds then to deal with three major aspects of the freedom we have in Christ: we are free *from* the well-deserved condemnation of the law, free *unto* willing compliance with the law, and free *in* "matters indifferent." Freedom is not, however, an impulse acting on its own. True freedom is integrated dynamically into the concentric-circle-like context of neighborly love and faith in God. For "as freedom must be subordinated to love, so in turn ought love to abide under the purity of faith" (*Institutes,* III,19,13).

Expanding on these thoughts, Ridderbos holds that "every consideration of the Christian life must find its point of departure" in this, that "the kingdom does not close the world to believers, but opens it." For "the earth is once again opened for believers through the coming of Christ and of his kingdom. Not only are all nations again involved in the salvation of the Lord, but the whole of life in all its dimensions as well" ("The Kingdom of God and Our Life in the World," p. 4). This redemptive reopenedness is the key to Christian freedom. Sin closed the world down. Christ's liberating mission opens it up. Christian communities can now bless their nations with life-renewing programs of kingdom service, sharing freely the healing power of the gospel with a broken and bleeding humanity.

Clearly, then, "the Christian life is the opposite of narrowness, limitation, and restrictedness." For it is defined by the perspectives of the kingdom, and "the kingdom is not narrow, but [as] broad" as creation. At the same time, however, this reopened freedom is "the opposite of licentiousness, autonomy, or neutrality (if the last indeed exists)" (Ridderbos, "The Kingdom of God and Our Life in the World," p. 7). Nonetheless, when motivated by faith and love, our Christian calling lies "in all that is created." This means that believers are "free in Christ to participate in all of life, to eat and drink, to marry, to buy and sell." It means also that "inherent in Christian liberty there is a Christian commission." Ridderbos then adds reflectively, "I am conscious of drawing the circles here very large indeed, but surely not larger than Scripture itself" ("The Kingdom of God and Our Life in the World," pp. 4-5). As Paul declares so boldly, the freedom of the body of believers is bounded only by the cosmic rule of Christ its Head. For "all things are yours, whether . . . the world, or life, or death, or things present, or things to come, all are yours; and you are Christ's; and Christ is God's" (1 Corinthians 3:22-23). Authentic freedom is christologically anchored. It is "a matter of faith, proceeding from the knowledge of the Lord Jesus."

By virtue of this knowledge we know that there is but one God and, whatever mention there may still be of "gods" and "lords," for the church there is but one God the Father and but one Lord Jesus Christ [1 Corinthians 8:1-13], and that there is therefore liberty to eat everything that is sold in the market-halls, for the earth is the Lord's, and the fullness thereof (I Corinthians 10:23-26). (Ridderbos, *Paul: An Outline of His Theology,* p. 302)

III. 6. 3. 2. Call to Holiness

It is important for the Christian community to be clear about the biblical meaning of holiness. We get off on the wrong foot if we allow the hymn, "Take time to be holy. . . ," to sing its way into our hearts and lives. We must, of course, take time to eat, to rest, to relax, to pray, to "go to church." But when it comes to holiness, like spirituality, we are on very different footing. It is utterly misleading to think we can "take time" to be holy or to be spiritual. For neither one is bound to time or place. Both are more than pious moods which may legitimately come and go. Spirituality raises the question of the driving force which moves and gives direction to our lives — is it the Holy Spirit or some unholy spirit? So holiness, too, is a basic quality of Christian living. It is holist in its thrust. Scripture points to it as a full-bodied reality, the all-pervading orientation which must mark the personal and communal life of the Church. Its fundamental meaning is "dedication." For "inseparably connected" with Christian freedom, and "just as central," is "the viewpoint of holiness, the submission of life to the lordship of Christ, the dedication of the whole of life to God" (Ridderbos, "The Kingdom of God and Our Life in the World," p. 6).

Just as with freedom, holiness too, like a two-edged sword, cuts both ways — negatively as well as positively. Already in Israel holiness called for separation from the profane things of the "world" so that the covenant people might be wholly dedicated to the Lord. Not only were the adornments of the priest to be engraved with the words, "Holy to the Lord" (Exodus 28:36-38), but the bells on the horses and every kitchen pot in Jerusalem, as symbols of the daily labors of God's people, were to bear the same inscription, "Holy to the Lord" (Zechariah 14:20-21).

The biblical call to holiness has a radically vertical, transcendent reference point. For "as he who called you is holy, be holy yourselves in all your conduct; since it is written, 'You shall be holy, for I am holy'" (1 Peter 1:15-16). As God opposes all that is evil and sides unalterably with the cause of righteousness, so his people are set apart wholeheartedly for a similar service. As Paul puts it, "present your bodies [our whole bodily existence] as a living sacrifice, holy and acceptable to God, which is your spiritual worship" (Romans 12:1). Then, as Ridderbos says,

> the commandments follow for life in the world (Romans 12, 13, 14). Here sacrifice and service — sanctification — are brought outside the temple. The new liturgy or service does not limit itself to Sunday or to the church in her own life. It consists rather in the daily, natural life of the members of the church: in marriage, but also in society, in their relationship toward the government, in intercourse with the neighbor who is not a Christian. ("The Kingdom of God and Our Life in the World," p. 6)

In every age, perhaps especially in our highly secularized times, the Christian community must resist the besetting sin of an accommodated Christianity — a sense of freedom unqualified by holiness. Such a compromise blurs the antithesis between two kingdoms in mortal conflict. Paul states the case bluntly, "Do not be mismatched with unbelievers."

> For what partnership have righteousness and iniquity? Or what fellowship has light with darkness? What accord has Christ with Belial? Or what has a believer in common with an unbeliever? What agreement has the temple of God with idols? For we are the temple of the living God. (2 Corinthians 7:14-16)

"Do not be mismatched," that is, "do not be unequally yoked." This metaphor suggests the idea of two different animals performing a common task; being so utterly unlike, they bear unequal yokes. This means, according to Ridderbos, that "because of this fundamentally different approach to life in believers and unbelievers, . . . [they] cannot form a team" (*Paul: An Outline of His Theology*, p. 305).

The answer to an enculturated freedom, however, is not a world-withdrawing brand of holiness. In the words of Ridderbos, "one sickness can never be healed by another" ("The Kingdom of God and Our Life in the World," p. 8). Yet this remains a difficult lesson to learn. For with monotonous regularity Christian communities tend to swing back and forth pendulum style between these opposing options, or they try to avoid this false dilemma by creating a dialectical middle ground between them. A biblically balanced view of freedom and holiness does indeed bring with it some very agonizing tensions (cf. Romans 14 on the "weaker brother"/"stronger brother" issue, and on "giving offense" and "taking offense"). Yet Scripture never pictures freedom and holiness as mutually exclusive. They are meant to go hand in hand. For an opened-up view of the world makes the practice of holiness viable, while a dedicated life-style keeps freedom authentically Christian. As the Church heeds the call to "practice Christian liberty and holiness in those areas of life where the great decisions are made for man and society," it comes to realize increasingly that there is "no longer any neutrality, . . . no longer a profane area in human life, of which one can say: here I am outside the sphere of influence of the kingdom" (Ridderbos, "The Kingdom of God and Our Life in the World," pp. 6, 10).

III. 6. 4. Church/church and Kingdom

The most central, all-embracing unifying theme running throughout the Scriptures is that of the coming kingdom. For "from every standpoint the kingdom of God retains its essential priority over the human community. Thought must therefore move essentially in one direction: from the kingdom of God to the heirs and sons of that kingdom" (Minear, *Images of the Church in the New Testament*, p. 124). Nothing matters but the kingdom, but because of the kingdom everything matters — especially the ministries of the church and the Church's daily living. Kingdom, Church, and church are not three separate realities. They are interdependent, but they stand in a certain unique relationship to each other. For in Scripture Church/church derives its meaning from kingdom, and not vice versa. It is possible to visualize this interrelatedness along the lines of the following unfolding concentric circle:

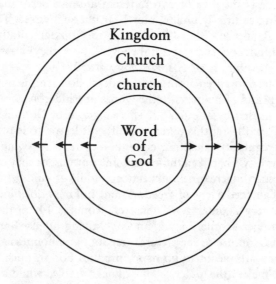

God's Word is the central dynamic for all life in the world. The ministries of the church as institute proclaim that Word within the fellowship of the worshiping community. The Church as the body of Christ is then called to translate that Word into concrete forms of Christian witness in every sphere of life. The goal of this ever widening outreach is the coming of the kingdom (note the unique combination of "waiting for and hastening the coming of the day of God . . ." in 2 Peter 3:12).

Thus, in the words of Bavinck, "the church is the means by which Christ distributes the benefits of the kingdom of God and prepares for its consummation" (*Gereformeerde Dogmatiek*, Vol. IV, p. 281). Christ is Lord of all, Head of the church and King of the Church. Thus, though "the kingship and the headship of Christ are inextricably bound up together," yet "the latter is subservient to the former." Willing kingdom citizenship is coextensive with membership in the Church. But the kingdom's "field of operation . . . is wider . . . since it aims at the control of life in all its manifestations. . . . It represents the dominion of God in every sphere of human endeavor" (Louis Berkhof, *Systematic Theology*, pp. 409-10, 570). According to Ridderbos, "the gospel does not contain any passage in which the word *basileia* is used in the sense of 'church.'" Yet "the idea of the *ekklesia* [as people of God] is a very essential element in the scope of Jesus' preaching and self-revelation." For "the *ekklesia* is the people elected and called by God and sharing in the bliss of the *basileia*." Thus, "the *ekklesia* is the fruit of the revelation of the *basileia;* and conversely, the *basileia* is inconceivable without the *ekklesia*." For "the concept of a Messiah without a people is unthinkable." Church and kingdom are therefore "inseparable . . . without, however, the one merging into the other" (*The Coming of the Kingdom*, pp. 348-55).

In our commonly held submission to the Word of God, the church must minister to the needs of all its ministers, the entire congregation, so that they as Church, the body of Christ in the world, may serve the cause of the coming kingdom.

The kingship of Christ embraces "all authority in heaven and on earth." As the realm over which he rules, it covers all creatures great and small. For the restoration of creation and the coming of the kingdom of God are one and the same. Accordingly Jesus viewed "every normal and legitimate province of human life as intended to form part of God's kingdom" (Geerhardus Vos, *The Kingdom and the Church*, p. 88). Moreover, his reign encompasses not only willing citizens who have been born anew into the kingdom (John 3:5), but also unwilling subjects who resist his rule. This sets the stage for the antithesis — two kingdoms in conflict. For "there is something totalitarian about the claims of both Satan and Christ; nothing in all creation is neutral in the sense that it is untouched by the dispute between these two great adversaries." We must therefore resist the "almost ineradicable tendency [which] exists among Christians to restrict the scope of the kingdom, . . . the persistent inclination to divide the world into sacred and profane realms" — whether by limiting the kingdom of God to "personal piety," "the institutional church," "the eschatological future," or humanitarian aspirations (Wolters, *Creation Regained*, pp. 60, 61, 65).

III. 7. The Christian Life

In the words of Bavinck, "grace restores nature." Being a Christian is therefore the most "natural" thing in the world. Accordingly, "Bavinck insists that the Christian is . . . truly human."

> Directed to non-Christians this means: to be truly human, in accordance with your Creator's purpose, you must have faith! Directed to his fellow Christians, it means: if you are a Christian, a Christian in the full sense of the word, then you are no peculiar, eccentric human being, but you are fully human. . . . Because [one] is a Christian, he is a man in the full and truest sense. (Jan Veenhof, *Nature and Grace in Bavinck*, pp. 23-24)

III. 7. 1. "What's in a Name?"

"In Antioch the disciples were for the first time called Christians" (Acts 11:26). There, in that fledgling congregation, the life-renewing Word reaped an early harvest. Establishing this gospel beachhead involved all three persons of the Trinity. For by "the grace of God [the Father] . . . a great number that believed turned to [Christ] the Lord." The Holy Spirit then prompted this community of faith to "set apart [emissaries] for the work" of an expanding gospel witness. One of those "sent out by the Spirit" was Paul. In the unfolding drama of redemption history, it was his ground-breaking mission which propelled the gospel outward from its original Hebrew base into the Greco-Roman culture of the day. He was a man with a plan. In Jewish synagogues he would appeal to the written Word of the prophets to demonstrate that Jesus is the promised Messiah (Acts 17:1-3). In addressing Gentile audiences his appeal was to God's Word for creation: "He did not leave himself without a witness . . ." (Acts 14:16-17). Paul's clarion calls to Christian faith, in his preaching campaigns as in his letters to the young churches, all focus centrally on Jesus Christ, the Word incarnate, crucified, resurrected, glorified: "all things" *(ta panta)* hold together "in Christ" *(en Christō)* (Colossians 1:15-20). "In Christ" is not

> a phrase that captures an incidental, side issue of Christian life, alongside of which man's real life is lived. It exposes the very root of life, the new life as it is created by and experienced in Jesus Christ. . . . The whole of life, from its fundamental being to its discrete actions, is surrounded by the reality of Christ. The pilgrim journey is not a burdensome trudge up a lonely road. . . . [For] life begins, proceeds, and ends in Christ. He is the route and the country through which the route crosses. The Christian is always "in Christ." (Lewis Smedes, *All Things Made New,* pp. 81-82)

Bearing the stigma "Christian" is therefore unthinkable apart from Christ. Credit goes to the townspeople of Antioch for this perceptive insight — however deviously intended. To them we owe this enduring nomenclature. Keeping it alive, the Heidelberg Catechism continues to confront heirs of the Reformation with the pointed question: "But why are you called a Christian?" In answer it then teaches us to confess that "by faith I am a member of Christ and so I share in his anointing . . ." (Q. & A. 32). Our anointing in Christ means, as Paul says, that we were "crucified with him" and thus "united with him in a death like his"; that we were "buried with him by baptism into death," so that "if we have died with Christ" we shall also "live with him"; being "united with him in a resurrection like his," we may now also "walk [with him] in newness of life" (Romans 6:1-11).

How is it possible for us, children of our times, to be contemporaries of Christ? Addressing this question, Calvin sums up the witness of the Scriptures: "the Holy Spirit is the bond by which Christ effectually unites us with himself." He is the "second Mediator." By his indwelling work Christ "shares with us what He has received from the Father" (*Institutes,* III,1,1). From start to finish, therefore, the Christian life is grounded in the saving intervention of Father, Son, and Holy Spirit. In the genial idiom of popular pulpiteering: the Father *thought* it ("God so loved the world"), the Son *bought* it (giving "his life as a ransom for many"), the Spirit *wrought* it ("testifying with our spirit"). Thus we *sought* it ("seek and you shall find"). But the devil *fought* it ("going about as a roaring lion"). That adds up to a lifetime of very intense spiritual struggle (Romans 7). Only by grace, through faith, can pilgrims make progress.

III. 7. 2. Steps in Faith

In traditional theology it is customary to analyze the Christian life in terms of the *ordo salutis* ("the order of salvation"). A great deal of mental energy has gone into sorting out and lining up in proper sequence the various developmental stages in Christian living. What comes first, regeneration or effectual calling? How is internal calling related to external calling? Being justified by faith within history, are we also justified from eternity? Is conversion once for all or daily or both? How is faith related to repentance? Mortification to vivification? How are sanctification, perseverance, and glorification connected? And where does election fit in? In much of this painstaking discussion *salus* ("salvation") gets sacrificed on the altar of *ordo* (concentration on logical "order").

All these concepts arise from theological reflection on biblical revelation. But nowhere does Scripture lay out a fully and precisely delineated *ordo*. It is not a handbook on dogmatics. Its closest approach to disclosing orderly steps in faith-life is in Romans 8:28-30: "Those whom [God] foreknew he also predestined, . . . and those whom he predestined he also called; and those whom he called he also justified; and those whom he justified he also glorified." In this listing, however, regeneration, sanctification, and perseverance are notably absent. In other passages, moreover, we encounter a different sequence: "But you were washed, . . . sanctified, . . . justified in the name of the Lord Jesus Christ and in the Spirit of our God" (1 Corinthians 6:11; cf. 1 Corinthians 1:30; Titus 3:5). In Scripture, therefore, "it is not the order as such that is decisive," but the richly diversified reality of a unified Christian life. For "the entire way of salvation is meant only to illumine *sola fide* and *sola gratia*. Only thus can it be confessed that Christ is the way" (Berkouwer, *Faith and Justification,* pp. 29-33).

The richly variegated emphasis of Scripture is reflected in the evangelical theology of the Reformers. In Calvin, for example, we find a certain loosely arranged orderliness. He speaks of "our regeneration by faith: repentance" (*Institutes,* III,3). His work comes up short, however, of the highly structured *ordo salutis* of later Protestant scholastic theology. This leads Kuyper to speak of an "unfinished conception" in the Reformers (*The Work of the Holy Spirit,* p. 294). Calvin's strength lies, however, in his emphasis on the unity of the way of salvation, not its complexity. Together with other Reformers, he was reacting against the "worthless distinctions" of the medievalists. By distinguishing between "implicit and explicit faith" and between "formed and unformed faith," they "draw a veil over Christ to hide him." For "unless we look straight toward him, we shall wander through endless labyrinths" (*Institutes,* III,3,2). This, then, is a basic motif in Calvin's theology: Fellowship with Christ means participation in all his benefits.

Some may regard this as "a defect" in Calvin (Louis Berkhof, *Systematic Theology,* p. 417), due to his alleged subjectivity and lack of clear and precise definitions. Such charges are more traceable, however, to reading the works of Calvin and other Reformers through glasses ground and polished by the later scholastic tradition. Accordingly, Kuyper says that "the operations of grace are riveted together as links of a chain" (*The Work of the Holy Spirit,* p. 297). Yet most seasoned scholastic theologians acknowledge ultimately that the Christian life is "a unitary process"; they "simply stress the fact that various movements can be distinguished in the process and that the application of redemption proceeds in a definite and reasonable order" (Louis Berkhof, *Systematic Theology,* p. 416).

Certain distinctions are indeed crucial to any well-ordered theology. Christian living includes "various experiences which, though they may never be separated, must be distinguished. . . ." Thus, "the various phases in the way of salvation are not to be thought of as a series of successive steps, each of which replaces the preceding, but rather as various simultaneous aspects of the process of salvation which, after they have begun, continue side by side" (Hoekema, *Saved by Grace,* pp. 15, 16). Similarly, John Murray holds that the way of salvation takes place "in a certain order, and that order has been established by divine appointment, wisdom, and grace" (*Redemption — Accomplished and Applied,* p. 98). Calvin already recognized this. The "mother church," he held, was guilty of confusing justification and sanctification, as though a life of good works were in part the ground for getting right with God. "Repentance" (meaning sanctification) and "forgiveness" (meaning justification), Calvin argues, are interrelated. "Though they cannot be separated, they ought to be distinguished." Accordingly, "we see that the Lord freely justifies his own in order that he may at the same time restore them to true righteousness by sanctification of the Spirit" (*Institutes,* III,3,5; 19). Thus, as Calvin was wont to say, "right order of teaching" has a primarily apologetic purpose — to foster sound doctrine and thereby to avoid misrepresenting the truth of Scripture. Though an obsessive emphasis on the order of salvation "may satisfy an appetite for logical construction," it has "no independent significance." For "if it is given any independence, the most highly developed and neatly systematized *ordo salutis* will lose all connection with Christian piety and will lend credence and assistance to the devaluation of dogma and dogmatics" (Berkouwer, *Faith and Justification,* p. 27).

III. 7. 3. Living as Persons in Community

As out of many grains one meal is ground and one bread baked, and out of many berries, pressed together, one wine flows and is mixed together, so shall we all who by true faith are incorporated in Christ be all together one body. . . .

These lines from a classic "Form for the Lord's Supper" employ rich biblical imagery to echo Paul's strong emphasis on the unified diversity of life in the Christian community (1 Corinthians 12:12-31). The apostle reminds us that "just as the body is one and has many members, and all the members of the body, though many, are one body, so it is with Christ. For by one Spirit we were all baptized into one body . . ." (verses 12-13). Again, "as in one body we have many members, and all the members do not have the same function, so we, though many, are one body in Christ, and individually members one of another" (Romans 12:4-5; cf. Ephesians 4:4, 16; 5:30; Colossians 2:19). For us today this means finding our places and playing our roles within a framework of interrelated subcommunities (households, churches, school circles, social action agencies, support groups) as part of the larger Christian community. Sustained by our involvement in these networks, we are also equipped for our tasks within society at large.

This pluralist view of the interrelatedness of "the one" and "the many" stands in sharp contrast to the two prevailing modern views on life in the world. The democracies of the West have fallen prey to individualism. At a fundamental level they absolutize individual existence. Western Christianity is not immune to this virus. Its publications are heavy on personal ethics, much lighter on social ethics. Gospel outreach often fails to get beyond the typical attention getter, "Brother, is your soul saved?" Sermons concentrate on the marks of personal spirituality. Such absence of communal consciousness leads Ridderbos to comment that "our power as the body of Christ is often so small because we so easily let go of the body and again and again attempt as separate members to make ourselves strong. . . . It must be affirmed," on the contrary, "that everything which results from the work of Christ and from the Spirit of Christ bears primarily a communal character" ("The Church and the Kingdom of God," p. 17; "The Kingdom of God and Our Life in the World," p. 11). The Eastern bloc is guilty of the opposite error, collectivism, also known as communism or socialism. It tends to absolutize the idea of human solidarity. Mass movements and class actions subordinate the interests of "the one" to some envisioned larger good of "the many." However divergent, both of these philosophies betray the humanist influence of the Enlightenment movement.

Scripture reveals a "third way," a better, more normative pattern for living together in God's world. As a genuine alternative, it offers healing in a world of broken relationships. And the Christian community is the right place to actualize it. "I am the true vine," says Christ, and "you are the branches" (John 15:1-5). Each branch has an identity of its own; yet the many branches draw their life from a common source. Together they are grafted into the vine with a view to jointly bearing good fruit. So we, too, act as persons, but never as isolated individuals. Christian living comes to its most meaningful expression within a dynamic web of human relationships. Accordingly, the gospel addresses us consistently as the people of God, the body of Christ, and individualizes its message within this context. For "a person is a true individual only in the Community. . . . The Community makes him truly an individual, in that God's call integrates him into a whole" (Weber, *Foundations of Dogmatics,* Vol. II, p. 505). Covenant, kingdom, church, and Church — all these central biblical realities are communal. The church is "the mother of believers," and we together are her children. Within this "family of God" we learn to image our Maker and Redeemer and to exercise our offices. Where this vision is lost, the company of believers becomes "entirely or mainly an aggregate of individuals and a product of personal faith." The antidote is to recognize that "humanness is always fellow-humanness." Therefore "people can fully experience their participation in the covenant event only with a community in which they support and mutually enrich each other" (Hendrikus Berkhof, *Christian Faith,* pp. 340-41).

III. 7. 4. The Pilgrimage

Pilgrims (from *paroika,* 1 Peter 2:11, from which we derive our word "parish") are people on the move — not meandering aimlessly, like hobos, displaced persons, or sluggish tourists, but people with a fixed destination. They are bound to "inherit the earth" (Matthew 5:5). In joining the pilgrim band, we are well advised to travel lightly, shedding the encumbrances and besetting sins which hold us back from running the good race (Hebrews 12:1-2). For we must be freed up so we can take "the glory and honor of the nations" with us into the New Jerusalem (Revelation 21:26).

The route we follow is not a trackless wilderness. The light of Scripture charts the course. Reillumined creational signposts mark the way. Others have gone before, leaving their footprints in the sands of time. And we have a sure Guide, Jesus, "the pioneer and perfecter" of our faith. He is the goal of the pilgrimage as well as the way to that goal. Sometimes pilgrims are forced to go it alone, not by choice, but pressured by severe opposition and adversity. The designated plan, however, calls for traveling in company with others — as marriage partners, families, a circle of friends, congregations, fellow workers, student bodies, and in other social, economic, and political associations.

Whatever the circumstances, we are called to live "by grace, through faith" — the grace of God on the revealing side and faith on the responding side. These deeply religious resources converge dynamically to shape the "correlation motif" (Berkouwer) which lends impetus and direction to the pilgrimage. Grace is that free sovereign gift of God by which he arouses a saving faith within us. As an older generation was therefore wont to say, "It is all of grace." At the same time it is also "all by faith." Faith is indeed a divine gift, without strings attached. For

> there is nothing in man that could possibly succeed as a condition. Nor is saving faith a particular form of general human faith; "faith in God" and "faith in my friend" are not two species of the same genus. . . . [For] faith is defined and determined in its totality and root . . . by its object. The act of faith is as much being held by God as holding him. . . (Berkouwer, *Faith and Justification,* p. 190)

Faith is thus the "beggar's hand" (Luther), empty of self-adulation, awaiting a divine filling. But it is also an urgent mandate. For Scripture excludes all notions of "cheap grace," which begins and ends with merely receiving. God's grace calls forth a "costly faith" (Bonhoeffer). To the pressing question, "What must I do to be saved?", Scripture responds, "Believe!" Faith is active. We must seek if we would find. But faith claims no merit for its actions. For believers seek their salvation, not in themselves, but in Jesus Christ alone. By their participation in God's way in Christ they also participate in God's way with Israel and the early church. The past witness of the prophets and apostles to God's abounding grace creates within them a new song of hope for the future. Thus covenant history lives on. King Jesus continues to enlist his followers in the program of the coming kingdom.

From beginning to end, therefore, pilgrims make progress "by grace alone"/"through faith alone." For faith is not just "one of the steps in the order of salvation; it must continue to be exercised throughout the believer's life" (Hoekema, *Saved by Grace,* p. 14). Grace and faith are therefore not independent chapters in the journal of life. They interact, yet in such a way that each retains its own divine and human integrity. They may not be reduced, however, to "objective" and "subjective" factors which stand in a competing or a half-and-half cooperating relationship. Nor are they caught in a bipolar dialectical tension. Rather, grace and faith, centered in God's mediating Word, intersect fully and freely at every turn along the way. This dynamic interaction is strongly emphasized in the "correlation motif" which pervades Berkouwer's works on justification, sanctification, and perseverance. As he puts it, "faith resolves all tensions between objectivity and subjectivity." This is so because the objectivity/subjectivity distinction does not hold for God's relationship to man. It applies only to intracosmic realities. For God is not "an Object." Yet faith does involve "a certain subjectivity." For as believers we are fully involved, acting in subjection to God's Word. It is therefore "a subjectivity which has meaning only as it is bound to the gospel." For "all the lines in the life of faith must meet at the center, the grace of God" (*Faith and Justification,* pp. 29-30).

Scripture employs a rich variety of images to depict the Christian life — "adoption," "ingrafting," "transformation," "conformity to Christ," "putting on the new nature," and once the very startling expression: becoming "partakers of the divine nature" (2 Peter 1:4). Even the most sure-footed pilgrims will be slow to see themselves in these awesome word pictures. Yet we do not lose heart, remembering that we walk, not by sight, but by a hope-filled faith. For the pilgrimage is not "the prerogative of a special category of people: monks, martyrs, ascetics, or itinerant preachers. It is the privilege of every recipient of grace" (Berkouwer, *Faith and Sanctification,* p. 149).

Drawing on the richly variegated witness of the Scriptures, we turn now to a brief theological reflection on key aspects of the Christian life.

III. 7. 4. 1. Regeneration: A New Lease on Life

Among the Reformers the biblical doctrine of regeneration took on an evangelical scope far more inclusive than the narrower focus of later theologies. It was related closely to other aspects of the Christian pilgrimage, such as justification, repentance, conversion, and sanctification (cf. Calvin, *Institutes,* III,3). In the first of his Ninety-Five Theses, Luther accordingly describes the penitent spirit which marks a regenerate person as a lifelong process of renewal: The entire life of the believer is repentance. This largely undifferentiated view is echoed in the confessional reference to our "regeneration by faith" (Belgic Confession, Article 24). In more recent times, however,

> the word "regeneration" is generally used in a more restricted sense, as a designation of that divine act by which the sinner is endowed with new spiritual life, and by which that new life is first called into action. So conceived, it includes both the "begetting again" and the "new birth." (Louis Berkhof, *Systematic Theology,* p. 467)

This more sharply focused usage undoubtedly reflects the influence of Protestant scholastic theology. It is nonetheless not without merit, inasmuch as it stresses the need for some clear theological distinctions. It should not be so pressed, however, as to fragmentize the one way of salvation. For while

> regeneration is the unrepeatable, once and for all, historical beginning of the new life, . . . the beginning of both justification and sanctification, . . .

it is no independent event alongside others, such as calling, justification, or sanctification. . . . [For] in regeneration the justification of the sinner by grace alone is being consummated. (Helmut Burkhardt, *The Biblical Doctrine of Regeneration,* pp. 22, 26, 29)

Regeneration points to a depth dimension of all the other aspects of Christian living. As such it opens up the very heart of the gospel.

In reaction to subjectivist excesses in some pietist circles, to Pharisaical tendencies by some to force quick and easy divisions between regenerate and unregenerate people, and to elitist notions of being "born again Christians," many mainline modern theologies tend to shy away from the biblical idea of regeneration. They capitalize on the allegedly "objective" doctrine of justification in Paul's letters at the expense of the supposedly "subjective" emphasis on rebirth in John's gospel. This leads Otto Michel to observe that "Reformation theology has tended to push justification into the foreground and append rebirth to it." But "this detracts from the significance of Johannine theology, which speaks deliberately and insistently of God's begetting" ("Regeneration," *Basic Christian Doctrines,* p. 189). On this issue once again we must be careful not to lock the God/man relationship into debilitating "objectivity"/"subjectivity" straightjackets. For regeneration and justification go hand in hand. Justification points to the radical reversal in our *status* before God — no longer "under judgment," but now recipients of the verdict of mercy, "no condemnation." At the same time, regeneration refers to a profound change in our *condition,* its fundamental redirection, the starting point of a renewed life. It is born of the overpowering initiative of the sovereign grace of God, for as Berkouwer puts it, "the womb of the heart is empty — it resists conception" (*Faith and Sanctification,* p. 190). In this new beginning a true faith is born which reaches out to embrace God's justifying grace. Both justification and regeneration emphasize decisively the priority of God's electing love. Paul himself links them closely together, grounding them jointly and exclusively in the mercy of God. "The saying is sure," he says, that God saves us "by the washing of regeneration and renewal in the Holy Spirit, . . . so that we might be justified by his grace." Personal boasting is completely ruled out. It all rests on a single foundation, the undeserved blessing which God "poured out upon us richly through Jesus Christ our Savior" (Titus 3:5-8). The entire way of salvation is centered in the Christ who came in fulfillment of the Messianic promise, "You are my son, today I have begotten you" (Psalm 2:7). Our "begetting" is based on his being "begotten" of the Father and being sent into the world, anointed by the Spirit. Appealing to Christ's earthly mission, Peter testifies that "we have been born anew [begotten] unto a living hope through the resurrection of Jesus Christ from the dead" (1 Peter 1:3). Fellowship with Christ therefore means, as Calvin says, participating in all his benefits, including the implantation of this new life principle.

Our Lord stresses the primordial importance of this inner transformation in unequivocal terms. "Unless one is born anew," he says, "he cannot [so much as] see the kingdom of God" (John 3:3). This decisive turnaround is a result of the unfathomable work of the Holy Spirit. As with the mysterious movement of the winds, "so it is with every one who is born of the Spirit" (John 3:8). Calvin accordingly calls the Spirit "the key that unlocks for us the treasures of the kingdom of heaven" (*Institutes,* III,1,4). We are afflicted with a "sickness unto death" (Kierkegaard). He makes us "new creatures" — our old nature has been buried with Christ and we are now raised with him to newness of life. The life-renewing Spirit enlightens our blinded minds. He liberates our enslaved wills. And what he begins, he also continues — from conception, to birth, to the signs of new life. Just as we are wholly unable to induce our own natural conception and birth, so also with this rebirth. As sanctification calls for "growth," so regeneration points to "birth." It is a miracle of divine grace. "God seeks covenant fellowship with man as he is; but for the sake of such fellowship, God cannot leave us as we are" (Hendrikus Berkhof, *Christian Faith,* p. 425). As a result, we can never be the same again.

Regeneration may be an undateable event. Its time and place may escape us. Yet it marks the dawn of a new day. With it comes a new lease on life. Like a seed sown in the ground, it may remain hidden for a while. But eventually it germinates and bears fruit. Rebirth therefore is "a total root-and-branch renewal of the whole person, . . . the decisive change of direction brought about by the work of the Spirit of God" (Burkhardt, *The Biblical Doctrine of Regeneration,* p. 23). But the Spirit does not work empty-handedly. In his regenerating actions he joins forces with that dynamic, healing power of God's Word which stands from the beginning. As Peter says, "You have been born anew . . . through the living and abiding Word of God" (1 Peter 1:23; cf. James 1:18).

So now the road ahead stretches out before us, trouble-free and under cloudless skies? On the contrary, Scripture offers no such "health and wealth" gospel. Rebirth does indeed engender a deep-seated, resilient peace, as Christ promised (John 14:27), even in the face of severe tribulations. It imparts a solid sense of good cheer, knowing that he has overcome the enmity of the world (John 16:33). But it offers no false promises of smooth sailing. In fact, regeneration marks the beginning of the real battle. It sets the scenes for sharing with Paul that ongoing spiritual struggle which pits the new self against the old (Romans 7:13-25). This about-face serves as a full-fledged introduction to Luther's description of the Christian life as *simul justus et peccator.* The battle lines are then also drawn between those "born of God" (1 John 5:18) and those born of "the father of lies" (John 8:44). There is no need, however, for a defeatist spirit. We can fall back again and again on the sure promises of God sealed in our baptism, the "washing of regeneration" (Titus 3:5). Thus cleansed, we are adopted as sons and daughters into the renewed family of faith, joint heirs in our heavenly Father's household. We may still betray our fraternal vows, or dash the sorority's hopes. But we cannot escape these spiritual ties. For our membership was decided for us. Come what may, therefore, within this fellowship we may always cry out, personally and communally, "Abba! Father!"

All believers are born-again Christians, not just a select circle of spiritually advanced saints. Moreover, we are not to rest content with merely basking in our rebirth as a personal blessing. This renewal must work itself out in reborn marriages, reborn friendships, even reborn work habits and reborn politics. Then one day we will hear the call to join in the final regeneration of the whole creation (Romans 8:18-25).

III. 7. 4. 2. Justification: Right with God

Since Christ was "raised for our justification" (Romans 4:25), the unfriendly jury is no longer out, weighing our case. The liberating verdict is in. In Christ God lifts the sentence of death which otherwise rests heavily and deservedly on us as sinners. He justifies the ungodly. For "while we were [yet] enemies we were reconciled to God by the death of his Son" (Romans 5:6-11). By this ultimate act of divine acquittal the grace of justification is brought home to us by faith as a present reality. Prodigals are forgiven and welcomed back into the Father's household (Luke 15:20-24). Estranged children are made "heirs of God and fellow heirs with Christ" (Romans 8:17). Justification is God's declaration of unmerited righteousness freely given to the penitent publican, sending him "down to his house justified," while the Pharisee, seeking to justify himself, remains unjustified (Luke 18:9-14). Whereas regeneration takes place *in nobis* ("within us" — by the Spirit), justification, as its deeper background, takes place *extra nobis* ("outside us" — in Christ). It, too, takes place once and for all. It is not a process. Yet "the believer must continue to appropriate his or her justification by a continuing exercise of faith . . . [as] a never-ending source of comfort, peace, and joy" (Hoekema, *Saved by Grace,* p. 173).

That "great exchange" is now an accomplished fact — before the tribunal of divine judgment, and also within the ambiguities of our tangled life stories. Christ became vicariously what he was not, the world's great Sin-bearer (Isaiah 53:4-6, *pro nobis* — "for us"), in order to make us what we by nature are not, righteous in the sight of God. In this stupendous transaction we sense the very heartbeat of the gospel. For the Reformers, this Word of reconciliation epitomized the many words of Scripture. It literally throbs throughout Paul's letter to Christians in Rome. Little wonder that this epistle has repeatedly played a decisive role in the reforming life of the church. Its liberating message evoked Luther's feisty "Here I stand!," shattering the centuries-old fetters of unbiblical tradition. In his "Preface to the Latin Writings" he recounts his "tower experience," which overwhelmed him while hiding away as a friendly hostage in the Wartburg. This turning point on the road to reformation was triggered by his reflections on Romans 1:16: "He who through faith is righteous shall live." Luther recalls that "this place in Paul was for me truly the gate to paradise. . . . Here I felt I was altogether born again. . . . There a totally other face of the entire Scripture showed itself to me" (Dillenberger, *Martin Luther,* pp. 11-12). Relieved of his unrelenting, fruitless devotion to works righteousness, he captured the full impact of Paul's teaching by penning boldly in the margin of his Bible the word *sola* — justified "by faith alone." For the righteousness proclaimed in the gospel is not an attribute of God, nor a righteousness which God demands of us, but one which he freely bestows for Christ's sake, wholly and solely through grace, but also wholly and solely by faith. Luther discovered that "the absolute antithesis which Paul insists on between the two ways of becoming righteous in God's sight coincides with the two epochs in his own life: before and after he met Christ." Like Paul, "before his conversion he worked for his own righteousness; afterward he accepted that of Christ" (Berkouwer, *Faith and Justification,* p. 78).

Such a radical and total reliance on the sovereign grace of God, which lies beyond our ability to earn it, stands, however, as a "stumbling block" and a "rock of offense" to Jews and Gentiles alike, and no less so to modern man. We are all addicted to the seductive, seemingly irresistible power of self-help programs of religion. Sensing this, Luther is reported to have commented dolefully near the end of his life that after his death this doctrine would become thoroughly obscured. Subsequent history confirms this dire prediction. Reflecting on the reason for such departures from reformational belief, Hendrikus Berkhof says that "to live as a sinner from the faith that salvation is purely God's free gift is something which in the long run proves too demanding." For the message of justification by faith alone "does not arise out of ourselves." In fact, in it "we receive the opposite of what we experience." Therefore, "in the face of an entirely opposite experience, we need to be told this ever and again" (*Christian Faith,* p. 438).

Calvin found himself in full agreement with Luther on this basic article of the Christian faith. "There is in justification no place for works," he says. We must rather be "clothed with the righteousness of Christ," and "the instrument for receiving [this] righteousness" is faith (*Institutes,* III,11,6). Further clarifying this idea, Berkouwer adds that "it is not faith itself that justifies; faith is only the instrument with which we embrace Christ who is our justification" (*Faith and Justification,* p. 45). Calvin appeals to the analogy of faith as an empty vessel in excluding every notion of self-justification: "for unless we come empty and with the mouth of our soul open to seek Christ's grace, we are not capable of receiving Christ" (*Institutes,* III,11,7). The point is not that faith is passive, but that it is devoid of all personal merit. Faith is indeed receptive, but it is an active and urgent receptivity. For "decision must be made, decision of frightening consequences" (Berkouwer, *Faith and Justification,* p. 186). "To walk in the way of faith," therefore, "is simply to admit that Christ is the way" (Berkouwer, *Faith and Justification,* p. 43). In him we are assured not only of the forgiveness of all sins past and present, but also of the redemptive ground for forgiveness in the future.

In recent times Hans Küng has reopened the sixteenth-century case of Rome versus the Reformation. Interpreting reformational thought through the eyes of Barth's theology, he holds that this long-standing conflict represents a great misunderstanding. Basically the faith of the Reformers is not at odds with the decrees of the Council of Trent on justification. "On the whole," Küng argues, "there is a fundamental agreement between the theology of Barth and that of the Catholic Church. Within this area of discussion," therefore, "Barth has no valid reason for separation from the ancient Church." For "living Catholic theology does take justification seriously as God's act of sovereignty in Jesus Christ" (*Justification: The Doctrine of Karl Barth and Catholic Reflection,* pp. 276, 282). Responding to this startling thesis in his prefatory letter to the author, Barth states that if Küng has faithfully transmitted the Catholic position, "then, having twice gone to the Church of Santa Maria Magiore [site of the Council of Trent] to commune with the genius loci, I may well have to hasten there a third time to make a contrite confession — 'Fathers, I have sinned' " (*Justification,* p. xx). Clearly Barth, and others as well, remains unconvinced. For it seems indisputable that traditional Catholic theology does not view the faith of justification as the decisive step which opens the entire way of salvation, but only as an initial stage along the way, needing additional stages to supplement it.

There are other representations of justification by faith which reformational theology finds unacceptable. Roman Catholic theology has long labeled the Reformer's doctrine of justification "fictitious," since it allegedly leaves the sinner unchanged. The Heidelberg Catechism answers this charge, however, by confessing that "it is impossible for those grafted into Christ by true faith not to produce fruits of gratitude" (Q. & A. 64). What about our continuing sins and shortcomings? To live by faith in God's justifying grace means simply yet profoundly daring to accept the divine verdict of our righteousness in Christ even in the face of this contrary evidence. Arminians also raised objections. The Reformed doctrine of justification, they charged, reduces the believer to a wholly passive recipient of God's favor. Appealing to a semi-Pelagian view of free will, they advocated instead an active, cooperative, and decisive role for human involvement in salvation. In its "rejection of errors" the Synod of Dordt saw in the Arminian position a serious infringement on the biblical doctrine of *sola gratia* ("grace and free choice [as] concurrent partial causes," Main Points Three/Four, IX). Believers can make no personal contribution to their justification. Nor is faith a prior condition to be met. It is rather our way of experiencing God's justifying grace.

Barth's theology presents its own unique challenge. Out of concern for honoring the reformational idea of faith as an "empty vessel" over against the subjectivizing tendencies of modern liberalism, Barth turns faith into a sovereign act of God which radically excludes all human participation. It is not we who believe in God, but God who believes in us. God is "the Subject" of faith, and man "the object." Faith is therefore "repeatedly a leap into the unknown, into darkness, into empty air." Accordingly, "the I is not its subject." For faith is "absolute otherness," and "this radically Other stands opposed to everything I am" (*Römerbrief*, pp. 73, 125). In Scripture, however, faith is a thoroughly human, though nonmeritorious act. It is nonetheless a powerfully charged response to God's grace. "O woman," says Jesus to the Canaanite mother who is willing to eat scraps from the Jewish table for the sake of her daughter's health, "Great is your faith! Be it done for you as you desire" (Matthew 15:28). To the woman bold enough to believe that a timid touch of the Messiah's garment would bring healing, Jesus declared, "Daughter, your faith has made you well" (Mark 5:25-34; Matthew 8:10). Justification is therefore not a divine monologue. Covenant partnership creates an arena for divine-human dialogue. There faith responds to God's Word of grace, which reconciles the estranged and justifies the unjust. Yet we are obliged to join in Barth's repudiation of religious propagandists who offer seductive, self-reliant schemes of justification. They are nothing but empty promises. Even the most orthodox systems of doctrine cannot set us right with God. As Berkouwer reminds us, "we are not justified by sound theology; faith alone saves us" (*Faith and Justification*, p. 201).

Justification rests on the unshakable foundation of Christ's vicarious atonement. He was "put to death for our trespasses and raised for our justification" (Romans 4:25). In the sight of God there is therefore now "no condemnation for those who are in Christ Jesus" (Romans 8:1). Being thus justified by faith, "we have peace with God" (Romans 5:1) and can revel in our "adoption as sons" (Galatians 4:5). Scripture abounds in judicial imagery to describe God's declaration of justification: the just demands of the law are satisfied, the Mediator took our judgment on himself, the sentence is lifted, we are acquitted of our guilt. Thus, "in the passive obedience of Christ . . . we find the ground for the forgiveness of sins; and in his active obedience . . . the ground for our adoption as children, by which [we] are constituted heirs of eternal life" (Louis Berkhof, *Systematic Theology,* p. 523). As Abraham "believed the Lord" and this act of faith was "reckoned to him as righteousness" (Genesis 15:6; cf. Romans 4:3, 9, 22), so now in Christ we, too, are "alive because of his righteousness" (Romans 8:10). His merits are credited to our account.

In this "great exchange" we hear the echoes of a courtroom scenario. The language of jurisprudence is very much at home in this setting. Based on imputed righteousness, the gracious Judge declares that the costly ransom has been paid. The Father exacts no double indemnity. Christ took our full penalty on himself. The Spirit testifies to our innocence. To reject these legal metaphors is to shortchange the reality of the substitutionary atonement. For the idea of forensic justification honors the gospel of *sola gratia* and *sola fide* in all its decisiveness. Satan may take the stand against us. And he is at his devilish worst, says Luther, when he sits on our shoulder and whispers in our ear, Your sins are too great! But then a voice sounds, "The Lord rebuke you, O Satan! The Lord who has chosen Jerusalem rebuke you! Is not this a brand plucked from the fire?" (Zechariah 3:2). Our conscience, too, may rise up to accuse us (Heidelberg Catechism, Q. & A. 60). But God's verdict lays even our conscientious objections to rest. These many accusations are real enough, "secured by incontrovertible facts." They are in fact "so irrefutable that the sinner can do nothing but admit the justness of the charges." Yet, because "the phrase *in Christ* is included in the declaration of personal justification," we are, as it were, "conducted into a court of law to hear a merciful declaration of pardon," there to acknowledge "the unique character of this declaration" (Berkouwer, *Faith and Justification,* p. 41).

By faith we embrace this Word of "alien righteousness." It is not of our doing. It originates in divine initiative. Justification is the good news that God's liberating verdict which he will pronounce over us for Christ's sake in the day of judgment has been brought into the present. It accentuates the priority of God's electing love. We learn this from Isaiah. There God first unburdens himself before his chosen people. He then issues his summons: "Set forth your case!" Yet, in the very midst of these protestations, the word of pardon resounds: "I, I am He who blots out your transgressions for my own sake" (43:25). That Old Testament assurance still stands, leaving the New Testament to fulfill it by adding "in Christ." He covers for us so completely "as if I had never sinned nor been a sinner, as if I had been as perfectly obedient as Christ was obedient for me" (Heidelberg Catechism, Q. & A. 60). This phrase, "as if," is an expression of comfort. Yet many find it troublesome, incredible, too good to be true. For such people the good news is this: Justification is not "fiction." It has nothing to do with make-believe. In justification something very real *act*-ually happens. There is, indeed, an opposite, a truly troubling "fictitious" way of life — "the 'as if' of unbelief (Luke 18:9, cf. Luke 20:20)," which is "to walk the way of self-justification" (Berkouwer, *Faith and Justification,* pp. 88-89). But for all who walk by faith, what is by nature unreal *in* us becomes real *for* us in Christ. He is our justification.

III. 7. 4. 3. Sanctification: Keeping the Faith

Nearly every issue in sanctification hinges on its relationship to justification. Scripture views these two dimensions of the Christian faith as holist realities which go hand in hand through life, inseparably connected. Justification is not a way station which believers can conveniently leave behind as a pleasant memory as they seek to make progress along the road of sanctified living. In the words of Berkouwer, "There is never a stretch along the way of salvation when justification drops out of sight" (*Faith and Sanctification,* p. 77). We are indeed justified by faith alone. But faith does not remain alone. It works. Good works are "the lived out reality of faith" (Barth). For "the faith that justifies is a faith that is fruitful in good works" (Louis Berkhof, *Systematic Theology,* p. 521).

Recall Abraham's pilgrimage. The heartbeat of the patriarchal covenant was the good news of justification by faith: Abraham "believed the LORD, and he reckoned it to him as righteousness" (Genesis 15:6). This sure word of promise then came to fruition in Abraham's act of sacrificial obedience (Genesis 22). In light of covenant history, therefore, the sharp tension which Luther felt between Paul and James is greatly relieved. For while "Abraham our father [was] justified by works when he offered his son Isaac upon the altar," so that "a man is justified by works and not by faith alone," yet "that faith was active along with his works, and faith was completed by works," and thus "scripture was fulfilled" (James 2:21-24). In the words of Louis Berkhof, "the justification of the just by works confirms the justification by faith" (*Systematic Theology,* p. 521).

The indicative ("being justified by faith") and the imperative ("now walk in love") are therefore like the two sides of a single coin. As unbreakable links in the chain of life, justification (the divine indicative) and sanctification (the divine imperative) stand in mutually reciprocating relationships to each other. God works saving grace in us, enabling and obliging us to work this salvation out in a life of faith (Philippians 2:12). Obedience to the imperative even serves as a touchstone for testing the reality of the indicative (note the conditional "if" of the gospel, 1 Corinthians 3:12-17; Galatians 5:25; Colossians 3:2). Basically, however,

> the imperative rests on the indicative, and this order is not reversible. . . . [For the imperative] is grounded in the reality that has been given with the indicative, appeals to it, and is intended to bring it to full development. . . . The indicative is [therefore] to be accepted once and for all and time and time anew. (Ridderbos, *Paul,* pp. 254-56)

Being adopted as children, we are now called to live as adopted children. Indeed, "good works do not make a man good, but a good man does good works" ("The Freedom of a Christian," *Martin Luther,* ed. Dillenberger, p. 69). The "transition" from justification to sanctification does not take place, however, as an automatic follow-through. For though "everywhere justification and sanctification are presented [in Scripture] as belonging together," yet this is not "a self-evident matter, because for the transition from the first to the second admonition and exhortation are constantly necessary" (Hendrikus Berkhof, *Christian Faith,* p. 454). Sanctification is, therefore, not

> a mere supplement, an appendage, to the salvation given in justification. The heart of sanctification is a life which feeds on this justification. The contrast is not between justification as an act of God and sanctification as an act of man. [For] the fact that Christ is our sanctification [as he is also our justification] is not exclusive of, but inclusive of a faith which clings to him alone in life. Faith is the pivot on which everything revolves. Faith, though not itself creative, preserves us from autonomous self-sanctification and moralism. (Berkouwer, *Faith and Sanctification,* p. 93)

Justification, as the reassuring declaration of God's gracious act of reinstatement, accompanies us throughout our Christian pilgrimage. Living by faith therefore means laying claim constantly to the Word which cannot fail. There are, however, two pitfalls we must avoid along the way. To play justification off against sanctification is to embrace "cheap grace," to indulge in "reckless living," or to minimize the struggles of living by faith — a charge often leveled against the Reformers, especially Lutherans. On the other hand, to emphasize sanctification at the expense of justification opens wide the door to legalism, a refined Pharisaism, and anxiety — an opposite criticism of the Reformers, especially Calvinists. *Sola gratia* and *sola fide* is the single antidote to both dangers.

In seeking to honor this central biblical teaching with its balanced emphasis, Calvin relates justification and sanctification in an unusual way. Appealing to "right order of teaching," he holds that both "newness of life" (sanctification) and "free reconciliation" (justification) "are conferred upon us by Christ, and both are attained by us through faith." Accordingly, they belong together. Reversing the normal order, however, Calvin turns first to a discussion of "repentance" (sanctification) before discussing "forgiveness of sins" (justification). For thus "it will better appear," he argues, that "man is justified by faith alone." But more pointedly, he chooses this sequence in order to forestall the charge that the doctrine of justification by faith alone, apart from works, leads to debauchery, by making clear that "actual holiness of life" (sanctification) cannot be "separated from the free imputation of righteousness" (justification) (*Institutes,* III,3,1).

God's justifying and sanctifying grace opens the door to a life of renewed obedience. Sanctification is therefore "the comprehensive objective of the Pauline imperative" — namely, a "whole new life." The origin of this new way of life lies in "the free, electing grace of God." Thus secured, "the religious, theocentric character of this new obedience finds its most pregnant expression in the concept of sanctification" (Ridderbos, *Paul,* pp. 264-65). It embraces all of life, in its total extent and in all its parts. We can therefore speak meaningfully of political sanctification, academic sanctification, economic sanctification, and all the rest. Nothing is beyond the reach of the life-renewing power of faith. It touches even the most mundane bread-and-butter, dollars-and-cents issues of daily living. For, as Paul says, "this is the will of God: your sanctification" (1 Thessalonians 4:3) — including, as the context indicates, the intimate human relationships of courtship and marriage. A sanctified life-style is "man's spontaneous response of gratitude, not egocentrically, but ex-centrically directed to the honor of God and the good of the neighbor" (Hendrikus Berkhof, *Christian Faith,* p. 451). The biblical horizons of sanctification are even cosmic in scope. For "Paul's doctrine of the new life does not find its determinative point of departure in the new 'creature' but in the new 'creation.'" The "redemptive-historical categories of old and new" in biblical revelation do not "speak in the first place of personal, individual regeneration. . . . What predominates is [rather] the inclusion and participation [of believers] in the new creation that has taken effect with Christ and is represented in him" (Ridderbos, *Paul,* p. 206).

The summons to sanctified living calls, therefore, not for superficial moralistic acts of self-exertion, but for a sturdy kind of "worldly" holiness, rooted in wholehearted dedication to the Lord in all our Christian callings. It calls for covenant faithfulness, kingdom loyalty, in full reliance on an unfailing divine initiative. Such a life of obedience is motivated and directed by a faith which finds in God's grace its source of strength. It is therefore utterly misleading to distinguish justification as an act of God from sanctification as human activity, as though faith picks up where grace leaves off. Life cannot be parcelled out that way — "partly this" and "partly that." Scripture allows for no such 50/50 cooperation. Such synergism is contraband. Sanctification as well as justification is wholly by grace and wholly by faith simultaneously and unceasingly. In calling Israel to continuing obedience, God declares, "Sanctify yourselves, . . . [for] I am the LORD who sanctifies you" (Leviticus 20:7-8). God's ever-ready grace and our responding faith fully qualify every move God's people make. Fortified by this "correlation motif," we with Israel can throw ourselves completely into the daring venture of taking possession of the "promised land."

This was the kind of courageous outlook which prompted Luther's controversial utterance, "Sin bravely!" What can we make of this crass expression? As is well known, Luther had a strong propensity for such jarring and provocative "table talk." Impetuous statements like this must indeed be taken with a grain of salt, sifting them critically for their moment of truth. Our post-sixteenth-century sensitivities are inclined to say with Berkouwer that "Luther might have been more cautious" (*Faith and Sanctification,* p. 34). Yet he was certainly not issuing a license to indulge sinful practices with reckless abandon. For as Luther himself says, "Our faith in Christ does not free us from works, but . . . from the foolish presumption that justification is acquired by works" ("The Freedom of a Christian," *Martin Luther,* ed. Dillenberger, p. 81). Such affirmations must be kept clearly in mind in listening to other jolting expressions by this feisty Reformer: "If it were possible to commit adultery in faith, it would not be sin!" This must be taken as a rhetorical statement, implying the impossibility of such promiscuous activity. In challenging Christians to "sin bravely," Luther, in a left-handed way, is therefore urging the fainthearted to "live bravely." Live by faith, he would say, in radical reliance on the grace of God, even though such a vigorous way of life involves falling repeatedly into sin. For in this life an end to sinning would mean an end to living. So let us keep going, knowing that nothing can separate us from Christ Jesus, even if — another shocking statement! — we were "to fornicate a thousand times a day and commit murder." Luther himself puts the best possible face on these provocative expressions when he explains, "I am a sinner and I sin bravely, but I am even braver in faith and joy in Christ who is victor over sin and death

498

and the world." In weighing such typically unsettling words by Luther, let it be said that they can hardly be condoned, let alone emulated; nor does it make sense to roundly condemn them; they are rather to be understood. Rightly understood, they represent a radical appeal to the gospel of *sola gratia, sola fide,* intended to liberate us wholly from reliance on works of personal merit or demerit.

Luther's legacy, with its highly charged dialectic, carries echoes of Paul's picture of the "battling believer" (Berkouwer) in Romans 7. The agonizing paradox of "willing the good, but not doing it" and "not willing evil, yet doing it" confronts us forcefully in this passage. Paul's discourse is punctuated heavily with the idiom of inner struggle — a motif which resounds throughout the Scriptures. But who is the subject in this intensely captivating intrapersonal dialogue? Is it the pre-Christian Paul or Paul the Christ-believer? The weight of contextual evidence, the dynamic flow of thought in chapters 5 through 8, favors the latter viewpoint. These soul-searching notes of internal conflict are not the voice of the "old man." The "natural man" is a stranger to such discord. These are true confessions which arise from the hearts of embattled believers, members of the church militant. For the indwelling work of the Spirit marks, not the end, but the beginning of this "spiritual warfare." A battle rages within believers which is foreign to unbelievers. Christians sense keenly the competing claims of the "mind of the flesh" and the "mind of the spirit" (Romans 8:7, 8). A radical antithesis cuts through our very hearts and lives. The result is a lifelong struggle. It calls for daily conversion, moved by a penitent spirit. Repentance means assuming blame for our failures. It pulls the rug out from under our feet. Thus unsettled, we are led to seek our salvation outside ourselves in Jesus Christ.

In Romans 7, therefore, we meet not two Pauls speaking, but one. To suggest an "apparent dualism" here, as though "two entirely different persons are speaking" (Hoeksema, *Reformed Dogmatics,* p. 535), poses formidable anthropological and religious problems. It is better, therefore, not to speak of a "dual ego," two selves carrying on this war of words like the antiphonal sounds of one "part" of our inner life contradicting another "part." We are not "partly a new self and partly an old self — something like a Dr. Jekyll and Mr. Hyde" (Hoekema, *Saved by Grace,* p. 209). These clashing notes are joint expressions arising from the heart of the "new man" in Christ who is *simul justus et peccator* — at once both wholly sinner and wholly saint. Security and struggle, self-denial and self-realization, mortification and vivification (Calvin, *Institutes,* III,3,3) go hand in hand in the Christian life.

The believer, says Luther, is like the sufferer of some disease who has been told by his physician that he will surely be cured. Hence the believer is

499

both ill and well — but well only in the prediction of the doctor.
(Berkouwer, *Faith and Sanctification*, p. 72)

Only by prediction? Clearly Scripture holds out a greater promise. The
contest is indeed real between the "old" and the "new," but the scales
are tipped toward the "new." For "believers are not the old selves they
once were, . . . [not] both old and new selves, but are indeed new selves
in Christ" (Hoekema, *Saved by Grace*, p. 212). As Christians we are to
become what we are: being Christians, we are to become that more and
more. For with the Heidelberger we confess that a deepening sense of
our sin and guilt, of our salvation in Christ, and of the debt of gratitude
we owe as a fitting response — all three convictions go together and
grow together across the length and breadth of our pilgrimage. Thus
"the better we get to know ourselves, the less we expect from ourselves,
and the more we fall back on God's grace as the decisive foundation of
our life" (Hendrikus Berkhof, *Christian Faith,* p. 471).

Our sanctification is indeed "in Christ." The outcome is therefore
no longer in doubt (Romans 7:25; 1 Corinthians 15:57). Victory is not
left hanging in the balance (Romans 8:37). This is our source of comfort
in the midst of conflict. But it is not an excuse for complacency. For "in
this life even the holiest have only a small beginning" of the obedience
to which we are called (Heidelberg Catechism, Q. & A. 114). Yet that
"beginning," however small, is decisive. It provides the foothold we need
for "fighting the good fight" of faith. It is, moreover, the pledge of the
promised payment in full. Again and again, therefore, Scripture focuses
our attention on "the double viewpoint of battling on the basis of victory,
and of gaining the victory on the basis of the battle" (Ridderbos, *Paul,*
p. 267). God's faithfulness arouses ours, and in our "small beginnings"
his faithfulness takes over.

III. 7. 4. 4. Perseverance: No Turning Back

Set right with God by faith, given a new lease on life, living now by the
law of love — is it possible to move along in the assurance that God's
grace will not let us down? Yes! There is no turning back. For "no one
shall snatch [you] out of my hand," says the Lord (John 10:28). Nothing
"will be able to separate us from the love of God in Christ Jesus our
Lord" (Romans 8:39). "And I am sure," says Paul, "that he who began
a good work in you will bring it to completion at the day of Jesus Christ"
(Philippians 1:6). Picking up on this biblical theme in its teaching concerning "the holy catholic church," the Heidelberg Catechism prompts
its heirs to confess that "of this community I am and always will be a

living member" (Q. & A. 54). The biblical doctrine of perseverance assures us "that God by his power keeps his people from falling away from him, that Christ will never permit anyone to snatch them out of his hand, and that the Holy Spirit seals them for the day of redemption" (Hoekema, *Saved by Grace*, p. 255).

In the confessions of the church (The Canons of Dort: The Fifth Main Point of Doctrine), and in theological reflection on it, this doctrine is called "the perseverance of the saints." Only saints can persevere. This article of faith includes all believers. Persevering in faith is possible, moreover, by drawing steadily on the boundless resources of God's preserving grace. Apart from his unchanging faithfulness, perseverance degenerates into the pursuit of an ever receding mirage. This is the hard lesson to be gleaned from covenant history in Israel. It is only because "I change not," says the Lord, that "you, O sons of Jacob, are not consumed" (Malachi 3:6). The tempered impatience of a persevering remnant looking for "the consolation of Israel" (Luke 2:25) is eloquent testimony to the steadfastness of God in keeping his Messianic promises. "For the gifts and the call of God are irrevocable" (Romans 11:29).

When in the fulness of the times the Messiah appeared, he revealed the widening scope of God's preserving/persevering grace in the parable of "the merciful Father" (Luke 15:11-32). Only the magnetic drawing power of the Father's compassionate love tugging persistently, irresistibly at the prodigal's heartstrings cleared the way for his homecoming. Penitent believers can now persevere in the confidence that the door to the Father's home always stands open.

Perseverance is not a status symbol but a dynamic reality, anchored securely in the sovereign grace of God, experienced by faith alone. It is worlds removed from self-righteousness and spiritual complacency. There is nothing presumptuous or rationally predictable about it. It offers no automatic guarantees of unbroken continuity in our lives. Nor does it grasp prematurely a glory reserved for the future. It is rather "in the thick of the actual struggles of life that Scripture speaks of perseverance in grace" (Berkouwer, *Faith and Perseverance*, p. 99). Persevering believers can only rely wholly on the miracle of divine continuity, the mystery of God's steadfastness. Relentlessly "the Hound of heaven" (Francis Thompson) shadows us down our labyrinthine ways, through all the ups and downs of the often zigzag course of our pilgrimage. For "the believer would fall away if he were left to himself" (Louis Berkhof, *Systematic Theology*, p. 546). Because persevering faith is not

> a human contribution to salvation, but the state of being oriented to God's grace; because it is not a grasping, but rather a being grasped; because it is not a conquest, but rather a being conquered — therefore, in light of

God's grace, there is a foundation for permanency. (Berkouwer, *Faith and Perseverance,* pp. 112-13)

The biblical witness is clear: perseverance is real, sinless perfection is a myth. Some Christian traditions nevertheless draw straight-line conclusions from the one to the other. We are indeed called to "be perfect as [our] heavenly Father is perfect" (Matthew 5:48). In context, however, Christ is not summoning us here to a God-like sinlessness but to spiritual wholeness, to personal integrity as opposed to hypocrisy and duplicity. Still, holiness movements argue from the imperatives of the central law of love to our ability to live up to the high standard of perfectibility. God would not ask the impossible. Within the full sweep of Scripture, however, as Louis Berkhof rightly concludes, "the measure of our ability cannot be inferred from the Scriptural commandment" (*Systematic Theology,* p. 538). Neither perfection nor perseverance may be viewed as a theological deduction. Nor may the claims of God's Word be tailored to the projected potentials of human response. Yet appeals are made to 1 John 3:9 in support of perfectionist doctrines: "No one born of God commits sin; for God's nature abides in him, and he cannot sin because he is born of God." Careful analysis of this passage, however, yields the following reading: Those born of God are not stranded in sinful practices as a settled way of life. This pastoral letter sheds an even fuller light on this question of sinlessness/sinfulness: The blood of Jesus Christ "cleanses us from all sin"; such cleansing is as necessary as daily conversion, for "if we say we have no sin, we deceive ourselves, and the truth is not in us" (1 John 1:5-10). Therefore, the biblical call to "be perfect" is not an "evangelical counsel" for some special class of believers. All are "perfect" who appropriate "the content of the Christian faith in the right way" (Ridderbos, *Paul,* p. 271). But there is no crown without cross-bearing. Christians suffer from within and from without, not in spite of the renewing power of Christ's triumph, but precisely because of it. "The newness of the new life," therefore, "is not static, but dynamic, needing continual renewal, growth, and transformation" (Hoekema, *Saved by Grace,* pp. 212-13).

Calvin already challenged perfectionist tendencies in his day. Though we are "freed through regeneration [sanctification] from bondage to sin," he says, we are not yet in "full possession of freedom so as to feel no more annoyance from the flesh." For while "sin ceases to reign" in believers, "it does not also cease to dwell in them" (*Institutes,* III,3,10-11). God's grace enlists us in lifelong "military service." For we are ever in "a threatened position." So we may never act as though we had "left sin behind as ground already conquered" (Ridderbos, *Paul,* pp. 267, 269). The "new man" in Christ has not yet vanquished the "old man" in Adam. We still live "by faith," not yet "by sight." Instead of striving for sinless perfection as a "second blessing," we must learn by faith to draw our strength continuously from the original, abiding blessing of the justifying and sanctifying grace of God. To seek total and final separation from sin in this life is to seek separation from life itself. To insist on "evangelical perfection" here and now is futile, says Calvin, for then "all would be excluded from the church" (*Institutes,* III,6,5).

The possibility of sinless perfection is plausible only by lowering the standards of God's Word, or by minimizing the effects of our fallenness, or by externalizing the reality of sin, or by overestimating personal virtue. Scripture calls us away from such mystical introspection. Only in Christ are we "perfect" — now "already," but at the same time "not yet." Therefore, as Weber puts it, "perfectionism, . . . if only in the form of an unfulfilled longing for it, is at its root an illusion" (*Foundations of Dogmatics,* Vol. II, p. 287).

Perseverance in faith also comes under attack from another quarter — an opposite reaction. In certain revivalist circles Christian living is reduced to a ceaseless cycle of capricious backslidings accompanied by repeated conversions. Whereas perfectionists cherish the ideal of sinless stability, for voluntarists salvation teeters constantly on the brink of disaster. Though diametrically opposed, these two extreme positions arise from a common faulty impulse — arriving at theological conclusions on the basis of spiritual introspection, some doing so optimistically, others pessimistically. The gospel certainly imparts a resilient faith to the Christian community (1 Corinthians 15:58). But such steadfastness is rooted only in the continuity of God's grace. Our security lies therefore in knowing that "the reality of salvation transcends by far any subjective, incidental experiencing of it" (Berkouwer, *Faith and Perseverance,* p. 79). Again and again God's irresistible grace overcomes our resistance. As the prophet testifies, "Thou art stronger than I, and thou hast prevailed" (Jeremiah 20:7). As we embrace by faith God's preserving grace we may rest assured that "the transition from death to life [is] irreversible" (Berkouwer, *Faith and Perseverance,* p. 238). Such assurance of a deep-seated durability is of utmost importance, for Christians

> cannot and they may not be faced continually with an either-or, with a possible back-and-forth movement, from life unto death and then perhaps again from death to life. . . . There is but one road they must travel without turning back. (Berkouwer, *Faith and Perseverance,* p. 119)

Scripture never minimizes the power of personal and communal temptations. The way of the church through world history, like that of Israel, is beset by demonic principalities and power. Accordingly, the gospel punctuates its good news regularly with urgent warnings against "falling away" (1 John 2:19; Hebrews 6:4-8). But its positive intent is equally clear: "Hold fast" to the faith. For "he who endures to the end will be saved" (Matthew 10:22). The enemy persistently disputes Christ's claim on us. This is not a contest, however, whose outcome remains undecided (John 10:18). In the midst of its earnest admonitions to persevere ("work out your own salvation with fear and trembling") Scripture affirms the Father's unfailing grace ("for God is at work in you" — Philippians 2:12-13). Basically, therefore, "We don't persevere, but He perseveres by constantly calling us, disturbing us, inspiring us" (Hendrikus Berkhof, *Christian Faith,* p. 477).

The plan of salvation is directed toward creating a renewed humanity perfectly at home on a renewed earth. That end lies secure in God's promise of a twofold preservation: He safeguards both the heirs of salvation and their inheritance (Matthew 25:34; John 14:1-4; 1 Peter 1:4). Thus God's people are assured of a permanent place in the sun. This outlook lends a steady course to our Christian pilgrimage. For perseverance is not

> an experience of consolation that flickers and dies and then flickers again in the shadows of life's uncertainties, . . . that tomorrow could be partially, and later even totally, threatened and destroyed; but it is a continuity amidst all the transitoriness of our lives, as we proceed by devious paths through numberless circumstances and dangers toward the consummation, toward the day of Jesus Christ. (Berkouwer, *Faith and Perseverance,* p. 10)

III. 7. 5. *"Pray Constantly"*

In an appendix to his doctoral dissertation of 1953, Edwin Palmer offered the following thesis: "It must be considered a serious omission in most Reformed systematic theologies that they devote little or no attention to prayer" (*Scheeben's Doctrine of Divine Adoption,* "Stellingen," no. VIII). A quarter century later Hendrikus Berkhof surveyed the field, including several more recent works, and came to a similar conclusion (*Christian Faith,* pp. 495-96). There are, however, some notable attempts to fill that void (cf. Berkouwer, "Perseverance and Prayer," *Faith and Perseverance,* pp. 127-53, where the author discusses "the prayers of believers, the intercession of Christ, and the prayer of the Holy Spirit"; Hendrikus Berkhof, "Prayer," *Christian Faith,* pp. 490-97; Thielicke, "Empowering for Prayer by the Pneuma," *The Evangelical Faith,* Vol. III, pp. 83-89). These dogmatic studies reflect a return to Calvin's strong emphasis on "Prayer [as] the Chief Exercise of Faith" (*Institutes,* III,20,1-52). Commenting there on Paul's exhortation to "pray constantly" (1 Thessalonians 5:17-18), Calvin says that

> the reason why Paul enjoins us both to pray and to give thanks without ceasing . . . [is] . . . that he wishes all men to lift up their desires to God, with all possible constancy, at all times, in all places, and in all affairs and transactions, to expect all things from him, and give him praise for all things, since He gives us unfailing reasons to praise and pray. (*Institutes,* III,20,28)

Prayer is "the perpetual exercise of faith." Paul is therefore not urging on the Thessalonian Christians "a prayer-mysticism, an attitude which suppresses ordinary life. In fact, . . . it is in their daily round that they are to pray without ceasing" (Berkouwer, *Faith and Perseverance,* p. 129). In prayer the entire multifaceted scope of the biblical worldview comes into play. For praying is not an occasional "sacred" activity alongside the regular "secular" affairs of life. It is holist in its outlook: it brings all of life to bear on this human-divine dialogue.

Prayer is trinitarian. As our Lord taught us, even our communal prayer has a very personal address: "our Father in heaven." For "just as faith is born from the gospel, so through it our hearts are trained to call upon God's name" (*Institutes,* III,20,1). In prayer, as in all else, moreover, "Christ is the eternal and abiding Mediator" (*Institutes,* III,20,20). For he is not only "the Preparer of the way: He is himself the way." Therefore, "our own praying is nothing other than our uniting ourselves with the prayer of Christ" (Wilhelm Niesel, *The Theology of Calvin,* p. 154). His mediation follows in a direct line of continuity with all covenant history. For "as sacrifice made prayer effective in the Old Testament, so the sacrifice of Christ makes his intercession for us at the right hand of God for ever effective" (Ronald Wallace, *Calvin's Doctrine of the Christian Life,* p. 275). "To pray rightly," Calvin holds furthermore, "is a rare gift." Such weakness of faith, however, should not cause us to "vegetate in that carelessness to which we are all too prone," but rather, "loathing our inertia and dullness, we should seek the aid of the Holy Spirit" (*Institutes,* III,20,5). For "He alone is the proper teacher of the art of prayer. He not only inspires in us the words, but guides the movements of our hearts" (Niesel, *The Theology of Calvin,* p. 155).

Fervent prayer arises thus from the heart, the religious unifying center of our entire personhood. Like converging lines of communication it draws together into concentrated moments of highly focused conversation the many outward expressions of daily living. Prayer is "the disburdening of the heart before God" (Wallace, *Calvin's Doctrine of the Christian Life,* p. 281) — "an emotion of the heart within," says Calvin, "which is poured out and laid open before God, the searcher of hearts" (*Institutes,* III,20,29). Viewed anthropologically, prayer is centered in the heart; but it must not be self-centered in its coverage. Think of the Lord's Prayer. It is our decisive introduction to prayer inasmuch as it encompasses [according to Luther] the whole span of possible situations out of which we pray. It focuses on the coming of the kingdom and the hallowing of the divine name, but also on the supply of daily bread, on all that the body needs — food, drink, clothes, shoes, house, farm, fields, money, property, a devout wife and devout children, devout companions, a devout and loyal master, good government, good weather, peace, health, order, honor, good friends, true neighbors, and the like. (Thielicke, *The Evangelical Faith*, Vol. III, p. 88)

"To every Christian," therefore, "Christ commits the welfare of the Church by committing to him the vital task of interceding for the Church and the Kingdom" (Wallace, *Calvin's Doctrine of the Christian Life*, p. 288).

Many today experience a "crisis in prayer." Does it really "pay" to pray? In such times it is important to remember that all our praying, together with hearing and answering on God's part, hinges crucially on his mediating Word. That Word, first spoken with the creation, then inscripturated in the Bible and incarnate in Christ, is the religious lifeline of our fellowship with God. God holds himself to that Word. We may therefore appeal incessantly to his covenant promises. As in the parable of the persistent widow and the obstinate judge (Luke 18:1-8), so, says Calvin, believers ought to "harass God the Father till at length they wrest from him what He would otherwise appear unwilling to give." For "God wills to be, as it were, wearied out by prayers" (Wallace, *Calvin's Doctrine of the Christian Life*, p. 291). There is accordingly in Scripture "a great emphasis on perseverance and continuity in prayer" (Berkouwer, *Faith and Perseverance*, p. 129).

In its parables, but elsewhere too, Scripture is clearly speaking analogically. It uses language accommodated to our creaturely level of understanding. The reality of the analogy is nonetheless securely anchored in the mediating Word of God. For not only does God bind himself covenantally to that Word, but he holds us to it as well. In praying, therefore, the heart moves the tongue to find words in answer to God's Word. Our approach to God is always motivated by his first coming out to us. His covenant Word seeks conversing partners. For prayer is "a meeting, not a monologue" (Hendrikus Berkhof, *Christian Faith*, p. 496). Thus, "one who is convinced of the genuineness and the decisive nature of the covenant encounter has no doubt that God reacts to his partner — more so than we dare pray for or imagine. . . . Outside this partnership [there is] no ground for this belief. . . . Inside [there is] no more ground for doubt" (Hendrikus Berkhof, *Christian Faith*, p. 497). In his winsome exposition on prayer under the caption "The Christian under the Universal Lordship of God the Father," Barth says that by coming before God as one who asks, [the Christian] magnifies God and abases himself. . . . [For] by his Word this great and holy and rich God draws . . . so near with the nearness of Father and child that in face of Him man now finds himself in the nearness of child and Father, . . . so that he may receive that which . . . only God can really give him. (*Church Dogmatics,* III/3, no. 49, pp. 268-70)

III. 7. 6. Elect in Christ

Why this unusual arrangement of doctrines — reserving a discussion of predestination in general, especially election and reprobation, to the close of the way of salvation? Is this "delay" meant to suggest that these truths are merely an afterthought? Certainly not that, for these manifestations of God's will are a fundamental and comprehensive expression of his sovereign rule in our world from beginning to end. They are woven inextricably into the very fabric of the unfolding biblical story line. How we think about this doctrine, and what we say about it, is obviously therefore very important. But where we locate it in our theology is hardly less important. In placing this doctrine here we are following Calvin's lead in the definitive edition of the *Institutes.*

In editions 1539-1554 Calvin treated the topics of providence and predestination in the same chapter. In the final edition [of 1559] they are widely separated, providence being set here in the context of the knowledge of God the Creator, while predestination is postponed to [Book III], where it comes within the general treatment of the redemptive work of the Holy Spirit. (John T. McNeill, ed., *Institutes,* I,16,1, footnote 1, p. 197)

Handling this decree in its original place lent it a rather abstract, scholastic, nonhistorical character. Calvin's later striking shift in location lends it a much more concrete, experiential, confirmational impact. It is designed to reassure believers that their salvation has a deeper background. It is securely anchored in the abiding and ever faithful Word of God. From start to finish, therefore, salvation was and is and ever will be in "good hands."

It is the prerogative of Scripture, Calvin holds, to establish the terms for theological reflection on the doctrine of predestination/election/reprobation. On the one hand, we must seek to say no more than is revealed in the Bible, lest we fall into idle speculation. He therefore warns against "human curiosity" which "will leave no secret to God that it will not search out and unravel." Such probing recognizes "no restraints" to "hold it back from wandering into forbidden bypaths and thrusting

507

upward to the heights." One who indulges such "audacity and impudence
. . . will enter a labyrinth from which he can find no exit" (*Institutes,*
III,21,1). On the other hand, says Calvin, we must try to say no less than
Scripture, lest we impoverish its message. Here Calvin has in mind those
who "require that every mention of predestination be buried; indeed they
teach us to avoid any mention of it, as we would a reef" (*Institutes,*
III,21,3). Thus Calvin concludes that "the Word of the Lord is the sole
way that can lead us in our search for all that is lawful to hold concerning
him, and is the sole light to illumine our vision of all that we should see
of him." Accordingly he commends "a certain learned ignorance" (*Institutes,* III,21,2). In passing it must be noted that, as with all of us, so
too with Calvin, theological reflection on this doctrine often fails to live
up to these sound principles of interpretation. In Calvin this arises largely
from his adherence to Augustine's idea of "double predestination," which
is traceable in turn to the influence of neo-Platonic thought.

In spite of this shortcoming, Calvin still represents a radical departure from the scholastic approach of medieval thinkers. In refuting
them, Calvin holds that "we ought not to rack our brains about God,"
as they do, "but rather we should contemplate him in his works"
(*Institutes,* I,5,9). The crucial question is therefore not "who is God in
himself?" but "who is he in his relationship to us"? All knowledge of
God's decrees is relational. And the *relatio* which binds God and man
together as covenantal *relata* is God's mediating Word. These freshly
evangelical insights of Calvin were soon lost, however, on his followers.
They recast the medieval tradition which Calvin had abandoned into a
Protestantized form of scholasticism with its decretal theology. This
brought about a return to two-factor theologizing with its far-reaching
consequences. It opened the door to very intricate speculations about
the order of the decrees in the eternal mind of God. Heated debates
arose between infra- and supralapsarians — posing false and cruel
dilemmas, and imposing on Reformed communities an irresolvable
problem. As a result, dark and ominous shadows were cast over biblical
teachings on the way of salvation. The sovereign grace of God engendered a gnawing sense of anxiety instead of hope and comfort and
security. The seasoned end product of this scholastic tradition comes to
expression in the following syllogism:

> The doctrine of reprobation follows naturally from the logic of the situation. The decree of election inevitably implies the decree of reprobation. If
> the all-wise God, possessed of infinite knowledge, has eternally purposed
> to save some, then He *ipso facto* also purposed not to save others. If He
> has chosen or elected some, then He has by that very fact also rejected
> others. (Louis Berkhof, *Systematic Theology,* pp. 117-18)

The question arises now, Is it possible to shed the unbearable weight of this troublesome caricature? Is there a better way of "handling aright the Word of truth"? Can we take this *decretum horribile* ("the awesome decree"), as Calvin called it, and make it more believable, preachable, teachable, and livable? Turning to Scripture, we read that in the very context of gospel outreach "as many as were ordained to eternal life believed, . . . [and the disciples] were glad and glorified the Word of God" (Acts 13:48). It would be sheer pretense, of course, to think that by putting our minds to it we can penetrate the mysterious depths of God's sovereign acts in history. The mystery stands, captured eloquently in the words of the familiar hymn:

> I sought the Lord, and afterward
>   I knew
> He moved my soul to seek him,
>   seeking me.

Thus, "Election is the first word in God's activity and the last in the confession of believers" (Hendrikus Berkhof, *Christian Faith,* p. 480).

Predestination/election/reprobation, accordingly, is not an independent, isolated doctrine. It is part and parcel of an overall perspective on life. Quoting Hendrikus Berkhof once again, "Election is not only the final resting place of the heart in the ups and downs of the spiritual struggle, it is also the basic word, which is as comprehensive as salvation itself because it characterizes the totality of God's dealings with his people, his church, his world" (*Christian Faith,* p. 479). Only a three-factor worldview — God/his Word/the world — can help relieve the tensions created by scholastic thinking and renew our vision. Election is rooted in God's Word, and never stands apart from it. That mediating Word, given with creation and reaffirmed in Scripture and in Christ, is the abiding standard for covenant-keeping and covenant-breaking. By honoring its central normative role in our theology, we can enrich our understanding of the urgency, profundity, and surety of our ongoing responses to that Word. We can then reflect more concretely on God's steadfastness: He remains true to his electing and reprobating Word. We can then also speak more experientially about covenant faithfulness/election and covenant unfaithfulness/reprobation on our part in responding to it.

From the beginning God by his mediating Word maintains his electing/reprobating claim on all mankind. That original Word embraces both his "Yes" and his "No," expressing both acceptance and rejection. Reprobation is not a Word added later, after the fall. It, too, is original. "Obey me!" God said — his Word of election. "Or else!" God said in the same breath — his Word of reprobation. Reprobation is the "or else" side of God's love command. Recall the Genesis story: "Eat freely of every tree" — God's electing Word. But the shadow side is also real: "In the day you eat of the [other tree] you shall die" — God's reprobating Word. From the dawn of history onward God's two-in-one Word is ever active and decisive. It encompasses all the vital elements of the covenantal relationship: the promise, the condition, the reward, and the penalty. Response to that Word is a matter of life (election) or death (reprobation). As it turned out, in Adam as our representative head we were all plunged into a state of reprobation. This divine judgment required no added decree. It was a consequence already given in and with God's original Word. God was simply implementing its abiding terms. True to that once-for-all Word, God rejects those who (continue to) reject him. Condemnation fell on all men: hence, by way of contrast, we now experience the enormous relief of Romans 8:1 — "no condemnation."

In Christ election is now a reality greater than our reprobation in Adam. For in his electing grace God the Father reaffirms the original intent of his Word. He does not (continue to) reject all who reject him. In the Christ of Scripture he reiterates the "Yes" side of his decreeing Word. And through the enabling work of the Spirit that Word takes hold in our hearts and lives. Its life-affirming side overcomes the death-dealing effects of the "No" which God pronounced on our reprobating choices. But why then do some continue to live under the heavy cloud of God's "No"? That is the enigma of reprobation. And why do others embrace his "Yes"? That is the mystery of election. Both responses find their ultimate reference point in the Word which stands forever. There is therefore mystery enough on the side of our response to God's Word without the urge to explore the mystery which lies on God's side, beyond the Word which he has given. Looking around in every direction, even beyond the horizons of our life in the world today, we may claim election as a present historical reality. And that confidence need not be eclipsed by foreboding thoughts about "election from eternity."

What, then, are we to make of those biblical passages which refer to "pretemporal" acts of God? Scripture speaks of "the kingdom prepared for you from the foundations of the world" (Matthew 25:24), of the "good works, which God prepared beforehand, that we should walk in them" (Ephesians 2:10), and of "being elect in Christ from before the foundation of the world" (Ephesians 1:4). Do these passages, then, thrust us back after all to a set of eternal decrees in the mind of God? They certainly confirm the Christian conviction that there is a deeper background to life's drama. But is a decretalist interpretation our only choice? In light of the biblical worldview, it may be said that the claim that such biblical passages make on us can be meaningfully satisfied by appealing to the originating, mediating Word of God. That Word is God's standing decree. It is neither necessary nor possible to reach back beyond it into the inner recesses of God's mind. As Niesel puts it in restating Calvin's thought,

> It is certainly not the will of God that by the process of our thinking we should seek to raise ourselves up to [God] in order to become clear about our destiny. . . . [For] when Christ confronts us in his Word and we become his own, then there is for us no longer any mysterious counsel of God which might become the object of our brooding and the source of our uncertainty. (*The Theology of Calvin,* p. 163)

The fully manifested Word of God is decisive for all men and for all time. Election echoes its overtone ("come unto me") and reprobation its undertone ("depart from me"). That single Word reveals both God's justice and his mercy.

In Jesus Christ, the Word incarnate, God's justice and mercy meet and embrace each other. This revelation of sovereign grace shapes all of covenant history. In choosing for a fallen Adam, in calling father Abraham, in re-creating Israel as a chosen nation, God was displaying his electing love with a view to the coming Messiah. So now, in electing Christ as Redeemer of the world (1 Peter 1:20; 2 Peter 2:4), God is electing a new humanity to carry out the creational mandate as our Christian calling. Drawing on an analogy going back to Augustine, Calvin, and others, we may look on Christ as "the mirror of our election." He reflects fully and clearly the Father's heart and will. He is God's final and ultimate Word on election/reprobation. We have no Word, and no need of any Word, beyond him. He is God's first and also his last Word for the world. He who has seen Christ has seen the Father (John 14:6-11). "Hence Christ is the mirror in which we must and certainly may behold the fact of our election" (Niesel, *The Theology of Calvin,* p. 163). Our answer to the question, "Where do we stand with Christ?" also settles the question of our election, one way or another. For by God's sovereign grace, just as we are justified by faith, so we are also elect by faith in Christ.

> Election/reprobation is therefore not an "eighth question" to be settled after the "first seven" are settled. It is not as though, having faced up to the questions of believing in Christ, loving him, seeking to serve him, and all the rest, there is still that final, haunting, gnawing, nagging "eighth" question hanging over one's head: "But am I elect?" Election/reprobation is not an extra, separate issue over and above the others. Rather, the fundamental issue of our relation to God is settled in the process of

511

answering the question, "What then will you do about Jesus?" For we are "elect in Christ." And no one can snatch the elect out of his hand. We need not, nor can we, reach behind the will of God in Jesus Christ in an effort to discover a higher or deeper will of God embedded in his eternal decree. Either he is our "rock and our redeemer," or he is our "stone of stumbling." It is impossible to go over Christ's head directly to the Father, as though there were some way of "going to the top" by making "an end run" around the Mediator. What more could God say or do than he has said and done in him? Christ is God's only interface with the world. (Gordon Spykman, "A New Look at Election and Reprobation," *Life Is Religion,* Henry Vander Goot, ed., pp. 181-82)

Election in Christ is therefore the firm foundation undergirding the certainty of our faith and our assurance of salvation. For "certitude of salvation in Christ is also certitude of election, and vice versa: certitude of election is only to be found in Christ" (Niesel, *The Theology of Calvin,* p. 165). This leads Berkouwer to comment pastorally that

The election of God is an election of mercy, precisely because it is election in Christ. That is why the Bible shows us the way of belief, and why "in Christ" can become the foundation of a pastoral message that points at Christ as *speculum electionis.* This is not meant as an escape, a rock to which we must cling in the face of the tremendous fact of election; no, the very structure of that election is revealed in Christ. There is election only in Christ, and for that reason we may look up to Him. . . . No theological reflection can by itself lead to this insight. It can only serve the preaching of the gospel by indicating the way of faith. This way can now be traveled because the inscrutability of election no longer poses a threat. Since election is election in Christ, the light of the message shines clearly. Because this light shines, the gospel may be preached, not as a proclamation regarding an accomplished state of affairs, but as a call and summons. He who travels the way of faith and puts his trust in Jesus Christ alone, will understand that beyond Him there arises no new, ultimate problem, but that in Him this problem is solved. God's election is election in Christ. (*Divine Election,* pp. 149, 162)

PART FIVE
THE CONSUMMATION

Transitional Comments

The central plot in the biblical story line continues to unfold. The final chapter is already being written into the annals of redemption history. Traditionally it bears the title "Eschatology." All too often, as Barth comments wryly, it is assigned the role of "a short and perfectly harmless chapter" (*Epistle to the Romans*, p. 500) reserved for the final week in a course of study, leaving little time to deal with it seriously. Such practice shortchanges biblical teaching. For the doctrine of "last things" is "interpretation [of these 'end times'] from the perspective of the central point of Scripture" (Weber, *Foundations of Dogmatics*, Vol. II, p. 667). The eschatological drama is already being enacted. It introduces no totally new, unheard-of themes and characters. It makes no clean break with the past and present. Yet there is advance. For this "end time" history carries the biblical story line of creation, fall, and redemption forward, drawing all its diverse elements together into a breathtaking array of culminating acts. In the doctrine of the consummation of all things we are dealing, therefore, with surprising discontinuities within the continuity of God's way with the world. In the words of Bavinck, "the first and second comings of Christ stand in the closest possible relationship to each other. It is a single work, entrusted by the Father to Christ, and that work reaches out to all ages and includes the entire history of mankind" (*Magnalia Dei,* p. 630).

There is then one more clearly marked red letter date on the divine calendar — our final rendezvous with the ultimate destiny of men and nations. How shall we greet this great "day of the Lord"? There is no need for nervous, fearful, fingernail-biting anxiety. We can approach it in the confidence of faith, knowing — as a familiar adage puts it — that "though life is short, and will all too soon be past, yet whatever is done for Christ will last."

Chapter I

The Home Stretch

I. 1. A Fascinating Universe of Discourse

The stunning, sometimes even fantastic imagery which Scripture employs to illumine this "end-time" epoch makes heavy demands on our sanctified imagination. Its visionary symbols and word pictures tax our theological vocabularies to the limit. The caption itself, "Eschatology," long used to cover these closing episodes in the biblical story, sometimes stops us in our tracks. It results from a combination of *eschaton* and *logos,* meaning a study of "last things." At its center stands Christ, the *Eschatos* (the "End" of all things), the *Omega* (the final letter in the Greek alphabet), and the *Telos* (the "Goal" of all creation). The events related to his return are referred to as the *epiphany* (his "appearance"), the *apocalypse* (his "revelation"), and the *parousia* (his "return," "arrival," or "coming again," not merely as a "second coming," which allows for the possibility of yet another, a third "coming," but his "last coming," just as Christ himself is the "last Adam"). All the days of man's life in the world converge with finality in the dawning of this great "day of the Lord," which will come when the appointed "time" *(chronos)* has run its full course, and "the hour is at hand" *(kairos).*

These biblical perspectives confront us with "an incomparable multiplicity of aspects" (Herman Ridderbos, *Paul,* p. 562). A kaleidoscopic picture emerges which defies even the most dogged attempts at reconstructing these richly diversified elements into a closed system of doctrines — let alone calculated timetables and precise blueprints. In the words of Ridderbos, this colorful collage simply will not yield "a doctrine that in fixed order and piece by piece indicates the component parts of the picture." For "every programmatic description of a sequence of events and how it is going to happen is lacking" (*Paul,* pp. 554, 555). This

516

panoramic vision of things to come reflects, once again, the kind of book the Bible is. Its center of gravity lies in the here and now. Even when its light penetrates the future it addresses us consistently with present urgency: Since "the promise of entering [God's] rest remains," he "sets a certain day, 'Today,'" saying, "Today, when you hear his voice . . ." (Hebrews 4:1-10). In the words of Berkouwer, "the proclamation of the future is always existential; it calls forth from within the structure of the coming kingdom" (*The Return of Christ*, p. 12).

For now we must be content with a "sneak preview" of the *eschaton*. Wait and see, says Scripture. It is better than you think! As it is written,

> . . . no eye has seen, nor ear heard,
> nor the heart of man conceived,
> what God has prepared for those who love him. (1 Corinthians 2:9)

Therefore, do not consume your precious resources on stargazing or apocalyptic speculation. The details of the coming "day of the Lord" belong to the mysteries held in store in the counsel of God. The full picture lies on the "other side" of God's abiding Word. In "pious ignorance," therefore, we can face the future with that uniquely believing combination of knowing "already" and "not yet" knowing. For, "we are God's children now; it does not yet appear what we shall be, but we know that when he appears we shall be like him, for we shall see him as he is" (1 John 3:2). In taking to heart Christ's promise of the "nearness" of his coming, we are called to support one another with the gospel's "urgent insistence on the certainty of things to come" (Ridderbos, *The Coming of the Kingdom*, pp. 524-25). For "it is not so much the proximity as the certainty of the *parousia* that dominates Jesus' eschatological pronouncements" (Ridderbos, *The Coming of the Kingdom*, p. 521). Scripture imposes "a ban on every form of calculation," says Adrio König, for "every form of calculation misreads its message" (*The Eclipse of Christ in Eschatology*, p. 198).

Biblical perspectives on the consummation are regularly couched in apocalyptic language. They draw on seemingly unreal and out-of-this-world scenarios to disclose the real movements of history in the world. Many of the highly concentrated apocalyptic metaphors of the New Testament (Matthew 24–25; 1 Thessalonians 4–5; 2 Thessalonians 2; Revelation) are redemptively updated replays of themes borrowed from Old Testament prophecy (Ezekiel, Daniel). These "boundary line" figures of speech point to actual events, past, present, and future. But they are veiled in mystery. Such biblical imagery is worlds removed, however, from Greek mythologies with their exposés of deceit and intrigue in the arena of the gods. The apocalyptic symbols of Scripture are rather concealed revelations of real down-to-earth crisis points in the eschatological drama. They touch on real historical life-and-death issues in language which skirts the outer edges of reality. They illumine the present from the viewpoint of "end-time" expectations. It is important accordingly to interpret them as we would Rembrandt's "Night Watch," not scrutinizing the fabric of the canvas or examining each stroke in the painting, but stepping back to catch a view of the picture as a whole. Since such "imagery is the language that comes closest to what eternity is like, together with the language of music" (such as in Handel and Bach), we may well ask with Hendrikus Berkhof, "Should not the dogmatician yield here to the poet?" (*Christian Faith,* p. 533).

I. 2. A Doctrine on the Move

In the ancient world the Hebraic-Christian tradition was unique in its goal-directed view of history. The prophets and apostles measured the great events in covenant history — past, present, and future — as moments within an interconnected linear movement, teleologically directed toward a divinely appointed "end." Among surrounding peoples a cyclical view of time prevailed. Jewish and Christian communities were therefore blessed with the opportunity of offering badly needed answers to the perennial questions of human existence: Where do we come from? How did we get to be the way we are? Why are we here? What lies ahead? In its address to these issues, the witness of the Old and New Testaments lays a firm foundation for a Christian eschatology. For already in the cross and resurrection "the mystery of the kingdom is most impenetrably veiled as well as most gloriously revealed. Now at last that which had been whispered into the ear can be preached from the house tops." In fact, "the parousia of the Son of Man is even provisionally fulfilled in his resurrection" (Ridderbos, *The Coming of the Kingdom,* pp. 465, 468).

In this reformational dogmatics the theology of the sixteenth-century Reformers has served as an historical point of departure. On the doctrine of "last things," however, a critical comment by Hoeksema must be taken into account. "At the time of the Reformation," he says, "eschatology did not receive its proper place and attention in dogmatics" (*Reformed Dogmatics,* p. 730). In reflecting on this theme, therefore, the writings of the Reformers offer only a limited source of appeal. In Anabaptist circles biblical visions on the future kingdom were exploited heavily. Luther, however, dealt with the doctrine of "last things" in only fragmentary ways. Calvin, too, gave it only passing attention. Noteworthy among his voluminous writings is the absence of a commentary on the book of Revelation. Far-reaching conclusions are often drawn from this omission, including indictments of an alleged eschatological impoverishment in the Calvinist tradition.

This shortfall in the theological legacy of the Reformers is better understood, however, when viewed against the background of the development of this dogma during the preceding centuries. A hasty review must suffice to make this clear. Many early church fathers already set out to probe the "end-time" mysteries revealed in Scripture. Recall the millennial views of Irenaeus and Tertullian, and the crass speculations of Origen. For generations eschatological reflection remained in a state of high flux. Eventually a consensus developed around Augustine's portrayal of the ultimate triumph of "the City of God" over "the city of the world." In the main, however, early Christians were sustained in their faith by a practical piety which looked to Jesus Christ as their hope of glory in facing the pressures of a pagan world.

During the medieval era eschatological attention became focused strongly on otherworldly pursuits. It fostered the saintly ideal of the "beatific vision." At the same time it troubled the conscience of common believers with the haunting specter of purgatorial fires.

Responding to these developments, the Reformers introduced a radical shift in emphasis. In the deeply spiritual struggles of that momentous century the most urgent, immediately pressing issue was walking the way of salvation here and now in the certainty of faith. This quest for assurance of salvation took center stage so completely that it left eschatological issues waiting in the wings. We must not forget, moreover, that this was still the sixteenth century. Not until the eighteenth century did a deeply ingrained sense of historical development emerge forcefully in the West. To think about issues eschatologically depends strongly on thinking historically. This set in with a vengeance in the wake of the Enlightenment. The Reformers' neglect of "the question of the future of the world" can be attributed to their failure to "perceive time as a process" (Weber, *Foundations of Dogmatics,* Vol. II, p. 672). During the first millennium and a half of the Christian era, therefore, while the eschatological vision of the church was often blurred, it was never eclipsed. The hope of believers in a reality transcending the present life strengthened them along the pilgrim way.

With the advent of modernity revolutionary changes set in. The transcendent vision faded. New eschatologies were born, based on the idea of "the unfolding of immanent forces" (Hendrikus Berkhof, *Christian Faith,* p. 522). Historicism arose, absolutizing a secularized progress ideal. Life was reduced to historical process, replacing biblical eschatology with humanist utopias. The social gospel of modern liberalism proclaimed the possibility of a "heaven on earth" if reasonable men of goodwill would rally to the cause. Evolutionism, social Darwinism included, rode in on this bandwagon. Existentialism absorbed future horizons into a succession of ever present moments. A host of conflicting futurologies arose, some optimistic in outlook, others pessimistic. Meanwhile science and technology held out the promise of instant transformations.

Reacting to these trends, neoorthodoxy helped to recover a profoundly eschatological awareness of God's dealings with the world. It tended, however, to stress the present reality of biblical eschatology at the expense of its historical extension, collapsing its horizontal dimension into crisis moments of vertical encounter. An even stronger reaction to nineteenth-century futurism arose in modern fundamentalism, especially in its dispensationalist wings. Sparked by the appearance of the Scofield Bible in 1909, masses of evangelical Christians set out to recover lost ground. They now confront us daily with prophecies of an impending rapture, accompanied by great tribulations, ushering in the millennium and the reestablishment of Israel as a theocracy.

These hasty strokes describe roughly the situation in which we find ourselves today. We face futurologies of the left, the right, and the middle. In the midst of these contrary winds of doctrine, biblical eschatology occupies a strategic place on our theological agendas. It is a highly problematic, critical venture, perhaps more so than ever before, and for that reason perhaps also a matter of increasingly high priority. A reformational dogmatics may not turn a deaf ear to the urgent questions of our generation: What is the destiny of man and the world? Is there still hope of a "happy ending"? Or must we brace ourselves for an impending "doomsday"? Is the "apocalypse now" perhaps already on us? These are issues we must keep in the forefront of our minds as we explore the contours of biblical eschatology, recognizing that dogmatics, as all else in life, is itself an eschatological undertaking. It, too, is "on the way," with "not yet" as well as "already" aspects. We must therefore remain keenly aware of our engagement in an "eschatological dogmatics."

I. 3. Last Things/First Things

As mediating Word of God, Christ is identified repeatedly in John's vision as both the absolute Alpha (the "Beginning") and Omega (the "End") (Revelation 1:8, 11; 21:6; 22:13). He is the Mediator not only of creation and redemption, but also of the consummation. For in him "the mystery of [God's] will" is revealed as "a plan for the fulness of time, to unite all things in him, things in heaven and things on earth" (Ephesians 1:10). He is "the Man for all seasons." Protology (the doctrine of "first things") and eschatology (the doctrine of "last things") in their full cosmic scope are both centered in Christ — and everything in between as well. Through all the twists and turns of covenant history, all across the wide-embracing sweep of the coming kingdom, Christ remains God's first Word and his last Word for the world. For

> the most profound link between creation and consummation lies in Jesus Christ himself, who is the beginning and the end, the first and the last, the Creator and the Consummator. In his own person he unites creation and consummation. In him they are not two events infinitely separated from each other in time, but a single reality bound together in him, the living Lord, by whose power creation proceeds to consummation and consummation comes forth from creation. All is created by him, and by him all is renewed. (König, *The Eclipse of Christ in Eschatology*, pp. 62-63)

The eschaton (the consummation) and the Eschatos (the Consummator) are therefore inextricably connected. As in the beginning, so also in the end, event and Person, history and kerygma, go hand in hand. For "all *things*," without exception, are "in *Christ*." In his person and work every created thing is infused with God-given meaning. Life does not merely *have* meaning as one among several of its attributes. Life *is* meaning. Since all of life, life in its entirety, is religion, it is therefore meaning-full, filled full with meaning. So it was in the beginning: creation was cosmos, not chaos. The meaning-full-ness of life was decisively restored in the cross and resurrection, where Christ overcame the absurdities of sin and evil. In this "new age" he continues his work of renewing the meaning of life: "Behold, I am making all things new" (Revelation 21:5). From this viewpoint "eschatology is teleological christology — goal-directed christology." Not that "eschatology is coextensive with christology." Still, "in order to understand eschatology . . . we must focus on [Christ] and determine who he is" (König, *The Eclipse of Christ in Eschatology*, pp. 37-38).

The consummation points to the final restoration of our life in the world to all it was and still is meant to be. Even now all world history is unfolding eschatologically toward its appointed Christ-centered eschaton. This is the comprehensive witness of Scripture. Our knowledge of God's "end times," like our knowledge of his "creating time," is wholly dependent on biblical revelation. Since therefore at both ends of the eschatological drama we "see through a glass dimly," our eschatology as well as our protology must be graced with a healthy dose of "pious ignorance." It is ours simply to search the Scriptures humbly and submissively as we keep our lives open to the great "day of the Lord." As we move on toward it, this conviction carries us along, that Christ is not only the Archē (the "starting point") of all creation, but also its Telos (its "Goal"). His parousia brings about "the end, when [the Son] delivers the kingdom to God the Father. . . ." For "when all things are subjected to [Christ], then the Son himself will also be subjected to him who put all things under him, that God may be everything to every one" (1 Corinthians 15:24-28). Then "every eye will see at last that our world belongs to God" (*A Contemporary Testimony,* stanza 58).

I. 4. Two Points of View

Eschatology is not a divine afterthought, like an item tucked away in the back pages of the newspaper, lost among the obituary columns and the advertisements. Its theme, "the King is coming," is front-page headline news, unfolding section by section from page one onward. It is not an appendix, but "an integral aspect of all biblical revelation" (Anthony Hoekema, *The Bible and the Future,* p. 3). From beginning to end the history of redemption is eschatological — moving toward its appointed "end." It is teleological — directed toward its goal. From the "mother promise" onward, through the call of Abraham, the creation of a "chosen people" to inherit the "promised land," through the era of the kings, the captivity, and the return from exile, and finally through the preservation of a faithful remnant — God's way with Israel held its course. This older phase in covenant history reached its eschaton, for the time being, in the appearance of the Messiah as "the consolation of Israel" (Luke 2:25).

The incarnation does not mark the end of the story, but another new beginning in the biblical story line, but then decisively new. God's way with the world exceeds Israel's expectations. In his life, death, and resurrection Christ inaugurates the final phase in kingdom history. The apostles, commissioned by him, pioneered the "end times." We with them have now entered the "last days." These are the contours of the biblical drama, leading us to read the history of redemption eschatologically, as a two-part drama. Let us pause now to differentiate these two points of view, standing first where the prophets stood and then taking our stand beside the apostles.

I. 4. 1. Tunnel Vision

Until the dawning of the great "day of the Lord," neither Israel nor the church can say, We have arrived! Together we are "on the way." The "not yet" factor is ever with us. Even in these latter days we are called to live by faith, not by sight. But in the midst of our provisional way of life we are sustained by God's "already" in Jesus Christ. For Israel, however, things were very different. Their eschatological vision was even more provisional, and their faith even more tentative. They had less to go by, and certainly less to see. They lived in the shadows of an exclusively "not yet" stage in redemption history, with no "already," no Messianic reality to which they could appeal. Faith in Israel was oriented to a distant promise.

As the prophets, therefore, looked beyond their "present age" toward the "age to come," their outlook on the future was understandably shortsighted. From our vantage point it is possible to differentiate the two comings of the Messiah. The prophets, however, suffered from "tunnel vision." Within their limited field of vision these two eschatological horizons merged into a single cataclysmic crisis (Luke 3:9, 17). This expectation of judgment and deliverance represented the full scope of their Messianic hopes, concentrated intensely in a coming "day of the Lord." The coming of the Messiah and the end of the age were viewed as coinciding (Isaiah 65:17-25). Yet even within this limited vision there is evidence of "a growing enrichment in eschatological expectation" (Hoekema, *The Bible and the Future,* p. 11).

This idea of eschatological convergence is echoed belatedly in the disciples' question concerning "the sign of your coming" and "the close of the age" (Matthew 24:3). Their minds were still shaped by the prophetic viewpoint in which the two appearances of Christ are drawn so close together that events related to the final coming are compressed into "one picture with the first coming" (Bavinck, *Gereformeerde Dogmatiek,* Vol. IV, p. 667). This merging perspective, collapsing the final consummation into its interim fulfillment, carried Old Testament believers halfway home. The New Testament offers us a more clearly differentiated viewpoint. However different the older and newer perspectives, yet they in their day and we in ours walk the same way of salvation and await the same eschaton, even though the "present age" of the prophets is now "times past" for us, and their "age to come" has been transformed into "these last days" (Hebrews 1:1-2). The prophetic and apostolic eras are now distinguishable as the "introduction" and the "conclusion" to this final phase in the single unfolding eschatological drama.

I. 4. 2. "Between the Times"

The New Testament believer is conscious, on the one hand, of the fact that the great eschatological event predicted in the Old Testament has already happened, while on the other hand he realizes that another series of eschatological events is still to come. (Hoekema, *The Bible and the Future*, p. 13)

These parameters define the "in-between times" in the life of the Christian community. The first "fulness of the times" created the conditions for our present witness in the world. It underscores the continuity of God's work of redemption. For precisely in its discontinuity — as with all other mighty acts of God, past, present, and future — Christ's first coming assures the eschatological continuity of the way of salvation, serves it, and stands decisively as its historical center.

With Christ's exaltation the teleological movements which shape kingdom history now move onward with quickened pace. The three earth-shaking days from Good Friday to Easter Sunday set the stage for the Messianic expectations of the prophets to reach their crowded climax in that provisional "end." From that moment on Christ's resurrection (the "already") and his return (the "not yet") stand out with finality as the two overpowering events which together define the opening and closing acts in the ongoing eschatological drama. Whereas the prophets envisioned fulfillment and consummation as a single highly compressed event, the apostles clarify these pro-visional anticipations by recognizing that they happen in sequence, thus creating space for present history, bounded by the first and last comings of the Lord. These two crucial events serve as a set of "book ends" holding together the gospel message. From where we stand, the fulfillment motif points back to the inauguration of these "last days." The consummation motif points forward to their culmination in the great "day of the Lord." The presence of Christ, even now during this period of his absence, unifies the outcome of these two events. Though separated by centuries in the march of time, Christ's first and last comings represent the "firstfruits" and the "final harvest" of covenant history. During this interim "Christ gives the reconciled creature time and space in order that he may participate in the harvest, not as a mere spectator, but as a co-worker" (Berkouwer, *The Return of Christ*, p. 135).

The eschatological "not yet" is not the norm for Christian living, as though we may appeal to it as an alibi for our shortcomings. Our norm is obedience to the "already" of the creation order, redemptively updated in the cross and resurrection. For, as Paul says, since "Christ was raised from the dead," we are now called to "walk in newness of life" (Romans 6:1-4). The approaching parousia stands as a constant reminder that we, together with all creation, are "not yet" the fully restored creatures we shall one day become. "The road of the 'not yet' can only be a road to glory," however, "if constructed with the permanent perspective supplied by the 'already' " (Berkouwer, *The Return of Christ*, p. 138). For the window to the future is kept free of cloudiness by the breezes which blow through from the open door of the past. This "relationship between the 'already' and the 'not yet' constitutes the hallmark of the community of believers" (Berkouwer, *The Return of Christ*, p. 113).

The cross and resurrection marks the abiding turning point in history. Therefore "the center of time no longer lies in the future . . . as it does in Judaism, but in the past, i.e. in Christ's coming and action" (Ridderbos, *The Coming of the Kingdom*, p. 466). That decisive past is related to the promised future as "the way to the end" (Hoeksema, *Reformed Dogmatics*, p. 772). As we walk this way, there is such "a close nexus between present and future" (Geerhardus Vos, *Pauline Eschatology*, p. 51), along with the past, that the New Testament writers often prompt us, as it were, to turn our eyes forward and backward simultaneously in order to view more clearly the "middle ground" where we now stand — to do so from both "ends" in a single glance. Our "in-between times" are therefore not a christological vacuum, a lonely interlude between the past reality of Christ, viewed as the prelude, and his future reality, viewed as a postlude. For "always and in all the events of history . . . Jesus is coming, and He is coming quickly" (Hoeksema, *Reformed Dogmatics*, p. 775). The Heidelberg Catechism bears witness to this "ever present absence" of our Lord: For "in his human nature Christ is not now [with us] on earth; but in his divinity, majesty, grace, and Spirit he is not absent from us for a moment" (Q. & A. 47).

This perspective also opens up cosmic vistas. For since we are now already participating in "a provisionally realized final state, . . . the whole surrounding world has assumed a new aspect and complexion" (Vos, *Pauline Eschatology*, pp. 38, 47). Every moment is therefore eschatologically pregnant: the whole creation, and we with it, is in labor, "groaning in the travail" of its birth pangs, eagerly awaiting its final redemption (Romans 8:18-25). We may therefore state with confidence: Nothing in all of life is religiously neutral. The myth of neutrality stands forever exposed for the lie that it is.

The "last days" are therefore already with us. They are clearly not "last" in the sense of introducing new things which are to happen only after everything past is forgotten. Nor may we view them as "last," after which nothing more can happen. Their "lastness," their finality, points rather to the measured unfolding of eschatological history, which with gathering momentum eventuates crescendo-like in the consummation of all things. Right living in these "last days" means reaching out expectantly to that great approaching "day of the Lord" in the very midst of all our ordinary everydays. For the ultimate kairos (the time of Christ's return) does not reduce the importance of our daily chronos (calendar time), but lends it penultimate meaning. All time is God's time. His kairos shapes our chronos. We are to open ourselves up to the coming eschatological kairos in the midst of our routinely experienced chronos. That ultimate "end time" lends both chronological and eschatological urgency to our daily work.

As we move along "between the times," generation after generation, Scripture assures us that our salvation is "nearer at hand than when [we] first believed" (Romans 13:11) — a passage which influenced Barth to build into his earlier radically vertical view of eschatology a larger measure of horizontal movement. Our direction into the future is set by a divinely appointed linear time line. But this "nearness" involves more than chronological temporality. It also impinges on us with the full weight of a kairos-laden existential decisiveness. Ours is crisis time — time measured out by the standards of the coming kingdom. The "end" is therefore always at hand. For by his Word and Spirit the King is always near.

Because "the Lord is at hand," we can live relaxed, carefree lives (Philippians 4:5-6; Matthew 6:25-34). For the outcome is "already" assured. At the same time, the "not yet" aspect of these in-between times arouses us to active expectancy. The "already" aspect does not relieve but intensifies the awesome reality of kingdoms in conflict in every sphere of life — in politics, international law, social relationships, education, labor, and all the rest. For "alongside the growth and development of the kingdom of God in the history of the world since the coming of Christ, we see also the growth and development of the 'kingdom of evil' (Matthew 13:24-30, 36-43)." Thus, as Hoekema goes on to say,

> Here again we see the ambiguity of history. History does not reveal a simple triumph of good over evil. . . . Evil and good continue to exist side by side. Conflict between the two continues during the present age, but since Christ has won the victory, the ultimate outcome of the conflict is never in doubt. The enemy is fighting a losing battle. (*The Bible and the Future*, p. 35)

Borrowing Oscar Cullmann's well-known analogy, we live between D-day and V-day. God's great "day of Decision" took place in the cross and resurrection. It stands as a once-for-all event, unrepeatable. The final "day of Victory" hovers on the horizon. With tempered impatience and in the certainty of faith we journey toward that coming apocalypse. For "the hope of the final victory is so much the more vivid because of the unshakably firm conviction that the battle that decides the victory has already taken place" (Cullmann, *Christ and Time,* p. 87). Christ's return will clarify fully the mystery and hiddenness which still cling to our understanding of his first coming. For the consummation is the completion of the fulfillment. In the meantime, the Christian community lives "on the basis of the *parousia* and toward the *parousia*" (Weber, *Foundations of Dogmatics,* Vol. II, p. 682).

I. 5. The "Great Delay"

"Surely, I am coming soon!" (Revelation 22:20). With these parting words resounding apocalyptically across the island of Patmos near the close of the first century, Christ bids his church a final farewell. No new note was being struck, however. What John heard echoes faithfully what Jesus had proclaimed during his earthly mission: ". . . You know that [the Son of Man] is near, at the very gates" (Matthew 24:33). This imminent eschatological outlook also entered into the witness, proclamation, and teaching of the apostles. Though Paul's concern was not "to fix the time," yet "there is every reason to believe that [he] lived in the expectation of a soon-to-be-realized *parousia*" (Berkouwer, *The Return of Christ,* p. 92; see also Ridderbos, *Paul,* pp. 487-88; Hoekema, *The Bible and the Future,* p. 123).

Many early Christians, it appears, took Christ's prophecies at face value. But before long questions arose. How soon is "soon"? "The Lord is at hand!" (Philippians 4:5) — certainly that must mean "within reach." "The time is near" (Revelation 1:3) — but what are we to think when "near" turns out to be far away? Had not Jesus himself declared emphatically and repeatedly that the first generation of his disciples would live to see "all these things take place" (Matthew 24:34; 10:23; Mark 9:1; 13:30)? Some members of the Thessalonian congregation concluded that since "the end" was just around the corner, the appropriate response was to withdraw from their vocations. Paul rebukes this attitude. He calls them back to order: "Do not be weary in well-doing" (2 Thessalonians 3:6-15). Adding to this eschatological tension was the scoffing of the skeptics: "Where is the promise of his coming?" (2 Peter 3:4). Christ's first coming, they argued, has made no difference. His return is nowhere in sight. Nothing ever changes.

So doubts arose. Was the original faith of the disciples misplaced? Had Jesus miscalculated? Was God stalling? Down through the ages the experience of this "great delay" cast its disquieting shadows over the eschatological hopes of many Christians. Others accommodated these feelings of disillusionment by reading a prolonged period of time into the New Testament writings as a "make-shift solution" to the crisis of postponed expectations. The hermeneutics of modernity, with its secular worldviews and critical tools of analysis, has turned this problem of faith into a radically altered theological construct — a completely open-ended future.

Fundamentally Peter's response (2 Peter 3:1-13) must still carry the day. It is God who metes out the times and seasons. His way of counting "nearness" differs from ours — "a thousand years . . . one day." As a result of the momentous impact of the "already," a sweeping change has taken place in the eschatological relationship of promise and fulfillment to the "not yet." For "because salvation has already come through the death and resurrection of Christ, the problem of the date of the *parousia* can no longer be of decisive importance" (Berkouwer, *The Return of Christ*, p. 74). Within these new horizons "nearness" remains "an absolutely essential component of the eschatological proclamation of the New Testament" (Berkouwer, *The Return of Christ*, p. 84). Therefore the theme of "nearness" in the impending parousia confronts us not as "an increasing crisis in the expectation of faith, but an urgent call to watchfulness" (Berkouwer, *The Return of Christ*, p. 94). The "problem of the delay" can become an occasion for spiritual estrangement only when the "already" is not fully honored.

Even now, after two thousand years have elapsed, and as we anticipate the frenetic speculations which seem always to accompany the approaching end of a century, the biblical reminder is once again in order: what is most decisive is not the proximity or remoteness of the consummation, but its certainty. The gospel bars all attempts to calculate the time and place (Matthew 24:23-28). It is therefore "preferable not to use the term 'delay' at all — since its very usage implies calculation" (König, *The Eclipse of Christ in Eschatology*, p. 200). The detailed outworkings of the eschaton lie solely in the hands of the Eschatos. As Calvin would say, "Both the beginning and the ending of the new life are at [God's] disposal" (Niesel, *The Theology of Calvin*, p. 130). The experience of "delay" does not indicate a real mistake in the biblical witness or a real eschatological impasse. For

> in the final analysis the "at hand" does not involve a question of the importance of the intervening period, but of the inseparability of the future from the present. . . . The meaning of the interim time is not to start from "the problem of the delay of the *parousia*," but from the all-embracing motif of fulfillment. (Ridderbos, *Paul*, p. 496)

The *chrono*-logy of the interim is charged with opportunity *(kairos)*. It creates time and space for the empowering work of the Spirit, for covenant living, for gospel outreach, for kingdom projects. We must therefore be busy "making the most of the time" (Ephesians 5:15-16). We must live with "a sense of urgency, realizing that the end of history as we know it may be very near, but at the same time [we] must continue to plan and work for a future on the present earth which may last a long time" (Hoekema, *The Bible and the Future,* p. 52). We are called to "an attitude that does not *reckon,* but constantly *reckons with* the coming of the Lord." Then, while "unexpected," it will not be "un-expected" (Berkouwer, *The Return of Christ,* pp. 84, 85).

I. 6. How Then Shall We Live?

The New Testament addresses this question with eschatological insistence. The time is short; therefore "conduct yourselves wisely," "continue steadfastly in prayer," treat others "justly and fairly," be "watchful" and "thankful" (Colossians 4:1-6). The watchword is *semper paratus* (cf. Matthew 25:1-13), which does not mean being always out looking for Christ's return. But it does imply a state of readiness for this future, undergirded by a clear recollection of the past. A sense of fulfillment and expectancy go hand in hand. For "the church is the church of the future"; but its expectation is "based on the fact that the fulfillment has come" (Ridderbos, *The Coming of the Kingdom,* pp. 519-20). As the future penetrates the present, we are to scan the horizon, as it were, with one eye alert to the Lord's promised return, while keeping the other eye fixed on the tasks at hand.

The apocalypse will catch most people off guard, breaking in like a thief in the night (1 Thessalonians 5:2; Luke 12:35-40). The element of surprise is never absent (Revelation 3:3; 16:15). But the measure of our shock will be in inverse proportion to the measure of our watchfulness, wakefulness, and workfulness. Readiness calls for no new decision, however, beyond the standing call of obedient response to the Christ of the gospel.

Biblical eschatology is therefore no excuse for an otherworldly retreat from our God-given callings. It does not have "a negative, but a positive significance for life in the present time" (Ridderbos, *Paul,* p. 495). The expectation of the future reinforces our present mandate. For the norms of God's Word do not change. They are the same from creation to consummation. Between God's past and his future, our present life has a provisional character. But it brings with it no new set of "interim ethics" which departs from the cultural mandate. We are indeed called to "set [our] minds on things that are above" (Colossians 3:2), remembering, however, that this command is not structural in its thrust, telling us "where" to live our lives, but directional, telling us "how"/"in whose Name" to do so. The best way to seek the things above is to participate in God's mission in his world. For "the tie between eschatological expectation and the call to mission is essential and indissoluble" (Berkouwer, *The Return of Christ*, p. 132). "Holy worldliness" is what counts, not an obsessive concern with our own anticipated "state of eternal bliss." For "without a view of the world, the Christian expectation is blind and lame, and the Christian presence is pharisaically separatistic or mystically sunken into itself" (Weber, *Foundations of Dogmatics*, Vol. II, p. 684). "Nothing in the gospel forbids [Christians] to be faithful to life, to the earth, to culture." Rather, the gospel urges us to "accept life for the time God gives us to enjoy it" (Ridderbos, *The Coming of the Kingdom*, p. 471) — as active peacemakers, earthkeepers, advocates of justice, and agents of neighborly love.

Chapter II

The Millennium

To be forewarned is to be forearmed. We are entering a "war zone." A word of caution is therefore in order.

> The battles of theology too often have been fought not only in . . . a "condition of low visibility," but also against opponents who are dead and whose literature has been relegated to the back shelves of the libraries or to the trash heap. This is especially true of the millennial controversy. (A. J. McCain, in Charles L. Feinberg, *Millennialism*, p. 13)

II. 1. One Voice, Many Echoes

In our Western Christian tradition a veritable avalanche of theological literature has been unleashed by the idea of Christ's "thousand-year reign." Fascinating, often fanciful, sometimes even fantastic views of world history have sprung up around the single biblical passage on the millennium — Revelation 20:1-6. There in six brief verses we find five references to *(ta) chilia etē*, "(the) thousand years" — from which the concept "chiliasm" is derived.

Over the centuries a polyglot of chiliast theories has arisen, eschatologies which cover the entire destiny of the cosmos and the human race. In secularized forms chiliast ideas have shaped both fascist dreams of a "final solution" to the human problem (Hitler's "Third Reich") and Marxian ideas of a utopian society. In many Christian circles this passing reference in John's vision functions as the hermeneutic keyhole through which to envision and reconstruct the entire biblical drama from Genesis through Ezekiel and Daniel to Revelation. Four major schools of thought have emerged, ranging from amillennialism, postmillennialism, and historic premillennialism to dispensational premillennialism, all rooted in differing interpretations of the biblical meaning of "millennium" — from the Latin *mille,* meaning "a thousand," and *annus,* meaning "year."

Repeatedly Christian communities have endured painful schisms over these differing interpretations. At stake is not only the nature of the millennium, but also the historical sequence of events related to it. When and where are we to locate this "golden age"? How are the "rapture," the "double resurrection," and the "great tribulation" connected? These considerations lead Berkouwer to say that "chronology is what is really at issue in the interpretation of Revelation 20" (*The Return of Christ,* pp. 307-8). Exegetical disagreements over whether the parousia will take place before, during, or after the "great tribulation" have triggered the emergence of rival "pre-trib," "mid-trib," and "post-trib" camps. Clearly the church lacks a unified voice. Its trumpet issues an uncertain sound.

Such lamentable splits are part of a larger picture, however. For a community's biblical hermeneutic goes hand in hand with its worldview. "The exegetical aspects of the discussion," therefore, "often take a back seat to more general arguments about the structure of the world" (Berkouwer, *The Return of Christ,* p. 293). Even a cursory exposure to the millennial landscape therefore underscores D. H. Kromminga's comment that "of varieties of eschatological views there is no dearth." This state of affairs is all the more serious because "one's eschatological outlook determines one's estimate of his own times. This is just as true of the Amillenarians and Premillenarians as of the Postmillenarians" (*The Millennium in the Church,* pp. 113, 114).

II. 2. In Retrospect

Millennial expectations were already widespread in the early church. Most of the early fathers envisioned some form of cosmic restoration. Origen is remembered for his highly speculative idea that this creation is but one in a "series of worlds." Use of Scripture by the fathers in support of their views was, however, often unconvincing, betraying the influence of allegorical methods of interpretation. The views of Irenaeus are fairly representative. Citing Genesis 27:27-29, he explains that the blessing bestowed by Isaac on Jacob "indisputably refers to the time of the kingdom, when the righteous shall rise from the dead and reign; when creation, renewed and liberated, shall produce food of every kind in abundance. . . ." Appealing to apostolic tradition, Irenaeus continues:

The days will come in which vines shall grow, each with ten thousand shoots, each shoot with ten thousand branches, each branch ten thousand twigs, each twig ten thousand clusters, each cluster ten thousand grapes; and each grape when pressed shall yield twenty-five measures of wine. And when any of the saints shall take hold of one of the clusters, another cluster shall call out, "I am a better cluster; take me, and bless the Lord through me." Likewise a grain of wheat shall yield ten thousand ears, each ear ten thousand grains, each grain ten pounds of pure white flour. And fruits, seeds, and grass shall yield in like proportion. And all the animals, enjoying these fruits of the earth, shall live in peace and harmony, obedient to man in entire submission. (Henry Bettenson, *The Early Christian Fathers,* pp. 99-100)

Tertullian holds out similar hopes:

For we also hold that a kingdom has been promised to us on earth, but before (we attain) heaven: but in another state than this, as being after the (first) resurrection. This will last for a thousand years, in a city of God's making, Jerusalem. . . .

For indeed it is right and worthy of God that his servants should also rejoice in the place where they suffered affliction in his name. This is the purpose of that kingdom, which will last a thousand years; during which period the saints will rise sooner and later, according to their degrees of merit; and then when the resurrection of the saints is completed, the destruction of the world and the conflagration of judgement will be effected; we shall be "changed in a moment" into the angelic substance, by the "putting on of incorruption," and we shall be transferred to the celestial kingdom. (Bettenson, *The Early Christian Fathers,* p. 164)

Such chiliast outlooks continued to be widely held among early Christians, it seems, until the "Augustinian misinterpretation" arose. In his City of God/City of the World thesis the bishop of Hippo leans toward a view of the millennium as a present kingdom reality. "After Augustine," Kromminga says, "chiliasm seems to have disappeared from the church." His exegesis of Revelation 20 "tended to wean even the common people away from chiliasm." From then on the church suffered from "a lack of great exponents of chiliasm" (*The Millennium in the Church,* pp. 29, 112, 113). An accommodated, highly ecclesiasticized form of Augustinian millennialism prevailed during the medieval era. During the age of the Reformation, Luther, Calvin, and other Reformers recovered the more original amillennial views of Augustine. Harking back to chiliasts who "limited the reign of Christ to a thousand years," Calvin contends that "the Apocalypse, from which they undoubtedly drew a pretext for their error, does not support them. For the number 'one thousand' (Rev. 20:4) does not apply to the eternal blessedness of the church, but only to the various disturbances that [from John's viewpoint] awaited the church, while still toiling on earth" (*Institutes,* III,25,5).

The radically changed circumstances which followed in the wake of the Renaissance and Reformation — the rise of democratic ideals, religious pluralism, and the secularization of mainline churches during the modern period — created a climate conducive to the rise and spread of a host of updated millennial theologies. These developments have continued at an undiminished pace into this last decade of the twentieth century. With few exceptions all these chiliast views of history conform to one or another of the basic and sharply contrasting types already mentioned: postmillennialism, premillennialism in either its historic or dispensational form, or amillennialism.

II. 3. Basic Types of Eschatology

Each of these major millennial theologies calls for at least a brief discussion.

II. 3. 1. Postmillennialism

This view, sometimes called "chiliasm of the present church age," looks for a "future maximum development of the power of Christ and the Spirit within this dispensation" (Hendrikus Berkhof, *Christ the Meaning of History,* p. 166). The "social gospel" of modern liberalism represents a radical revision on the biblical idea of the millennium. Its spokesmen introduced a "shift from catastrophe to development." They held that "evolution will gradually bring [about] the millennium" (Louis Berkhof, *Systematic Theology,* p. 717). Committed to notions of cultural optimism linked to Darwinian views of history, liberals projected the ideal of continuing evolutionary progress as the outcome of human achievement apart from any notion of divine cataclysmic intervention. In its more historic, orthodox forms postmillennialists anticipate the emergence of a "golden age" ushering in the return of Christ "without any catastrophic events," but by "the mere operation of the Gospel and the Spirit" (Kromminga, *The Millennium in the Church,* p. 298). Accordingly, as Loraine Boettner, an advocate of postmillennialism, puts it:

> The postmillennialist looks for a golden age that will not be essentially different from our own so far as the basic facts of life are concerned. This

534

age gradually merges into the millennial age as an increasing proportion of the world's inhabitants are converted to Christianity. . . . Present heresies will disappear as did those of the past. . . . [Thus] the coming of the millennium is like the coming of summer, although ever so much more slowly and on a much grander scale. ("Postmillennialism," in Robert G. Clouse, *The Meaning of the Millennium,* pp. 120-21, 129, 133)

On the way to the parousia evil will be reduced to "negligible proportions, Christian principles will be the rule, not the exception" as the gospel steadily permeates the world, and "Christ will return to a truly Christianized world" (Boettner, *The Millennium,* p. 14). Anthony Hoekema, an amillennialist, regards this view as "a romantic oversimplification of history not warranted by the biblical data. To be sure," he adds, "Christ has won a decisive victory over sin and Satan, so that the final outcome of the struggle is never in doubt. Yet the antithesis between Christ and his enemies will continue until the end" (*The Bible and the Future,* p. 180).

As cherished hopes of peace are repeatedly dashed in our times, and because "it offers no living voice in its own defense," Lewis Sperry Chafer, an ardent proponent of dispensational premillennialism, declares that "postmillennialism is dead" (in Charles L. Feinberg, *Millennialism,* p. 14).

II. 3. 2. Premillennialism

As the name indicates, premillennialists believe that Christ will return prior to the millennium to inaugurate a "thousand-year reign of peace upon the earth." Berkouwer refers to this anticipated golden age as a "temporary eschaton," an "intermezzo in history" (*The Return of Christ,* p. 292). Ridderbos regards this concept of a "millennial interlude" as a major stumbling block on the path of a biblical eschatology. For the New Testament view of redemption history offers "no ground for the idea that with the parousia only a provisional objective has as yet been reached" (*Paul,* p. 559). On premillennial premises, the resulting view of this present age is burdened with "a very somber view of historical development." In sharp contrast to postmillennialism, "it cherishes no expectation of a rule of peace coming along evolutionary lines; rather, it expects a demonic evolution to be interrupted transcendently by Christ coming in his kingdom of glory" (Berkouwer, *The Return of Christ,* p. 297). Accordingly, historic premillennialists "look for a reign of Christ on earth for a period of a thousand years after his return, and before the ushering in of the final state" (Hoekema, *The Bible and the Future,* p. 180).

As the parousia approaches, however, several events must take place first: "the evangelization of the nations, the great tribulation, the great apostasy or rebellion, and the appearance of a personal antichrist." Then comes the visible rule of Christ over the entire world — "a kingdom which will last approximately a thousand years," with "his redeemed people [reigning] with him. . . . The unbelieving nations which are still on the earth at this time are kept in check and ruled over by Christ with a rod of iron" (Hoekema, *The Bible and the Future,* pp. 180-81).

This millennial expectation is "something of a theological anomaly," however. "It is neither completely like the present age nor is it completely like the age to come" (Hoekema, *The Bible and the Future,* pp. 180-81, 186). Viewed within the context of the comprehensive witness of the New Testament, premillennial eschatology has built into it an enormous ambiguity: "On the one hand is the triumph [of Christ], the binding of the strong man; on the other hand is the continuing activity of evil, the presence of the devil" (Berkouwer, *The Return of Christ,* p. 306). A related ambiguity is implied in the premillennial view of the imminent "rapture." Its view of the "thousand years" has a very earthy cast to it. Yet the "rapture" is often pictured in otherworldly escapist terms — as openly displayed on bumper stickers: "In case of rapture, this car will be driver-less." The impression is often left of Christ catching his followers up with him to heaven. Yet when Scripture speaks of our "assembling to meet [Christ]" (2 Thessalonians 2:1) and our "[appearing] with him in glory" (Colossians 3:4) and "God [bringing] with him those who have fallen asleep" (1 Thessalonians 4:14), the thrust of such passages is earthward. For "Christ's parousia is directed [precisely] toward the earth." Accordingly, "this going of believers to meet the Lord has the meaning of being placed at Christ's side at his coming, the open demonstration of belonging to him and being his people, . . . of being included in his company, moving in his retinue, coming with Christ in his glory" (Ridderbos, *Paul,* p. 536).

Once a premillennial interpretation of Revelation 20 is accepted as the hermeneutic key to the full meaning of Scripture, the temptation is almost irresistible to read all the Pauline writings in this light. As Ridderbos says regarding 1 Corinthians 15, however, the idea of an "intermediate kingdom" is not there, but is "clearly read into it" (*Paul,* p. 558). Similarly, says Berkouwer, to read this passage as "a Pauline reference to a millennium smacks of being too much influenced by Revelation 20" (*The Return of Christ,* p. 302).

Premillennialism in its more thoroughgoing dispensational forms, often rising to fever-pitched popularity, was stimulated by the appearance of the Scofield Bible early in this century. With it came a sweeping reconstruction of redemption history. The basic principle in dispensationalism is its sharp distinction between Israel and the church. God has two purposes in history, embodied in these two peoples, and they remain distinct throughout all history and into eternity. Its hermeneutic involves "the meaning and significance of the entire Bible, defines the meaning and course of the present age, determines the present purposes of God, and gives both material and method to theology" (John Walvoord, *The Millennial Kingdom,* p. 15). Accordingly, its "concept of the present age makes the inter-advent period unique and unpredictable in the Old Testament." During this dispensation "the world becomes . . . increasingly wicked as the age progresses" (Walvoord, *The Millennial Kingdom,* p. 134).

On this view, the biblical story line is generally divided into a series of seven dispensations from the creation of the first Adam to the parousia of the last Adam. For "God deals with the world of humanity in the course of history on the basis of several covenants." Each of these dispensations represents a "different test of the natural man; and since man fails to meet the successive tests, each dispensation ends in judgment." Thus dispensationalists arrive at a "new philosophy of the history of redemption, in which Israel plays a leading role and the church [age] is but an interlude" (Louis Berkhof, *Systematic Theology,* p. 710). They drive a wedge between the Old and New Testaments. The former is viewed as the book of past manifestations of the kingdom, the latter the book for the present life of the church. The kingdom in its restored glory awaits the future millennium. For "millennium and kingdom indicate exactly the same ideas" (Feinberg, *Millennialism,* p. 184). Even the sympathetic critic cannot suppress the question: What, then, becomes of the oneness of the way of salvation?

II. 3. 3. Interim Comments

Postmillennialism is often regarded as a "church-historical" and premillennialism an "end-historical" eschatology. These two views of redemption history are generally taken to be diametrically opposed to each other, even mutually exclusive. Yet they share a common concern with chronology. Both view the millennium as a rather specifically definable "thousand-year" time span, a "golden age," though oriented to very different timetables. But both are inclined to devote a great deal of attention to "reportorial eschatology" (Berkouwer). The error of chiliasts in general is that they regard Revelation as "history written in advance" on the faulty assumption that "by decoding Revelation correctly we can write history in advance" (König, *The Eclipse of Christ in Eschatology,* p. 135).

The element of truth in chiliasm in its postmillennial form is its strong commitment to the present creation and its fervent hope for the renewal of God's world. This "burning, passionate expectation for this earth and earthly existence" is fueled by an "anti-spiritualistic motive" often coupled with a "utopian aspect" (Berkouwer, *The Return of Christ*, pp. 308, 296). Premillennialism, on the other hand, holds out little hope for this present age, only the prospect of continuing trials and temptations, and eventually a time of severely intensified tribulation at the hands of satanic powers. These two eschatologies therefore part ways mainly over questions of timing, whether the anticipated reign of peace will be established during this dispensation or the next.

Are we then left with no biblically warranted alternative? Is there no option other than choosing between the cultural optimism of the one and the cultural pessimism of the other? Fortunately there is an authentic "third way." We are not compelled to cast in our lot with the vision of either an intrahistorical realization of the kingdom or the deferred hope of an exclusively posthistorical expectation. As Berkouwer argues, "to reject both the certainty of a transcendent millennium and the certainty of an evolutionary penetration into the millennium" does not mean facing the future with less "assurance and hope." Moreover, such "lesser certainty" does not involve "a weaker eschatological expectation." Nor does it "limit this expectation, but stimulates it." For faith always relies on "the certainty that God's ways are and will remain inscrutable" (*The Return of Christ*, p. 321).

II. 4. Hermeneutic Decisions

Sifting through the millennial options available to us, and taking a stand, involves a number of basic hermeneutic choices. Not surprisingly, the principles of interpretation which shape the entire course of this dogmatic study tip the scales decisively in favor of an amillennial eschatology. The "analogy of Scripture" which undergirds this biblical story-line approach must also be honored in seeking to clarify the meaning of Revelation 20. Accordingly, the millennium forms an integral aspect of the unfolding central plot — creation, fall, redemption, and consummation — in the biblical drama. Just as creation has a definite beginning, so it is also moving toward a decisive eschaton — not a provisional "thousand-year" interlude between the present "end time" and the final "day of the Lord." The full sweep of covenant/kingdom history is the enduring context for reading Revelation 20, and thus for understanding its place and meaning within the ongoing flow of redemption history. The biblical worldview must inform our interpretation of Revelation 20.

This classic passage on the millennium also calls for decisions regarding its literary genre. John writes while "in the Spirit on the Lord's day" (Revelation 1:10). Thus inspired, his visions begin to unfold. As exiled bishop of a cluster of early churches, he is on "the island called Patmos" (Revelation 1:9). This is his base of operations. But the revelations he receives come in the form of apocalyptic imagery. What he left us is therefore "a highly symbolic book" (Louis Berkhof, *Systematic Theology*, p. 715). This is evident from the repeated use of number values, such as "seven," all of them laden with symbolic significance: seven lampstands, stars, and churches; a book sealed with seven seals, seven angels blowing seven trumpets, seven thunders, seven bowls of wrath, seven kings. A similar apocalyptic play on numbers is evident in the three woes and three foul spirits, the twenty-four elders on thrones, the 144,000 elect, the City with twelve gates, the tree of life with twelve fruits, and the number of the beast, 666. So also the concept "times and time and half a time," that is, three and a half years or 42 months, refers symbolically to an appointed period of time. The idea of a "thousand years" falls into the same typology.

John writes to the church during its second great persecution — under the Emperor Domitian around the year A.D. 95. Given the trying circumstances which led to John's banishment, the message of Revelation takes on a deep sense of heightened urgency when read as a coded message to early believers. The language is cryptic, even secretive, with its mysterious metaphors and in-house imagery — in case it should fall into wrong hands. Outsiders would be baffled by it. Christians, however, familiar with the apocalyptic prophecies of Ezekiel, Daniel, and Jesus' eschatological discourse (Matthew 24), had at their disposal the clues needed to decipher this coded message.

For the early Christian community, therefore, Revelation served as a book of comfort and security in the face of opposition and martyrdom. It reassured them that God has not abdicated his throne. The Lamb of God is now the Lion of the tribe of Judah. "Only because He is the Lamb of God can He become the King of Kings" (George E. Ladd, *The Last Things*, p. 56). This is John's message to the "seven churches," which are symbolic of the church universal. Through these revelations to his original readers John still speaks to us today.

Accepting this perspective settles the basic hermeneutic decision which we face today, as posed by four major ways of interpreting Revelation 20. There is, first, the school of "realized eschatology," which holds that these things have already been fulfilled. There is also the "futurist" viewpoint of premillennial theologies. Again, many contemporary theologies seek to distill from the events described here universal "myths" without any real historical points of reference. In contrast, the hermeneutic implied throughout this dogmatic study views the "thousand years" as a visionary commentary on this present age, from Christ's first coming (Revelation 12) to his return (Revelation 22:16-20). This is the so-called amillennial position. Such a reading of Revelation lends it a very practical, down-to-earth relevance for our life in God's world today. Then we need no longer shy away from it as a foreboding book or as a bewildering puzzle to be solved. It offers us instead a biblical view of redemption history presently in the making.

II. 5. Promillennialism

It is time now to introduce a new concept — a switch from amillennialism ("a-" meaning "non-," or worse still "against") to *pro*millennialism ("pro-" meaning "for," in the sense of "in favor of"). Many commentators agree that "the term amillennialism is not a very happy one" since it is not an "accurate description" of this view (Hoekema, *The Bible and the Future,* p. 173). It reflects a purely and baldly negative stance. It suggests that amillennialists do little more than set themselves off against other millennial views. They then give the appearance of allowing pre- and postmillennialists to stake out their claims, while they are content with merely reacting negatively. Yet this dubious concept continues to hold a respected place in the vocabularies of Reformed theologians. "The amillennial view is, as the name indicates, purely negative," says Louis Berkhof in justifying its use, since it holds that there is "no sufficient Scriptural ground for the expectation of a millennium" (*Systematic Theology,* p. 708). Similarly, according to Hoeksema, "amillenarians . . . believe that scripture does not teach a millennium in any form" (*Reformed Dogmatics,* p. 816). In rejecting the alternative concept, "realized millennialism" as being "a rather clumsy one," Hoekema opts to continue using "the shorter and more common term, amillennialism" (*The Bible and the Future,* pp. 173-74).

But surely it is not amiss to ask whether we must continue to live under the cloud of a purely negative, defensive reputation. Is amillennialism the last word on the matter? Jay Adams calls it "a misnomer for the biblical system of eschatology" (*The Time Is at Hand,* p. 107). He concedes that "it is easy enough to criticize the term, but not quite so easy to offer a satisfactory substitute" (p. 8). To acknowledge this difficulty, however, is to accept it as a standing challenge. For it is not enough simply to say "no" to the idea of a "thousand years" in Revelation 20. It is incumbent on us to sound a more positive note. For "when amillennial books do little more than refute premillennialism, they give substance to the opposing charge of repudiating a clear Biblical teaching." The task of amillennialism is "not to 'explain away' the millennium, but to explain it" (Adams, *The Time Is at Hand,* p. 7). The term *pro*millennialism is therefore intended to eliminate the negative and accentuate the positive.

Often it is argued that amillennialism, now rechristened promillennialism, represents a relatively new and untried theology. On the contrary, says Louis Berkhof, it is "as old as Christianity." It is the "most widely accepted view, . . . the only view that is either expressed or implied in the great historical confessions of the church" (*Systematic Theology,* p. 708). Reformational theology is therefore in a position to make a positive contribution to a renewed understanding of the "end times," both present and future. With the biblical story line as our revelational grid, we are offered a vantage point for grasping, dimly at least, the mysteriously ongoing course of events which shape our lives. All human and cosmic history is eschatological. Both Old and New Testaments hold out constantly the hope of bigger and better things to come. A forward-looking perspective is never absent from the unfolding biblical drama. Our entire life together in God's world is teleologically directed toward one "day of the Lord" after another on the way to the coming great "day of the Lord." Through a succession of provisional "end times" we have now entered the present decisive "end times" heading for the final "end time."

Within these biblical perspectives, eschatology is inseparably related to protology. In God's way with the world, the prospect of the full realization of all things in the consummation is present from the beginning as a potential in the creation. Already in the fall God announces a coming redemptive triumph in the midst of enmity (Genesis 3:15). The heartbeat of Israel's legacy is its Messianic expectation. In the gospel record of what took place in the "fulness of the times," the life, death, resurrection, and ascension of Christ open the door to kingdom living as a present reality, now already during these "last days," and consummately at Christ's parousia. The outpouring of the Spirit at Pentecost represents a crucial turning point within the discontinuous continuity of salvation history. It is "the beginning of the future." For

> . . . the activity of the Spirit of God is a present manifestation of the eschatological rule of God. The Spirit is the dynamic of the kingdom and, as such, eschatological power. . . . The empowering presence of the Spirit is eschatological presence. . . . [The Spirit's presence] is the down payment on the eschaton, which down payment is itself a realization, in anticipation, of the eschaton. The Spirit is the first installment of eschatological existence. . . . In a word, then, life in the Spirit is eschatological life. (Richard Gaffin, "Life in the Spirit," in *The Holy Spirit: Renewing and Empowering Presence,* pp. 46-48)

This, then, is the revelational context for a promillennial view of the "thousand years." It covers a real historical, down-to-earth time span. It extends from Christ's first advent to his final advent. Like the other number values in Revelation, it carries full weight, but expressed in apocalyptic symbols. It is designed to "create a picture rather than give an exact sum. Already the 'millennium' has lasted almost two thousand years" (Adams, *The Time Is at Hand,* p. 86). The present millennial age signals Christ's conquest of the opposing "principalities and powers," his "binding of the strong man" (Matthew 12:29; cf. Luke 10:18), whom John identifies as "the dragon, that ancient serpent [of Genesis 3], who is the Devil and Satan." He it was that the heaven-sent angel "bound . . . for a thousand years" (Revelation 20:2).

The decisive turning point lies behind us. Cross power and resurrection power are now also eschatological power — the beginning of "the end." The forces of darkness are defeated, though not yet vanquished. In terms of Cullmann's analogy, during this "showdown" time in redemption history between "D-day" (God's day of Decision) and "V-day" (his day of Victory) life is filled with mixed blessings — the triumphs of God's grace mingled with his judgments which are also still in the earth. All around us "there are enigmas; there is mystery. . . . This is probably the deepest mystery of eschatology: that the joy of this eschatological outlook goes hand in hand with this suspense" (Berkouwer, *The Return of Christ,* p. 322). This is the picture which emerges from John's visions of the "seven seals" (5:1–8:5) disclosing the meaning of history, the gospel call heralded by the "seven trumpets" (8:6–11:19), and the "seven bowls" pouring out final judgment on the earth (15:1–16:21). These sevenfold signs of the times follow a parallel but interacting course through history. "Each spans the entire new dispensation, from the first to the second coming of Christ." Together they reveal "a progress in depth or intensity of conflict" (William Hendriksen, *More than Conquerors,* pp. 28, 30). Read contextually, therefore, Revelation 20 is not "a narrative account of a future earthly reign of peace at all, but the apocalyptic unveiling of the reality of suffering and martyrdom that still continues as long as the dominion of Christ remains hidden." Such a promillennial hermeneutic "not only conform[s] to the nature of the Book of Revelation but [is] also consistent with the clarity of the contrast between cross and glory" (Berkouwer, *The Return of Christ,* p. 307).

There is therefore no room for easy triumphalism in kingdom living. For "until Jesus comes, resurrection-eschatology is eschatology of the cross. . . . The sign of inaugurated eschatology is the cross. Believers suffer not in spite of or alongside of the fact that they share in Christ's resurrection, but just because they are raised up and seated with him in heaven" (Gaffin, "Life in the Spirit," in *The Holy Spirit: Renewing and*

Empowering Presence, p. 54). As with the conflict between the dragon's hosts and Michael's angelic band (Revelation 12), so also with the "thousand years" (Revelation 20) — both span this entire present dispensation. For the book of Revelation as a whole is an "illumination of history from the viewpoint of the as-yet-hidden triumph of the Lord who is coming" (Berkouwer, *The Return of Christ,* p. 313).

II. 6. An Unsealed Message

"Do not seal up the words of the prophecy of this book," so the angel instructs John, "for the time is near" (Revelation 22:10). These apocalyptic visions come to us as an urgent message of ever current relevancy for millennial living. Accordingly, the angelic instruction leads immediately to stern exhortations and reassuring comfort. Revelation is an existential book. It is therefore fully readable, teachable, preachable, and livable in these "last days." For "it is not a discourse about the future provided to satisfy our curiosity, but a message that proclaims and directs us to the incontrovertible salvation of God" (Berkouwer, *The Return of Christ,* p. 314). The basic choice facing us is not "between interpreting the millennium as a feature of church history and interpreting it as something to be awaited at the end of history. Rather, it is the choice between apocalyptic comfort and a strictly chronological narrative account." On promillennial grounds it offers us "a view of reality seen in eschatological perspective in these last days" (Berkouwer, *The Return of Christ,* p. 315).

Chapter III

Eschatological Countdown

III. 1. Signs of the Times

All the roads we travel converge in the parousia, which looms like a summit along the horizon of this "end-time" history. Only faulty vision, however, pictures this eschatological drama as "an historical development from a lower to a higher stage." No evolutionary worldview can account for "the end" or the way which leads to it. Both result from "the powerful action of the Son of Man" (Ridderbos, *The Coming of the Kingdom,* p. 469.) For the future of the world is not unrelated to its past and present state of affairs. It has its precursors that point the direction and herald the coming of the King.

Scripture opens our eyes to a number of such antecedents. Only once are they referred to as "the signs of the times" (Matthew 16:3). In scattered New Testament passages, however, we find allusions to these eschatological signs, identifying them more clearly. They come in various forms: persons, powers, events, movements. In his sermon on "last things," Jesus mentions "wars and rumors of wars," "famines and earthquakes," "tribulation," "false prophets," and the worldwide proclamation of "the gospel of the kingdom" (Matthew 24:3-14) — all very familiar signs of our times! Paul speaks even more concretely. He warns believers about surging "rebellion," the appearance of the "man of lawlessness," the "son of perdition" — hostile forces held in check for a while by a "restraining" presence (2 Thessalonians 2:1-12). In John's epistles the powers of darkness become incarnate in "the antichrist"/"antichrists" (1 John 2:18, 22) and deniers of Jesus Christ who breath "the spirit of the antichrist" (1 John 4:3).

What are we to make of these signs of our "end times"? Both Ridderbos (*Paul,* p. 528) and Berkouwer (*The Return of Christ,* p. 243) caution us with good reason against "reportorial eschatology." Moreover,

as Weber puts it, "the hope of the world" rests not in "Christian penetration of reality," but in "the Parousia (return) of the Resurrected One"
(*Foundations of Dogmatics,* Vol. II, p. 680). These signs are for all times.
They are an urgent summons to readiness, for believers then and there,
but also here and now. So much so that "Jesus could have come at any
moment in the past nineteen centuries and no sign would have been
unfulfilled." In every age, therefore, "any view of the signs which makes
it impossible to preach Christ's near return is a distortion" (König, *The
Eclipse of Christ in Eschatology,* pp. 191, 193).

For a good grasp on the biblical teachings concerning these signs,
Hoekema's analysis is very helpful. Summarizing his discussion, both its
negative and positive points, we are first introduced to the following four
"mistaken understandings."

1) Thinking of "the signs of the times as referring exclusively to
. . . the period immediately preceding the Parousia," having "nothing to do with the centuries preceding. . . ."

2) Thinking of the signs "only in terms of abnormal, spectacular,
or catastrophic events."

3) Thinking of them "as a way of dating the exact time of Christ's
return."

4) Thinking of them as a way "to construct an exact timetable of
future happenings."

In five points Hoekema then discusses the "proper function" of the signs.

1) They "point first of all," not to "the future," but to "what God
has done in the past."

2) "The signs of the times also point forward to the end of history,
particularly to the return of Christ."

3) They reveal "the continuing anthithesis in history between the
kingdom of God and the powers of evil."

4) "The signs of the times call for decision."

5) They "call for constant watchfulness" (*The Bible and the Future,*
pp. 130-35).

The roadway of the coming kingdom is lined with these eschatological signposts. They are on open display. Only those with Spirit-
illumined eyes, however, are able to see them for what they are and read
them aright — though, even with the eyes of faith, only dimly and from
a distance. They stand, nevertheless, as forceful reminders that God's just

judgments are present in the world as awesome realities, as "fire upon the earth" (Luke 12:49). But his forbearance and longsuffering mercy is no less real, calling all men to repentance since God has appointed a day of reckoning (Hebrews 9:27). Knowing this, the church, "by schisms rent asunder, by heresies distressed," can keep its windows open to the future, confident that the history of our times is still on course and that the way to "the end" is clear and open. As construction signs along the highways alert travelers to "Men at Work," so the signs of the times confirm "the unmistakable fact that God is at work" in the world (Ridderbos, *Paul*, p. 522).

Perhaps the most telling aspect of all the signs is this, that they are out for all to see but we fail to take note of them. We are like traveling salesmen, driving home near midnight at the end of a long day, along an avenue ablaze with neon lights but oblivious to it all, because our minds are miles away, plotting our next day's sales pitch. We hear it said that these are "changing times." But when it comes to human response, so little has really changed. "As were the days of Noah, so will be the coming of the Son of Man." People will be "eating and drinking, marrying and giving in marriage" — all the good and ordinary things of life. But who is sensitive to the eschatological pointers (Matthew 24:37-39)? This is the tragic fate of our rapidly secularizing, post-Christian societies, that "in spite of all the signs of the approaching end, people will continue to live in false peace of mind [1 Thessalonians 5:3] and in unwillingness to be converted" (Ridderbos, *The Coming of the Kingdom*, p. 480).

III. 2. The Antichrist(s)

We meet the ominous figure of the antichrist/antichrists in Scripture as both the ultimate and immediate enemy of the reign of Christ. Both pictures emerge, the former especially in Paul, the latter in John. In writing to early Christians Paul warns against disturbing rumors to the effect that "the day of the Lord has [already] come." For "that day will not come," he says, until the antichrist — the "man of lawlessness," the "son of perdition" — puts in his appearance as a belligerent pretender to the throne of divine glory. His coming to usurp Christ's dominion, motivated by "the activity of Satan," will be accompanied by "all power" and "pretended signs and wonders" (2 Thessalonians 2:1-11). As a substitute Christ the antichrist represents a counterfeit incarnation. He is the absolutely negative image of the Christ of God. The antichrist is the supreme parasite, the demonic alter ego of Christ himself. He can therefore rise to his full stature only in a world where "the gospel of the king/kingdom" has taken root.

In Paul this decisive antithesis is reserved largely for the twilight zone which announces the dawning of the great "day of the Lord." The antichrist will burst on the scene as an ultimate pseudo-apocalypse, as God's appointed apocalypse in reverse. Knowing that his time is running out, as a diehard he will launch his final desperate, diabolically inspired counteroffensive. The battle lines will be drawn within the earthly arena. But fighting on all fronts will spread steadily into an all-out, ever expanding eschatological encounter. This decisive warfare will be waged along the very outer boundaries of our world of experience and far beyond (Revelation 12:7-9).

The antichrist's ID card carries the number "666" (Revelation 13:18). His power is great, but always short of "seven." He is therefore doomed to defeat. As long as the conflict lasts, however, it is in the antichrist that "the humanity hostile to God comes to definitive eschatological expression." For "the figure of 'the man of lawlessness' is clearly intended as the final eschatological counterpart of the man Jesus Christ."

> His coming, just as that of Christ, is called a *parousia;* it is marked by all manner of powers, signs, and wonders, like those of Christ in the past. . . . The man of sin is the last and highest revelation of man (humanity) inimical to God. (Ridderbos, *Paul,* pp. 514, 515)

The antichrist is therefore more than an individual rival. He represents mankind in revolt against God. But he also embodies suprahuman powers. He is evil incarnate — enlisting and mobilizing in his cause the alien hosts of darkness. He is more than an "it," however, more than a seductive strategy or an impersonal force. However much our modern mind resists the idea, Paul indicates that eventually everything anti-Christian will come to a head in a personal antichrist. For just as

> the organic and corporate unity of human life finds its bearer and representative . . . in Adam and Christ, so also in the antichrist, in a specific person. The antichrist would be no antichrist if he were not the personal concentration point of lawlessness, if he were not *the man* of lawlessness. (Ridderbos, *Paul,* p. 516)

Paul mentions in passing that this eschatological confrontation is not reserved exclusively for the very "last days." For "the mystery of lawlessness is already at work" (2 Thessalonians 2:7). This passing reference in Paul becomes a major theme in John. In his letters the scene shifts from a more distant future to the present. "Children," John writes, "it is the last hour." He recalls Paul's emphasis, "that the antichrist is coming." He then adds quickly that "many antichrists have [already] come." The enemy is not only singular but plural. He is legion, and his accomplices are too near for comfort. In fact, in John's day these surrogate christs arose within the very ranks of the faithful. "They went out from us," but "they were not of us." Like their father the liar, they, too, were living the lie — denying that "Jesus is the Christ." In John's scenario the spirit of antichrist appears clothed in the garments of heresy. For "this is the antichrist, he who denies the Father and the Son" (1 John 2:18-25). These "false prophets" had apparently fallen victim to Gnostic rejections of the reality of the incarnation. To deny that Jesus Christ is "of God" and that he has "come in the flesh" is to break the bond of fellowship with both the Father and the Son (1 John 4:1-3). Those who embody the spirit of the antichrist break faith with the great love command which is the very heartbeat of John's message. Many anti-Christian turncoats have "gone out into the world" — into our world too — "men who will not acknowledge the coming of Jesus Christ in the flesh." Anyone who embraces this heresy is "the deceiver and the antichrist" (2 John 6-7).

The antichrist wears many masks. He is one and he is many. He rears his ugly head in every age. For

> the sign of the antichrist, like other signs of the times, is present throughout the history of the church. . . . Every age will provide its own particular form of antichristian activity. But we [also] look for an intensification of this sign in the appearance of *the* antichrist shortly before Christ's return. (Hoekema, *The Bible and the Future*, p. 162)

III. 3. The Restrainer and His Restraints

With this masked "man of lawlessness" on the loose, this bedeviled "son of perdition," the antichrist and his diabolical cohorts; with the cumulative power of these antichrists and their anti-Christian accomplices laying their ambushes along the way of the coming kingdom — how then is it possible, in the face of all this, that for many people life is still livable, even enjoyable and productive? In answer to this pressing eschatological question Paul points to the presence of a restraining force in world history. For the time being the "mystery of lawlessness" is being held in check by a counter-acting power. Some day, however, this restraint will end. To be forewarned is to be forearmed (2 Thessalonians 2:6-8)!

"It is difficult to get at Paul's meaning here," as Berkouwer says, "because he was addressing the believers in Thessalonica on an issue that was familiar to them" (*The Return of Christ,* p. 125) — but not to us. Questions abound, with few satisfying answers. Only time will tell.

This much we can say: Paul refers to this restraining influence both as a power and as a person. You know, he reminds his readers, "*what* is restraining" the full unleashing of the antichrist's diabolical fury. There is, as it were, a dam holding back the torrent of raging waters the antichrist is about to unleash on the world. This ultimate showdown is being held in abeyance "so that [the antichrist] may be revealed in his time." When the time of this holding action has run its full course, then the final life-and-death struggle will take place. This confrontation will then settle decisively the antithesis which reaches all the way back to Genesis 3 between the kingdom of light and the kingdom of darkness.

Almost in the same breath, Paul goes on to identify this restraining power as a person. "The mystery of lawlessness is already at work" in the world. But "he who restrains it" is also active. A measure of love and justice and peace is still present among men and nations — more here, less there. Constructive work is still possible. This will last, says Paul, until the restrainer himself gets "out of the way." For eventually he will step aside, pull back, and withdraw his restraining hand. When this happens the destructive power of evil will be free to run rampant over the world. Then the powers of "the lawless one will be revealed" in their unmitigated fury.

The general contours of the picture are fairly clear, though it is difficult to fill in the details. "A case can undoubtedly be made," according to Berkouwer, "for a retardation of the coming of the man of lawlessness through the activity of some temporary force in history, even though we do not know the nature of this force" (*The Return of Christ,* p. 127). As Ridderbos sees it, this eschatological prospectus points not so much to "specific historical phenomena or events, but speaks in apocalyptic language of supernatural factors that determine the restraining of the last things" (*Paul,* p. 525). One idea suggests itself: Is it possible to see in the withdrawal of the restrainer and his restraints an eschatological pointer to the withdrawal of the restraining, preserving, conserving influences of God's "common grace"? That would set the antithesis between good and evil in stark and untempered relief, the antithesis between those "for me" and those "against me," between covenant keepers and covenant breakers, between the kingdom of light and the kingdom of darkness.

III. 4. The "Intermediate State"

Around the world countless tombstones are engraved with the words "Asleep in Jesus" and "Rest in Peace." An almost impenetrable mystery surrounds such memorials. They are primarily testimonies to the life which was lived, but also to the hope which extends beyond these "threescore years and ten." A certain grave marker bears witness reflexively to one man's living faith in the eloquently simple yet profound confession, "Forgiven." This much is clear: Where the tree falls, there it remains. But what lies beyond death confronts us as a paradoxical reality. In this transaction which awaits us all we pay the final installment on "the wages of sin" (Romans 6:23). The grim reaper is our "last enemy" (1 Corinthians 15:26). But there is also a bright side to the story. "Death is for us who are in Christ not a satisfaction for sin: It was that for Christ, but not for us. . . . For Christ death was part of the curse; for us death is a source of blessing" (Hoekema, *The Bible and the Future*, p. 84). We face death, therefore, as the transition from seemingly irrevocable defeat to victory in the company of "the spirits of just men made perfect" (Hebrews 12:23). This outlook leads Paul to declare that "to live is Christ, to die is gain" (Philippians 1:21).

But once the funeral is over, after the parting eulogies have been spoken, when the flowers have faded and the lingering salty tears are dried — what then? Can we say anything meaningful about the immediate hereafter? Scripture speaks only in a "whisper" (Berkouwer) about this state of existence. Already in Calvin we find a similar hermeneutic restraint. "Let us be content with the limits divinely set for us," he says, and "not transgress" them; let us refrain from "superfluous investigation," but rather "be satisfied with the 'mirror' and its 'dimness' until we see [God] face to face (I Corinthians 13:12)" (*Institutes*, III,25,6, 11). Many questions may therefore remain unanswered. Yet we are not left totally in the dark. For in death as well as in life, we are "with Christ" — "this is all Paul knows about the intermediate state" (Hoekema, *The Bible and the Future*, p. 104). That reassurance is ultimately what matters most — "the promise of continuing communion" with Christ (Berkouwer, *The Return of Christ*, p. 52). As Calvin says, "Scripture goes no farther than to say that Christ is present with them and receives them into paradise" (*Institutes*, III,25,6).

Though Scripture offers no "theoretical explications of the intermediate state" (Berkouwer, *The Return of Christ*, p. 51), no detailed analysis of it, its reality is a basic biblical presupposition. With the kind of cumulative clarity which typifies its unfolding story line, Scripture posits as a fundamental premise our continuing creaturely existence as human beings. It never stops to "prove" it, however, just as at another level it offers no rational arguments for the existence of the Creator God. An afterlife as the continuing reality of this life is an unquestioned axiom in the teleologically directed drama of eschatological history. The here and now is not a dead-end street. At the far end is a gate which opens to a mysteriously continuous yet also discontinuous hereafter which is at once both more and less than our present life. As Calvin puts it, the struggle against sin and evil is then over. But the everlasting crown is still outstanding. In the intermediate state there is still an anticipation of more to come. It has a precursory character, marked by a provisional glory, awaiting the parousia (*Institutes,* III,25,6). For Calvin "the whole intermediate state is focussed on the expectation of what is to come — Christ's coming." Therefore, since Christian hope "extends beyond the grave and ultimately to the parousia itself, . . . the tension between the 'already' and the 'not yet' must remain even for those who, in death, await the coming of the Lord" (Berkouwer, *The Return of Christ,* pp. 49, 34). Thus, this way of being with Christ does not diminish but intensifies the eschatological expectation of those who cry out, "How long!" How long until the final resurrection? From where we now stand, therefore, we are not to view the intermediate state and the parousia as two separate expectations but as two phases in a single eschatological movement. "Death is not the eschaton in an absolute sense, but it is *an* eschaton" (Weber, *Foundations of Dogmatics,* Vol. II, p. 665).

Death is not the doorway to a geriatric waiting room, where life is suspended and everything held in abeyance. Our "translation" does not consign us to a state of dormancy, soul sleep, or unconscious existence — certainly not to extinction or annihilation. For Paul "to depart and be with the Lord" could hardly be envisioned as personally "far better" under such uninviting circumstances (Philippians 1:23-24).

Though there is "no doubt of the reality of believers being with Christ immediately after death," yet "the significance of this reality and what place it occupies in the whole of salvation" is far less clear (Ridderbos, *Paul,* p. 506). Yet this is "our comfort in life and death," that even the disruptions of death cannot sever the ties which unite Christ and his body. For "if we live, we live to the Lord, and if we die, we die to the Lord; so then whether we live or whether we die, we are the Lord's. For to this end Christ died and lived again, that he might be Lord both of the dead and of the living" (Romans 14:8-9). His life is the sure pledge of ours. As our life before death is centered in Christ, so, too, our life after death. Nothing in all creation can break this bond (Romans 8:39). Life in the intermediate state therefore has no "independent existence." Nor does it offer "a separate ground of comfort." It is "taken up entirely in the hope of the resurrection and would not exist without it" (Ridderbos, *Paul,* p. 506).

What it means, however, to be alive spiritually, apart from our present historical existence, baffles our minds. To live beyond the present bodily life but short of the state of glory is "an inconceivable mode of existence" (Ridderbos, *Paul,* p. 507). In every attempt to describe it structurally and functionally, words fail us. We have no anthropological clues. But the direction is not hidden. Life after death is not a setback. At the same time, it is "not yet" all we are meant to be and become. It is a "provisional and incomplete" state (Bavinck, *Magnalia Dei,* p. 634). But it is the next move in our eschatological pilgrimage. Amid the many ambiguities which bridge the here and the hereafter, we are always in "good hands." And for now, that is enough.

III. 5. The Resurrection Life

Sunday after Sunday countless worshipers, from cathedrals to under-ground churches, recite the article of faith: We believe "the resurrection of the body." This is a uniquely Christian confession. Greek philosophers (Acts 17:30-32) and Enlightenment thinkers advocated theories of the "immortality of the soul." They based this doctrine on a quality of durability which allegedly inheres invincibly in the human spirit. Unfortunately, this very dubious, alien notion has also made its way into historic Christianity. At best, however, it is a "mixed article of faith" (Bavinck, *Gereformeerde Dogmatiek,* Vol. IV, p. 567). For, as Hoekema says, "the concept of the immortality of the soul is not a distinctively Christian doctrine. Rather, what is central in biblical Christianity is the doctrine of the resurrection of the body" (*The Bible and the Future,* p. 91).

In sharp contrast, therefore, to Hellenist, Gnostic, and some humanist traditions, Scripture emphasizes the integrity of bodily life. Its creational and redemptive importance is supremely manifest in the in-carnation — "the Word became flesh and dwelled among us, . . . like unto us in all things." This biblical teaching commits us now already to promote the full-bodied well-being of all human life and other creaturely reality. Beyond our present history, moreover, it holds out the firm es-chatological promise of complete restoration to newness of life — our resurrection and the restoration of the entire creation. For personal eschatology goes hand in hand with cosmic eschatology (Romans 8:18-25). In Scripture "the one expectation is not played off against the other" (Berkouwer, *The Return of Christ,* p. 36).

Death remains a foreign, antinormative intruder into the life of creation. Resurrection points to the final restoration of all things to a state of normalcy. It sets our sights beyond the hazy prospects of the intermediate state to a much more recognizable future. The resurrected world has a very familiar, down-to-earth ring to it. For "in my flesh shall I see God" (Job 19:26) on "a new earth in which righteousness dwells" (2 Peter 3:13). The eschaton will certainly result in dramatic changes. A "glorified body" will rise from the grave (Philippians 3:21). A renewed world will emerge, purged by fire (2 Peter 3:10-13). Yet these eschatological discontinuities presuppose an equally real continuity with our present earthly life. As Hoekema puts it, we now live in "a state of psychosomatic unity. So we were created, so we are now, and so we will be after the resurrection of the body" (*Created in God's Image*, p. 218). Perhaps the faith language of the church is helpful at this point. Our forefathers often pictured the resurrection as our "translation" to glory. Think of it as a book, faithfully translated, say, from German to English: in reading it we find continuity in substance within the very flow of lingual discontinuity.

Scripture regularly describes the resurrected life in negatives: bodies without pain, eyes without tears of grief, life without corrupting influences. But how can we give positive expression to these enticing expectations? We do so knowingly, yet with limited foresight. It is a restrained hermeneutic of faith which shapes our vision of the future. We anticipate "the perfect that is coming," after "the imperfect passes away" (1 Corinthians 13:10), by faith not by sight. We do not know with full clarity "what we shall be"; but we do know that "when [Christ] appears we shall be like him, for we shall see him as he is" (1 John 3:2). Pious ignorance therefore befits the expectations of the Christian community. This is clear from Paul's analogy of the seed and the plant (1 Corinthians 15:35-50). For "just as there is continuity between the seed and the plant, so there will be continuity between the present body and the resurrection body." Yet, "just as one cannot tell from the appearance of the seed what the future plant will look like, so we cannot tell by observing the present body exactly what the resurrection body will be like" (Hoekema, *The Bible and the Future*, p. 248).

The reality of our resurrection hope, like every other hope, is centered in Christ. Apart from him, as Calvin argues, "it is too hard for men's minds to apprehend." Recognizing that "it is difficult to believe that bodies, when consumed with rottenness, will at length be raised up in their season," Calvin holds that "one of the helps by which faith may overcome this great obstacle" is "the parallel of Christ's resurrection" (*Institutes*, III,25,3). The reality of our "not yet" resurrected life is anchored securely in the empowering reality of Christ's "already" resurrection (Romans 8:11; 1 Corinthians 6:14; 2 Corinthians 4:14). Our resurrection is embodied in his, and his resurrection authenticates ours.

The renewing work of the Spirit in our lives is now already an eschatological beginning of our future resurrected life (2 Corinthians 3:18; 4:10-11; Philippians 3:10-11). Since we as "genuinely new persons" shall someday be "totally new," we may embrace "the soteriological blessings we receive in this life" as "a foretaste of the greater blessings to which we look forward in the age to come" (Hoekema, *The Bible and the Future,* p. 9).

This foretaste of ultimate renewal, which "comes from the Lord who is the Spirit," is the pledge and guarantee of its final consummation. The here and the hereafter in our bodily history, therefore, "do not stand over against each other as the lower and higher in the sense of a dualistic anthropology, but as two modes of bodily existence, of which the resurrection of Christ forms the turning point" (Ridderbos, *Paul,* p. 543).

As we await the sound of the trumpet, we may anticipate a real anthropological identity. The opening of the graves will signal a restoration of the various aspects of our way of being human. We will "fully understand" as we are "fully understood." In moving from the "now" to the "then," says Paul, "faith, hope, and love abide" (1 Corinthians 13:12-13). This presupposes that we shall continue to believe, hope, and love. Jesus Christ is the archetype. He who arose was the same as he who died and was buried. "See my hands and feet" — with these challenging words of invitation he reinvigorated his downhearted disciples. "It is I myself: handle me and see; for a spirit has not flesh and bones as you see that I have" (Luke 24:39). In another appearance we read that "none of the disciples dared ask him, 'Who are you?' They knew it was the Lord" (John 21:12). Yet in his glorified body closed and locked doors were unable to bar his entry. Perhaps a crude analogy from the physical sciences may be helpful in picturing this spectacular transformation: a given object, when operating on an unusual frequency, displays extraordinary patterns of behavior. Still, we continue to see through a glass dimly.

This much we can say, however: The article of faith concerning "the resurrection of the body" refers to "man as he has been created by God, for God's glory, and to his service, and thus also as he is raised from the dead and saved by God" (Ridderbos, *Paul,* pp. 548-49). We may therefore affirm wholeheartedly that "it is and remains we ourselves who arise. . . . It is not another human being that is brought into existence; it is this human body that is changed" (Hendrikus Berkhof, *Christian Faith,* p. 527).

III. 6. The Last Judgment

From the original creation to the renewed creation God's Word for the world is ever the same: "Let justice roll down like waters, and righteousness like an ever-flowing stream" (Amos 5:24). In the beginning the created order was marked by such shalom — "It is very good!" But then "righteous blood" was shed (Hebrews 11:4). Along the way of redemption history the prophets therefore declare relentlessly, "Do justice" (Micah 6:8). In the fulness of the times Christ blesses those who "hunger and thirst for righteousness" (Matthew 5:6). In the end God will judge the world justly. Righteousness will then be fully vindicated. But God's Word also has an "or else" side, the righteous Judge "inflicting vengeance upon those . . . who do not obey the gospel of our Lord Jesus" (2 Thessalonians 1:5-8). Mankind's standing appointment at Christ's return to appear before the tribunal of divine judgment represents the final public vindication of God's unchanging Word. In the end

> . . . a political reckoning must occur, and the power that has been misused in political history must be handed back to its proper source. And this must be in some sense a "public" event. The corrupt rulers of history must stand trial — the unrighteous kings of Israel and Judah, the Egyptian pharaohs, the rulers of Assyria and Syria, the Roman caesars, Hitler, Stalin, Idi Amin, the corrupt politicians of the so-called "free world." The abuse of power cannot go unchecked in the final settling of accounts. (Richard Mouw, *When the Kings Come Marching In,* p. 31)

God's judgments are indeed now already at work in the world (Romans 1:18-32). But beyond the present a final day of reckoning awaits all mankind. "For we must all appear before the judgment seat of Christ, so that each one may receive good or evil, according to what he has done in the body" (2 Corinthians 5:10). Life and death verdicts are handed down decisively in this ultimate hall of justice, ruling out any higher court of appeals. The standard of judgment will be the same then as now — whether our life is "hid with Christ in God" or whether we are "still in our sins." There will be no surprisingly new standards. Yet there will be expressions of surprise (Matthew 25:31-46).

This eschatological picture of the final judgment is the biblical counterpart to the classic moral argument for the existence of God. The existence of a "moral world order" needs no rational proof. In Scripture its reality is self-evident. Especially in the Pauline writings it is axiomatic that "God will one day judge the world" (Ridderbos, *Paul,* p. 552). As long as the present "end times" last, God continues to temper his pent-up righteous indignation by his longsuffering mercy, calling insistently for repentance. But when at last the day of grace has run its course, when the world's cup of iniquity runs full, then Christ will appear to set the record straight once and for all.

In this life already, however ambiguously, our "sins will find us out" (Augustine). Now already good and evil are their own reward. In the end, however, to cap it off, the Judge of all will take his seat to settle these many open and closed accounts with an air of finality. And he will judge righteously, in keeping with the degree of revelational light which people receive and their response to it (Matthew 11:20-24). This gospel teaching has far-reaching implications for the mission mandate of the church. But among us, where the Light has shone so brilliantly, "how shall we neglect so great a salvation?" (Hebrews 2:3). Ultimately, then, in answering the call of the gospel, all men get what they want most out of life. To proclaim judgment, therefore, both present and future, is to proclaim the Word incarnate, crucified, risen, and now exalted. His return will consummate the "great reversal" inaugurated at his first coming. He will unmask all deception and disrobe all hypocrisy (Luke 11:37-52). He will bring about a final rectification in the affairs of men and nations — exposing our deepest impulses, clarifying the ambiguities of history, and putting on open display the secret files of international intrigue. We must be careful, however, says Paul, to honor God's forbearance during these "last days" and not "pronounce judgment before the time, before the Lord comes." His coming "will bring to light the things now hidden in darkness, and will disclose the purposes of the heart. Then every man will receive his commendation from God" (1 Corinthians 4:5). As Berkouwer puts it,

> no longer will evil be called good and good evil; no longer will darkness be turned into light and light into darkness; no longer will bitter be made sweet and sweet bitter (Isaiah 5:20). This is the inevitable radical end of all human deceptions. The conflict between good and evil will come to an end, as will all arguments about motives, intentions, and the nature of good. . . . Error will be exposed: real error, turning away from the Lord. This exposure will be clearer, fairer, truer, and more thorough than any [anathemas, condemnations, or rejection of errors ever pronounced] in the annals of the church. . . . All pretended motives will count for nothing and the route of sophistry made impassable. It will be revealed who really believed that giving was more blessed than receiving (Acts 20:25) and who closed his heart to the needs of his brother (I John 3:17). (*The Return of Christ,* p. 160)

The crooked will at last be made straight, the unrequited wrongs made right — the unresolved crimes against humanity, the defamation of God's name, the wanton slaughter of the unborn, indifference to the crying needs of the poor and oppressed. For "too much injustice remains unpunished, too much goodness unrewarded, to allow our conscience to rest content with conditions as they are in this present dispensation" (Bavinck, *Magnalia Dei,* p. 641). In the end "we shall all stand before the judgment seat of God; for it is written, 'As I live, says the Lord, every knee shall bow to me, and every tongue shall give praise to God.' So each of us shall give an account of himself to God" (Romans 14:10-12).

There are but two exits leading from this eschatological courtroom — the "broad way" which leads to death and the "narrow way" which leads to life. Both destinies, heaven as well as hell, are as real as the fallen and redeemed creation itself. Hell — only with deep-seated reluctance can we speak of this terrible prospect, with fear and trembling. Yet we must do so, lest we suppress the awesome witness of Scripture and become accomplices in the condemnation of others to eternal misery (Ezekiel 3:16-21). When people cry out in desperation, "War is hell!"; or, on the other hand, when they compliment a host on serving a "heavenly meal," something in us resonates to such hyperboles. Such overstatements fall short, however, of capturing the intensely urgent meaning which Scripture ascribes to heaven and hell. Their full reality cannot be collapsed into our contemporary life experience as two historical horizons in conflict. We do indeed experience a foretaste of both eternal life and eternal death already in this present age. But only Christ our Substitute endured the full weight of "the anguish and torment of hell" here on earth (Heidelberg Catechism, Q. & A. 44). And he alone experiences now the full glory of the heavenly estate. For the rest of humanity the full reality of hell and heaven awaits the day of judgment. Then the blurred antithesis of the moment will be fully revealed as a fixed contradiction.

The Christian community must also appear before the divine tribunal. For "the church, the *ecclesia militans,* with all its dividedness, its discipline and insubordination, its preaching, its love, must remember that judgment begins with the household of God" (Berkouwer, *The Return of Christ,* p. 160). And "if it begins with us, what will be the end of those who do not obey the gospel?" (1 Peter 4:17). The church is not exempt from this final adjudication (1 Corinthians 3:10-15). For "every one to whom much is given, of him much will be required" (Luke 12:48). Moreover, as Kuyper sometimes put it, "the world is often better than we might expect, and the church worse." The believer may nevertheless confess: "I turn my eyes to the heavens and confidently await as judge the very One who has already stood trial in my place before God" (Heidelberg Catechism, Q. & A. 52). Though the failures of Christians will "enter the picture on the Day of Judgment, . . . the important point" is this: "the sins and shortcomings of believers will be revealed in judgment as forgiven sins" (Hoekema, *The Bible and the Future*, p. 259). As now already, so also in "the end," there is no condemnation for those who are in Christ. For the Judge is our Savior and Lord. "And just as it is appointed for men to die once, and after that comes the judgment," so for the Christian community, Christ "will appear a second time, not to deal with sin but to save those who are eagerly waiting for him" (Hebrews 9:27-28).

III. 7. "All in All"

In "the end" the biblical story line comes full circle — not as the dizzy outcome of a vicious cycle of ever recurring events, but as the teleologically directed consummation of redemption history. Broken covenant relationships will then be completely healed. The kingdom will reach its uncontested fulfillment. In its opening scenario Genesis leaves us with the picture of a Garden — God at work creating the heavens and the earth. In John's apocalypse that original vision returns: God is still and again at work re-creating all things, but with a decisively eschatological advance: the Garden has become a City! Between these two great epochs, and binding them together, is the gospel of the coming kingdom which sweeps the redeemable aspects of human culture along into the "new Jerusalem."

Our view of "the end" settles once and for all our view of "beginnings." Either we envision the creation as restored or we view it as superseded. Bavinck rightly rejects the idea of "repristination" — a simple return to Eden, as though God's future plan calls for wiping the slate clean of everything that happens in between. He also rejects the idea of "destruction." For Christ came not to destroy the works of his Father or the obedient acts of his followers, but only the works of the devil and those who serve his diabolical cause. Instead, God is the great Restorer of creation (Veenhof, *Nature and Grace in Bavinck*, pp. 19-20). Calvin already held to this view, stating that "Christ came not for the destruction of the world, but for its salvation" (*Institutes,* III,25,9). Others followed in this line. Expectation of "the renewal of the present creation is favored by Reformed theologians," says Louis Berkhof (*Systematic Theology,* p. 737). Hendrikus Berkhof also affirms this eschatological vision, holding that "Reformed orthodoxy generally thought in terms of a re-creation" in which "the coming world would be the renewal and consummation of this one" (*Christian Faith,* pp. 520, 529). For John's vision of "a new heaven and a new earth," where the root word for "new" is *kainos* (Revelation 21:1), rather than pointing to "the emergence of a cosmos totally other than the present one," points to "the creation of a universe which, though gloriously renewed, stands in continuity with the present one" (Hoekema, *The Bible and the Future,* p. 280). Even "the fire will not do away with the universe." For "after the fire there will still be the same 'heaven and earth', but gloriously renewed . . ." (William Hendriksen, *The Bible on the Life Hereafter,* p. 205).

The parousia, therefore, does not introduce a radical break with the past. The full sweep of the ground we have covered in this study, its many themes in their basic unity and their rich diversity, converge in the reality of the coming age. The familiar contours of the created order, with its divinely given structures and functions, give shape and form to the life of a resurrected humanity in God's renewed world where everything will be thoroughly redeemed, completely redirected to its appointed end. Isaiah's prophecy (chapters 60 and 65) of a time of "beating swords into ploughshares" will come to final fulfillment in the new earth.

Is it possible now already to envision a world in which "righteousness dwells" (2 Peter 3:13)? John's apocalyptic imagery helps in bringing it home to us: streets of gold, the river of life, ever bearing trees, city gates standing wide open day and night. It is a picture of Paradise regained, with shalom as the order of the day! These earthy concepts were very familiar to early Christians: The "new Jerusalem" recalled the geographic Jerusalem they knew so well, the historical redemptive center of their christological hopes. Because the eschaton belongs to the Eschatos, the Lord they knew so well, therefore "the future can never be labeled *terra incognita,* 'the realm of the unknown.'" Though life on the renewed earth baffles our senses and exceeds our wildest expectations (1 Corinthians 2:9), yet it is not "the unknown of the future but the known in the future that is decisive for eschatological reflection" (Berkouwer, *The Return of Christ,* p. 13). Of the glorified humanity we read that "their deeds shall follow them" (Revelation 14:13). Even "the kings of the earth shall bring their glory" into the City: "nothing unclean shall enter it," but only "the glory and honor of the nations" (Revelation 21:24-27). Therefore,

> the Holy City is not wholly discontinuous with present conditions. The biblical glimpses of this City give us reason to think that its contents will not be completely unfamiliar to people like us. In fact, the contents of the City will be more akin to our present cultural patterns than is usually acknowledged. (Mouw, *When the Kings Come Marching In,* pp. 6-7)

But what about us, late twentieth-century Christians? We sometimes repaint John's picture in such otherworldly terms ("beyond the blue horizon"), as a faraway place ("beautiful isle of somewhere") with strange-sounding names ("Beulah land"), that we can hardly conceive of it as real, let alone want it very much. Such ethereal projections lead Hoekema to ask pointedly:

> . . . does such a conception do justice to biblical eschatology? Are we to spend eternity somewhere off in space, wearing white robes, plucking harps, singing songs, and flitting from cloud to cloud while doing so? On the contrary, the Bible assures us that God will create a new earth on which we shall live to God's praise in glorified, resurrected bodies. On that new earth, therefore, we hope to spend eternity, enjoying its beauties, exploring its resources, and using its treasures to the glory of God. (*The Bible and the Future,* p. 274)

Bavinck emphasizes this same point of continuity in the midst of discontinuity:

> We are not to think in terms of a completely new creation. For heaven and earth as they presently exist will indeed come to an end in their present form (I Corinthians 7:31), and will be burned and purged by fire (II Peter 3:6, 7, 10), just as the ancient earth was deluged by the flood. Yet, just as human beings are renewed by Christ, but are not destroyed to be created again (II Corinthians 5:17), so essentially the world will be preserved, even though it will experience such a great change in form that it is called a new heaven and a new earth. (*Magnalia Dei,* p. 644)

We must therefore try to rehabilitate for our times the vivid expectation of the early Christians. For beleaguered communities of believers today, hard-pressed by poverty, oppression, and persecution, the consummation holds out hope for a "sabbath rest" (Hebrews 4:9-10). But the "new order" also offers abundant opportunities for a renewed pursuit of the cultural mandate. There will be times of exuberant worship, face to face with our Lord, no longer restricted to a temple (Revelation 21:22), thus resolving forever the competing claims of church membership. But there will also be time for gardening in this Paradise, for constructive activities in this City, time for reading those good books we somehow never get around to, for finishing those half-written letters, for removing the incompletes on our academic transcripts. As my chemistry professor once put it: an eternity to continue running laboratory experiments, probing the unfathomable wonders of creation. Perhaps we may even join Barth in listening to more of Mozart's music. In Christ "all things are [ours]" (1 Corinthians 3:21-23). For "the meek . . . shall inherit the earth" (Matthew 5:5). Now already all this, and more, is ours in hope — and someday in perfection.

Bibliography

Abbott, W. M., and J. Gallagher. *The Documents of Vatican II*. New York: Herder & Herder, Association Press, 1966.

Adams, Jay. *The Time Is at Hand*. Nutley, N.J.: Presbyterian and Reformed Publishing Company, 1970.

Augustine. *The Confessions of St. Augustine*. London: Dent & Sons, 1946.

Barth, Karl. *The Word of God and the Word of Man*. Boston/Chicago: Pilgrim Press, 1928.

———. *The Epistle to the Romans*. London: Oxford, 1950.

———. *Church Dogmatics*, I/1, III/3, III/4. Edinburgh: Clark, 1955.

Bavinck, Herman. *De Katholiciteit van Christendom en Kerk*. Kampen: Zalsman, 1888.

———. *Christelijke Wereldbeschouwing*. Kampen: Kok, 1913.

———. *Gereformeerde Dogmatiek*, Vols. I, II, III, IV. Kampen: Kok, 1928.

———. *Magnalia Dei*. Kampen: Kok, 1931.

Bavinck, J. H. *The Impact of Christianity on the Non-Christian World*. Grand Rapids: Eerdmans, 1948.

———. *The Church between Temple and Mosque*. Grand Rapids: Eerdmans, 1966.

Berkhof, Hendrikus. *Christ the Meaning of History*. Richmond: John Knox Press, 1966.

———. *Christelijk Geloof*. Nijkerk: Callenbach, 1973.

———. *Christian Faith*. Grand Rapids: Eerdmans, 1979.

———. *Essays on the Heidelberg Catechism*. N.p., n.d.

Berkhof, Louis. *Introductory Volume to Systematic Theology*. Grand Rapids: Eerdmans, 1932.

———. *Systematic Theology*. Grand Rapids: Eerdmans, 1947.

————. *The History of Christian Doctrines*. Grand Rapids: Eerdmans, 1949.

Berkouwer, G. C. *Faith and Sanctification*. Grand Rapids: Eerdmans, 1952.

————. *The Providence of God*. Grand Rapids: Eerdmans, 1952.

————. *De Sacramenten*. Kampen: Kok, 1954; English translation *The Sacraments*. Grand Rapids: Eerdmans, 1969.

————. *Faith and Justification*. Grand Rapids: Eerdmans, 1954.

————. *The Person of Christ*. Grand Rapids: Eerdmans, 1954.

————. *General Revelation*. Grand Rapids: Eerdmans, 1955.

————. *The Triumph of Grace in the Theology of Karl Barth*. Grand Rapids: Eerdmans, 1956.

————. *Faith and Perseverance*. Grand Rapids: Eerdmans, 1958.

————. *Divine Election*. Grand Rapids: Eerdmans, 1960.

————. *Man: The Image of God*. Grand Rapids: Eerdmans, 1962.

————. *The Work of Christ*. Grand Rapids: Eerdmans, 1965.

————. *Sin*. Grand Rapids: Eerdmans, 1971.

————. *The Return of Christ*. Grand Rapids: Eerdmans, 1972.

————. *The Church*. Grand Rapids: Eerdmans, 1976.

Bettenson, Henry. *The Early Christian Fathers*. London: Oxford, 1956.

————. *The Later Christian Fathers*. London: Oxford, 1970.

Beuker, G. J. *Umkehr und Erneuerung*. Uelsen, Germany: Synode der Evangelisch-altreformierten Kirche in Niedersachsen, 1988.

Blocher, Henri. *In the Beginning*. Downers Grove, Ill.: InterVarsity Press, 1984.

Bloesch, Donald. *Essentials of Evangelical Theology*. San Francisco: Harper & Row, 1978.

Boer, Harry R. *Pentecost and the Missionary Witness of the Church*. Franeker: Wever, 1955.

Boettner, Loraine. *The Millennium*. Grand Rapids: Baker, 1958.

Bonhoeffer, Dietrich. *Letters and Papers from Prison*. New York: Macmillan, 1972.

————. *Ethics*. New York: Macmillan, 1975.

Braaten, Carl. *History and Hermeneutics*. Philadelphia: Westminster, 1966.

Bruce, F. F. *The Spreading Flame*. Grand Rapids: Eerdmans, 1958.

Bruggink, Donald. *Guilt, Grace, and Gratitude*. New York: Half Moon Press, 1963.

Brunner, Emil. *Dogmatics*, Vol. II. Philadelphia: Westminster, 1950.

————. *The Mediator*. Philadelphia: Westminster, 1957.

Bultmann, Rudolf. *Jesus and the Word*. New York: Scribner, 1958.

————. *Jesus Christ and Mythology*. New York: Scribner, 1958.

Burgsmüller, Alfred. *Die Barmer Theologische Erklärung.* Neukirchen-Vluyn: Neukirchener, 1983.

Burkhardt, Helmut. *The Biblical Doctrine of Regeneration.* Downers Grove, Ill.: InterVarsity Press; Exeter, England: Paternoster, 1978.

Calvin, John. *Commentary on Ephesians.* Grand Rapids: Eerdmans, 1948.

————. *Commentary on (I Peter) the Catholic Epistles.* Grand Rapids: Eerdmans, 1948.

————. *Commentary on Jeremiah.* Grand Rapids: Eerdmans, 1950.

————. *Commentary on (Amos) the Twelve Minor Prophets.* Grand Rapids: Eerdmans, 1950.

————. *The Institutes of the Christian Religion.* ed. John T. McNeill and Ford Lewis Battles. Philadelphia: Westminster, 1960.

Clouse, Robert G. *The Meaning of the Millennium.* Downers Grove, Ill.: InterVarsity Press, 1977.

Corduan, Winfred. *Handmaid to Theology.* Grand Rapids: Baker, 1981.

Cullmann, Oscar. *Christ and Time.* Philadelphia: Westminster, 1950.

Daane, James. *The Freedom of God.* Grand Rapids: Eerdmans, 1973.

Darwin, Charles. *The Origin of the Species.* New York: P. F. Collier, 1909.

de Dietrich, Suzanne. *God's Unfolding Purpose.* Philadelphia: Westminster, 1974.

De Ridder, Richard. *My Heart's Desire for Israel.* Nutley, N.J.: Presbyterian and Reformed Publishing Company, 1974.

————. *God Has Not Rejected His People.* Grand Rapids: Baker, 1977.

De Graaf, S. G. *Promise and Deliverance,* Vol. I. St. Catharines: Paideia, 1977.

De Graaff, Arnold, and James H. Olthuis. *Toward a Biblical View of Man.* Toronto: Association for the Advancement of Christian Scholarship, 1978.

Diemer, J. Heinrich. *Nature and Miracle.* Toronto: Wedge, 1977.

Dillenberger, John, ed. *Martin Luther: Selections from His Writings.* Garden City, N.Y.: Anchor Book, 1961.

Dooyeweerd, Herman. *A New Critique of Theoretical Thought.* Philadelphia: Presbyterian and Reformed Publishing Company, 1953-58.

————. *Christelijke Perspectief,* No. 1. Amsterdam: Buijten and Schipperheijn, 1962.

————. *In the Twilight of Western Thought.* Nutley, N.J.: Craig Press, 1968.

Dowey, Edward. *The Knowledge of God in Calvin's Theology.* New York: Columbia University Press, 1952.

Feinberg, Charles. *Millennialism.* Chicago: Moody Press, 1982.

Fowler, Stuart. *What Is Theology?*. *Blackburn, Australia: Foundation for Christian Scholarship, n.d.*

————. *On Being Human*. Blackburn, Australia: Foundation for Christian Scholarship, 1980.

————. *The Church and the Renewal of Society*. Potchefstroom: Potchefstroom University Press, 1988.

Gilkey, Langdon. *Maker of Heaven and Earth*. Garden City, N.J.: Doubleday, 1959.

Greidanus, Sidney. *The Modern Preacher and the Ancient Text*. Grand Rapids: Eerdmans, 1988.

Gutiérrez, Gustavo. *We Drink from Our Own Wells*. Maryknoll, N.Y.: Orbis Books, 1984.

Hendriksen, William. *More than Conquerors*. Grand Rapids: Baker, 1939.

————. *The Bible on the Life Hereafter*. Grand Rapids: Baker, 1959.

Henry, Carl F., ed. *Basic Christian Doctrine*. New York: Holt, Rinehart, and Winston, 1962.

————. *God, Revelation, and Authority*. Waco, Tex.: Word, 1976.

Hoekema, Anthony. *The Bible and the Future*. Grand Rapids: Eerdmans, 1982.

————. *Created in God's Image*. Grand Rapids: Eerdmans, 1986.

————. *Saved by Grace*. Grand Rapids: Eerdmans, 1989.

Hoeksema, Herman. *Reformed Dogmatics*. Grand Rapids: Reformed Free Publishing Association, 1966.

Holmes, Arthur. *Contours of a World View*. Grand Rapids: Eerdmans, 1983.

Holwerda, David. *Neo-Pentecostalism Hits the Church*. Grand Rapids: Christian Reformed Church Board of Publications, 1968.

Jewett, Paul. *Emil Brunner's Concept of Revelation*. London: J. Clarke, 1954.

Jüngel, Eberhard. *Karl Barth: A Theological Legacy*. Philadelphia: Westminster, 1986.

Kalsbeek, L. *Contours of a Christian Philosophy*. Toronto: Wedge, 1975.

Kant, Immanuel. *Religion Within the Bounds of Reason Alone*. New York: Harper, 1960.

————. *The Conflict of the Faculties*. New York: Abaris, 1979.

————. *The Critique of Judgement*. Indianapolis: Hackett, 1987.

Kelly, J. N. D. *Early Christian Doctrine*. London: Black, 1958.

Kline, Meredith. *Treaty of the Great King*. Grand Rapids: Eerdmans, 1963.

————. *By Oath Consigned*. Grand Rapids: Eerdmans, 1968.

Klooster, Fred. *Quests for the Historical Jesus*. Grand Rapids: Baker, 1977.

König, Adrio. *The Eclipse of Christ in Eschatology*. Grand Rapids: Eerdmans, 1989.

Kraus, H. J. *The People of God in the Old Testament*. New York: Association, 1958.

Kromminga, D. H. *The Millennium in the Church*. Grand Rapids: Eerdmans, 1948.

Kuitert, Harry. *Wat Heet Geloven?*. Baarn: Ten Have, 1977.

Kuyper, Abraham. *The Work of the Holy Spirit*. Grand Rapids: Eerdmans, 1941.

———. *Christianity and the Class Struggle*. Grand Rapids: Piet Hein, 1950.

———. *Principles of Sacred Theology*. Grand Rapids: Eerdmans, 1965.

———. *Lectures on Calvinism*. Grand Rapids: Eerdmans, 1970.

———. *Souvereiniteit in Eigen Kring*. Amsterdam: Kruyt, 1880.

Küng, Hans. *Justification: The Doctrine of Karl Barth and Catholic Reflection*. New York: Nelson, 1964.

———. *The Church*. New York: Doubleday, 1976.

Ladd, George E. *A Theology of the New Testament*. Grand Rapids: Eerdmans, 1974.

———. *The Last Things*. London: Scripture Union, 1978.

Langer, Susanne K. *Philosophy in a New Key*. Cambridge: Harvard University Press, 1951.

Machen, J. Gresham. *The Virgin Birth of Christ*. New York: Harper, 1930.

Maier, Gerhardt. *The End of the Historical-Critical Method*. St. Louis: Concordia, 1977.

Mann, Thomas. *Joseph the Provider*. New York: Knopf, 1944.

Minear, Paul S. *Images of the Church in the New Testament*. Philadelphia: Westminster Press, 1960.

Moltmann, Jürgen. "Theological Basis of Human Rights." Neukirchen-Vluyn: World Alliance of Reformed Churches, 1977.

Mouw, Richard. *When the Kings Come Marching In*. Grand Rapids: Eerdmans, 1984.

Murray, John. *Redemption — Accomplished and Applied*. Grand Rapids: Eerdmans, 1955.

Niesel, Wilhelm. *The Theology of Calvin*. Philadelphia: Westminster Press, 1956.

Olive, Don H. *Wolfhart Pannenberg*. Waco, Tex.: Word, 1975.

Palmer, Edwin H. *Scheeben's Doctrine of Divine Adoption*. Kampen: Kok, 1953.

Pannenberg, Wolfhart. *History and Hermeneutics*. New York: Harper and Row, 1967.

———. *Revelation as History*. New York: Macmillan, 1968.

————. *Basic Questions in Theology.* Philadelphia: Fortress Press, 1970-71.

————. *Jesus — God and Man.* Louisville: Westminster John Knox, 1982.

Pelikan, Jaroslav. *The Riddle of Roman Catholicism.* New York: Abingdon Press, 1959.

————. *The Emergence of the Catholic Tradition — 100-600.* Chicago: University of Chicago Press, 1971.

Prenter, Regin. *Creation and Redemption.* Philadelphia: Fortress Press, 1967.

Rahner, Karl. *Foundations of Christian Faith.* New York: Seabury Press, 1978.

Richardson, Don. *Eternity in Their Hearts.* Ventura, Cal.: Regal Books, 1984.

Richardson, Herbert. *Toward an American Theology.* New York: Harper & Row, 1967.

Ridderbos, Herman N. *Matthew's Witness to Jesus Christ.* New York: Association, 1958.

————. *The Authority of the New Testament Scriptures.* Grand Rapids: Baker, 1963.

————. "The Church and the Kingdom of God," *International Reformed Bulletin,* No. 27, October 1966.

————. "The Kingdom of God and Our Life in the World," *International Reformed Bulletin,* No. 28, January 1967.

————. *The Coming of the Kingdom.* Philadelphia: Presbyterian and Reformed Publishing Company, 1975.

————. *Paul: An Outline of His Theology.* Grand Rapids: Eerdmans, 1975.

Robertson, O. Palmer. *The Christ of the Covenants.* Grand Rapids: Baker, 1980.

Runia, Klaas, ed. *The Church and Its Social Calling.* Grand Rapids: Reformed Ecumenical Synod, 1980.

Schaeffer, Francis. *Death in the City.* Chicago: InterVarsity Press, 1969.

Schilder, Klaas. *Christ in His Suffering.* Grand Rapids: Eerdmans, 1938.

————. *Christ on Trial.* Grand Rapids: Eerdmans, 1939.

————. *Licht in de Rook.* Delft, Netherlands: Meinema, 1951.

Schleiermacher, Daniel F. E. *Christian Faith.* Edinburgh: T. & T. Clark, 1928.

————. *On Religion: Discourse to Its Cultured Despisers.* New York: Harper, 1958.

Smedes, Lewis B. *All Things Made New.* Grand Rapids: Eerdmans, 1970.

————. *Ministry and the Miraculous.* Pasadena, Cal.: Fuller Theological Seminary, 1987.

Smith, Ronald G. *The Whole Man: Studies in Christian Anthropology.* Philadelphia: Westminster, 1969.

Spykman, Gordon J., ed. *Testimony on Human Rights.* Grand Rapids: Reformed Ecumenical Synod, 1983.

———. "Christian Philosophy as Prolegomena to Reformed Dogmatics," *'N Woord op sy Tyd.* Pretoria: NG Kerkboekhandel, 1988.

Temple, William. *Readings in St. John's Gospel.* London: Macmillan, 1949.

Thielicke, Helmut. *The Evangelical Faith*, Vols. I, II, III. Grand Rapids: Eerdmans, 1974.

Torrance, Thomas. *Calvin's Doctrine of Man.* Grand Rapids: Eerdmans, 1957.

Vander Goot, Henry, ed. *Life Is Religion.* St. Catharines: Paideia, 1981.

Vander Stelt, John. "Theology or Pistology?", *Building the House: Essays on Christian Education.* Sioux Center, Iowa: Dordt College Press, 1980.

Vander Velde, George, ed. *The Holy Spirit: Renewing and Empowering Presence.* Winfield, B.C.: Wood Lake Books, 1989.

Van Der Walt, B. J. *Being Human: A Gift and a Duty.* Potchefstroom: Institute for Reformational Studies, 1990.

———. *A Christian Worldview and Christian Higher Education for Africa.* Potchefstroom: Institute for Reformational Studies, 1991.

Van Ruler, A. A. *Religie en Politiek.* Nijkerk: G. F. Callenbach, 1945.

———. *The Christian Church and the Old Testament.* Grand Rapids: Eerdmans, 1971.

Van Til, Cornelius. *The Doctrine of Scripture: In Defense of the Faith*, Vol. I. Ripon, Cal.: den Dulk Christian Foundation, 1967.

Veenhof, Jan. *Nature and Grace in Bavinck.* Toronto: Institute for Christian Studies, n.d.

Vos, Geerhardus. *The Teaching of Jesus Christ Concerning the Kingdom and the Church.* Grand Rapids: Eerdmans, 1958.

———. *Pauline Eschatology.* Grand Rapids: Baker, 1979.

Wallace, Ronald. *Calvin's Doctrine of the Christian Life.* Tyler, Tex.: Geneva Divinity School Press, 1982.

Walvoord, J. *The Millennial Kingdom.* Findlay, Ohio: Dunham, 1959.

Walsh, Brian J., and J. Richard Middleton. *The Transforming Vision: Shaping a Christian Worldview.* Downers Grove, Ill.: InterVarsity, 1984.

Weber, Otto. *Groundplan of the Bible.* Philadelphia: Westminster, 1959.

———. *Foundations of Dogmatics*, Vols. I, II. Grand Rapids: Eerdmans, 1981/83.

Wolters, Albert M. *Creation Regained: Biblical Basics for a Reformational Worldview.* Grand Rapids: Eerdmans, 1985.

Zylstra, Henry. *Testament of Vision.* Grand Rapids: Eerdmans, 1961.

Index of Subjects

Given the rather elaborate Table of Contents at the beginning of this book, this Index of Subjects is kept quite compact, thus minimizing overlap and duplication. On a given topic the reader is therefore advised to consult these two registries in combination as a guide to studying this work.

Index of Persons

Aalders, G. C., 262
Adams, J., 540-41, 542
Anselm, 34, 382
Apollinaris, 402-03
Aquinas. *See* Thomas Aquinas
Arius, 401-02
Athanasius, 401-02
Augustine, 6, 19, 26, 116, 155, 204,
 268, 309-10, 316, 323-26, 433,
 455, 519

Barth, K., 31-36, 43, 45-48, 49, 53-
 54, 56-58, 101, 169, 172-76, 218,
 248, 293-94, 370, 386-88, 414-15,
 493, 495, 506-07, 515
Bavinck, H., 6, 69-70, 87, 94-95, 97-
 98, 111, 188-89, 223, 224-25,
 238, 263, 271, 272, 290, 291,
 294, 304, 307, 421-22, 441, 444,
 448, 452, 454, 455, 462, 465,
 466, 469, 479, 480, 515, 523,
 552, 557, 558
Bavinck, J. H., 426-27
Berkhof, H., 3, 29, 52-55, 58, 94,
 159, 190-91, 196-97, 201, 274,
 275, 305-06, 310, 311, 318, 322,
 340-41, 343, 345, 347, 353, 365,
 369, 373, 374-75, 385-86, 396,
 397, 399, 418, 420, 422, 423,
 424, 432, 439, 446, 453, 454, 457-
 58, 459, 467, 485, 489, 491, 496,
 497, 500, 504, 506, 509, 518,
 519, 534, 554, 558
Berkhof, L., 6, 7, 141, 235, 241,
 276, 288, 295, 311, 320, 342,
 357, 362, 411-12, 418, 420, 421,
 424, 429, 432, 439, 443, 444, 452-
 53, 455, 466, 479, 482, 483, 487,
 494, 495, 501, 502, 508, 534,
 537, 539, 540, 541, 558, 560
Berkouwer, G. C., 51-52, 170, 197,
 206, 221-22, 225, 227-28, 236,
 242, 248, 273, 290, 292, 304,
 305, 307, 308, 320, 339, 343-44,
 345, 346, 401, 402, 404, 406,
 407, 409, 411, 413, 414, 415,
 416, 438, 442, 443, 444, 445,
 446, 448, 449, 450, 451, 453,
 455, 457, 458, 460, 482, 483, 486-
 87, 488, 491, 492, 493, 494, 495,
 496, 498, 499-500, 501-02, 503,
 504, 505, 506, 512, 517, 524,
 525, 527, 528, 529, 530, 532,
 535, 536, 537, 538, 542, 543,
 549, 550, 551, 552, 556, 557, 559
Bernard of Clairvaux, 6
Beuker, G. J., 461
Beza, T., 23
Blackman, B., 313-14
Blocher, H., 308
Bloesch, D., 450
Boer, H., 422

574

Index of Scripture References

577